Tanna dĕḇe Eliyyahu

TRANSLATED FROM THE HEBREW BY

William G. (Gershon Zev) Braude

AND *Israel J. Kapstein*

Philadelphia 5741 / 1981

TANNA DĚBE ELIYYAHU

The Lore of the School of Elijah

The Jewish Publication Society of America

Manufactured in the United States of America

Library of Congress Cataloging in Publication Data

Tanna debe Eliyahu. English.
Tanna dĕḇe Eliyyahu - The lore of the school of Elijah.

Includes also chapters 39–41 of Pirke de-Rabbi Eliezer.
Includes index.
I. Pirke de-Rabbi Eliezer. Chapters 39–41.
English. 1980. II. Braude, William Gordon, 1907–
III. Kapstein, Israel James, 1904–
IV. Title. V. Title: Lore of the school of Elijah.
BM517.T4E5 1980 296.1'4 80–10805
ISBN 0–8276–0174–3

Designed by Adrianne Onderdonk Dudden

My share in this work is dedicated to my beloved children, Joel Isaac and Ruth Rita, Benjamin Meir and Lois Carol, and Daniel, and grandchildren, Yosef Zvi Braude and Yonatan Ezra Braude.

W. G. B.

To my grandchildren, Frances Martha Brodsky and John Bernard Brodsky, and Helen Sarah Kapstein and Adrienne Susan Kapstein, whose love has been a blessing to me, I dedicate my part in this work.

I. J. K.

CONTENTS

---

*In *Eliyyahu Rabbah* the chapter numbers in parentheses refer to the chapter numbers in editions preceding Friedmann's; the absence of parentheses indicates that Friedmann's numbering of a chapter agrees with that of the earlier editions.

Eliyyahu Zuṭa

---

*In *Eliyyahu Zuṭa* the square brackets enclosing chapter numbers indicate that in Codex Vatican 31, the prime source of Friedmann's text, these numbers are not given and Friedmann supplied them.

Pirḳe Hay-Yĕridot

ACKNOWLEDGMENTS

First to be thanked for his generous help to the translators is Leon Nemoy, who with unruffled equanimity has worked his way through every word, phrase, and sentence of the manuscript. His great learning, his close critical reading, and his editorial skills have contributed immeasurably to improvement of the translation both in substance and style.

Heartfelt thanks also go to the following scholars whose command of various areas of Hebraic study has through correspondence resolved many knotty problems presented by the text: Professors Chaim Zalman Dimitrovsky, Louis Finkelstein, David Weiss Halivni, Max Kadushin, Saul Lieberman, and Dov Zlotnick of the Jewish Theological Seminary; Professor Jehuda Feliks of Bar-Ilan University; Professors Jonas Greenfield, Gershom Scholem, and Ephraim E. Urbach of the Hebrew University; Professor Sid Z. Leiman of Yeshiva University; Professor Jakob J. Petuchowski of the Hebrew Union College-Jewish Institute of Religion; and Rabbi Mordecai Savitsky of Boston.

Also to be thanked is the study group composed of the Most Reverend Dom K. Ansgar Nelson and Dom Caedmon Holmes, and Rabbis Eli A. Bohnen, Leslie Y. Gutterman, Alvin Kaunfer, Saul Leeman, Lawrence M. Silverman, and Nancy Wellins. From week to week this group made valuable suggestions in regard to the interpretation of a number of passages, and helped in collating Friedmann's edition of *Tanna dḇe Eliyyahu* with Codex Vatican 31 and Parma MS 2785. For help in collation, the late Rabbi Israel M. Goldman is also to be thanked.

For their aid in bibliographical matters, the translators are grateful to Herbert Zafren, Dr. Israel O. Lehman, Susan Tabor, Carole Weiner, and Patricia Gordon of the Library of the Hebrew Union College-Jewish Institute of Religion; Dr. Menahem Schmelzer, Dr. Herman Dicker, and Mrs. Rosalyn Remer Friedman of the Library of the Jewish Theological Seminary of America; Dr. Leonard Gold of the New York Public Library; Professor Elazar Hurvitz of Yeshiva University; and Professor Benjamin Meir Braude of Boston College.

With characteristic energy, unfailing precision, and devotion, Esther (Mrs. Philip) Kaplan typed successive revisions of the manuscript and prepared the index of subjects and names; Phoebe (Mrs. Sidney) Nulman prepared the indexes of passages and authorities cited; and Meta (Mrs. David J.) Cohen, Gladys (Mrs. Sherwin) Kapstein, and Pen (Mrs. William G.) Braude read copy.

Finally, the translators wish to thank Pen Braude and Stella (Mrs. Israel J.) Kapstein for their iron patience and steady encouragement.

"The words are ancient and sweeter than honey and the honey comb. The beautiful parables charm a man's heart, restraining him from doing any kind of evil, and directing him to the doing of good."

From the title page of the Venice edition, 1598

"His holy words burn like flaming coals setting hearts afire. Yet from under his tongue, a tongue of gold, a tongue of healing, come honey and milk.

"Happy is he who is ever at study. Happy is he in whose home are heard the words of this weighty and sacred volume."

From the title page of the Sudzilkow edition, 1833; the Jozefow edition, 1833; and the Lemberg edition, 1850

INTRODUCTION

I. The Text: Author; Time and Place of Composition; History

Except for an abridged translation into Yiddish, the work now in the reader's hand has never been translated from the original Hebrew. It has most often gone under the Hebrew title *Tanna dĕḇe Eliyyahu*[1] or *Seder Eliyyahu,* although it has been conjectured that the two titles refer to two separate works, one of which, the *Seder,* is no longer extant. A literal translation of the first title would be "The Lore of Elijah" or "The Lore of the School of Elijah," and of the other title "The Work of Elijah"; but none of these translations attests to the vitality and scope of the work.

Tanna dĕḇe Eliyyahu has a unity of thought and feeling, of style and structure, that makes it seem the work of a single individual. Even if it be considered the product of a school, it is still likely that the text as we have it came from the head of the school, possibly a school named for him. In any event, he was a man of so strong a spirit as to impress it deeply upon the work, no matter how many of his disciples may have participated in its composition.

There is, indeed, a detailed legendary account of the work's origin, an account which has prefaced every edition of the work, that attributes it to an individual named Elijah, that individual no other than the prophet Elijah himself. According to the legend, the prophet dictated the two parts of the work over two separate periods to R. Anan, a Babylonian teacher and judge who lived in the third century C.E. During the earlier period Elijah dictated the first and larger portion termed the *Rabbah* (i.e., "the Greater") and some time afterward, during the second period, dictated the second and briefer portion termed the *Zuṭa* (i.e., "the Lesser").

One day, so the legend begins, a man brought a catch of small marsh fish to R. Anan. R. Anan asked why the man was presenting the fish to him, and the man replied that he had a lawsuit coming up before the rabbi. Thereupon R. Anan declined the gift, adding that he was simultaneously disqualifying himself as a judge in the man's case.

The man answered that he would not plead with R. Anan to hear his case, but would ask him, nevertheless, to accept the fish as an offering of first fruits, on the ground that it was proper, in the absence

1. The work is also referred to as *Tĕni Eliyyahu* (Gen. Rabbah 54:4), *Elijah* (Num. Rabbah 4:20), and *Tanna dĕḇe Eliyyahu Rabbati* (Eleazar ben Judah of Worms [*ca.* 1165–1230], *Roḳeaḥ* [Jerusalem, 5727 (1967)], §329, §361).

of a priest, to present such an offering to a Sage.[2] Agreeing that the man had a point, R. Anan accepted the gift. He then sent the man to a colleague, R. Naḥman, to whom he also sent a private message explaining that he had disqualified himself from trying the man's suit and asking R. Naḥman to adjudicate it in his stead.

Because of the message, R. Naḥman reasoned that the man must be a relative of R. Anan's. It happened just then that a trial involving some orphans' property was being conducted before R. Naḥman, but he postponed it. He told himself that although sitting in judgment in a matter involving orphans was a religious duty, showing respect for a man learned in Torah, as was R. Anan, was also a religious duty, and therefore, out of respect for Torah, the man's case should take precedence over the orphans'. Accordingly, he asked that the man's suit be called up at once. When the other man involved in the suit observed R. Naḥman's deference to his opponent, he became too upset to argue his case properly and presumably lost it.

Up to this time, the legend goes on, the prophet Elijah in the guise of a teacher had been visiting R. Anan regularly and had already instructed him in the *Rabbah* portion of the work. But when R. Anan allowed himself to be so cunningly manipulated in the matter of the lawsuit, Elijah abruptly ceased to visit him. Thereupon R. Anan fasted and prayed until Elijah appeared to him again. Awestruck, however, the rabbi was at first unable to grasp what Elijah was telling him. It was not until R. Anan had performed further acts of penitence that the prophet reappeared, allayed his fear, and instructed him in the *Zuṭa* portion of the work.[3] Thus, according to tradition, it would seem that the work was transmitted orally for some time until it was finally in the days of R. Anan (third century C.E.) set down in writing.[4]

As to scholarly speculation concerning the author of the work and the time and place of its composition, we have what at one time was thought to be the earliest reference to the work in R. Nathan's *'Aruḵ* (eleventh century C.E.).[5] The *'Aruḵ* states that the titles of the two portions of the work are *Seder Eliyyahu Rabbah* and *Seder Eliyyahu Zuṭa,* as mentioned in the Talmud, and goes on to say that the *Rabbah* portion is made up of three "gates" or parts comprising thirty chapters and that the *Zuṭa* portion comprises twelve chapters.

---

2. See Exod. 23:19 and 2 Kings 4:42. In the latter passage, Elisha, described as a man of God, had first fruits, barley, and fresh ears of corn presented to him, even though Elisha of the Tribe of Gad was not a priest. See B.Keṯ 105b and Pes 68a.

3. B.Keṯ 105b–106a in the version of *Re'šiṯ ḥoḵmah* (see Friedmann, Introduction, p. 1, n. 1).

4. In the Vatican Codex 31 (1073 C.E.) the scribe placed it after the Sifra, which might suggest that he regarded the work as of Tannaitic origin. See below, n. 56.

5. *S.v. "seder."* In fact, R. Nathan quotes R. Naṭronai, a Babylonian gaon of the ninth century C.E.

To this identification and description of the work, however, Solomon Rapoport[6] (1790–1867), the first modern scholar to consider the time and place of its composition, takes strong exception. He asserts that the text we have in hand is not the *Seder Eliyyahu* referred to in the Talmud and in the *'Aruk̲,* that the first printed edition (Venice, 1598) is entitled not *Seder Eliyyahu* but *Tanna dĕb̲e Eliyyahu,* that its *Rabbah* is not divided into three parts and contains not thirty chapters but thirty-one, and that its *Zuṭa* contains not twelve chapters but twenty-five. Finally, from the dates referred to in the *Tanna,* Rapoport concludes that it was composed in the middle or latter part of the tenth century C.E.

In refutation of Rapoport, Meir Friedmann (1831–1908), editor of the text on which this translation is based, asserts that his text is the very one referred to in the Talmud[7] and R. Nathan's *'Aruk̲* as *Seder Eliyyahu,* and in full faith takes the account of its supernatural origin to be not legend but fact. The dates on which Rapoport bases his views of the time and place of the text's composition are not authentic, says Friedmann, because they were introduced into the text by later scribes.[8] Furthermore, in a valiant effort to restore what he believes were the original parts of the text as given in the *'Aruk̲,* he renumbers the chapters in the *Rabbah*[9] and separates from the *Zuṭa* its last ten chapters (Chapters 16–25).

In Friedmann's edition these ten chapters, along with three others from Parma MS 1240, comprise the third and concluding portion of the text. He calls them "Supplements to Seder Eliahu Zuṭa" or "Pseudo-Seder Eliahu Zuṭa." He divides the ten chapters further into two sets, and groups each set under a separate title: to the first three chapters (Chapters 16–18) he assigns the general heading "Pirḳe Derek̲ 'Ereṣ," and to the next set of seven chapters (Chapters 19–25) he assigns the general heading "Pirḳe R. Eliezer."[10] To these ten chapters

---

6. Solomon Rapoport, in *Tolĕdot̲ R. Nathan (Bikkure ha-'ittim, 10* [1829], 43–44, n. 43), cited by Friedmann, Introduction, pp. 91–93.

7. Friedmann, however, agrees with Zĕ'eb̲ Jawitz that ER, 89–118 is an interpolation, and was composed in the seventh century (Introduction, p. 101).

8. See his Introduction, pp. 46 and 86. Already R. Elhanan of Dampierre (d. 1184) regarded the date in ER, 7 as a later interpolation. See Tosafot̲ on B.AZ 9a, as quoted in Raphael Rabbinovicz, *Diḳduḳe sofĕrim* (Jerusalem, 1960), p. 22, n. 40, *ad loc.*

9. Asserting that Chapters (15) 16 and (16) (ER, 72–83) are really one (see Friedmann's note on ER, 80), Friedmann reduces the number of chapters in the Venice edition from thirty-one to thirty, the number given by R. Naṭronai (Introduction, p. 91).

10. The name "Pirḳe R. Eliezer" for this portion of the work, as Friedmann points out (*Nispaḥim lĕ-seder Eliyyahu Zuṭa* [Vienna, 5664/1902], Introduction, p. 20), had already been used by R. Eleazar ben Judah of Worms in his *Roḳeaḥ. Hilk̲ot̲ Ro'š haš-šanah.* (Jerusalem, 5727 [1967]), §206, p. 98.

But if the last ten chapters are not part of the original text of the *Seder,* why did the Venice printer or the scribe whose manuscript he used include them? Perhaps he added "Pirḳe Derek̲ 'Ereṣ," which deals primarily with right conduct, to round out the work which at its beginning asserts the priority of right conduct. So Friedmann might have argued, and by the same token might have argued further that to round out the work

Friedmann adds three more chapters under the general heading "Pirḳe hay-Yĕriḏoṯ"; these he took from Parma MS 1240, where they serve as a sequel to "Pirḳe R. Eliezer." With these thirteen chapters Friedmann concludes the "Pseudo-Seder Eliahu Zuṭa," and thus, by his renumbering and rearranging of the chapters in the work as a whole, makes his edition of the text correspond to R. Nathan's description of the text in the *'Aruḵ*.

The sharp difference of opinion between Rapoport and Friedmann concerning the identity of the text and its author, contents, and time and place of composition is but one example of the continuing disagreement in these matters among scholars over the last one hundred and fifty years. No other Midrash has engaged scholars as deeply, and yet the results of their research are so inconclusive and contradictory as to cancel one another out. For proof, one has only to summarize the views of four modern scholars who have worked in detail on the problems posed by the text and to mention in passing the opinions of other scholars. The four are Meir Friedmann, Avigdor Aptowitzer (1871–1942), Moshe Zucker (1904–), and Mordecai Margulies (1910–68).

Friedmann[11] in entire faith regards the *Seder Eliahu* as having been communicated by the prophet Elijah in the guise of a scholar to a Rabbi Anan, who presumably passed on to his disciples what he had been taught by Elijah. The "I" who occasionally speaks in the text is the prophet himself speaking, Friedmann maintains. He concedes, however, that the work may not have been first communicated to R. Anan, but may have been in existence long before his time and was at length edited by the school he headed. Hence the title *Tanna dĕḇe Eliyyahu* may refer either to the pious men who were instructed by Elijah in his guise of teacher, or to a school *(dĕḇe)* named for him in Jerusalem or Jabneh where his teachings were studied.

In order to show further the antiquity of the text, Friedmann examines a number of parallels between the *Seder* and the Babylonian Talmud (closed about 500 C.E.), and concludes that neither borrowed from the other and that both used common earlier sources. In short, he considers the *Seder* to be an independent work compiled before the close of the Talmud[12] and after the composition of the Mishnah—hence

---

which at its beginning speaks of Israel's distinction as the people of Torah, the Venice printer or the scribe before him added "Pirḳe R. Eliezer," which speaks of Israel's distinction as the people of God.

11. For a superb and richly detailed account of Friedmann's views, see Max Kadushin, *The Theology of Seder Eliahu* (New York, 1932), pp. 6–12.

12. Besides Friedmann's arguments, other details possibly point to the work's pretalmudic provenience:

(a) A curriculum of studies to be pursued begins with Scripture, goes on to Mishnah, and ends with Halaḵoṯ, a term referring to the legal lore, which, on being edited, came to be known as "Talmud" (ER, 31; EZ, 198). Elsewhere in the work, Halaḵoṯ is referred to in the phrase *Midraš Halaḵoṯ wĕ-'Aggadoṯ* (ER, 37, 88, 91 [twice], 100, 155, and *passim*).

compiled before the fifth century C.E., and most likely in the third century.

Aptowitzer[13] disagrees with this dating of the work and proposes instead the first half of the ninth century C.E. as the time of its composition. He also insists that the work was composed in Babylonia, because Jews and non-Jews mingled so freely there that *Tanna dĕḇe Eliyyahu* again and again warns Jews against close social relations with non-Jews, which might lead to lapses in right conduct[14] (ER, 43, 46, 48, 116).

In further support of Babylonia as the place of composition, Aptowitzer points to the work's more lenient attitudes in such matters as conversion to Judaism[15] (ER, 146), Judaism's liturgical formulas[16] (ER, 31) and practices[17] (ER, 140), and so on.[18] He then goes on to argue that the work could not have been composed in Palestine in talmudic times because it so strongly favors the Jewish community in Babylonia, all but saying that it has become the new "Zion" for Jewish learning in contrast to the Jewish community in Palestine (ER, 98, 129). Aptowitzer concludes with refutation of the idea that certain Palestinian practices in such matters as payment of tithes, ritual cleanliness, and the like were not followed in Babylonia, insisting that they were in fact followed there[19] and so confirming it as the place of the *Tanna*'s composition.

Aptowitzer's essay seems to have been ignored by Moshe Zucker,[20] who makes no reference to it in his discussion of *Tanna*

The exceptional reference to Talmud (ER, 106; EZ, 167) should accordingly be regarded as a scribal interpolation.

(b) The reference to Mishnah as the source of a statement, such as "If a heathen comes to be converted, a hand of welcome is held out to him to draw him under the wings of the Presence" (ER, 35), may well be to a Mishnah such as R. Meir's, which was current before R. Judah's edition became normative, or was possibly contemporaneous with it.

(c) The listing of a series of worthies which begins with Abraham, Isaac, and Jacob, goes on to, among others, Moses, Hezekiah, Ezra, Hillel, and Rabban Johanan ben Zakkai, and ends with R. Meir and his company (ER, 36), men of the second century.

13. Avigdor Aptowitzer, *Jewish Studies in Memory of George Alexander Kohut* (New York, 1935), "Seder Elia," pp. 5–39.

14. *Ibid.*, pp. 10–11, 16–17.

15. Those who wished to convert in order to wed a Jewish spouse were accepted in Babylonia but not in Palestine. For the Palestinian practice, see Ger 1:3.

16. The use of the phrase *'ahăḇaṯ 'olam* (Babylonian) and *'ahăḇah rabbah* (Palestinian).

17. "A man who says the *Tĕfillah* loud enough so that he hears himself, [is praying as though God were hard of hearing, and hence] is bearing false witness against Him" reflects the Babylonian attitude. In Palestine the *Tĕfillah* was uttered aloud.

18. Thirty days of celebration of a wedding (seven days of feasting, followed by twenty-three additional days) is referred to only in the Babylonian Talmud (B.Keṯ 8a).

19. Aptowitzer, pp. 26–31. Anan's "tithe of metals" *(ma'ăśer mattaḵoṯ),* or money tax, would thus have been no more than an adaptation to urban life of agricultural levies which had been current in Babylonia. See Zvi Ankori, *Karaites in Byzantium* (New York-Jerusalem, 1959), p. 182, n. 52.

20. Moshe Zucker, *'Al Targum RaSaG lat-Torah* (Brooklyn, 5719/1959), pp. 116–27, 205–19.

dĕbe Eliyyahu. His dating of the text is based on what he considers its polemics, pointing out, to begin with, that it attacks the heretical writings of Ḥīwī al-Balkhī (ninth century C.E.). Other passages in *Tanna dĕbe Eliyyahu* are directed against the Karaites,[21] Zucker maintains, even though he concludes that the author blunted the polemical point of the work in order to keep the contemporary reader from realizing that the work was written by a contemporary author and to make the reader believe that it was written much earlier.[22] On the basis of its polemics, Zucker sets the date of *Tanna dĕbe Eliyyahu*'s composition as between 850 and 860 C.E. since it attacks the Karaite Daniel al-Ḳumīsī, who flourished in the middle of the ninth century. It could not have been composed after 860, Zucker concludes, because R. Naṭronai, writing in 860, refers to the work as already extant.[23]

Mordecai Margulies[24] brings us back full circle to Friedmann in his reassertion of some of Friedmann's arguments against Rapoport. Agreeing that the number of chapters in *Eliyyahu Rabbah* and *Eliyyahu Zuṭa* does in fact correspond to the number ascribed to them in the *'Aruk,* Margulies goes on to maintain that the dates which seem to indicate their composition in the ninth or tenth centuries are scribal interpolations, and concludes from a comparison of similar passages in the two works that *Tanna dĕbe Eliyyahu* is at least as ancient as the Talmud. Turning to other ascriptions of the time and place of the text's composition, Margulies attacks the view of Jacob Mann (1888–1940)[25] that the political background in the *Tanna* is the persecution of the Jews in the Sassanid empire during the second half of the fifth century. Margulies' refutation is simple: Were not hostile decrees and persecutions recurrent events in Jewish history? If so, the fact of political persecution cannot serve to determine the time of composition. Margulies takes much the same stand against Aptowitzer's view that the *Tanna*'s warnings against easy social relations with non-Jews points to its composition in the early part of the ninth century in Babylonia, for warnings against such relations are to be found also in much earlier periods of Jewish history.

---

21. *Ibid.,* pp. 203–19. At least three scholars preceded Zucker in describing *Tanna dĕbe Eliyyahu* as an anti-Karaite work: (1) Wilhelm Bacher, *MGWJ, 23* (1874), 266–94; (2) Ḥayyim Oppenheim, *Beṯ Talmud, 1* (1881), 265–70, 304–10, 337–46, 369–77; and (3) Jacob Samuel Fuchs, *ham-Maggid lĕ-Yiśra'el, 11* (1897), 22–23, 34–35, 45–46, 57–58. Fuchs even identified Anan, the founder of Karaism, with the R. Anan mentioned in the Talmud.

22. Zucker, p. 205, n. 797.

23. *Ibid.,* p. 219. It is puzzling that so eminent a contemporary as R. Naṭronai should have been unaware of the pseudepigraphic character of the work, a fact which had to wait for its disclosure by a man of the twentieth century.

24. Mordecai Margulies, *Sefer Asaf* (Jerusalem, 5713 [1943]), pp. 370–90.

25. Jacob Mann, *HUCA, 4* (1927), 305.

Margulies then considers the argument of Jacob N. Epstein[26] (1878–1952), who takes R. Anan to be the compiler of an earlier version of *Tanna dĕḇe Eliyyahu,* a version that was augmented in the fifth century C.E. when the Jews were being persecuted in the days of King Peroz. Margulies' reply is that the work's uniformity of style proves it to be all of a piece and not a compilation or a miscellany.

In conclusion, Margulies asserts that the author of *Tanna dĕḇe Eliyyahu* was a certain Abba Eliyyahu[27] who lived in the first half of the third century during Yezdegerd I's persecution of the Jews. The work leads us to believe that Eliyyahu's home was Jabneh in the Land of Israel, that he studied and taught in Jerusalem, and that he also traveled in Babylonia and Persia, instructing Jews in prayer and Torah (ER, 63).

Ephraim Urbach (1912–)[28] all but dismisses Margulies' arguments as unconvincing, and concludes from internal linguistic and literary evidence that the work was composed in the ninth century C.E. Like Urbach, a number of other scholars making use of particular allusions in the text have also ventured to supply a date to the work: e.g., the third century in the time of Jezdegerd I;[29] the first half of the fourth century in the time of Constantine the Great;[30] the latter half of the fourth century in the time of the Emperor Julian;[31] the fifth century in the time of Jezdegerd II;[32] the seventh century in the time of the Emperor Heraclius;[33] the ninth century in the days of the Nestorian Patriarch Yeshu bar Nun of Baghdad;[34] and the tenth century when Hungarian hordes ravaged Europe.[35]

---

26. Jacob N. Epstein, *Maḇo' lĕ-nusaḥ ham-Mišnah* (Jerusalem, 1948), pp. 1302, 762.

27. Abba Eliyyahu is mentioned in EZ, 197. But in the parallel in Parma MS 2785 the sobriquet "Abba" is missing.

Long ago, Isaac Abravanel (1437–1508) identified the author as a Sage whose name was Eliyyahu, and more recently Zĕ'eḇ Jawitz identified him as Abba Eliyyahu. See his *Tolĕdoṯ Yiśra'el* (Jerusalem, 5698 [1938]), *9,* 225; first published in *Kĕneseṯ Yiśra'el, 1* (1887), 382–86.

28. *Lĕšonenu, 21* (1957), 183–97.

29. Margulies, pp. 279–80.

30. Samuel Klein, *ha-Hed, 7* (5692 [1932]), 18.

31. Eliezer Atlas, *hak-Kerem* (5648 [1888]), 100, and Isaac Dov Ber Markon, *Mis-Sifraṯenu ha-'attiḳah* (Wilno, 1910), p. 42.

32. Mann, p. 305.

33. Jawitz, p. 231.

34. Aptowitzer, p. 17, and Zucker, p. 219. The latter, as already stated, contends that the work is a polemic against the Karaite Daniel al-Ḳumisi, who flourished in the middle of the ninth century.

35. Leopold Zunz (*had-Dĕrašoṯ bĕ-Yiśra'el* [Jerusalem, 5707/1947], p. 53) takes the author to be a Babylonian. Heinrich Graetz (*Geschichte der Juden,* 3rd ed., *5,* 274, as cited by Friedmann, Introduction, p. 99, n. 3) takes the work to have been written in Rome. Moritz Guedemann (in his *Geschichte des Erziehungswesens . . . der Juden in Italien* [Vienna, 1884], Note (i.e., Appendix) II, pp. 300–303, as cited by Friedmann, Introduction, p. 99, n. 3) takes the author to be an Italian. The work, he says, breathes the spirit of Europe. Graetz and Guedemann, according to Friedmann, have been misled by Solomon Judah Rapoport's erroneous dating of the work as of the tenth century.

This diversity of opinion as to the date of composition is matched by the diversity as to the place of composition, given variously as Palestine, Babylonia, Italy, or Byzantium. A similar diversity of opinion exists in regard to the style of the text; some scholars view it as genuinely contemporary with the style of the Mishnah, others as imitative, contrived, or pseudoclassic.

The fact is that *Tanna dĕḇe Eliyyahu* refuses to yield the secret of its origin—it is almost as though it were deliberately concealing its supernatural origin from mortal eyes. We may surmise, indeed, that the legendary account of the work's origin is closer to the truth than the common sense of scholars is willing to accept.[36] We have had testimony again and again, over the centuries, from men of all religious faiths of their direct mystical experience, of an Eternity above and beyond mortal time and space.[37] This direct experience of the Divine is nothing strange in Jewish religious history. One need only read Gershom Scholem's brilliant study of Jewish mysticism[38] to realize what a force it has been in the lives of individual Jews and in general Jewish history. If R. Anan was a man open to such direct experience of the supernatural, he would have had no doubt that it was Elijah the prophet in person who, in the guise of a scholar, was visiting and instructing him in wisdom from above.

At a lower flight of imagination we may surmise that R. Anan, in his reverence for the prophet, may have given Elijah's name to his school and to the discourses comprising *Tanna dĕḇe Eliyyahu.* At a still lower level, we may imagine that an Abba Eliyyahu lived in the third century and headed a school to which he gave his name and in which the discourses that make up our text originated. It is further possible that since the prophet's reputation far outshone his own, as time went on, people came to attribute the authorship of *Tanna dĕḇe Eliyyahu* not to him, Abba Eliyyahu, but to Elijah the prophet. Subsequently, in order to explain in part the origin of a work bearing the prophet's name, people may have attached to it a popular yarn about a cunning litigant and a naive judge in order to bring the work down to earth, so to speak.

In any event the mystery of the origin of *Tanna dĕḇe Eliyyahu* remains unsolved. If the scholarly investigations of its authorship and

---

36. Friedmann cites numerous rabbinic and kabbalistic passages which speak of encounters between individuals and Elijah, who appears in guises as varied as an Arab merchant, a Roman dignitary, a slave, an old man, a Sage, and so on (Introduction, pp. 27–44).

37. See R. J. Z. Werblowsky, *Joseph Karo, Lawyer and Mystic* (Oxford, 1962).

38. Gershom G. Scholem, *Major Trends in Jewish Mysticism,* 3rd rev. ed. (New York, 1954).

its time and place of origin cancel one another out, then imagination[39] in these matters may indeed serve us as well as reason.

Even the bibliographical history of the text has an air of the supernatural about it. As we have noted, over the centuries it has led some of the scholars who occupied themselves most deeply with it to believe in its supernatural origin. Thus Meir Friedmann, in his 1902–4 edition[40] of the text based on a Vatican MS dated 1073,[41] unequivocally declares the legend to be fact. He has no doubt whatever about the supernatural source of the work.

Neither had Samuel Haida before him. Haida worked on the text as published in its first printed edition (Venice, 1598), based on a manuscript dated 1186. In his preface the printer says that he was under great stress in the production of the book and apologizes for its many errors. The errors were indeed so numerous as to drive Haida nearly to distraction, and he resorted finally to asking Heaven's help in solving the textual problems. After a series of prayers, fasts, and vigils, during which he entreated the prophet Elijah's aid, Elijah appeared to him, so Haida tells us, and revealed to him the authentic text, as Elijah had dictated it centuries before. So, in 1677, Haida was able to issue in Prague what he called a new and correct version of the original text. Before each chapter of his version he put the corresponding chapter of the Venice edition, perhaps with a view to letting the reader see how much superior was his restored text. He prefaced the work with two lengthy introductions and added a prolix and occasionally quite useful commentary. Since his version of the text was so much more readable and comprehensible than the Venice text, it became the standard version of the text for the next two hundred years.[42]

---

39. Not only imagination! Certain literary forms in *Tanna dĕḇe Eliyyahu* may have congeners in texts of the late second or early third century, as Professor Jonas Greenfield of the Hebrew University points out. He cites the periodic style, the use of a succession of adjectives in describing God, as traits which mark both *Tanna dĕḇe Eliyyahu* and Heḵaloṯ hymnology. See Gershom G. Scholem, *Gnosticism, Mysticism, and Talmudic Tradition* (New York, 5720/1960), pp. 24, 42; and Johann Meier, "Serienbildung und 'Numinoser' Eindrukseffekt in den Poetischen Stücken der Hakhalot-Literatur," *Semitics* (University of South Africa), *3* (1973), 36–66.

40. The work first appeared in 1900 in Vienna as a supplement to the seventh *Jahresbericht der Israelitisch-theologischen Lehranstalt,* and was reviewed by J. Theodor in *MGWJ, 44* (1900), 380–84; upon its republication in 1902–4, J. Theodor reviewed it again in *MGWJ, 47* (1903), 70–79.

41. See below, p. 35.

42. Among the reprints of Haida's text (without the Venice edition text) were the following: Zolkiew, 1796, 1798, 1805, 1808; Minkowce, 1798; Lemberg (Lwow), 1799, 1826, 1850, 1859, 1862, 1865, 1867; Hrubieszów, 1817; Polonnoye, 1818; Sudzilkow (Sudilkov), 1833; Ostrog, 1838; Józefow, 1838, 1852; Warsaw, 1857, 1874, 1876, 1880; Königsberg (?), 1863—all with commentary by Jacob ben Naphtali Hirz of Brody, who was assisted by Shalom ben Jacob.

Sudzilkow, 1834; Lemberg, 1864, 1869; Warsaw, 1873; Jerusalem, 1972—all with

During this time, Haida's version was reprinted without the Venice text and without his commentary, so that it bred new commentaries based largely on his text alone. Not until 1880 did a printer in Warsaw reprint both the Venice text and Haida's text in parallel columns. In the same year an abridged Yiddish translation was published by Judah Reuben Tsinkes in Wilno.

That the idea of the supernatural source of *Tanna dĕḇe Eliyyahu* has persisted for centuries and has evoked such complete belief in those who have been engaged most deeply with the work attests, if nothing else, to its extraordinary power. This power owes as much to the literary quality of the work as it does to the ideas it expresses.[43]

---

commentaries by Abraham Schick *(Mĕ'ore 'eš)* and, except for the first, by Jacob ben Naphtali Hirz.

Ostrog, 1838; Wilno, 1839, with two commentaries by Isaac Landau *(Ma'aneh Eliyyahu* and *Śiaḥ Yiṣḥak)*.

Wilno, 1880, 1900; Warsaw, 1883; Jerusalem, 1956, with abridged translation into Yiddish, published by Judah Reuben Tsinkes and his son Abba Saul (?). The first two have commentary by Jacob ben Naphtali Hirz.

Przemysl, 1887, with commentary by Joshua Alexander *(Yĕšu'oṯ Yiśra'el)*.

Jerusalem, 1900, 1906, with commentaries by 'Aḳiḇa Joseph ben Jehiel *(Tosafoṯ ben Jehiel)* and Jacob ben Naphtali Hirz.

Lublin, 1896, 1907, 1927; Jerusalem, 1960, 1967, with commentaries by Ḥayyim Isaiah hak-Kohen *(Ṭuḇe ḥayyim)* and Jacob ben Naphtali Hirz.

Vienna, 1902–04 (facsimile, Jerusalem, 1960, 1967, 1969), ed. Meir Friedmann, with commentary entitled *Me'ir 'ayin.*

Warsaw, 1912, with commentaries by Aaron Śimḥah of Gumbin *(Rimze 'eš)* and Jacob ben Naphtali Hirz.

Jerusalem, 1959, with commentaries by Jacob Meir Schechter *(Mišpaṭ u-ṣĕḏaḳah)* and Jacob ben Naphtali Hirz.

Anastatic reprint of Warsaw, 1874 edition, with commentary by Jacob ben Naphtali Hirz, Bergen-Belsen (1945 or shortly thereafter).

The Haida and Venice texts reprinted in parallel columns, with Haida's commentary *(Sifra' zikḳukin dĕ-nura u-bi'urin dĕ-'ešša)*, Warsaw, 1880; Lublin, 1924; Jerusalem, 1970.

Luaḥ 'erez, a widely ranging commentary which cites only the passages commented upon, by Abraham Palache (Falaggi, 1788–1869), Smyrna, 1881.

Warsaw, 1908; Jerusalem 1966 (facsimile), with *Ramaṯayim ṣofim,* a Hasidic commentary by Samuel Shinwa, drawn from the teachings of the Hasidic Rabbis of Lublin, Przysucha, Kotzk, and Gora Kalwaria. The "commentary" does not expound the text, but merely uses it for homiletic purposes on sundry themes.

At the end of every Sabbath in the year, Hungarian and Galician Hasidim read designated portions of *Tanna dĕḇe Eliyyahu* divided to correspond to the weekly pericope. The title pages of several editions of the work (Polonnoye, 1818; Brooklyn, post–World War II; and the Yiddish translation) encourage this practice, particularly during the month of Elul. Such reading, it is affirmed, will give success in study of Torah, health of body, prosperity in enterprise, and for the soul a "garment" in the world-to-come.

43. Section I of the Introduction was presented on 18 June 1978 at the Hebrew Union College-Jewish Institute of Religion, Jerusalem, as part of the Adam and Gideon Weiler Memorial Lecture.

II. Doctrines

The reader will quickly recognize in *Tanna dĕḇe Eliyyahu* the basic doctrines of Judaism: God is one, the Creator and Preserver of the world, whose word, the Torah, is intended to serve as the guide of Israel's conduct along the way to their redemption by the Messiah and their eternal residence with God in the time-to-come. Redemption is to be the reward of the righteous for their performance of good deeds in obedience to Torah's precepts and commandments by which, in the unending conflict within man's divided nature, the Inclination to good triumphs over the Inclination to evil. Though God's justice is strict—"as a man measures, so it is measured out to him"—His chastisement of the transgressor is a chastisement of love meant to bring him to repentance. In His mercy, He is ever ready to forgive and receive the penitent and welcome him among the righteous who "abide in the house of the Lord for ever."[43a]

So tightly are these doctrines interwoven in his work that Elijah can scarcely speak of God without involving Torah and Israel in his discourse; he cannot speak of God apart from His people Israel; he cannot speak of Israel apart from the conduct enjoined upon them by Torah; he cannot speak of Torah apart from its author, the Holy One. The shuttle of his thought weaves these three major threads of Elijah's discourse into a tight and iridescent fabric whose colors are ever changing but whose stuff is always the same.

In his handling of these doctrines, however, Elijah is inclined to linger on certain matters whose significance in the life of Israel makes a particular appeal to him. His emphasis on these matters—among other things, the dramatic presentation of his ideas and their suffusion by his radiant spirit—serves to set off *Tanna dĕḇe Eliyyahu* from all other Midrashim.

Consider, for example, his emphasis on the universal rule of the Holy One. As His rule is universal, so the rules of Torah have universal application: it sheds its light, Elijah declares, from one end of the world to the other (ER, 17). God had first intended to give the Torah to all the nations of the earth (EZ, 191), but when He offered it to them, they refused to accept it. Indeed, after Adam's fall, He had revealed to mankind the Torah's teaching (the so-called Noahide commandments) that the way of right conduct is to refrain from idolatry, blasphemy, bloodshed, unchastity, and robbery, and to institute civil courts for the maintenance of justice and order in the world. God's presence would

---

43a. More eloquently and emphatically than any other rabbinic text, *Tanna dĕḇe Eliyyahu* endeavors to demonstrate God's forbearance and mercy. See particularly ER, 3–6, 8–9, and 15.

then have rested among the nations: "I call heaven and earth to witness," says Elijah, "that whether it be a heathen or a Jew . . . the holy spirit will suffuse each of them in keeping with the deeds he or she performs" (ER, 48). Even when God gave the Torah to Israel at Sinai, He meant it to be a book open to all the peoples of the world. Elijah quotes the words of the prophet through whom God declares, *I have not given it in secret* (Isa. 45:19) (ER, 11).

Nor did God turn away from the nations after they rejected Him. If they would not accept His teaching, He saw to it that seven Prophets rose among them to admonish them; these were Shem, Eliphaz, Zophar, Bildad, Elihu, Job, and Balaam (ER, 35, 142). Only when Balaam, the greatest of these, disgraced himself (ER, 142; EZ, 191) did God allow prophecy to cease among the nations. Even then God did not forsake them, for among the heathen there were those who became converts to Judaism and thus represented the word of God among their countrymen. On this account, Elijah tells us, when a heathen comes to be converted, a hand of welcome is held out to him to draw him under the wings of the Presence (ER, 35).[44] Should the motives of a convert prove unworthy and he be about to revert to his former practices, Israel must strive to keep him. Even as he was drawn to you, says Elijah, so you are to draw him to you, for God declares, *Love ye . . . the convert* (Deut. 10:19) (ER, 146).

In further emphasis of his conviction that all men are children of God,[45] Elijah points out that heathen are permitted to bring offerings to Him in the Temple, and should they fail to provide money for the libations required with the offerings, the libations are to be paid for out of Israel's public funds (ER, 34).

As for the conduct of Jews toward Gentiles, Elijah reminds Jews that the precepts of Torah are to be observed not only by Jews dealing with Jews, but by Jews dealing with all men. "A man should keep away from dishonesty in dealing with Jew or Gentile" (ER, 140), he says, and declares further that a man's neighbor, whoever he may be, is to be treated like a man's own kin and that his kin are to be treated like his neighbor (ER, 75).

By the same token God shows His appreciation of any act of goodwill performed by Gentiles in Israel's behalf. Thus, because the Canaanites Sheshai and Talmai showed kindness to the Israelites who had been sent from the wilderness to spy out their land, God spared many other Canaanites whom He had otherwise doomed (ER, 145). Furthermore, those Gentiles who allow Jews dwelling among them to renew their

---

44. In sharp contrast to the opinion which asserts: "Evil upon evil comes upon those who receive proselytes" (B.Yeḇ 109b).

45. Even in their present state, Elijah declares, "the greatness of [God's] name is noted among the nations speaking the seventy languages of the world" (ER, 34).

devotion to Torah, God treats as He does the firstborn of Israel (ER, 93).

Finally, Elijah assures us, in regard to God's sovereignty over all mankind, that Israel's exemplary devotion to Torah will someday bring the nations to study and understanding of its precepts and so to love of God (ER, 37). At that time the nations will pay homage to Israel and with them will make pilgrimage to Jerusalem in acknowledgment of His universal rule (ER, 81).

God holds both Jew and Gentile equally responsible for obedience to His precepts and judges all mankind impartially. Because it was the people of Israel, however, who alone accepted Him as their King and the Torah as their guide, He promised them a land of their own, promised them redemption by the Messiah, promised them resurrection and residence with Him in eternal life. But these rewards are to be earned, for God holds Israel responsible for their transgressions and hence punishes them according to the measure of justice—punishes them both as individuals and as a people. He afflicts the transgressor not only in this world; sometimes He condemns him to Gehenna, and sometimes, most severe punishment of all, denies the unrepentant sinner life in the world-to-come. In His punishment of Israel as a people He has them enslaved, banished, exiled, tortured, slaughtered by the nations whom He uses as His instruments.

This view of God as a God of justice is familiar enough, and Elijah is set upon not only asserting it, but also meeting the skeptic's questioning of it, and so he considers special cases of individuals who at first glance seem not to deserve God's affliction of them. Among these are the poverty-stricken; the infants who, fresh out of the womb, come crippled into the world; and the righteous whom adversity befalls. The degree of poverty a man suffers, says Elijah, is the consequence of his wickedness; he brings his poverty not only upon himself but upon succeeding generations of his family (ER, 120; EZ, 181). As to the person afflicted from birth by blindness, deafness, or the like, Elijah is consistent in viewing him as a transgressor, arguing that had God not disabled him, he would have been guilty of even more heinous crimes than those his Inclination to evil leads him to commit. One of the longest and most dramatic stories in *Tanna dĕḇe Eliyyahu* is given over to proof of God's exercise of foresighted judgment in this special case (S, 41). And as in His affliction of the seemingly innocent, so is God's justice at work in His affliction of the righteous who "through poverty . . . come to fear the Lord. . . . For they who act out of love come to it only through poverty; they who bestow many kinds of charity come to it only through poverty. And they who fear Heaven come to it only through poverty" (EZ, 181).

Transgressors are punished not only in their lifetime; for some of them God has set aside Gehenna as a place of punishment after they have perished out of this world. According to legend, immediately after He composed the Torah (ER, 160), He created Gehenna as a warning to mankind that disregard of Torah's commandments would bring down His punishment. He did not light the fire of Gehenna, however, until after Adam had sinned (ER, 3), and even then intended its fire not to punish men but only to make them fearful of the consequences of sin (ER, 6). Gehenna keeps seething, nevertheless, until transgressors are consigned to it; to punish them, it alternates between heat and cold. Elijah specifies some of those who are sent down to Gehenna: men who honor unworthy teachers (S, 5), men who are flippant (ER, 61), slanderers (ER, 108), idol worshipers (S, 35), and the wicked among the nations (EZ, 192).

Yet Gehenna is not a place coeval with heaven. It is not a place of eternal punishment. The only ones to be destroyed in it are the people of the nations that have always been set upon the destruction of Israel (EZ, 192). As for Gehenna's other denizens, release and redemption are open to them.[46] The prayer of a child uttering praise of God can intercede for a transgressor and free him (S, 23). At the close of the Day of Judgment, even Gehenna's most hardened sinners who can hear the discourses and prayers in the Garden of Eden and say "Amen" to them will be allowed to enter the Garden and sing in God's presence (S, 33).

What mankind comes to, then, Elijah would have us know, is God's mercy by way of His justice. He does not rejoice in the suffering of the transgressor. On the contrary, He weeps for the man whom the measure of justice compels Him to punish (ER, 87). To Him chastisement is not an end in itself, an exact balancing of suffering against sinning; to Him, chastisement is an act of love (EZ, 191) meant for Israel's good (ER, 96). It is intended to make them repent their sins and bring them to righteousness and the performance of good deeds, so that God will welcome them to eternal life.

If a man dies unrepentant, however, he is to be wept for (ER, 18) because on the Day of Judgment God will banish him from Israel; he will never be allowed to return and will have lost for ever his chance to win eternal life. But even if, with his last breath, the transgressor repents, God's hands are spread out to receive him (S, 37) and to make him an inheritor of the world-to-come (ER, 117). Hence, says Elijah, repentance is greater than prayer and greater than charity (S, 37)—it is the healer of Israel's iniquities. For God, therefore, the Day of Atonement is a day He rejoices in, for it brings the sinner to Him in repentance (ER, 4).

---

46. Unlike St. Augustine, who says that the bodies of the wicked will be given over to everlasting suffering.

Having reconciled God's justice with God's mercy, Elijah pushes his faith in God's love of man to its ultimate conclusion: there ought to be joy in the world, he asserts, because whatever exists in it, no matter how frightening, how hostile, how disgusting it may appear, attests His love (ER, 81). When a disciple asked, "My master, why do you rejoice because of the angel of death?" Elijah answered, "My son, but for [our fear of] the angel of death, what might we not be making our Father in heaven [do to us]?" *(ibid.)*. "[Upon] the first ten generations of mankind . . . God lavished such kindness as to give them a happy foretaste of the world-to-come. [However, when the generations no longer lived in fear of death, they came to the wickedness that] nearly brought about the destruction of the world [by the flood]" (ER, 81).

Elijah's disciple next asked him why he rejoiced in the existence of the Inclination to evil. Elijah replied that if it did not exist, Israel would not have the opportunity of proving themselves capable of overcoming wicked inclinations and thus leading lives of righteousness. Furthermore, by their conquest of the Inclination to evil, Israel will win the homage of the nations of the world and will bring them to acknowledge God as their sovereign. Indeed, Israel will then be the nations' offering to God, as is said, *And they shall bring all your brethren out of all the nations for an offering unto the Lord* (Isa. 66:20) (ER, 81).

To the disciple's question as to how there can be any joy with regard to the necessity of sitting in the privy, Elijah has two answers. One is that the call of nature reminds Israel that God will eventually redeem them from where they now sit as in a privy amidst the idolatry of the nations and will bring Israel the days of the Messiah and the world-to-come. The other answer is that the call of nature serves to remind men that in this regard they are no better than animals and thus to teach them humility and obedience to the precepts of Him who made them more than animals *(ibid.)*.

When we keep in mind, concludes Elijah, that even these three hard facts of life in this world serve God's good purposes and bring us joy, we are also to remember that having served their purpose in this world, they will not exist in the world-to-come (ER, 7).

As Israel puts its faith in God, so God puts His faith in Israel. He made Israel—indeed, all mankind—able to prove itself worthy of having been given life in this world and in the world-to-come. In the endless conflict within man between the Impulse to good and the Impulse to evil, God would have the good triumph. To this end, He offered all mankind the Divine support of Torah, but it was Israel alone who accepted it and has suffered anguish for its sake (EZ, 173). Were it not for Israel, there would be no Torah in the world (ER, 112), and without Torah neither earth nor heaven would endure (ER, 105).

As Israel has preserved Torah, so Torah, like bread and water, like milk and wine (EZ, 195), has preserved and nourished Israel. Of all Israel's occupations, only their unremitting study of Torah gives God contentment (ER, 4). Hence a man is to put himself to the work of understanding it as an ox puts itself to the yoke (ER, 8). His labor will bring him blessing in this world (*ibid.;* S, 24) and life in the world-to-come (S, 24).

In study of Torah man abides with God (ER, 137); study of Torah relieves him of preoccupation with trivial things (S, 2, 15); study of Torah conquers man's Impulse to evil (EZ, 167); study of Torah gives a man true freedom (S, 17); study of Torah is like immersion in a pool of purifying water (ER, 105); study of Torah can even give a man supernatural powers—can enable him to shake the firmament and bring down rain (ER, 92).

Since the study of Torah is man's supreme occupation—Elijah ranks it above priesthood and royalty (S, 18)—he should come to it with trepidation and awe, and as he labors in it he will become more and more fearful of falling into iniquity (ER, 37). On the other hand, intermittent study of Torah leads to rapid forgetting and confusion of mind, and entire neglect of study brings Divine censure (S, 17) and makes God wish to destroy the world (ER, 11). It was Israel's neglect of study of God's word that made the wicked kingdoms prosper (ER, 95) and all but brought about Israel's destruction (ER, 96).

In Elijah's emphasis on study of Torah, one hears the urgent voice of a teacher. Like a schoolmaster, he points again and again to the importance of study, the steady pursuit of understanding the Torah's doctrines. These lend support to man's Inclination to good and to his performance of good deeds; they enlist him in the fellowship of the righteous.

His righteousness brings him no small rewards. Though he may be afflicted with adversity and be punished for trivial offenses (ER, 11), and though he may know discord in the earlier years of his life, he can expect serenity in his later years (EZ, 191). Joy will be his in this world (ER, 26). He will be granted a share of God's power (ER, 8), and no enemy will be able to prevail against him (ER, 94). Dwelling in humility and in love of God brings the reward of resurrection from the dust of the earth and the dust of the dead (ER, 22; S, 31). Entering into eternal life, he will be welcomed by God Himself (ER, 11) and will have come to the end of his journey in space and time.

We are on the way, Elijah points out in his overview of history (ER, 160), from time to eternity, to a future existence which he refers to as "the world-to-come" or as "the time-to-come." He is definite about the periods of history in Israel's mortal life, even tells us that the Messiah will appear during the fifth era of the creation (ER, 160) and will reign for two thousand years[47] (ER, 6). His coming will be preceded by a seven-year period of afflictions, and he will appear in a generation whose leaders will be dog-faced brutes (S, 11). At some time during the Messiah's reign all those who rise from the dust to life again will assemble in the Land of Israel and will never again return to the dust (ER, 164). Israel will rejoice in a double portion of Torah in those days (EZ, 196). The nations will bestow riches upon Israel, and those nations that never afflicted her will serve as her farmers and vintagers (ER, 121).

One cannot be precise about Elijah's idea of the days of the Messiah. On the one hand, he tells us that Israel's dead, wherever they are buried, will be raised and will return to the Holy Land, where they will never go back to the dust (ER, 164). But, we may ask, if they are resurrected and their mortal life and death are ended, what need would they have of the riches and services of the nations? Or, likewise, what need would they have of eating or drinking (ER, 26)?

It is also difficult to distinguish the reign of the Messiah from the state of being that Elijah refers to as "the time-to-come" or "the world-to-come." If "the time-to-come" refers to eternity and "the world-to-come" to heaven, and if both together suggest man's eternal life with God, then the two-thousand-year reign of the Messiah followed by the seventh millennium[48] is to be the prelude to man's admission to this life.

Though Elijah ventures few details about the kind of life man will lead in the world-to-come, he is specific about who will be admitted to it and who will not. No uncircumcised person will be admitted (ER, 121); neither will the unrepentant sinner (EZ, 194). The righteous, on the other hand, will be welcomed by God (ER, 26) to His house, where the Inclination to evil will not exist (ER, 81) and death will be no more (ER, 7). In His house men who were possessed of good deeds but were unlettered in Torah will minister to the righteous (EZ, 194) who, possessed of both Torah and good deeds (ER, 20), will have heavenly radiance shining from their faces *(ibid.)*.

---

47. "The world as we know it was intended to exist for two thousand years in desolation [without Torah], two thousand years with Torah, and two thousand years of the Messiah's reign," followed by the seventh millenium, during which there is to be neither death, nor sin, nor iniquity (ER, 6–7). The scheme of six thousand years which is quoted in the Talmud (B.Sanh 97a; AZ 9a) is also found in the writings of St. Augustine (354–430) (see Friedrich Ueberweg, *A History of Philosophy* [London, 1972], *1,* 345–46), and became so well known that it may even have influenced James Ussher (1581–1656), the Anglican archbishop whose chronology was placed in the margin of many reference editions of the Authorized Version (see Saul Leeman, "Was Bishop Ussher's Chronology Influenced by a Midrash?" *Semeia, 8* [1977], 127–29).

48. See n. 47.

One other striking detail of Elijah's account of the time-to-come is notable: in acknowledgment of God's universal kingship, during Sukkot the nations will go up as pilgrims to Jerusalem, taking Israel with them (ER, 81). This detail seems to suggest that the world-to-come may not be a heaven distinct from man's world, but rather man's world transformed by the presence of God in it, the Garden of Eden once again where man will be forever happy, forever free of the weight of his mortality.

Wherever and whenever the Garden exists, Elijah has no doubt that it does exist. It exists for him because God exists for him. It is God's world whether in this time or in the time-to-come, and it is therefore a spiritual world, a moral world. If man lives in the way God asks of him, his reward is redemption from the evil within him and from affliction without; his reward is resurrection from the dust of his mortality; his reward is the joy of dwelling in the house of the Lord forever.

III. The Midrash as Literature

A summary of the doctrines of *Tanna dĕḇe Eliyyahu* gives no more than the bare bones of the work. Even to the reader who has no more than a casual acquaintance with Jewish religious thought, most of its leading ideas are familiar: the uniqueness and sovereignty of God; Israel as His chosen people; His gift of Torah as the guide of their conduct and hence their prime object of study; His chastisement of them for their surrender to the evil Impulse; the mercy He shows them when they repent; His promise of a Messiah to redeem them and His assurance of eternal life with Him in the world-to-come.

What animates and gives life to these concepts is the artistry with which they are fleshed out. Not the least of the attractions of the work is Elijah's own presence in it. Although he speaks but rarely in the first person, his presence is a radiant one that shines from all its pages. His love of God reveals itself in the prayers and blessings that burst from him in the very midst of his precise exegesis of some matter of Torah, and his yearning for God's redemption of Israel leads him again and again to plead with them to follow the path of righteousness.

But what we know of him—this Elijah, whoever he was—we know, for the most part, only by inference. He is not concerned with telling us about himself; he is no St. Augustine or Jean Jacques Rousseau making public confession of his inner turmoil and his struggle to find peace of mind. Such peace our Elijah has already found. His faith is firm and certain, and the meaning and purpose of life are clear to him. If he tells us very little about himself, it is because his focus is not on himself but on the One beyond him. Because his perspective is true, his is a true humility. He sees himself, sees the people of Israel, sees all men only in relation to the One who created them, who gave them life in this world and has promised them residence with Him in the world-to-come.

He tells us that he came from a place called Jabneh (ER, 95; EZ, 168), near Jerusalem; that he wandered from place to place in Babylonia and Israel, and perhaps other eastern lands; that in his wanderings he taught unlettered Jews how to pray and gave them instruction in Torah. In short, he was a wandering preacher and teacher who took upon himself the sacred duty of teaching the word of God. His adventures in his wanderings are not the adventures of the hero whose great strength enables him to overcome every physical obstacle in his way—mountain, river, wild beast, or outlaw. Elijah's adventures are adventures of the mind and spirit, tests of faith. He meets and is challenged by the questions and doubts of the ignorant, the half-educated, the skeptic, the near-heretic, the Parsee priest, the Roman official, even the Sages of the academy in Jerusalem, and he disposes of their questions with learning and logic—disposes of them without condescension, patiently and politely.

In these debates we are aware of the literary skill, conscious or not, that gives life to this work. The debates are not merely summarized for us: they are reported directly in the words of the speakers and have the dramatic force of living voices. Some chapters are given over almost entirely to these debates. In Chapter (14) 15, for example, we find the following discourse: "Once," says Elijah, "while I was traveling from one place to another, I came upon a man who had learning in Scripture but not in Mishnah. The man said, 'My master, there is a certain thing I want to say to you, but I am afraid to say it because you may be angry with me.' I replied, 'If you ask me something pertaining to words of Torah, why should I be angry with you?' Whereupon the man said . . . ," and the reader is thereupon launched on the lengthy debate that follows (ER, 70).

The dramatic sense that reveals itself in the dialogues and debates, however, is little in comparison with its far richer development in the varieties of narrative that give vitality and force to the moral and religious ideas in the work. Consider first the drama inherent in the *Tanna:* it begins with God's departure from earth after the fall of man out of the Garden of Eden and ends with man's return to the earthly paradise in the time-to-come; it begins with man's separation from God and ends with his reunion with Him; it begins in time and ends in eternity. Between these two poles of man's existence lies the way, the way man is to travel from the depths to the heights.

The intention of *Tanna dĕbe Eliyyahu* is to point the way for man, to show him how he must conduct himself in order to reach his destination. It is a struggle all the way, for what he must contend with is not only the enemy whom he encounters from without but also the enemy within whom he must overcome. In the conflict between the two sides of his nature, the good against the evil, he has the help of a just and merciful God whose Torah is his guidebook.

So *Tanna děḇe Eliyyahu* is dramatic in a way that a piece of fiction or a play is dramatic: it presents us with a plot, the essence of which is a conflict that rises to a climax and comes to a conclusion. However, here the drama does not develop in a straight line as it usually does in a novel or play, for the work's intention, as we already have reason to understand, is didactic. We are given the drama not for its own sake, as a vicarious experience, entertaining and thrilling, but rather for what it teaches.

Like any good teacher, Elijah makes use of any literary device that will move his audience to accept his teaching. In considering his artistry, we must remember that he was a religious teacher, very likely a man who had disciples and just as likely also considered Israel at large as his pupils, laymen who knew less than he, understood less than he, and needed his instruction to help them along the way of deliverance from bondage and exile to freedom and home. So the teaching devices he uses are all common and familiar ones—homilies or sermons, for example, making their appeal to reason or to common sense. But their intention is also to simplify moral problems and make them understandable to the layman. As might be expected, Scripture as the source of morality is called to aid, and its stories, prophecies, poems, and precepts are summoned in support of the teacher's analysis of abstract moral and religious concepts. As an example, consider a brief passage from "Eliyyahu Rabbah" (ER, 3):

> In His wisdom and with His understanding God created His world and set it on its foundation. He then created Adam and had him lie prone before Him. As He scrutinized him till the end of all the generations that would come from him, He foresaw that his descendants would provoke His wrath. Hence He said: If I hold mankind to account for its successive misdeeds, the world will not endure; I must therefore have its successive misdeeds pass out of mind. And He had them do so. As for the proof, you can readily see it for yourself. When Israel were in the wilderness, they befouled themselves with their misdeeds. Thereupon He proceeded to have all that they had done pass out of mind, as is said, *The Lord passed before him* (Exod. 34:6). Do not read *passed* but "had pass"—that is, He had all their evil pass away from before Him, so that He was able to proclaim Himself *Lord, Lord* [*of mercy*] *(ibid.).*
>
> Men are likewise to have pass from their minds . . . the offenses of others.

That this is a sermon there is little doubt. But it should be noted that Elijah's sense of the dramatic turns its moral theme into dramatic narrative, even discovers God's thinking to us, and thus makes a lively appeal to imagination as well as to reason.

Even more common than the narrative element in the passage above is the parable, the sort of story that makes its moral or religious point in terms of everyday people and their actions. Sometimes the point of the parable is given in advance so that the story serves as down-to-earth illustration, an acting-out of the point. At other times the parable is given first, with its point held off to the end. In any event, the teacher takes no chance that his audience will miss the point. Most often in *Tanna dĕḇe Eliyyahu* the parable serves to dramatize and explain God's actions by analogy with the actions of a mortal king. In this way God is brought down to earth, so to speak, and the awesome, remote Being is made understandable in terms of mortal speech and action. Indeed the opening sentence of many a parable seems to be a familiar folktale formula: "Once there was a king who lived in a city far across the sea"—a formula that suggests not only the sovereignty of Israel's King, but also the mystery of His power, remote and awesome.

Sometimes the parable is no more than a simple analogy, an idea presented in the briefest narrative. For example, a homily on the beauty of creation points out that the beauty of the stars comes as much from the way they are arranged in the heavens as from the stuff they are made of, and then continues with "the parable of a king who had a solid ingot of gold. If he had put the solid ingot as an ornament on his head, would it have become him? His wisdom and understanding made him think otherwise. So he took a half-*sela*'s weight of gold from the ingot and had it made into a linked chain which he hung around his neck. Such transformation is the way of beauty. Even so did the Holy One, may His great name be blessed for ever and ever and ever, arrange the stars in the sky, giving to each its proper place and thus creating their beauty" (ER, 9).

The parable is often far more elaborate than the one just quoted. It may involve great detail, extended action, and realistic dialogue, as in this example:

By what parable may the relationship between Israel and their Father in heaven be understood? By the parable of a mortal king one of whose servants ran away from him time and again. But the king kept searching for him through land after land until the servant fell into his hand and was brought back into his presence. When the servant was thus taken and brought into the king's presence, the king took him by the hand, brought him into his palace, showed him silver and gold, precious stones and pearls, and the other valuables he had in his palace. Later he took him outdoors and showed him the gardens and orchards and all the other good things he had growing in his fields. Then he showed him his sons, both the older and the younger ones, and his other servants, both the older and younger ones. After the king had shown the runaway servant everything, he said to him: "Do you see now that I have no need of you for anything? Nevertheless, come and do my work alongside my sons and my servants, both the older and the younger ones. Accord me honor and show me respect the way other men accord me honor and show me respect."

[Like the runaway servant, Israel keep leaving their King, but He seeks them out nevertheless and brings them back into His presence even though He has no need of them.] He expects from them only the honor due Him, honor equal to that due a father and a mother, as is said, *A son honoreth his father, and a servant his master. If then I be a father, where is the honor due Me, and if I be a master, where is the respect due Me?* (Mal. 1:6) [ER, 136].

Elijah's lively imagination and his natural skill as a storyteller carry him beyond the composition of parables. As one might expect from a person so steeped in Scripture, he makes use not only of verses from Scripture but its stories as well. He does not merely cite these in support of the idea he is enforcing, but often expands them with realistic dialogue, such as the dialogue between God and Moses on the occasion of Israel's worship of the golden calf and God's consequent anger (ER, 17–18). The dialogue serves to show God's merciful restraint after hearing Moses' plea in Israel's behalf, and His willingness to be reconciled with Israel despite the enormity of their sin. It is typical of Elijah to stress in this dialogue, as he does again and again throughout the work, God's love and compassion for Israel and His willingness to forgive the repentant sinner.

Similar elaboration of scriptural narrative is to be found throughout the work in its stories of Abraham and the king of Sodom (ER, 128), Deborah and Barak (ER, 48–49), Mordecai and Esther (ER, 3–4), and in a number of others as well.

Elijah is not content to stop with stories expanded from Scripture. He draws also on the rich and exciting legends associated with Scriptural characters and Scriptural events. In some instances, as in the legend of Abraham and the idols, there seems to be little basis in Scripture for the legends. Nevertheless, they have such vitality, display such fantasy, and are so richly ornamented with detail and occasional touches of humor that we can readily understand Elijah's inclusion of them. Notable among them for its sharp characterization and its brisk, realistic dialogue is the story of Abraham as a seller of idols and his ironic treatment of those, including king Nimrod himself, who put their faith in idols. Again Elijah turns the story to moral account: God protects men like Abraham, who was willing to die at Nimrod's hands rather than bow down to his idols (ER, 27–28; S, 47–49).

Along with elaboration of Scriptural narrative and legend go stories from Jewish postbiblical history, stories of Jewish heroism and of Jewish martyrdom. Sometimes these stories are no more than realistic anecdotes, poignant and pointed, as is the "story of a maiden whose father was very friendly with a heathen. As they ate and drank and made merry, the heathen said to the maiden's father: 'Give your daughter to my son for a wife.' Though the father consented, he said nothing to her of the matter until the time of her wedding came. When the time came, and she was told, she went up to the roof, jumped off, and died. A Divine voice was heard saying: Because of such as she, Scripture says,

Who can reckon the purity of the couchings of Israel? (Num. 23:10)" (ER, 116).

Elijah goes beyond such terse anecdotes and occasionally gives us an extended, carefully worked-out short story complete with several characters, a lively plot, and circumstantial details, a story that dramatically projects a difficult moral problem and its solution. Such is the story given in reply to the skeptic's question concerning God's justice: Why does God bring into the world infants who are born deaf or mute or lame or blind, suffering affliction even before they are capable of sin?

The story is of a man born blind, a man who turns out in the course of the plot to be a thief, a liar, and a lecher. The story has its moral, of course: God knows what He is doing even when He afflicts those who appear to be innocent of wrongdoing (S, 41–42).

In addition to the varieties of story we have already noted, Elijah's dramatizing imagination, ranging from the time before creation to the time of the Messiah and of the world-to-come, ventures into prophetic narrative: "At some time in the days of the Messiah . . . all those who rise to life again will go to the Land of Israel and never again return to the dust. . . . [In the Land, the Holy One Himself will receive the righteous who will come into His presence] like children coming into the presence of their father . . . and like disciples coming into the presence of their teacher" (ER, 164–65).

Another way, an expository rather than a dramatic way, by which Elijah seeks to engage the reader is exegesis, interpretation of the meaning of words, verses, and passages from Scripture. Such dependence on Scripture for their existence is the very essence of Midrashim. Because commentaries of this kind have only a contingent existence, some scholars do not consider them as belonging to even a subordinate order of literature, and regard them merely as adjuncts, classifying them with dictionaries, encyclopedias, thesauri, and similar works. Some Midrashim can be described as miscellanies or anthologies made up of separate discourses on a variety of moral and religious topics. Others are made up of sermons or homilies on special subjects: *Pĕsiḳta dĕ-Rab̲ Kahăna,* for example, is a compilation dealing with Israel's festive days and special Sabbaths. While each chapter or discourse in such works centers on a particular topic, the work as a whole does not pursue a single theme and therefore lacks the unity of structure and sharpness of focus that give a literary work much of its effectiveness.

Among the Midrashim, *Tanna dĕb̲e Eliyyahu* shines with a far brighter luster than any other. In the eyes of many students and scholars it is unique, a masterpiece.[49] Not that its subject matter is notably

---

49. Meir Friedmann spoke of it as "the jewel of Haggadic literature" (*Seder Eliahu rabba und Seder Eliahu zuṭa* [Vienna, 1900], Foreword, p. v.

In a letter Leon Nemoy writes that the author of *Tanna dĕb̲e Eliyyahu* was "blessed by the Muse of poetry more than any other midrashic author that I have read. Who

different—not at all, for in this respect it is largely traditional. What has made it so highly regarded over the centuries and what still gives it its power to move the contemporary reader is its dramatic unity, its singleness of purpose, its variety of expression—in short, its quality as a work of art. Its intention to show mankind in general and Israel in particular the way to eternal life controls and focuses its traditional ideas and its traditional modes of expression, and the same intention governs the interpretation of the language of Scripture. For Elijah the exegesis is useful only when it serves his purpose in the work as a whole.

The exegetical norms[50] he follows are traditional, but Elijah seems not inclined to use them all. With his audience—the common run of Israel—in mind, he is more prone to use the simpler norms and these far more sparingly then do most other composers of Midrash. Aware that understanding of the word of God leads to acceptance of the word of God, wherever it is necessary to clarify meaning for his audience he does so with ingenuity and precision. The reason is simple: the language of the Torah is God's language, and like Him it is infinite, limitless. No man can ever exhaust its meaning no matter how deeply he probes it. Indeed, in the time-to-come, Elijah tells us, God Himself will sit down with the righteous and they together will probe the depths of Scripture and Mishnah to make revelation reveal itself (ER, 14; S, 32–33).

Since every word, every phrase, every verse of Scripture is open to interpretation, the surface meaning of a word, phrase, or verse may be only one of other meanings that lie beneath it. Hebrew is a language that lends itself easily to the discovery of such multiple meanings because as written its words are composed only of consonants. In a Hebrew text in which the vowel sounds are not indicated, the reader or speaker comes to know them because he has been taught them orally. As every Jewish schoolboy knows, however, these vowel sounds, though not represented by letters, can be indicated for the reader by a set of signs—dots and dashes variously combined under or over the consonants—to indicate the standard pronunciation of the word, as in printed editions of Scripture, prayer books, or other Hebrew works. In the absence of a vowel letter or a sign standing for the vowel, the reader of an English word made up of two consonants such as *m* followed by *t* could supply the vowel *a* and read the word as *mat.* Supplying a different vowel sound, one could read *met, meat, meet,* or *moat,* or with a mute *e* added at the end, *mate, mite, mote,* or *mute.* Similarly, a variety of meanings is theoretically possible for every syllable and word of

---

knows, he might have, in a different milieu, written a Hebrew Divine Comedy to rival Dante's."

50. For a discussion of the norms of exegesis see *Pĕsiḳta dĕ-Raḇ Kahăna* (Philadelphia, 1975), pp. xxvii–xlv.

Scripture, so that the Sage or scholar who gives himself over to the study of Torah—as the "ox to the plow" (ER, 8; EZ, 198), so Elijah tells us—discovers levels of meaning that lie below the customary standard reading or pronunciation of the Hebrew syllable or word.

This is not to say that every word of Scripture is examined by the commentator for double or multiple meanings. Generally speaking, his focus is on those words or phrases or verses whose surface meaning is not clear because of what appears to be vagueness, incoherence, obscurity, contradiction, needless repetition, redundancy, or any other such stylistic failures. It is such seeming failure that catches the eye of the exegete. He knows that God's words are perfect as He is perfect. They cannot be otherwise, for if they were truly marred by error, the blasphemous conclusion would be that He Himself was in error. The exegete's responsibility, then, is to explain or clarify what appears to be a defect in the text. Unless it be the error of a scribe or copyist, the commentator takes it for granted that there is no real error, and hence the apparent error can be corrected by a searching examination of the text.

One of the commonest norms of exegesis by which the scholar works his way to the more precise or fuller meaning of Scripture has its English equivalent in the pun, a play on words which exploits the different meanings of two or more words with the same or similar sounds or exploits two or more meanings of the same word. Nowadays in English the pun is used for humorous effect, but in English literature of the sixteenth and seventeenth centuries in particular, it was a serious literary device as it is in the Midrashim. To see the device carried to its extreme, one has only to look at a page of James Joyce's *Finnegans Wake* (1939), where individual words not only suggest multiple meanings, but also are fused from several languages so as to constitute a separate language of their own. This tour de force of rhetoric is sustained throughout the entire work, and contemporary scholars have toiled at unraveling the multiple meanings of its words much as scholars have toiled at unraveling the meanings of the language of Scripture.

The interpreter of Scripture during the centuries long past was just as ingenious in his exploitation of the pun as the twentieth-century novelist. It should be remembered that in the pun the different meanings of the word are not regarded as being in conflict with one another: each meaning simply adds its own level of significance to the other meaning. Consider the following example: In the story of Esther and Mordecai, Mordecai has occasion to become angry at Esther because she has been evasive about going to king Ahasuerus in behalf of Israel. At the same time, he was about to pray to God to forgive Israel for their sins. So, as Scripture tells us, Mordecai *went his way* (Esther 4:17). This simple statement of fact in regard to the situation is not enough for Elijah. He reads *way-yaʿăḇor,* "went his way," with a slight change of vowel as *way-ya'ăḇer,* "caused to pass," and thus takes the verse to mean, "So Mordecai caused his anger at Esther to pass out of mind" (ER, 3–4). What Elijah is pointing out by this reading of the verse is that Mordecai could not in all conscience ask God to forgive Israel unless he could first bring himself to forgive Esther. Throughout *Tanna dĕḇe Eliyyahu* a good number of other such plays on individual words add new levels of meaning to otherwise simple statements of fact.

A more ingenious and more complex play on words results from the transfer of the meaning of a word from one context to another. The exegetes of Torah, having long ago discovered that the meaning of a word is largely defined by its context, do not hesitate to transfer the meaning of a particular word in one context to another context so as to add richer significance to the verse or passage that makes up the word's context. A case in point: In David's question to God, *Who am I, O Lord God, and what is my house that Thou hast brought me hitherto (hălom)?* (2 Sam. 7:18), Elijah loads *hălom* with much greater significance and force than it possesses as an adverb. He finds it used elsewhere in a tight and dramatic context which defines it as signifying "the royal estate" or "the royal presence," when king Saul, speaking imperiously to his chiefs as they were drawing away from him, says, *Draw near hălom*—[i.e., to the royal presence]—*all ye chiefs of the people* (1 Sam. 14:38). With this sense of *hălom* in mind, Elijah takes David to be saying in the verse cited above, *Who am I, O Lord God, and what is my house that Thou hast brought me to royal estate?* (ER, 90).

Occasionally, as in the following instance, the exegesis combines the play on words by a change of vowels with the transfer of meaning from one context to another. The verse *Beside them dwell the fowl of the heaven, from among the branches they sing* (Ps. 104:12) seems to the average eye to be no more than a commonplace observation; but its very obviousness seems to challenge Elijah, for he sets out to show that what the Psalmist had in mind was something far more significant than the fact that birds sit on branches and sing. To this end, the exegesis proceeds dramatically to pick up a verse from the scriptural account of the plague of frogs in Egypt: *the frog came up* (Exod. 8:2). We are told that the puzzling singular of "frog" *(ṣĕfarde'a)* in this context is not meant to indicate that there was only one frog, but rather to point up the striking fact that the frog is the birds' intelligencer. For proof, Elijah takes *ṣĕfarde'a* to be made up of two words, *ṣippor,* "bird," and *de'ah,* "knowledge," thus signifying "conveyor of knowledge to birds," or "birds' intelligencer." When birds sit hesitating to drink from a watering place, the frog calls out to them, "Be not afraid, come and drink." Getting the frogs into the verse from Psalms presents no problem to Elijah: the word *'ăfa'im,* usually translated "branches," can also be taken as a derivative of *ta'ufah,* "darkness," referring to the blackish green coloration of frogs (ER, 48). So the statement *Beside them dwell the fowl of the heaven* is transformed into *The birds of heaven sit above the watering places until from the dark-hued ones* (i.e., the frogs) *comes the call to drink,* and turns out to be a proof of God's love and concern for the lives of all His creatures, great and small.

As Elijah turns a general and abstract concept into the specific and dramatic terms of narrative, so he reverses the process and makes specific and concrete terms stand as symbols of general concepts. For example, in his reading of Jeremiah's statement that God will bring *the blind and the lame* (Jer. 3:7) into the life of the world-to-come, he enlarges the meaning of the phrase to signify Jews who are unlettered in Torah but nevertheless conduct themselves uprightly: they are blind to temptation and do not run after what is forbidden. In another sense, *the blind* is taken to mean the Sages and their disciples who shut their eyes to temptation and devote themselves to study of Torah. In still another reading *the blind and the lame* is taken to refer to men who possess knowledge of Torah but are morally crippled by their indecent behavior (ER, 69–70).

Elijah as exegete seems reluctant to use the more complicated modes of interpretation which are part of the tradition and are common enough in other Midrashim. One senses that he uses such relatively simple modes as have been illustrated above for the same reason that he dramatizes his moral and religious ideas in so many ways: he never forgets that his audience is the generality of Israel and not the specialist, the scholar in the academy. Deliberately he keeps things simple, forceful, dramatic; he wants even the humblest of men, the ignorant, the illiterate, the half-educated, the poverty stricken, to lay hold of the grandeur of God and His precepts, to understand them and live by them. Learned as he is, the scholar in him gives way to the preacher and the teacher.

IV. The Translation

The intention of *Tanna dĕḇe Eliyyahu* and the audience the work is aimed at have together determined the level of English diction in the translation. Elijah's imagery is drawn from the objects and events of everyday life in a largely pastoral society. The Torah is life-giving water (ER, 93); it is a mother's breast at which infants suck (ER, 22); teachers are like cedars that stand on the banks of the life-giving stream of Torah and draw strength from it (ER, 117); the transgressor is like a man whose body is marred by spots of leprosy (ER, 77; EZ, 175); there ought to be joy in the world even because of the necessity of sitting in the privy (ER, 81); a leaf from the tree of life, Torah, opens the mouth of Jews for fluent discourse on it (ER, 93); happy is the man who depends on God for his protection because he is like a man armed with shield and buckler *(ibid.);* disciples of the wise are as happy as the olive tree whose leaves do not fall during either the sunny season or the rainy season (ER, 91); a chaste wife is like a vine that brings forth fruit (ER, 92); as a certain variety of nut has four segments, so each Sage in Israel has four qualities of spirit: wisdom, understanding, knowledge, insight (ER, 93); a man's good deeds are like the budding of the vine and the flowering of the pomegranate *(ibid.);* if a thorn pricks a man in a fleshy part of the body and not in a part where there are blood vessels and bones, he should thank God (ER, 97); even as a spice seller carries with him a hundred kinds of spices, so every Sage in Israel has in his heart a hundred thoughts about Scripture (ER, 106); as water goes into a river and never returns, so a man who has had a quarrel with his fellow should not harbor anger in his heart against him, but should let ill feeling drain out of his heart never to return (ER, 105).

Diction such as this is not the diction of formal theological discourse heavy with abstract terms; on the other hand, it is not the colloquial, often slangy, language of everyday life. Like standard English, it occupies a middle ground between these two extremes: it is simple, rooted as it is in the everyday objects and events of a people's everyday life; it is often lyrical in the imagery by which it weds abstract moral and religious ideas to the daily conduct of Israel; it is, in summary, wholly appropriate to the purpose that animates it and the audience it addresses.

If the reader finds that he is taking in this translation with some ease and even, so the translators hope, with some pleasure, he ought not to be misled into thinking that the translation has sacrificed the literal sense of the Hebrew in order to achieve idiomatic standard English. In emulation of God—if one dare speak thus—who, we are told, selected, scrutinized, and analyzed every word of the Torah before putting it in its place (EZ, 190), so the translators have examined every word of the original again and again for its exact meaning and for each word have labored to find an exact English equivalent. They are well aware that their efforts have not been fully rewarded if only because some flavor, some overtone, of the original is inevitably lost in its conversion into another language. The poet Shelley, speaking of the task of translation, says that it is like casting violets into a crucible: one may thus extract the violets' essence, but one has also killed the violets in the process.[51] How can English "pity" or "compassion" convey the full emotive power of the Hebrew *raḥămanuṯ,* whose literal meaning is "a trembling of the womb," suggesting an inner agitation far stronger than is suggested by either of the English equivalents?

In short, no translation can be an exact equivalent of the original,

---

51. The all but impossible task of the translator is described by R. Judah as follows: "If one translates a verse literally, he is a liar; if he adds thereto, he is a blasphemer and a libeller" (B.Ḳid 49b).

and so all that translators can do is attempt the impossible. Since they always fail, their only consolation must be their success in coming close. This is also to say that translators must show respect not only for the language they are translating from, but also for the language they are translating into. What is good idiom in Hebrew may not have a close English equivalent and could, if translated literally, make awkward English at best. Let not the reader assume that the awkwardness he finds in a translation is somehow a guarantee that the translation is a good one. What the awkwardness proves is that the translation is a bad one, and the present translators pray that such awkwardnesses are few and far between in the *Tanna.* To this end they have not hesitated, when the occasion has so demanded, to use an English equivalent which may not contain a literal translation of even a single word in the original Hebrew phrase, or clause, or sentence, but yet conveys the sense of the original as fully and precisely as possible.

Once an English equivalent has been used in the translation of a Hebrew term, it does not necessarily follow that the term will be translated in precisely the same way when it recurs in the text. In a manner of speaking, words are soft around their edges: it is the pressure of the context—the phrase, clause, sentence, paragraph, sometimes even the chapter in which the word occurs—that shapes its exact meaning. Hence the reader who is following the Hebrew text as he reads the English translation ought not be surprised at finding some slight yet precise differentiation of the meaning assigned, for example, to a word like *kašer,* which is variously translated "spotless" (ER, 31), "pure" (ER, 32, 33, 34), "of immaculate character" (ER, 36), "noble" (ER, 125), and "virtuous" (ER, 128). Similarly, *nitgalgĕlu* is variously rendered "welled up" (ER, 27; EZ, 181), "flooded up" (ER, 80), "overflowed" (ER, 154), "flooded over" (ER, 112), and "crested like a wave" (ER, 129). More freely translated, perhaps, is one of God's names, *Maḳom.* Its literal meaning is "place," a term which seems to be a metaphor for the idea of God as the ground of existence or ground of being, and it is therefore translated in one context as "the Preserver of the world" (ER, 3) and in another context as "He whose presence is everywhere" (ER, 35).

What is true of individual words whose meaning is determined by context is also true of phrases, and in rendering certain of these the translators have not hesitated to find more than one equivalent for each phrase. Hence the phrase *'am ha'areṣ,* whose literal meaning is "people of the earth," is translated in one place as "unlettered" (ER, 48), in another as "unlettered in Torah" (ER, 48), in another as "clod" (ER, 155), and in still another as "ignoramus" (S, 8). Similarly, according to the circumstances in which the phrase is being used, *šalom 'al nafši* (literally "peace to my soul") is variously translated "this is the life for me" (ER, 56), "take it easy" (EZ, 198), "let my soul remain at peace" (ER, 128), "as for me, let my soul remain untroubled" (ER, 167), and "all is well with you, my soul" (ER, 112).[52] Another case in point is the phrase *derek 'ereṣ,* literally "the way of the world." In one context it is used in reference to moral conduct, to the way one conducts oneself in the world, and is necessarily translated "the way of right conduct" (ER, 3, and n. 7). In another context, however, the phrase is noncommittal as to morality and refers simply to everyday patterns of behavior; hence it is translated "how things go in the world" (ER, 30, 59; EZ, 185) or "worldly things" (S, 56).[53]

One encounters a similar problem in the translation of other phrases of general significance. Elijah, a stylist who is often original in his use of Hebrew, coins phrases of this kind whose significance depends almost entirely on their immediate context.[54] Thus the phrase *dĕbarim yĕterim,* translated literally "excessive things," comes to signify "things, words, or acts that exceed the limits of decency or good taste." In specific contexts, the phrase is translated "arrogant words" (ER, 49), or "things that should not be said" (ER, 115), or "things that are uncalled for" (EZ, 176); in one instance the idea of the overstepping of bounds is so strong as to require translation of the phrase into "went ahead and persisted" (EZ, 194). Another phrase, *dĕbarim še-'enan rĕ-'uim,* whose literal meaning "words, or acts, that are improper" roughly parallels *dĕbarim yĕterim,* is translated under pressure of its context as "indecencies one dare not record" (ER, 101), or "indecencies one dare not give a name to" (ER, 56, 69), or "deeds that are unutterable" (ER, 87). In both Hebrew phrases just cited a strong sense of propriety seems to be at work, as though Elijah were avoiding, by a loose euphemism, any specific terms that might offend or shock the prudish or the innocent. But in other places in the text Elijah does not hesitate to speak frankly about sexual matters, and one can only infer therefrom that he deliberately uses the euphemisms to let the reader's imagination work on, and recoil from, the excesses that presumably he, Elijah, cannot bring himself to specify.

Certain phrases presented particular problems for the translators. For example, the phrases "time-to-come" and "world-to-come" stand for a doctrine that does not present a firm outline of its meaning even

---

52. An utterance such as *modeh 'al ha-'ĕmet wĕ-dober 'ĕmet bi-lĕbabo* appears to have two meanings. In describing a man "who reveres Heaven," the utterance is translated "he acknowledges the truth of [Torah] and will speak its truth in his heart" (ER, 118, 138). On the other hand, in instances where a man's relations with his fellow man are set forth, the utterance is translated "he should be ready to acknowledge truth; ready to acknowledge openly what he has committed himself to in his heart" (ER, 63, 104).

An utterance such as *lo' šimmeš talmide ḥăkamim* is translated at times "put himself under the guidance of the Sages" (ER, 17, 91, 100), at times "ministered to scholars" (ER, 23), and at other times "attend on Sages" (S, 18).

53. On the term *derek 'ereṣ,* see Friedmann in his Introduction to the Supplements to *Eliyyahu Rabbah* and *Eliyyahu Zuṭa,* pp. 3–6.

54. See Friedmann, Introduction, pp. 119–29.

in a close context. In some places the phrases seem to be referring to a specific time, namely the two thousand years of the Messiah's presence in the world in the third cycle of the six thousand years of the world's existence as reckoned by man. At times the phrases seem to point to a seventh millennium, to a world redeemed "when there will be neither sin nor iniquity, neither affliction nor chastisement" (ER, 7). At still other times, however, the phrases seem to refer not to this world transformed and redeemed, but to eternity, to endless life in God's presence. The translators were unable to resolve these ambiguities in the two phrases "world-to-come" and "time-to-come."

For the sake of clarity as well as accommodation to their contexts, certain technical terms have been translated rather freely. The word *Ḳabbalah,* for example, does not in Elijah's, or indeed in rabbinic, usage, refer to the mystical doctrines which this term came to signify in later centuries, but rather refers to the "received parts of Scripture," entitled "Prophets" or "Writings," and consequently is translated "post-Mosaic Scripture" (ER, 4, 14, 23, 75). As teacher, preacher, and scholar, Elijah was necessarily also something of a dialectician, as the several debates in his work indicate, and therefore, in order to climax a point in his argument, he adduces the operating principle of *ḳal wa-ḥomer.* The technical definition of the term is usually given as "a conclusion *a minore ad majus,*" or "an inference from the lesser to the greater" (S, 18), a translation which itself requires translation, namely "a conclusion arrived at by inference from a minor premise to a major premise." Since this definition may ask for still further definition, the translators, for the sake of clarity, ease of understanding, and accommodation to the context, have translated the term variously as "inference" (ER, 75, 93, 147), "all the more certain" (EZ, 161), "may not the matter be strongly argued?" (S, 15), or even "now to the point" (ER, 148).

Yet, though the translators insist that they have been as scrupulous as possible in their faithfulness to the text, they have presumed to add some material to the English that is not in the Hebrew. Such addition was thought necessary in those passages in which the Hebrew text is defective and makes no sense whatever, perhaps because of a copyist's error in transcribing or omitting a phrase, clause, or sentence. Rather than leave a blank in the English version, the translators, on close examination of the Hebrew context in which a defect occurs, have supplied what they consider to be the intention of the original word, phrase, or clause. In order not to mislead the reader, the translators have not only enclosed such corrections in square brackets, but have called his attention to them in the footnotes accompanying each page.

In his editing of the text, Friedmann made up for apparent defects in the Hebrew by supplying such Hebrew words and phrases as he considered necessary for the clarity of the work. He enclosed the supplied material in brackets, and this is indicated by angular brackets which enclose the translation of the material interpolated by Friedmann.

Again, for the sake of the reader's understanding of the work, the translators have gone still further in making additions to it. In places where the Hebrew text fails to connect events or ideas from sentence to sentence, from paragraph to paragraph, or from section to section of a chapter, places where the reader is left hanging, so to speak, the translators have ventured to add such connective material as to provide continuity in the exposition of ideas or the flow of the narrative. The gaps in continuity seem often to result from the fact that Hebrew supplies many fewer directive or transitional words and phrases than English employs to indicate concession, condition, exception, contrariety, possibility, and the like—words such as "although," "however," "nevertheless," "unless," and phrases such as "on the other hand," "in addition to," "on the contrary." Instead, Hebrew relies heavily on context, the sentence or the paragraph, or even the more general context of the section or chapter to indicate the turns of thought or narrative which English usually supplies by its connective words or phrases or sentences.

Sometimes Elijah, like many authors of Midrashim, seems simply to have taken it for granted that his audience was so familiar with the subject of his discourse that it was not necessary for him to supply such connective material. Hence, where the translators have considered it absolutely necessary for the reader's understanding of the text, they have presumed, again taking into account the context, to supply the connective material. This material is also enclosed in square brackets, so that the reader will be fully aware that it is not in the original Hebrew. To decide for himself whether the translators were justified in taking such action, the reader may omit the bracketed material as he reads. By adding it, however, the translators hope that they will have helped him to greater appreciation of a masterpiece of Jewish thought and therefore that he will forgive their presumption. It is taken, after all, on his behalf, not on theirs. Also in his behalf, for each chapter the translators have supplied a title and a summary,[55] a map, so to speak, to make easy his journey along Elijah's way.

---

55. In the summaries the abbreviations "ER," "EZ," and "S," followed by page numbers, indicate material just preceding the abbreviation. In the text of the translation the abbreviations are placed in the margins and indicate the material that follows.

The chapter numbers enclosed within parentheses refer to the chapter numbers indicated in Haida's edition (Prague, 1677) and in subsequent reprints of this edition preceding Friedmann's edition (Vienna, 1902–4).

V. *The Manuscripts*

Codex Vatican 31,[56] the oldest rabbinic manuscript extant, completed in 1073, is the prime source of Friedmann's text. This is the text used for the present English translation. The MS contains only the *Eliyyahu Rabbah* and Chapters 1 through 15 of the *Eliyyahu Zuṭa.* A word-for-word collation of Friedmann's text with this codex shows his faulty transcription of at least three words[57] and omission of a number of lines as well.[58]

Two other MSS of parts of *Tanna dĕḇe Eliyyahu* are extant: Parma MS 2785[59] and Parma MS 1240. The first of these, which was completed in 1290 by Samuel bar Joseph of *'wn ḳstyl* (possibly Uncastello, in northern Spain), includes the text of *Eliyyahu Zuṭa* in a recension which differs from Codex Vatican 31.[60] Friedmann did not obtain a copy of this text until he had completed his edition.[61] His notes, however, list variants that appear in the Parma MS. The translators have followed the MS's variant readings in EZ, 173, 174, 190, and 191.

The second manuscript, Parma MS 1240,[62] was completed in 1270 by Menahem ben Jacob, a scribe living in a town in the Rhineland. The MS is made up of texts of *Pĕsiḳta Rabbati, Tanḥuma,* and eleven other Midrashim, including *Pirḳe R. Eliezer* and *Pirḳe hay-Yĕriḏoṯ.* The latter

---

56. The manuscript is described by Umberto Cassuto, *Codices Vaticani Hebraici* (Rome, 1956), pp. 38–41.

A facsimile which contains the Sifra as well as *Eliyyahu Rabbah* and *Eliyyahu Zuṭa* was published by the Maḳor firm in 5732 (1972) in Jerusalem. Ninety years earlier, in 1882, Ḥayyim Meir Horowitz published the *Eliyyahu Zuṭa* of the manuscript in his *Beṯ 'eḳeḏ ha-'aggadoṯ*, Frankfurt am Main, part 3, pp. 31–64. Not until the completion of his edition of the work did Friedmann learn that Horowitz had, in part, preceded him (see the Preface to his Introduction, p. 7, n. 1).

57. The word *wĕ-hišliḵo* (ER, 1) is transcribed *wĕ-hišliṭ;* the word *bwšth* [*bŏštah*] (ER, 27) is transcribed *mišteh;* and the phrase *kĕ-'oḇ 'aḇ zar* (=*kĕ-'oḇde 'ăḇodah zarah*) is transcribed *kĕ-'oḇre 'ăḇerah* (ER, 153).

58. See ER, 31, 79, 96, 101, and elsewhere.

Friedmann frequently disregards the plene spelling of the original; he also disregards the joining of the particle *šel* with the noun that follows it. (On this phenomenon see Ḥanoḵ Yalon, *Maḇo' lĕ-niḳḳuḏ ham-Mišnah* [Jerusalem, 5724/1964], pp. 26–27.) But the mistakes in copying and the omission of lines may have been due to the fact that when Friedmann began his work on the *Tanna* he was already in his late sixties and presumably no longer superb master of the editorial precision which marked all his earlier works.

59. See Giovanni Bernardo de Rossi, *MSS Codices Hebraici* (Parma, 1803), *1,* 182, No. 2785.

60. The order of the chapters is different. This MS begins in the middle of EZ, Chapter 1, and ends with two stories that are found in EZ, Chapter 1. Unlike Codex Vatican 31, which has fifteen chapters in *Eliyyahu Zuṭa,* Parma MS 2785 has only twelve.

61. See Friedmann's brief but thorough note in ER, 165–66.

62. See de Rossi, *3,* 116, No. 1240.

two, as previously noted, were added by Friedmann to his edition as *Nispaḥim,* or Supplements. He also refers to variant readings in his notes.[63]

Aside from the value of Codex Vatican 31 as the prime source of Friedmann's edition, the best of all the printed editions, the MS contains some touching rhymed prayers which the copyist Mošeh (*mšh,* Moses) added to the text. His name appears as an acronym in the first three words of the verses at the beginning of the Sifra and at the beginning of *Eliyyahu Rabbah* and of *Eliyyahu Zuṭa,* as well as at the conclusions of these two portions of the text.

Mošeh's prayer for Divine help at the beginning of *Eliyyahu Rabbah* reads as follows:

May He who is uniquely One,
The majesty of His glory matched by none,
Acclaimed by a people uniquely one,
Help me from start to finish, I pray,
Through Eliyyahu Rabbah to make my way.

A prayer for the restoration of Jerusalem and a prayer of thankfulness at the conclusion of *Eliyyahu Rabbah* reads thus:

May You set before You, O Lord, our God,
The resolve to let us see
The rebuilding of Jerusalem—
Oh, so may it be!

With the help of Him supreme, who
By a myriad of angels is attended,
My copy of Eliyyahu Rabbah
Was begun and now is ended.

Mošeh asks again for Divine help in his prayer preceding *Eliyyahu Zuṭa:*

May He who made soft His firmament
And over Sinai had it bend,
Help me copy Eliyyahu Zuṭa
From beginning to end.

Finally, Mošeh pleads at the conclusion of *Eliyyahu Zuṭa* for God's help in continuing his work, a plea which the present translators of *Tanna dĕḇe Eliyyahu* devoutly echo:

---

63. In the edition printed in Venice (1598) and in Prague (1677), and in all subsequent editions, *Pirḳe R. Eliezer* is deemed part of *Tanna dĕḇe Eliyyahu.* See Friedmann's Introduction to the *Nispaḥim lĕ-Seder Eliyyahu Zuṭa,* pp. 20–21; S, 26, n. 1; and *passim.*

With the help of Him who has given men
The talent for beauty of expression,
May we return to you, Eliyyahu Zuṭa,
For another study-session![64]

'Ereb̲ Šabbat̲ ḥol ham-Mo'ed̲ Sukkot̲, 5738
30 September 1977

William G. Braude
Israel J. Kapstein

---

64. The prayer ends with the words "blessed be He who gives strength to the weary" (see Hertz, *APB,* p. 23).

ELIYYAHU RABBAH

CHAPTER 1

Why God does not make use of Gehenna

Summary

The work begins with an account of God's withdrawal from earth to heaven because of Adam's transgression. At the same time He withdrew, God brought Gehenna's fire into existence in order to assure man's obedience to the precepts of Torah. Nevertheless, those whose transgressions make them deserve to be punished in Gehenna are rarely punished therein. For He who knows the beginning and the end of all things, foreseeing that the descendants of Adam would provoke His wrath, resolved to put their misdeeds out of mind: He chose to see the good in mankind and not the evil. And as He is merciful to men, so He would have them be merciful to one another, as Mordecai, for example, was merciful to Esther (ER, 3).

What day did God provide for Israel to assure that He would put out of mind their offenses against Him? He provided them with the Sabbath day, a day set aside for the study of Torah and hence a day for men to make their peace with God and with their fellow men. In the study of Torah they tremble in their anxiety to grasp its sense so exactly as never to feel shame or embarrassment when they are told to set forth a text from Scripture or from Mishnah.

The day that God provided for Israel may also be taken to refer to the Day of Atonement, the day on which God rejoices as He pardons Israel's iniquities (ER, 4). Such is the mercy God bestows upon Israel that their iniquities in this world are swept away in order to assure that no charges will be made against them in the world-to-come. Thus He removes their names from the book of death and puts them in the book of life.

The day that God provided for Israel may also be taken to be the day of Gog, the day when the nations of the world who put forth their hands against Israel will be sentenced to go down to Gehenna. They will suffer His vengeance because they did not heed the precepts of Torah governing right conduct, and because they afflicted Israel (ER, 5). Yet so great is God's mercy not only toward Israel but toward all mankind that even though Jews and Gentiles alike deserve to be annihilated for their misdeeds, He spares them, saying that if He allows life to beasts and even to reptiles and creeping things, He can do no less than allow life to mankind as well. For this reason it may be said that man owes his life on earth to reptiles and creeping things.

Despite the evidence of God's mercy, however, there are those who dare to say that God is a devouring fire, quoting from Torah the words *fire eternal* (Lev. 6:6) as referring to Him. But these words are to be rightly understood as meaning that fire, like Gehenna, is an instrument in God's hand which He keeps by Him always as a threat of punishment for those who do not turn away from sin and repent, as is said, *By fire will the Lord threaten judgment* (Isa. 66:16) (ER, 6).

Chapter 1

p. 3 *And He separated Adam*[1] (Gen. 3:24),which is to say that the Holy One gave Adam a bill of separation such as is given to a woman who has been divorced. Thereupon God, [withdrawing from His earthly domicile], *had His presence dwell* [*in the first heaven*] *with the cherubim,*[2] [*whom He had created*] *prior to* [*His creation of*] *the Garden of Eden*[3] *(ibid.),* for, as the text implies, the cherubim were among those angels who had come into being before the entire work of creation.[4] [Also, at the time of His withdrawal, God made dwell in Gehenna][5] *the heat of the flame that alternates* [*with the cold of ice*][6] *(ibid.),* by which Gehenna is *to assure obedience to the way (ibid.).* By *way* here is meant the way of right conduct, the revelation of whose specific commands,[7] as the text further implies, had preceded all [others,[8] indeed had preceded the revelation of] *the tree of life (ibid.),* the tree of life being Torah, of which Scripture

---

1. JV: *So He drove out the man.* But since Scripture has already said, *The Lord God sent him forth from the Garden of Eden* (Gen. 3:23), ER regards the meaning "drove out" for *grš* as repetitive; hence *separated.*

2. The cherubim are frequently referred to as part or support of God's seat in heaven (see 1 Sam. 4:4; 2 Sam. 6:2; 2 Kings 19:15; Isa. 37:16). The firmament, that is the first heaven, is likewise described as set "over the head of the cherubim" (Ezek. 10:1). Consequently, here in the reference to angels known as cherubim, ER sees an allusion to the tradition that upon Adam's sin, God, separating Himself from Adam, withdrew to the first heaven. See Tanḥuma, *Pĕḵuḏe,* 6; *ibid., Naśo',* 16; Tanḥuma B, *Naśo',* 24; PR 5:7 (YJS, *18, 1,* 105); PRKM 1:1, p. 2; and Haida.

3. JV: *and He placed at the east of the Garden of Eden the cherubim.* But *miḵ-ḵeḏem,* "at the east of," may also mean "prior to"; and the particle *'eṯ*, generally a sign of the accusative, may also mean "with"; hence *with the cherubim.* And since *way-yaśken,* "He placed," no longer has "the cherubim" as the object, the commentator takes *šĕḵinah,* "the Presence," a nominal form of *way-yaśken,* to be the object implied.

4. Apparently ER reads Gen. 1:1, "In the beginning He created Elohim," that is, angelic powers including those known as cherubim (see ER, 160; *Midraš han-ne'ĕlam* as quoted in *Torah šĕlemah, 1,* 35; Gen. Rabbah TA, 21:9, p. 203; and The Syriac Apocalypse of Baruch 21:6). The *'ofannim* were on the palace's second level; above it, on the third level, were the ministering angels (ER, 160).

5. According to ER, early in creation in the first era of the history of the world, He made six special things—the Torah, Gehenna's bastion, the Garden of Eden, the throne of glory, the name of the Messiah, and the Temple—before proceeding to His creation of the physical world and all the work of His hands including man. Gehenna's fire came into being on the sixth day following Adam's offense (see ER, 160).

6. JV: *the flaming sword which turned every way.* But *ḥereḇ,* "sword," may also mean "heat," as in Deut. 28:22 and Lam. 5:9 (NJV). In Gehenna, heat alternates with cold as punishment for transgressors. See PRKM 10:4, p. 165 (PRKS, pp. 189–91), and Tanḥuma B, *Bĕr'ešiṯ,* 25.

7. Adam was given six commands: to refrain from idolatry, blasphemy, bloodshed, unchastity, and seizure of another's property, and to institute civil courts. See PRKM 12:1, p. 202 (PRKS, pp. 226–27).

8. Presumably, commands such as the one given to Noah not to eat flesh cut from a living animal, the one given to Abraham concerning the circumcision of Isaac, the one given to Jacob forbidding the eating of the sinew of the thigh vein, and the one ordained for Judah concerning the obligation to marry a brother's wife who is widowed and childless. See PRKM 12:1, p. 203 (PRKS, pp. 227–28).

says, "She is a tree of life to them that lay hold upon her" (Prov. 3:18).

Blessed be the Preserver of the world, blessed be He![9] Though He knows both beginning and end and can tell from the beginning what the end of anything is to be[10] long, long before it has been made; though He knows what has been made and what is yet to be made, still [in whatever is made] He chooses to see the good and chooses not to see the evil.[11] Thus, because He is content with His portion, He is rich.[12]

In His wisdom and with His understanding God created His world and set it on its foundation.[13] He then created Adam and had him lie prone before Him.[14] As He scrutinized him till the end of all the generations that would come from him, He foresaw that his descendants would provoke His wrath. Hence He said: If I hold mankind to account for its successive misdeeds, the world will not endure; I must therefore have its successive misdeeds pass out of mind. And He had them do so. As for the proof, you can readily see it for yourself. When Israel were in the wilderness, they befouled themselves with their misdeeds. Thereupon He proceeded to have all that they had done pass out of mind, as is said, *The Lord passed before him* (Exod. 34:6). Do not read *passed,* but "had pass"[15]—that is, He had all their evil pass away from before Him, so that He was able to proclaim Himself *Lord, Lord* [*of mercy*] *(ibid.).*

Men are likewise to have pass from their minds, as in the story of Mordecai, the offenses of others. When Esther said to him something that she should not have said, he became angry at her. Now what was the thing that she should not have said? She should not have said, *But I have not been summoned to visit the king* (Esther 4:11). And what was Mordecai's reply? *If thou altogether holdest thy peace at this time* [*and goest not to the king*], *thou and thy father's house will perish* (Esther 4:14). Thereupon she turned and spoke to him in the way she should have

---

9. Cf. Mid 5:4; MTeh 90:10 (YJS, *13, 2,* 92–93); and Louis Jacobs, *A Jewish Theology* (New York, 1973), pp. 142–46.

10. Cf. Isa. 46:10.

11. See Gen. Rabbah 8:4; PR 40:2 (YJS, *18, 2,* 703–4); and MTeh 1:22 (YJS, *13, 1,* 33).

12. Cf. Ab̲ 4:1; and "The glory of the Lord endures for ever, because the Lord rejoices in His works" (Ps. 104:31).

13. Cf. Prov. 3:19.

14. Thus apparently R which, like V, reads *wĕ-hišlik̲o lĕ-fanaw,* "He had him lie prone before Him," the implication being that Adam, containing within his person all of mankind, lay stretched from end to end of the world (PR 23:1 [YJS, *18, 1,* 472] and MTeh 139:5 [YJS, *13, 2,* 345]). Apparently conflating the letters *kaf* and *waw* at the end of *wĕ-hišlik̲o* into one letter, the letter *ṭet,* Friedmann read the first word *wĕ-hišliṭ,* "made him master over that which is before him." E. E. Urbach in *Lĕšonenu, 21* (1957), 186, calls attention to Friedmann's probable misreading.

15. A slight variation in vowels changes *wa-ya'ăb̲or,* "He passed," into *wa-ya'ăb̲ir,* "He had pass."

spoken, so that he praised her words ungrudgingly. And, under the circumstances, what were the words she should have spoken? At once she should have said, *Go, gather together all the Jews . . . and fast ye with me*[16] (Esther 4:16). Thereat he had pass out of his mind what she had
ER, *p.* 4 first said, | as is said, *And Mordecai caused to pass out of mind*[17] (Esther 4:17). [In short, he acted forgivingly toward her, as he hoped God would act toward the Jews who had stuffed themselves and guzzled at the feast of Ahasuerus], for, as is said to Him, *Who is a God like unto Thee that lifteth an act of iniquity* [*from the pan in the scale of justice by which Thou weighest men's acts and, even more forgivingly*], *has pass altogether out of mind the defiance of His sovereignty among the remnant of* [*Israel who are*] *His heritage?*[18] (Mic. 7:18). [Indeed, from the very beginning of time, God made known His mercy, for], according to the Psalmist, Adam declared to God, *Thine eyes did look kindly upon my flawed substance* (Ps. 139:16), and in this verse further declared, *In Thy book only those acts which are unblemished are to be written down*[19] *(ibid.).* How are we to understand these words? That when the Holy One is seated in His court of inquiry with the righteous of the world seated in His presence, He will say to them: My children, such-and-such a generation observed the Torah, and I bestowed upon them what they merited; and such-and-such a man observed the Torah, and I bestowed upon him what he merited. But the iniquities of Israel, I cannot remember; they do not even come to mind, as is said, *Dwell not on former* [*offenses*] (Isa. 43:18), and also [*Offenses*] *gone by shall not be remembered, nor even come to mind*[20] (Isa. 65:17).

[What did God provide for Israel in order to have them act in such a way as to cause Him to put out of mind their offenses against Him?]

---

16. "By *fast ye with me,* she meant 'Fast ye because you ate and drank at the feast of Ahasuerus.' " See MTeh 22:5 (YJS, *13, 1,* 301).

17. A slight variation in vowels changes *way-ya'ăbor,* "went his way," to *way-ya'ăbir,* "caused to pass [out of mind]." NJV: *So Mordecai went* [*about the city*]. Cf. B.Meg 15a.

The Jews of Persia who, as stated in the preceding note, participated in the banquets of Ahasuerus, shared also in the immorality which attended them (see Ginzberg, *Legends, 4,* 370), and so by fasting three days they asked God to forgive them. But before Mordecai could summon the people to beg God's forgiveness, he himself had to forgive.

18. JV: *Who is a God like unto Thee, that pardoneth the iniquity, and passeth by the transgression of the remnant of His heritage.* But the literal meaning of *nośe',* "pardon," is "lift up," and the literal meaning of *peša',* "transgression," is "rebellion," or "defiance of God's sovereignty."

19. JV: *but in Thy book they were all written down.* But apparently ER takes *kullam,* "all of them," to mean "those acts which are whole."

20. So also understood by Samuel Laniado in his commentary *Kĕli paz,* Venice, 1657.

Promises of physical renewal—a way in the wilderness, rivers in the desert (Isa. 43:19), new heavens and a new earth (Isa. 65:17)—are made in both passages. The fulfillment of these promises resulting from God's not having former offenses come to mind are thus given a spiritual interpretation: the radiance in a world where sin is no more—not even remembered—will make heaven and earth appear new.

He provided Israel with the Sabbath: *Among the days that were to be fashioned, one of those days was to be wholly His* (Ps. 139:16). In what sense is it to be wholly His? Say, a man who labors for six days, rests on the seventh, and so finds himself at peace with his children and the other members of his household. Likewise, a man may labor all six days in the presence of people who are hostile to him, but then, as he rests on the Sabbath, he forgets all the vexation he had previously had. Such is the nature of man: the day of rest brings about his forgetting of evil, and a day of trouble brings about his forgetting of good.[21] The nature of man being what it is, the Holy One said to Israel: My children, have I not written for you in My Torah, *This book of Guidance shall not depart out of thy mouth* (Josh. 1:8)? Although you must labor all six days of the week, the Sabbath is to be given over completely to Torah.[22] Accordingly, it is said that a man should rise early on the Sabbath to recite [Mishnah] and then go to the synagogue or to the academy where he is to read in the Five Books and recite a portion in the Prophets. Afterwards, he is to go home and eat and drink, thus fulfilling the command *Eat thy bread with joy, and drink thy wine with a merry heart,* [*for God hath already accepted thy works*] (Eccles. 9:7). [Thus the man who avails himself of the Sabbath to make his peace with his fellows, at the same time is making his peace with God.] For the contentment of the Holy One comes only from those who are busy with Torah, as is said, *For the sake of all these things*—[*the ordinances and laws of Torah*]—*hath My hand made* [*the world*][23] (Isa. 66:2).

From this very verse in Isaiah [which goes on to say, *The man I have regard for . . . trembles in his anxiety (to grasp the exact meaning) of My word*], the following is inferred: When a man reads [a text] he should have so good a grasp of it that no shame or embarrassment will overcome him when he is told, "Stand up and set forth in proper fashion the Scripture you read," or when he is told, "Stand up and set forth in proper fashion the Mishnah you recited." The point is made plain by David, king of Israel, in post-Mosaic Scripture: *O Lord, in the morning mayest Thou be pleased to hear my voice; in the morning I am at once ready to set forth in proper fashion the words which are Thine—indeed I look forward* [*to having men ask me questions about Thy words*] (Ps. 5:4).[24]

In another interpretation, the verse *Among the days that were to be*

---

21. Cf. Ben Sira 11:25.

22. ER apparently construes Josh. 1:8a as applying to the Sabbath and 1:8b, *and meditate therein day and night,* to weekdays, when saying the Shĕma' morning and evening is regarded as fulfillment of the command to meditate in Torah during the day and during the night. See MTeh 1:17 (YJS, *13, 1, 23*), and cf. P.Shab 15:3, 15a and PR 23:9 (YJS, *18, 1,* 490–91).

23. The preceding verse asks, *Where is the place that may give Me contentment?* (Isa. 66:1).

24. So Landau. JV: *O Lord, in the morning shalt Thou hear my voice, in the morning will I order my prayer unto Thee, and will look forward.*

fashioned, one of those days was to be wholly His (Ps. 139:16) is taken to mean that God provided Israel with the Day of Atonement, a day of great joy[25] for Him at whose word the world came into being, for He gave the day to Israel with abounding love. A parable will explain how God regards the day. There was a mortal king whose servants and members of his household, [after cleaning up the palace], used to take the refuse and throw it out before the king's private doorway. When the king left the palace and saw the refuse, great was his rejoicing, [for he knew that the palace was clean]. Thus we are to understand the Day of Atonement which the Holy One bestowed with abounding love <and joy>. Nay more! As God pardons the iniquities of Israel, great is His rejoicing: He has no misgivings. To the mountains and to the hills, to the streams and to the valleys,[26] He says, Come and join Me
ER, *p.* 5 | in My great rejoicing, for I am about to pardon Israel's iniquities.

Hence in the spirit of the verse *Remember these things, O Jacob* (Isa. 44:21), a man should remember all the favors and mercies which God has bestowed upon Israel continually from the day He chose Abraham until the present hour, He having assured Israel *I sweep away as a thick cloud, thy transgressions* (Isa. 44:22). Even as clouds are swept away by wind, so the iniquities of Israel are swept away in this world and have no power to stand up [and make charges against Israel] in the world-to-come, for, [as God affirms, "Your transgressions, though] *thick as a cloud, I sweep* [*utterly*] *away."* What is meant by the words *For I have redeemed thee (ibid.)* which conclude this verse? They mean, In redeeming you, I have removed your name from the book of death and put it in the book of life.[27] Hence it is said, *For I have redeemed thee.* And what follows? *Sing, O ye heavens* (Isa. 44:23), [and join in My rejoicing].[28]

In still another interpretation, the verse *Because among the days that were to be fashioned, one of those days was to be wholly His* (Ps. 139:16) is taken to mean that in the time-to-come [God will set aside] the day of Gog.[29] In the eyes of Him at whose word the world came into being, the present time is to be compared with a householder who hired workmen and kept his eye on them to see which of them did their work faithfully, as is said, *The eyes of the Lord run to and fro throughout the whole earth,* [*to show Himself strong in the behalf of him whose heart is faithful*

---

25. "There were no more joyous days for Israel than the 15th day of Ab and the Day of Atonement" (R. Simeon ben Gamaliel in Ta 4:8).

26. See Ezek. 36:4, 25 and R. 'Akiba's comment on the latter verse in Yoma 8:19; Ezek. 36:29, 8. These verses taken together account for God's bidding the mountains and the valleys to rejoice in the pardon extended to Israel on the Day of Atonement. So Urbach, p. 191.

27. See B.RH 16b and Ar 10b.

28. For if mankind were not pardoned, heaven and earth would be destroyed.

29. See Ezek. 38.

toward Him (2 Chron. 16:9).[30] The one who did his work faithfully and the one who did not do his work faithfully—what each one has coming to him will be ready at "the feast."[31] [On the day of Gog], accordingly, the [heathen] nations of the world, because they put forth their hand against Israel and Jerusalem and against the Temple, will be sentenced to be swept away, to perish from the world and go down to Gehenna. And the proof? You can see it for yourself. When Nebuchadnezzar, king of Babylon, came and encompassed Jerusalem, the nations of the world spoke up, saying with one voice: Why should we have ever considered that we would have to reckon with Him whose city and Temple we are about to capture so easily?[32] Thereupon the holy spirit responded, saying to them: You cocksure fools, until this hour you had not been sentenced to go down into Gehenna. Now, it is of this very hour that Scripture speaks, saying to you, *Your mother shall be sore ashamed, she that bore you shall be confounded*[33] (Jer. 50:12).

So, too, at the very time Gog and his allies gather into many armies with a view to helping themselves to the possessions of Israel, the Holy One, for His part, will have Gog and his allies gather for judgment upon the mountains of Israel, [judgment which] will wreak harsh vengeance upon them because, disregarding Torah's commands, they will not restrain themselves [as God's agents in punishment of Israel], but will seek instead to exterminate Israel.[34] Therefore, God is quoted as saying, *I am very sore displeased* [*with the nations*][35] (Zech. 1:15); and so *I will execute vengeance in anger and fury upon the nations, because they hearkened not*[36] (Mic. 5:14); then, when *The day of the Lord cometh* (Zech.

---

30. Instead of Zech 4:10 (as in V and R), where the identical expression occurs. The substitution was suggested by Professor Dov Noy of the Hebrew University.

31. Cf. Ab̲ 3:16 and Meiri's comment: "Just as a man finds prepared for his feast only such things as he took the trouble to buy and bring home—meat and cheese or any kind of food—so shall souls find a feast prepared for them in the world-to-come, made up of what they have 'purchased' in this world. For some [the food] will be bitter, for some sweet." Cited from *The Living Talmud*, ed. Judah Goldin (New York, 1957), p. 147.

32. Or, [Why should we pay regard to Him? We have as good as conquered His city and His Temple? L. N.] Cf. MTeh 79:2 (YJS, *13, 2,* 44).

33. In the two preceding verses it is said, *Chaldea shall be a spoil . . . because you rejoiced, O ye that plundered My heritage* (Jer. 50:10–11).

34. [Literally "because in disregard of the words of Torah they oppressed Israel." L. N.]

35. In Moffatt's translation (New York, 1954) Zech. 1:14b–15 reads: *I am stirred, deeply stirred, on behalf of Jerusalem and Zion; I am deeply wroth with the arrogant nations. For while I was slightly angry with Israel, they have pushed My anger for their own evil ends.* "As God's instruments for the correction of Israel, [the nations] had gone far beyond what they had been commissioned to do. [They] were appointed as a rod of chastisement to punish and discipline, but not to exterminate" (Eli Cashdan in the Soncino Commentary on the Twelve Prophets, p. 275). Cf. Isa. 10:5ff and 47:6–7.

36. "Not only did the nations refuse the Torah; they would not even put up with the seven laws given to the descendants of Noah, which the nations accordingly cast off." See Sif Deut. 343 (ed. Finkelstein [Breslau, 1936–39], p. 396).

14:1), *I will gather all nations against Jerusalem to battle* (Zech. 14:2); and at once I, *The Lord, shall go forth and fight against those nations*[37] (Zech. 14:3).

[But why does God put off the day of vengeance against Gog and his allies? Listen]: One day as I was walking through the greatest city of the world,[38] there was a roundup and I was roughly seized and brought into the king's house where I saw divans lavishly spread and silver vessels and gold vessels set out [in great number]. So, [in resentment of having been seized], I said, *The power of vengeance, the power of vengeance, O Lord, shine forth*[39] (Ps. 94:1). Presently a Parsee priest came to me and asked me, "Are you a scholar?" I replied, "A bit of a one." He said, "If you can answer the particular question I am about to ask, you may go in peace." I replied, "Ask." He then asked <"Why did God create loathsome reptiles and creeping things?"[40] I replied>:
ER, *p.* 6 "God is a judge who is indeed holy and just, | but He is also loving because He is perceptive [of man's condition] for ever and ever and

---

37. As He did when He intervened on behalf of Israel at the Red Sea. Cf. Exod. 14:25ff and 15:3ff; and PRKM 9:11, p. 159 (PRKS, p. 183).

Paralleling Exod. 15:18, Zech. 14:9 reads: *The Lord shall be King over all the earth: in that day shall the Lord be One, and His name one.* The parallel is noted and included in the morning service. See Hertz, *APB,* p. 104.

38. Probably Ctesiphon, capital of the Sassanids. See Jacob Mann, "Date and Place of Redaction of Seder Eliahu Rabba and Zuṭṭa," *HUCA, 4,* 302–10, particularly n. 137. [To a Babylonian Jew, Ctesiphon no doubt seemed the largest city in the world. L. N.]

39. JV: *O Lord, Thou God to whom vengeance belongeth, Thou God to whom vengeance belongeth, shine forth.* But *'el,* "God," may also mean "power."

The vengeance of God, as apparent from 2 Thess. 1:7–8 and Jude 7, is conceived in the imagery of Isa. 66:15–16, which describes the final judgment. At that time God is to reveal Himself in flaming fire, taking vengeance upon them who refuse to know Him.

So the author of ER, distraught by the indignity imposed on him, may at first have entreated God that in the words of Isa. 66:16, *the Lord is to contend* with his captors at once *by fire,* the fire of final judgment. Only as, reasoning with the Parsee priest, he comes to see creation in a larger perspective, does the author relent, saying at the end of the chapter, as he had at the beginning, that by fire the Lord does no more than threaten judgment.

Another explanation of ER's cry for vengeance is linked with the fact that Psalm 94 is the Psalm for the fourth day in the week, the day the sun and the moon were created (Gen. 1:14–19). Even symbolic worship of these luminaries, as practiced by Zoroastrians, was to be punished (B.RH 31a). Hence here the words *The power of vengeance, the power of vengeance, O Lord, shine forth* may have a dual thrust. They are directed, to begin with, at the authorities who seized and restrained the author. But they may also be directed at the Manicheism of Zoroastrians for whom Ormazd is light and life, the creator of all that is pure and good in the world; and for whom the antithesis, Ahriman—darkness, filth, and death—produces all that is evil in the world. See *Encyclopaedia Britannica,* 14th ed., *s.v.* "Zoroastrianism." For the author of ER, for the Jew, however, both realms—light and darkness—are one, since the one God, their Creator, "forms light and creates darkness." See Hertz, *APB,* p. 108.

40. In Zoroastrian teaching such creatures are the work of Ahriman, the god of darkness and evil. But for ER, as will become evident, such creatures serve an admirable purpose.

"<'Why did God . . . ?' I replied>"—P.Ber 9:3, 13c.

ever. He knows both beginning and end, and can tell from the beginning what the end of anything is to be long, long before it has been made; though He knows what has been made and what is yet to be made, still [in whatever is made] He chooses to see the good and chooses not to see the evil. Thus, because He is content with His portion, He is rich. In His wisdom and with His understanding He created His world and set it on its foundation. Then He created Adam and brought him into the world. And He created him for no other purpose than to serve Him with a whole heart and He would thus find contentment in him and in his descendants after him until the end of all generations. But then after Adam complied with the command to be fruitful and multiply, one [descendant] worshiped the sun and the moon, another worshiped wood and stone, and thus every day Adam's descendants came to be deemed by Him as deserving annihilation. Nevertheless, upon considering all the work of His hands in the world of His creation, God said: These—[human beings]—have life, and those—[other creatures]—have life. These have breath and those have breath; these have desire for food and drink, and those have desire for food and drink. Human beings ought to be deemed as important as cattle, as beasts, at least as important as the variety of loathsome reptiles and creeping things which I created upon the earth. At once He felt some measure of contentment and resolved not to annihilate mankind. And so you see that reptiles and creeping things were created in the world as a means of mankind's preservation."

Then the Parsee priest brought up another matter saying, "You assert that fire is not God. Yet is it not written in your Torah *fire eternal*[41] (Lev. 6:6)?" I replied: "My son, when our forebears stood at Mount Sinai to accept the Torah for themselves, they saw no form resembling a human being, nor resembling the form of any creature, nor resembling the form of anything that has breath which the Holy One created on the face of the earth, as is said, *Take ye therefore good heed unto yourselves—for ye saw no manner of form on the day that the Lord spoke unto you in Horeb* (Deut. 4:15); they saw only God, the one God—*He is God of gods and Lord of lords* (Deut. 10:17)—whose kingdom endures in heaven and on earth as well as in the highest heaven of heavens. And yet you say that God is fire! Fire is no more than a rod to be used upon men on earth. Its use is to be understood by the parable of a king who took a lash and hung it up in his house and then said to his children, to his servants, and to the members of his household, 'With this lash I may strike you, may smite you, may even kill you'—threatening them, so that in penitence they would turn away from sin. If they do not repent, do not turn back, then God says, 'I will have to strike them with the

---

41. According to one tradition, the fire seemed to rise as though the altar itself were aflame. See Lev. Rabbah M, 7:5, p. 159.

lash, will have to smite them, will even have to kill them.' Hence *fire eternal* is to be read in the light of the verse *For by fire will the Lord threaten judgment* (Isa. 66:16)."

Of course you might attempt to refute me by quoting the words *The Lord thy God is a devouring fire* (Deut. 4:24). But a parable will explain the intent of these words. The children, servants, and members of the household of a mortal king did not behave properly. So he said to his children, to his servants, and to the members of his household, "Because of your ways I will growl at you like a bear, roar at you like a lion,[42] seem to be coming at you like the angel of death." Such is the intent of *The Lord thy God is a devouring fire.*[43]

---

42. Cf. Lam. 3:10. [Literally, "I will ambush you like a bear, like a lion, indeed like the very angel of death." L. N.] But the use of "growl" and "roar" implies the threat which God intended.

43. Cf. Saadia Gaon, *The Book of Beliefs and Opinions* (YJS, *1,* 114, 265–66).

CHAPTER 2

God's decision to give Torah to the Jews and their being tested before the Messiah's coming

Summary

The day which is to be wholly His (Ps. 139:16), construed in the previous chapter as the Sabbath, the Day of Atonement, and the day of Gog, respectively, is in the chapter in hand construed as the world's seventh "day," a "day" lasting a thousand years (ER, 6). During this "day" mankind will be released from affliction and will be suffused with the spirit of holiness. To be sure, the coming of this "day" has been delayed, but come it will. In the meantime, we have had intimations of its character in the life of David (ER, 7). Indeed, every Jew who, like David, digs deep into Torah may anticipate and savor the sweetness and power of that "day" (ER, 8).

Eager for the song of praise which Jews utter as they occupy themselves with Torah, God changed His original plan of the order of creation and brought about His revelation of Torah earlier than He had intended. The heavens, indeed, are fit to declare the glory of God and to praise Him: they both witness and help bring about the annual growth of crops; even a small part of them overlooks all of mankind; the stars are arranged in them with consummate beauty (ER, 9); the speed and silence of the sun in its course through them inspires awe; the variety of creatures they behold below them is infinite. By their mere presence, the heavens testify to God's glory. But just as God had previously changed the order of creation in order to give the Torah earlier than He had planned, so, in order to help Israel achieve victory, on three different occasions God halted the course of the stars in the heavens and their praise of Him.

Still, God's glory which the heavens proclaim is not the creation's variety or the stars' beauty, but man's study of Torah and his obedience to its precepts (ER, 10), whereby God's great name will soon be hallowed among all peoples to the very ends of the world.

Until that day comes, nothing is spared the heat of God's anger: the righteous are punished in this world even for trivial offenses, while the wicked are punished in this world only for the most grievous ones.

Should Torah, God forbid, be completely neglected, the Holy One may spurn mankind and destroy the entire world (ER, 11). Such is the threat voiced at the beginning of Psalm 29, which goes on, according to ER, to plead that in order to prevent the world's destruction men should engage themselves in matters of Torah. Even before they worship, they should utter at least one precept of the Oral Law or one verse of Scripture, making certain that either one is completely accurate, lest they who hear these words be led astray and assert something not in accord with Torah.

Even as in His utterance of Torah God thundered but at the same time was gentle, so in his study of Torah a man should be vigorous but at the same time gentle and unassuming.

As for him who, satisfied with his worldly achievements, does not concern himself with Torah, he will be broken. Likewise, he who refuses to understand the meaning of chastisement will suffer doubly for his rejection of the instruction that chastisement intends (ER, 12).

Yet, severe as God is with people who in their prosperity become complacent or in obtuseness refuse to heed the meaning of chastisement, He is gentle with the man who is unable to study Torah himself, but sees to it that his child does; or with another man who is unable to study Torah, but mornings and evenings in the synagogue reads the Shĕma' and devoutly recites the *Tĕfillah.* Such men as these will not be charged with neglect of Torah, whose flames of fire light up men's hearts in numberless ways.

It should be remembered, however, that Israel's acute suffering in the world as we know it is not altogether the result of chastisement, but also of the throes which attend the Messiah's coming into the world. Soon the nations will be agitated with fear of annihilation, but God will reassure them that His intention is not to annihilate the world but rather to bring the Messiah and thus assert His sovereignty (ER, 13).

Chapter 2

ER, *p.* 6 *cont'd* Another comment: Among [God's] days—each of which is equivalent to a thousand years—*one of those days was to be wholly His* (Ps. 139:16), namely the world's seventh "day." For the world as we know it was intended to exist for six thousand years—two thousand years in desolation [without Torah], two thousand years with Torah, and two thousand years of the Messiah's reign. Because of our many, many sins ER, *p.* 7 enslavement has come upon us during the two thousand | years which God had intended to be the Messiah's. Indeed, more than seven hundred of his years have already passed,[1] as is said, *The Lord would have done what He devised, but had to cut back the promise which He had uttered in the days of old*[2] (Lam. 2:17). Soon, however, just as we carry out the stipulation that one year in seven be a year of release, so the Holy One will provide a day of release, a "day" lasting a thousand years. That God's "day" is of such length is implied in *A thousand years in Thy sight are but as yesterday when it is past* (Ps. 90:4). *The one day which shall be known as the Lord's, not day and not night* (Zech. 14:7) thus refers to the world's seventh "day," the kind of "day" on which *light will continue even though evening has come (ibid.),* the "day" we speak of as [precursor of] the world-to-come, the "day" when *from one New Moon to another,*

1. The age of Torah is said to have begun with the fifty-second year in Abraham's life, when he began converting non-Jews (B.AZ 9a), and to have come to an end in the one hundred and seventy-second year after the Temple's destruction by the Romans. See B.Sanh 97a and Rashi, *ad loc.* The phrase "more than seven hundred years" may be specifically seven hundred and forty-four years (see ER, 37), and hence the scribe's chronological note may refer to the year 986 C.E.

2. A poignant overtone for the reader of Lamentations on the ninth of Ab. JV: *The Lord hath done that which He devised; He hath performed His word that He commanded in the days of old.* But *biṣṣa',* "performed," may also mean "cut back" or "canceled."

and from one Sabbath to another shall all flesh come to worship before Me (Isa. 66:23), the "day" of *A Psalm, a song for the Sabbath day* (Ps. 92:1) for a world wholly suffused with Sabbath. Another comment on *A Psalm, a song for the Sabbath day* [stresses not the holiness with which God will suffuse the Sabbath year of days, but] the disappearance[3] from the world, at that time, <of the destructive forces> that afflict mankind. Or else the repetition in the words *A Psalm, a song* intimates [the holiness as well as the absence of all affliction that will mark this "day"], the seventh year of days, in the world.

At the end of this Sabbath year of days, there will be ushered in the time of the world-to-come when death will never, never be again.

[In the meantime, however, before the arrival of the world-to-come], during the world's Sabbath year of days, there will be neither sin nor iniquity, neither affliction nor chastisement. Each and every man will rejoice in his absorption of Torah and his understanding of it. As for the proof of what that "day" will be like, you can readily find it for yourself. You need only draw the inference that [such joy will be manifold] in the "day" that is certain to come from the way the Holy One showed His joy <in David> in the days of this world. Such joy is implied in the verse *These are the latter words*[4] *of David*[5] (2 Sam. 23:1) [which may be read, "These are the words of David, referring to the latter[6] 'day' "—that is, the "day" which will follow upon the six thousand years of the world's existence as reckoned by man].[7]

[There are, to be sure, other comments on 2 Samuel 23:1.] In one such comment the verse is read, *These words of David concern latter doings (ibid.),* implying that David pleaded with God: Master of the universe, even as You forgave me my former sins, forgive me also my latter sins.[8] Hence *These words of David concern latter doings.*

In another comment the verse is read, *These are the last words of*

---

3. The stem *šbṭ* means "rest," and also "make cease, cause to disappear."

4. JV: *These are the last words.* Since subsequently David is recorded as conversing with Joab (2 Sam. 24:2), with Gad (2 Sam. 24:14), with an angel of the Lord (2 Sam. 24:17), with Araunah (2 Sam. 24:21), with Bath-sheba (1 Kings 1:29–30), and with Solomon (1 Kings 2:1–9), the words referred to in 2 Sam. 23:1 cannot be David's last words. Hence the comments that follow.

5. David's Psalm goes on to say, *The righteous shall be . . . as the light of the morning . . . a morning without clouds* (2 Sam. 23:2–3).

6. So, too, Targum Jonathan, *ad loc.* In Hebrew, *the latter* may be an adjective or a prepositional phrase.

7. In one of the verses of 2 Sam. 23 which will be quoted below, the righteous are described as achieving a share of God's power. Hence the time referred to, a time when the righteous will flourish like the palm tree (Ps. 92:13), ER in this comment takes to be the world's seventh "day."

8. The earlier sins were against Saul, of whom God said to David: If Saul's fate had been thy fate, or if thy fate had been his fate, how many Davids would I have caused to perish for his sake (MTeh 7:3 [YJS, *13, 1,* 104]). See also B.Yoma 22b. The latter sins were the seizure of Bath-sheba and the murder of Uriah (2 Sam. 11).

David (ibid.). It is said that for twenty-two years the holy spirit was taken away from David,[9] king of Israel, and that in his grief he shed a cupful of tears every day and ate his bread sprinkled with ashes, as is said, *I have eaten ashes like bread,* [*and mingled my drink with weeping*] (Ps. 102:10). Hence *These are the last words of David . . . the saying of the man* [*once more*] *raised on high*[10] *(ibid.):* [not only did David's repentance serve to have him raised once more on high; it also provided proof to all sinners of the power of repentance, as evident from] further comment on the verse *These are the last words of David.* What exactly were these last words? [It may be inferred that they were as follows]: "Master of the universe," David pleaded with God, "because of my full repentance receive me into Your presence. Thereby You will make the wicked worthy of the world-to-come, for You will be able to say to them: 'David, king of Israel, committed a grave offense in My eyes, but as soon as he came to full repentance, I received him because his repentance was complete. Surely, then, if you come to full repentance, I will receive you.' " And the proof that David put his case before God in this way is in the words *For Thee, Thee only, have I sinned and done that which is evil in Thy sight;* [*that Thou mayest be justified when Thou speakest of repentance*] (Ps. 51:6). Such is the implication of *These are the last words of David . . . of the man through whom the yoke* [*of repentance*] *was raised on high* [*for all to see*][11] (2 Sam. 23:1).

ER, *p.* 8 | Finally, in still another comment, [which concerns itself with the conduct of men during the "day" following the six thousand years of the world's existence as reckoned by man], the verse is read, *These are the latter deeds of David:* Even as in David's former deeds there was neither sin nor iniquity,[12] so in his latter deeds there was neither sin nor iniquity. Such is the implication of *These are the latter deeds of David,* as further intimated by the words that follow, *The saying of David the son of Jesse, the man willing to have the yoke* [*placed upon him*], the yoke, that is, of Torah and the yoke of commandments. And for such willingness what, [God asked David], is to be your reward? You will be known as

---

9. In the seventeenth year of his reign, during his campaign against Ammon, he took Bath-sheba. And the next twenty-two years until the day of his death he spent in penitence. See 2 Sam. 11:2–17 and 12:15–23; 1 Chron. 3:5; Abrabanel on 1 Kings 3:7; and EB, *2,* 634 and 641–42, *s.v.* "David."

According to another account, the holy spirit was taken away from David for only six months. See B.Yoma 22b and Sanh 107a–b.

10. The holy spirit having been restored to him. See Ps. 51:13–14.

11. JV: *of the man raised on high.* But *'ol,* "on high," may also mean "yoke." Cf. MTeh 51:3 (YJS, *13, 1,* 472–73).

12. The comment, exculpating David from blame for the rape of Bath-sheba and the murder of Uriah, seems to disagree with the two preceding comments. Presumably, in keeping with R. Samuel bar Naḥmani, it is held that Uriah was a rebel against royal authority and that, following the prevailing practice of men who set out for war, he had given his wife Bath-sheba a bill of divorce before he set out against the Ammonites. See B.Shab 56a.

The anointed of the God of Jacob, the sweet singer of [*the Psalms of*] *Israel*[13] *(ibid.).*

Blessed is the man who makes himself submit like an ox to the yoke and like an ass to the burden;[14] the man who makes himself sit and meditate every moment of every day upon words of Torah. Forthwith the holy spirit suffuses the man whose Torah has taken root deep within him. [Of such a man it is said], *Blessed are ye that sow eagerly beside all waters* (Isa. 32:20). By *waters* is meant Torah, of which Scripture says, "Ho, every one that thirsteth, come ye to the waters"[15] (Isa. 55:1). What is implied by the word *all* in the phrase *all waters?* That a man is to read [all of Scripture]—the Five Books, the Prophets, and the Writings; that he is to recite Halakot and Midrash;[16] that he is to spend as much time as he can in the company of scholars and spend as little time as he can in the company of tradesmen. Forthwith the holy spirit will suffuse him to his very depths, and God's word will come readily to his tongue, as David went on to say, *The spirit of the Lord spoke by me, and His word was upon my tongue* (2 Sam. 23:2).

The man who works himself to the bone in study of words of Torah, who steadily makes his way through them like oxen plowing a field, is a man who is blessed. [Nay more: The words of Torah which he masters will be deemed his.] As the Holy One said to David: My son, My earlier words [which you voiced in Torah] as well as My later ones [to you] will all be deemed yours, for David testifies that *The God of Israel said: The word of the Rock of Israel is to be mine*[17] (2 Sam. 23:3).

[Still speaking to the man who attains mastery of Torah], God

---

13. Cf. MTeh 1:6 (YJS, *13, 1,* 10).

14. The reference to the yoke of an ox and the burden of an ass, ER finds in the conclusion of Isa. 32:20, which he reads, "who in your eagerness to sow beside all waters, send yourselves forward as cattle and asses to the field." See Yalkuṭ Isa. 437.

ER's interpretation of Isa. 32:20 provides a noble climax for the Messianic passage 32:15–20, which in verse 17 declares, *The work of righteousness shall be peace; and the effect of righteousness quietness and confidence for ever;* ER also avoids repetition, *peaceable habitation* and *quiet resting places* having already been promised in verse 18.

Verse 19, which reads, *And it shall hail in the downfall of the forest; but the city shall descend into the valley,* is obscure and appears to be irrelevant to the Messianic vision. Our author may therefore have construed the verse as follows: *For hail will come down only in the forest, and any lowliness ascribed to the city* [*of Jerusalem*] *will be solely in allusion to that part of it which lies on low ground.* So Ḳimḥi.

15. That here *waters* means Torah is made clear by the call in a succeeding verse (Isa. 55:3), *Hear, and your soul shall live.*

16. The probable meaning of Halakot is traditional statements of laws in general, such as the Mishnah, but without their exegetical derivation from Scripture. Midrash, exegesis, may refer to Sifra and Sifre, which contain the laws derived from the Five Books and the manner of such derivation.

To the question "What is Mishnah?" R. Meir replies, "Halakot," and R. Judah [b. Il'a'i], "Midrash." See B.Ḳid 49a and H. Freedman's notes in Soncino tr., p. 246.

17. JV: *The Rock of Israel spoke to me.* But ER reads not *dibber,* "spoke," but *dĕbar,* the construct of *dabar,* "word, utterance." See Gesenius-Brown, p. 184, on the suggested emendations of Jer. 5:13. On the theme that Torah is named after he who meditates upon it, see MTeh 1:16 (YJS, *13, 1,* 22–23).

went on to say to David: *The righteous who rules over the all too human in him shares rule with the Awesomeness of God (ibid.).* [18] What is it in the righteous man that gives him the power to rule thus? The righteous man whose self-rule overcomes the evil Impulse within him achieves a share of God's power and rules alongside *the Awesomeness of God.* [19]

Blessed be the Preserver of the world, blessed be He in whose presence no man is favored more than another, from whose presence clear shining and light [come] to the world, from whose presence rains come to the world and tender grass comes into the world. The reward of the righteous who wear themselves out in study of words of Torah is that Scripture regards them as though it is they who bring clear shining and light into the world, as though it is they who bring rains and blades of tender grass into the world. Hence it is said, [*Because of the righteous*] . . . *clear shining, rain, even tender grass springeth out of the earth* (2 Sam. 23:4).

[Having in mind the people of Israel from whom come those who can achieve righteousness through their mastery of Torah], king David went on to say: I will declare the Holy One's acts of mercy and loving-kindness which He performs for the people of Israel each and every hour, each and every day. Every day a man [of Israel] sells himself to evil, but is redeemed;[20] every day in the evening his spirit is taken from him and deposited with the spirit's true Owner and in the morning it is restored to him, as is said, *Into Thy hand I commit my spirit, and then Thou dost release it to me, O Lord God, Thou who art to be relied on*[21] (Ps. 31:6). Every day miracles are performed for a man [of Israel] as great as the ones performed for those who went out of Egypt; every day redemption is bestowed upon him like the one bestowed upon those

ER, *p.* 9 who went out of Egypt; | every day such sustenance is given him [as was given him] on his mother's breast; and every day the same punishment is inflicted upon him for his misdeeds as is inflicted upon a child by his teacher. But why should God have such concern for the children of Israel? Because, as you can see for yourself, it is the seed of Abraham, Isaac, and Jacob [who declare His glory, the seed concerning] whom God asked [in eager anticipation of their coming], When will these

---

18. JV: *Ruler over men shall be the righteous, even he that ruleth in the fear of God.* Cf. EZ, 167.

19. In order to account for the extraordinary power bestowed upon the righteous, our author will soon expound upon Psalm 19 to prove that what God desires is not that the heavens declare His glory, but that Israel do so by word and deed. Cf. Deut. Rabbah 10:3.

20. The comment is based on *With Him is plenteous redemption, and He will redeem Israel from all his iniquities* (Ps. 130:7–8).

21. Thus, according to ER, the Psalmist surrounded by enemies demonstrates that God is indeed men's *stronghold* (Ps. 31:5). JV: *Into Thy hand I commit my spirit, Thou hast redeemed me, O Lord, Thou God of truth.* Cf. Luke 23:46.

appear so that I may hear words in praise of Me from their mouths? [So desirous was God of hearing such words that] nine hundred and seventy-four generations before He created the world, He made great changes in His original plans for mankind [and waited for only twenty-six generations before giving the Torah to Israel].[22]

[It may be asked, however, why God took the trouble to change His plans in regard to mankind, particularly since], according to a Psalm of David, *The heavens* [*themselves*] *declare the glory of God* (Ps. 19:2). The answer may be, of course, that the heavens are incapable of speech and so could not actually voice the glory of God.[23] Nevertheless, the fact that the heavens were created at the very beginning of time shows that they are indeed fit to declare the glory of Him who spoke the word that brought the world into being. Remember that the world, all of it—man and beast and the fowl of heaven—is sustained in life only through the interaction of heaven and earth which makes crops grow during the six months of winter and makes them ripen during the six months of summer. All of the inhabitants of the world live on these crops—indeed, all of God's handiwork does.

[Another reason that the heavens are fit to declare God's glory is that even one small sector of them overlooks, so to speak, all of mankind.] The entire inhabited world, I once heard the Sages say, occupies an area corresponding to the region in the heavens between Ursa Major and Scorpio.[24] Whereupon I asked, "My Masters, may I who am no more than dust under your feet say something in reply to you?" They answered, "Say it." I then said, "My Masters, all the inhabitants of the world reside under a single star." They said, "Prove what you say," and I replied, "Yes, I will," and went on: "My Masters, let two men take up a position anywhere in the Land of Israel and take note of a star directly above their heads at sunrise or sunset on the first, fifth, or fifteenth day of the month. Let them then travel to the great city of Rome. Will not the star that they saw rise directly above their heads in the Land of Israel be the very same one that rises above the great city of Rome? In short, as I said, all the inhabitants of the world reside under a single star."

---

22. God's original plan as indicated in the verse *The word which He was to command after a thousand generations* (Ps. 105:8; 1 Chron. 16:15) was that one thousand generations should pass before He gave the Torah. Foreseeing their wickedness, however, He changed His plan; sweeping away nine hundred and seventy-four generations that were to have been created, He gave the Torah to Moses in the twenty-sixth generation from Adam. See MTeh 90:13 and 105:3 (YJS, *13, 2,* 95 and 181).

Again ER emphasizes not the punitive aspect of God but the love that is His.

23. "The answer may be . . . could not actually declare the glory of God" is a paraphrase of what more literally may be translated: "But since the heavens are incapable of narrating the work of creation, why does Scripture say, *The heavens declare the glory of God?*"

24. Heat is said to emanate from the first, and cold from the second. See B.Ber 58b and Pes 94a.

[Another reason that the heavens are fit to declare the glory of God is the beauty in the arrangement of the stars.] Is it not of great significance that the beauty of the seven stars of the Pleiades derives from their having been arranged in the heavens in a fixed relation to one another? By such arrangement, says Scripture,[25] the generations of mankind are taught appreciation of how art gives beauty to substance.[26] A man should not say, therefore, Why is not the entire sky paved solid with stars? [For him to understand that the beauty of the Pleiades comes from the way they are arranged as well as from the stuff they are made of], let him consider the parable of a king who had a solid ingot of gold. If he had put the solid ingot as an ornament on his head, would it have become him? His wisdom and understanding made him think otherwise. So he took a half-*sel'a*'s weight of gold from the ingot and had it made into a linked chain which he hung around his neck. Such transformation is the way of beauty. Even so did the Holy One, may His great name be blessed for ever and ever and ever, arrange the stars in the sky, giving to each its proper place and thus creating their beauty.

ER, *p.* 10 | [Still another reason that the heavens are fit to declare the glory of God is the presence of the sun in them, the sun whose speed is awesome, whose silence is utter, and whose disappearance at nightfall is complete.] Consider, said the Sages, that every day the sun travels a distance that at an ordinary pace would require five hundred years. Consider, furthermore, that in its journey from the remote place where it rises to the remote place where it sets, not a sound is heard in its journeying and its going down, nor is it seen after it sets and before it rises. Moreover, the velocity of the sun in its journey through the heavens, every day traveling a distance that at an ordinary rate of speed would require five hundred years, is so precisely adjusted to the circumference of the tree of life—[the earth, that is—as to enable the sun to circle the entire tree in one day].[27] Hence it is said, *How great are Thy works, O Lord,* [*their precise adjustment shows how*] *very deep are Thy thoughts* (Ps. 92:6).

A further comment on *How great are Thy works, O Lord*—[how great is their infinite variety]! Just think how many kinds of cattle there are in the world, how many kinds of beasts there are in the world, and

---

25. Job 38:31 reads, *Canst thou bind* (or *link*) *the chains of the Pleiades?* On the number of stars in the Pleiades, see W. M. Feldman, *Rabbinical Mathematics and Astronomy* (London, 1931), p. 214.

26. "Of how art gives beauty to substance" is an extended paraphrase of the literal "The proper [or desirable] way on earth."

27. The tree of life is said to extend over an area of five hundred years' journey (Gen. Rabbah 15:6), corresponding in size to the entire earth out of all of which (see Gen. 2:9) presumably it was made to grow. Hence here the tree is understood as a metaphor for the earth.

how many kinds of fish there are in the sea! And within each kind is there even one whose voice is like another's, or whose look is like another's, or whose disposition is like another's, or whose flavor is like another's? [Indeed, only to think of the variety of mankind itself, as] the Sages taught in a Mishnah, "is to proclaim the greatness of the King of the kings of kings, the Holy One, blessed be He. For if a man strikes many coins from one die, they all resemble one another—in fact, they are all exactly alike. But, though the King of the kings of kings, the Holy One, blessed be He, fashioned every man in the stamp of the first man [Adam], not a single one of them is exactly like his fellow" (Sanh 4:5). Hence it is said, *How great are Thy works, O Lord,* [in their infinite variety]! (Ps. 92:6).

Another comment on *For the Leader. A Psalm of David. The heavens declare the glory of God* (Ps. 19:2): Do they not always hold the same course,[28] a course from which they never depart? Nevertheless, great as is His joy in their unswerving obedience to His will, an obedience true of all the work of His hands, His supreme joy is not so much in the heavens as it is in the seed of Abraham, [for whose sake, on two separate days, He actually changed the heavens' unaltering course. In fact, the first of these two days heralded another like it], as we are told in the very next verse: *One day heralds another*[29] (Ps. 19:3). What are the two days that Scripture refers to here? The first was a day in the life of Moses, a day which heralded a particular day in the life of Joshua. Of another day [of victory] in Moses' life, it is said, *By means of this day,* [*O Israel*], *I will begin to stir up dread of thee . . . among the peoples under the whole extent of heaven* (Deut. 2:25). If you ask: But since the Holy One extirpated [the kingdoms of] Sihon and Og, who was present there to declare Moses' victory to the peoples of the world? It was the sun standing still in the heavens[30] [that proclaimed his victory throughout the world]. And where do we find it intimated that the sun did, in fact, stand still for Moses? In an earlier verse which tells us that during his war against Amalek, *Moses' hands were heavy . . . and Aaron and Hur stayed up his hands . . . until the going down of the sun* (Exod. 17:12). By the words *until the going down of the sun* can Scripture be saying that the sun stood still for Moses until[31] he had vanquished Amalek [and that only

---

28. "The coursing of the sun is its praising Him." See MTeh 19:1 (YJS, *13, 1,* 281).

29. JV: *Day unto day uttereth speech.* Cf. MTeh 19:8 (YJS, *13, 1,* 278).

30. Moses is said to have made the sun stand still on three occasions: (1) during the battle with Amalek, (2) during the war against Sihon and Og, and (3) at the time when Moses commanded heaven and earth to stand still and listen to him, saying *Give ear, ye heavens, and I will speak and let the earth hear the words of my mouth* (Deut. 32:1). See Ginzberg, *Legends, 6,* 45–46.

31. [Perhaps the reasoning is based on the basic meaning of *'ad* (from *'adah,* "to advance, to pass over"), so that *until the going down of the sun* could be rendered "the

then did it go down]? Yes, for it was this day of Moses' victory that passed on the word to a day in the life of Joshua of a victory when the sun would stand still for him also. Such is the intimation of the words *Whisper into Joshua's ears the prayer* (Exod. 17:14), by which Scripture meant: May it be the will of God that as the sun stood still for me, [Moses], so may it stand still for you, [Joshua]. Where, indeed, do we find it intimated earlier in Scripture that the sun was to stand still for Joshua? In the verse *Joshua said in the sight of Israel: Sun, stand thou still upon Gibeon,* does not the verse go on to say further *Is this not written in the Book of Jashar,* [*the Upright One's Book*],[32] *that the sun would stay in the midst of heaven* (Josh. 10:12–13)?

[God's joy, we thus see, is not so much in the heavens' declaration of His glory as it is in the seed of Abraham's preoccupation with His Torah.] Hence, in extended comment, [what the heavens specify in their declaring God's glory is] not only, as previously asserted, the [plain] fact that *One day heralds another* (Ps. 19:3). But what these words, when read *Day uttereth speech to the day,* further suggest is that the daytime is the proper time for the study of Torah—study of the Five Books, the Prophets, and the Writings. And the conclusion of the verse *Night declareth knowledge to the night (ibid.)* is taken to mean that the nighttime is the proper time for study of rabbinic exposition of Torah.[33] In addition to Torah and exposition of Torah, the Halaḵoṯ, [those unwritten laws which govern the daily conduct of Jews], are to be studied, the laws of which it is said, *There is no speech* [*concerning them*], *there are no words* [*concerning them*], *neither is there heard the Voice that*
ER, *p.* 11 *validates them*[34] (Ps. 19:4). | For all such studies, *The gathering*[35] [*that occupies itself*] *with them is gone out all over the world* (Ps. 19:5)—that is to say, all over the world Jews gather in academies where during

---

setting of the sun having been advanced, deferred, passed over, in favor of a later hour." L. N.]

32. Targum Jonathan, on 2 Sam. 1:18, translates Book of Jashar as "the Torah." See also B.Az 25a and Gen. Rabbah 6:9.

33. Interpolating the word *midrašan,* "exposition of," before *šelkĕṯuḇim,* which is taken to mean "all of Scripture," hence "Torah." So Louis Ginzberg in *OT,* p. 282, n. 274. Ginzberg's proposed reading follows Rabbinic association of the day's brightness with Scripture and the night's mystery with its Oral Exposition. See MTeh 19:7 (YJS, *13, 1,* 276–77); PR 15:6 (YJS, *18, 1,* 314); and PRKM 5:6, p. 88.

Friedmann interpolates the word *lelan,* "during the night of," and reads the passage, "*And declareth knowledge* (Ps. 19:3), those parts of the writings—[Ezra, Nehemiah, and Esther]—composed *during the night (ibid.)* of exile."

34. Those laws which are said to be "like mountains hanging by a hair, for Scripture's teaching thereon is scanty and the rules many" (Ḥag 2:8). Thus the many kinds of work prohibited on the Sabbath are not even referred to in the Five Books, in which only plowing and sowing (Exod. 34:21), kindling fire (Exod. 35:13), and gathering sticks of wood (Num. 15:32) are expressly prohibited.

35. JV: *Their line.* But apparently the commentator takes *ḳw,* "line," as a nominal form of *ḳwh,* "collect"; hence "gatherings of people in academies." So Schick.

discussion everyone is given the opportunity to voice his agreement [or dissent],[36] thus causing people to listen attentively to discussion of words of Torah. [Nevertheless, the greatest understanding of Torah, of rabbinic exposition of Torah, and of Halakot is to be attained] in the Land of Israel, as is said, *But their words are in the Land which is uppermost* [37] *(ibid.).* As the Land of Israel has all six kinds of terrain,[38] and so is described as "The Land which is supreme in terrain among all other lands"[39] (Prov. 8:26), [so the Land of Israel presents supremely all modes of study and hence is supreme among all other lands in understanding of Torah].

In another comment the words previously read *Their words are in the Land which is uppermost* (Ps. 19:5) are now read *Their words to the world's uttermost ends,* and are taken to refer to the study of 'Aggadot whereby God's great name is hallowed to the ends of the world.[40]

For them hath He set out a tent in the sun (ibid.), [which is to say that to house the words of Torah, the Holy One set out the Tent of Meeting in the open]. A parable will explain further how the verse is to be understood. There was a mortal king who kept precious stones and pearls of purest ray in his palace, and the people of the kingdom offered to buy them for a goodly sum—[that is, for their complete loyalty]—<provided the gems would be their own private property>. The king told them: I will let you buy them; not, however, to be hidden away for the exclusive use of one people, but open to all the peoples of the world. Likewise, when the Holy One—may His great name be blessed for ever and ever—gave the Torah to Israel, He meant it to be left open for all the peoples of the world,[41] as is said, *I have not given it in secret* (Isa. 45:19). [Yet, though the Torah was given in the open, mankind rejected it, so that as the verse from the Psalm cited above continues, *The sun is*] *as a bridegroom coming out of his chamber* (Ps. 19:6)—that is, like a bridegroom entering the bridal chamber clean and coming out of it unclean,[42] so the sun's disk is clean upon entering the world and unclean upon coming out. Therefore, [because of the sun's reluctance to enter the world],[43] rays of light like arrows are sent before it to point

---

36. See Rashi on B.Soṭ 27a.
37. JV: *And their words to the end of the world.*
38. Tilth, soil, sod, valley, desert, and earth's foundation. See PRKM 23:10 and Sif Deut. 37 (ed. Finkelstein [Breslau, 1936–39], p. 70).
39. JV: *The beginning of the dust of the world.*
40. In the spirit of the utterance, "If you wish to come to know Him by whose word the world came into being, study 'Aggadah. For you will thus come to know Him by whose word the world came into being and you will also cleave to His ways" (Sif Deut. 49 [ed. Finkelstein, p. 115]).
41. Cf. Mek, *2,* 198.
42. See Lev. 15:18 and Šulḥan 'aruk, Oraḥ ḥayyim, 88.
43. Interpolated as in parallel in MTeh 19:11 (YJS, *13, 1,* 281). See Hab. 3:11.

its way into the world, while at the same time it is admonished: "Is it for your own pleasure that you go forth [or is it to serve Me]?" Hence [*The sun*] *is as a bridegroom,* etc.

[Righteous men sent forth into the world may, like the sun, be reluctant to live in it because of the sins committed therein. Let them remember, however, that in time God] <*will rejoice as a mighty man to run* [*to welcome*] *His guest*[44] *(ibid.)*>. A parable will explain how these words are to be understood. For a period of seven—some say a period of thirty—days,[45] a mortal king had his servants and the officers of his household feasting at a banquet in his presence. At the end of the seven, or the thirty, days each of the guests took his leave and returned to his domestic duties in peace. After a time, however, one of the guests came back to the palace and the king was told, So-and-so has come back. Thereupon the king enfolded himself in his robe, and went out to meet him, saying, "Enter in peace," and then continued, "Stay until the time of the [great] feast comes." So it is with the righteous in this world. For when they take leave to go to their eternal world, [the Holy One], like a mighty man receiving his guests with joy and friendly countenance, says of each of them, *Let him come in peace, let them rest on their couches* [*and await My kingly feast*][46] (Isa. 57:2). Such is the significance of *He rejoiceth as a mighty man,* etc.

<But in the meantime, *His going forth* [*to judge*] *is a decision in heaven—the fierceness of His anger is upon the most distinguished of men, but ultimately none are hid from the heat thereof*[47] (Ps. 19:7).> Hence the righteous are punished [in this world] even for trivial offenses while the wicked are punished only for the most grievous ones. The truth of this statement can be illustrated from the lives of Moses, Aaron, Nadab, and Abihu,[48] who were punished for trivial offenses. And the proof that the wicked are punished only for their grievous offenses? From the lives of Jeroboam, Ahaz, and Manasseh,[49] who were not condemned until they filled the entire world with their transgressions. A parable will

---

44. *Oraḥ,* "course," may also mean "guest."

45. See B.Keṭ 8a.

46. See PR 2:3 (YJS, *18, 1,* 52–53). On God's feast for the righteous, see Moore, *Judaism, 2,* 363–65.

47. In JV, Ps. 19:7 reads, *His going forth is from the end of the heaven, and his circuit unto the ends of it, and there is nothing hid from the heat thereof.* But apparently, according to Friedmann, ER takes *ḳṣh,* "end," to denote "cut"; hence "cutting, decree, decision." Furthermore ER takes *tĕḳufah,* "circuit," to be a form of the Aramaic *tuḳfa',* "fierce reproof," and takes *ḳĕṣoṭam,* "the ends of it," to mean "the innermost quarters," hence "the most distinguished of men." Cf. Raṣhi on Num. 11:1.

48. Moses and Aaron were punished for failing to sanctify God's name (Exod. 32:23–24; Num. 20:11). Nadab and Abihu were punished even though they intended the strange fire they brought for the worship of God (Lev. 10:1).

49. Jeroboam sinned and made Israel sin (1 Kings 14:16). Ahaz closed schools to prevent the study of Torah (MTeh 2:10 [YJS, *13, 1,* 42]). And Manasseh set the graven image of Asherah in the Temple (2 Kings 21:7; ER, 47, 111).

explain how the matter may be understood. A mortal king was seated on his throne with the elders of his realm seated in his presence. As soon as one of them said something that was not right, he was slapped down at once in reproof, whereas any one of those who, [not being elders], stood outside the throne room was allowed to stand unreproved for an offense until the time of his punishment in Gehenna came. Hence it is said, *His going forth [in instant reproof] . . . is upon the innermost quarters of heaven* (Ps. 19:7)—[that is, His reproof falls[50] upon the righteous, those who are seated in His very presence]. And why such immediate reproof? Because of [the enormity of their transgression against] *The Torah of the Lord which is perfect, restoring the soul; the testimony of the Lord which is sure, making wise the simple. The precepts of the Lord which are right,* [and by which, as it is said, *Thy servant is warned*] (Ps. 19:8–12). That is, say the Sages, whenever men, [who are God's servants, neglect His warning and] cease to concern themselves with Torah, the Holy One wishes to destroy the entire world, | so that He ER, *p.* 12
[turns away from mankind and][51] says, *Give praise unto the Lord, ye Divine beings* (Ps. 29:1), the *Divine beings* being the ministering angels. The very fact, says the Holy One, that I multiplied men like the birds of heaven and the fish of the sea,[52] led them to choose not to obey My wish with regard to the precepts of Torah, and so I hid My face from them. <[Hence, O mankind, take heed]. *Ascribe unto the Lord the glory of strength (ibid.)*>, such *glory* being Torah, as intimated in the verse "Let them set before the Lord glory"—[that is, His glory comes from men's obedience to Torah] (Isa. 42:12). And elsewhere Scripture enjoins us, "To the Lord your God give glory, [obedience to Torah], before it grow dark, and before your feet stumble upon the mountains of twilight" (Jer. 13:16). Moreover, we are told, *Worship the Lord only after savoring the awe of that which is holy*[53] (Ps. 29:2). Hence it is said: A man should not stand up even for the *Tĕfillah* unless he has first uttered at least one Halakah or one verse of Scripture.[54] Such is the implication of *Worship the Lord only after savoring the awe of that which is holy.* [And in uttering the Halakah or the verse from Scripture, the worshiper should be sure that he is uttering the Halakah or the verse correctly, since] *The voice of the Lord is concerned for the waters* (Ps. 29:3)

---

50. See above, n. 47.

51. Implying that God has given up hope of hearing such praise from mankind.

52. Only the birds of heaven and the fish of the sea had, like mankind, the blessing "Be fruitful and multiply" bestowed upon them. See Gen. 1:22, 28.

53. JV: *Worship the Lord in the beauty of holiness.* But in keeping with R. Joshua ben Levi (B.Ber 30b), ER apparently reads *hadrat,* "beauty," by metathesis, as *ḥerdat,* "awe."

54. In the course of the years this requirement before the morning *Tĕfillah* was expanded to include selections from Scripture, Mishnah, and pertinent comments thereon from the Talmud. See Hertz, *APB,* pp. 14–43.

—that is, for Torah['s being quoted correctly]. Watch your words, said the Sages, lest you assert something not in accord with Torah and thus incur from Heaven the penalty of death.[55] Should you make such an assertion, the disciples who listen to you may also assert something not in keeping with Torah, and thus they, too, may incur from Heaven the penalty of death. May there never be such assertions—[not even before the *Tĕfillah*][56]—as a result of which the name of heaven will be profaned!

In the verse *The God of* [*Torah's*] *glory thundereth, but also the Lord upon many waters (ibid.),* [the word *many* is taken to be referring to liquids besides water]. For your sake, says God, in accompaniment of My thunder, I caused to rain words of Torah as gentle as milk and oil, so gentle that they can be poured from one vessel into another without making a sound. [Likewise, in study of Torah a man should be vigorous, yet gentle.][57] Such is the meaning of *The Lord of glory thundereth, but also The Lord upon many waters,*[58] [a meaning echoed in the words that follow], *The voice of the Lord is powerful, yet the voice of the Lord is also gentle*[59] (Ps. 29:4).

A parable will explain how the first part of the verse just cited is to be further understood: A mortal king had notable sons; some came to possess Torah [on their own],[60] others came to possess Mishnah [on their own], still others came to possess skill in honorable dealing with their fellows [on their own]. Then the king took another wife, a humble woman, by whom he had several children. He sent them to be taught Scripture, to be taught Mishnah, and to be taught honorable conduct. He then sat back to wait, saying: How long will it be until these boys are like my notable sons? After some time, he went to visit them—they were not engaged with Scripture, nor with Mishnah, nor in honorable conduct. He sat down on the ground in front of them and clapped his hands in grief, saying: To what end did I build houses for these boys? To what end did I buy fields for them? To what end did I plant vineyards for them?

In the sight of their Father in heaven [the notable children were the Patriarchs,[61] whereas] the children of Israel in the world as we

---

55. Cf. Ab 1:11.

56. Since such assertions, being private, are not intended for instruction.

57. Cf. B.MK 16a–b.

58. Cf. Song Rabbah 1:2 and MTeh 1:18 (YJS, *13. 1,* 24–25).

59. JV: *The voice of the Lord is powerful, the voice of the Lord is full of majesty.* But ER apparently takes *hadar,* "majesty," as though written *ḥazar,* "restorative," hence "gentle"; or perhaps as though it were the Aramaic *hadar,* "restorative." Cf. R. Ḥama bar R. Ḥanina's statement, "The voice of the Lord was powerful for the young and 'restorative' (or 'gentle') for the old." See Num. Rabbah 10:1 and Mah, *ad loc.;* and Song Rabbah 5:13.

60. So Schick.

61. So Schick.

know it who do not concern themselves with matters of Torah are like the king's children by his second wife. And against those who are not thus concerned, says the Psalmist, *The voice of the Lord is powerful . . . the voice of the Lord breaketh cedars* (Ps. 29:4–5). By *cedars* is meant self-satisfied people who have prospered in the world, but do not concern themselves with matters of Torah. The Psalmist likens them to cedars because, like cedars, those who have no Torah bring forth no [edible] fruit. Of such it is said, *I destroyed the Amorite whose height was like the height of cedars . . . and I destroyed his fruit from above, and his roots from beneath* (Amos 2:9). [The Lord breaks such "cedars" now, even as in the past.] *The Lord broke in pieces the cedars of Lebanon* (Ps. 29:5), the term *Lebanon* suggesting that these "cedars" were men of the First Temple[62] who, with hair trimmed and coiffed, set themselves up in the Land, but had no concern for matters of Torah. It is [worldly] men such as these who are referred to as cedars in the words *The voice of the Lord breaketh the cedars (ibid.).*

Further on in the Psalm the Psalmist refers to another kind of worldly men of the First Temple *whom He observed kick like a heifer* (Ps. 29:6). As the following parable will make clear, the Psalmist refers to the kind of man who stubbornly refuses to learn from chastisements, and hence must suffer doubly for his stubbornness. Consider: A householder had a stubborn heifer [which kicked up continually]. He thought to restrain it with a rope ten cubits long, but it continued to kick up. So he tried to restrain it with a rope twenty cubits long, and it stubbornly continued to kick up. Even with a rope forty cubits long the heifer kept on kicking up, until finally the householder subdued it with the weight of a fifty-cubit rope. *Like a stubborn heifer, Israel has proved stubborn* (Hos. 4:16), [even while suffering for their stubbornness]. Such stubbornness, furthermore, bodes ill for any man. Not only | do his iniquities [remain unforgiven],[63] as the Sages tell us, but he **ER, *p.* 13**
is brought to commit such indecencies as one cannot even give a name to,[64] and thus he uproots himself by his own hand from both this world and the world-to-come. If you would learn My ways of dealing [with men, says the Lord], stop and consider on the other hand what was done to the generation of the wilderness. Because[65] they had heeded Torah throughout their days, the moment they said something before Me that was not proper,[66] I smote them—at once I smote them. Such

62. *Lebanon,* "that which whitens *(malbin)* the sins of Israel," is a term often used to designate the First Temple, which Solomon built with cedars of Lebanon. See B.Yoma 39b and 1 Kings 5:22–25.

63. Cf. B.Ber 5a–b.

64. See Louis Ginzberg's n. 367 in *OT,* p. 311.

65. ["Although." L. N.] But at times *'af 'al pi* seems to mean "because."

66. Apparently ER exculpates Israel from the sin of the golden calf, presumably regarding it as the brainchild of the "mixed multitude"—the Egyptians, who at the

is the sense of the verse *The Lord shook in convulsions*[67] [*the generation of*] *the wilderness, the Lord shook in convulsions* [*the generation of*] *the wilderness which was holy*[68] (Ps. 29:8).

[*The voice of the Lord is also gentle* (Ps. 29:4)]: The Holy One then went on to reassure Israel, saying to them: My children, I swear by My throne of glory that [the father of][69] a boy who is busying himself for My sake with Torah in his teacher's house will receive the reward which I already have at hand for such a father, for [by his concern for his child's instruction], he will have avoided the transgression of [neglect of Torah]. Even for a man who knows no more than how to behave properly and who has only a slight acquaintance with Scripture, the reward he is to receive lies before Me already, for [by his behavior and by his minimal acquaintance with Scripture] he will have avoided the transgression [of neglect of Torah].[70] Even for a man who has neither Scripture nor Mishnah but comes early, mornings and evenings, to the synagogue or to the academy where having in mind My great name he reads the Shĕma' and having in mind My great name recites the *Tĕfillah,* the reward he is to receive lies before Me already, for [by such awareness of My name] he avoids the transgression [of neglect of Torah. It is thus possible for every man in his own way to avoid the transgression of neglect of Torah], for *The voice of the Lord heweth out* [*numberless*] *flames of fire* (Ps. 29:7).

In the sight of their Father in heaven, to what may we compare Israel in this world? To a hind who is in pain while pregnant and in pain while giving birth, all calvings being difficult. Thus the words *The voice of the Lord that maketh the hinds to calve* (Ps. 29:9) [signify that Israel's travail will be followed by the coming of the Messiah].[71]

[When the Lord's voice is heard] at the time [of the Messiah's coming], the whole world will be agitated, saying: Is it possible that God is coming to the world to destroy it? The holy spirit will reply saying: The King of the kings of kings, blessed be He, is coming only to join in a feast with His children. He will say to them, I have come to be sovereign. Over whom am I to be sovereign? [Over you.] And

---

exodus joined Israel for wrong reasons. The one sin ER charges Israel with is that after the spies had returned with an adverse report concerning the Land, the entire community railed against Moses and Aaron and said, "Let us head back for Egypt" (Num. 14:4). See Haida and ER, 122–24.

67. Throughout the year, according to R. Nathan, they retched until on the ninth of Ab they died (see MTeh 78:7 [YJS, *13, 2,* 27]). JV: *shaketh.*

68. JV: Kadesh. But Kadesh may of course be taken to mean "holy" (*ḳadoš*).

69. "[the father]"—as construed by Haida.

70. So Haida, who bases his interpretation on MTeh 1:17 (YJS, *13, 1,* 23). But see Louis Ginzberg's n. 350 in *OT,* p. 310.

71. See PR 15:14/15 (YJS, *18, 1,* 327–28).

why am I willing to be your sovereign? Because you are adorned with good deeds and with study of Torah. Hence *Is the Lord again enthroned for a flood?* No, *Even as the Lord has given [Torah's] strength to His people, the Lord is now about to bless His people with peace* (Ps. 29:10–11).[72]

---

72. Cf. PR 20:1 (YJS, *18, 1,* 398).

CHAPTER 3

The radiant countenance of the Sages foreshadows the bliss of the world-to-come

Summary

David's crying out, "My awe of God arises from my joy in Him, and my joy in Him arises from my awe of Him, but my love of Him is stronger than both," caused God to make a covenant with him, giving him exceptional insight into Torah's entire range, bestowing upon him radiance of countenance, release from sorrow, release from enslavement to the Impulse to evil, and the kind of strength and glory which are associated with, indeed foreshadow, the bliss of the world-to-come (ER, 13).

Disciples of the wise, it is observed, do not prosper greatly, lest riches lead them to rebel against the precepts of Torah. In other respects, the lives in this world of disciples of the wise, like the life of David, foreshadow the bliss of the world-to-come, for they are even able to bring the dead to life (ER, 14) and can behold now and then the downfall of Israel's oppressors.

When Israel's sinners in the time-to-come are brought before the Holy One to be sentenced, the righteous, by reminding Him of the sinners' occasional deeds of merit, will bring about the raising of the sinners from the dust to which they had been reduced.

David, the exemplar of disciples of the wise, remarkable in self-abnegation and in humility, is deemed to surpass in worth the three Patriarchs, to have authority next to God's, and to be exalted always as chief of Israel during their pilgrimages to Jerusalem.

David's distinction as a scholar stemmed from his capacity to lend delicacy and subtlety to words of Torah (ER, 15) and from his willingness to yield to others in the academy. Yet at the same time, as a warrior, he was unyielding on the battlefield. There he was greatly successful, though, to be sure, because of his sin with Bath-sheba—of which he quickly repented—his victory on one occasion fell short of what God had promised to the completely righteous. David's quick repentance again sets the example for disciples of the wise whose love of Torah moves them immediately to repent their failings. Hence one ought to refrain from gossiping about their occasional slips.

In the world-to-come different kinds of radiance will be vouchsafed to disciples of the wise; the greatest of these will shine with the radiance of the firmament's atmosphere when it is clear of clouds. As for transgressors who repented before they died, they too will share in the radiance of the time-to-come. On the other hand, in the time-to-come, some sinners, such as the four notorious kings, will have faces not shining but black as the bottom of a pot (ER, 16).

Though the source of radiance in the countenances of disciples of the wise is Torah, which gives light from one end of the world to the other, nevertheless response to the guidance of Sages and the heeding of chastisements are likewise deemed obedience to the will of God and worthy therefore of the reward of radiance of countenance (ER, 17).

Chapter 3

King David said further: I, in this world, what am I? What is there to say of myself except that my awe of God arises from my joy in Him, and my joy in Him arises from my awe of Him,[1] but my love of Him is stronger than both? Because David spoke thus, the Holy One made a covenant with him, assuring him that he would be completely at home in Scripture, in Mishnah, in Halakot, and in 'Aggadot. With regard to this covenant David said: *An everlasting covenant He hath made with me* (2 Sam. 23:5)—made, that is, a covenant of knowledge of Torah, such as is referred to in the verse "My covenant was with him[2] . . . concerning the Torah of truth" (Mal. 2:5–6). And David went on to say, [*a covenant*] *set up with everything* (2 Sam. 23:5)—with Scripture, with Mishnah, with Halakot, with 'Aggadot; and *safeguarded (ibid.),* that is, words of Torah were safeguarded <within him> for ever and ever and ever. The words that follow are usually read, *So that all my deliverance, and everything precious He will not make it grow* [*like a plant that soon withers*] *(ibid.),*[3] but here do not read the verse thus; read it rather, "So that for the sake of my complete deliverance and for the sake of everything precious, [He sees to it] that I make not myself grow [in material riches]." Whenever a disciple of the wise—so it is said—engages much in business and does not do well at it,[4] it speaks well for him because | the Holy One loves the Torah within him, and so does not permit him to grow rich, lest growing rich he will rebel against the precepts of Torah. By the same token, whenever a disciple of the wise engages much in Torah and does not get much worldly profit from it, it speaks well for him because the Holy One loves the Torah within him and takes care that the disciple of the wise grow not rich and then rebel against the precepts of Torah. In post-Mosaic Scripture, similar concern is explicitly voiced by Solomon king of Israel: *Two things have I asked of Thee. . . . Give me neither poverty nor riches . . . lest I be full, and deny, and say: "Who is the Lord?"* (Prov. 30:7–9).

ER, *p.* 13 *cont'd* — ER, *p.* 14

Blessed be the Preserver of the world, blessed be He who has chosen the Sages and the disciples of their disciples until the end of

---

1. The utterance paraphrases *Serve the Lord with fear, and rejoice with trembling* (Ps. 2:11).

2. The words *life and peace,* which appear in ER, are deleted.

3. So interpreted by Ḳimḥi. JV: *For all my salvation and all my desire will He not make it grow?*

4. [Rather "immerses himself in business"; the implied approval of a disciple of the wise devoting himself to the chase of the almighty dollar raises my eyebrow, and makes me wonder if the correct text is *še*['*eno*] *marbeh bĕ'esek,* in which case the accurate, and logical, translation would be, "who does not make business his main preoccupation, and does not derive most of his livelihood *(mitparnes)* from it." If I am not mistaken, most of the Sages, except those born into wealthy families, earned their bread in skilled or unskilled trades like cobblery, tailoring, etc. L. N.]

<all generations>, He who in their behalf fulfills the saying "As a man measures, so it is measured out to him": they sit in synagogues and academies, indeed wherever a place is available, and, with the fear of Heaven within them, read Scripture for the sake of Heaven, recite Mishnah for the sake of Heaven; by the utterance of their mouths they give duration to matters of Torah, and consequently matters of Torah are not and will not be forgotten in their mouths or in the mouths of their children for ever and ever and ever, an assurance voiced in the words: *This is My covenant with them, saith the Lord; My spirit that is upon thee, and My words which I have put in thy mouth, shall not depart out of thy mouth, nor out of the mouth of thy seed, nor out of the mouth of thy seed's seed, saith the Lord, from henceforth and for ever* (Isa. 59:21). But transgressors in Israel have no such assurance. Their children[5] are gentle enough in their youth, but in their old age they are sure to harden:[6] what is to be the requital of such transgressors? Their children will be made to ascend [to heaven] and there be burned in the great court of inquiry —in the great assize.[7] [Through their heritage], such children *are worthless,*[8] as Scripture says, and hence *like thorns must go up* [*in flame*]*—root, stock, and stem*[9] (2 Sam. 23:6). *They shall be utterly burnt with fire in the* [*heavenly*] *assize*[10] (2 Sam. 23:7), says the very next verse.

Because what is to befall the children of transgressors is implicit in what they are now,[11] it may be inferred that all which is to befall in the time-to-come has <already> been foreshadowed to some degree <in this world. (1) That at some time in [the days of the Messiah and in] the time-to-come> there will be a seat for the Holy One in His great court of inquiry with the righteous of the world seated in His presence has already been foreshadowed by the seat that the righteous in this world occupied in the presence of David king of Israel. (2) That at some time in the days of the Messiah and in the world-to-come the righteous will have radiance of countenance is foreshadowed by the radiance of countenance that the righteous already possess, to some

5. "Their children," etc. So Haida. R and V read "They—the transgressors—are gentle enough," etc.

6. Cf. *Man looketh on the outward appearance, but the Lord looketh on the heart* (1 Sam. 16:7); and Sanh 8:5, which asserts, "A stubborn and rebellious son is condemned because of what he is certain to become in the end." On the other hand, Ishmael was spared from death by thirst because at the time Ishmael was righteous, and God said, "I do not judge a man except for what he is at the time I am judging him." See MTeh 5:8 (YJS, *13, 1,* 88–89).

7. Gehenna being above the firmament. So B.Tam 32a citing TE.

8. For another rabbinic view, see above, n. 6.

9. JV: *But the ungodly, they are as thorns thrust away, all of them.* But *bĕliyya'al,* "the ungodly," means literally "worthless," and *kullaham,* "all of them," may also mean "in their entirety"; hence "root, stock, and stem."

10. JV: *in their place.* But *baššab̲et* literally means "in the session"; hence "in the [heavenly] session" or "assize."

11. "Because what is to befall . . . in what they are now" paraphrases the cryptic *mikkan,* "from this."

degree, in this world. (3) That at some time in the days of the Messiah and in the world-to-come the lives of the righteous will not be subject to sorrow or to the Impulse to evil has been foreshadowed to some degree in this world in the lives of the righteous—men such as Abraham, Isaac, Jacob, Jabez,[12] Jethro,[13] and all others like them—who, in some measure, were not subject to sorrow or to the Impulse to evil. (4) That at some time in the days of the Messiah and in the world-to-come there will be a revival of the dead by the Holy One has been now and then foreshadowed in this world in the revival of the dead by such righteous men as Elijah, Elisha, and Ezekiel the priest the son of Buzi.[14] (5) That at some time in the days of the Messiah <and> in the world-to-come the righteous will taste strength and glory has been foreshadowed in this world by the taste of strength and glory given in no small measure to the righteous such as Jehoshaphat, king of Judah.[15] (6) That at some time in the days of the Messiah and in the world-to-come the righteous will enjoy eating, drinking, <and merrymaking> in cool comfort[16] has been foreshadowed in this world by the eating, drinking, and merrymaking in cool comfort that Solomon, the son of David, king of Israel, enjoyed in no small measure in this world.[17] | (7) That at some time in the time-to-come [upon **ER,** ***p.*** **15**
Israel's mountains] an unremitting calamity of [spilt] blood, [torn] flesh, and broken [bones] will be Gog's[18] has been foreshadowed in this world by the intermittent calamities of [spilt] blood, [torn] flesh, and broken [bones] our eyes behold befalling our oppressors every day without fail.

---

12. Jabez, "the good and worthy man, the man of truth and saint" (ARN, chap. 35 [YJS, *10,* 145]), was delivered from the Impulse to evil which ceased to trouble him (1 Chron. 4:9–10). He is taken to be identical with Othniel, who was Joshua's successor and the first of the judges. "He was called Othniel because God answered him *('anah 'El),* and Jabez because he counseled *(ya'aṣ)* and fostered Torah in Israel" (B.Tem 16a).

13. "Jethro's transformation from an idolatrous priest into a God-fearing man is conveyed by his seven names. He was called Jether, because the Torah contains an 'additional' section about him; Jethro, [because] he 'over-flowed' with good deeds; Hobab, 'the beloved son of God'; Reuel, 'the friend of God'; Heber, 'the associate of God'; Putiel, 'he that renounced idolatry'; and Keni, 'he that was zealous' for God and 'acquired' the Torah." See Ginzberg, *Legends, 2,* 290.

14. See 1 Kings 17:18–24; 2 Kings 4:32–37; Ezek. 37:5–10; and PRKM 9:4, p. 152 (PRKS, p. 176).

15. Of Jehoshaphat it is said, *And his heart was lifted up in the ways of the Lord* (2 Chron. 17:6), which is taken to mean that he appointed judges who knew how to walk in the ways of the Lord (Tanḥuma B, and Tanḥuma, *Šofĕṭim,* beginning); hence "strength and glory."

The name Jehoshaphat may be taken to suggest "justice *(shaphat)* carried out in the Lord's *(Jeho)* name."

16. Friedmann emends *ṣinnah,* "cool comfort," into *rinnah,* "singing."

17. At the dedication of Solomon's Temple, which took place during the month of Tishri, the time when days grow cooler, the Hebrews "celebrated" the Day of Atonement by eating, drinking, and merrymaking (see 1 Kings 8:2, 65 and 2 Chron. 7:9), activities which were suffused so greatly with the love of God that they pleased Him more than the customary fasting (Gen. Rabbah 35:3).

18. See Ezek. 38.

If you wish to study and take delight in matters of Torah, then draw the proper inference from the first item in the series above, namely, that the Holy One will sit in His court of inquiry and the righteous of the world will sit in His presence. They will enjoy the give-and-take of discussion of Scripture, Mishnah, Halakot and 'Aggadot. They will determine whether a thing is ritually unclean or whether it is ritually clean; the unclean will have been determined properly as unclean and the clean will have been determined properly as clean.[19] Then the wicked will be brought [in for judgment] and in the presence of the righteous will be sentenced. Some of the wicked will be sentenced [to Gehenna] for thirty days, some for sixty days, some for three months and some for six months. The rule of the matter our Masters taught in a Mishnah: "The sentence of the wicked in Gehenna is to endure no more than twelve months" (Ed 2:10). At the time of sentencing, the righteous will stand up before Him at whose word the world came into being and will dare to say to Him, "Master of the universe, at the time we dwelt in this world, these very men [whom You have just sentenced] would get themselves to the synagogue morning and evening, read the Shĕma', say the *Tĕfillah,* and observe a number of commandments."[20] God will respond, "If they did indeed do so, go and bring healing to them." At once the righteous will go and, standing upon the dust to which the wicked had been reduced [by the Holy One], will entreat mercy for them. Then, out of the dust they were reduced to, the Holy One will have the wicked stand up on their feet, as is said, *The wicked, who under the soles of the feet of the righteous will be no more than ashes, you,* [*the righteous*], *will make* [*rise to life again*][21] (Mal. 3:21).

As for the righteous such as David, king of Israel, there is no doubt that they occupied seats of learning in this world. What was notable about such seats? For example, as Scripture says, *Among David's deeds of heroic abnegation was his sitting down upon the ground* [*when he studied*][22] (2 Sam. 23:8). While all the people occupied comfortable seats before

---

19. See Landau, and Louis Ginzberg's n. 74 in *OT,* p. 272. [The Hebrew says, "they will declare the unclean unclean, and the clean clean; they will declare that a certain thing is unclean under only certain circumstances, or clean only under certain circumstances." L. N.]

The discussions in heaven of cleanness and uncleanness appear to have metaphysical meaning, as though cleanness and uncleanness were elements in the universe itself.

20. They may have been a group of Jews who were "flexible" in the observance of commandments, heeding some and ignoring others.

21. JV: *Ye shall tread down the wicked, for they shall be ashes under the soles of your feet.* But *wĕ-'asoṯem,* "ye shall tread down," is apparently read *wĕ'asoṯom* [*la'amoḏ 'al raglehem*], "you will make them [stand up on their feet]."

22. JV: *These are the names of the mighty men whom David had: Josheb-basshebeth a Tachkemonite.* For ER, however, *Josheb-basshebeth* is not a proper name but a phrase describing the manner in which David studied, "sitting in session," hence "sat on a seat." *Gibborim,* "mighty men," ER construes as "specific deeds of heroic abnegation,"

him, king David sat neither on a bolster nor even on a stool but on the bare ground and from this uncomfortable position he taught Torah, in Heaven's name, to multitudes. The Presence then came and, standing above David, joined in the session, saying finally to him: My son, you know, of course, whence come the words you utter: they come from Me. Therefore, you prove yourself to be like the *taw,* the first letter of the word Torah—[in you the Torah lives]. Hence *Tachkemoni (ibid.)* —[an attribute of David—is read as made up of the letter *taw,* symbolic of Torah's very essence, combined with *chkemoni,* "man's innate wisdom"].

In further comment on *Tachkemoni* it is to be noted that God says, You, David, [who in your reverence for Torah] choose to sit on the bare ground with nothing to lean back on for your comfort—indeed, as has been often said, most people would rather stand than sit without a back support[23]—you, David, *tĕhe kamoni:* You are like Me, [with authority equal to Mine].[24]

Further on in the verse in hand, what is meant by *Leader of the three (ibid.)?* That you, David, have become the leader in study of all three parts of My Torah, [the Five Books, Prophets, and Writings].[25]

In another comment on the phrase it is read *Heir*[26] *together with the three (ibid.)* and is taken to mean: Your portion, David, will be equal to the portions of the three righteous, Abraham, Isaac, and Jacob.

<In another comment the phrase is read *Chief of the three (ibid.)* and is taken to mean: You, David, will be chief of the Patriarchs>.[27] [That is, you will have extended the line of the Patriarchs down

---

which were typical of David. See PR 49:2 (YJS, *18, 2,* 831) and B.MḲ 16b.

Perhaps the fact that 2 Sam. 23:8 describes Adino the Eznite before mentioning his name is taken by ER as an intimation that, in addition to listing David's heroes, the text subtly continues to enumerate David's other virtues. So Josiah Pinto on 'En Ya'ăḳoḇ, MḲ 16b.

Besides, in Samuel the name of the first of David's three "mighty men" does not correspond to the parallel in 1 Chron. 11:11, nor does the number slain by him at one time. Hence, ER interprets 2 Sam. 23:8 as a kind of cipher for the merits, distinctions, and exploits of David.

Other rabbinic commentators construe 2 Sam. 23:8 as referring to Joab. See Num. Rabbah 23:13; Tanḥuma, *Mas'e,* 12, and *Dĕḇarim,* 3; Tanḥuma B, *Mas'e,* p. 83, and *Dĕḇarim,* p. 2; and PR 11:3 (YJS, *18, 1,* 204).

23. See B.Keṯ 111a, bottom, and Leḳaḥ Ṭoḇ, ed. Buber (Wilno, 1884), on Gen. 27:19.

24. "With authority equal to Mine"—B.MḲ 16b. The authority to annul God's decrees. Rabbi Mordecai Savitsky elucidated the meaning of the paragraph.

25. See PRKM 12:13 (PRKS, pp. 237–38).

26. Apparently *ro'š,* "chief," is read as though spelled *roš,* "heir." See Deut. 2:24, 31.

27. In fulfillment of the verse *David My servant shall be their prince for ever* (Ezek. 37:25). Samuel Edels (on B.MḲ 16b) suggests the meaning to be that David will lead in the saying of Grace.

through the generations]—*The threefold cord is not quickly broken* (Eccles. 4:12), Scripture tells us—[and indeed you will have surpassed them in worth].

In another comment the phrase is read *Chief during the triad [of festivals]* (2 Sam. 23:8) and is taken to mean: You, David, will be chief of all the children of Israel when they make their pilgrimage to Jerusalem to celebrate the festivals,[28] with regard to which Scripture commands, *Three times in the year all thy males shall appear before the Lord God* (Exod. 23:17).

[In further exposition of 2 Sam. 23:8], the question is asked: To what may words of Torah be likened? To a hide given to a man who would tan it: he smooths it out and stretches it until he brings it to a delicate finish. Therefore in the verse in hand David is given the appellation *Adino the Eznite,* and is identified as *One who gives delicacy (Adino) to the rough bark of the tree (Eznite) [of Torah]*[29] (2 Sam. 23:8).

In another comment on *Adino the Eznite,* the appellation is applied
ER, *p.* 16 to David in a different sense: | when you sit in the academy, make yourself as yielding *(adino)* as a worm, but when you go forth to wage war be as unyielding as the wooden shaft *(eznite)* [of a lance].[30]

When you waged war, what was your reward? You *killed eight hundred men in one onset (ibid.)*—two hundred short [of the thousand I promised I would rout before only one of the children of Israel (Deut. 32:30)].[31] David spoke up: "Then why, O Master of the world, was I denied the killing of the two hundred?" God replied: David, my son, have I not written in My Torah, "Even when the children of Israel do not know how to expound Torah, but know only right conduct and Scripture, *Five of you will be able to rout a hundred* (Lev. 26:8)? But if the children of Israel obey Torah to the exclusion of all else, one of you alone will be able to rout a thousand. To be sure, you, David, have done My will, *but in the matter of Uriah the Hittite* (1 Kings 15:5) you did not fully do My will.[32] Therefore you were denied two hundred [of the thousand I promised]."

Hence it is said: If you see a disciple of the wise, [such as David], committing a transgression one day, do not think evil of him the day

---

28. Passover represents the Temple Service; the Feast of Weeks, Torah; and Sukkot, deeds of mercy. The three elements—worship, Torah, and deeds of mercy—were united in the person of David. So Landau.

29. JV: *The same was Adino the Eznite.* The translation—highly tentative—takes *Adino* to be a nominal form of the verb *'dn,* "give delicacy," and *Eznite* to be related to *'ṣ,* "tree"; hence "tree [of Torah]."

30. Cf. the *ḳĕri* in 1 Sam. 17:7.

31. See Sif Deut. 323 (ed. Finkelstein, [Breslau, 1936–39], p. 373).

32. On David's blame with regard to Bath-sheba, see PR 11:3 (YJS, *18, 1,* 203); B.Shab 56a; MTeh 3:3, 4:2 (YJS, *13, 1,* 53, 61); the present work, chap. 2, n. 12; and Ginzberg, *Legends, 7, s.v.* "Bath-sheba."

after. Very likely, he repented during the night,[33] as did David, saying to himself, *The Torah of Thy mouth is better unto me than thousands of gold and silver* (Ps. 119:72). As Scripture says, *Hatred* [*of Torah*] *stirreth up rebellions, but love*—that is, Torah—*leads to repentance for all kinds of transgressions*[34] (Prov. 10:12). [Such repentance through Torah is as certain as that] *Clouds full of rain empty themselves upon the earth* (Eccles. 11:3). You may thus infer that he who gossips about the failings of disciples of the wise is as one who gossips about the Presence: [he does not understand that through Torah such men come to repent their failings].

At some time in the days of the Messiah and in the world-to-come the righteous will have radiance of countenance. To what degree? <There are some> who will be given radiance of countenance such *as the sun's when he goeth forth* (Judg. 5:31) in the day's first hour *before he attains the full might of his radiance (ibid.).*[35] There are some who will be given radiance such as the sun's in the first two hours of the day; some, its radiance in the first three hours; some, its radiance in the first four hours; some, its radiance in the first five hours; some, its radiance in the first six hours. And some will be given radiance such as the sun's throughout the entire day. There are others who will be given radiance of countenance like the radiance of the moon at the time of the New Moon. Others will be given radiance such as the moon's on the fifth day in the month. Others such as the moon's on the tenth in the month. Others such as the moon's on the fifteenth day of the month. There are still others whose radiance will be like the great stars, and others like the small stars. There are still others who will be given the radiance of the firmament's atmosphere when it is clear <of clouds>. But there will be others, alas, whose faces will be as black as the bottom of a pot.

The fact is that he who lifts his face to the goodness [of Torah] deserves to receive the radiance of the Presence upon him. But he who is befouled and soiled will not be permitted to recline on a couch in the presence of the King. This is true only of one who has not repented. But if he repents and then dies, he is regarded in every respect like the world's righteous.

[Concerning such men as resist repentance] the Sages taught: "Four kings—Jeroboam, Ahab, Ahaz, and Manasseh[36]—have no portion in the world-to-come." Indeed, I say that whoever practices idolatry, whether in his youth or old age, and [unrepentant] dies an idolater,

---

33. Leon Nemoy suggests an alternate translation: ". . . do not suspect him of the same the day after—he may have repented during the night."

34. Literally, *love covereth all transgressions.*

35. Judg. 5:31 reads *They that love Him be as the sun when he goeth forth in his might.*

36. Tos Sanh 12:11. For Jeroboam, see 1 Kings 13:34; for Ahab, 1 Kings 21: 21–22; for Ahaz, 2 Kings 16:2–4; for Manasseh, 2 Kings 21:2–9 and ER, 111.

even if he were qualified to serve as High Priest, has no portion in the world-to-come, as is said, *They that swear by the sin of Samaria, and say: "As thy God, O Dan, liveth" . . . shall fall and never rise again* (Amos 8:14).

All the commandments which a man obeys in this world radiate no more light than the light of a single lamp, but the Torah gives light
ER, *p.* 17 from one end | of the world to the other.[37] [There is still another source of light for mankind]: whoever responds to the guidance of the Sages and their disciples, it is imputed <to him> as though he had actually done the will of his Father in heaven.[38] As for him who knows how to provide guidance and does provide it to multitudes, such a man gives delight to Him at whose word the world came into being, for it is said, *As for them who provide guidance, every one of them gives delight, and so the blessing of the Good comes upon them*[39] (Prov. 24:25). The text does not say "blessing . . . upon him [who provides guidance]," but *blessing . . . upon them,* that is, upon him who provides guidance and also upon him who is willing to receive it.

Then, too, he who acknowledges the justice of chastisements which he receives and indeed even manages to rejoice in them, is given life without end both in this world and in the world-to-come, for it is said, *The commandment is,* [*to be sure*], *a lamp, and the Torah is light, but the way to life* [*eternal*] *is through heeding of chastisements* (Prov. 6:23).[40]

---

37. *A commandment is but one lamp, but the Torah is light* (Prov. 6:23). See B.Soṭ 21a.

38. An intermediate comment made by way of expounding Prov. 6:23b (JV: *Reproofs of instruction are the way of life*) as "heeding the Sages' instructive guidance is the way of life."

39. JV: *But to them that decide justly shall be delight, and a good blessing shall come upon them.* But *mokiḥim,* "they who decide justly," can also mean, "they who provide guidance"; *yin'am,* "shall be delight," can also be construed as "gives delight"; and *birkat tob,* "a good blessing," may also be rendered as "the blessing of the Good."

40. Cf. Ber 9:5; Sif Deut. 42 (ed. Finkelstein, p. 57); B.Ber 5a; and ER, 12.

CHAPTER 4

God's reward of the righteous; His compassion for the repentant; His requital of the wicked

Summary

Following the incident of Israel's worship of the calf, Moses agonized over the profanation of God's and Israel's glory. But after God had put to death the three thousand worshipers of the golden calf, Moses persuaded God that His slaying of the entire people of Israel because of the three thousand offenders would be too severe a penalty, and thus Moses succeeded in reconciling God to Israel (ER, 17). Thereupon God, suddenly made aware of the dreadful act He might have committed had not Moses intervened, bestowed upon Moses everlasting radiance of countenance—the kind of radiance which He will give to the countenances of the righteous in the time-to-come.

Not only Moses but every disciple of the wise who busies himself with Torah does not really die: he is treasured in life for ever and ever. Accordingly, mourning for the dead is to be restricted to the measure and pattern prescribed by the Sages. Only for sinners who are unrepentant is one to mourn sorely (ER, 19).

The true disciple of the wise needs no sword, no javelin, nor any other kind of weapon, for the Holy One guards him. In the days of the Messiah and in the world-to-come he will have a life without distress, a perfect life no longer subject to the Impulse to evil. At that time all men will have a *new heart—a heart of flesh* (Ezek. 36:26), not of stone.

The reptition in the verse of these two phrases maintains the pattern set in the Five Books of Moses, where time and again precepts are repeated to intimate that they are to be obeyed time and again. Unfortunately Israel, instead of affirming Torah's twice-tempered strength, has regarded precepts as no precepts, so that God has come to regard Israel's gatherings as no gatherings (ER, 19). Still, though God punishes Israel severely, He cannot bring Himself to withhold His compassion for them: again and again He delivers them from the Impulse to evil and from oppression by the peoples of the world. For these two God has no compassion at all: He requites them sevenfold for the acts of seduction and hostility that led to the destruction of the First and Second Temples (ER, 20).

Chapter 4

Why did Moses merit in this world the radiance of countenance which God is to give the righteous only in the time-to-come? Because Moses carried out the will of the Holy One all of his days, and because he agonized over [the profanation of][1] the glory of the Holy One and of ER, *p.* 17 *cont'd*

1. "the profanation of"—Landau.

the glory of Israel, and because what he hoped for and looked forward to—indeed, what he craved—was the reconciliation between Israel and their Father in heaven. And the proof of what he craved? See it for yourself. When Israel during their stay in the wilderness behaved so indecently [in the matter of the golden calf], the Holy One said to Moses, *Now, therefore, let Me be* (Exod. 32:10). [Since up to this point, Moses had not interceded for Israel but had let God be, Moses understood God's words as] a hint to take hold of Him, so to speak, in behalf of Israel.[2] Hence, as Scripture says, at once *Moses besought the Lord his God, and said: . . . Wherefore should the Egyptians speak, saying: "For evil did He bring* [*the children of Israel*] *forth to slay them?" . . . Remember Abraham, Isaac, and Israel . . . to whom Thou didst swear . . . I will multiply your seed as the stars of heaven* (Exod. 32:12–13). Immediately, as we are told, Moses had God's [favorable] response: *The Lord repented of the evil which He said He would do unto His people* (Exod. 32:14). Thereupon Moses said: Master of the universe, right now is there anything of greater concern to You than the measure of justice You extend to any and all the world's inhabitants, the work of Your own hands which You created in this world? And so let me go down from Your presence and carry out upon Israel the measure of justice, whatever its consequences, so that if they indeed[3] worshiped the calf with a whole heart, they will, all of them, die in one day.

Thereupon Moses went down from God's presence, took the calf, and burned it in fire, as is said, *He took the calf, and burnt it with fire. . . . Then Moses stood in the gate of the camp . . . and said unto them: "Thus saith the Lord"* (Exod. 32:20, 26, 27). I call heaven and earth to witness, however, that the Holy One said to Moses no such thing as that he was to stand at the gate of the camp and ask, *Whoso is on the Lord's side?* (Exod. 32:26), [and then, when only *the sons of Levi gathered themselves together unto him (ibid.)*], go on to declare to them, *Thus saith the Lord, the God of Israel* (Exod. 32:27). Moses, righteous man that he was, justified [his attribution to God of his command to the sons of Levi] in this way:[4] If, on my own, I were to say to Israel, *Slay every man his brother, and every man his companion, and every man his neighbor (ibid.),* Israel would say, "Did you not teach us, 'A Sanhedrin that puts even one man to death in a week [of years][5] is called a tyrannical tribunal?' (Mak 1:10). Why, then, are you about to slay three thousand men in a single

2. Cf. B.Ber 32a.

3. In ER, the locution *mah 'im* may mean "if indeed, perhaps." So Mordecai Margulies in Lev. Rabbah M, p. 54, n. 1.

4. Moses' inference went as follows: If danger to the life of a single Israelite supersedes all negative commands in the Torah, all the more are such commands superseded by danger to the life of the entire people of Israel. And so he deliberately told an untruth. See *Torah šĕlemah, 21,* 143.

5. See Dan. 9:24.

day?" Therefore, [in order to avert Israel's reproach of him, he attributed his command to the sons of Levi to slay the worshipers of the golden calf] to the Glory that is above, by saying, *Thus saith the Lord, the God of Israel* (Exod. 32:27). [Indeed, that it was not God who had spoken to Moses] is evident from the next verse which reads, *The sons of Levi did according to the word of Moses* (Exod. 32:28).

[After they had done as he commanded them], Moses, the righteous one, returned and stood in entreaty before the Holy One, daring to say to Him: Master of the universe, You are just, yet merciful, and all Your deeds are performed with scrupulous care! But now, because of three thousand who worshiped [the calf] with a whole heart, do You desire that six hundred thousand adults[6] shall die, and, in addition, those who are only twenty years old and those even younger—eighteen, fifteen, ten, two, and even one, and, besides, an endless number of strangers and slaves, ever so many, who have attached themselves to the people of Israel? At these words, the mercy of the Holy One welled up, and in that instant He became reconciled with Israel. By what parable | may God's change of heart be understood? By the **ER, *p.* 18**
parable of a mortal king whose oldest son had acted offensively in his presence. The king took hold of his son, turned him over to the steward who was in charge of the household, and said to him, "Take him out, slay him, and give his body to beasts and dogs." What did the steward do? He removed the son from the king's presence and put him up <in his own home, and then hastened back> to attend the king. After thirty days, when the king was disposed to be merry, his servants and members of his household assembled to recline for a meal in his presence. But when lifting his eyes, he did not see his first-born, he let sorrow and sighing enter his heart. No mortal was aware of his grief, however, except his steward, the master of the household, who forthwith ran and brought back the king's son and had him stand in his usual place. A beautiful crown was lying before the king, and the king took it and placed it upon the head of his steward, the master of his household.

Since on four and five occasions Moses rose up in entreaty to God and delivered Israel from death as the king's steward had delivered the king's son, the Holy One said to Moses: Because on four and five occasions you have appeared before Me[7] and thus saved Israel from death, the beautiful crown which they acquired because of their acceptance of Torah, the crown that was to have been worn by the people of

---

6. See Num. 1:45–46.

7. ER apparently refers here to the ten trials whereby the children of Israel tried God (see Num. 14:22 and Ab̲ 5:4). In nine of these, Moses saved Israel from death. Cf. below ER, 33 and 159.

Why "four and five" instead of "nine" is not clear.

Israel, by their children and their children's children, is from now on the crown you will wear for all time,[8] [its radiance shining forth from your face], as is said, *The children of Israel saw the face of Moses, that the skin of Moses' face sent forth beams* (Exod. 34:35). Lest you suppose that after Moses had come into his eternal abode, the radiance of his face vanished, Scripture assures us, *There hath not arisen a prophet since in Israel like unto Moses, whom the Lord had continued to know face to face* (Deut. 34:10). Even as the Face on high shines for ever and ever and ever, so, too, the radiance of Moses' face entered with him into his eternal abode [and remained with him for ever], as is said, *Moses was a hundred and twenty years old; at his death his radiance did not dim because the life-force in him had not departed*[9] (Deut. 34:7).

Not only Moses, but every disciple of the wise who from youth to old age busies himself with Torah until he dies, does not really die: he is treasured in life for ever and ever and ever, as is said, for example, of David, *The life-force of my lord shall be kept in the treasury of life with the Lord thy God* (1 Sam. 25:29), which, by analogy, implies: As the Lord your God, whose great name is blessed for ever and ever and ever, [lives for ever], so every disciple of the wise who from youth to old age busies himself with Torah until he dies, lo! he still lives—he is deathless, he is in life for ever and ever and ever. Where is his soul? Under the throne of glory. Hence it is said: A man should not multiply weeping and lamentation, sorrow, and sighing for the dead beyond the measure which the Sages have prescribed: three days for weeping and lamentation, seven days for mourning, and thirty days of refraining from cutting the hair, from putting on freshly pressed garments, and from certain other customary acts.[10] He who afflicts himself beyond these limits is guilty of injury to himself, as is said, *Weep not for the dead* [*in excess*] (Jer. 22:10). Surely you are not more grief-stricken on the deceased's account than I, [your God].[11]

[No, weep not overlong for the dead but weep for the unrepentant transgressor.] When a man engages in a quarrel with a friend and goes by himself to make his peace with his friend, he finds that the other refuses to be reconciled. Not until the man gets together a good number of people[12] [and takes them along to witness his apology] will his friend consent to be reconciled.[13] And even then, though the friend

---

8. Literally, "for the world-to-come."

9. JV: *Moses was a hundred and twenty years old when he died; his eye was not dim, nor his natural force abated.* But see Rashi, *ad loc.*

10. Such as saluting one's friends, shaving, combing the hair, participating in festivities, or taking a wife. See Sem 6–7 (YJS, *17,* 48ff) and Šulḥan 'aruk̠, Yoreh de'ah, 389–92. Note that there is no reference to a year of mourning.

11. Cf. B.Ta 27b.

12. Ten men are required. See PR 38 (YJS, *18, 2,* 692).

13. See B.Ta 27b.

consents to make peace with the man, the friend still feels some resentment toward him. But I, [says God], am not like that. When a man commits a transgression against Me and then repudiates it and repents of it, at once I feel compassion toward him and receive him in his repentance. And once I receive him in his repentance, I choose not to remember even the least part of his transgressions. Hence it is said, *Weep not [in excess] for the dead, neither bemoan him, but weep sore for him that keeps going away (ibid.).* Who is meant in the words *him that keeps going away?* He who commits a transgression, commits it a second time, and then a third time—transgresses three times, yet has no misgivings and does not resolve upon repentance. For such a man you are to weep sore: he is uprooted from the world. *He shall return no more, nor see his native country*[14] *(ibid.).*

| [In contrast to the transgressor and his fate, consider the righteous man and his reward.] The reward of Moses, the righteous man, who on four and five occasions[15] pleaded with God on Israel's behalf and thus saved them from death—of him Scripture speaks as though it was he who had created them. Hence it is said of God, *Then He remembered the days of old, Moses and his people*[16] (Isa. 63:11). Like Moses, each and every Sage in Israel who truly has the word of Torah within him, who throughout his days agonizes over [the profanation of] the glory of the Holy One and [the profanation of] the glory of Israel, who craves, hopes for, and looks forward to the [restoration of the] glory of Jerusalem and the glory of the Temple, and to the deliverance that it might soon sprout, and to the ingathering of the dispersed—in his utterances is the holy spirit: *He puts His holy spirit within him (ibid.).* Accordingly, it is said: Every disciple of the wise who every day without fail busies himself with Torah in order to increase the glory of Heaven needs no sword, no javelin, no spear, nor any other kind of weapon, for the Holy One Himself guards him, and the ministering angels stand around him, all of them with swords in their hands, and they, too, guard him, for it is said, *When the high praises of God are in men's mouths, it is as though a two-edged sword were in their hands* (Ps. 149:6). **ER**, *p.* 19

[Furthermore, there will be for the disciples of the wise] "a life without distress in the days of the Messiah and in the world-to-come." What will that life be like? The Holy One will be seated in His great academy and seated in His presence will be the righteous of the world, they, their wives, their sons, their daughters, their menservants and their maidservants, the needs of their households all being provided for them. Thus it is said, *And it shall come to pass afterward, that I will pour*

14. The world of souls out of which he came. So Landau.
15. See above, n. 7.
16. JV: *Then His people remembered the days of old, the days of Moses.*

out My spirit upon all flesh, and your sons and your daughters shall prophecy . . . also upon the servants and upon the handmaids in those days will I pour out My spirit[17] (Joel 3:1–2). And it is said further, *Rise up, ye women that are at ease, and hear My voice*[18] (Isa. 32:9).

[And in the days of the Messiah and in the world-to-come the righteous] "will not be subject to the Impulse to evil." What will that time be like? *A new heart will I give you* (Ezek. 36:26) then, a "new heart" signifying the Impulse to good. *And a new spirit will I put within you (ibid.)* then [to move you to] good deeds. *And I will take away the stony heart out of your flesh (ibid.),* "stony heart" signifying the Impulse to evil. *And I will give you a heart of flesh (ibid.),* "heart of flesh" [signifying the Impulse to good. The repetition of "new heart" and "heart of flesh"][19] maintains the pattern set in the Five Books of Moses where time and again precepts are repeated [to intimate that they are to be obeyed time and again].[20] And the proof that they are repeated? The verse *I am the Lord thy God* (Exod. 20:2) at the beginning of the Ten Commandments as they were uttered at the foot of Mount Sinai is repeated in the Ten Commandments given [again in Deuteronomy] in the Book of Admonitions. The laws concerning torts[21] were given at the foot of Mount Sinai, and the laws concerning torts were given again in the Book of Admonitions. Thus the precept beginning *If thou buy a Hebrew servant* (Exod. 21:2) given at the foot of Mount Sinai is repeated in the verse beginning *If thy brother, a Hebrew man . . . be sold unto thee* (Deut. 15:12) in <the Book of> Admonitions, as are repeated many, many[22] other laws in the category of torts. The law that forbids sowing a field with two kinds of seed was given at Mount Sinai (Lev. 19:19), and the law that forbids sowing a field with two kinds of seed is repeated in the Book of Admonitions (Deut. 22:9). The law *Thou shalt not seethe a kid in its mother's milk* was given at Sinai (Exod. 23:19), and the law *Thou shalt not seethe a kid in its mother's milk* is repeated in the Book of Admonitions (Deut. 14:21), and so, too, are repeated many, many[23] other laws in the category of statutes. So, too, the signs [of ritual

---

17. Immediately before this verse Joel says: *Ye shall eat in plenty and be satisfied . . . and My people shall never be ashamed* (Joel 2:26–27).

18. Instead of regarding Isa. 32:9 as the opening verse in the next paragraph, ER construes it as the conclusion of Isa. 32:1–8, a passage with messianic overtones. He thus demonstrates that in the days of the Messiah, men's wives, not referred to in Joel 3:1–2, will also hear God's voice.

19. "signifying . . . 'heart of flesh' "—Louis Ginzberg. See *OT,* p. 274, n. 109.

20. Cf. PRKM 10:4, pp. 165–66 (PRKS, p. 191). The repetition may also, according to Landau, be taken to indicate God's reaching out to man as at Sinai, and man's reaching out to God as besought by Moses in the Book of Deuteronomy. To ER the repetition intimates that the two, God and man, will come together in entire compatibility.

21. These are set forth in Exod. 21:1 through 22:23.

22. Literally, "a hundred."

23. See n. 22.

cleanness and uncleanness] in domestic and wild animals were designated at the foot of Mount Sinai (Lev. 11:1–31), and then these signs in domestic and wild animals are designated again in the Book of Admonitions (Deut. 14:3–19). At the Tent of Meeting at Horeb all communal and private offerings were prescribed, and the communal and private offerings were again prescribed shortly before Aaron's death, and then again after his death.[24] I made a covenant with you, [God declares], when you went forth out of Egypt and again made a covenant with you, as is told in the Book of Admonitions.[25] I had you utter a song when you went forth out of the land of Egypt and again had you utter a song as is told in the Book of Admonitions.[26] Thus you see that words of Torah are time and again said twice.

Yet you do not affirm Torah's twice-tempered strength. You regard Torah's walls as daubed with unseasoned plaster.[27] You scorn <My> words as though they had no substance, and so you come to regard a precept as no precept, and you turn My having gathered you together into no gathering. When you went forth out of Egypt I gave you precepts; then again in the Book of Admonitions I gave you precepts. For 480 years before the Temple was built[28] I kept you gathered; then again I kept you gathered for 410 years after the Temple was built;[29] as is said, *But each precept [uttered once] became no precept, each precept [though uttered a second time] became no precept; [the first] gathering no gathering, [the second] gathering* | *no gathering*[30] (Isa. 28:10). Neither before the Temple was built did I find satisfaction in you, nor thereafter, when the Temple was built, have I found satisfaction in you. What, then, is to be your wage from Me? The answer may be given by means of a parable. A mortal king became angry at his servant, and he

ER, *p.* 20

24. At the Tent of Meeting the offerings—public and communal—are mentioned in Lev. chaps. 1–7; 12:6–8; 14:1–32; 15:14–15, 29–30; chap. 16; 22:26–30; chap. 23. Then shortly before Aaron's death, they are mentioned in Num. chaps. 28–29, his death being recorded in Num. 33:38–39. Then they are mentioned again after Aaron's death in Deut. 12:11–29; 15:19–23, and *passim.*

25. See Exod. 24:8 and Deut. 29:11.

26. See Exod. 15 and Deut. 32.

27. Cf. Ezek. 13:11.

28. See 1 Kings 6:1.

29. "Rabbinic tradition has decided that the First Temple could only have stood 410 years, for when added to the seventy years during which there was no Temple, the total equalled, i.e., was symmetrical with, the 480-year period from the exodus to the building of the First Temple." H. L. Ginsberg in an oral communication to Gerson Cohen. See the latter's *The Book of Tradition* (Philadelphia, 1967/5728), p. 192.

30. JV: *For it is precept by precept, precept by precept, line by line.* But ER reads *ṣaw leṣaw,* "precept by precept," as though written *ṣaw lo' ṣaw,* "precept [became] no precept"; and associates *ḳaw* not with "line" but with *ḳwh,* "gather." So Louis Ginzberg in *OT,* p. 274, n. 110, and Professor Saul Lieberman in a private communication. [It seems to me . . . that *ḳawwa'ah* is . . . derived from *ḳaw,* "line," i.e. rule, commandment (as we use it in "party line," "official line"). This would accord with the proof verse Isa. 28:10 . . . *ḳiwwiṭi* would thus mean "I kept you in line." L. N.]

gave these orders concerning him: first, that he be bound in chains, and next, that the chains be pulled from behind in such a way as to make him fall face up and then be kicked in the face and the kidneys,[31] as is said, *And so the word of the Lord is unto them . . . that they may go, and fall backward, and may be broken, and snared, and taken* (Isa. 28:13). Now, on a hundred occasions, you have committed such indecencies before Me as one cannot even give a name to, [but I have not punished you as you have deserved]. On the contrary, every day, without fail, My compassion goes out first to you, as is said, *Lord . . . who deliverest the poor from him that is too strong for him* (Ps. 35:10). Wherein poor? Is it not in his deeds? *Lord . . . who deliverest the poor and the needy from him that spoileth him (ibid.).* Wherein *needy?* Is it not in his deeds? Nevertheless, of this verse you must say that the words *Lord . . . who deliverest the poor from him that is too strong for him* mean that Thou deliverest the poor in deeds not only from the Impulse to evil [*that is too strong for him*], but also from the peoples of the world. [With regard to the man poor in good deeds], it is said, *For the Lord hearkeneth unto the man in need* [*of good deeds*] (Ps. 69:34); and [with regard to the man whose plight is poor because of oppression by peoples of the world], it is said elsewhere, *He will regard the prayer of the man who raises a cry*[32] (Ps. 102:18), the cry of the average man [who has no particular merit, but cries mercy].

Two afflictions I will requite: the Impulse to evil I will requite sevenfold, even as I requited it of you sevenfold in the past; and those who seek your hurt I will requite sevenfold even as I requited sevenfold any hurt to you in the past.[33] Thus it is said, *It shall come to pass in that day, that the Lord will punish the host of the high heaven on high, and the kings of the earth upon the earth* (Isa. 24:21), "host" and "kings" referring to those who sought to destroy you in this world. Sevenfold also will be the requital of the Impulse to evil because it led you so far astray that Torah did not flourish in this world; as is said, *Now Joshua was clothed with filthy garments . . . and he showed me Joshua the High Priest. And the Lord said unto Satan: "The Lord rebuke thee, O Satan* [*for the hurt thou hast done Joshua and the people of Israel*]" (Zech. 3:3, 1–2). What is to be Satan's punishment from Me? Since he made My land and My possession barren and desolate in order that no soul shall rise to any height in it, I, says God, according to Scripture, *will remove far off from you the hidden one*[34] (Joel 2:20)—that is, the Impulse to evil that lies hidden in you to bring you to disaster, I will remove far from you; *and will drive*

31. [to make him fall down upon his face . . . and in the bowels. L. N.]
32. Rashi on the verse and on Isa. 15:5 associates *'r'r* (in JV, "destitute") with *yĕ'o'eru,* "raise."
33. Cf. PRKM 3:6, pp. 44–45 (PRKS, pp. 48–49).
34. EV: *the northern one.* But *ṣĕfoni,* "northern," may also mean "hidden."

[*Satan*] *into a land barren and desolate because he set his face against the eastern sea (ibid.)*—against the First Temple[35] which he caused to be destroyed, slaying the Sages that had been in it; *and his hinder part against the western sea (ibid.)*—against the Second Temple which he caused to be destroyed, slaying the Sages that had been in it. *For his stink had come up, and his ill savor, engaged as he was in* [*what he deemed*] *mighty deeds (ibid.):* he let be all the peoples of the world and came and attached himself to the children of Israel in order <to turn them aside> from obedience to the precepts of Torah.[36]

---

35. The Temple wherein all manner of people gather is taken to be symbolized by the sea. So Rashi on B.Suk 52a.

36. The preceding comment on Joel 2:20 is paralleled in B.Suk 52a.

CHAPTER 5

Why most of those who die will be resurrected; and why Elijah, Elisha, and Ezekiel were able to quicken the dead

Summary

In the days of the Messiah and in the world-to-come Israel will be saluted, albeit reluctantly, by the ministering angels and the nations of the world (ER, 21): the angels will have overcome their envy of Israel, and the nations will have admitted that they themselves rejected the Torah when God offered it to them.

In the world-to-come not only the righteous of Israel will be seated in God's presence. They who were poor in good deeds, but who, just before they died, yearned for repentance will also be raised up out of the dust and brought into the life of the world-to-come. All of life came from the Root of all being who established Himself in all His holiness in the middle of the Temple. And so, even a last-minute repentance manifesting a spark of holiness in transgressors will serve to raise them from the dead (ER, 21). Now if the promise of being gathered up from the grave is made to transgressors who have done no more than yearn for repentance, it is all the more certain that the righteous, whose hearts have ever been willing, will be gathered up from the grave.

The dust of a man who made himself dwell in humility in the dust will be awakened, but the dust of a man who did not make himself dwell in humility in the dust will not be awakened.

In this world the resurrection of the dead by God serves to hallow His name. And Elijah, because he did the will of God and because he voiced his anguish that God had withdrawn His glory from Israel and that the glory of Israel was gone, was enabled to bring a dead man back to life. Because Elisha did the will of God (ER, 22), cared not at all for what he owned, and ministered to Elijah, he was enabled to bring two dead men back to life. Elijah's and Elisha's continuous discussion of matters of Torah leads to the observation that no harm can befall a man thus engaged. Hence Elijah did not die, but *went up by a whirlwind into heaven* (2 Kings 2:11).

Because each and every hour Ezekiel's concern was wholly for Israel, he was enabled to bring the dead in the valley of Dura back to life (ER, 23)—even though while they were alive, the willingness to obey God's commands had dried up in them, and they had been guilty of the sin of idolatry.

As for the oppressors of Israel, their lot will be the unremitting calamity of spilt blood, torn flesh, and broken bones upon Israel's mountains. That they have been and are our oppressors, we have ourselves to blame because we failed to heed the precepts of our Teacher.

Still, God bestows His blessing upon Israel who remain at the center of His concern. Even when He smites Israel, He refrains from smiting them heavily (ER, 25).

As for the righteous in Israel, in the world-to-come they will enjoy eating and drinking, merrymaking, and singing. In the radiance of heaven's luminaries couches will be spread for them. And because of their righteousness, in this world also they will have enjoyed in some measure the eating and drinking and the joy of the world-to-come (ER, 26).

Chapter 5

"The righteous will have strength and glory in the time-to-come and ER, *p.* 20 *cont'd* in the world-to-come." For example? The Holy One will be seated in His great academy with the righteous of the world seated in His presence; and each and every one of the righteous will be given a radiance of countenance in keeping with the Torah in him. But the ministering angels standing round about will be weeping inwardly even as they say: Blessed are Israel because all the oppression, affliction, and grief they endured in this world are over and gone.[1] Now great good is theirs.

[How explain the angels' weeping?] To begin with, when the Psalmist says | *Angels*[2] *of ministry yiddoḏun, yiddoḏun* (Ps. 68:13), do ER, *p.* 21 not read *yiddoḏun, yiddoḏun,* "they flee, they flee," but *yiddēḏun, yiddēḏun,*[3] "they remonstrate, they remonstrate," for the angels had remonstrated with Moses, father of wisdom, father of Prophets, when he went up to the heavenly heights and therefrom brought down the Torah.[4] But what has the angels' remonstrance to do with their weeping? Because [their remonstrance had been to no avail]. Hence they will say, "This great good of Israel's came to them [and not to us] because of their acquisition of Torah."

In this world, all the peoples of the earth used to ridicule Israel [in regard to their possession of Torah]. The nations used to say to Israel: "We possess silver and gold, and Israel possess silver and gold. We possess fields and vineyards, and Israel possess fields and vineyards. We possess food and drink, and Israel possess food and drink. We possess comely garments, and Israel possess comely garments. So what reward can Israel derive from their possession of words of Torah, which, in fact, have brought them nothing but distress?" In the course of time, however, when the days of the Messiah will have come and the angel of death will have vanished from the earth, all the peoples of the world will have to say: Blessed is this people Israel whose lot turned out to be good. Blessed is this people whose Lord God is their portion, as is said, *When He maketh death to vanish in life eternal*[5] . . . *the ridicule*

---

1. See Song 2:11.
2. MT reads *malḵe,* "kings," but the word is read as though written *mal'aḵe,* "angels." Psalm 68 is interpreted as an account of the revelation at Sinai. Cf. MTeh 8:2 (YJS, *13, 1,* 123).
3. ER associates *yiddēḏun* with the root *dwn,* "remonstrate, debate, dispute." [*Yiddēḏun* cannot be derived from *dwn.* . . . The only escape I can think of, and a very narrow one, is the Aramaic *did* (in *diḏi, diḏaḵ,* etc.); the sense then would be "they 'mined-and-thined' with Moses," which is near enough to the idea of the angels claiming prior right to the Torah and opposing its surrender to Moses and Israel. L. N.]
4. In PR 25:3 (YJS, *18, 2,* 520–22) and MTeh 8.2 (YJS, *13, 1,* 122–23) also the angels are not fully reconciled to God's giving the Torah to Israel. In B.Shab 89a and PR 20:4 (YJS, *18, 1,* 409–10), they fully accept God's decision.
5. Slightly changed from Hertz, *APB,* p. 1099. JV: *He will swallow up death for ever.*

of His people He will take away from off all the earth (Isa. 25:8).

Hence in the days of the Messiah, this is what will happen: The peoples of the earth will cry openly because [when given the chance], they had refused to hearken to the words of Torah,[6] and the ministering angels will weep secretly[7] because they had not been granted the privilege of earning the goodness and greatness which are Israel's, as is said, *Behold the [nations'] men of war cry openly, and in bitterness the angels of peace weep [secretly]*[8] (Isa. 33:7).

Furthermore, in the days of the Messiah and in the world-to-come, along with the righteous, *God . . . will raise up out of the dust the poor* (1 Sam. 2:8), [*the poor* here signifying the poor in good deeds. Why should He raise these up], since they had been guilty of many transgressions and had had the penalty of [premature] death imposed upon them and their children over a span of four generations, as is said, *I visit the iniquity of the fathers upon the children unto the third and fourth generation of them that [continue to] hate Me*[9] (Exod. 20:5)? [Nevertheless, He will raise these transgressors up], if, just before they died they had turned about, had yearned for repentance, yearned to read Scripture and to recite Mishnah. God's distress on their account[10] will allow Him no comfort until He will have raised them out of the dust onto their feet, <seated them> between His knees, taken them into His arms, held them close, kissed them, and brought them into the life of the world-to-come. Hence it is said, *He will raise up out of the dust the poor [in good deeds], and from the dung-hill He will lift up the needy, [those in need of good deeds to their credit], that He may set them with those whose hearts have ever been willing* (Ps. 113:7).[11]

[Surely God will raise the dead, even those who at the end of their days merely yearned for repentance, for it was] He *who set the Root in the House*[12] (Ps. 113:9)—that is to say, He, the Root of all being,

6. See PR 15:2, 21:3 (YJS, *18, 1,* 307, 417).

7. ["Openly" and "secretly" would be usually expressed by *bĕ-ḳol—bĕ-leḇ,* rather than by *ba-ḥuṣ—bi-fnim.* I think the meaning is that the nations are crying from *outside* heaven, while the angels are weeping *inside* heaven. L. N.]

8. The preceding two verses speak of God's filling Zion with justice (verse 5) and of the full flowering of Torah reflected in the six orders of Mishnah. Verse 6 is interpreted by Resh Laḳish as follows: *Faith,* the Order of Seeds; *Times,* the Order of Seasons; *Strength,* the Order of Women; *Deliverance,* the Order of Torts; *Wisdom,* the Order of Things Holy; and *Knowledge,* the Order of Things Pure (B.Shab 31a). Hence both warriors and angels are induced to weep. In JV, Isa. 33:7 reads, *Behold, their valiant ones cry without; the ambassadors of peace weep bitterly.* But see Landau.

9. When the descendants continue, in their own lives, in the ways of their wicked forebears (B.Ber 7a; Sanh 27b).

10. [At the lateness of their repentance, which allowed them no time in this world to put it into execution. L. N.]

11. The parallel in 1 Sam. 2:8 reads, *to make them sit with those whose hearts have ever been willing and inherit the throne of glory.* The word *nĕḏiḇim,* "princes," may also be read, "those whose hearts have been ever willing." Cf. ER, 117.

12. JV: *Who maketh the barren woman dwell in her house. 'Aḳereṯ,* "barren woman," may also mean "root." [I wonder if you are right in referring *'Aḳereṯ* to the Deity. I think

established Himself in the middle of the Temple [site] and therefrom created the entire world, from world's end to world's end,[13] as affirmed in the verse *The Lord by wisdom founded the earth; by understanding He established the heavens; by His knowledge*[14] *the depths were broken up* (Prov. 3:19–20).

In another comment, the verse from Psalms quoted above is read *The Lord . . . who sets one in authority over the house* (Ps. 113:9), *the house* standing for this world, and the verse as a whole signifying that the Holy One, having proceeded to create the world—all of it—from world's end to world's end, [set man to rule over it], as is said, *I have made the earth, and over it man*[15] (Isa. 45:12).

The "mother" of children [in Israel] rejoices (Ps. 113:9). Blessed be the Preserver of the world, blessed be He whose joy on account of Israel is ever great: As Israel obey the Torah in this world | and **ER, *p.* 22** rejoice in it, so, in return, Torah, [the mother],[16] rejoices in them for ever, as is said, *The "mother" of children [in Israel] rejoices.* Hence and thereafter He finds His joy in us.[17]

[A verse from Hosea confirms the assurance in the words] *God . . . will raise up the poor out of the dust* (Ps. 113:7), which is to say that in the days of the Messiah and in the world-to-come God will raise up the righteous. If it be asked how we know that He will do so, the answer [as given in a comment just above] is this: A man guilty of many transgressions will have had the penalty of [premature] death imposed upon him and his children over a span of four generations, in keeping with the verse *I visit the iniquity of the fathers upon the children unto the third and fourth generation of them that [continue to] hate Me* (Exod. 20:5). But, the comment goes on, if the transgressor has had a change of heart [even just before he dies], and begins yearning for repentance, yearning to read Scripture, the Prophets, and the Writings, yearning even to recite Mishnah and Midrash of Halakot and 'Aggadot, and to wait

---

rather the *root* refers to all creation: "who maketh the root [of all creation] to dwell in the House" (so JV), that is the source or beginning of the creative process. I doubt if the Deity would be designated by a feminine noun. . . . As your note explains, God stood on the Temple site when He did His work of creation, hence that site is the fountainhead of all creatures. L. N.]

13. Both earth and heaven, according to one opinion, were made out of Zion, the site of the Temple (B.Yoma 54b)—hence out of holiness. And so all life, even that which has no more than a spark of holiness, will be raised from the dead.

14. The Tabernacle and the Temple were built by Bezalel and Hiram, men filled with wisdom, understanding, and knowledge (see Exod. 31:3 and 1 Kings 7:14), the very qualities God invoked in the making of heaven and earth. And the building of the prototype of the Temple, be it noted, preceded the making of heaven and earth. See below, ER, 160, and PRE, chap. 3.

15. JV: *and man upon it.*

16. Torah is referred to as "mother," as in *Forsake not the teaching of thy mother* (Prov. 1:8).

17. At the suggestion of Leon Nemoy, the obscure *'im banu* is read *'alenu,* "over," or "in us."

upon the Sages, then even if a hundred penalties[18] had been decreed against him, the Holy One will rescind them. This conclusion is confirmed by the verse in Hosea usually read, *Yea, though they hire (yitnu)*[19] *among the nations, I will now gather them up* (Hos. 8:10), but [in connection with the verse *God . . . will raise up the poor,* etc.] is to be read, *Yea, if among the nations they aspire even to Oral Torah (yišnu),*[20] [*after they die*], *I will forthwith gather them up.* [Now if the promise of being gathered up from the grave is made to transgressors who have done no more than yearn for repentance, all the more is being gathered up from the grave certain for those, the righteous, whose hearts have ever been willing.]

In this world the resurrection of the dead by the Holy One serves to hallow His great name. But at some time in the days of the Messiah the resurrection of the dead by the Holy One will serve also to reward in the world-to-come those who have loved Him and revered Him. Such is the assurance in the words *Let Thy dead revive* (Isa. 26:19), referring to the dead in the Land of Israel;[21] a like assurance is in the words *let corpses arise (ibid.),* referring to the dead in Babylonia.[22] Hence David said: May my portion be [life eternal] with those who all but consume themselves for the sake of words of Torah: *Among those who all but slay themselves for the sake of that which came from Thy hand . . . but whose portion is in life* [*eternal*][23] *. . . may I be satisfied, when I awake, with Thy likeness* [*before me*] (Ps. 17:14–15).

[In further allusion to the resurrection of the dead], Isaiah goes on to say, *Awake and sing, ye that dwell in the dust* (Isa. 26:19b). The inference to be drawn from the verse is that the dust of a man who made himself dwell in humility in the dust will be awakened, but that the dust of a man who did not make himself dwell in humility in the dust will not be awakened.[24] Note a further inference from *Awake and sing, ye*

---

18. Two more than the ninety-eight curses or denunciations in Deut. 28.

19. In biblical Hebrew, and often in rabbinic Hebrew, the word *yitnu* from *tnh* sometimes means "recount, rehearse, learn," or "teach by word of mouth." See Judg. 5:11 and Ps. 8:2 (cf. B.BB 8a; PR 16:7 [YJS, *18, 1,* 354]; and PRKM 6:3, p. 118 [PRKS, p. 133]).

[ER regards *yitnu* as derived not from the Hebrew *tnh,* "to hire, to conclude a hiring agreement with someone," but from the Aramaic *tny,* "to study Mishnah." L. N.]

20. See n. 19.

21. The Land of Israel is described as *The Land which the Lord your God looks after* (Deut. 11:12). Hence the dead buried in it are referred to as *Thy*—God's—dead, so to speak.

22. Cf. PR 1:6 (YJS, *18, 1,* 45). [I suspect that this is a word-play *nBLh=BBL;* just as the second-person suffix in *meteka* indicates Palestine, so the letters *bl* in *nĕbelah* indicate Babylonia. L. N.]

23. JV: *From men, by Thy hand, O Lord . . . whose portion is in this life.* But *mĕtim,* "men," may be read *metim,* "who all but slay themselves."

24. ER thus construes Isa. 26:19b not as a repetition of 26:19a but as a call to humility. See B.Soṭ 5a.

that dwell in the dust: the text does not speak of the dead as simply lying in the dust, but says "ye that *dwell* in the dust,"[25] signifying that in their lifetime in this world the dead were content to have themselves and their flesh dwell in the dust for the sake of study of Torah. Over the dust of such men the Holy One will throw a light as of sparkling dew drops, will lift them up between His knees, put His arms around them, hold them close, and kiss them, and thus usher them into life in the world-to-come, as is said, *A light as of sparkling dew drops is Thy light (ibid.).* But as for the nations of the earth who used to say, "We are mighty, we are the ones who know how to wage war. Who can stand up against us?"—against them You will carry out great acts of vengeance, as You promised Your children concerning the nations: *The land of* [*the formidable*] *Rephaim Thou wilt cause to fall*[26] *(ibid.)* before Your children.

How did Elijah gain such merit as to enable him to bring a dead man back to life?[27] Because he did the will of Him at whose word the world came into being—the Holy One, blessed be He. And because every day without fail he voiced his anguish that the Holy One had withdrawn His glory from Israel and that the glory of Israel was gone: indeed, it seemed to him as though Israel—may such an end befall its enemies—were about to perish from the world.[28] Hence in each and every generation, whenever Elijah would find men who were righteous, he would at once take them into his arms, hold them close, kiss them, and bless, exalt, praise, magnify, and hallow the name of Him at whose word the world came into being—the Holy One, blessed be He.

But why did Elisha gain such merit as to enable him to bring [not one, but] two dead people back to life?[29] Because he did [more than

---

25. [There isn't any real difference between *lying* and *dwelling* in the dust. The real difference is indicated by the following *maškinin: šĕkene* is passive, while *šokĕne* is active. The text, according to ER, thus implies that the dead were not passively deposited ("made to dwell") in the dust, but while still living had *made themselves dwell (maškinin)* in the dust out of sincere humility. L. N.]

26. JV: *And the earth shall bring to life the shades.* But *tappil,* "bring to life" (literally "cause to fall out"), is here understood as "cause to fall"; and *rephaim,* "shades," as "[the doughty] Rephaim" whom the Ammonites ousted. See Deut. 2:20.

27. The son of the woman of Zarephath (1 Kings 17:17–24).

28. Literally, "as though Israel's enemies were to perish." The concern expressed here, however, is not for Israel's enemies, but for Israel itself. In other words, the clause is a euphemism which avoids putting into words even the possibility of Israel's perishing, and so it is translated "as though Israel—may such an end befall its enemies—were about to perish from the world." Cf. below, ER, 43, 44.

29. The son of the great woman of Shunem (2 Kings 4:32–37), and the man whose body, thrown during an emergency into Elisha's grave, touched Elisha's bones and as a result was brought back to life (2 Kings 13:21). This man is said to have been Shallum the son of Tikvah, who had led a life of loving-kindness. He would, for example, go daily outside of his city, bearing a pitcher of water to provide drink for travelers. His wife was Huldah the prophetess (2 Kings 22:14). See Ginzberg, *Legends, 4,* 246.

was required by] the will of Him at whose word the world came into being. The facts of the story of Elijah and Elisha, anyone can find for himself in Scripture: *Go, return on thy way to the wilderness of Damascus,* the holy spirit told Elijah, *and Jehu the son of Nimshi shalt thou anoint to be king over Israel; and Elisha . . . shalt thou anoint to be prophet in thy stead . . . So he departed thence, and found Elisha the son of Shaphat of Abel-meholah*[30]
ER, *p.* 23 (1 Kings 19:15–19). Elisha had great skill[31] | in plowing—indeed he had as many as *twelve yoke of oxen before him* (1 Kings 19:19). *But when Elijah passed over unto him, and cast his mantle upon him* (1 Kings 19:20), at once Elisha left all that he owned and ran after Elijah, as is said, *he left the oxen (ibid.).* Thereat he renounced ownership[32] of all that he had, indeed he salted his entire field [so that it became barren.[33] Then to show further how little he now cared for all that he had owned, when Elisha] *returned from following* [*Elijah*], *he took a yoke of oxen and slew them,* etc. (1 Kings 19:21). Thereupon, Scripture continues, *Elisha . . . ministered unto Elijah (ibid.).* Note that it is not said, "Elijah taught Elisha," but *Elisha . . . ministered unto Elijah.* Hence it is said: Ministering to a scholar can teach us more than studying with him.[34]

But[35] it is also said, [in connection with the discourse between Elijah and Elisha], that one man should not take leave of another without bringing up some matter of Halakah,[36] in order that the former may be able to say, "May So-and-so be remembered for good, for he was the cause of fixing this particular matter of Halakah in my memory." Of the discourse between Elijah and Elisha Scripture says, *And it came to pass, as they went on walking (holĕkim), they kept on (ḥalok)*[37] *talking*[38] (2 Kings 2:11). Here *talking* must refer to talk of Torah, as

---

According to another tradition, the second miracle took place when Elisha healed Naaman, the Aramean commander, of his leprosy (2 Kings 5:14), a leper being regarded as one dead (B.Sanh 47a).

At all events, Elisha's last entreaty to Elijah, *Let a double portion of thy spirit be upon me* (2 Kings 2:9), was thus fulfilled: the master brought only one person back to life, and the disciple, two.

30. The words *of Abel-meholah* are not in MT [here, but are given in verse 16 as Elisha's birthplace. L. N.]

31. For *kal,* in the sense of "skilled," cf. Lieberman, *TKF, 4,* 23, and *5,* 87. These references were provided by Professor Saul Lieberman in a private communication.

32. So, apparently R, which reads *hifkir,* "gave up ownership," and not, as in Friedmann, *hifkid,* "turned over [to others]."

33. To indicate the irrevocability of his resolve to join Elijah. Cf. Judg. 9:45.

34. The disciple is thus constantly with the master who instructs by example as well as by word. Cf. B.Ber 7b.

35. See Louis Ginzberg in *OT,* p. 284, n. 306.

36. See B.Ber 31a and Ta 10b.

37. In *ḥalok,* ER seems to find an intimation of Halakah.

38. "What specifically did they talk about? The reading of the Shĕma', of which it is said, *Thou shalt talk of them* (Deut. 6:7), says R. Aḥawa bar R. Ze'era; the creation of the world, of which it is said, *By the word of the Lord were the heavens made* (Ps. 33:6),

in the verse " 'Is not My talk like as fire?' says the Lord" (Jer. 23:29). Therefore, when an angel was sent out over Elijah and Elisha to destroy Elijah[39] and arrived to find the two engaged in discussion on matters of Torah, he said to the Holy One, "Master of the universe, they are engaged in discourse on matters of Torah, and so I cannot take dominion over them." [Thereupon God sent the angel back], for the verse goes on to say, *Behold,* [*the angel was confronted by*] *a chariot of fire, and horses of fire, until finally the two,* [*Elijah and Elisha*], *were parted asunder* (2 Kings 2:11). By *chariot of fire* is meant the Five Books, the Prophets, and the Writings; by *horses of fire* is meant Mishnah [which includes] Halakot and 'Aggadot. That here "fire" does indeed refer to Torah, [which tempers a man's soul and makes it proof against death and Gehenna's fire],[40] is shown in the verse "the Torah of the Lord being perfect, tempers the soul" (Ps. 19:8). What, then, can we conclude, is meant by the words *until finally the two were parted asunder?* That the angel [again] turned back and stood before the Lord, telling Him directly: "Master of the universe, just now I have given You all the satisfaction I could in the world [of the living]. The indignity I inflicted upon Elijah and Elisha in rudely pushing them apart [while they were engaged in study of Torah] should be sufficient deprivation for them. [Do not ask me to impose death on Elijah]." Such is the implication of *until finally the two were parted asunder.* [Thus it came about that Elijah did not die, but *went up by a whirlwind into heaven* (2 Kings 2:11).]

Hence it is said: When two men are walking along engaged in discourse on matters of Torah, no harm can befall them, as implied in the passage cited earlier, which says that the two men kept right on walking and talking.

[In further reference to the power of a mortal to resurrect the dead], how, it may be asked, did Ezekiel gain such merit as to enable him to bring many corpses back to life? Because each and every hour his concern was wholly for Israel.[41] Thus in the verse *Son of man, wilt thou judge, wilt thou judge the bloody city* (Ezek.

---

says R. Judah ben Pazzi; the comforting of Jerusalem, of which it is said, *Talk to the heart of Jerusalem* (Isa. 40:2), says R. Yudan son of R. Aibu; of the chariot, for the verse goes on to speak of *a chariot of fire and horses of fire* (2 Kings 2:11), say the Rabbis." See P.Ber 5:1, 8d.

39. R reads "to destroy them," perhaps a miswriting for "him."

40. The clause within brackets is interpolated on the basis of a parallel: "*Nothing is hid from the heat of judgment's sun* (Ps. 19:7). Still, in the time-to-come, asks R. Aḥa, who will be hid from the sun's fiery heat? And answers: He who occupies himself with Torah, for the very next verse in the Psalm says, *The Torah of the Lord being perfect restores the soul* (Ps. 19:8)" (Yalkuṭ Ps. 674).

[The author may regard *měšibat,* "restores," as equal to *mě'ěšibat,* "makes fireproof." L. N.] Hence "tempers."

41. In the course of his activities as prophet, Ezekiel, more than any other prophet, subjected himself to deprivation and discomfort. See Ezek. 4:4–6, 9, 16.

22:2), what is implied in God's saying *wilt thou judge* twice? That the Holy One was saying to Ezekiel: For you as for Me, both of us concerned alike for Israel, it is proper to judge Israel.[42]

In another comment the words are read *Son of man, wilt thou reprove, wilt thou reprove?* and God is considered to be saying to Ezekiel: If you are ready to reprove Israel [as harshly as they deserve], then reprove them. But if you cannot bring yourself to reprove them thus, then I will subject them to chastisement.[43] [But of what use your reproof of them?] You are like a song whose melody people generally delight in, but whose words they rarely heed and so do not delight the singer: *Lo, thou art unto them as a love song of one that hath a pleasant voice, and can well play on an instrument; so they hear thy words, but they heed them not* (Ezek. 33:32).[44] And the proof that they did not heed [Ezekiel's
ER, *p.* 24 words], you can see for yourself: | When Nebuchadnezzar, king of Babylon, came and made Jerusalem go into exile and made its inhabitants go down into Babylon, at first he set them up as princes over his entire kingdom.[45] But then, when they gave offense by their deeds, he took them out into the valley [of Dura (Dan. 3:1), where, even though they were willing to worship an idol], Nebuchadnezzar had them slain nevertheless.[46] And as they were being slain, they cried out: Woe unto us! *Our bones will be dried up, and our hope is lost; we are clean cut off* (Ezek. 37:11). Hence it is said: A man is capable of knowing whether or not he is to be a dweller in the world-to-come. For if he is guilty of such an enormity [as idol worship], it is as though he were thereby rooting himself out of the world-to-come.

Now, [since Ezekiel's sole care was always the lot of his people], the Holy One brought him to Israel, indeed carried him to them, as Ezekiel himself said: *The hand of the Lord was upon me, and the Lord carried me out upon the wind and* [*said*] *He would have me rest in the midst of that*

---

42. ER thus takes the repetition of *wilt thou judge* as God's inquiry of Ezekiel: "Will you judge in your own behalf? Will you judge as well in My behalf?" (Professor Saul Lieberman in a private communication.)

43. Ezekiel consented to utter such reproofs. Thus ER accounts for the paradox of Ezekiel's willingness to undergo painful deprivations for Israel's sake and the harshness of his utterances to them.

44. The next verse reads, *When this cometh to pass—behold, it cometh—then shall they know that a prophet hath been among them,* that is, one whose words they should have taken to heart, not just dismissed as no more than a song which titillates the hearer.

45. See Dan. 2:49.

46. After Hananiah, Mishael, and Azariah were saved from death (see Dan. 3:26–30), Nebuchadnezzar spoke as follows to those Jews who had obeyed his command to worship the idol in the valley of Dura: "You know that your God can help and save. Why, then, have you forsaken your God and worshiped idols which have no power to deliver? This wickedness proves that as by your deeds you have destroyed your own land, now with your iniquity you would also destroy my land" (PRE, chap. 33, and B.Sanh 92b).

From the above it is clear that the people of Judah refused to heed the words of Ezekiel.

valley[47] (Ezek. 37:1). Here by the word *rest* Ezekiel is referring to the repose of death, as in the verse "Let him come in peace, let them rest on their couches" (Isa. 57:2). The valley, Ezekiel goes on, *was full of bones ('ṣmwṯ)* (Ezek. 37:1), but note that *'ṣmwṯ,* "bones," can also be read *'ṣ mwṯ,* "tree of death." [Hence Ezekiel had in mind the fact that the men whose bones lay in the valley were not only descendants of] Adam who had eaten of the forbidden tree and that therefore they would have to suffer the penalty of death until the end of all generations [but also Ezekiel had in mind that on account of the enormity of their sins they would be *clean cut off* (Ezek. 37:11) from the world-to-come]. Such was Ezekiel's train of thought upon his viewing the valley full of bones.

Ezekiel then went on to say, *He took me to them* [*in a place*] *"encompassed"* (Ezek. 37:2), a word he had previously used in describing a place befouled by images of idols: *I went in and saw; and behold every detestable form of creeping things and beasts, and all the idols of the house of Israel portrayed upon the wall "encompassing" the area* (Ezek. 8:10). Now in using the word again, he was intimating that the valley was likewise a place befouled with the images of idols. [To Ezekiel, so many bones in this valley signified that many of the children of Israel had been guilty of idolatry because the willingness to heed God's commands had dried up in them]:[48] *Behold, there were very many in the open valley; and lo, they were very dry* (Ezek. 37:2). And Ezekiel cried out: These—perchance such [was the enormity of the transgression of these] whose bones lie here that they are utterly perished from the world [and will not live again]! Thereupon the Holy One said to Ezekiel: *Son of man, these bones are the whole house of Israel* (Ezek. 37:11).

The Holy One said further to Ezekiel, *Son of man . . . prophesy over these bones* (Ezek. 37:4), and then, according to the prophet, continued: *Prophesy, son of man, and say to the breath* [*of life*]: *Thus saith the Lord God: Come from the four winds, O breath, and breathe upon these slain, that they may live* (Ezek. 37:9). [Ezekiel's use of the word "slain" proves that the dead whose bones lay in the valley had not died naturally, but that Nebuchadnezzar had, in fact, taken their lives]. Indeed, according to the Sages, because he had done so, ten ministering angels were ap-

---

47. A great deprivation. For "he who dies outside the Land has two agonies to contend with—the agony of dying itself and the agony of burial outside the Land. . . . In the days of the Messiah the dead of the Land of Israel are to be [at once] among the living; and the righteous [dead] outside the Land are to get to it and come to life upon it" (see PR 1:6 [YJS, *18, 1,* 44–45]). The traditional burial place of Ezekiel is at Kefil near Birs Nimrud in Babylonia (see *JE, 5,* 316). Thus he was like Moses who was buried in the wilderness, so that in the time-to-come he would be the one to lead to the Land the generation that died in the wilderness. See Exod. Rabbah 4:2 and PR 50:4 (YJS, *18, 2,* 848).

48. "To Ezekiel . . . dried up in them"—Landau's comment.

pointed to attend [to the punishment] of this wicked man,[49] as described in the following words addressed to him: *Thou art thrown up from thy grave like an abhorred monster, draped with the bodies of those thou hast slain, those that were thrust through with the sword, and consequently* [*thou wilt be in the company of those*] *that are sent down to the very bottom of the pit, as a carcass trodden under foot* (Isa. 14:19).[50]

As for the dead in the valley, they were brought back to life! Again they stood up on their feet, again they begot children, and thus it was that the name of the Holy One was magnified in the world from one end of the world to the other. Of this event, the resurrection in the valley, Ezekiel tells us that God Himself declared: *I magnified Myself, and sanctified Myself, and made Myself known in the eyes of many nations* (Ezek. 38:23).

Hence the answer to the question asked above—[How did Ezekiel come to such merit as that through him so many dead were brought back to life?]—is that Israel and Israel's lot were ever his sole care.

[As for the oppressors of Israel, it has been previously said]: "In the time-to-come upon <Israel's> mountains the unremitting calamity of [spilt] blood and [torn] flesh, and broken [bones] will be Gog's."[51] Because the nations of the earth [would exterminate Israel, first having] oppressed and tortured them, ground their bones and flesh until their souls departed from them, and not had a care whatever for them, the Holy One will gather Gog and his allies for judgment on Israel's
ER, *p.* 25 mountains | and will feed their flesh to the birds of heaven and to the beasts of the field and will not have a care whatever for them, as is said, *Now then, O son of man, thus saith the Lord God: Speak unto the birds of every sort, and to every beast of the field: . . . Gather on every side to My feast that I do prepare for you, even a great feast, upon the mountains of Israel, that ye may eat flesh and drink blood* (Ezek. 39:17).

Indeed, "in this world, every day, without fail, our eyes behold the intermittent calamity of [spilt] blood and [torn] flesh befalling our oppressors." How did they come to be our oppressors? [Because we failed to heed the precepts of our Teacher.] Consider [Israel and Judah as] two young children who, having studied Scripture in the house of their teacher, presently grew up and became disciples of the wise. Now whenever they pass the doorway of their teacher's house and see the strap he used to chasten them with, they say jokingly to each other, "There is the very strap he used [to make us heed his teachings!" But

---

49. Nebuchadnezzar was driven from the society of men and made to dwell with wild beasts. See Dan. 4:28–30.

50. ER appears to take the five nouns and five adjectives in the Hebrew of Isa. 14:19 to intimate the presence of ten angels of punishment.

In the passage beginning "Ezekiel's use of the word 'slain' " and ending with *"trodden under foot"* the translators follow Edds.

51. See ER, 14–15.

because Israel and Judah still fail to heed their Teacher's instruction], the peoples of the world, [the instrument of God's chastisement, determined to exterminate Israel], oppress and torture them, grind their bones and flesh until life leaves them, and have not a care whatever for them. However, in the event, they, [the enemy nations], are to be dispersed on the mountains and on the hills, as is said to them, *Thou hast forgotten the Lord thy Maker that stretched forth the heavens, and laid the foundations of the earth* (Isa. 51:13). [The verse goes on to say to Israel, *Thou fearest continually all the day because of the fury of the oppressor (ibid.).*] Had the verse gone on to say, "As I make ready to destroy," one might have taken the words to be asserting "As I, [your God], make ready to destroy you, [Israel]." But since Scripture actually says, *As he makes ready to destroy,* it follows that the verse refers to Babylon [and not to Israel; that is, Babylon thought he would devastate Israel but he was to be disappointed]. And so[52] when Scripture asks, *Where is the fury of the oppressor? (ibid.),* the answer is that it has vanished among the mountains and the hills where the birds have consumed the flesh from off the Babylonians.

What blessing [God bestows] upon Israel! Despite the fact that wherever they dwell in the four corners of the earth they have been harried north to south, south to north, east to west, west to east, they still are at the center [of God's concern]. For, as the Lord has said: *Lo, I will command, and I will cause to move to and fro the house of Israel among all the nations, as a sieve is moved to and fro* (Amos 9:9). Had this verse gone on to say, "and the pebble shall fall to the earth," my heart would

---

52. In the passage "As I, [your God], make ready . . . refers to Babylon . . . disappointed]. And so"—a very difficult passage—Leon Nemoy's rendition is followed. He suggests that *bĕ-'eyneḵa*, a corrupted word, must refer to Israel, that *lĕḇaḇo* is a dittography of *lĕ-baḇel*, and that *hemennu* is to be equated with *mimmenu*.

In a private communication Professor Saul Lieberman suggests the following emendations: The word *bĕ-'eyneḵa*, "visibly," or "in your eyes," he associates with *'oyen*, "eyed with hostility" (1 Sam. 18:9); hence "your enemies." The word *lĕ-baḇel* he regards as a corruption of *lĕḇaḇĕḵa*, "your heart, your courage." The word *lĕḇaḇo*, "his heart," he regards as a gloss which attempted to cope with the difficult *lĕ-baḇel*. Finally *heymennu*, an Aramaic word which appears out of place in ER, he takes to be a corruption of *ha'ăminu*, "believe, be confident."

Following Professor Lieberman's emendations, the passage would read: "Had the verse read 'I make ready to destroy,' one might have taken it to mean 'I, your God, make ready to destroy you through your enemies.' Thereupon your hearts would have left you in terror. But be reassured, for the verse reads *As he*—meaning the enemy—*maketh ready to destroy. And where, now, is the fury of the [inimical] oppressor?"*

Another possible rendition, one which resorts to no emendations, follows: "Eventually, therefore, Israel find themselves dispersed on the mountains and the hills, as is said to them, *Thou hast forgotten the Lord thy Maker that stretched forth the heavens, and laid the foundations of the earth* (Isa. 51:13). The verse goes on to say to Israel, *Thou fearest continually all the day because of the fury of the oppressor,* concluding *as [I] make ready to destroy (ibid.),* so that one might take the words to be saying 'As [I your God] make ready to destroy you.' If this were God's meaning, then your heart might well fail you. But have no fear, for in saying *make ready to destroy,* God had in view not the present destruction of His people Israel, but the future destruction of their oppressor Babylon."

be broken within me and all my bones would grow weak.[53] I would have said: When a pebble falls to the earth, in the nature of things it is lost. But the text reassures me, *Yet shall not the least pebble fall upon the earth (ibid.):* As grain which a man shakes back and forth in a sieve always ends up with a pebble at the center of the sieve, so, too, Israel —may I make atonement for them![54]—are at the center [of God's concern]. Despite the fact that wherever they dwell in the four corners of the earth they have been harried north to south, south to north, east to west, west to east, Israel still are at the center [of God's concern]. Such is the Holy One's concern for Israel, as is also averred in post-Mosaic Scripture by Your servants, the Prophets: *For I the Lord change not; therefore ye, O sons of Jacob, are not consumed* (Mal. 3:6). And in further proof of the Holy One's concern for Israel it is said: Once I have had occasion to smite a nation, I have not had to smite it again—*I the Lord have not had to do it again*[55] *(ibid.).*

[But in His smiting of Israel, He has always refrained from smiting them heavily.] Thus, for example, of the "seventy-two colors" mentioned in the Torah <"as signs of leprosy">[56] (Neḡ 1:4), He who sits on the throne of the Judge of mercy—may His great name be blessed for ever and ever and ever!—said: "If I bring out upon them who are of Israel all the seventy-two signs of leprosy, Israel will be deemed the most repulsive among the nations, so that the peoples of the world will exclaim, 'How repulsive it is!' " [Therefore God brings out upon Israel no more than] one or another of only four colors among all the seventy-two signs of leprosy spoken of in the Torah. And if you should see a man in Israel who has upon his person one of those colors which are signs of leprosy, that man is an altar of atonement[57] for Israel wherever they dwell. And further, if you should see a man in Israel who is afflicted by only one plague of all the plagues mentioned [in Scripture],

53. Cf. Jer. 23:9.

54. That is, "May I be allowed to make atonement for any transgressions they may be guilty of." See Neḡ 2:1.

55. The word *šaniṯi,* "change," may also mean "do it again, do it twice." Israel, on the other hand, is always smitten gently, so that the verse concludes, *Ye, O sons of Jacob, are not consumed.*

56. So Neḡ 1:4, citing 'Aḳaḇiah ben Mahalalel. Since each of the four kinds of leprosy (Lev. 13) has eighteen variant colors, the total 72 is taken to represent the word *ḥsd,* "mercy," the numerical value of whose letters is 72. Thus the varieties of leprosy are construed as "chastisements inflicted with mercy." Cf. ER, 86.

In his commentary on Neḡ 1:4, Maimonides accounts differently for 'Aḳaḇiah's seventy-two signs: eight signs [shades of white] of plague in the skin of a man's body; eight signs respectively in (a) a boil or a burning in the skin, (b) a scall, and (c) the bald part in the front or the back of the head. Thus thirty-two signs. To these 'Aḳaḇiah adds the reddishness and greenishness in (a) men's garments (Lev. 13:49) and (b) houses (Lev. 14:37)—four more signs, which bring the total to thirty-six. Since a priest is called upon to examine all such signs twice, once at the end of the first week and again at the end of the second week, 'Aḳaḇiah comes to a total of seventy-two signs. See also Midraš hag-Gaḏol on Leviticus, ed. Adin Steinsaltz (Jerusalem, 5736/1975), pp. 332–33.

57. Cf. B.Ber 5b.

that man is to be deemed a scapegoat for Israel wherever they dwell. Thus, to the Holy One, one man of Israel [who is capable of achieving expiation for the entire people] is equal in importance to all the peoples of the world.[58] The proof | you can see for yourself. When the Holy One carried out His sentence against wicked Rome, what does Scripture say? *I have trodden the small winepress alone, because among the peoples there was not even one man who was with Me*[59] (Isa. 63:3). On the other hand, when Pharaoh-necoh slew Josiah, king of Judah,[60] what does Scripture say? *As in a large winepress the Lord hath trodden the virgin daughter of Judah* (Lam. 1:15). Since the large nations [such as Rome] are referred to as a "small winepress," and the small nation Israel is referred to as a "large winepress," you can judge for yourself their relative worth in the eyes of God. ER, *p.* 26

Such is Israel's worth to Him that the Holy One proceeds slowly with the chastisements He brings upon Israel and refrains from punishing them as much as they deserve.

[As for the righteous in Israel, how great is their reward!] "In the days of the Messiah and in the world-to-come, the righteous will enjoy eating and drinking, merrymaking, and singing." In the radiance of heaven's luminaries[61] there will be spread couches for the righteous who will eat and drink and know great joy—[yes, "joy of heart" for the righteous, but "sorrow of heart" for the wicked], as is said, *Therefore, thus saith the Lord God: Behold, My servants shall eat, but ye,* [*the wicked*], *shall be hungry; behold, My servants shall drink, but ye shall be thirsty; behold, My servants shall rejoice, but ye shall be ashamed; behold, My servants shall sing for joy of heart, but ye shall cry for sorrow of heart, and shall wail for vexation of spirit* (Isa. 65:13–14). [And so it should be.] For in the sight of heaven and earth, of sun and moon, of stars and planets, indeed in the sight of all the works of creation—all without exception—plain are the deeds of the righteous. In the sight of heaven and earth, of sun and moon, of stars and planets, indeed in the sight of all the works of creation—all without exception—plain are the deeds of the wicked. The righteous will collect the reward for their deeds, and the wicked will collect the reward for their deeds. [So it will be in the days of the Messiah and in the world-to-come], when *the light of the moon shall be as the light of the sun, and the light of the sun shall be sevenfold, as the light of the seven days* (Isa. 30:26). Then, says Isaiah, *The sinners in Zion will be afraid; trembling will seize the ungodly* (Isa. 33:14). Each and every one of them will be led forward, seated, and told: You utter fools, until this

---

58. Cf. MTeh 119:2 (YJS, *13,* 21, 264).
59. JV: *And of the peoples there was no man with Me.*
60. 2 Kings 23:29–30.
61. The reference may be either to *But unto you that fear My name shall the sun of righteousness arise with healing in its wings* (Mal. 3:20) or to *I, saith the Lord, will be unto her a wall of fire round about* (Zech. 2:9).

hour you were unable to recognize the worth of one who lives rightly in the world, he of whom it is said, *He that walketh righteously, and speaketh uprightly; he that despiseth the gain of oppressions, that shaketh his hands from holding of bribes, that stoppeth his ears from hearing of blood, and shutteth his eyes from looking upon evil* (Isa. 33:15). As for you, the utterly righteous men who [in this world] every day without fail do My will as set forth in My Torah, what does Scripture say of you? *Unto you that fear My name shall the sun of righteousness arise with healing in its wings* (Mal. 3:20).

Indeed "In this world the righteous will enjoy in some measure the eating and drinking [and the joy of the world-to-come]." How can that be? He who reads Scripture for the sake of Heaven and recites Mishnah for the sake of Heaven, and eats what he has earned himself, and takes pleasure in his own labor, "of him the Psalmist says, *When thou eatest the labor of thy hands, happy shalt thou be, and it shall be well with thee* (Ps. 128:2)—*happy shalt thou be,* in this world; *and it shall be well with thee,* in the world-to-come"[62] (Ab̲ 4:1). As the Song of Songs says, *How fair and how pleasant art thou, O love, for delights* (Song 7:7)[63]—when a man is delighted with what he owns [and seeks not what others own].[64]

I call heaven and earth to witness that any disciple of the wise who reads Scripture for the sake of Heaven and recites Mishnah for the sake of Heaven, and eats what he himself has earned, and is content with the fruit of his labor [will never be forsaken]—of such as he the Psalmist says, *I have not seen the righteous forsaken, nor his seed begging bread* (Ps. 37:25). Nay more, the people in his household will revere him, and the Holy One will love him with an all-encompassing love. Of him Scripture says further, *All the peoples of the earth shall see that the name of the Lord is called upon thee* (Deut. 28:10); and [the Holy One assures him], *When thou passest through the waters, I will be with thee, and through the rivers, they shall not overflow thee* (Isa. 43:2).

---

62. "Because in this world you will not be dependent upon human beings; and being satisfied with what is yours, you will not embezzle [what belongs to others] and therefore will be deemed worthy of life in the world-to-come" (*'Ẹs Yosef* on Ab̲ 4:1).

63. "*Behold thou art fair, My beloved, behold thou art fair* (Song 1:15). . . . Behold thou art fair in this world, behold thou art fair in the world-to-come" (Song Rabbah, 1:15).

64. See ER, 91.

CHAPTER (5) 6

Why Abraham, Jacob, Jethro, and Jabez came to have a life with no Inclination to evil

Summary

Abraham came to have in this world a life with no distress, no Inclination to evil—a life such as God bestows upon the righteous only in the world-to-come —because he was willing to give up his life in the fire of the Chaldees (ER, 27). After his deliverance, Abraham, old and white-haired as he was, found his hair turning black and he recovered the vigor of his youth. Abraham became a young man again and Sarah became a young woman. Awed by such wondrous rejuvenation, the peoples in Canaan made him king over them. Thereupon all the kings of the east pressed an attack upon the kings that were on the side of Abraham. Abraham intervened when he learned that his own flesh-and-blood had been seized. He was victorious. But he stopped his pursuit of the invading kings at a point in the north where, so God told him, his own descendants, the Danites, would worship idols.

To assure the world that in his foray he was not after booty, Abraham had his soldiers wearing a variety of precious ornaments as they went into battle (ER, 28).

With all kinds of blessings, with wisdom, with wealth, with children, with length of days did God bless Abraham even though he observed no commandments of Torah other than the belief in one God. How much more and more does He love Abraham now that his children are in possession of the entire Torah!

Jacob also came in this world to merit the kind of life God bestows upon the righteous only in the time-to-come. Because of his immersion in Torah and because of the effort he made to instruct his children, God rewarded him by making him the begetter of the Fathers of the Twelve Tribes. Then, too, his misgivings about his own conduct (ER, 29) won him, as a further reward, well-being for seventeen years before he reached old age.

Jethro, a non-Jew by birth, also came to have the kind of life God bestows upon the righteous only in the world-to-come. Although his conversion came about as a result of shrewd calculation, he ultimately arrived at the essence of true faith, and so his children are always to be found in academies of learning.

The example of Jethro who gave his daughter in marriage to a man of learning should be heeded.

Jabez, an unassuming but conscientious teacher of the people of Israel, also came to have the kind of life God bestows upon the righteous only in the world-to-come (ER, 30). Nevertheless, despite Torah's infinite worth, a man should do good deeds first and only then ask for the gift of Torah; a man should hold fast to the way of humility and only then ask understanding from Him whose presence is everywhere (ER, 31).

Chapter (5) 6

ER, *p.* 27 How did Abraham come in this world to merit a life with no distress, with no Inclination to evil—a life, indeed, such as God bestows upon the righteous only in the world-to-come? Because for the sake of Heaven he was willing to give up his life in the fire of the Chaldees. And whenever a man is willing to give up his life for the sake of Heaven, he is given back not only his life in this world but full and long life, endless life, in the world-to-come. The proof you can see for yourself. Keep in mind that the household of Abraham's father, idolaters all, used to make idols and go out to sell them in the marketplace. One day, when it was Abraham's turn to sell the idols, a man came up to him and asked, "How much is this idol?" Abraham replied, "Three minas," and then went on to inquire, "How old are you?" The man replied, "Thirty." Abraham exclaimed, "Thirty! At your age don't you know any better than to worship this thing which I turned out just today?" Thereupon the man was abashed and went away.

Shortly, another man came and asked Abraham, "How much is this idol?" Abraham replied, "Five minas," and then asked, "How old are you?" The man answered, "fifty." "Fifty!" exclaimed Abraham. "At your age don't you know any better than to worship this thing which my father's household turned out just today?" The man was abashed and went away. When what Abraham was saying to would-be buyers came to Nimrod's ears, he sent men to fetch Abraham and had him appear before him. Nimrod then said to him, "Son of Terah, make a beautiful god for me, one which will be uniquely mine." So Abraham went back to his father's house and said, "Make a beautiful idol for Nimrod." When Terah's household got the idol finished, they put a cincture around it and painted it a variety of colors.[1] [After Abraham brought the image to Nimrod, he said to him, "You are a king, and yet you are so lacking in a king's wisdom as to worship this thing which my father's household has just turned out!"] Thereupon Nimrod had Abraham taken out [to be consumed] in a fiery furnace. In tribute to Abraham's righteousness, however, the day turned cloudy, and presently rain came down so hard that Nimrod's men could not get the fire started.

Next, as Nimrod sat [in his throne room], surrounded by the entire generation that was to be dispersed [for its transgressions], Abraham was brought in and put in their midst. He approached[2] Nimrod and again voiced his contempt of the king's idol. "If not this idol, whom shall I worship?" Nimrod asked. Abraham replied, "The God

---

1. Here in R there is a lacuna.

2. Literally, "went down," perhaps "went down" in the bowing and prostration required in addressing a king.

of gods, the Lord of lords, Him whose kingdom endures in heaven and earth and in the uppermost heaven of heavens." Nimrod said, "Nevertheless I will rather worship the god of fire, for behold, I am going to cast you into the very midst of fire—let the god of whom you speak come and deliver you from the fire."

At once his servants bound Abraham hand and foot and laid him on the ground. Then they piled up wood on all sides of him, [but at some distance away],[3] a pile of wood five hundred cubits long to the north, a pile five hundred cubits long to the south, a pile five hundred cubits long to the west, and a pile five hundred cubits long to the east. Nimrod's men then went around and around setting the wood on fire.[4]

At that time the entire household of Terah were idolaters; not one of them acknowledged his Creator. And so all of Terah's neighbor <s> came and jeeringly tapped him on the head, saying to him: "You have been put to bitter shame![5] That son of yours, of whom you have been saying that he was to be heir of this world and of the world-to-come, Nimrod is having him consumed by fire!"

At once the compassion of the Holy One welled up, and the holiness of His great name came down from the upper heaven of heavens, from the place of His glory, His grandeur, and His beauty and delivered our father Abraham from the taunts and the jeers and from the fiery furnace, as is said, *I am the Lord that brought thee out of the fire*[6] *of the Chaldees* (Gen. 15:7).

And after God performed His miracle in behalf of our father Abraham, then and there Terah's household had good excuse to open their mouths and return jeer for jeer to the generation that was eventually to be dispersed [for its transgressions]. To Terah and to his son Abraham applies the verse *My son, be wise and make my heart glad, that I may answer him that taunteth me* (Prov. 27:11). The words *him that taunteth me* would thus apply to the generation that was to be dispersed, a generation which if it had had its way | would have slain his son **ER, *p.* 28** Abraham and had him perish in this world as well as in the world-to-come.

[After Abraham's deliverance], Terah, for the sake of Heaven, proceeded to quit his dwelling place, as is said, *And Terah took Abram his son,* etc. (Gen. 11:31). As a reward for Terah's having quit his

---

3. Nothing defiling, certainly not a corpse, may according to the Zoroastrians be put into fire. And so Nimrod arranged to have the burning wood piled at a distance from Abraham so that he would not die quickly from the fire itself, but slowly from the heat thrown off by the flames. So Friedmann, Introduction, p. 82.

4. A further precaution by fire worshipers against their own "contamination" through proximity to a corpse.

5. Thus R, which reads *bwšth.* Apparently conflating the letters *beṯ* and *waw* at the beginning of *bwšth* Friedmann read the word *mšth.* The line would then read, "A celebration? No, a bitter shame!"

6. JV: *Ur.*

dwelling place, for the ensuing thirty-five years of his life[7] he had the honor and distinction of having had his son Abraham established as king by the Holy One.

And Abraham and Sarah went to the land of Canaan, as is said, *Abram took Sarai his wife . . . and they went forth to go into the land of Canaan* (Gen. 12:5). Abraham grew old and white-haired[8] and abstained from the way of husband and wife in the world; Sarah, too, grew old and white-haired and abstained from the way of husband and wife in the world. True, it is said, *Now Sarah and Abraham were old* (Gen. 18:1), but then Abraham, old and white-haired as he was, found his hair turning black, and he recovered the vigor of his youth. Sarah, likewise, old and white-haired as she was, found her hair turning black. Abraham became a young man again and Sarah became a young woman again.[9] Thereupon, just about everyone in the world gathered around them and asked, "What was so unusual about you both as to have such extraordinary things befall you?" So Abraham sat down, and beginning with his deliverance from the fire of the Chaldees, told everything that had happened to him in the world up to that very hour. Of the things that befell Abraham, it is said, *Who hath raised up one*[10] *from the east? At whose steps does victory attend? He giveth nations before him, and maketh him rule over kings* (Isa. 41:2). And as soon as the gathering heard words of Torah from Abraham, they made him king over them.

Right away, in that very hour, all the kings of the east banded together, and they came and pressed an attack upon the kings that were on the side of Abraham. But he did not move against the hostile kings until they seized his own flesh-and-blood, as is said, *And when Abram heard that his kinsman was taken captive,* [*he led forth his trained men . . . and pursued as far as Dan* (Gen. 14:14), and freed his kinsman]. It was at Dan that the Holy One revealed to Abraham that his descendants[11] would one day worship idols there, as is said "And the children of Dan set up for themselves the graven image" (Judg. 18:30), and when Abraham heard this, his strength left him.[12] Hence Scripture

---

7. After the birth of Isaac, who was Abraham's heir, Abraham was king. Since Terah was 70 when Abraham was born, and Abraham was 100 at Isaac's birth, Terah was then 170, and he lived to 205 years (Gen. 11:32). Hence for thirty-five years he saw his son Abraham rule as king.

8. Until the time of Abraham men did not grow old. See Gen. Rabbah 65:8 and B.BM 87a.

9. Had she not become youthful, Abimelech would not have taken her. See B.BM 87a and PR 42:3 (YJS, *13, 2,* 740).

10. [*one*—here understood as referring to Abraham. L. N.]

11. R reads "two of his descendants." But since a reference to only two Danites who would worship idols makes no sense, the suggestion that *šene,* "two," is a miswriting of *bĕne,* "descendants," is followed (see Friedmann, Introduction, p. 139).

12. *"And pursued as far as Dan* (Gen. 14:14). As yet the Tribes had not come into the Land, and the Land of Israel had not been apportioned among the Israelites. Why

says, *During the night they were divided—Abraham from his servants* (Gen. 14:15), [who continued the pursuit].[13] [In another comment], there are those who take *Night* to be the name of the angel who came down to help Abraham, and hence the verse is read " 'Night,' together with his servitors [the stars], took up the fight against Abraham's enemies"[14] *(ibid.)*.

With what did Abraham make his trained men glitter?[15] With silver and gold, precious stones and pearls, and with all kinds of costly ornaments from all over the world. He did so to make known to just about every one in the world that he was very rich, and hence people would not be likely to say, "Abraham proceeded to slay the kings for no other reason than to get hold of the valuables that were on them."

As for the proof that our father Abraham was made a king in the world, he is so addressed in Scripture: *Thou art a prince of God among us* (Gen. 23:6). Elsewhere in the Five Books, the term "prince" occurs in the phrase *When a prince sinneth* (Lev. 4:22). In the Prophets, Zedekiah is addressed as *Profane, wicked prince of Israel* (Ezek. 21:30), and Israel's rulers of the future are told *Let it suffice you, O princes of Israel* (Ezek. 45:9). And even as the term "prince" in reference to rulers of the kingdom of Israel means a ruler who has no one over him save the Lord his God, so the term "prince" in reference to rulers of the kingdom of Judah means a ruler who has no one over him save the Lord his God. From the preceding we may infer that this sense of the word applies also to the term "prince" when used in the Five Books, and thus the term "prince" when used of Abraham also means a ruler who has no one over him save the Lord his God.[16] Hence we conclude that our father Abraham was a kingly ruler in the world for seventy-five years —thirty-five years during Terah's life and forty years after his death.

And what was distinctive about the coins he issued? [Because of the change in Abraham and Sarah from old age to youth], Abraham's coins had stamped on one side the images of an old man and an old woman | and on the other the images of a young man and a young woman. ER, *p.* 29

---

then does Scripture say, *as far as Dan*? Simply because God had said to Abraham our father: In the future your children will worship idols in this place. Whereupon Abraham's strength left him" (Mek, *2,* 154–55). See also PRKM 3:12, 49–50, (PRKS, pp. 53–54).

13. Without Abraham, who was unable to continue in pursuit.

14. "and hence the verse is read . . . against Abraham's enemies" is transposed from ER, 28, line 9 f.b. See Friedmann's n. 14 and B.Sanh 96a, where in support of this reading of Gen. 14:15, R. Isaac Nappaḥa cites *They fought from heaven; the stars in their courses fought against Sisera* (Judg. 5:20).

15. The question, as phrased in ER, derives from the meaning of *way-yareḳ* (JV: "led forth") in Gen. 14:14. ER, however, defines the word, as does R. Simeon ben Laḳish, "he made them glitter with precious stones and pearls, *way-yareḳ* meaning 'glitter,' as in *With the glitter (yĕraḳraḳ) of gold* (Ps. 68:14)." See Gen. Rabbah 43:2.

16. ER thus seems to read Gen. 23:6 "Thou art a prince under God among us." Cf. Sif Lev. 4:22 (ed. Weiss [Vienna, 1862], p. 19c) and B.Hor 10b, 11a–b.

There was not a single blessing in the world which the Holy One omitted to bestow upon Abraham. He blessed him with wisdom, with understanding, with knowledge, and with prudence. He blessed him with money and with goods. He made him possessor of heaven and earth and appointed him lord over all His world, as is said, *Blessed by God Most High be Abram who has come to possess heaven and earth*[17] (Gen. 14:19). And He blessed him with children and children's children, and He had him come to possess length of days in this world and also in the world-to-come, for it is said, *As Abraham grew old, he came into days*[18] (Gen. 24:1). Scripture does not refer here [only] to Abraham's earthly days: it has reference not only to a day in this world but also to a day in the days of the Messiah, and to still another day, [a day without end], in the world-to-come. And as the Holy One blessed Abraham, He said: Ten generations came [after Adam], and then I destroyed My world and drove man out of it. What comfort was it to Me to have done so? But now that Abraham has come, My heart is with My world again, as is said, *Thou hast won My heart, O beloved* [*Abraham, who in proclaiming God's oneness*], *gave oneness to My world;*[19] *Thou hast won My heart with one of thine eyes* (Song 4:9). We are reminded here of the parable of a mortal king who wed a woman after having beheld only one of her eyes, [the other being veiled]. Nevertheless he loved her with an exceeding love, he took great delight in her, he yearned over her. You can imagine therefore, how much more and more she would have been loved had the king seen both of her eyes. Even so, the Holy One loved our father Abraham with utter love, took delight in him, and yearned over him for the one reason that he opened the eyes of mortals to their need of Him[20] and thereby brought them under the wings of the Presence. Now if God so loved Abraham for the one reason that he opened [the eyes of] mortals to their need of Him and thereby brought them under the wings of the Presence, all the more and more will He love him for a second reason—that is, when his children will have

---

17. JV: *Blessed be Abram of God Most High, Maker of heaven and earth.*

18. JV: *And Abraham was old, well stricken in age.*

19. JV: *Thou hast ravished my heart, my sister, my bride.* But in this comment, *'aḥoṭi,* "my sister," is taken to be derived from the root *'ḥḥ,* "to sew together, to unite"—hence Abraham "the sewer," who proclaimed "the unity and oneness of God, the corollary of which is the unity and brotherhood of man" (J. Theodor in Gen. Rabbah 39:3, Soncino tr., p. 313); and "my bride" is taken in its generalized meaning of "my beloved"—hence Abraham, beloved of God.

20. Abraham, it is implied here, observed no commandments of Torah other than the belief in God. Elsewhere in tradition Abraham is said to have kept the entire Torah. See MTeh 112:1 (YJS, *13, 2,* 110). Instead of *'ene,* "eyes," all other editions of ER—beginning with Haida—read *'inyĕne,* "matters, needs." In the translation, both readings are taken into account. Hence, "Abraham . . . opened the eyes of mortals to their need of Him."

acquired [the merit of having performed] major precepts <and> bundles upon bundles [of less weighty ordinances] of Torah. Such is the implication of the verse *Thou hast won My heart . . . with one of thine eyes.*

Even the almost fatal wounds which the Holy One visited upon Israel because of their sins in this world will be a healing for them in the world-to-come, as is said, *Come, and let us return unto the Lord, for He hath torn us, and He will heal us. . . . On two days He will revive us* (Hos. 6:1–2). The first of the days the verse refers to is life in this world; the second of the days is life in the time of the Messiah. And *on the third day,* the verse concludes, *He will raise us up (ibid.),* "the third day" referring to life in the world-to-come.

How did our father Jacob come in this world to merit a life with no distress, with no Inclination to evil—a life something like the life that God bestows upon the righteous only in the time-to-come? Because from his youth to his old age he frequented the house of study, familiarizing himself with Scripture, Mishnah, and Midrash of Halakot as well as of 'Aggadot, as is said, *Jacob was an ideal man—he sat in tents* [*of study*] (Gen. 25:27). And [because his care was instruction of children], to him apply the verses *As arrows in the hand of a mighty man, so are children instructed from their youth* (Ps. 127:4), and *To whom is he most likely to give instruction? Whom is he likely to make understand the message? Those newly weaned from the milk, just taken away from the breast* (Isa. 28:9). And [because of his care for children], when Jacob left his father's house to go to the house of Laban, the Presence came and stood over him and spoke to him as follows: My son, lift up your eyes and look toward heaven, and there behold twelve stars and signs of the Zodiac twelve hours in the day and twelve hours in the night—to the number of these will correspond [the number of your sons], the Twelve Tribe-fathers whom I shall give you. [And such was his love for his children] that later, after Jacob returned [from the house of Laban] and Joseph was sold, Jacob mourned and wept for him twenty-two years,[21] as is said, *Jacob . . . mourned for his son many days. And all his sons and all his daughters rose up to comfort him; but he refused to be comforted. . . . And his father wept for him* (Gen. 37:35). [Jacob mourned for Joseph], but did he also weep for him? [Read not *wept for him,* but *wept for himself*], for he said: "Have I incurred guilt for having married two sisters?[22] Or because I craftily profited from the wealth of Laban?[23] Or because

21. Joseph was 17 when he was sold into slavery and 30 when he was presented to Pharaoh. Then came the seven years of plenty, and after two years of famine Jacob arrived in Egypt—hence twenty-two years. See Rashi on Gen. 37:34.

22. See Lev. 18:18.

23. See Gen. 30:25–43.

ER, *p.* 30 I unprotestingly profited from the wealth of | Shechem?[24] If so, then the covenant that the Holy One made with me has been annulled." Hearing these words, the Holy One at once was moved to compassion and decreed well-being for Jacob for the seventeen years before he reached old age. Hence, it is said: It is considered an auspicious sign for him whose well-being extends to the year before he reaches old age [because it is a foretaste of the heavenly reward he is to receive], and it is considered an inauspicious sign for him to whom adversity comes a year before he reaches old age [because it is a foretaste of the heavenly punishment he is to receive].[25] Accordingly, the fact that our father Jacob experienced well-being for seventeen years [before he reached old age] means that the Holy One intended to compensate him so abundantly as to make it seem as though all of his days had been spent in well-being. Note that the words *And Jacob lived in the land of Egypt seventeen years* are followed directly by *so the days of Jacob, the years of his life, were a hundred forty and seven* (Gen. 47:28).[26]

How did Jethro come in this world to merit a life with no distress and with no Inclination to evil—a life something like the one God bestows upon the righteous only in the world-to-come? Because through his shrewdness he managed first [to get himself accepted as a convert][27] and ultimately arrived at the essence of true faith. During all the years that Moses dwelt in the house of Jethro, Jethro saw all the good deeds that Moses was doing, deeds which made no impression whatever on Jethro[28] until Moses came to Egypt where through his efforts a great deed, [the exodus], came to pass. Then Jethro said: Woe is me![29] All the good deeds that this man Moses has done while he was dwelling in my house are gaining him life in the world-to-come; but as for me, I do not know what [my end is to be]. Thereupon, of his own volition, he ventured to do a great thing, as is said, *Jethro, Moses' father-in-law, took Zipporah, Moses' wife . . . and her two sons . . . and pleaded with Moses* (Exod. 18:2–3) [in his characteristically clever way] by having the messenger whom he sent to Moses speak as follows:[30] "I

---

24. See Gen. 34:28–29.

25. So *MS*. [The Hebrew says: "an auspicious sign if one has (at least) one good year just before he reaches old age . . . an inauspicious sign if one has (even) one bad year," etc. L. N.]

26. R. Judah [I] the Patriarch, who spent seventeen years in the salubrious climate of Sepphoris, compared them with the seventeen good years Jacob spent in Egypt. See Gen. Rabbah 96:5.

27. So Landau. ["Shrewdness" and "managed" imply a rather cynical and insincere attitude, whereas Jethro was more or less sincere in his behavior (he thought of his own salvation first, but that is surely no sin). I'd say "Because he proceeded to act with wisdom for its own sake." L. N.]

28. Or: "which netted Moses nothing at all."

29. Reading not *'elu,* "these," but, as in V, *'oy li,* "Woe is me!"

30. Since Exod. 18:7 says, *Moses went out to meet his father-in-law,* earlier communi-

adjure you by [the names of] your two sons to heed my plea: when people asked you, 'Why did you call the one son Gershom?' you said [as I say to you now], 'I want to become a convert *(ger)* to Israel there *(shom)* [at Sinai], in a land where I am a stranger' *(ibid.)*.[31] And when people inquired of you further, 'Why did you call the other son Eliezer?' you said [as I say to you now], 'May the God *('El)* whom I would have as my Father be my help *('ezer)'* (Exod. 18:4).[32] And so I adjure you by the God of your father that you come to meet me and receive me with friendly countenance." Yet Moses would not go out to meet Jethro until the Holy One said: Moses, Moses, go out to meet Jethro and receive him with friendly countenance. It was only then that Moses went out to meet Jethro, as is said, [*Finally*] *Moses went out to meet his father-in-law, and bowed down and kissed him* (Exod. 18:7).

Thereat, He who examines the hearts and reins of men said: Jethro, because you came to pay your respects to [Moses], that righteous man, [and became a convert to Israel], academies of learning will never be without the presence of your seed, as is said, *And he looked on the Kenite . . . and said: Enduring shall be thy seat* [*of learning*][33] (Num. 24:21).

---

cations between them, such as those mentioned in Exod. 18:6, must have been indirect —through a messenger or a letter. See Mek̲, *2,* 172.

Concerning converts of varying motivations, cf. ER, 146.

31. Moses used to account for Gershom by saying (as in JV) *I have been a stranger in a strange land.* Jethro cleverly turns Moses' own words against Moses. For a somewhat similar turn in interpretation, see *Torah šelemah, 15,* 8. On Jethro's wit and presence of mind, see PRKM, *1,* 36 (PRKS, p. 42).

ER's explanation of the two names as Jethro's witty and effective plea to Moses serves to account for the occurrence of the two names as well as their etymologies in an otherwise unexpected context.

32. JV: *The name of the other was Eliezer: for the God ('El) of my father was my help ('ezer).*

[It seems to me that the intent of the passage is logically simple: Jethro says to Moses: When you sojourned in Midian, you indicated your sincere desire to become a faithful citizen of that country by giving your sons symbolic names indicative of that desire. Now I have come to join my future with that of your people Israel. I have no newborn sons to give them names symbolic of the sincerity of my desire to become a citizen of Israel, but I adjure you to accept my sincerity on faith, and to welcome me, as Midian had welcomed you before. (Thus *ger* would refer, as logic demands, to Midian [*shom*] not to Israel.) L. N.]

In a similar vein, Sid Z. Leiman writes: "I agree with Leon Nemoy's less elaborate reconstruction, and even consider his interpretation to move beyond the plain sense. Jethro swears to Moses an oath of loyalty, as it were. He swears by those items most sacred to Moses, namely Moses' sons and Moses' God. The author of the Midrash knows this because of the sequence of the verses in Exodus 18. How else account for verses 18:3–4?"

Still, V, introducing the entire passage, says of Jethro, "he proceeded to act with wisdom not for its own sake," clearly implying that he began as an opportunist. Moreover, the ingress among the worthies—Abraham, Isaac, and Jabez—of Jethro who arrived at the true faith by a circuitous route enhances the narrative's dramatic quality.

33. On the Kenites, descendants of Jethro, see PRKM, *1,* 36 (PRKS, p. 42); Mek̲, *2,* 187; Sif Num. 78 (ed. Horovitz [Frankfurt am Main, 1917], p. 73).

Hence, [because Jethro had given his daughter to be the wife of Moses], it is said: A man should give his daughter in marriage to a disciple of the wise, <even if he has to give up all of his wealth for her sake, as did Jethro, with the result that through Moses he came to acquire merit. Indeed, a man ought to marry the daughter of a disciple of the wise>,[34] even if he has to put up a large sum to get her.

The proof you can find for yourself if you will go out and see the way things go in the world. When a man marries the daughter of a disciple of the wise and after a time dies <or> is banished, no matter what, he will still have fathered sons who are disciples of the wise.[35] But if a man marries the daughter of someone unlettered in Torah, then, if the man dies or is banished, he will have fathered sons unlettered in Torah. Consider by way of analogy that a grape-bearing vine intermingled with a berry-bearing bush,[36] or a berry-bearing bush intermingled with a grape-bearing vine, makes an ugly sight and one that is unseemly. But a grape-bearing vine intermingled with another grape-bearing vine, or a berry-bearing bush intermingled with another berry-bearing bush, makes a beautiful sight and one that is seemly.[37] Such, indeed, is the way things go in the world.

How did Jabez come in this world to merit a life with no distress and with no Inclination to evil—a life something like the one God bestows upon the righteous only in the time-to-come? Because for the sake of Heaven he traveled throughout [the Land of] Israel and taught Torah to many of the people of Israel.[38] And he who teaches his fellow one verse of the Written Law, or one precept of the Oral Law, or indeed even one word of either, is to be regarded as though he had bestowed life upon his fellow, as is said, *hearkening to His voice . . . is thy life, and the length of thy days* (Deut. 30:20), and as is said further, *Length*
ER, *p.* 31 *of days is in* [*Wisdom's*] *right hand* (Prov. 3:16), | and *She is a tree of life to them that lay hold upon her, and every one that props up* [*her laden branches*] *will himself stand firm* (Prov. 3:18). Nevertheless, note what is said: A man should do good deeds first and only then ask for Torah from Him whose presence is everywhere.[39] A man should first emulate the deeds of men whose lives are righteous and spotless and only then

---

34. The passage "even if he has to . . . disciple of the wise" is based on a parallel in Yalkuṭ, *2, Yiṭro,* 268.

35. Because the wife will see to it that the children are properly taught Torah.

36. The *rubus sanctus.*

37. See B.Pes 49a.

38. Jabez is taken to be another name for Joshua's successor Othniel, who fostered Torah in Israel. See ER, chap. 3, n. 12, and 1 Chron. 2:55, where families of scribes are said to have sat in the presence of Jabez.

39. Cf. "He whose fear of sin comes before his wisdom, his wisdom shall endure" (R. Ḥanina ben Dosa in Aḇ 3:11).

ask for grasp of the reasoning in Torah from Him whose presence is everywhere. A man should first hold fast to the way of humility and only then ask understanding [of Torah] from Him whose presence is everywhere. Thus it is said: *Ask ye of the Lord rain in the time of the latter rain* (Mal. 10:1).

Hence it is said of the study of Scripture: When a man has studied <the Five> Books, the Prophets, and the Writings and knows how to reply to questions concerning them, let him keep [in mind what he has learned from these books], and let him bless, praise, magnify, exalt, and hallow the name of Him by whose word the world came into being, the Holy One, blessed be He. When a man has studied one or two divisions of Mishnah and knows how to reply to questions about them, let him keep [in mind what he has learned from these divisions], and let him bless, praise, magnify, exalt, and hallow the name of Him by whose word the world came into being.[40] Needless to say, the same applies even more to the man who has studied the entire range of Oral Law. When a man takes a wife and has one son or two sons by her, let him bless, praise, exalt, hallow, and magnify the name of Him by whose word the world came into being, the Holy One, blessed be He, so that his marriage bed remain pure, and that he acquire [life in] this world, in the days of the Messiah, and in the world-to-come. Thus it is said, *And Jabez called on the God of Israel, saying: Oh that Thou wouldst bless me indeed* (1 Chron. 4:10)—that is, bless me in the study of Torah; *and enlarge my bounds (ibid.)*—that is, enlarge the bounds of my understanding through disciples of the wise; *and that Thy hand might be with me (ibid.)*—that is, keep me from forgetting what I have learned; *and provide me with friends*[41] *(ibid.)*—that is, provide me with friends who will study with me; *that it may not torment me (ibid.)*—that is, may the Impulse to evil not so torment me as to prevent me from studying. *And God granted him that which he requested (ibid.).* Hence, to Jabez applies the verse *Grant thee according to thine own heart, and fulfill all thy counsel* (Ps. 20:5), and the verse *We will triumph in Thy salvation, and in the name of our God we will set up our banners; the Lord fulfill all thy petitions* (Ps. 20:6).

Another interpretation of the verse from Chronicles quoted above: *And Jabez called on the God of Israel, saying: Oh that Thou wouldst bless me indeed*—that is, bless me with sons and daughters; *and enlarge my border*—that is, enlarge my family with further offspring; *and that Thy hand be with me*—that is, Thy hand aid me in the give and take of

---

40. "When a man has studied one or two . . . came into being"—R. This passage is not in Friedmann's edition.

41. JV: *And Thou wouldst work deliverance from evil.* But here ER appears to read *me-ra'ah,* "from evil," as though vocalized *me-re'ah,* "friend, friends."

business; *and that Thou wouldst work deliverance from evil*—that is, [in the years of] life Thou hast set for me I experience neither headache, nor eye ache, nor bellyache: in short, *that no ailment torment me. And God granted him that which he requested,* for he found contentment in his old age.[42]

42. See Mek, *2,* 189–91, and B.Tem 16a.

CHAPTER (6) 7

Torah is God's innermost sanctum; Prophets plead for mercy in Israel's behalf; decisiveness of offerer's motivation determines God's acceptance of offerings

Summary

Because God's love for Israel is enduring (ER, 31), He drew Israel into His inner sanctum, a counterpart of which is the inner sanctum of Torah: into it disciples of the wise flee, even as they rejoice that God had left His myriads of angels and come to cleave to Israel, speaking to Israel with unbelievable affection, and thus giving them assurance of the redemption to come.

God, taking note of the deeds of the righteous, such as Jacob, bemoans the absence of such righteous whenever Israel, despite miracles performed in their behalf, befoul themselves with misdeeds: though He performed no miracles for Jacob, yet throughout his days—God muses—Jacob retained his uprightness.

And so Amos asked (ER, 32): If there is no one like Jacob, is the world indeed to be destroyed? God reassured Amos at once that He would relent.

Prophets, Moses in particular, know well how to pour out pleas for mercy. Hence God credits the writing of the Torah as though it had actually been wrought by Moses.

Though it is clear that God was willing to bring Moses into the innermost sanctum of the innermost chambers of Torah, yet Moses did not venture to enter until invited (ER, 33).

God's regard for His messengers is shown likewise in the kinship, compassion, and love He expressed in speaking to Ezekiel. Moreover, in the vision of the chariot, God showed Ezekiel that His dwelling had nowise been diminished by the expulsion of Israel. Then, too, the number of those who worship Him—whether angels in heaven or nations on earth—continues undiminished. Still, though Israel spurn Him, He acts compassionately in their behalf for the sake of His great name.

Heathen may bring burnt offerings to the Temple (ER, 34), and if they do not send the money for the required libations, an exception is made for them in that their libations are paid for out of public funds. In the observance of religious rites, proselytes are fully equal to native Jews. In fact, now that there are no more Prophets among the heathen nations, the proselytes of each succeeding generation are there to admonish their fellow countrymen.

A variety of offerings is acceptable from Israel's sinners, many of whom, because of their weakness of will, are duped by temptation. But no offerings are accepted from apostates and the like.

The righteous of former generations obeyed the Torah, whose specific injunctions they anticipated (ER, 35).

Leviticus 1:11 is construed as implying that when the daily sacrifices are offered upon the altar, God brings to remembrance the binding of Isaac son of Abraham or, as another comment would have it, the deeds of Israel's worthies from Abraham through subsequent generations.

Observations follow on regulations concerning the manner of bringing offerings. Thus the fact that the obligation of carrying the limbs of a bullock to the altar is not stated in Leviticus is taken to downgrade the full-fleshed bullock which a sinner may bring to God as a kind of bribe. Accordingly, a man should do good deeds, devote himself to study of Torah, and content himself with bringing a lean ram (ER, 36). Similar observations are made with regard to a meal offering baked on a griddle with but a touch of oil, and the one made in a stewing pan with as much oil as the meal can absorb. The "oil" that God desires is Torah and good deeds. If the nations were to comprehend Torah's wisdom, they, too, whatever their lot, would come to love God. They would do so, to cite one example, because of the provision of Jubilees whereby wrongs and inequities are redressed.

Torah's hidden meaning is attained not through study alone: ministering to the Sages is also required. And when Torah is deep in a man, he trembles lest he come under the influence of sin (ER, 37).

Returning to the theme of offerings, it is again stated that it is not the offering—its size or number—but the offerer's motivation which is decisive in having God say to Himself: I shall look upon the offerer with compassion and accept him in repentance.

God knows that man is incapable of committing no sins at all. What He desires therefore is contrition, and an awareness that one is innocent and guilty at the same time (ER, 38).

Chapter (6) 7

ER, p. 31 *cont'd* *Draw me, we will run after Thee*[1] (Song 1:4).Thus speaks the congregation of Israel which, letting herself be drawn along, walks behind her Husband, as is said, *"From afar the Lord appeared unto me." "Yea, I love thee with an everlasting love; therefore with affection have I drawn thee"* (Jer. 31:3). Lest you might say that the love the Holy One bestowed is a love of three years, or a love of ten years, or a love of a hundred years, note that the text does not say "long-lasting love," but says *everlasting love.* It is a love that is to endure for ever and ever and ever, which is precisely what God meant when He said, *I love thee with an everlasting love.* By way of analogy consider a mortal king who sat on his throne with his servants standing in front of him. When he fixed his eyes on **ER, *p.* 32** the one he favored most, | he took hold of his hand and drew him into his inner chambers [to talk with him alone]. Thus the verse *Draw me, we will run after Thee* (Song 1:4) implies that the congregation of Israel says of God: The Holy One drew me alone into His inner sanctum; He did not draw in any other people or kingdom, as is said, *The King brought me* [*alone*] *into His innermost chambers (ibid.).*

Another comment on *The King brought me into His innermost chambers:* As the Holy One has an innermost sanctum in the innermost chambers of the Torah which He had composed, so disciples of the wise

---

1. On the allegorical interpretation of Song of Songs, see Gerson D. Cohen, "The Song of Songs and the Jewish Religious Mentality," reprinted in *The Canon and Masorah of the Hebrew Bible,* ed. Sid Z. Leiman (New York, 1974), pp. 262–82.

—each and every one of them—have an innermost sanctum in the innermost chambers of the Torah which they have learned. Thus should you see afflictions creeping up nearer and nearer to you, run to words deep within Torah, and the afflictions will at once flee from you, as is said, *Come my people, enter thou into thy chambers . . . until wrath has gone by* (Isa. 26:20). Such is the meaning of *The King brought me into His innermost chambers.*

We will be glad and rejoice in Thee (Song 1:4). In that You have magnified us, hallowed us, extolled us, and exalted us, and from world's end to world's end You have bound us with a great knot to words of Torah. [*We . . . rejoice in Thee*] because You left[2] the four billion nine hundred and sixty million[3] ministering angels and came and cleaved to us—to Israel—for ever; because You, who say of Yourself, *I am God, and there is none else* (Isa. 45:22), did, nevertheless, address us as "Gods," "My children," "My servants";[4] because You, who say of Yourself, *Before Me there was no God formed, neither shall any be after Me* (Isa. 43:10), did, nevertheless, address us as "My brothers," "<My people>";[5] because You, who say of Yourself, *A just God and a Savior; there is none beside Me* (Isa. 45:21), did, nevertheless, liken Your great name <to> the name of Israel and the name of Israel to Your great name.[6] [Because You have so favored us, we look forward to that time of redemption which is promised us in Your words], *I sleep, but My Heart waketh*[7] (Song 5:2), a festive time when, as said in the preceding verse, God will say to Israel: *Eat, O friends; drink, yea, drink abundantly, O beloved* (Song 5:1).

We will take note of Thy love more than of wine (Song 1:4): The Holy One Himself—may His great name be blessed for ever and ever and ever—[takes note of] the deeds of the righteous and the pure, by clapping His hands together, one against the other, saying sadly: Why

---

2. So V, which reads *šebinnaḥta,* "You left." R reads *šebiṯnah,* "who stipulated," or, as emended by Friedmann, *šebiṯneṯa,* "You stipulated"—God stipulated that is, that He would allow the world to continue to exist only if Israel accepted the Torah.

3. The absolute *'lfym,* "thousands," is at the suggestion of Leon Nemoy read as a construct *'lfe,* "thousands of"; hence "thousands of myriads," each of which is a billion.

The integers 4, 9, and 6 in the number designating the angels may, according to Friedmann (n. 3), correspond to the numerical value of the letters in *malḵuṯ,* "Dominion," the tenth Sefirah "in which the will, the plan, and the active forces become manifest." On the Sefiroṯ, see Louis Ginzberg in *JE, 3,* 474–75. Although formulation of the Sefiroṯ is posttalmudic, still the correspondence in numbers is a striking coincidence.

4. See Ps. 82:6, Isa. 43:6, and Lev. 25:42.

5. See Ps. 122:8 and comment thereon in MTeh 15:4 (YJS, *13, 1,* 190); Exod. 7:16, and *passim.*

6. See PR 1:2, 11:7 (YJS, *18, 1,* 38, 215) and Ginzberg, *Legends, 3,* 96.

7. In the verse *God is the rock, my heart, and my portion for ever* (Ps. 73:26), God, says R. Ḥiyya bar Abba, is actually identified as the heart of Israel. See PRKM 5:6, p. 87 (PRKS, p. 98).

is not the world full of men like Jacob? Why not full of men like Moses? Why not full of men like David? [As God takes note of righteous men], so should men, wherever they are, [take note of] words of Torah and words of wisdom, for then their awareness of Him who is everywhere will increase, as is said, *Whoso seeketh wisdom [in Torah] will come to know [the Lord's ways], whoso is prudent will get to understand them, [and will acknowledge] that the ways of the Lord are right* (Hos. 14:10).[8]

When, for example, did the Holy One take note of the deeds of righteous and pure men, [such as Jacob], and sadly clap His hands together, one against the other? <When Israel> in the wilderness had befouled themselves with their misdeeds, the Holy One, saying, How many miracles and mighty deeds have I done for them, and still they are unwilling to put themselves under the wings <of the Presence>! And He went on: But Jacob, for whom I never performed a miracle, was, nevertheless, upright before Me throughout his days, as is said, *And Jacob was an innocent man* (Gen. 25:27)—innocent of dishonest dealing, innocent of [sexual] transgression, innocent of any kind of loathsome behavior. <And so the Holy One>, taking note of Jacob and rejoicing in him, would clap His hands together, saying, *Israel,* [by whom He meant Jacob], *dwells in trust only of Him who is called Eye of Jacob . . . O happy Israel*[9] (Deut. 33:28–29).

Hence when the prophet Amos, [aware that God had taken note
ER, *p.* 33 of Jacob's righteousness], besought | the Holy One's compassion in Israel's behalf, he said, "Master of universes, just because there is no one like Jacob in all the world, is the world to be entirely destroyed?"

Our Father in heaven, may Your great name be blessed for ever and ever and ever, and may You have contentment from Israel Your servants wherever they dwell, for You did not keep Amos waiting but answered him at once by means of a vision, as is said: *Thus the Lord God showed me; and behold, He formed locusts. . . . As they were devouring the last of the herbage in the Land, I said: "O Lord God, forgive, I beseech Thee; how shall Jacob['s people], unworthy, to be sure, stand? [It will soon be made an end of]." Then the Lord relented, and said: "This shall not happen"* (Amos 7:1–3). Such was Amos' first version of what God said to him. But his second version of what God said to him was as follows: *This was what the Lord God showed me: The Lord God called upon fire to contend [against*

---

8. JV: *Whoso is wise, let him understand these things, whoso is prudent, let him know them. For the ways of the Lord are right.*

[I don't see how you can squeeze your interpretation out of the Hebrew, which is probably irreparably corrupted. In any case *lfny hmkwm* cannot mean "awareness of God." The parallelism calls for something like "Why is not the world everywhere full of Torah and wisdom?" Hence the JV of Hos. 14:10 would fit here better than your version of it. L. N.]

9. JV: *And Israel dwelleth in safety, the fountain of Jacob alone. . . . Happy art thou, O Israel.* But *'eyn,* "fountain," also means "eye."

the world], *and it devoured the great deep, and would have eaten up the Land. Then said I: "O Lord God, cease, I beseech Thee: How shall Jacob*[*'s*] *people*], *unworthy, to be sure, stand?* [*It will soon be devoured*]." *The Lord relented and said: "This also shall not happen"* (Amos 7:4–6). <He thus revealed Himself> through a vision which Amos set forth in the two versions quoted above, and then, [having repented of His resolve to destroy the world and Israel along with it], said to Amos: Amos, Amos, have I not by the hand of Moses your teacher written how it is to be with Israel: *Happy art thou, O Israel, who is like unto thee?* (Deut. 33:29) —under all circumstances whether you are wicked or pure, *a people saved by the Lord (ibid.).* It was thus that Moses spoke to Israel, [for he surpassed all others in his intercession in Israel's behalf]. Indeed, in the days of Hosea the son of Beeri, in the days of Joel the son of Pethuel, in the days of the prophet Amos, in the days of Micah the Morashtite, and in the days of all other Prophets there were none who knew how to pour out [pleas for] mercy and utter supplications as did Moses. Hence it is said, *Remember the Torah of Moses My servant* (Mal. 3:22). But is it Moses' Torah? Is it not Yours, kept by You for nine hundred and seventy-four generations before the world was to be created,[10] was it not You who refined it, and then gave it to Israel Your servants? Why, then, is it said, *Remember the Torah of Moses My servant?* Because on four and five occasions Moses stood up in prayer and saved Israel from death,[11] the Holy One credited him with the writing of the Torah as though it had actually all been wrought by him—as though, in fact, it belonged to him. Hence *Remember the Torah of Moses My servant.*

[Likewise, as Scripture tells us, the Holy One speaks of the Tabernacle as though it were David's.] In the days of the kings of Israel and in the days of the kings of Judah the notables of the realm used to go and seat themselves close to the royal presence. When a person of lower rank would fix his eyes upon one of higher rank than he, [and say]: "Although what you say is in keeping with the law, and I speak not in keeping with the law, your words are to be passed by and mine be accepted, even if the result were the destruction of the entire world."[12] Of those sinful kings [who permit such arrogance and yet assert that evil will not overtake them], Amos declares, *All the sinners of My people shall die by the sword, that say: "The evil shall not overtake nor confront us"* (Amos 9:10). And what follows directly upon this verse? God's promise *In that day I will raise up the Tabernacle of David . . . and close up the breaches thereof . . . and I will build it as in the days of old* (Amos 9:11).

---

10. See ER, 9.
11. See above, ER, chap. 4, n. 7.
12. See Landau. Ezekiel condemned prophets who *have been like jackals in a ruin . . . who never ventured into the breach, who never bothered to fortify the House of Israel* (Ezek. 13:4–5).

Another comment on the verse *We will take note of Thy love more than of wine* (Song 1:4): Taking note anywhere of words of Torah and words of wisdom has a finer savor than a king's vintage wine that has to be stored in the innermost chamber of the inner chambers of his chambers [in order to preserve its savor]. Hence *We will take note of Thy love more than of* [*vintage*] *wine.*

The King hath brought me into His innermost chambers (Song 1:4), says Scripture. The chamber the Holy One brought Moses into is only one of a thousand times thousand times thousand and myriad times myriad of innermost chambers of the inner chambers of His chambers that the Holy One has in His Torah. From the instruction given to Israel [it is clear] which chamber it was: *Out of the Tent of Meeting the Lord called out to Moses* [*to enter,* showing that at that time the Presence had His chamber in the Tent of Meeting], *and then told him to speak* [*to Israel*][13] (Lev. 1:1). In connection with Moses' conduct on this occasion—[that is, not entering the Tent of Meeting unbidden]—it has been said, "If a disciple of the wise lacks a sense of propriety,[14] an animal is better than he is." The truth of this you can see for yourself. Just go and infer it from the conduct of Moses, father of wisdom and master of Prophets. It was he who brought Israel out of Egypt, and through him miracles were performed in Egypt, "wondrous works in the land of Ham, terrible things by the Red Sea" (Ps. 106:22). Moreover, he went up to the high heavens, brought down the Torah from heaven, and busied himself with the making of the Tabernacle. Yet he did not presume to enter into the innermost part of the Tabernacle until God called him into it. This is what we are to understand by the verse *Out of the Tent of Meeting the Lord called out to Moses* [*to enter*], etc. Elsewhere[15] Scripture says, *And*
ER, *p.* 34 *when the Lord saw* | *that he turned aside to see, God called unto him out of the midst of the bush, and said: Moses, Moses* (Exod. 3:4). When God spoke to Moses from out of the midst of the burning bush, He had set a wall [of fire] between them. But at the Tent of Meeting there was no such wall as there had been at the burning bush.[16] [How can the difference be explained?] By means of the parable of a king who having become angry at his servant put him behind prison walls. Accordingly, when he charged his messenger [to see to it that his servant be freed], he charged him, it goes without saying, from outside the prison wall. But in the tent where the king held audience [with no wall between

---

13. JV: *And the Lord called unto Moses and spoke unto him out of the Tent of Meeting saying: Speak unto the children of Israel.*

14. *De'ah* generally means "knowledge, reason, sense."

15. ["Elsewhere" is factually correct, but the Hebrew says expressly *wlhln,* "Further on"—presumably an error due to citation from memory. L. N.], or a copyist's miswriting.

16. In Egypt the Hebrews are said to have rebelled against God, having persisted in defiling themselves with the Egyptian idols. See Ezek. 20:5–9, and also Haida, and *MṢ.*

him and his children and the members of his household], he rejoiced in them all, even as they rejoiced in him. Thus when he had occasion to charge his messenger, having seated him between his knees in the way a man acknowledges his son, he charged him [not from the outside of the tent] but from the inside. Such is the significance of the verse *Out of the Tent of Meeting the Lord called out to Moses* [*to enter*].[17]

[God's regard for Israel is also shown in the verse] *Speak unto the children of Israel, and say unto them: When any man ('adam)* (Lev. 1:2). Here the use of the word *'adam* [instead of *'iš*] suggests feelings of kinship, compassion,[18] and love.[19] Accordingly, when the Holy One addressed Ezekiel son of Buzi the priest as *son of 'adam* (Ezek. 2:1), He was implying that Ezekiel was a descendant of men who were pure, a descendant of men who were virtuous, a descendant of men who were charitable, a descendant of those who were willing to abase themselves[20] throughout their days for the sake of God's glory and Israel's glory.

In further comment the word "man" *('adam)* is construed in connection with *son of man* (Ezek. 2:1), [as referring to the people of Israel.[21] The phrase *son of man* appearing at the beginning of Ezekiel's vision] is to be understood by means of a parable. A mortal king had a wife and sons who acted offensively toward him. Consequently, he proceeded to keep after them until he expelled them from his palace. After a while he sent for one of his sons, had him fetched from his mother's side, and said to him: "Son of such-and-such a woman, come and I will show you my palace of which the dwelling I built for your mother [is a counterpart].[22] Will my glory be the least bit diminished [as a result of my having expelled her and her children from] the palace I built for her, [a palace which is soon to be destroyed]?" The parable leads us to understand Ezekiel's vision, which begins as follows: *Now it came to pass in the thirtieth year,* [23] *in the fourth month,* [24] *in the fifth day*

---

17. Cf. Lev. Rabbah M, pp. 32–33.

18. The word *'tyrh* may mean "entreaty," or "yielding to entreaty"; hence "compassion." See PR 11:3 (YJS, *18, 1,* 209).

19. [In classical Arabic *'adama,* whose basic meaning is "to make bread more palatable by adding seasoning to it" (*'idām* = seasoning, condiment), has come to mean "to associate or to unite a person with one's own family, to induce affection or agreement among several individuals" (see E. W. Lane, *Arabic-English Lexicon,* Book I, part 1, pp. 35–36). L. N.]

20. A play on *Buzi,* taken here to be a form of *bzh,* "to abase."

21. Cf. *And ye* [*Israel*] *My sheep, the sheep of My pasture, are men ('adam), and I am your God, saith the Lord God* (Ezek. 34:31).

22. On the Sanctuary below as the counterpart of the Sanctuary above, see Mek, *2,* 78 and MTeh 30:1 (YJS, *13, 1,* 386).

23. The vision of the *Merkabah* came to Ezekiel before the final exile in 586, during the thirtieth year of the last Jubilee (593 or 592 B.C.E.) which was observed in the Land of Israel.

24. Tammuz, an ominous month, during which the first breaches in Jerusalem's walls were made.

of the month . . . the heavens were opened, and I saw visions of God. In the fifth day of the month, which was the fifth year of King Jehoiachin's captivity, the word of the Lord came expressly unto Ezekiel . . . and the hand of the Lord was there upon him (Ezek. 1:1, 2, 3). In the first version of what God said to him, [Ezekiel speaks generally of his seeing *visions of God*]. In the second version, however, with what particulars does he describe the visions? *And I looked, and behold, a stormy wind came out of the north*[25] . . . *And out of the midst thereof came the likeness of four living creatures* (Ezek. 1:4–5). After God had shown Ezekiel the chariot in heaven, He said: Son of man, was [Israel's offensive behavior] the honor to be accorded Me for having raised them above the other peoples of the earth? Do you, [Israel], think that My glory will be the least bit diminished because of [what is about to happen to] the House I built for you [as a counterpart to Mine]? You will know otherwise, for the time will come when it will be possible to say of Israel *Now that they are ashamed of all that they have done,* [*I will instruct thee, Ezekiel, to*] *make known unto them the form of the house* [*in heaven*], *and its fittings,* etc. (Ezek. 43:11). Perhaps you will say [that in the meantime, before Israel in shame will have repented], there is <no> one who will worship Me? But have I not four billion nine hundred and sixty million ministering angels[26] who stand before Me and every day continually hallow My great name from the rising of the sun until the setting of the sun, saying before Me, *Holy, Holy, Holy* (Isa. 6:3); and from the setting of the sun to the rising of the sun saying, *Blessed be the glory of the Lord wherever His place may be*[27] (Ezek. 3:12)? And is not [the greatness of My name noted] among the nations speaking the seventy languages of the world?[28] Why, then, do you continue to follow ways that are loathsome and to do things that are unutterably vile? Why do you spurn the chastisements that come to you? What then am I to do? No matter what, I will act [lovingly in your behalf] for the sake of My great name which is spoken in connection with you, as is said, *I will act for My name's sake, that it should not be profaned in the sight of the nations* (Ezek. 20:14).

[In further discussion of what people are included in the term *'adam* as connoting affection, the following verse is cited]: *When any man ('adam) of you bringeth an offering unto the Lord* (Lev. 1:2). Why does not the text read here as of a similar injunction in Exodus: *Speak unto all the congregation of Israel, saying: In the tenth day of this month they shall*

---

25. The storm betokens the final expulsion in the days of Zedekiah, culminating with the burning of the Temple in 586 B.C.E. See 2 Kings 25:1–11.

26. See above, n. 3. Or, "four hundred and ninety-three," the numerical value of *ṣb't*, "the hosts [of Israel]." Thus in heaven God has angelic hosts of which Israel is no more than a counterpart. See *Yĕde Mošeh* on Lev. Rabbah 2:8.

27. See PR 20:4 (YJS, *18, 1,* 407).

28. Cf. *From the rising of the sun even unto the going down of the same My name is great among the nations* (Mal. 1:11).

take to them every man ('iš) a lamb (Exod. 12:3)? And why, too, does not the text read *When any man ('iš) of you bringeth an offering unto the Lord,* instead of *When any man ('adam)?* Because *'adam* is a term that covers the proselyte as well as Israel. [It should be noted, however, that the phrase *of you,* following *'adam,* implies that only those who are born Jews or have become Jews can lay their hands upon the head of the animal offered for sacrifice. Hence, while] a heathen is permitted to bring burnt offerings,[29] [he cannot, during the ritual, lay his hands upon the head of the animal because he is not permitted to be present in the courtyard where the slaughter of the offerings takes place].[30]

Nevertheless, among the seven rulings which, according to Rabban Simeon ben Gamaliel,[31] the court pronounced, one made unique provision for a heathen: Should a heathen send his burnt offering from a city far beyond the sea and | send with it the money for the accom- **ER,** ***p.*** **35**
panying libations,[32] they are to be offered out of the money he has provided; but if he does not send the money for these libations, they are to be offered out of public funds.

[As for the court's other rulings concerning the use of public funds], there was, to be sure, the stipulation that upon a High Priest's death[33] his daily meal offering[34] was to be offered out of public funds, but R. Judah maintained, [and his ruling was accepted as law], that it was to be offered by his heirs out of his estate. [The court and R. Judah agreed that under these circumstances], the entire tenth of the ephah [for the meal offering, whether paid for out of public funds or by the heirs], was to be used up [in the morning as well as in the evening].[35] Only salt and wood, [which belonged to the Sanctuary but whose use was subsidiary in the ritual], were priests permitted to make free use of, [and even these they were permitted to use only when they were preparing the flesh of a sacrifice that they were permitted to eat].[36] And

---

29. Only burnt offerings were accepted from Gentiles—so R. 'Aḳiḅa. But according to R. Jose the Galilean, peace and thank offerings also were accepted. See B.Men 73b; Ḥul 13b; and Maimonides' Code VIII, v, iii, 2–3 (YJS, *12,* 171–72).

30. See Num. 1:51 and *passim.* The slaughtering of the sacrificial animal must follow immediately after the rite of laying the hands upon its head (Men 9:8).

31. "R. Simeon [b. Yoḥai]," according to Sheḳ 7:6.

32. For the wine and the oil used in such offerings.

33. And no successor had as yet been appointed.

34. After his ordination, the High Priest was to bring a daily meal offering at his own expense, as did Aaron. See Lev. 6:12–16.

35. Ordinarily each such offering was to consist of one-twentieth of an ephah, equal to the contents of 21.6 eggs. Thus when a High Priest died [or was deposed], the expense incurred was twice as great (cf. Men 4:5). Such expense presumably was a serious consideration in the latter days of the Second Temple, when "no High Priest completed a year in office" (B.Yoma 9a).

36. See B.Men 21b and Maimonides' Code VIII, IX, viii, 6 (YJS, *12,* 440). As for the use of the wood, the priests were permitted to kindle with it the hearth in the Chamber of the Hearth in order to keep warm. See Shab 1:11.

with regard to the Red Heifer, [only because of special circumstances][37] was <the law of sacrilege>[38] not invoked against those who made unauthorized use of its ash. As for bird offerings[39] which had become unfit for sacrifice, others were offered in their stead out of public funds. R. Simeon[40] taught, however—[and his ruling, too, was accepted as law]—that the dealer who supplied the bird offerings should be required to supply at his own expense the birds to be offered instead of the ones that had become unfit.[41]

One time, as I was walking along a road, a man accosted me. He came at me like a man aggressively encountering another, and said to me: "You say that seven Prophets[42] have risen to admonish the heathen nations of the world that they must [change their ways or else] go down to Gehenna. But the time of these seven Prophets being past, the peoples of the world can well say: 'You did not give us Torah as a guide, and no [later] Prophets have admonished us so far. Why, then, should we be doomed to go down to Gehenna?'" I replied to him, "My son, our Sages taught thus: If a heathen comes to be converted, a hand of welcome is held out to him to draw him under the wings of the Presence. And so, after no more Prophets appeared among the heathen nations of the world, the proselytes of each succeeding generation are there to admonish their fellow countrymen."

[In further comment on the term *'adam* as connoting affection, it is said], *Ye shall bring your offering of the cattle, of the herd, or of the flock* (Lev. 1:2). If the text specifies cattle, what need is there to identify the cattle further as of the herd or of the flock? If, on the other hand, the text specifies herd or flock, what need is there to identify them as cattle? Hence it is said: A variety of offerings is acceptable from Israel's sinners, [who, like cattle, are unconscious of their duty to God and men],[43] in order to make it possible for them to come back under the wings of the Presence; but no offering is acceptable from the [com-

---

37. The ash of the Red Heifer, according to Scripture, is not subject to the law of sacrilege (Lev. 5:14–16). The use of the ash for medical purposes, however, made the Rabbis at first invoke the law of sacrilege for such unauthorized use, whereupon priests fearful of violating the law of sacrilege were reluctant to administer lustrations of the ash mingled with water even when lustration was required. The court consequently had to introduce the rule that secular use of the ash of the Red Heifer was permitted.

38. For a definition of the law see *The Mishnah,* translated by Herbert Danby (London, 1933), p. 573, n. 2.

39. The Temple bought them with money placed in the chest for bird offerings (Sheḳ 6:5) by those who were obligated to bring such offerings.

40. "R. Jose," according to Sheḳ 7:7.

41. See Sheḳ 7:6–7. Clearly there was great reluctance to spend public funds for private purposes. Thus the special provision mentioned previously (n. 31), to purchase libations for a heathen who had not arranged for them, indicates an eagerness to encourage heathen to reach out to the one God of the universe.

42. Shem, Eliphaz, Zophar, Bildad, Elihu, Job, and Balaam. See below, ER, 142.

43. See parallel in B.Er 69b and Maimonides' Code VIII, v, iii, 4 (YJS, *12,* 172).

plete] apostate, from the [hardened] sinner, who [with malice aforethought] pours libations before an idol or publicly desecrates the Sabbath.

<Blessed be He whose presence is everywhere>: He is to be blessed because He has the righteous of former generations described by [the term "perfect"], a term that is usually applied only to Him. Thus, in thanks to the Holy One, Adam, [the first of the righteous of former generations], brought a young bullock, [created just a short time before he was],[44] to be sacrificed upon the altar, for David spoke of his own thanksgiving as an act that *shall please the Lord more than [Adam's] bullcalf that [first] had horns and [then] hooves*[45] (Ps. 69:32). Noah [anticipated and] did what was subsequently written in the Torah, as is said, *Noah understood what the altar of the Lord was to require*[46] (Gen. 8:20). Abraham [anticipated and] did what was subsequently required in the Torah, as is written, *Because that Abraham hearkened to My voice [that was yet to be heard]* (Gen. 26:5).[47] Isaac [anticipated and] did what was subsequently to be required in the Torah: like a lamb to be sacrificed he let himself [be bound] and cast down before his father.[48] Jacob [anticipated and] did what was subsequently required in the Torah: *And they gave unto Jacob all the foreign gods which were in their hand* (Gen. 35:4).[49] Judah [anticipated and] did what was subsequently to be required in the Torah, for he said: *Go in unto thy brother's wife, and perform the duty of a husband's brother unto her* (Gen. 38:8).[50] Joseph did all that Torah was to command—all: Honor thy father, thou shalt not murder, thou shalt not commit adultery, thou shalt not steal, thou shalt not bear false witness, thou shalt not covet.[51]

In the time of these men Torah had not yet been given, but on

---

44. He thus anticipated the injunction that a burnt offering should be *of the herd* and of the clean animals, as specified in Lev. 11:1–8.

45. The commentator regards the assertion that a bullock has horns and hoofs as self-evident and therefore seemingly superfluous. Hence he concludes that David speaks of a particular bullock, the one Adam offered up. The idea was that at creation animals emerged fully formed out of the ground, and so had horns a moment before they had hoofs. See Rashi on B.AZ 8a.

46. JV: *Noah builded an altar unto the Lord.* But the commentator apparently reads *way-yiḇen,* "builded," as *way-yoḇen,* "understood." And once he understood, he took the animals required, namely, clean beasts and clean fowl for the burnt offerings. Cf. MTeh 1:12 (YJS, *13, 1,* 15).

[Seems to me you're putting ideas into the author's mind. What the author means is that Noah was (if I am not mistaken) the first to build an altar to God, thus anticipating what God wished him (and the subsequent Patriarchs) to do. He did not read *way-yoḇen,* and the selection of only clean beasts for sacrifice is a secondary matter (even heathens used mostly clean sacrificial animal species so far as I can recollect). L. N.]

47. Cf. Gen. Rabbah 49:2 and MTeh 1:13 (YJS, *13, 1,* 17).

48. See ER, 138, 174, and G. F. Moore, *Judaism, 1,* 539.

49. See ER, 131, and Gen. Rabbah 81:3.

50. Cf. PRKM 12:1, p. 203 (PRKS, p. 227).

51. See ER, 131, and Meḵ, *1,* 180–81.

their own they obeyed it. Therefore the Holy One loved them with perfect love, and so applied to them a term such as honors His own great name, saying of them: *Blessed are they that are perfect in the way*[52] (Ps. 119:1); and of God, it is said, *The Rock, His work is perfect, for all His ways are exactly reckoned*[53] (Deut. 32:4); and *As for God, His way is perfect, the word of the Lord is proved* (Ps. 18:31).

ER, *p.* 36 | [In further discussion of the term *'adam* as connoting affection, the verse] *And he shall kill the bullock before the Lord* (Lev. 1:5) is cited. A little further on in the text, when the offering of a ram is spoken of, the same phrase *before the Lord* appears again, [but this time it does not stand alone but is conjoined with] the words *on the side of the altar northward before the Lord* (Lev. 1:11). These words are to be read with the fact in mind that as a memorial of the day our father Abraham bound his son Isaac on the altar, the Holy One ordained that two yearling rams be sacrificed, one in the morning and one in the evening. [Accordingly, the words just cited are not to be read *northward (ṣafonah) before the Lord,* but "it is seen before the Lord,"[54] as though *ṣafonah* were derived from the root *ṣfh,* "to see".] This is to say that when Israel offer the daily sacrifice upon the altar, and read the words "it is seen *(ṣafonah)* before the Lord,"[55] the Holy One brings to remembrance the binding of Isaac son of Abraham. So I call heaven and earth to witness! Whether a heathen or a Jew, a man or a woman, a manservant or a maidservant, recites the words *ṣafonah before the Lord,* [he should be aware that] that the Holy One remembers the binding of Isaac son of Abraham.

Another comment: The words *ṣafonah before the Lord* allude to the deeds of Abraham, Isaac, and Jacob which are laid up *(ṣĕfunin)* like treasure before Him. And the proof that *ṣafonah* here means "laying up of treasure"? The verse *New and old . . . I have laid up for Thee, O my Beloved* (Song 7:14). The *old* refers to Abraham, Isaac, and Jacob; the *new* refers to Amram son of Kohath and all the other men of immaculate character who were in Egypt; all alike are referred to in the phrase *new and old.* Or *the old* refers to the company of Moses, the company of Joshua, the company of David king of Israel, and the

---

52. Ezekiel's assertion *Thou wast perfect in thy ways* (28:15) is taken to have been addressed to Adam. Noah, Abraham, and Jacob are described as "perfect" (Gen. 6:9, 17:1, and 25:27), and Isaac, being an unblemished sacrifice, was, it goes without saying, "perfect."

53. ["exactly reckoned" for *mišpaṭ* raises my eyebrow; "impeccably just"? (JV: *are justice*). L. N.]

54. Cf. *The Lord seeth* (Gen. 22:14), the words Abraham used to name the place where he had offered a ram instead of his son.

55. On the reading of *ṣafonah* as associated with *ṣfh,* "see," see Mah on Lev. Rabbah 2:11. *Before the Lord* is thus construed here as not meaning that food is served up to God as though He were a mortal.

company of Hezekiah king of Judah. *The new* refers to the company of Ezra, the company of the elder Hillel, the company of Rabban Johanan ben Zakkai, the company of R. Meir and his colleagues.[56] Of them Scripture says, *New and old . . . I have laid up for Thee, O my Beloved.*

With regard to the offering of a bullock, Scripture says, *Its inwards and its legs shall* [*the priest*] *wash with water* (Lev. 1:9). But with regard to the offering of a ram, Scripture says, *The inwards and the legs shall he wash with water* (Lev. 1:13), [the definite article with each noun suggesting that before the actual offering a special purpose is served by each]. In reference to this special purpose note the difference in the gaits of the bullock and the ram: When the bullock is walking, its legs do not bear to left or right, but move straight ahead. But when the ram is walking, its legs bear inward from right to left and left to right in a sort of weaving motion. [Because of this motion the ram's inwards are more rapidly warmed and its food more quickly digested. Hence Scripture speaks of *the* inwards and *the* legs of the ram to signify the special process which the ram's gait starts off.][57]

[Likewise, when a man brings an offering he, too, like the ram, must be inwardly prepared. With the need for such preparation in mind], the Sages noted: From the rule that requires the carrying of the limbs of a sacrificial ram to the altar, we infer the same requirement in regard to a sacrificial bullock.[58] [It is important to note that the rule in

---

56. R. Meir, though rarely mentioned in the Mishnah by name, was in fact greater than his colleagues, such as R. Judah [I] the Patriarch, who were not always able to follow the subtlety of his arguments. See B.Er 13b.

57. This process is taken to symbolize man's preparation of himself through good deeds and proper attitude, preparation which the act of sacrifice to Him on high requires (see *MṢ* and Friedmann's n. 39). Hence it was a ram, not a bullock, which God provided for Abraham as a substitute for Isaac (Gen. 22). Hence, too, it is the yearling ram which is used for the daily offering. Hence, too, it is in connection not with the bullock but with the ram that the word *ṣafonah* (Lev. 11:11), suggesting "God sees" and "God treasures," occurs.

The literal translation of "In reference to this special purpose . . . the ram's gait starts off]" is: "And what is the difference between the ram and the bullock? The bullock lacks 'warp and woof,' but in the ram 'warp and woof' is not lacking."

Schick interprets this difficult passage as follows: "With regard to the offering of a bullock Scripture says, *Its inwards and its legs shall he* [*the priest*] *wash with water* (Lev. 1:9). But with regard to the offering of a ram, Scripture says, *The inwards and the legs shall he wash with water* (Lev. 1:13), [the definite article with each noun suggesting that the ram's body and legs are precisely differentiated from each other]. What is the difference between the ram and the bullock? [Unlike the ram], the bullock lacks precise differentiation, [so that the observer cannot say exactly where the body ends and the legs begin]. But the ram's configuration is such [that the point where the body ends and the legs begin can be readily seen. Hence Scripture speaks of *the* inwards and *the* legs to signify that both are precisely differentiated]." But Schick's version provides no link with the paragraphs that follow it.

58. The words which follow, "And from the rule that requires the carrying of the limbs of a sacrificial bullock to the altar, we infer the same requirement with regard to a sacrificial ram" are omitted (see note 1 in parallel in Lev. Rabbah M, p. 53). *Yĕfeh to'ar* emends the clause just cited to read, "And from the rule that requires the flaying

regard to the bullock is derived from the rule in regard to the ram and not the other way around.] Hence I said: My Masters, twelve princes were engaged in carrying out the dedication of the altar. In the account of the dedication, a burnt offering is mentioned as having been brought by one prince and then by each of the others, a sin offering <by one, then by each of the others>,[59] a peace offering by one and then by each of the others.[60] Among other details in the account, the carrying of the limbs of the offering to the altar is mentioned with regard to a bullock as well as to a ram. In Leviticus, however, the carrying of the limbs to the altar is mentioned with regard <to the ram>, not with regard to the bullock.[61] Why is the obligation to carry the limbs to the altar stated with regard to the ram, and not stated with regard to the bullock? So that no man should say to himself: "I will go and do vile things, things that one cannot even write down, and then bring a full-fleshed bullock and offer it up on the altar, so that the Holy One will be inclined to regard me with favor." Instead a man should do good deeds, [devote himself to] study of Torah, and be content to bring a ram that is lean, all of which will be consumed by the fire, as an offering <upon> the altar, [so that the Holy One will say]: "I shall regard him with compassion and accept him in his repentance." For good reason, therefore, in Leviticus, the obligation to carry the offerings to the altar is mentioned for the ram, but is not mentioned for the bullock.

ER, *p.* 37 | For the same good reason, meal offerings of two kinds, [each prepared in a different way, are brought to the altar, as specified in the two following verses]: *If thy offering be a meal offering baked on a griddle* (Lev. 2:5), and *If thy offering be a meal offering of the stewing pan* (Lev. 2:7). To both offerings apply the words *Thou shalt bring the meal offering that is made* [*on, or*] *in, these utensils unto the Lord* (Lev. 2:8). What is the difference between the meal offering baked on a griddle and the one made in a stewing pan? The first is made with merely a touch of oil, the second is made with as much oil as the meal can absorb.[62] In this connection the Sages taught in a Mishnah: "A stewing pan is deep, and what is prepared in it comes out soft; a griddle is flat, and what is prepared on it comes out firm" (Men 5:8). What lesson is taught by the contrast between the softness of the first offering and the firmness of

---

of a sacrificial ram we infer the same requirement with regard to a bullock," no such precept being stated with regard to the bullock.

59. Since the princes offered no guilt offerings, Friedmann omits the words which follow, "A guilt offering for one, then for each of the others."

60. See Num. 7, where all details pertaining to the sacrifices are repeated for each of the princes. In the account of the offerings presented by each of them, Scripture begins *he presented*—that is, carried to the altar—*his offering.*

61. With regard to the ram it is said, "the priest shall carry all [the limbs to the altar]" (Lev. 1:13), no such rule being stated concerning the bullock.

62. Cf. Lev. 2:5 and 2:7.

the second one? That a man should not say, "I will go and do vile things, unutterable things that one cannot even write down, and then bring a [soft] offering by way of avowing my love,[63] saying, 'I love Him whose presence is everywhere.' " The Holy One replies: My son, [if you mix so much oil into your offering], why do you not mix words of Torah with your actions?[64] By "oil," then, is meant Torah; and further by "oil" good deeds are meant, as is said, *Thine oil has a goodly fragrance* (Song 1:3)—that is, your good deeds have a goodly fragrance.

Thy name is as ointment poured forth (ibid.). [And because of your good deeds you will own a goodly name, as is said, *Thy name is as ointment poured forth*]. Our reward for coming to study Your Torah is that You pour out Torah for us as oil pours silently from vessel to vessel. Such is the further meaning of *Thy name is as ointment poured forth.*

Therefore, [*because of Torah*], *would worlds*[65] (*'ălamoṯ* usually read "maidens") *love Thee (ibid.)*—that is, if the nations of the world *('olam)* were to come to recognize the wisdom, the understanding, the knowledge, and the discernment of Torah, were, in short, to reach Torah's substance, they, too, would love You with utter love—no matter whether their ultimate lot were to be joy [as suggested by the happiness of maidens *('ălamoṯ)*], or were to be grief, [as suggested by the reading of *'ălamoṯ* as *'al muṯ,* "unto death"].

In another comment, the verse *Therefore do the maidens ('ălamoṯ) love Thee (ibid.)* is read [by the Sages], *Therefore do mankind love Thee because of long periods of time ('olamoṯ)*—[that is, love Thee because of the fifty-year periods You did ordain]. How did the Sages conclude that *'olam* stands for a span of fifty years? Because such is its meaning in the verse *But Hannah went not up,* [*saying*], *After the child is weaned, I will bring him that he may appear before the Lord, and there abide for 'olam*[66] (1 Sam. 1:22), that is, fifty years. This meaning of the word is confirmed by the fact that of a Hebrew slave who refuses to be freed, Scripture says, *His master shall pierce his ear with an awl; and he shall serve him for 'olam*[67] (Exod. 21:6). Even as *'olam* mentioned with regard to the prophet Samuel means fifty years, so *'olam* mentioned with regard to a Hebrew slave means fifty years. (Thus from the time the world was created until the present time ninety-four fifty-year periods and forty-four single

---

63. There may be a play on *maḥăḇaṯ,* "pan [with its soft contents]," and *mĕ-'ahăḇaṯ,* "pretended love," i.e., the hardened sinner pretending love of God brings the kind of offering which is actually hard.

64. The end of Lev. 2:5, *fine flour . . . mingled with oil,* is apparently understood to mean "the fine flour you offer is to be mingled with the teachings of Torah."

65. As though Scripture read *'olamoṯ,* "worlds." So Haida.

66. JV: *and there abide for ever.* As a Levite (1 Chron. 6:8), Samuel would have to retire from service upon reaching the age of fifty (Num. 4:23).

67. JV: *and he shall serve him for ever.* See Meḵ, *3,* 17.

years had gone by.)[68] Such is the meaning of *Therefore do mankind love Thee because of long periods of time* (Song 1:2)—[that is, because of the fifty-year periods spoken of in Scripture as *'olamoṯ*].[69]

In still another comment the verse is read *Therefore they who possess Torah's hidden*[70] *meanings love Thee* (Song 1:4). If a man has read Scripture but has not recited Mishnah [from memory], or has recited Mishnah [from memory] but has not read Scripture, he still stands outside [Torah]; even if he has read Scripture and also recited Mishnah, but has not yet under the guidance of the Sages [worked out the reasoning behind the dicta in Mishnah],[71] he is still one from whom <the substance> of Torah is hidden, as is said, *After I returned* [*to study Torah*], *I regretted*[*that I had not done so previously by first letting myself be guided by the Sages*][72] (Jer. 31:18). But when a man has read the Five Books, the Prophets, and the Writings, and in addition recited [from memory] Mishnah and Midrash of Halaḵoṯ and 'Aggaḏoṯ, and letting himself be guided by the Sages, [has worked out the reasoning behind the dicta in these works],[73] then, even if he has to die for Your sake, even if he has to let himself be slain for Your sake, it is to be remembered that he will abide in bliss for ever, as is declared: *Unto death*[74]*—they will be given the joy of loving Thee* (Song 1:3).

---

68. That is, 4744 A.M. or 984 C.E. The sentence is probably a copyist's or reader's interpolation.

69. Because at the end of each such period there comes the Jubilee, during which land is restored to its original owners and debts are canceled. See *JE, 10,* 605.

70. The word *'ălamoṯ* ("maidens" or "worlds") is now construed as a nominal form of the verb *'lm,* "hide, conceal"; and is also construed as *'al muṯ,* "unto death," meaning that he who understands Torah's inner meanings so loves Torah that he is willing to die for it.

71. Literally, "but has not yet ministered to the Sages," which is taken by commentators to mean attendance at gatherings of Sages whose discussion serves to clear up and illuminate matters of Halaḵah. See Rashi on B.Soṭ 22a and *hak-Koteḇ* on 'En Ya'a˘ḳoḇ B.Ber 7b. [Why not preserve the expressive brevity of the Hebrew, "but has not yet sat at the feet of the wise?" L. N.]

72. So Haida, and Lev. Rabbah, Soncino tr., p. 45, n. 4. "Personal attendance on scholars, constituting 'apprenticeship' to them, is considered superior even to study itself." See Aḇoṯ, Soncino tr., p. 84, n. 11; and ER, 23. [I'd say: *not done so before by sitting at the feet of the Sages.* L. N.]

Leon Nemoy suggests that the Soncino note is misleading in that it seems to imply "that serving the master his breakfast or attending to his laundry is more meritorious than study of Torah. This is surely not what *šimmuš ḥaḵamim* means; rather it means associating with one's master also outside class hours, since his *obiter dicta* and his daily actions are also full of Torah and instructive of it—indeed they demonstrate to the disciple how to translate Torah into daily practice and how to make it govern all his actions. I would cross the note out."

In JV, Jer. 31:19 reads: *Surely after that I was turned, I repented, and after that I was instructed, I smote upon my thigh; I was ashamed, yea, even confounded, because I did bear the reproach of my youth.* The words *reproach of my youth* are taken to mean failure to be guided in one's youth by the Sages. So Haida and *'Eṣ Yosef* on Lev. Rabbah 3:7.

73. [I'd say, "and 'Aggaḏoṯ, and has sat at the feet of the wise." L. N.]

74. *'Ălamoṯ,* "maidens," is now read *'al muṯ,* "unto death."

A stewing pan *(marḥešet)* is deep, and things cooked in it tremble *(roḥăšin).* And the point of this statement? That when there is Torah deep in a man, he trembles with apprehension lest he come under the influence of iniquity or sin. The Holy One says to him: My son, bless you! May contentment be yours in the world, and may words of Torah be well stored in your mouth for ever.[75] Blessed is the man within whom are words of Torah, lovingly stored deep within him, so that whenever called upon he is able to give a proper answer [to a question concerning Torah]. To him apply the words | *Counsel in the heart of a man is like deep water, and a man of understanding will draw it out* (Prov. 20:5); *Out of the depths [of knowledge] I call Thee, O Lord* (Ps. 130:1); and *A prayer of him who knows how to answer, because he had wrapped himself around [Torah]*[76] (Ps. 102:1). **ER, *p.* 38**

This is the teaching concerning the burnt offering (Lev. 6:2). AND[77] *this is the teaching concerning the meal offering* (Lev. 6:7); *This*[78] *is the teaching concerning the sin offering* (Lev. 6:18); AND *this is the teaching concerning the guilt offering* (Lev. 7:1).[79] AND[80] *this is the teaching concerning the sacrifice of peace offerings* (Lev. 7:11). Why does Scripture begin some of these regulations concerning offerings with the conjunction *And,* but does not use it to begin others?[81] Why, for example, does Scripture say, *This is the teaching concerning the burnt offering* [and not *And this is the burnt offering?* The answer: When a regulation does not begin with the *And,* it concerns a sacrifice not to be repeated, because it is not favored by God. When it begins with the *And,* it concerns a sacrifice to be repeated, one favored by God]. Thus a man should not say to himself, "I will go ahead and do vile things, even things that are unspeakable, then bring a burnt offering, all of it to be consumed by the fire, and

---

75. The word *roḥăšin,* previously taken to mean "tremble," is now understood as "full of, overflow" (Ps. 45:2)—hence "well-stored"—like a stewing pan.

[Your note sounds as if the Hebrew had *yirḥăšu,* whereas in fact it has the simple *yiṭmĕnu;* nor, so far as I can see, did the author have in mind the alternate meaning of *rḥš,* "to overflow" (actually, "to boil over"; Gesenius-Brown, p. 935, to Ps. 45:2, "is astir," [is] not very good in my judgment). All the Hebrew means to say is "May words of Torah be stored deep *(yiṭmĕnu)* in your mouth, as deep and secure from loss as in a deep pan." In other words, the comparison here is factual, and not etymological, between a deep mouth filled with Torah and a deep pan filled with cooking dough. L. N.]

76. JV: *A prayer of the afflicted, when he fainteth.* But *'ani,* "afflicted," may be a form of *'oneh,* "answer"; and *'ṭf,* "faint," may mean "wrap oneself." The reading of the verse was suggested by Leon Nemoy.

77. So MT; omitted in R.

78. So MT; R reads *And this.*

79. A guilt offering is not necessarily what the epithet "guilt" seems to connote. It was in fact quite often a voluntary offering not for a particular sin, but to appease the conscience of the scrupulously pious (Ker 6:3).

80. So MT; omitted in R.

81. Literally: "Why the difference between these and those, these having an extra letter, and those not having an extra letter?"

Professor Sid Z. Leiman suggested the interpretation of the preceding passage.

present it on the altar so that God will look on me with favor." Instead Scripture urges a man to do good deeds and [engage in] study of Torah. If he does so, it is enough for him to bring a meal offering, even if it is worth no more than a *sela'* or even an *'issar*[82] and present it upon the altar. [Thereat the Holy One will say]: I shall look upon him with compassion and accept him in repentance. With good reason therefore it is said, <*And*> *this is the teaching concerning the meal offering.* Again why is the regulation concerning the sin offering worded *This is the teaching concerning the sin offering* [and not *And this is the sin offering*]? In order to warn a man not to say, "I will go and commit a transgression, then bring a sin offering and because of the offering will be forgiven." For the Sages taught in a Mishnah: "If a man says, 'I will sin and repent, and sin again and repent,' he will be given no chance to repent" (Yoma 8:9). Hence with good reason it is said, *This is the teaching concerning the sin offering* [and not *And this is the teaching,* etc.].

[And with good reason is the following verse worded *And*] *this is the teaching concerning the guilt offering.* For this is what the Holy One said to Israel: My children, I am He who once said to you, "I desire no more of you than that you humble yourselves[83] and commit no sins." But then I retracted what I had said, and resolved as follows: "Even if a man should commit a hundred sins, each one more heinous than the one preceding, but then turn about, vow repentance, abase himself, regard himself as innocent and guilty at the same time, [so that any subsequent act of his can tip the scales one way or the other],[84] and every day believe himself liable for the kind of guilt offering one brings when in doubt as to the commission of a sin[85]—then I will feel compassion for him. I will accept him in repentance, give him male children who will grow to full stature, children who engage in study of Torah and fulfill its commandments, and finally I will see to it that the words of Torah [he acquires] will be securely stored in his mouth." Thus in the verse *Does it please the Lord to crush a man by disease?*[86] (Isa. 53:10), Scripture implies that the Holy One says to [a repentant] Israel: Do not charge

---

82. A *sela'* is a silver coin worth four denar; an *'issar* is a copper coin worth one twenty-fourth of a denar.

83. So Louis Ginzberg, who emends *bĕrakah,* "boon," to *bedaka',* "humbling"—a play on Isa. 53:10, *Yet it pleased the Lord to humble him.* The verse is later explained in the mode of 'Aggadah: God desires the humbling of the sinner, etc.; but also, God finds pleasure in the humble, i.e., the pious. "The correct reading as herein suggested by me [Louis Ginzberg] is found in *Menorat ham-maor* by al-Nakawa, ed. Enelow, *3,* 12, where this passage is quoted from Way-yikra' (Lev.) Rabbah" (*TSE,* p. 132, n. 86).

If the text is not emended, it reads, "I have no desire other than you bless Me with [your study of Torah and with good deeds], and that there be no sin in any one of you." [Seems to me the sense is rather "that you be worthy of being blessed by reason of your study of Torah," etc. L. N.]

84. For the words interpolated, see Tos Kid 1:11.

85. See Ker 6:3.

86. JV: *Yet it pleased the Lord to crush him by disease.*

Me[87] with wishing man to be like one diseased who is neither alive nor dead. If only a man abases himself and begins to speak as one ready, in the words of Scripture, *to lay upon his soul liability of guilt*[88] *(ibid.)*, if only, in other words, a man comes to feel that a burden of guilt rests upon him, then surely *he will have delight in his seed, and prolong his days (ibid.),* words which may also be taken to mean that he will *have delight in his seed* in this world, and that he will *prolong his days* in the world-to-come.

And why finally is the regulation concerning the peace offering worded AND *this is the teaching concerning the sacrifice of peace offerings* (Lev. 7:11)? Because by such wording the Holy One was saying to Israel: My children, do good deeds, bring peace offerings which are to be entirely eaten by their donors, except for the blood and the consecrated parts that are to be offered on the altar, and I shall ever rejoice in this offering, [even though it forms but a small part of the offering].[89] Hence, for good reason it is said, AND *this is the teaching concerning the sacrifice of peace offerings.*

When Israel were in their own Land, what did the Holy One say to them concerning their sacrifices? *Add your burnt offerings unto your sacrifices, and eat ye flesh*[90] (Jer. 7:21), *For I desire mercy, and not sacrifice* (Hos. 6:6). And so the Holy One bade Jeremiah: Jeremiah, go and say in reproach to them, to Israel: How long will you conceal the vile things, the unspeakable things you do, and at the same time dare to say of Me: In everything we have done God has acted with malice aforethought toward our fathers and toward us. Hence, *Go,* [*Jeremiah*], *and proclaim these words toward all the kingdoms of the*[91] *north,*[92] *and say: Return, thou backsliding Israel . . . I will not frown upon you; for I am merciful. . . . Only acknowledge thine iniquity, that thou hast transgressed against the Lord thy God* (Jer. 3:12–13).

---

87. Instead of *'al tĕśimuni,* "do not make Me," the text is read *'al ta'aśimuni,* "do not charge Me." For a similar elision involving the letter *he',* see Rashi on Deut. 1:33. So Louis Ginzberg in *TSE,* p. 132, n. 87.

[As the Hebrew stands, it can mean only one thing—"Do not regard Me as if I were a man prostrated by illness, neither fully alive, nor yet completely dead." That is the bricks-and-mortar that we have on hand to fit into the logical scheme of the whole passage. The only way I can fit it is to assume that it means "Do not regard Me, in your arrogant sinfulness, as if I were as helpless and ineffective as a gravely ill man—repent before I lower the boom on you!" L. N.]

88. JV: *To see if his soul would offer itself in restitution.*

89. [What counts is not the lavishness of God's share in the offering but the intention and the moral conduct of the offerer. L. N.]

90. "Burnt offerings were wholly consumed on the altar, whilst of other sacrifices parts were eaten by the priests and offerers. [Accordingly, Jeremiah is understood as saying]: There is no sanctity in offerings brought by guilty men; they are merely flesh, and so you might as well eat your burnt offerings too!" (H. Freedman, in *Jeremiah,* Soncino edition, p. 56).

91. *All the kingdoms of the,* which occurs in Jer. 1:15, is mistakenly inserted here, probably owing to quotation from memory.

92. That is, Assyria, whither the Ten Tribes had been deported.

CHAPTER (7) 8

The norm of God's judgments is measure for measure

Summary

The wise course that Elisha set out for the king of Israel had greater force than all of Joram's military stratagems. Likewise, the wisdom of David in his reply to Gad saved the people of Israel from the ravages of pestilence (ER, 39). As for the course God follows, He refrains from executing judgment upon Israel but hastens to execute it upon Israel's wicked foes—Egypt, for example, which was steeped in such iniquities as one cannot even give a name to. Indeed, Israel was the means by which He took the Egyptians as in a snare. The ten plagues He brought upon them were all by way of measure for measure (ER, 40–42).

So, too, by the norm of measure for measure, the Egyptians were drowned in the sea because God took vengeance on them for the decree that the children of Israelites be cast into the river, a decree in which all Egyptians had rejoiced. Previously, God had His angels deliver the Israelites' children (ER, 43). Pharaoh, it should be added, had also ordered that an Israelite who did not fill his required quota of bricks was to be put under the courses of bricks in the edifice being built.

As with Pharaoh, so it was with Sennacherib, who ordered his soldiers, each and every one of them, to bring him a handful of Jerusalem's earth so that the city's very name might be rooted out (ER, 44). His soldiers were so numerous that by the time they had crossed over the Jordan, they had soaked up all its waters. Yet in a single instant, every one of them died, except for Sennacherib and four others. Sennacherib was to be slain soon thereafter.

If it be asked why the people of Israel remained in Egypt not for four generations, as God had promised Abraham, but for seven, the answer is that Abraham had entered into partnership with a heathen and made a covenant with him. The ministering angels were so shocked by Abraham's act that they questioned his loyalty to God, a loyalty which God promptly proved when Abraham was willing, at God's behest, to sacrifice his only son (ER, 45). Partnerships and covenants with heathen should be avoided (ER, 46).

Chapter (7) 8

ER, *p.* 39 [The theme of wisdom, wisdom which is capable of bringing men into the innermost chambers of Torah—a theme set forth in the preceding chapter,[1] but interrupted by the discussion of sacrifices—is here resumed.]

Wisdom, says Scripture, *is better than weapons of war* (Eccles. 9:18). For example, the wise course[2] Elisha set out for the king of Israel turned

---

1. See ER, 33.

2. Instead of *pwsṭwn,* reading with parallel in Yalḳuṭ, Kings, p. 231, *pyskwn,* "sharp, well-aimed—hence wise—words," as in the description of the angel

out to be more effective than all the military stratagems Joram, son of Ahab, king of Israel, had devised. For, as we are told, *The king of Israel said unto Elisha, when he saw* [*the enemy within Samaria*]*: "My father, shall I smite them? shall I smite them?" And he answered: "Thou shalt not smite them. Wouldst thou smite those whom thou hast taken captive with thy sword?"*[3] (2 Kings 6:21–22). Thereupon, as the text goes on to say, [*Joram,* following the wise course suggested by Elisha], *prepared great provision (kerah) for them,* the term *kerah* holding out the prospect of peace, like a man who says to his fellow, "Peace upon you, my master, hail *(chaire)!*"[4] such being the implication of *Joram prepared great provision (kerah) for them.* You thus see that the wise course Elisha set out for the king of Israel turned out to be more effective than all the military stratagems Joram son of Ahab had devised.

A similar piece of wisdom was David's saying *The source of Thy word is truth* (Ps. 119:160). How did David come to say in his praise of the Holy One that the source of His word is truth? He reasoned a fortiori as follows: The Holy One spoke of Himself as truth—*The Lord* [*of mercy*], *God* [*of judgment*], *Truth* (Jer. 10:10), and *The Lord, Truth, hath sworn unto David* (Ps. 132:11). Hence I say to Him, *The source of Thy word is truth, and thereon is ever based Thy judgment and Thy mercy* (Ps. 119:160).[5]

In keeping with such firm belief in the enduring mercy of God was David's reply to [the prophet] Gad after *Gad came to David, and said unto him: "Thus saith the Lord: Take which thou wilt: either three years of famine; or three months to be swept away before thy foes . . . or else three days of . . . pestilence in the land"* (1 Chron. 21:11). Thereupon David reasoned as follows: If I say, "Let famine come," Israel will say of me, "He could rely on his own full storehouses, so naturally he said: 'Let famine come.' " If I say, "Let the sword come," Israel will say, "Because he could rely on his own fighting men, therefore he said: 'Let the sword come.' " [And so David concluded in wisdom]: I will ask for that which serves all alike—the poor and the rich, the young and the old—[pestilence]: *And David having said unto Gad: "I am in a great strait; let me fall now into the hand of the Lord; for very great are His mercies"* (1 Chron.

Gabriel's manner while pleading before the court in heaven (B.Sanh 44b).
Professor Morton Smith suggests that *pwsṭwn* may be a corruption of the Greek *epistasin,* "knowing observation"; hence "wise course."

3. The implied answer is "No." So how much lesser cause was there for slaying these men who were not captured in the ordinary way. See I. W. Slotki, *Kings* (London, 1950), p. 200.

4. [The author identifies the Hebrew word *kerah,* "provision, feast," with the Greek greeting *chaire,* "rejoice (=mayest thou rejoice)." L. N.]

5. Since the word *mšpṭ* means "judgment" and the word *ṣedek* means "mercy," ER finds the two notions inconsistent and the phrase "Thy judgment of mercy" an oxymoron; and so, taking the phrase to be a hendiadys, he renders it "Thy judgment, Thy mercy." JV: *The beginning of Thy word is truth; and all Thy righteous ordinance endureth for ever.*

21:13), *the Lord sent a pestilence upon Israel from the morning even to the time appointed* (2 Sam. 24:15). *And . . . the angel stretched out his hand toward Jerusalem to destroy it* (2 Sam. 24:16). *And David lifted up his eyes, and saw the angel of the Lord standing between the heaven and the earth*[6] (1 Chron. 21:16). As this verse implies, at that moment David lifted up his eyes and saw the iniquities of Israel heaped up to the very firmament. Hence, immediately after the words *And David lifted up his eyes, and saw the angel,* Scripture goes on, *Then David and the elders, clothed in sackcloth, fell upon their faces (ibid.).* Thereupon the angel came down from the heights of heaven and was about to slay[7] Gad the seer, four of the sons of David, and the elders who were with David. And when David saw the sword of the angel of death, terror and icy cold so pierced him that no more strength was left in him, as implied in the very next passage, *They covered him with clothes, but he could get no heat* (1 Kings 1:11).

Speaking in Israel's behalf, David said: *Thine eyes look kindly upon my flawed substance* (Ps. 139:16). Blessed be He whose presence is everywhere, blessed be He who made a promise to our forebears and gave the knowledge of His promise to their descendants: Therefore the **ER,** ***p.*** **40** Holy One, may | His great name be blessed for ever and ever and ever, puts off or puts out of His mind rancor or vengefulness and in no way harbors them, <thus refraining from executing judgment> upon Israel wherever they dwell,[8] even while He does not withhold from them the wisdom of Torah [as exemplified in the counsel of Elisha and David].

[But as for the wicked foes of Israel], the Holy One harbors fierce wrath in His heart in order to execute judgment upon them. And the proof you can see for yourself. You need only draw the right inference from the story of Pharaoh who was king of Egypt and also thought of himself as king of all the children of Israel, every one of them. Pharaoh and all his Egyptians, without exception, were filled with rancor and vengefulness toward Israel. Thereat the Holy One was filled <with fierce anger> and with vengefulness toward Pharaoh and toward his

---

6. MT: *between the earth and the heaven.*

7. Literally, "slew." But since in verses which follow this event (e.g., 2 Sam. 24:18), Gad is quite alive, the word is rendered "was about to slay." So Landau who cites as parallel Gen. 2:17 where Adam was told he would die on the day he ate of the fruit of the tree of knowledge. Actually he did not die on that day, but death was decreed for him. So, too, Schick.

In the event, the pestilence's sole victim was Abishai, deemed the equal of seventy thousand men of Israel who, according to 2 Sam. 24:15 and 1 Chron. 21:14, fell during the pestilence. The proof that such was the pestilence's outcome is taken to be intimated in the words *The Lord repented Him of the evil, and said to the angel that would have destroyed the people: It is the teacher* (i.e., Abishai); *now stay thy hand* (2 Sam. 24:16 and 1 Chron. 21:15). See MTeh 17:4 (YJS, *13, 1,* 207) and PRE, chap. 43.

Thus David's wise request led to a "merciful" outcome of the pestilence.

8. Cf. ER, 25.

entire encampment. Go forth and see for yourself that from the day the world was created until this very hour each and every person gets what is coming to him, whether good or evil, for God, as is said, is *Great in counsel and mighty in work; His eyes are open upon all the ways of the sons of men, to give every one according to his ways, and according to the fruit of his doings* (Jer. 32:19); and, as is said also, *Far be it from God, that He should do wickedness. . . . For the work of a man will He requite unto him* (Job 34:10–11); and, as is said further, *The Lord is a jealous and avenging God . . . The Lord taketh vengeance on His adversaries, and reserveth wrath for His enemies* (Nah. 1:2).

Why was Egypt dealt with differently <from all the other countries into which Israel had come? It is said: At that time Egypt ruled from world's end to world's end. It is further said: No people> in the world was as steeped in filthy ways and in iniquities such as one cannot even give a name to. None, <but Egypt>, for one example, were suspect of witchcraft and lewdness. Indeed, all sorts of evil deeds were done nowhere as much as in Egypt. Therefore, through Israel, the Egyptians were taken as in a snare, for it was through Israel that the Holy One sought to bring back respect[9] for His great name. In this connection, consider the parable of a king of kings who sat reviewing the armies of his vassal-kings as they paraded past him. In disorderly undress[10] the army of the first vassal-king came by, but the king of kings refrained from reproaching him—[in fact, found excuses for him]. But then in even greater disarray another army led by its vassal-king straggled by. Whereupon the king of kings, [aware of the deliberate insult to his majesty], was enraged [and ordered the execution of the vassal-king. Just so the King of kings put up with Egypt's contemptuous attitude toward Him until its affliction of Israel brought down His wrath upon Pharaoh and his people.][11] Hence it is said, *The burden of Egypt*—[that is, because of the burden of sins borne by Egypt]—*Behold, the Lord rideth upon a swift cloud, and cometh unto Egypt, and the idols of Egypt have been moved at His presence* (Isa. 19:1). But *The princes of Zoan were utter fools* [*unheedful of the Lord*]; *the wisest counselors of Pharaoh were a senseless counsel* (Isa. 19:11). *The Lord* [*found*] *that within* [*Egypt*] *was mingled a spirit of perverseness, that caused Egypt to stagger in all her doings as a drunken man staggereth in his vomit* (Isa. 19:14). Indeed, in the time-to-come, all the peoples of the world will stagger as under a

---

9. Literally, "comfort." [Comfort for God's indignation at the Egyptians' wickedness. . . . Egypt is still (or was at least until recently) regarded by other Arabs as a sink of immorality, and Cairo was (perhaps still is) known for its pandering to all sorts of natural and unnatural vices, far worse than Paris. L. N.]

10. Literally, "without personal arms."

11. Leon Nemoy's interpretation of the preceding parable and its meaning is followed.

crushing burden—under Israel, for it is said, *And it shall come to pass in that day, that I will make Jerusalem a stone of burden for all the peoples; all that burden themselves with it shall be lacerated* (Zech. 12:3).

The Holy One brought ten plagues upon the Egyptians, each of which came upon them only because of what they had devised and intended to carry out against Israel. Though [in the exercise of justice and the infliction of punishment], all His ways are ways of truth, still not one measure of evil issues from His presence—only all kinds of measures of good issue from His presence. Hence, [not from Him], but from men's foul deeds issues the measure of evil that befalls them—that befell the Egyptians, for example, upon whom came the plagues of blood and of frogs, of swarms of insects and of hordes of beasts, of murrain, boils, locusts, darkness, and the plague of the first-born.

The plague of blood—why did it come upon the Egyptians? Because observing that after intercourse the men of Israel immersed themselves to purify themselves and that after menstruation and after intercourse the daughters of Israel immersed themselves to purify themselves, the Egyptians denied them water so that the Israelites would be unable to immerse themselves and hence would not couch with their wives so as to be fruitful and multiply [as the Holy One had commanded them]. Therefore the Holy One turned the water of the Egyptians into blood, as is said, *He turned their rivers into blood* (Ps.
ER, *p.* 41 78:44).[12] | So when an Egyptian said to an Israelite, "Give me water," and the Israelite gave him water, it became blood. When the Egyptian then said to the Israelite, "You drink it," as the Israelite drank, the blood turned back to water. When thereupon the Egyptian said to the Israelite, "Let you and me drink out of the same vessel," the water was alternated, water staying water for the Israelite but becoming blood for the Egyptian. Hence were fulfilled the words of the Holy One: *That thou mayest tell in the ears of thy son, and of thy son's son, what I have wrought upon Egypt, and My signs which I have done among them; that ye may know that I am the Lord* (Exod. 10:2).

The plague of frogs—why did it come upon the Egyptians? Because the Egyptians said to the Israelites, "Go out and bring us loathsome reptiles and creeping things, so that, as the fancy strikes us, we can play tricks with them."[13] Therefore, the Holy One brought frogs upon the Egyptians until their croaking of *ḳaw lĕ-ḳaw*[14] ("tit for tat") was heard coming out of the bellies of the Egyptians. Nay more, as the

---

12. More aptly, V cites *He turned their waters into blood* (Ps. 105:29).

13. [The Egyptians' real purpose: to inflict through the loathsome reptiles uncleanness upon Israelites so that they would not couch with their wives to be fruitful and multiply. L. N.]

14. *Ḳaw lĕ-ḳaw* (Isa. 28:10, 13; JV: *line by line*) also means "measure for measure." So Haida.

Egyptians went to the privy to ease themselves, the frogs moved from the Egyptians' bellies into the passages of the penis and the anus and bit them from within—there is nothing to equal such degradation—as is said, *And the river shall swarm with frogs . . . and the frogs shall come up in thee, and in thy people* (Exod. 7:28–29). Then Pharaoh said to Moses, "Is it with such sorcery that you come at me? Summon even little children from school and they will match you," as is said, *Then Pharaoh called for the wise men and the sorcerers as well (g̱am)*[15] (Exod. 7:11). Thus Moses and Aaron made blood, and the sorcerers, too, made blood. Moses and Aaron made frogs, and the Egyptians, too, made frogs. But at that point they had to stop, because there is no one in the world capable of creating a creature smaller than a lentil seed, [and so Pharaoh's sorcerers could not make insects to match the insects that plagued his people].[16]

[Apropos of the plague of frogs], one verse says, *And the frog came up* (Exod. 8:2), while another verse says, *The river shall swarm with frogs* (Exod. 7:28). How are the two verses to be reconciled? There was only one frog to begin with, said R. 'Aḳiḇa, but as the Egyptians kept beating it with a stick [to kill it], it kept dropping frogs until all Egypt was filled with frogs. Thereupon, in reply to R. 'Aḳiḇa, R. Eleazar the Modiite said: What business have you with interpretation of 'Aggaḏah? You ought to give up this kind of exegesis,[17] and turn to study of the treatises "Signs of Leprosy" and "Tents"[18] [with which you are familiar]. And R. Eleazar went on: The singular of *ṣĕfarde'a,* "frog," in Exod. 8:2 does not intend to indicate that there was only one frog, but rather to point to a singular characteristic of the frog, namely, that the frog is the birds' intelligencer:[19] when birds are thirsty, but hesitate to drink water from certain rivers and ponds, the frog calls out to reassure them, "Come and drink, be not afraid." Of the frogs' call, Scripture says, *The birds of heaven remain above the water springs until from a dark-hued* [*frog*][20] *comes the call* [*to drink*] (Ps. 104:12).

---

15. [The word *g̱am* is seemingly superfluous unless one assumes that others, such as little children from school, had been summoned before the wise men. L. N.]

16. See Exod. 8:14, B.Sanh 67b, and Exod. Rabbah 10:7.

17. For had the miracle of the frogs been beyond dispute, as R. 'Aḳiḇa maintains, the Egyptians would have acknowledged it, as, in fact, they did acknowledge the miracle of the insects, saying of them, *This is the finger of God* (Exod. 8:15).

18. Two difficult treatises in the sixth order of the Mishnah: the first deals with the laws concerning the plague of leprosy, and the second with the laws relating to persons who have stayed under the same roof with something or someone unclean.

19. The word *ṣĕfarde'a* is taken as made up of two words: *ṣippor,* "bird," and *de'ah,* "knowledge"; hence "birds' conveyor of knowledge" or "intelligencer."

[Another explanation occurs to me: *ṣafar* is the same as the Arabic *ṣafara,* "to whistle," and, according to Gesenius-Brown, is the root of *ṣippor* ("peeper"). Hence *ṣĕfarde'a* would mean "he who conveys knowledge by croaking." The question is—is there other evidence of the compiler of TE being familiar with Arabic? L. N.]

20. JV: *Beside them dwell the fowl of the heaven, from among the branches they sing.* But

Fourteen kinds of insects the Holy One brought to plague the Egyptians: greenbottle flies, borers, fleas, chafers, mosquitoes, gnats in swarms, horned cockroaches, horned grasshoppers, large sluggish ants, small agile ants, tarantulas, ticks, yellow-jackets, and wasps with basket-shaped heads.[21]

The plague of insects—why did this plague come upon the Egyptians? Because they forced Israelites to be sweepers of houses, sweepers of pastures,[22] sweepers of roads, and sweepers of streets. Moreover,
ER, *p.* 42 men were forced to sweep the houses of women, and women | were forced to sweep the houses of men.[23] Therefore the Holy One turned the dust of Egypt into insects, as is said, *Aaron stretched out his hand, and . . . all the dust of the earth turned into insects throughout all the land of Egypt* (Exod. 8:13), so that the Israelites <found> no dust for them to sweep.

Hordes of beasts—why did this plague come upon the Egyptians? Because they ordered the Israelites, "Go out and get us wolves and lions and bring them into our arenas so that with these beasts we can stage contests of the kind we enjoy." But the Egyptians' purpose in so ordering the Israelites was to get them off into the uttermost parts of the desert, so that they could not readily return to their homes where they might couch with their wives and [thus heed the command of the Holy One to] be fruitful and multiply. Therefore the Holy One brought upon the Egyptians all the kinds of wild beasts in the world until the Egyptians said: "We have sinned," as is said, *There came hordes of beasts . . . in all the land of Egypt. . . . And Pharaoh called for Moses and for Aaron, and said: Go ye, sacrifice to your God . . . entreat for me* (Exod. 8:20–21, 24).

The plague of murrain—why did it come upon the Egyptians? The

---

'afa'im, "branches," may be a form of *ta'ufah,* "darkness." Mitchell Dahood takes *'afa'im* to be "ravens" (*'oreb̲,* from the root *'rb̲,* "to be black"). See The Anchor Bible, *Psalms* (New York, 1970), *3,* 38–39.

21. The names of the fourteen creatures represent an attempt to identify the obscure list, which literally translated might read: (1) greenies (or "glitterers"), (2) rotters, (3) leapers, (4) dancers, (5) hunger-makers, (6) hand-scatterers (or "fistfuls"), (7) antennaed house-bugs, (8) antennaed field-bugs, (9) slow-moving ants, (10) fast-moving ants, (11) tarantulas, (12) incisers, (13) rough stingers, (14) insects with basket-shaped heads.

In a private communication, Professor Yehuda Feliks conjectured highly tentative identifications of numbers 7, 8, and 11.

The number fourteen—*MṢ* suggests—is intimated in the words *Aaron stretched out his hand (yad̲o)* (Exod. 8:13), an expression not used in connection with the other nine plagues. The numerical value of *yod̲* being 10 and of *dalet̲* 4 (the two letters make up *yd,* "hand"), ER concludes that fourteen kinds of insects beset the Egyptians.

22. Presumably forced them to collect the dung.

23. [The Egyptians' intention was to expose Israelite men and women to the temptation of fornication and prevent them from couching with their own spouses to be fruitful and multiply. L. N.]

Egyptians had assigned Israelites to be herders of horses, herders of asses, herders of camels, herders of cattle, and herders of sheep, so that the Israelites would be in the outermost pastures and thus not be able to come to their wives, couch with them and be fruitful and multiply, [as the Holy One had commanded them]. Therefore the Holy One brought upon the Egyptians a murrain which slew all the animals that the Israelites might be ordered to take care of, as is said, *Behold, the hand of the Lord is upon thy cattle which are in the field, upon the horses, upon the asses, upon the camels, upon the herds, and upon the flocks; there shall be a very grievous murrain* (Exod. 9:3).

The plague of boils—why did it come upon the Egyptians? Because they had assigned Israelites to the task of making hot water for them[24] and cold water for them. Therefore the Holy One brought boils upon the Egyptians, so that the touch of water, whether hot or cold, was too painful for them, as is said, *Moses and Aaron . . . took soot of the*[25] *furnace . . . and Moses threw it heavenward, and it became a boil breaking forth with blains upon man and upon beast* (Exod. 9:10). And, in the meantime, what were the Israelites doing? They went and washed themselves in water [as the Egyptians could not], entered their houses with joy, [and couched with their wives].

The plague of hail—why did it come upon the Egyptians? Because they had assigned Israelites to be planters of gardens, orchards, and of all kinds of trees, all these located in the outermost parts of the wilderness, so that the Israelites would not be able to go to their homes where they could couch with their wives and be fruitful and multiply, [as the Holy One had commanded them]. Therefore the Holy One sent down hail which broke all the plants the Israelites had set out, as is said, *The hail smote throughout all the land of Egypt . . . smote every herb of the field, and broke every tree of the field. Only in the land of Goshen, where the children of Israel were, was there no hail* (Exod. 9:26–27). Whatever the hail smote was cut down, as is said, *He destroyed their vines with hail, and their sycamore trees with frost (ba-ḥanamal)*[26] (Ps. 78:47). [But *ba-ḥanamal* is also read here as being made up of the words *ba'*, "He came," *ḥan*, "He encamped," and *mal*, "He cut down."]

The plague of locusts—why did it come upon the Egyptians? Because they had assigned Israelites to be sowers of wheat and barley and of all kinds of pulse, so that the Israelites would have to be in the uttermost parts of the wilderness and thus be unable to go to their homes where they would couch with their wives and be fruitful and

---

24. So that while tending to such chores Israelites would scald themselves and be unable to couch with their wives.

25. The definite article is taken to intimate that the furnace was one Israelites knew well, the one in which they had to boil water for the Egyptians. So Landau.

26. See MTeh 78:13 (YJS, *13, 2,* 36).

multiply, [as the Holy One had commanded them]. Therefore the Holy One brought locusts which ate up all that the Israelites had sown, as is said, *They covered the face of the whole earth . . . and all the fruit of the trees which the hail had left* (Exod. 10:15).

The plague of darkness—why had it come upon the Egyptians? [Because in the darkness the Egyptians could not see the Israelites, whereas the Israelites could see the Egyptians.] Blessed be He whose presence is everywhere, blessed be He who thus showed that in His presence there is no favoring of [Israelites, even though it might appear so]. Since there had been transgressors in Israel, at the very time when
ER, *p.* 43 there was darkness for the Egyptians, there was light | for Israel by which to bury the transgressors in Israel.[27] The Egyptians, [unable to see what the Israelites were doing], could not say, "Even as there has been pestilence among us, so has there been pestilence among them." Hence, says Scripture, *The Egyptians saw not one another, neither rose any from his place for three days* (Exod. 10:23).

The first-born of the Egyptians—why did they die? Because <Pharaoh said>: *When ye do the office of midwife to the Hebrew women . . . if it be a son, then ye shall kill him; but if it be a daughter, then she shall live* (Exod. 1:16). [Thereupon the Israelites exclaimed]: "Some decree the Egyptians decreed against us! Had they said, 'If it be a daughter, then ye shall kill her, but if it be a son then he shall live,' Israel's numbers would then have been sadly diminished." For it is a man's way to wed ten wives and have many[28] sons, but it is not a woman's way to be wed even to <as few as two> men. As it was, *the midwives . . . did not as the king of Egypt commanded them, but saved the men-children alive* (Exod. 1:17). Nevertheless, God considered the decree as though it had been actually carried out. Hence it is said: The peoples of the world are held accountable for an [evil] thought <as though> it had, in fact, been carried out.[29] But Israel are not held accountable until the <evil> deed [resulting from the evil thought] has actually been committed by them.

And why were the Egyptians drowned in the sea? Because Scripture says, *And Pharaoh gave commandment to all his people, saying: Every son that is born ye shall cast into the river* (Exod. 1:22); in this context "commandment" implies a public proclamation, as it does also in the verse *Moses gave commandment, and they caused it to be proclaimed throughout the*

---

27. Their lives God brought to an end during the three days of darkness. See PR 15:11 (YJS, *18, 1,* 323).

28. At the suggestion of Leon Nemoy we read, as in V, *mĕrubbin,* "many," and not, as in R, *nimmolin,* "to be circumcised."

29. Perhaps because they are caught up in evil and ultimately will do what this time they intended, but did not do. Or, possibly, because as far as Pharaoh was concerned the deed had been done; he had no reason to suppose that he would be disobeyed.

camp (Exod. 36:6). In both verses the word "commandment" is used: even as in the latter verse a public proclamation was made, so in the former verse a public proclamation was made.[30]

Every son that is born ye shall cast into the river (Exod. 1:22). "Here again it was some decree they issued against us! Had they said: 'If it be a daughter, ye shall cast her into the river, but if it be a son, he shall live,' then—may such be the lot of Israel's enemies!—Israel's numbers would have been forthwith sadly diminished." For it is a man's way to wed ten wives [and so increase and multiply as the Holy One has commanded], but it is not a woman's way to be wed even to as few as two men. So, [in obedience to Pharaoh], what did the sons of the wicked Egyptians used to do? They used to go around in the villages of the Israelites until they heard the voice of a woman crying out in giving birth. Then they went and told their fathers who would come and take the sons of the Israelites and throw them into the river. To the events of that time apply the words *Take us the foxes*—the wily Egyptians; *the little foxes*—the children of the Egyptians; *that spoil the vineyards when our vineyards are in blossom* (Song 2:15)[31]—spoil the house of Israel which is likened to a vineyard, as is said, "The vineyard of the Lord of hosts is the house of Israel" (Isa. 5:7).

The elder R. Eliezer said, [with the nations of the world in mind]: Since the Holy One's vineyard is the house of Israel, do not peep into it. Even if you peep into it, do not enter it. If you enter it, do not breathe in its fragrance. If you breathe in its fragrance, do not eat of its fruit. But if you do peep into it, enter it, breathe in its fragrance, and eat of its fruit—the end of such as you is that you will be rooted out of the world.

[Subsequent verses in Scripture tell us still more of God's help to Israel at the time of the exodus.] Thus when the children of the Israelites were being thrown into the river, the Holy One said to the ministering angels: For this very moment I created you. Leave My presence and behold My children, My beloved ones, the children of Abraham, Isaac, and Jacob being thrown into the river. Thereupon the ministering angels went down precipitously from His presence, and standing up to their knees in the water, took hold of the children of Israel, and set them upon the rocks in the river. Forthwith, out of the rocks the Holy One brought forth nipples which suckled the Israelites, as is said, *He had him suck honey out of the rock* (Deut. 32:13).

| In another decree which Pharaoh issued, he said, "Whosoever does not complete his required quota of bricks will be put under the ER, *p.* 44

30. Thus, since all of Egypt knew of the decree to drown Jewish children, all Egyptians incurred a like fate—drowning.

31. Cf. Midraš zuṭa, ed. Buber (Berlin, 1894), pp. 27–28. See also Judah Goldin, *The Song at the Sea* (New Haven and London, 1971), p. 165.

courses of bricks in the edifice under construction." But the Holy One made His voice vibrate throughout Egypt, so that [the walls of the edifices were shattered and] the people of Israel could escape alive from the edifices like a bird escaping alive from a cage, as is said, *Our soul is escaped as a bird out of the snare of the fowlers. . . . Our help is in the name of the Lord, who made heaven and earth* (Ps. 124:7–8).

[Because the Egyptians cast Israel's children into the Nile],[32] it had been the intention of the Holy One to have the River Nile rise immediately in flood and destroy Egypt—every part of it. [Why then, much later, did He have the Egyptians drown in the Red Sea?][33] Blessed be He whose presence is everywhere, blessed be He for whom impartiality is the rule in His judgment of men. In Israel at the time of the exodus there were rebellious individuals who might have said skeptically: "We are simply fleeing for our lives the way people ordinarily do. As for God, power to save is not in Him." Thereupon the Holy One said to Moses: *Speak unto the children of Israel, that they turn back and encamp before Pi-hahiroth, before Migdol and the sea, before Baal-zephon, over against it shall ye encamp by the sea*[34] (Exod. 14:2). And with Israel thus encompassed, Hiroth on one side, Egypt on the other side, Migdol on the third side, and Baal-zephon on the fourth side, I, the Lord, shall show the rebellious ones in Israel whether or not the power to save is within Me.

At that time, Scripture goes on to say, *When Pharaoh drew nigh, the children of Israel lifted up their eyes, and behold, the Egyptians were marching after them; and they were sore afraid; and the children of Israel cried out unto the Lord* (Exod. 14:10). From this passage you learn that the Holy One does not need to be entreated by the great when the small will already have entreated Him. Therefore the Holy One reproached Moses: *Wherefore criest* THOU *unto Me?* (Exod. 14:15).[35] And what evil had the Egyptians devised for the children of Israel? They said, "We will pursue the children of Israel and overtake them—we will override them, triumph over them, and cast them into the sea.[36] [But the Holy One came to Israel's help], and it was then, as Scripture tells us, that *Moses sang: The Lord hath triumphed gloriously. . . . The Lord is my strength and might*[37]*. . . . The Lord is a master of war. . . . Who is like unto Thee, among the mighty?* (Exod. 15:1, 2, 3, 11).

---

32. The interpolation is made following Haida and Friedmann, n. 34.

33. See n. 32.

34. Not to continue into the wilderness beyond Etham at the wilderness's edge (Exod. 13:20), but to go back to settled Egyptian territory in order to lure Pharaoh to follow Israel and meet his death in a way that would manifest His power even to skeptics in Israel.

35. Cf. PR 9:4 (YJS, *18, 1,* 164).

36. See Exod. 15:9.

37. So NJV.

As with Pharaoh, so with Sennacherib, king of Assyria, who was filled with rancor and vengefulness against Israel, against all of them. In return, the Holy One was filled with rancor and vengefulness against Sennacherib and against his camp. [How do we know that God proceeds] with rancor, with vengefulness, with mighty acts, to a glorious triumph? With rancor: *God is rancorous and vengeful* (Nah. 1:2). With vengefulness: *The Lord is a God of vengeance* (Ps. 94:1). With mighty action: *The Lord . . . great in counsel, and mighty in action* (Jer. 32:19). And with glorious triumph: *I will sing to the Lord, for He hath triumphed gloriously* (Exod. 15:2). What was the scheme which wicked Sennacherib had devised? "Go forth, all of you," he said to his soldiers, "and each and every one of you bring me a handful of Jerusalem's earth, and thus its very name will be rooted out of the world." In reference to him, Scripture says to Nineveh: *Out of thee came he forth, that deviseth evil against the Lord, that counseleth wickedness* (Nah. 1:11). But could it be that the Assyrians presumed to take counsel against the Lord? No, but Scripture tells you that he who counsels evil against Israel is to be regarded as one who counsels evil against Him on high. Hence Scripture asserts, *Out of thee came he forth, that deviseth evil against the Lord.* In reaction to Sennacherib's wicked counsel, the Holy One who searches the hearts and reins of men said to him: You are the biggest fool in the world! Would I permit My children to be destroyed? Would I permit My people to be destroyed? Would I permit My flock to be destroyed? Would I permit My inheritance to be destroyed? Thus Scripture says: *What do ye devise against the Lord? He will make a full end* (Nah. 1:9)—[that is, He will give measure for measure], for it is said, *The Lord is a rancorous and vengeful God* (Nah. 1:2).

Blessed be the Preserver of the world, blessed be He who requited Israel's enemies. As it had been wicked Sennacherib's intention to root out Israel—may such be the lot of their enemies!—from the world, it was the intention of the Holy One to root out wicked Sennacherib and his camp from the world, and so, as is said, *It came to pass that night, that the angel of the Lord went forth, and smote in the camp of the Assyrians,* etc. (2 Kings 19:35). With what may one compare the world held in Sennacherib's hand? With a nest of abandoned eggs gathered up in a man's hand. As the king of Assyria, according to Scripture, said: *I was able to seize like a nest the wealth of peoples; as one gathers abandoned eggs did I gather all the earth* (Isa. 10:14). [Such was my power that] no mortal could say a thing to me: *nothing so much as flapped a wing, or opened a mouth to peep (ibid.).* And [to maintain Sennacherib's power], how many soldiers were there | in the Assyrians' camp? Two hundred and sixty myriads **ER,** ***p.*** **45**
and five thousand less one, [so many of them that by the time they had crossed over the Jordan, they had soaked up all its waters].

The first of them had to swim; the next got across it with the waters reaching only up to their heads; the next found the water only up to their loins; and the last sought water and could not find it,[38] saying *I had to dig in order to drink . . . water, for with the sole of my feet have I dried up all rivers of lands under siege*[39] (2 Kings 19:24). But why does Kings give one hundred and eighty-five thousand [as the number in Sennacherib's camp]? This was the number of only the leaders, captains, and men of valor who were with Sennacherib;[40] it goes without saying that with these, all the myriads of his common soldiers [were likewise smitten]. All of them died in a single night, in a single hour, in a single instant. No more than five of them were left—Sennacherib and his two sons, and Nebuchadnezzar, and Nebuzaradan. And of those five, Sennacherib was slain subsequently, as is said, *And it came to pass as he was worshiping in the house of Nisroch his god, that Adrammelech and Sarezer his sons smote him* (2 Kings 19:37). Of the Assyrians, the Psalmist says, *And yet a little while, and the wicked is no more* (Ps. 37:10); and *I have seen the wicked in great power. . . . But one passed by, and lo, he was not* (Ps. 37:35, 36); and *The wicked plotteth against the righteous* (Ps. 37:12), but, as the Psalmist goes on, *The Lord doth laugh at him* (Ps. 37:13).

[But why did the people of Israel remain in Egypt not for four generations, as God had promised Abraham (Gen. 15:16), but for seven,[41] and have to suffer oppression during their long stay? Because Abraham was guilty of an error.] As a Jew he was not to enter into partnership with a heathen[42] and certainly not make a covenant with him. But we find that our father Abraham entered into just such a partnership, and in the end made a covenant with a heathen king, as is said, *Abraham took sheep and oxen, and gave them unto Abimelech, and they two made a covenant* (Gen. 21:27). Thereupon, the ministering angels gathered before God and declared: Master of all the universes, the one man You have chosen <for Yourself> out of the peoples speaking the seventy languages of the world has made a covenant with the peoples of the world. God replied: When Abraham reached the age of one

---

38. Cf. Ezek. 47:3–5.

39. JV: *all the rivers of Egypt.* But *maṣor* may mean "Egypt," or "siege," the latter being a more apt translation since Sennacherib is not known to have invaded Egypt.

40. The parallel in 2 Chron. 32:21 reads, *The Lord sent an angel, who cut off all the mighty men of valor, and the leaders and captains, in the camp of the king of Assyria.* Cf. B.Sanh 95b.

41. Not during the lifetime of Joseph or Levi, who was in the fourth generation from Abraham, but in the time of Moses, who after Levi, Kohath, and Amram was in the seventh generation from Abraham.

42. "One is not to enter into a business partnership with a heathen, lest [in the event of a dispute], the heathen, obliged to take an oath, will swear by his idol, whilst the Torah says, *Let not an idol's name be heard because of thee* (Exod. 23:13)." So Rashi on the verse; B.Sanh 63b; and *Torah šĕlemah, 3,* 860, n. 123, and *19,* 197, n. 184.

Such prohibitions apply neither to Christians nor to Moslems, who are regarded as people who believe both in God and in the sanctity of Torah. See B.Bek̲ 2b, and Tosafot̲, *ad loc.*, which cites Rabbenu Tam; and Isserles' gloss Šulḥan ʿaruk̲, Yoreh deʿah, 156, 1.

hundred I gave him an only son, and said to him, *In Isaac shall seed be called to thee* (Gen. 21:12). Now I shall tell him to fetch Isaac as a burnt offering. If he brings him, I will feel assured [of Abraham's faithfulness]; if he does not bring him, you will have indicted him justly, as is said, *And it came to pass after these things that God set out to prove Abraham* [*'s faithfulness*], *for He said unto him: . . . Take now thy son . . . and offer him . . . for a burnt offering. . . . And Abraham stretched forth his hand, and took the knife to slay his son* (Gen. 22:1–2, 10).

Yet the covenant with a heathen king did Abraham no good, for the heathen Egyptians afflicted Israel and oppressed them for more than three hundred years. | Such was the requital Israel had to suffer for ER, *p.* 46
Abraham's having made a covenant with peoples of the world.[43]

Hence it is said: Whenever a man enters into a partnership with a heathen, he will end up by making a covenant with him and in effect will be led to idolatry. Furthermore, if the man is a disciple of the wise, he belittles his Torah, profanes the name of his Father <in heaven>, and wastes his patrimony. As for the fate of his sons, it is as though he had surrendered them to the sword, or had them exiled from their Land, or given them over to idolatry.

---

43. In the passage "Yet the covenant . . . with peoples of the world," an emended text as suggested in Friedmann's n. 42 is followed. R is unintelligible.

Abraham's use of seven ewe lambs in making his covenant with Abimelech was the cause of the bondage that Abraham's progeny were to suffer for seven generations. See Gen. Rabbah 54:4.

CHAPTER (8) 9

Why Hezekiah was given a wicked son and Elkanah a good one

Summary

Hezekiah's streak of arrogance showed itself when in a time of emergency his prayer to God sounded like that of a man speaking to his equal; it showed itself also in his determination not to wed because he presumed to foresee that his son would be wicked. He was therefore punished by grave illness. But then when he prayed properly, God heard his prayer (ER, 46) and even performed in his behalf a miracle which impressed the king of Babylon so greatly that he sent ambassadors with gifts to Hezekiah, whose confidence in his own mastery of Torah and other matters became once again overweening. He showed the ambassadors Temple treasures which he should not have shown, and sat with them—with heathen—at table. And so, in requital, a wicked son, Manasseh, was given him.

In contrast, Elkanah strove hard to keep away from heathen and their idolatrous ways (ER, 47), and did all he could to have his fellow Israelites do likewise by persuading them to accompany him on his pilgrimages to Shiloh. In reward he was given Samuel, a good son (ER, 48).

Chapter (8) 9

ER, *p.* 46 *cont'd* Among the things a man should keep in mind is taking care not to sit at table with a heathen.[1] For < we find >, as will be set forth concerning Hezekiah, king of Judah, that he sat at table with a heathen, and because he did, consequently had great punishment imposed on him. And the proof you can see for yourself. When Sennacherib, king of Assyria, came and encompassed Jerusalem, Hezekiah stood up in prayer before the Holy One: *O Lord of hosts. . . . Incline Thine ear, O Lord, and hear . . . Sennacherib, who hath sent* [*messengers*] *to taunt the living God. . . . Save us from his hand, that all the kingdoms of the earth may know that Thou art the Lord, even Thou only* (Isa. 37:15–20). [In his prayer] Hezekiah seemed to speak like a man who is conversing with a fellow mortal.[2] Thereupon the spirit of God rested upon Isaiah the prophet, the son

1. Somewhat similar injunctions are found in Jubilees 22:16; Tos AZ 4(5):6; B.AZ 8a; and ARN, chap. 26 (YJS, *10,* 112). "The purpose of such separation," so Maimonides explains (Code I, IV, ix, 15), "is to avoid idolatry, as it is said, *They will invite you, and you will eat of their sacrifices. Then you will take wives from among their daughters for your sons, their daughters will lust after their gods and will cause your sons to lust after their gods*" (Exod. 34:16).

2. Later, when Hezekiah took sick, it is said, *he wept sore* (Isa. 38:3). No such note of grief is evident in the prayer which Hezekiah uttered upon hearing Sennacherib's taunt. See B.Ber 10b.

of Amoz, [who at once went to Hezekiah and] said: "When a man addresses a mere mortal who is greater than he, his body is agitated and his limbs tremble. Surely, then, he who addresses the King <of the kings> of kings, blessed be He, should all the more speak with terror and trepidation, trembling and quaking."[3] In punishment for his effrontery, Hezekiah was stricken with a grave illness, as is said, *In those days was Hezekiah sick unto death* (Isa. 38:1). [Nay more! For Isaiah said to Hezekiah: *"Thou shalt die, and not live (ibid.)*]. *Thou shalt die* in this world; *and not live* in the world-to-come." Why did Isaiah say to Hezekiah that life in the world-to-come would be denied him? In order to induce him to take a wife and have children.[4] Now Hezekiah was convinced that he [had good reason for not being wed and having children, and so] did not deserve to be denied life [in the world-to-come].[5] Therefore he set himself before the Holy One to pour out [his plea for] compassion and let gush his supplication, [as is said, *Then Hezekiah turned his face to the wall, and prayed unto the Lord: . . . I beseech Thee. . . . And Hezekiah wept sore* (Isa. 38:2–3)]. Apropos of Hezekiah's turning his face to the wall while at prayer, the Sages set out the following four injunctions in regard to prayer: (1) A man should not stand and pray in a glen in the manner of the peoples of the world [who are given to idolatry]; (2) nor should a man stand in the midst of a crowd and pray, for it might seem that he wants people to know what he is doing;[6] (3) nor should a man stand among women and pray, because he is likely to be distracted by the presence of women; (4) [before he begins to pray], a man should see to it that an area four cubits to the north of him, four cubits to the south of him, four cubits to the east, and four cubits to the west is completely clean [of feces or urine], and he should further see to it, if he prays within a room, that the entire room, even if its area is a hundred cubits square, be likewise clean,[7] for it is said, *The Lord thy God walketh in the midst of thy camp . . . therefore*

---

3. See B.Ber 22a.

4. That Hezekiah did not wed until late in life is demonstrated as follows: Hezekiah was twenty-five when he became king, and he ruled for twenty-nine years (2 Kings 18:2). During the fourteenth year of his reign, when he was thirty-five, Sennacherib came up to attack Jerusalem. In that year Hezekiah took sick, recovered, and fifteen years were added to his life (2 Kings 20:6). Now since his son Manasseh was twelve when he became king (2 Kings 21:1), Manasseh's birth must have taken place during the last fifteen years of Hezekiah's life. See Friedmann's n. 2.

5. Hezekiah's reason for not marrying was his foreseeing that his son would be wicked (B.Ber 10a).

6. So Louis Ginzberg in *OT,* p. 279, n. 217. Or: "for he could be distracted by the presence of people." [The parallelism with women (which follows) suggests that the alternate translation (in this note) is to be preferred. L. N.]

7. See B.Ber 34b, 3a, 24a; Ber 3:5; and B.Ber 25b.

shall thy camp be holy (Deut. 23:15).[8] Moreover, from Hezekiah's example, the Sages inferred that a man should pray standing close to a wall ER, *p.* 47 of wood or stone,[9] as is suggested by the verse *Hezekiah turned* | *his face to the wall, and prayed unto the Lord* (Isa. 38:2). When the gracious and compassionate One whose compassion knows no limit [saw] Hezekiah's lips moving in sincerity, [saw] his lips comely with wisdom and understanding, knowledge and insight,[10] at once He heard his prayer, as is said, *And it came to pass before Isaiah was gone out of the inner court of the city, that the word of the Lord came to him, saying: "Return, and say to Hezekiah: I will heal thee; on the third day thou shalt go up to the house of the Lord"* (2 Kings 20:4–5). *And Hezekiah said unto Isaiah: "What shall be the sign that the Lord will heal me?" . . . And Isaiah said: "This shall be the sign unto thee from the Lord, that the Lord will do the thing that He hath spoken: shall the shadow go forward ten degrees, or go back ten degrees?" And Hezekiah answered: "It is a light thing for the shadow to lengthen ten degrees; nay, but let the shadow return backward ten degrees." And Isaiah the prophet cried unto the Lord; and He brought the shadow ten degrees backward* (2 Kings 20:8–11). Thereupon [the faces of] all the peoples of the world, particularly [the faces of] their wizards and sorcerers, were twisted [with shame], and they said: No one outside of [Jerusalem's] Sanhedrin knows how to do such a thing! At once a letter and a present were sent to Hezekiah, as is said, *At that time Merodach-baladan . . . king of Babylon, sent a letter and a present to Hezekiah. . . . And Hezekiah was glad of them, and showed [Merodach's ambassadors] his treasure-house, the silver, and the gold, and the spices . . . there was nothing in his house . . . that Hezekiah showed them not* (Isa. 39:1–2). Thereupon the spirit of God rested on Isaiah, and he demanded of Hezekiah: *"What said these men, and from whence came they unto thee?"* And Isaiah probed further: *"What have they seen in thy house?" And Hezekiah answered: "They have seen all that is in my house"* (Isa. 39:3–4). Why did Isaiah question Hezekiah so sharply on these matters?[11] The answer is implied in the next question Isaiah put to Hezekiah: "What brought you to disclose to the heathen the secret treasure of the Lord?[12] [Was it pride] because the heathen nations of

---

8. Both R and V cite *For the Lord thy God is devouring fire* (Deut. 4:24) as the proof text. But since such a verse seems irrelevant, Schick's suggestion that Deut. 23:15 be substituted is followed.

9. See B.Ber 5b.

10. See B.Ber 10b.

11. [Rather: "But was it about such (mundane) things (=silver, gold, etc.) that Isaiah questioned Hezekiah?" L. N.]

12. That Hezekiah showed everything, including the sacred vessels in the Temple and the Tables of the Law, to the ambassadors from Babylon is implied in the verse *There is nothing in my treasures that I have not shown them* (Isa. 39:5), and also in the verse *There was nothing in his house, nor in all his dominion, that Hezekiah showed them not* (2 Kings 20:13).

the world were asking in wonder why the Holy One had acted toward Hezekiah so differently from the way He had acted toward his father and his father's father—indeed, in Hezekiah's behalf, had actually changed the workings of heaven and earth?"[13] In any event, some said, Hezekiah, [in disclosing the secret treasure of the Lord], had not accorded proper respect to his Father in heaven, and therefore Isaiah declared to him: *Behold, the days come, that all that is in thy house, and that which thy fathers have laid up in store unto this day, shall be carried to Babylon* (2 Kings 20:17). Hence, say the Sages, a man should not take pride in his mastery of matters of Torah, nor assume that <[being so conversant with them] he may quarrel> with them. For if he deals in this way with them, he may find himself rooted out <of the world>. Indeed we find of the king mentioned just above that he took such pride in his mastery of matters of Torah as to presume to quarrel with them, and consequently was about to be rooted out of the world. For God in heaven knows[14] that despite the requital one might have expected for the sin of Hezekiah's saying *What shall be the sign that the Lord will heal me?* (2 Kings 20:8), the fact is that the workings of heaven were changed in his behalf. But because of the fact that the workings of heaven were changed in his behalf, the sense of his own importance grew overweening; and because the sense of his own importance grew overweening he sat at table with heathen. And because of having sat at table with heathen and shown each of them the Ark with the Tables of the Law, thus disclosing to each of the heathen the secret of those on high, Manasseh, a [wicked] son, was given in requital to him.[15]

In contrast to the story of Hezekiah, you will find in Scripture the story of Elkanah, as is said, *Now there was a certain man of Ramathaim-zophim . . . and his name was Elkanah* (1 Sam. 1:1). Now Elkanah used

---

13. [I do not see the logic of your translation, and the plural suffix of *še-šinnu* does not fit the context and must be erroneous. The situation seems to be this: Hezekiah exhibited to the Babylonian envoys not only his royal riches, but also the "secret of the Lord." Now what is this "secret"? From *še-šinnu* (read *še-šinnah,* referring to God) etc., it would seem that Hezekiah boasted to them that in answer to his prayer, "God reversed for him the normal course of heaven and earth," that is, miraculously cured him of a fatal illness. No such favor was vouchsafed to Hezekiah's father Ahaz and his grandfather Jotham, who did not deserve it anyway. Hence it would seem to me that Isaiah was asking him, "Why did you reveal God's secret (healing of you)? Was it because these heathens would otherwise have said, 'Is Hezekiah any more favored than Ahaz or Jotham, [whose royal riches were as great as Hezekiah's]?' Was it in order that they should say, '(How superior is Hezekiah to his sire and grandsire), in that for his sake God altered the normal course of nature!'?" L. N.].

14. So emended by Friedmann. R reads: "Let God in heaven know."

15. See B.Sanh 104a and Ginzberg, *Legends, 4,* 273–77.

to make a pilgrimage [to Shiloh] four times a year: *And this man went up out of his city from year to year to worship and to sacrifice unto the Lord of hosts in Shiloh* (1 Sam. 1:3)—he went three times as required by Scripture and one time in fulfillment of what on his own he required of himself.[16] Elkanah went up together with his wife, his sons, his daughters, his brothers, and his sisters, and with him all his other kin and members of his household—he had all of them accompany him to prevent their learning to follow the idolatrous ways of Canaanites and transgressors and to prevent their doing anything not in keeping with the precepts of Torah.

ER, ***p.*** **48** But there is another explanation of why Elkanah | had every one come up with him. When Elkanah and his retinue were on the way, they would lodge in the broad place of a city, where the men in his retinue would gather by themselves [with the men of the city] and the women by themselves [with the women of the city], for a man is likely to fall into conversation with a man, and a woman with a woman, a grown-up with a grown-up, and a little one with a little one. As a result the city was astir as people kept asking Elkanah's people: <"Where are Elkanah and all the rest of you bound?"> "To Shiloh, where out of the house of God comes Torah, whence come commandments. What do you say, why don't you come with us, and we'll all go together?" Thereupon tears came to the eyes of the questioners, and they said, "May we really go with you?" and Elkanah and his retinue answered, "Yes, of course." So the next year there were five more households [set on going to Shiloh]; the year after there were ten more households, and the year after that the entire city was astir, set on going up to Shiloh, so that as many as sixty households would go up. Moreover, the way Elkanah would go one year he would not go the following year, but would go another way instead. Thus Elkanah tipped the balance on the scales of merit in Israel's favor and trained them in the observance of the commandments, so that many people grew in virtue because of him. The Holy One, who examines the hearts and reins of men, said to him: Elkanah, you tipped the balance on the scales of merit in Israel's favor and you trained them in the observance of commandments, so that many grew in virtue because of you. Therefore I will see to it that you have a son who will likewise tip the balance on the scales of merit in Israel's favor and train them in the observance of commandments, so that many will grow in virtue through him.

---

16. That Elkanah would go up a fourth time during the year is, according to Haida, intimated in 1 Sam. 1:21, which speaks of the sacrifices required annually as well as of the vow which on his own he required of himself.

Thus you see that Samuel, [a good son], was the reward for Elkanah, even as Manasseh, [a wicked son], was the requital for Hezekiah.

Hence, to conclude as we began: He who sits at table with a heathen is on his way to heathen worship and to eat sacrifices made to lifeless idols. If such a man is a disciple of the wise, he belittles his learning in Torah, profanes the name of his Father [in heaven], wastes his possessions, turns his sons over to his enemies—indeed, fells them by the sword or causes them to be exiled from their Land.

CHAPTER (9) 10

Of Deborah and Jezebel, Omri and Ahab

Summary

Because of his aversion to the ways of idolatry, Elkanah merited becoming father of Samuel. Likewise, because of the deeds she performed, Deborah became judge and prophet even though Phinehas, also a judge and a prophet, was still alive. Deborah even brought it about that her husband, who had no learning whatever, came to be reckoned with men of worth (ER, 48).

By way of contrast to Deborah, there was Jezebel, who said in the very first year she entered the palace of Ahab, "Learn the ways of idolatry." Indeed, she brought Ahab to give himself over to idolatry, and ultimately he perished together with all his kin.

Ahab's father, Omri, was unique among the kings of Israel in that he was succeeded by a son and two grandsons who were likewise kings. Omri's further distinction was that he added a great city to the other cities of Israel. No man in the world was as powerful as Omri's son Ahab, but Ahab's son Joram was not to possess such power (ER, 49), defeated as he was by Mesha, king of Moab.

To return to Deborah: Her rank as prophet equaled Samuel's. In her day there were few disciples of the wise. Barak deserved to be her husband because for years he ministered humbly to the elders of Israel, as Zebulun and Naphtali had done in their time. (ER, 50).

The character of such women as Deborah and Jael serves to explain the meaning of the words *a help that makes him impressive* (Gen. 2:18), as a wife who helps a man stand up on his own two feet and who helps put a sparkle in his eye.

Yet when a woman's beauty changes, her husband may seek to wed another. God will never treat Israel so (ER, 51), for He harbors no rancor against her. Indeed, as the beauty of Asher's daughters, the oldest of whom looked like a maiden whose menses had not yet begun, was preserved, so God preserves the beauty of Israel. Thus it is a beauty which for Him never fades.

Happy the man who, married to a worthy wife, is never guilty of sexual transgression (ER, 52).

Chapter (9) 10

ER, ***p.*** **48** *cont'd* *Now Deborah, a prophetess . . . judged Israel at that time* (Judg. 4:4). In reference to this verse, it should be noted that Phinehas, the son of Eleazar, was still serving Israel in Deborah's time as judge and prophet. Hence it may be asked: What was the special character of Deborah that she, too, judged Israel and prophesied concerning them? In regard to her deeds, I call heaven and earth to witness that whether it be a heathen or a Jew, whether it be a man or a woman, a manservant or a maidservant, the holy spirit will suffuse each of them in keeping with the deeds he or she performs.[1]

Take it that Deborah's husband was completely illiterate [and so unable to study Torah]. So his wife said to him: "Come on, make wicks, and take them to the Holy Place in Shiloh. Your portion may thus be with men of worth [who will be studying by the light of your wicks], and you will have life in the world-to-come." And because he used to make thick wicks whose light was ample, he was called by the name Lapidoth, a name which means "Bright Lights." In fact, he had three names—Barak, Lapidoth, and Michael: Barak, because his face had the livid look of lightning; Lapidoth, because he used to make wicks which he took to the Holy Place in Shiloh; and Michael, which was his given name.

The Holy One, who examines the hearts and reins of mankind, said to her: Deborah, you suggested the proper thing [for your husband to do] and can be considered responsible for the fact that the light of his wicks was greatly enhanced by their thickness. And so I will enhance you in Israel and in Judah both—indeed throughout Israel's Twelve Tribes. And who brought it about that Lapidoth came to be reckoned with men of worth and to have life in the world-to-come? | His wife **ER, *p.* 49**
Deborah, of course. Of her, of those like her, of those who resemble her, and of one who performs deeds like hers, Scripture says, *The wise among women—each of them buildeth a house fit for her* (Prov. 14:1).

By way of contrast to Deborah, one may cite Jezebel, the daughter of Ethbaal, king of the Zidonians, the wife of Ahab, son of Omri (1 Kings 16:31–33). The very first year she entered the palace of Ahab, she said, "Learn the ways of idolatry," and it was through her that Ahab gave himself over to idolatry, as is said, *But there was none like unto Ahab, who did give himself over to do that which was evil in the sight of the Lord, whom Jezebel his wife stirred up* (1 Kings 21:25). And because of her deeds and the deeds of her husband they perished from this world and from the world-to-come, and their sons perished with them.[2] In regard to their destruction, one is reminded of the mortal king whose servant presented him with seventy jars of oil,[3] but at the same time addressed his master in such arrogant words that the king smashed the jars right before his servant's face.

And who caused Ahab to perish from this world and from the

---

1. Cf. Gal. 3:28.

2. Ahab had seventy sons all of whom Jehu ordered to be slain. See 2 Kings 10:1–14.

3. The jars of oil are "candles of the Lord," so to speak, *the spirit of man being the candle of the Lord* (Prov. 20:27). Thus, unlike Lapidoth and Deborah who enhanced light, Ahab and Jezebel, by their actions, diminished it.

world-to-come and caused his sons to perish with him? You must say: Jezebel his wife, of course. Of her, of the likes of her, of those who resemble her, and of those who perform deeds like hers, the verse in Proverbs, cited earlier goes on to say, *But the foolish plucketh it down with her own hands* (Prov. 14:1). Of such women, the Psalmist says, *And yet a little while, and the wicked is no more* (Ps. 37:10); *I have seen the wicked in great power, but one passed by, and lo, he was not* (Ps. 37:35, 36); *The wicked watcheth the righteous. . . . the Lord will not leave him in his hand* (Ps. 37:32); and [*The wicked plotteth against the righteous*]. . . . *The Lord doth laugh at the wicked* (Ps. 37:12–13).

One time I was seated in the presence of Sages in the great academy of Jerusalem, and I asked them: My Masters, what accounts for the fact that Omri, captain of the host of a king of Israel, was accorded a distinction not accorded [to any who had occupied the throne of Israel previously]? For before him, never had a king who was also the grandson of a king been enthroned, whereas after Omri three of his descendants—[a son and two grandsons]—came successively to the throne.[4] They replied: We have not heard why he was so honored. I said: My Masters, the reason for Omri's reward is that he added a large city[5] to the number of cities in Israel: his purpose was to establish Samaria for the kings of Israel as Jerusalem was established for the kings of Judah, for Scripture says, *He bought the hill Samaria . . . and called the name of the city which he built . . . Samaria* (1 Kings 16:24).

That Samaria was indeed a large city is shown by what God said to Ezekiel: *Son of man, there were two mother cities*[6] . . . *the names of them were Oholah* [signifying "a tent of her own—and not God's"] *the larger, and Oholibah* [signifying "My Tent is within her"] *her sister. . . . Samaria is Oholah, and Jerusalem Oholibah* (Ezek. 23:2, 4). Because Omri added a large city to Israel, his reward was that three of his descendants sat successively on his throne.

Speaking of Omri, no man in the world was as rich as [his son] Ahab, king of Israel. Two hundred and thirty-two kings served him, and there is no need to mention the house of ivory he built.[7] But when people learned of his [wealth], they rebelled against him. Thereupon he proceeded to have brought to him the son of each and every king who served him and had every one of the sons live in Jerusalem or in

---

4. Omri's son, Ahab, and Ahab's two sons, Ahaziah and Joram (1 Kings 16:29, 22:40; 2 Kings 3:1). Of Omri's predecessors, Jeroboam's and Baasha's sons, but not their grandsons, came to the throne. See 1 Kings 15:25–27 and 16:8–9.

5. Before Samaria, Tirzah, the capital, was presumably a city of lesser importance. See 1 Kings 14:17, 15:33, 16:6, 8–9, and *passim.*

6. The word *našim,* "women," is here understood as "mother cities."

7. See 1 Kings 22:39.

Samaria. All these sons, it is said, worshiped idols, but when they got to Jerusalem and to Samaria, they became "God-fearers."[8]

Blessed be the Preserver of the world, blessed be He, in whose presence no one is favored more than another, for their reward for having become genuine God-fearers was the great deliverance that came through them to Israel, as is said, *Behold, a prophet came near unto Ahab, king of Israel, and said . . . "All this great multitude . . . I shall deliver into thy hand." . . . And Ahab said: "By whom?" And* [*the prophet*] *replied: "By the sons of the rulers of the kingdoms."*[9] *. . . Then,* [*Ahab*] *numbered the sons of the rulers of the kingdoms, and they were two hundred and thirty-two* (1 Kings 20:13, 14, 15).

Now Mesha king of Moab [*one of the royal hostages*], *was a sheep master; and he rendered* | *unto the king of Israel the wool of a hundred thousand lambs* (2 Kings 3:4). But then, when Ahab died, the king of Moab rebelled against the king of Israel. Thereupon three kings—the king of Israel, the king of Edom, and Jehoshaphat, king of Judah—joined together and came up against the king of Moab. When he saw them [arrayed against him], he took his oldest son and presented him as a burnt offering upon the altar, saying to God: Master of universes, Abraham presented his son upon the altar, but did not slay him. I shall slay my son, however, and present him to You entire as a burnt offering, for all You say to me I am ready to do, as is said, *Then he took his eldest son that should have reigned in his stead, and offered him for a burnt offering on the wall* (2 Kings 3:27). In that instant Israel descended from a high rung to a low rung on the ladder of merit, for it is said, *And there came great wrath upon Israel because they departed from* [*Israel*], *and returned to their own land*[10] *(ibid.)*. That is, after Ahab died, the sons of the rulers of the kingdoms—each and every one of them—departed and went back to their own homes. **ER, *p.* 50**

Blessed be He whose presence is everywhere, blessed be He who requites the children of men, each of them, according to his conduct, each and every one—every single one of them—according to his deeds, proving the truth of the dictum "In the measure a man measures, it is measured out to him." Hence, [according to her deeds], *Deborah was a prophetess . . . she judged Israel* (Judg. 4:4).

And she sat under the palm tree of Deborah between Ramah and Beth-el (Judg. 4:5). Take note: As Samuel, [the prophet], sat in Ramah, so Deborah, [the prophetess], sat in Ramah. This is the point of the verse *She sat under the palm tree of Deborah between Ramah and Beth-el.*

---

8. Semi-proselytes. See William G. Braude, *Jewish Proselyting* (Providence, 1940), pp. 136–38.

9. JV: *By the young men of the princes of the provinces.* But see Rashi, *ad loc.*

10. Hence, unlike his father, Joram was not successful in the wars he waged.

There were then so few disciples of the wise in Israel that the few there were occupied no more than half the space of the shadow cast by a palm. Hence *She sat in the place of the palm*—[surrounded that is, by disciples of the wise].

In another comment, the point of the words *She sat under the palm tree of Deborah* is taken to be that since it is not proper for a woman to be alone in a house with a man, Deborah went outside and sat down under a palm tree where she instructed multitudes in Torah. This is how we are to understand the verse *She sat under the palm tree of Deborah between Ramah and Beth-el.*[11]

And she sent and called Barak the son of Abinoam out of Kedesh-naphtali, and said: "Hath not the Lord . . . commanded . . . : Go and draw toward Mount Tabor, and take with thee ten thousand men? . . . And I will draw unto thee . . . Sisera . . . and I will deliver him into thy hand" (Judg. 4:6–7). If it be asked how Deborah inferred that the Lord had commanded her to lead Israel against Sisera, the answer lies in the words of Torah that *The judges shall inquire diligently* (Deut. 19:18). Since Deborah was a judge in Israel, she took the passage immediately following to be the Lord's command to undertake the battle against Sisera: *When thou goest forth to battle . . . and seest horses, and chariots, and people more than thou, thou shalt not be afraid of them* (Deut. 20:1).

[As for her marriage], what connection was there between Deborah and Barak, and between Barak and Deborah, since, to begin with, they lived some distance from each other: Deborah in her place, [Mount Ephraim], and Barak in his place, [Kedesh-naphtali]? The answer is that Barak ministered to the elders during the life of Joshua and after Joshua's death continued to minister to them. Therefore it came about that he was fetched and joined in marriage to Deborah [who as an elder in Israel was worthy of his ministering to her]. At that time Deborah was shown the means whereby the Holy One delivers Israel from among the peoples. The means are men like Barak—ministrants—who, morning and evening, every day, go to the synagogue or the academy where, together with men like Joshua and with those who minister to them, they are continually engaged with matters of Torah.

Hence why ask how it was that of all the Tribes, Zebulun and Naphtali were singled out—singled out in preference to all the others
ER, *p.* 51 —so that a great deliverance came | to Israel through Zebulun and Naphtali? The facts are that Naphtali ministered to our father Jacob[12] and found great pleasure in the task; and Zebulun ministered to Issachar and provided him with hospitality.[13]

11. Cf. B.Meḡ 14a.
12. See Ginzberg, *Legends, 2,* 209.
13. See Ginzberg, *Legends, 7,* 512, column 1, *s.v.* "Zebulun, Tribe of, maintained the Tribe of Issachar."

Because Barak had faith in God and believed in the prophecy of Deborah, a portion was accorded him in the song she sang. Thus it is said, *Then sang Deborah and Barak the son of Abinoam* (Judg. 5:1), because previously he had expressed his faith in her in the words *If thou wilt go with me, then I will go* (Judg. 4:8). And she had replied: *I will surely go with thee* (Judg. 4:9).

For what reason was Jael, Heber's wife (Judg. 4:11–17), accorded a distinction not accorded to any other woman in that deliverance came to Israel through her? Because she was a woman of worth who did her husband's will.[14] Indeed it is well said that no woman is to be regarded as worthy unless she does her husband's will.

Once while seated in the great academy of Jerusalem in the presence of Sages, I said to them: My Masters, may I who am no more than dust under the soles of your feet say something to you? They replied: Say it. I began my answer with a blessing: My Father who is in heaven, may Your great name be blessed for ever and ever and ever, and may You have delight in Israel Your servants in all the places of their habitations. [Then I went on]: For all the boons and comforts which You promised them, Israel Your servants, You promised with wisdom and understanding, with knowledge and insight. Thus You said, *It is not good that the man should be alone; I will provide him a help that makes him impressive*[15] (Gen. 2:18). By *help that makes him impressive* is meant a wife who would help him stand up on his own two feet and would help put a sparkle in his eye. The Sages said to me: Explain further what you mean. I replied: I shall, and went on to say, My Masters, before wheat and barley are prepared and before they are ground in a mill, are they fit for anything else than tinder? They said: Well? I went on: Adam gave them to his wife who made them edible: she prepared the grains by sifting them and grinding them in a mill, and thus out of the grains made bread. Which is the most satisfying—bread, or tender meat, or rich fat, or any other kind of good things to eat in the world? They said: Bread is more satisfying than tender meat, or rich fat, or any other good things to eat in the world. I went on: Flax—its fibers are no more than grass, are they not? They said: Well? [Then I declared]: When Adam gave the flax to his wife, she wove a garment out of its fibers. <Nay more>! out of her he brought increase of mankind in the world. <And yet more>! because of his appreciation of her, he did not go about committing adultery.

---

14. The fact that she is identified as *Heber's wife,* ER construes as signifying that she did his will, specifically in consenting to leave fertile Jericho and follow him to arid Arad where, together with other Kenites, he was determined to study Torah with Jabez. See Yalḳuṭ and Rashi on Judg. 1:16.

15. JV: *help meet for him.* But *kĕ-negdo,* "meet for him," may also be derived from *ngd,* "to set in front, to make conspicuous"; hence "impressive."

These are the four things that a wife does for her husband: [She prepares his food, weaves his garments, gives him children, and keeps him from sexual transgression]. As for food, is it not provided for man as it is for cattle, for beasts, and for fowl? [I], Master of all the worlds, provide man, however, with something far more satisfying than food —*a help that makes him impressive,* a wife who helps him stand up on his own two feet, who helps put a sparkle in his eye.

Then I spoke in the presence of the Sages of another matter: My Masters, in the time-to-come, the Holy One will sit in the great academy with the world's righteous men sitting before Him. He will say to them: My children, though you are no more than flesh-and-blood, you are still My children. Now when a man weds a good and extraordinarily beautiful woman, he rejoices in her and desires her. But when her beauty changes, he seeks to wed another woman beside her. But you are not to be so treated. From the beginning you have been and will be Mine—[beloved][16]—for ever and ever and ever, as is said, *The Lord said unto me: "Go yet, love a woman beloved of her friend and an adulteress, even as the Lord loveth the children of Israel, though they turn unto other gods." . . . Afterward shall the children of Israel return; and seek the Lord their God* ER, *p.* 52 | (Hos. 3:1,5); and . . . *Saying: If a man put away his wife, and she go from him, and become another man's, may he return unto her again? But thou hast played the harlot with many lovers. . . . Didst thou not just now cry unto Me: "My father, Thou art the friend of my youth. Will He bear grudge for ever? Will He keep it to the end?" Behold,* God replies to Israel, *since thou spakest thus, though thou hast done evil, thou, nevertheless, prevailest* [*in retaining My love of thee*][17] (Jer. 3:1, 4). But are the gods Israel have taken as lovers to be considered as rivals to the Holy One or <have they such> substance to be spoken of as gods, that Jeremiah should have said to Israel, *Thou hast played the harlot with many lovers (ibid.)?* [It was not Jeremiah, however, but Israel who regarded their idols as lovers rivaling God.][18]

Blessed be the Preserver of the world, blessed be He, who has the iniquities of Israel pass out of mind, and does not harbor rancor and vengefulness against them wherever they dwell. Nor does He withhold words of Torah from them. As for their sins that go back a long, long way, He has them pass away from before Him, as is said, *Thus saith the Lord: If heaven above can be measured, and the foundations of the earth searched out beneath, then will I also cast off all the seed of Israel for all that they have done* (Jer. 31:36), and also *If these ordinances depart from before Me, saith the Lord, then the seed of Israel also shall cease from being a nation*

---

16. "beloved"—V.
17. JV: *Behold, thou hast spoken, but hast done evil things, and hast had thy way.*
18. "It was not Jeremiah . . . lovers rivaling God"—Haida.

before Me for ever (Jer. 31:35). By chastisements [shall their iniquities be purged].[19] For His deeds are not like your deeds: *Of Asher it was said: Blessed be Asher above* [*the other*] sons [*of Jacob*], and then Asher was told, *Like thy young shall thine elderly be*[20] (Deut. 33:24–25). Hence it was said <of Asher's daughters that the oldest one of them> looked like a maiden whose menses had not yet begun. [And what God did for the Tribe of Asher, He does, and will do, for all the Tribes of Israel], as is said, *Like thy young shall thine elderly be.*[21]

Scripture goes on, *There is none like God, O Jeshurun, who rideth upon the heaven as thy help* (Deut. 33:26). Happy is the man who has not been guilty of [sexual] transgression, has not been guilty of iniquity or sin, so that there has not come <out of him semen without issue. [Happy is the man] in whom there are words of Torah in all their truth>. Even if such a man be an ordinary Israelite, he is deemed worthy of bringing a burnt offering upon the altar, as is said, *And he sent the young men of the children of Israel who offered burnt offerings . . . unto the Lord* (Exod. 24:5). <But he who made> himself slothful when it came to [sexual] transgression and did not commit it, is deemed worthy <of receiving> the Presence as the ministering angels do, for it is said, *And upon the lazy ones*[22] *of the children of Israel He laid not His hand, and they beheld God* (Exod. 24:11).

---

19. "shall their iniquities be purged"—V.

20. JV: *And as thy days go shall thy strength be.* But *db'k,* "thy strength," may by metathesis be read *d'bk,* "thy sorrow"; hence "thy state of being elderly." See Naḥmanides, *ad loc.*

21. *Iron and brass shall be thy bars,* the first part of Deut. 33:25 quoted in ER, is deleted.

22. JV: *the nobles.* But ER reads *'aṣile,* "nobles," as though it were written *'aṣle,* "slothful."

CHAPTER (10) 11

The rewards of piety, honesty, and learning

Summary

Because there are men in Israel who morning and evening make up the complement of ten in a congregation and because there are men who provide for the disciples of the wise, requitals are visited upon the nations for their oppression of Israel (ER, 52).

The pious acts of such men as well as acts of mercy and kindness deliver the children of Israel from death—delivered even the descendants of the family of Eli who were all doomed to die young. These acts have the power, it is said, to ransom God from whatever place of exile His presence abides in.

Hence in her song Deborah calls upon the governors of Israel to be honest in their handling of public funds and to establish government on rational judgment (ER, 53). She calls also upon the Sanhedrin to meditate upon Torah and to make accurate distinctions in laws. Indeed, it is differences of opinion and discussion among scholars that lead to increase in knowledge of Torah.

Though Israel's dispersion among the nations makes it impossible for her enemies to bear down on her all at once and destroy her (ER, 54), Israel's best defense, nevertheless, is still her disciples of the wise even though there may be no more than two of them (ER, 55).

Chapter (10) 11

ER, ***p.*** **52** *cont'd* *Then sang Deborah and Barak . . . saying . . . When men let grow* [*their hair*] *in Israel* (Judg. 5:1–2). Why should Deborah have begun her prophecy with such a matter-of-fact statement? [The word *pr'*, "let grow," however, may also mean "requite," so that the statement can be taken as saying *When requitals were visited in Israel.*][1] Hence, Deborah's prophecy really began with this question: On what account did the Holy One, in Israel's behalf, requite the peoples of the world? On account of men who come without fail, morning and evening, to the synagogue, where they respond in the prayers with "Amen," just as their study of Torah in the academy is also a way of blessing the Holy One with "Amen,"[2] as is said, *When requitals were visited in behalf of Israel, it was because of those among the people who offered themselves willingly, saying, Bless ye the Lord* (Judg. 5:2). Of the men previously mentioned, those among the people of Israel who without fail, in one way or

---

1. So also Targum and Ḳimḥi.

2. [All the Hebrew says is "They respond with Amen to every benediction beginning with 'Blessed art Thou, O Lord.' " This refers not only to synagogal prayers but also to the blessings pronounced in the house of study at the conclusion of tractates, etc. L. N.]

another, eagerly bless the Holy One [with their Amens], the Psalmist says, *Because of full complements whereby many [Amens] come to be on my side, He redeems my soul from the battle against me*[3] (Ps. 55:19). The Psalmist refers here to a man who goes morning and evening to make up the complement [of ten[4] men, the least number by whom congregational prayers may be said]. This is the man the Psalmist refers to in the words, *Because of full complements whereby many [Amens] come to be spoken in my behalf, He redeems my soul from the battle against me.*

[In another comment the verse from Psalms is read *To reward me for bestowing charity,*[5] *God redeems me* (Ps. 55:19), and is understood to be spoken by the people of Israel as a whole as well as by individuals among the people. For an example of one who bestows charity], consider the man who has a disciple of the wise living in the same quarter and comes to know of him that he reads Scripture for the sake of Heaven and recites Mishnah for the sake of Heaven. Therefore, he feeds the disciple of the wise, sustains him, and provides for him, so that he supports not only the disciple of the wise, his wife, and his children, but, in effect, supports also all those who read Scripture and recite Mishnah with the disciple. Of the man who bestows such charity, the Psalmist says, *To reward him for the charity he bestows, God redeems me from death* (Ps. 55:19), | for there is no elixir as effective against death as **ER, *p.* 53**
an act of charity. Thus Moses, saying, *I was in dread of the Anger and the Fury*[6] (Deut. 9:19) [at the time God was about to destroy Israel, mercifully interceded in Israel's behalf and stayed the angel of death. Moses, indeed, saved an entire people, whereas the man who saves a disciple of the wise saves only one person]: nevertheless, as the Sages taught in a Mishnah, "If any one preserves a single soul,[7] Scripture ascribes it to him as though he had preserved the entire world" (Sanh 4:5). Of such an act of charity, Scripture says, *A gift in private, pacifieth Anger, and a present in the bosom strong Fury* (Prov. 21:14).[8]

[In connection with such prayers and acts of charity, consider] the story of two families of priests who came before Rabban Johanan ben Zakkai and said to him: Master, our sons die at the age of eighteen, at the age of fifteen, and even at the age of twelve. He replied: Such

---

3. JV: *He hath redeemed my soul in peace so that none came nigh me; for they were many that strove with me.* But NJV reads the last part of the verse *it is as though many were on my side;* and ER apparently takes *bĕ-šalom,* "in peace," to mean "complete"; hence *Because of full complements.* Cf. B.Ber 8a and Shab 119b.

4. Instead of "ten" (*'śrh*), R has "crown" (*'ṭrh*).

5. The word *šalom* may mean "peace," "requital," "reward," or "bestowal [of charity]." [I think the author read here not *shalom* but *shillum* (*shalom* as "charity" is rather stretching it an awful lot) = payment of one's moral debts: mercy, honesty, charity, etc. L. N.]

6. Cf. MTeh 7:6 (YJS, *13, 1,* 106–7).

7. Some texts add "of Israel."

8. Cf. B.BB 9b.

premature death can only mean that you are of the family of Eli's descendants to whom it was said, *All the increase of thy house shall die young men* (1 Sam. 2:33). They asked: Master, what are we to do? He replied: When any son [of yours] reaches puberty, estimate his worth in goods and money and then give all of both to charity, keeping in mind the verse *Charity delivereth from death* (Prov. 10:2). You will thus save from death [a descendant of Eli] to whom it was said, *All the increase of thy house shall die young men* (1 Sam. 2:33). So the families did as they were advised and thus delivered themselves from death.[9]

Nay more, of him who acts justly, [gives] charity, and thus preserves many lives, Scripture says, *He hath redeemed My soul [through such acts which lead to] peace* (Ps. 55:19). When such acts are performed, the Holy One says: Who is the man who ransoms Me from whatever place of exile <My> presence abides in,[10] and ransoms Israel from exile among the peoples of the world? It is the man giving charity and exercising justice who brings about[11] [harmony . . .].

When Israel act justly and [give] charity, what verse of Scripture applies to them? *When a man loveth charity and justice, the earth is full of the loving-kindness of the Lord*[12] (Ps. 33:5). But when Israel do not act justly and [give] charity, what is said of them? *Truth is lacking [in them]* (Isa. 59:15).[13]

My father in heaven, may Your great name be blessed for ever and ever and ever, and may You have contentment from Israel, Your servants. For it was You who said: "Who ransomed Me from the place where My presence must abide, and ransoms and delivers Israel from among the peoples of the world? The man who gives charity," etc. Is it not, in fact, You who redeem and deliver all the inhabitants of the world as well as Your handiwork in the world You created? For it is said, *Redeem Israel, O God* (Ps. 25:22), and it is also said, *He will redeem Israel* (Ps. 130:8).

[True, He will redeem Israel, but in the meantime Israel must do justice and save the oppressed.] And so, kindred of David, why are you sitting still? What is it that you are seeking? The days of the Messiah, the redemption? *O kindred of David, thus saith the Lord: Execute judgment in the morning, and deliver the spoiled out of the hand of the oppressor* (Jer. 21:12).

[To execute judgment and deliver the oppressed], said Deborah, is [obedience to Torah], bringing contentment on high and content-

---

9. Gen. Rabbah 59:1.
10. Cf. B.Ber 8a.
11. Lacuna in R.
12. Cf. B.Suk 49b.
13. The preceding verse reads *Justice is turned away backward, and charity standeth afar off.*

ment here below: Torah, as is said, *is a tree of life to them that lay hold upon her* (Prov. 3:18). Hence, in addressing the governors of Israel, Deborah describes them as *Ye that ride on white asses* (Judg. 5:10), signifying by *white* the purity of the governors in refraining from plundering [the public treasury]. And in addressing them further as *ye that sit in judgment*[14] (*ibid.*), she was praising them as men who establish government upon rational judgment. (The word *middin* here translated *in judgment* is usually translated "rich cloth," [*ye that sit on rich cloth*], but in the words from Isaiah "To turn aside the needy from judgment" [Isa. 10:2], the word is taken to be made up of *mid,* "from," and *din,* "judgment." As in the verse from Isaiah *middin* has to do with judgment, so in the verse in hand *middin* is also taken as having to do with judgment.[15]

Turning to the Sanhedrin, Deborah goes on to say, *And ye that walk by the right way, meditate upon it* (Judg. 5:10). At the beginning of her song, Deborah had hailed the Sanhedrin in the words *Hear, O ye kings* (Judg. 5:3), [you] upon whom the world | leans. Now she ad- **ER,** *p.* 54
monishes them, saying: Why are you sitting idle? *Meditate upon* Torah (Judg. 5:10)—any moment not given to such meditation is a moment of idleness.

[She exhorts the Sanhedrin further]: *Meditate* [*and speak*] *with the voice of those who make accurate distinctions*[16] (Judg. 5:11), those, that is, who determine whether a thing is ritually unclean or whether it is ritually clean—the clean will have been determined properly as clean <and the unclean determined properly as unclean>; [speak also with the voice of] those who make distinctions in the laws applying to the observance of the Sabbath, in the laws applying to festal offerings, in the laws applying to improper use of sacred property, and in the laws which govern disputes among human beings.

When Deborah goes on to speak of *the places where water is drawn* (*maš'abim*) (Judg. 5:11), it may be thought that she is using *maš'aḇim* in its literal sense of drawing water, as in the verse "and drew (*wat-tiš'aḇ*) for all his camels" (Gen. 24:20). In Isaiah, however, a different form of the word is used in an extended metaphorical sense in the verse "Therefore with joy shall ye draw (*u-šĕ'aḇtem*) water out of the wells of salvation" (Isa. 12:3). <It is this extended sense of the word that Deborah had in mind: Out of the wells of salvation—out of Torah, that is—the Sanhedrin are to draw up [and drink life-giving water].>[17]

In another comment, the words *Among places where waters are drawn*

---

14. So AV. JV: *Ye that sit on rich cloths.*

15. Cf. B.Er 54b.

16. JV: *archers.* But *meḥaṣĕṣim,* "archers," may also be derived from *ḥṣṣ,* "divide"; hence "those who make distinctions."

17. "It is this extended sense . . . life-giving water"—V.

(Judg. 5:11) are read "Out of disagreements in places where waters are drawn"—that is, out of disagreements among[18] scholars concerning the right interpretation, words of Torah are drawn. Indeed, sharp differences of opinion among scholars lead to great increase in words of Torah. Hence the words are read not "Among places," etc., but "Out of disagreements in places where waters are drawn."

[In the same verse in which the words just cited occur, Deborah goes on]: *There shall they rehearse the mercies of the Lord, the mercies in His dispersing*[19] *of Israel* (*ibid.*). The Holy One showed great mercy in dispersing Israel among the peoples of the world. [In connection with the dispersion], a story is told of a Roman commander and R. Judah [I] the Patriarch. The two men eating and drinking together got into a jovial mood, and the general said to R. Judah [I] the Patriarch: We Romans are more compassionate than you Jews. When you were given the authority to cut Edom down, you left only a single pregnant woman alive, as is said, *Joab and all Israel remained there six months until he had cut off all remembrance*[20] *of Edom* (1 Kings 11:16). [On hearing these words], R. Judah [I] the Patriarch remained silent; he said not one word. Then he stood up, went into the marketplace and passed on the commander's reproach to a disciple. Returning, R. Judah sat down in his place and said to the commander: Will you allow a disciple of mine to come in and tell us something that will engage us? The commander replied: Let him come in. Entering, the disciple remained standing and put the following question: Where is the master of a house to deposit his vessels, so that when he returns, his vessels will go back with him into the house? The disciple said it once, a second time, then a third time, until the commander got the point of the question.[21] Thereupon

---

18. The word *ben* may mean simply "among," or "out of encounters among"; hence "out of disagreements among." [I wouldn't go so far as to say that *ben* means "encounters." The author makes a semantic observation: *ben* has the basic meaning of "space, interval (between two or more things or individuals)." If the individuals bridge that interval, the result is agreement, if they do not, the result is disagreement. L. N.]

19. JV: *His rulers.* But *pirzono,* "His rulers," may also mean *pizrono,* "His scattering, dispersing." The Arabic *faraza,* Leon Nemoy points out, means "to separate, to set apart."

20. JV: *until he had cut off every male in Edom.* But apparently ER reads *zakar,* "male," as though vocalized *zeker,* "remembrance," or "memory." See B.BB 21a–21b, and Ginzberg, *Legends, 6,* 259.

Here Edom, Amalek's ancestor (Gen. 36:1, 12), is taken to represent Amalek whose remembrance from under heaven Israel were enjoined to blot out (Exod. 17:14). Possibly ER understands Joab to have acted thus in that part of Edom which was Amalek's territory (see 2 Sam. 8:14).

As for the one pregnant woman whom he spared, she may have been the mother of Hadad, the child who was enabled to flee to Egypt. Presently Hadad was to return to his native land and become "an adversary," a continuing threat to Solomon. See 1 Kings 11:17–22, 25.

21. Politely, the disciple says to the commander: We do not believe your professions of kindness. In fact, you do not act against us only because, like the weapons in the parable, we are dispersed, so that you cannot get to all of us at one time to destroy us.

he also stood up, lifted both of his hands to heaven, and said: Blessed be He whose presence is everywhere, blessed be He who chose you Jews out of all the inhabitants of the world, indeed took complete possession of you—both sons and servants who are His very own, called you people, inheritance, treasure which is His very own. In a hundred places we rehearse plans for disposing of you, but then we say: If we slay those of you in the Land of Israel, who will slay for us those in the north and in the south? Even if we slay those in the north and in the south, who will slay for us those who are in Babylonia and in Elam and in other countries? And thus our plans are defeated without our having achieved a thing. Indeed the Master of the house knows just how to go about depositing His vessels, so that when the Master of the house chooses to come back to His house, He will be able to take His vessels with Him back into the house.[22]

Another comment [on the concluding words of the passage from Deborah's song]: *There shall they rehearse the righteous acts of the Lord, even the righteous acts of those who disperse* [*gifts*] *in Israel* (Judg. 5:11). [In regard to Israel's rehearsal of the righteous acts of the Lord, consider] a small town in Israel where people proceeded to build themselves a synagogue and an academy. For the latter they engaged a Sage, for the former they engaged teachers of little children.[23] Thereupon, when the people of another city nearby saw [what their neighbors had done], they, too, proceeded to build a synagogue and an academy, and they, too, engaged for themselves teachers of little children, and in this manner there came to be many houses of study in Israel, as is said, *Then the people of the Lord went down to the gates* [*of learning*] (*ibid.*). | Blessed is he from whose mouth words of Torah are given new mean- ER, *p.* 55
ing[24] within academies grown numerous in Israel. It is as though such a man is given to hear the Holy One saying to him <from heaven>, "My son, My great academy is yours," as is said, *God then chooses the new* [*insights*] *brought forth out of the give-and-take of discussion in gates of learning*[25] (Judg. 5:8). In this connection it is said: If forty thousand men of Israel came together to go forth to war with no more than a single pair of disciples of the wise among them, it is likely that God would deliver the foe into the hands of that pair, for it is said, [*With such as these two*] *was there need for a shield or a spear to be seen among forty thousand in Israel?* (*ibid.*).

---

22. Cf. B.Pes 87b.
23. See Louis Ginzberg in *OT,* p. 281, n. 252.
24. "*Ḥaddeš*—to establish a new law or draw a new interpretation—is found already in the Mishnah, cf. Yaḏ 4:3, and is not rare in Talmud and Midrash" (Louis Ginzberg in *OT,* p. 275, n. 132).
25. JV: *They chose new gods; then was war in the gates.* But *yiḇḥar,* "they chose," means more accurately "He—God—chose." *Laḥem,* "war," is taken to mean "the conflict", or "give-and-take of minds in discussion."

CHAPTER (11) 12

On sundry events in the Book of Judges

Summary

Israel are not required to pay a penalty even of a penny without first having been brought to judgment, as is proved by the account in the Book of Judges of what befell Deborah and Barak, Ahab and Jezebel, Zebulun and Issachar, Jael, Phinehas, the sons of Eli, and the men of Beth-shemesh (ER, 58–59).

During the period of the judges' governance of Israel, the people so befouled themselves with their deeds that God was constrained to chastise them by having the surrounding nations set upon them again and again.

The forty-two thousand Ephraimites who were slain by Jephthah deserved their fate because of their ingratitude, their indifference to his plight (ER, 55), and their practice of idolatry. But since all Israel are responsible for one another, the man who was ultimately to blame for the death of the Ephraimites was Phinehas. He shirked his responsibility by not intervening to release Jephthah from his vow to sacrifice his daughter.

Similarly, the death of the seventy thousand Benjamites was the result of a shirking of responsibility on the part of the Sanhedrin. Upon the arrival of Israel in the Land, the members of the Sanhedrin should have gone about to all the cities and given their inhabitants instruction in proper conduct. Instead each member chose to go only to his own vineyard, saying, "May all go well with me" (ER, 56).

Incidentally, it should be noted that the incident in Gibeah, involving the concubine, the incident which led to the death of the seventy thousand Benjamites, took place shortly after Israel's conquest of Canaan. But the story was not put in its proper place in the Book of Judges; instead it was put at the end to avoid its being said that of their own volition, without following the example of the Canaanites, Israel managed to disgrace themselves by their sexual immorality.

To return to Phinehas: because of his neglect of the duties of his office, the High Priesthood was denied for seventy years to his descendants. The office was turned over to the descendants of Ithamar, Aaron's other son, and they held it until, in their turn, Ithamar's descendants in the persons of the sons of Eli, disgraced themselves. Thereupon God concluded that there being little to choose from either line, the High Priesthood should be restored to the line of Eleazar. But before the restoration, because of the misdeeds of Eli's sons, four thousand Israelites were slain in battle with the Philistines, and in another battle thirty thousand were slain, and the Ark of the Covenant was captured (ER, 57).

Chapter (11) 12

ER, ***p.*** **55** *cont'd* What parable applies to Israel in the days when the judges ruled? The parable of a mortal king who possessed <houses> and menservants. Some of the servants he had brought up at his table from the time they were six years old, some from the time they were five, some from the time they were four, some from the time they were three, some from the time they were two, some from the time they were one. All of them ate what he ate, all of them drank what he drank. After he had brought them up, he built houses for them, planted vines, trees, and shrubs for them, and instructed them: Take care of these shrubs, take care of these trees, take care of these vines. But after they had eaten and drunk, they proceeded to root up the vines, cut down the trees, and destroy the houses and the shrubs. Nevertheless, when the king came he was disposed to be indulgent,[1] saying: They are still behaving like school children. What can be done about them? Go, [he then said to his servants], fetch them, and spank them not once, but twice, and even thrice.

Thus in the days when the judges ruled were Israel regarded in the eyes of their Father in heaven. After they befouled themselves with their deeds, He turned them over to [an alien] kingdom [to be spanked]. When they turned about and promised to be good, He forgave them right away. You are thus to understand that Israel are not required to pay even the smallest fine without first having been brought to judgment, and that all that is then done to them is based on such judgment.[2]

Concerning the forty-two thousand slain in the days of Jephthah the Gileadite,[3] perhaps you may ask, why were they slain? Because Jephthah the Gileadite made a vow that was utterly improper, at a time when, [as High Priest], Phinehas the son of Eleazar was available to counsel him. Phinehas should have gone to Jephthah to release him from his vow, or Jephthah should have gone to Phinehas to have himself released from his vow. But neither went, Phinehas saying: I am the High Priest, son of a High Priest, and grandson of Aaron the [premier] Priest[4]—am I to go to such a clod? And Jephthah said: I, captain of all Israel, am I to go to such a man who is practically a has-been? Thus one fumed, and the other fumed. Thus one gave himself airs, and the other gave himself airs.[5] Woe unto self-pride which buries those possessed by it! Woe unto false pride which does no good in the world! When Jephthah the Gileadite made a vow that was utterly improper—a vow to offer up his daughter on an altar—the people of Ephraim gathered against him and got into a great argument with him.

---

1. Leon Nemoy suggested that "his mind was broadened in respect of them" means that "he was disposed to be indulgent."
2. The interpretation of the preceding passage was suggested by Leon Nemoy.
3. Judg. 12:6.
4. *Phinehas . . . was ruler . . . the Lord['s word] had been with him in the past.* See 1 Chron. 9:20 and Rashi, *ad loc.*
5. The two were thus a pair completely unlike the pair of disciples of the wise into whose hands, as stated at the end of the preceding chapter, God would deliver a foe.

Phinehas should have said to them: You did not come to offer him release from his vow. All you do is engage in an argument with him because he made it. For his part, however, Phinehas neither intervened
ER, *p.* 56 between the children of Ephraim [and Jephthah], | nor did he release Jephthah from his vow.

He who sits on the throne as the Righteous Judge—may His great name be blessed for ever and ever and ever—said [in defense of Jephthah]: After Jephthah took his life in his hand and set to and delivered Israel from the hand of Moab and from the hand of the children of Ammon, nevertheless the Ephraimites prepared for a great conflict with him. They moved to wage war, and so he went out and slew forty-two thousand of them, those who when told *Say now "Shibboleth," said "Sibboleth"* (Judg. 12:6). "Sibboleth," as it happened, includes the name of an idol among its syllables, so that the term was an approximation of the phrase *Śa' Bul,* "Lift up the idol Bul." In any event, when any one of the Ephraimites *could not frame to pronounce Shibboleth right, they laid hold on him, and slew him at the fords of the Jordan* (*ibid.*).

But, in fact, who slew all of the Ephraimites? You must admit that their slayer was none other than Phinehas son of Eleazar who had the opportunity to intervene but did not intervene, who had the opportunity to release Jephthah from his vow but did not release him from his vow. Phinehas shirked his responsibility, and no man should do so. Whenever a man has the opportunity to intervene in a quarrel and does not intervene, or has an opportunity to bring Israel back to the right way and does not take advantage of the opportunity, the blood spilt in Israel is spilt by him, as is said, *So thou, son of man, I have set thee a watchman . . . when I say unto the wicked: O wicked man, thou shalt surely die, and thou dost not speak to warn . . . his blood will I require at thy hand. Nevertheless, if thou warn the wicked . . . he shall die in his iniquity, but thou hast delivered thy soul* (Ezek. 33:7–9). In short, all the children of Israel are responsible for one another. With what may this responsibility be compared? With a ship in which one compartment has split apart. Of something like this, people do not say, "A compartment in the ship has split apart." What they say is, "The entire ship—the whole thing—split apart." Thus it is said, *Did not Achan the son of Zerah commit a trespass concerning the devoted thing, and* [*in consequence*] *wrath fell upon all the congregation of Israel?* (Josh. 22:20).[6]

Concerning the approximately seventy thousand[7] of the children of Benjamin who were slain in Gibeah, perhaps you will ask why were they slain? Because the [members of the] Great Sanhedrin, which Moses, Joshua, and Phinehas the son of Eleazar had left with Israel,

---

6. See Tanḥuma Deut., *Niṣṣaḇim,* 2.

7. The actual total was 65,130. [Since it is over 65,000, the next round figure is 70,000. L. N.]

should have bound chains of iron around their loins, should have rucked their garments up above their knees, and labored to go about to all the towns in Israel, spending a day in Beth-el, a day up in Hebron, a day up in Jerusalem, and continuing in this way for a year, or two, or even three, until Israel had settled down in their Land and had been taught proper conduct. [Had the Sanhedrin done so], the name of the Holy One would have been magnified and hallowed in the world—in all of it, from end to end—which He created. But they did not do so. When they entered the Land, each member of the Sanhedrin went to his own vineyard and to guzzling his wine, saying, "This is the life for me!" not intending to take on any burdens but his own. [Besides, he argued], the Sages taught in the Mishnah: "Engage only a little in business, but be busy with Torah. Be of humble spirit before all men. If you have neglected the Torah, many reasons for further neglect of it will present themselves to you" (Aḇ 4:10). When in Gibeah, which belongs to the children of Benjamin, the Benjamites followed filthy ways and committed such indecencies as one cannot even give a name to, then and there the Holy One was about to destroy Israel,[8] all of it. God said: I gave My Torah to these people <only in order> that they read and study it and learn right conduct from it. Moreover, have I not written in My Torah that even if they do not know how to expound Torah, but know only Scripture and right conduct,[9] *Five of you shall give chase to a hundred* (Lev. 26:8), and if you heed the Torah zealously, *one* [*of you*] *will chase a thousand, and two put ten thousand to flight* (Deut. 32:30)?[10] On the other hand, when the Benjamites, [lacking knowledge of Scripture, of exposition of Scripture, and of right conduct] mustered and went forth to war, | seventy thousand of them were ER, *p.* 57
slain. And who slew all of these? It was no other than the Great Sanhedrin which Moses, Joshua, and Phinehas son of Eleazar the [High] Priest left [to the children of Israel].

The incident of the concubine in Gibeah (Judg. 19–21) took place in the days of Cushan-rishathaim.[11] Now what was there about the story

---

8. Literally, "the world," a term frequently applied to Israel alone. See *OT,* p. 284, n. 318.

9. R reads *mid-dereḵ 'ereṣ.* But Louis Ginzberg's suggestion that the phrase is a contraction of *miḳra',* "Scripture," and *dereḵ 'ereṣ,* "right conduct," is followed. See *OT,* p. 300, n. 160.

[The text yields good sense without emending (rather fancifully) *mid-dereḵ 'ereṣ* into *m*(*iḳra' wĕ*)*-dereḵ 'ereṣ.* The author interprets *My statutes and . . . My commandments* in Lev. 26:1 as referring to the laws of *dereḵ 'ereṣ,* while Deut. 32:30 refers to the laws of Torah: "Did I not . . . that even if they do not cultivate the Torah, but are guided only by *dereḵ 'ereṣ* . . . ? But if you cultivate the Torah with zeal," etc. L. N.]

10. Cf. above, ER, 16.

11. The incident took place shortly after the conquest of the Land (see Judg. 3:8), and not at the end of the period of the judges, as one might suppose from the place of the story in the Book of Judges. So also Josephus, *Antiquities, 5, 2,* 8 (Loeb ed. *5,* 62–63, n. b): "It is incredible," writes Dr. G. F. Moore (*International Critical Commentary* [New York, 1895], p. 405), "that the Tribe of Benjamin was almost exterminated only a

of the concubine that caused it to be inserted [toward the end of Scripture's account of the period] when judges ruled Israel? The story was put there because the compassion of the Holy One for Israel is ever constant. Lest the peoples of the world should say that Israel had disgraced themselves by sexual immorality almost as soon as they entered the Land, He had the story of the concubine put off to the very end of the account of the judges' rule of Israel, [so as to make it appear that Israel had learned such immoral practices from the Canaanites long after Israel had entered the Land]. Blessed be the Preserver of the world, blessed be He whose bountiful compassion for Israel is ever constant, and who is concerned for their honor wherever they dwell.

At the time of the judges' tenure [it was decreed] that for seventy-two years the [High] Priesthood should succeed to the descendants of Ithamar the son of Aaron[12] until such time as the sons of Eli would undo the succession of Ithamar's descendants.[13] Forthwith the Holy One said: Why should one line of descent continue to be favored over the other? Was not Eleazar a son of Aaron even as Ithamar was a son of Aaron? [There was not much to choose between the descendants of either.] As Scripture says, *I looked, and there was none to help, and I beheld in astonishment, and there was none to uphold*[14] (Isa. 63:5). Nevertheless, said the Holy One, the [High] Priesthood should be restored to its original possessor. Hence the man of God said to Eli: *Thus saith the Lord of hosts:*[15] . . . *I said indeed that thy house, and the house of thy father*—by which Aaron and Ithamar are meant—*should walk before Me for ever; but now the Lord saith: . . . thou shalt behold a rival in My habitation . . . and I will raise Me up a faithful priest . . . and he shall walk before Mine anointed for ever* (1 Sam. 2:27, 30, 32, 35). [And so it turned out], for Zadok the Priest[16] was to walk before king David.

Because of the misdeeds of the sons of Eli, Israel went forth to war,

---

generation or two before the time of Saul; but the events related in these chapters probably fall in a much earlier period."

12. The decree was actually carried out after the death of Jephthah in whose days Phinehas the son of Eleazar was still alive. See Gen. Rabbah 60:3 and 1 Chron. 9:20, a verse which is taken to imply that the spirit of God had departed from Phinehas. So for the next seventy-two years descendants of Ithamar served in the High Priesthood. The change in families—so Friedmann suggests in n. 16—is intimated in the lacuna of six generations—Amariah, Ahitub, Zadok, Ahimaaz, Azariah, and Johanan—in the genealogy of Ezra the Priest (Ezra 7:1–6) of the line of Eleazar and Phinehas. Cf. the genealogy in 1 Chron. 5:28–41, where there is no such lacuna.

13. In the days of Solomon, Zadok, a descendant of Eleazar, became High Priest, displacing Abiathar (1 Kings 2:26), who was of the family of Eli (see *EB, 1,* 35, *s.v.* "Abiathar").

14. V quotes Isa. 63:5, which Landau interprets thus: Phinehas, who failed to go around the Land to teach, gave no active help; but the sons of Eli did not even offer support. R seems to quote Isa. 59:16.

15. *Of hosts* is not in MT.

16. A descendant of Eleazar. See 1 Chron. 6:35–38.

and four thousand of them were slain. Thereupon Israel asked: *Wherefore hath the Lord smitten us today before the Philistines? Let us fetch the Ark of the covenant of the Lord out of Shiloh . . . that He may . . . save us out of the hand of our enemies* (1 Sam. 4:3). The Holy One replied: When the sons of Eli were provoking Me in the court of Israelites and in the court of women, you did not ask to know where the Ark resided. But now that Israel has gone forth to war, you say, *Let us fetch the Ark of the covenant of the Lord out of Shiloh unto us* (*ibid.*). And the people sent and fetched the Ark of the Covenant of the Lord, as is said, *So the people sent to Shiloh, and they brought from thence the Ark of the covenant of the Lord of hosts . . . and . . . all Israel shouted with a great shout* (1 Sam. 4:4–5). But the great shout Israel raised had no genuine feeling;[17] it was the kind of shout of which God was to say, "She hath [merely] raised her voice at Me; therefore have I hated her" (Jer. 12:8). On the other hand, the Philistines said: *Woe unto us! who shall deliver us out of the hand of these mighty gods? . . . Be strong and quit yourselves like men, O ye Philistines* (1 Sam. 4:8–9). Hence when Israel went forth into battle, thirty thousand of them were slain, and the Ark of the Covenant was captured and brought to Ashdod, to the house of Dagon, god of the Philistines. However, *When they of Ashdod arose early on the morrow, behold, Dagon was fallen upon his face to the ground before the Ark of the Lord* (1 Sam. 5:3). When the men of Ashdod saw what been meted out to them, | *They* **ER, *p.* 58**
sent and gathered all the lords of the Philistines . . . and they resolved: Let the Ark of the God of Israel be carried about unto Gath (1 Sam. 5:8). But there, too, it caused great havoc, as is said, *And it was so, that after they had carried it about, the hand of the Lord was against the city with a very great discomfiture* (1 Sam. 5:9). When the men of Gath saw what had been meted out to them, they sent the Ark to Ekron, as is said, *So they sent the Ark of God to Ekron* (1 Sam. 5:10). There, too, the Ark caused great havoc, as is said, *The Ekronites cried out, saying: They have brought the Ark of God . . . over to us, to slay us and our people* (*ibid.*). When the Ekronites saw what had been meted out to them, they took it into the open field, as is said, *And the Ark of the Lord was in the open field of the Philistines* (1 Sam. 6:1). And there, too, it caused such great havoc that *The Philistines called for the priests and the diviners* (1 Sam. 6:2). Though idolaters, the priests did have a sense of what was proper in regard to the Ark. And what did their sense of what was the proper thing to do lead them to say? *If ye send back the Ark of the covenant of the Lord God of Israel,*[18] *do not let it go without a gift* (1 Sam. 6:3).

In the meantime, what was <the> plague the Holy One brought

---

17. Such shouting prevailed at Jericho (Josh. 6:5), but because of the sins of the sons of Eli, such shouting did not prevail at Aphek.

18. JV: *If ye send away the Ark of the God of Israel.*

upon the Philistines? He brought upon them mice who slew among the Philistines men, women, and little children. Out of the Philistines' houses, the mice then ran into the open field where they ate the wheat, the barley, the beans, the lentils, and every kind of pulse, as is said, *Wherefore shall ye make images of your emerods, and images of your mice that mar your land; and ye shall give glory unto the God of Israel. . . . Wherefore then do ye harden your hearts, as the Egyptians and Pharaoh hardened their hearts?* (1 Sam. 6:5–6). Forthwith the Philistines hastened to fill the Ark with silver and mounted it upon the wagon. And as they walked on the way the heifers drawing the wagon lifted their voice in song [in praise of the Ark]:

Sing, O sing, Ark of acacia wood,
Ascend in all thy grace and good,
Thou art enmeshed in woven gold,
In the Tent's Holy Place art thou extolled,
Thee, the wings of cherubim enfold,[19]

as intimated in the verse *The heifers sang on the way*[20] *to Beth-shemesh* (1 Sam. 6:12). When they were two thousand cubits by measure from Beth-shemesh, the Philistine lords said: We will take the official vestments [of the Ark] and put them in an out-of-the-way place and see what these people do for their god whom we have so honored and who has done such extraordinary things. Thereupon they took the vestments and put them in an out-of-the-way place.

Now upon seeing the Ark, the people of Beth-shemesh should have taken their garments, put them over their faces,[21] and only then have come forward and for an hour or two or even three prostrated themselves before the Ark until the Ark was properly covered: by such conduct, the name of the Holy One would have been magnified and hallowed from world's end to end. But they failed to conduct them-

---

19. See *And they shall make the Ark of acacia wood* (Exod. 25:10); *He overlaid [the Ark] with pure gold within and without* (Exod. 32:2); *And he prepared the Sanctuary in the midst of the House within, to set there the Ark of the covenant of the Lord* (1 Kings 6:19); and *The cherubim spread forth their wings over the place of the Ark, and the cherubim covered the Ark and the staves thereof above* (1 Kings 8:7).

See Gen. Rabbah TA 54:4, pp. 581–82, and B.AZ 24b for parallels to the Song which, according to *Yĕfeh to'ar,* extols the Ark for its material (acacia), its workmanship, its appearance, its purpose (study of Torah), and its Divine authority, prophecy being voiced from between the cherubim's wings that cover it.

20. JV: *And the heifers took the straight way.* But *way-yiššarnah,* "took the straight way," is grammatically a form of the verb indicating its subject to be both masculine and feminine in gender. Besides, later in the verse, we are told that the heifers *turned not aside to the right hand or to the left.* Hence ER associates the *šarnah* of *way-yiššarnah* with *šir,* "sing."

21. In keeping with the practice prescribed for the Levites who were told not to go in *to see the holy things as they were being covered, lest they die* (Num. 4:20).

selves properly. When they saw the Ark, they laughed and stood up, and once they were standing, they began to dance around and even say things that were utterly inappropriate,[22] as is said, *And they of Beth-shemesh were reaping their wheat harvest in the valley, and they lifted up their eyes, and gazed shamelessly at the Ark and their joy at seeing it was unseemly* (1 Sam. 6:13). The people of Beth-shemesh did not know of course who had left the Ark there. Thereat the Philistine lords took <the Ark's vestments they had previously hidden> and proceeded to leave the place, as is said, *And when the five lords of the Philistines had seen it, they returned to Ekron the same day* (1 Sam. 6:16).

Because of their irreverent staring at the Ark, there fell fifty thousand of Israel and with them the Great Sanhedrin, as is said, *He smote of the men of Beth-shemesh, because they had gazed shamelessly upon the Ark of the Lord, even He smote of the people, the seventy men [of the Sanhedrin, and] fifty thousand fighting men* (1 Sam. 6:19). And who was responsible for the slaying of all these people? It was none other than the people of Beth-shemesh who did not know how to conduct themselves properly. What has been said above is meant to teach you that not even a penny is taken from Israel without Israel's having been first brought to judgment—all that is done to them <is based strictly on judgment of them>. God in heaven knows that judgment decreed a reward for Deborah and her prophecy and for Barak and his prophecy | in that ER, *p.* 59
there came a great deliverance [for Israel] through them. Judgment decreed that as requital for the misdeeds of Ahab and Jezebel, they perished from this world and from the world-to-come, and with them there perished their children. [Judgment decreed that] as a reward for the Tribe of Zebulun and the Tribe of Naphtali who did the will <of their Father in heaven and the will> of their father Jacob,[23] there came a great deliverance [for Israel] through them. [Judgment decreed that] as a reward for Jael, wife of Heber the Kenite, who did the will of her husband, there came a great deliverance [for Israel] through her.[24] [Judgment decreed that] as requital for Phinehas' misdeed, the children of Ephraim went forth to war, and forty-two thousand of them were slain; and as requital for [the misdeeds of] the Great Sanhedrin whom Moses left [with Israel] and [requital for the misdeeds] of Joshua, and of Phinehas the son of Eleazar, Israel mustered and went forth to war against the children of Benjamin, and seventy thousand of Israel were slain.[25] And [judgment decreed that] as requital for the

---

22. Such as "Who embittered You that You were thus embittered [and did not release Yourself from the Philistines], and what has come upon You that You are now appeased?" (B.Soṭ 35b).
23. See Ginzberg, *Legends, 2,* 209, and *7,* 512, column 1.
24. See Judg. 4–5, and above, chap. (9) 10, n. 14.
25. See Judg. 19–20.

[misdeeds of] the sons of Eli, Israel went forth to war, and four thousand of them were slain.[26] [Judgment decreed that] as requital for [the misdeeds of] the elders, Israel went forth to war, and thirty thousand of them were slain,[27] and the Ark of the covenant was captured. [Judgment decreed that] as requital for the misconduct of the men of Beth-shemesh, there fell fifty thousand men of Israel and with them the Great Sanhedrin.

Hence it is said: In the measure a man metes out, it is meted out to him. Most assuredly, Master of all the worlds, *Thy mercy is like the mighty mountains, and Thy judgments are like the great deep* (Ps. 36:7).[28]

---

26. See 1 Sam. 4:2.
27. See 1 Sam. 4:3–10.
28. Cf. PRKM 9:1, p. 146 (PRKS, p. 165).

CHAPTER (12) 13

Dining with the right kind of people

Summary

One should not dine with men unlettered in Torah, but try to dine with Sages as did Abraham with the angels who visited him. Not wishing to part even for an instant from his guests, Abraham dared ask God to wait a while until he was done entertaining them.

Those who provide for the Sages are greatly rewarded (ER, 59). Thus in reward for Abraham's hospitality to the angels whom he regarded as Sages, his children in the wilderness were given the well, the seven clouds of glory, the manna, and God Himself as escort.

On the other hand, one should take care not to dine with men unlettered in Torah as may be learned from the example of the angels who would not partake of the food offered them by Gideon and Manoah, both of them unlettered in Torah. The denial, however, of a piece of bread to one who is hungry may lead to the slaying of Israel's notables, even though, as Scripture tells us, the giving of it may cause the Presence to rest on false prophets (ER, 60).

In conclusion, it may be said that all kinds of calamities are likely to befall the man who persists in dining with men unlettered in Torah (ER, 61).

Chapter (12) 13

A man should keep in mind certain rules about dining: he ought not sit at table with men unlettered in Torah, nor make a habit of dining with them anywhere, because such men stint the payment of tithes and do not make available to all the produce of every seventh year. [In short, a man should not associate with his inferiors in learning.] As Scripture, quoting God Himself, puts it: *What hath the straw to do with the wheat?* (Jer. 23:28); and as wise men declare: "Every fowl dwells with its kind, let man dwell with his equal" (Ben Sira 13:15).[1] Likewise David said: *I do not consort with men given to cheating. . . . I detest the company of dishonest men* (Ps. 26:4–5). *O Lord, I love the habitation of Thy house* (Ps. 26:8), *where I may wash my hands in innocence, and walk around Thine altar* (Ps. 26:6); *Do not allow me to be reckoned among the ranks of sinners*[2] (Ps. 26:9). Hence it is said: A man should make a habit of dining with disciples of the wise so as to learn Torah from them. Rarely should he dine with men unlettered in Torah because they are likely to speak ill of him afterwards, [saying that he guzzled and stuffed himself.[3] That

ER, *p.* 59 *cont'd*

---

1. Cf. B.BḲ 92b.
2. JV: *Gather not my soul with sinners.* But *te'ĕsof,* "gather," may also mean "allow to be reckoned among."
3. See B.Pes 49a.

one ought to make a habit of dining with Sages] we learn from Abraham who prepared a meal for angels; [though angels require no food], they made themselves enjoy the meal [because he had prepared it. Such was Abraham's desire to please those who share in Divine wisdom that he asked God, who had come to visit him after his circumcision, to wait while he dined with the angels], saying, *My Lord, if now I have found favor in Thy sight, please wait a while for Thy servant*[4] (Gen. 18:3). Hence it is said: In order to try and be hospitable to disciples of the wise who have come to dine with him, a man may ask permission to put off <even his Sovereign>. It took courage indeed on Abraham's part to say to God: *My Lord . . . wait a while for Thy servant* (*ibid.*).[5] As for anyone who says that the ministering angels ate nothing at our father Abraham's, he is talking nonsense. For in acknowledgment of the righteousness of that righteous man and as a reward for the trouble he went to [in the angels' behalf], the Holy One saw to it that they opened their mouths and ate, as is said, [*Abraham*] *stood by them under the tree, and they did eat* (Gen. 18:8).[6]

Blessed be the Preserver of the world, blessed be He who rewards those who love Him and fear Him: such is the way He now has things go in this world, but in the world-to-come a much more enduring reward awaits him who both loves and fears God. As a reward for Abraham's providing a mere cruse of water so that the angels could wash their hands,[7] the Holy One gave Israel the well which for forty years [accompanied them and] provided them with water in the wilderness. And how did the well work? As long as Israel obeyed the will of
ER, *p.* 60 the Preserver of the world, | the water would begin welling up early in the morning wherever Israel were camped; but when Israel did not obey the will of the Preserver of the world, it would delay welling up for as much as an hour, or two, or three, or four, or even five until little children and disciples of the wise would go out to the wellhead and say: Spring up, O well, because of the merit of Abraham, Isaac, and Jacob; spring up, O well, because of the merit of Moses, Aaron, and Miriam. At once the well would start gushing in a spot between the Tribe of Judah and the Tribe of Issachar,[8] as Israel prayed in the song they sang: *Spring up, O well . . . the well, which the princes digged, which the nobles of*

---

4. JV: *pass not away, I pray Thee, from Thy servant.*

5. For parallels, see B.Shab 127a and MTeh 18:29 (YJS, *13, 1,* 259–60).

6. See Ginzberg, *Legends, 5,* 236, n. 143.

7. "their hands"—R and V; Haida and Friedmann emend "their feet," as in Gen. 18:4. But *Midraš hab-be'ur,* a Yemenite Yalḳuṭ, speaks of the angels' washing as the washing of hands required before a meal. See *Torah šĕlemah, 3,* 746.

8. Judah was princely in royal power even as Issachar was princely in his knowledge of Torah. Hence, ER infers that the well would gush up in the area where these two Tribes camped alongside each other.

the people had delved[9] (Num. 21:18). And when the water gushed up, there was great joy in Israel among their grown-ups and little ones alike.

As a reward for the shade of the tree under which our father <Abraham> had seated the ministering angels, the Holy One had seven clouds of glory hover for forty years over Israel in the wilderness. <As a reward for the morsel of bread which our father Abraham fed the ministering angels, the Holy One fed Israel with manna for forty years in the wilderness.>[10] And besides providing Israel with the manna, what did God do about its taste? Blessed be the Preserver of the world; blessed be He in whose presence no man is favored over another, [where every man is treated with complete fairness]. Even as our father Abraham had provided several kinds of food[11] to the ministering angels, so [God provided for Israel]: <he> who sought the taste of bread in the manna found the taste of bread in it, he who sought the taste of meat in the manna found the taste of meat in it, he who sought the taste of honey found the taste of honey in it, he who sought the taste of milk found the taste of milk in it, he who sought the taste of butter found the taste of butter in it, as is said, *The people went about, and gathered it, and ground it in mills, or beat it in mortars, or seethed it in pots, or made cakes of it. However it was prepared, its taste was like the taste of rich cream from the breast* [*of a nursing mother*][12] (Num. 11:8). And as a reward for the calf which our father Abraham had the ministering angels eat, the Holy One on two occasions provided Israel with quail —once before the revelation of the Torah and once after the revelation of the Torah.[13] In reference to the second occasion, the word *ślyw,* "quail," which has the overtone of *slyw,* "thorn,"[14] marks the great miracle associated with the pestilence <which came> through the eating of the quail. [While Israel ate the quail and suffered no discomfort thereby, the "mixed multitude"—that is, the Egyptians who for

---

9. ER takes the phrase *nobles of the people* to refer to Abraham, Isaac, Jacob, Moses, Aaron, and Miriam, whose merit *had delved* the well. So Haida. See also Ginzberg, *Legends,* 6, 21, n. 129.

10. "As a reward for the morsel of bread . . . with manna for forty years in the wilderness"—V.

11. [Literally, "had provided bread," but here evidently referring to the several courses (cakes, curd, milk, and a calf) offered by Abraham to the angels (Gen. 18:6, 8). L. N.]

12. The point is that from day to day her infant tastes in her milk the varied flavors of the food she has eaten. JV: *and the taste of it was as the taste of a cake baked with oil.* But ER apparently construes *lĕ-šaḏ,* "dainty bit" or "cake," as "from the breast" (*šaḏ*); and construes *šamen,* "oil," as "rich cream." Cf. Sif Num. 87, 89 (ed. Horovitz [Frankfurt am Main, 1917], pp. 86–87, 89); B.Yoma 75a; and PRKM 12:25, p. 224 (PRKS, p. 249).

13. See Exod. 16:13 and Num. 11:31–35.

14. [There really is no such word as *slyw* = "thorn"; I'd say, "which has the overtone of *sylwn,* "thorn." L. N.]

unworthy motives had joined Israel in the exodus—lusting for meat, suffered such discomfort from eating the quail as though thorns had pierced their guts.][15]

Finally, as a reward for our father Abraham's having escorted the ministering angels, the Holy One escorted His children for forty years in the wilderness, as is said, *The Lord went before them by day in a pillar of cloud* (Exod. 13:21). Had Scripture not stated it, it would have been impossible to utter such a thing. He went before them, if one dare speak thus, in the manner of a father walking before his son, in the manner of a master carrying a lantern before his servant—indeed as a father carries his son, or as a mother carries her infant. As God Himself said to Moses, *Thou mightest even say to Me: Carry them in Thy bosom, as a nursing-father carrieth the sucking child* (Num. 11:12).

[To return to the matter of not sitting at table with men unlettered in Torah], we learn from the story of Gideon, [who, though no Sage, was not altogether unlettered in Torah],[16] that when he prepared food for an angel, the angel did permit himself to taste it. Gideon said: *If now I have found favor in thy sight . . . Depart not hence . . . until I bring forth my present and lay it before thee. And Gideon went in, and made ready a kid and unleavened cakes. . . . Then the angel . . . touched the flesh and the unleavened cakes* (Judg. 6:17–21). From the story of Manoah, on the other hand, [a man totally unlettered in Torah],[17] we learn that when he prepared food for the angel of the Lord, the angel did not permit himself as much as to touch it, saying: *Though thou detain me, I will not eat of thy bread* (Judg. 13:16).

Take note of the punishment for denial of a piece of bread: on the one hand, the denial of it led to the slaying of Israel's notables; on the other hand, the giving of it caused the Presence to rest on false prophets. And the proof that denial of bread led to the slaying of Israel's notables you may infer from what befell the city of Nob and from what befell Saul and Ahimelech the son of Ahitub who had severe punishment imposed on them [because Jonathan denied David two loaves of bread].[18] As for the proof that the giving of a piece of bread even caused the Presence to rest on a false prophet, you may infer from the

---

15. Cf. B.Yoma 75b. The "mixed multitude" who had a gluttonous craving for meat are here identified as Egyptians who at the time of the exodus joined Israel not out of conviction but merely to get "on the bandwagon," so to speak (Sif Num. 86 [ed. Horovitz, p. 86]; and Rashi on Num. 11:1, 4). So Ben Yeḥiel.

16. Gideon was head of the court, and as such was to be accorded the deference given to Moses in his day. See Tos RH 2:3 (Lieberman, *TKF, 4,* 311) and Midraš Šĕmu'el, chap. 15.

17. Manoah was an utter ignoramus. See B.Er 18a.

18. "Had Jonathan given David but two loaves of bread, Nob, the city of priests, would not have been put to the sword, Doeg would not have been banished from his portion of life in the world-to-come, and Saul and his three sons would not have been slain" (B.Sanh 104a).

story of the true prophet who came to [Jeroboam] king of Israel. To that prophet, the Holy One said: Accept no benefit from Jeroboam. If you accept any benefit from him, you <will not be buried in the sepulcher | of your fathers>. Then a false prophet came and lied to the true prophet, saying: *I am also a prophet as thou art; and an angel spoke unto me by the word of the Lord, saying: Bring him*—[i.e., *the true prophet*] —*back with thee into thy house, that he may eat bread, and drink water* (1 Kings 13:18). And though the false prophet had lied, the holy spirit did come to rest upon him, as is said, *And it came to pass, as they sat at the table, that the word of the Lord came unto the "prophet"* (*ibid.*).[19] ER, *p.* 61

From the foregoing it follows that he who eats bread with men unlettered in Torah and gets used to dining with them more and more frequently will find that his words are not heeded, and eventually that dissension results through him, as is said, *They snatched on the right, but remained hungry, and consumed on the left without being sated . . . Manasseh against Ephraim*[20] (Isa. 9:19–20). It also follows that he who eats with men unlettered in Torah and gets to feast more and more frequently with them is like a man who worships idols;[21] if he happens to be a disciple of the wise, <he> comes to belittle <his Torah>, desecrates the name of his Father <in heaven>, widows his wife, orphans[22] his children, having not lived out his days, and, in conclusion, brings a contemptuous epithet upon himself, upon his children, and upon his children's children unto the end of all generations.[23]

---

19. "A mouthful of food may alienate those who are near, draw near those who are distant . . . and make the Presence rest even on the prophets of Baal." So R. Johanan in the name of R. Jose b. Ḳisma (B.Sanh 103b).

20. The lines that follow are omitted as a copyist's doublet of "From the foregoing it follows . . . *Manasseh against Ephraim.*"

21. "R. Simeon said: If three have eaten at a table and have spoken there no words of Torah, it is as if they had eaten of sacrifices to lifeless idols" (Aḇ 3:4).

22. Isa. 9:15–16 reads: *That people's leaders have been misleaders. . . . Hence my Lord will not spare their youths, nor show compassion to their widows and orphans.*

23. The epithets, according to the parallel in B.Pes 49a, are "oven stoker, tavern dancer, plate licker."

Rashi and Samuel Edels explain the downfall of such a disciple of the wise: "His fondness for feasting elsewhere leads him to do the same in his own home, and to make it possible he must sell his furniture, etc. Seeing himself on the road to ruin, he wanders into exile, leaving his wife and children widowed and orphaned. He wastes his time, so forgets his learning. This involves him in disputes on learning. Or his poverty involves him in disputes with tradesmen because he cannot settle his bills. Again, the banqueting table itself is a fruitful source of quarrels" (H. Freedman's n. 7 in B.Pes, Soncino tr., p. 235).

CHAPTER (13) 14

The hazard of flippancy

Summary

Jesting, idle talk, or flippancy may lead to lewdness, to idolatry, to shedding of blood, and to a double portion of punishment in Gehenna. God, engaged in serious business, has little time for laughter (ER, 61). Laughter serves Him for only one brief hour—when the peoples of the world give themselves to boasting, or when He derides the wicked among Israel, although even for them His mercies are ever abundant. His laughter is also bittersweet at the Impulse to evil, which He regrets having created, even as He notes with satisfaction the doorways of mercy opening up for those whom the Impulse to evil has beguiled. When jesters enter their eternal abode, God Himself asks: Did you not learn from Me that I do not laugh except for the one brief hour when the nations boast that they will overcome Me? And so He asks Israel: From the age of thirteen on, what serious business have you engaged in?

In regard to the serious business of life it is said: There are two kinds of toil—toil in matters of Torah and toil in worldly affairs. He who chooses to toil in worldly affairs finds that worldly affairs take their toll of him. He is like a bag filled with water: once the water is spilt and gone, nothing is left in the bag. On the other hand, he who labors in Torah (ER, 62) may be compared to a tree into whose shade all people come, or to a lamp which provides light for the eyes of many.

To make amends for what befell Israel because of him, Aaron dedicated himself to labor in Torah, teaching people to recite the Shĕma', to say the *Tĕfillah,* and to know the ABC's of Torah, tasks which all people should undertake.

A man should guide himself by twelve rules of conduct in his day-to-day life (ER, 63) and by four rules of conduct in the academy.

In further discourse on the theme of joking and flippancy, it is said that these bring down burning wrath upon the world: crops are diminished, trials and tribulations befall the world. The frivolous end up by affirming under oath that which is false, by subverting justice, and by bringing about exile (ER, 64). Prophets, priests, and princes who do not reprove Israel's frivolity bear the burden of blame.

A man should always take care not to yield to sin, even the most trivial kind of sin, for the consequences may well prove incalculable—witness Abraham's thoughtless remark and Moses' and Aaron's act at the waters of Meribah. What God asks of a man is that he live according to the eleven attributes of mercy, which out of the infinite number of His attributes He has chosen to display to mankind.

There follow two stories, one to illustrate the requital for jesting and flippancy (ER, 65), the other to illustrate the reward for humility and reverence. Another story is told to illustrate the punishment visited upon a priest for improper, indeed frivolous, use of the heave offering (ER, 66).

Incidentally, it is implied that without adequate knowledge of Torah, one is not to presume to give instruction in it. With such knowledge, it is added, one must go and do good deeds. One should also remember that chastisement comes upon a man only to do him good and purge him of his inclination to wrongdoing.

As for those who cannot contend successfully with their fellows (ER, 67), God steps in to help them and also to help those who though innocent are deprived of their rights by those with whom they live.

God also encourages all those who would live together in amity as well as those whose lives are notable for admirable conduct. Ultimately there will be a great reward for such men: like God they will endure and reap His loving-kindness for ever and ever (ER, 68).

Chapter (13) 14

A man ought to keep certain restraints in mind, such as not making a habit of jesting,[1] idle talk, or flippancy, for jesting, idle talk, and flippancy lead to lewdness. "As R. 'Aḳiḇa put it: 'Jesting and levity lead a man to lewdness' " (Aḇ 3:17). Jesting also leads to idolatry: Scripture tells us that *The people [who were about to make the golden calf] sat down to eat and to drink, and rose up to jest* (Exod. 32:6). Jesting also leads to the shedding of blood, as on the occasion when *Abner said to Joab: Let the young men, I pray thee, arise and do things to make us laugh. . . . And they caught every one his fellow by the head, and thrust his sword in his fellow's side* (2 Sam. 2:14–16). Jesting thus leads to grave transgression, as is said, *Therefore, refrain from mockery, lest your bonds be tightened* (Isa. 28: 22). Finally, jesting leads to a double portion of punishment in Gehenna, as is said, *Wherefore hear the word of the Lord, ye . . . makers of jests. . . . Because ye have said: We have made a covenant with death, and with the nether world are we at agreement. . . . When I make justice the line, and righteousness the plummet . . . your covenant with death shall be annulled, and your agreement with the nether world shall not stand* (Isa. 28:14–15, 17–18). **ER,** ***p.*** **61** *cont'd*

[The Holy One Himself has little time for laughter, for He has much serious business in hand.] Am I not the one, He said to Israel, who for nine hundred and seventy-four generations[2] before the world was created used to sit examining, analyzing, testing, and refining all the words of the Torah—every one of them? And from the day the world was created until the hour [of the Torah's revelation], I have been sitting on My throne of glory for a third of the day | reading Scripture and reciting Mishnah, for a third of the day imposing judgment, and for a third of the day according mercy, feeding, sustaining, and providing for the entire world—every part of it—and for all My handiwork in the world I created. **ER,** ***p.*** **62**

For Me laughter serves for only one brief hour. When is there to be laughter for Me? When the peoples of the world give themselves to boasting, saying: With how many mighty men will He come at us?

---

1. Cf. B.Ber 31a.
2. See ER, 9.

Let Him come at us with even a thousand thousand mighty men! With how many horsemen will He come at us? Let Him come at us with even a thousand thousand horsemen! With how many swords will He come at us? Let Him come at us with even a thousand thousand swords! Then shall I laugh [at the nations], says God, as Scripture declares, *Why are the nations in an uproar, and peoples utter vain things . . . against the Lord? He who is enthroned in heaven laugheth, the Lord hath them in derision* (Ps. 2:1–2, 4).[3]

In some circumstances laughter for Me is bittersweet,[4] [expressing both My delight and My derision]. Thus when Scripture says, *The Lord said unto Moses: Take unto thee sweet spices, stacte, onycha, and galbanum* (Exod. 30:34), [note that stacte and onycha are indeed sweet-smelling], but is not galbanum foul-smelling? [Why, then, is it included with the others? Because it stands for the Holy One's derision of the wicked among Israel just as the sweet spices stand for His delight in the righteous among them]: <for both nevertheless—for the wicked and the virtuous—at one and the same time, the mercies of the Holy One are ever abundant>.[5]

Again, when is my laughter bittersweet?[6] When transgressors in Israel set out to destroy the virtuous among them, as is said, *The wicked plotteth against the righteous, and gnasheth at him with his teeth* (Ps. 37:12). And what does the next verse say? *The Lord doth laugh at him, for He seeth that his day is coming* (Ps. 37:13).[7]

On another occasion, the reaction of the Holy One to the presence of the Impulse to evil was [bittersweet—satisfaction mixed with] regret. What a breach I brought about within man! He said. How I regret having created this Impulse in My world, an Impulse of which it is said, *Would the* [*beguiling*] *serpent ever dare bite without a whisper from above?* (Eccles. 10:11).[8] At the very same time, however, it gave Him satisfaction to have opened a doorway of mercy for those who had been beguiled, the transgressors in Israel, to be received in repentance. For, under the circumstances, they could dare say to Him: Master of the universe, it is known and plain to You <that [You created] the Impulse to evil that beguiled us>.[9] Therefore in Your great compas-

---

3. Cf. B.AZ 3b.
4. Literally, "laughter and not laughter."
5. "for both . . . the mercies of the Holy One are ever abundant"—parallel in Yalkut, *2, Ki tiśśa'*, 390, which cites ER. See also B.Ker 6b.
6. See n. 4.
7. "He Himself does not rejoice—He causes others to rejoice, a fact clearly indicated in the verse *And it shall come to pass, that as the Lord rejoiced over you to do good . . . so will the Lord cause rejoicing* (*yaśiś*)—not 'the Lord will rejoice' (*yaśuś*)—*over you by destroying you* (Deut. 28:63)." So R. Jose ben Ḥanina in B.Sanh 39b. See also B.Meg 10b.
8. JV: *If the serpent bite before it is charmed.* See PRKM 4:2, p. 58 (PRKS, pp. 62–63).
9. "that [You created] the Impulse to evil that beguiled us"—V.

sion receive us in wholehearted repentance into Your presence.[10]

For he who engages much in jests, idle talk, or flippancy will have them accompany him until the time he enters his eternal abode. And when he enters his eternal abode, the Holy One will say to him: My son, did you not learn from your Father in heaven who, seated on His throne of glory, recites Mishnah and reads Scripture a third of the day, imposes judgment a third of the day, and a third of the day bestows mercy as He feeds, sustains, and provides for all the inhabitants of the world and for all His handiwork in the world He created—did you not learn from Him that in His presence there is no laughter except for one brief hour? Now tell Me, [what serious matters have you been engaged in] from the age of thirteen on? Have you acquired Torah? Have you done good deeds? I, *who form the mountains . . . ask man what hath he done with his thought* (Amos 4:13).[11]

[In regard to the serious business of life] it is said: There are two kinds of toil—<toil> in matters of Torah and toil in worldly affairs. He who chooses to toil in worldly affairs finds that worldly affairs take their toll of him.[12] Of this sort of man, Scripture says, *Man is born for toil* (Job 5:7). With what may he be compared? With a leather bag filled with water: once the water is poured out and gone, nothing is left in the bag. On the other hand, to him who chooses to toil in matters of Torah applies the verse *For the soul that labors [in Torah], Torah labors for him*[13] (Prov. 16:26). With what may this sort of man be compared? With a threshold upon which all step; with a plank | over which all **ER,** ***p.*** **63**
pass; with a tree into whose shade all come; with a lamp which provides light for the eyes of many.[14]

Aaron knew that because of him a great pestilence befell Israel, [and so to make amends he dedicated himself to labor in Torah]. He bound a chain of iron about his loins and made the rounds of Israel's thresholds. Any one who did not know how to recite the Shĕma', he taught to recite the Shĕma'; any one who did not know how to say the *Tĕfillah,* he taught to say the *Tĕfillah;* any one who did not know the ABC's of Torah, he taught him to know them. Such labor in Torah need not be true only of Aaron. It is true of any one who, for the sake of Heaven, teaches Torah to multitudes in Israel and does not favor either the rich or the poor, but has both alike read Scripture and has both alike recite Mishnah. Because of his labor the Holy One has compassion for

---

10. Cf. B.Ber 31b–32a.

11. At the time of death even the most trivial conversation is recalled to him (Ka, chap. 3 [ed. Higger (Jerusalem, 5730), p. 213], and B.Ḥaḡ 8b).

12. Cf. Aḇ 3:6. [I think that *noṯĕnin 'alaw 'amal dereḵ 'ereṣ* means not that worldly affairs take their toll of him, but that his reward is nil, in the end he is as empty (of reward) as an empty water-skin. Not so with *'amal Torah,* etc. L. N.]

13. JV: *The hunger of the laboring man laboreth for him.* But *nfš,* "hunger," may also mean "soul."

14. Cf. DEZ 58b, chap. 3 (Soncino tr., p. 577), and P.Sanh 6:3, 23b.

him and gives him a spirit of wisdom and understanding, of knowledge and insight, gives him his portion with the three righteous men, Abraham, Isaac, and Jacob. Of him Scripture says, *Of the toil of his soul he shall see to the full, even My servant, who by his knowledge did justify the righteous to the many* (Isa. 53:11).

Hence it is said that a man should guide himself by <twelve>[15] rules of conduct: He ought to be (1) affable on entering [a house]; (2) modest in the seat he takes;[16] (3) resourceful in the fear of God;[17] (4) discerning in Torah; (5) alert to do <good> deeds; (6) courteous and therefore welcomed by his fellow men; (7) willing to acknowledge truth; (8) resolved to acknowledge what he has committed himself to in his heart;[18] (9) quick to confess [his failings] and forsake them;[19] (10) eager to love the Holy One—whether in kindness He rewards him or in justice punishes him—with a complete love;[20] (11) agonizing all his days over [the profanation of] the Holy One's glory and of Israel's glory;[21] (12) and craving, yearning for, and looking to the honor of Jerusalem, to the honor of the Temple, to the deliverance soon to sprout up, and to the ingathering of the dispersed. When these yearnings are satisfied, the holy spirit will dwell in a man's words, for it is said, *There is to be vision yet again at the appointed time . . . wait for it, because it will surely come* (Hab. 2:3), and *Therefore turn thou to thy God, keep mercy and justice, and wait for thy God continually* (Hos. 12:7).

If "a man ought be affable on entering [a house]," he ought to be all the more so when he enters the academy; he will then be beloved on high, well-liked here below among his fellows, and the days of life allotted to him will be completed. "He ought to be modest in the seat he takes"—in the seat he takes in the academy, so that he be beloved on high, well-liked here below among his fellows, and the days of life allotted to him will be completed. By such conduct a man will increase [his sensitivity] to words of Torah, there being no greater reward than [sensitivity to] them. He should, while seated in the academy, [take an

---

15. "Twelve"—Friedmann; R and V: "eighteen."

16. He does not rush to occupy a front seat or a seat of honor.

17. He endeavors to find new ways to attain it. Cf. EZ, 167.

18. Literally, "speaketh truth in his heart." As did R. Safra, an eminent scholar who lived in Caesarea, where he carried on an extensive trade. One day, while R. Safra was reciting the Shĕma', someone offered him a sum of money for an article in his possession. Though willing to sell, R. Safra would not speak during the recital of Shĕma'. The would-be purchaser, interpreting R. Safra's silence as refusal, kept increasing the offer. After R. Safra finished the Shĕma', he explained the reason for his silence and indicated his willingness to sell the article at the price originally suggested. (See Samuel ben Meir [RaSHBaM] on B.BB 88b, also B.Ḥul 94b.)

19. See Prov. 28:13.

20. See Rashi on Deut. 6:5.

21. Literally, "to be sighing over the glory," etc., which, according to Landau and Louis Ginzberg, is a euphemism for the glory that is no more. See *OT,* p. 278, n. 190. Cf. ER, 17.

active part in its proceedings], asking questions and replying to questions, | thereby <increasing> his wisdom, thereby, too, keeping ER, *p.* 64
himself from dozing—<*Dozing is apt to lead to patchwork* [*knowledge*] (Prov. 23:21)>.[22] Indeed no flaw in man's nature is worse than his inclination to doze off in the synagogue or in the academy. But there is more to be said on this matter.[23] The verse from Proverbs cited just above begins by asserting that the student in the academy who eats and drinks too much will be inclined to doze.[24] Indeed in the verse *Lest when thou hast eaten so much that thou art sated . . . thou mayest forget the Lord thy God* (Deut. 8:12), a man is told: Even as you ask God in His mercy to put words of Torah inside you, better ask His mercy for the sins [of putting too much food and drink inside you] and hope that these sins be forgiven you.[25] Moreover, a man, [seated in the synagogue or in the academy], should not hesitate to ask the meaning of a verse even if every one ridicules him, or ask the meaning of a Halaḵah even if every one ridicules him. And if a man is not at all at home in Halaḵah, he should bring himself into the text of Torah [learning it by rote, if need be], as is said, *If thou art humiliated, a lifting* (Prov. 30:32)—that is, if in your attempt to understand Torah you are willing to be humiliated, you will be lifted up. *But if thou muzzlest thyself, thy hand will ever be over thy mouth*[26] *(ibid.)*—[that is, if you are not willing to endure humiliation by asking questions, your hand will always be over your mouth, and you will never come to understanding of Torah]. Out of your willingness to be humiliated,

---

22. "For *Dozing is apt to lead to patchwork* [*knowledge*]"—B.Sanh 71a.

23. Literally, "not only this, but." Here Friedmann follows V in interpolating "not this" and "but." [I don't see any need for the *three* interpolated words: "or in the academy, especially (*bi-lĕḇad,* "only") because, having eaten and drunk (too much) he succumbs to drowsiness." It is only here that the author takes up the proof-verse of Deuteronomy, "as is said, *Lest when thou. . . .* Let him find the answer *(yiš'al 'aḏam)* in this verse, even though every one derides him; let him find the answer in the Halaḵah, even though every one derides him; let him immerse himself in the *corpus* of Torah, even if he is not expert in it," etc. . . . L. N.]

24. *The drunkard and the glutton shall come to poverty* [*in their understanding of Torah*] (Prov. 23:21).

25. The words "a man is told . . . that these sins be forgiven you" are transposed to follow Deut. 8:12 in keeping with Louis Ginzberg's suggestion (*OT,* 278, n. 196); and the phrase "not in order" is deleted as a scribe's gloss which asserts that the text is in disarray *(ibid.).* [This passage belongs (as in the Hebrew) before the last sentence ("Out of your willingness to be humiliated," etc.) in the paragraph: "One should be told: While you implore mercy so that words of Torah might enter your inwards, you might very well also implore mercy for your transgressions. Who knows but that *(mah 'im)* they may be forgiven (in consideration of your effort to learn Torah), to wit (your misdeeds) that were improper" (*še-lo' kĕhogen,* in note rendered "not in order"); I see no need to insert *hizzaher me-'aśoṭ.* L. N.]

26. JV: *If thou hast done foolishly in lifting up thyself, or if thou hast planned devices, lay thy hand upon thy mouth.* But *naḇalta,* "thou hast done foolishly," may also mean "thou art humiliated"; and *zammoṭa,* "thou hast planned devices," may also mean "thou muzzlest thyself." See B.Ber 63b and Gen. Rabbah 81:2.

[and][27] out of minding the first four of the rules of conduct listed above, you will come to understand and remember Torah.

Keep in mind also that with all of the twelve rules of conduct listed above, there goes with each a quick reward for its being observed and with each a quick punishment for its being disregarded.

Remember that he who makes a habit of jesting, idle talk, or flippancy brings burning wrath down upon the world: because of him crops come to be diminished, <and because of these vices> many <tribulations and evils>[28] befall the world: harsh decrees are issued again, Israel's young men are put to the sword, orphans and widows cry out and receive no reply, as is said, *Therefore the Lord shall have no joy in their young men, neither shall He have compassion on their fatherless and widows, for . . . every mouth speaketh wantonness* (Isa. 9:16). Nay, more! he who makes a habit of jesting, idle talk, or flippancy, <comes to> *swearing and lying and killing and stealing and committing adultery* (Hos. 4:2), comes to affirming by oath that which is false and hence to subversion of justice.[29]

Such a man, if he lives with a family whose members delight in him, in the end will cause the family to be exiled. If he lives in a cluster of houses, and the residents of the cluster of houses delight in him, in the end he will cause the residents of the cluster of houses to be exiled. If he lives in a lane, and the residents of the lane delight in him, in the end he will cause the residents of the lane to be exiled. If he lives in a courtyard and the residents of the courtyard delight in him, in the end he will cause the residents of the courtyard to be exiled. If he lives in a city and the inhabitants of that city delight in him, in the end he will
ER, *p.* 65 cause the inhabitants of the city to be exiled, as it is said, | *For all this His anger is not turned away, But His hand is stretched out still* [*against the frivolous person*][30] (Isa. 5:25). Because of him, *doth the Land mourn, and every one that dwelleth therein doth languish* (Hos. 4:3). Whose is the blame? Those who should reprove the frivolity of Israel, but do not do so at all, as is said, *No man strives, no man reproves* (Hos. 4:4). Even when a priest comes upon a frivolous person, he joins in laughter with him and therefore must share in his punishment. <Even if a prophet or a prince comes upon a frivolous person, he joins in laughter with him and therefore must share in his punishment, as Hosea says, *Therefore shalt thou stumble in the day, and the prophet also shall stumble with thee in the night* (Hos. 4:5).

---

27. "and"—Ginzberg, *OT,* p. 278, n. 196.
28. Friedmann interpolates on the basis of V.
29. Cf. B.Shab 33a.
30. In two preceding verses Isaiah denounces *Those who call evil good and good evil, who present darkness as light and light as darkness . . . those who are so wise—in their own opinion; so clever in their own opinion* (Isa. 5:20–21).

A man should always take care not to yield to the power of sin, even the most venial kind of sin. Remember that our early forebears came down to Egypt only because of [a venial sin], the thoughtless remark that Abraham made—*O Lord God, whereby shall I know that I can take possession of the Land?* (Gen. 15:8). On the other hand, as a reward for the no more than slight token of respect which Ishmael showed his father,[31] the Holy One did not give to any people or kingdom the authority to rule over Ishmael's children. And as a reward for the scant two tears that Esau shed, he was given Mount Seir upon which rains of blessing never cease to fall. And for having out of deference to Jacob picked up his weapons and gone away, he was given one hundred provinces as a reward.[32] Yet take note that as requital for Jacob's having heeded Joseph [and shown him preference over Joseph's brothers, a minor sin], he was punished twenty-two years therefor.[33] Likewise, because [of their minor sin in regard to the waters] of Meribah,[34] Moses and Aaron were punished. In regard to severe punishment for minor sins, the Sages said, [citing a popular proverb]: If fire seizes what is moist, what may one expect it to do to what is dry? It was at the time of God's punishment of him that Moses composed *The Prayer of Moses* (Ps. 90:1).[35] In reply, the Holy One turned to placate Moses, saying: Am I not He whose sons are you and the children of Israel, sons whose Father I am? You and they are My brothers and I am your Brother. You are My friends and I am your Friend. You are My beloved and I am your Beloved. Have I ever had you deprived of anything? Since I examined My attributes of mercy and found eleven to be the number of such attributes,[36] I ask of you only that your lives display these eleven attributes of mercy: Let each of you be one (1) *who lives without blame,* (2) *who does what is right,* (3) *and in his heart acknowledges the truth* that I am God; (4) one *whose tongue is not given to evil,* (5) *who has never done harm to his fellow,* (6) *or endured reproach for* [*mistreatment of*] *his neighbor;*

---

31. He repented while his father was still alive. See Gen. Rabbah 59:1.

32. See MTeh 80:4 (YJS, *13, 2,* 50).

33. Here ER departs from the usual assertion that Jacob's mourning, which lasted twenty-two years, corresponded to the number of years he had dwelt apart from his parents and had not fulfilled the duty of a son toward them (Ginzberg, *Legends, 2,* 31). So Jakob J. Petuchowski in a letter.

34. See Num. 20:1–13.

35. There is a tradition that Moses composed Ps. 90 at the time of his sin in regard to the waters of Meribah. Thus R. Alexandri is quoted as saying that David composed Ps. 102 *(A Prayer of the afflicted . . . when he pours forth his plea before the Lord)* as a kind of analogue of *The Prayer* [*of Moses*]. See *Yelammĕdenu* on Deut., ed. L. Grünhut (Frankfurt am Main, 5601 [1901]), p. 97. The reference to R. Alexandri and the interpretation of his comment were provided by Professor Chaim Zalman Dimitrovsky of the Jewish Theological Seminary.

36. ER ascribes to God not thirteen qualities of mercy, but eleven, which is also the opinion of Rab. See MTeh 93:8 (YJS, *13, 2,* 129). Cf. PR 16:1 (YJS, *18, 1,* 343–44) and B.RH 17b. See also B.Mak 24a.

(7) one to *whom a contemptible man is abhorrent,* (8) *but who honors those who fear the Lord,* (9) *who stands by his oath even to his own hurt;* (10) *who has never lent money at interest,* (11) *or accepted a bribe to the hurt of the innocent* (Ps. 15:2–5).

Then the Holy One continued to placate Moses, saying to him: Do I show any partiality as between a heathen and an Israelite, between a man and a woman, or a manservant and a maidservant? The fact is that when any sort of person obeys a Divine command, the reward therefor is immediate, as is said, *When Thou rewardest the righteous, Thou lovingly exaltest him like the mighty mountains* >,[37] [*but when in justice, Thou dealest with the wicked, Thou dost cast him down to the uttermost depths*] (Ps. 36:7).[38] Hence it is said, when a man thinks much of the glory of Heaven, the glory of Heaven is magnified and his own glory is likewise magnified. When a man thinks little of the glory of Heaven, however, and much of his own glory, the glory of Heaven remains undiminished, but his own glory is diminished.[39]

[To return to the matter of requital for flippancy]: A story is told of a man who was standing with his son in a synagogue. When all the congregation responded to the reader with "Hallelujah,"[40] the man's son responded with some flippant words. "Look," the people said to the man, "your son is responding with flippant words." He replied: **ER,** ***p.*** **66** "What am I to do | with him? He is only a child, let him amuse himself." The next morning the same thing happened: When all the congregation responded to the reader with "Hallelujah," the man's son again responded with flippant words. "Look," the people said to the man, "your son is once more responding with flippant words." He replied again: "What am I to do? He is only a child; let him amuse himself." During all the eight days of the Festival,[41] the son kept on responding with flippant words, and the father did not say anything to stop him. It is reported: Not one year passed by, nor two, nor three, but that the man died, his wife died, his son died, his grandson died, and all together fifteen souls departed from his house. <Only two> sons were left, one lame and blind, the other half-witted and malicious.

---

37. The passage beginning "A man should always take care not to yield" and ending with *"the mighty mountains,"* was interpolated by Friedmann from Yalḳuṭ *1, Lek̲ lĕk̲a,* 77, which cites ER.

38. Both the interpolation of Ps. 36:7b and the translation were suggested by Professor Jakob J. Petuchowski. JV: *Thy righteousness is like the mighty mountains; Thy judgments are like the great deep.*

39. In striking the rock Moses made it appear that through his power and not through God's the rock gave forth water. Thus in this instance Moses failed to sanctify and magnify God. See Naḥmanides on Num. 20:1.

40. The response after each verse in the Psalms of *Hallel* (Pss. 113–18).

41. Sukkot (Tabernacles).

Another story is told of a man who always regretted his not having read Scripture nor recited Mishnah. Once, as he and I were standing in the synagogue and the reader reached the Sanctification of the Divine Name,[42] the man raised his voice, responding loudly to the reader, "Holy, holy, holy is the Lord of hosts."[43] People asked him: "What impelled you to raise your voice?" He replied: "Is it not regrettable enough that I never read Scripture and never recited Mishnah? So when I get the opportunity, should I not raise my voice so that my troubled spirit be calmed?"[44] It is reported: Not one year passed by, nor two, nor three, but that [good fortune came to this man]. He went up from Babylonia to the Land of Israel, was made a deputy of the emperor, and was appointed supervisor of all the castles in the Land of Israel. He was also given a section of land where he built himself a city in which he lived all the rest of his life, then left it for his children and his grandchildren until the end of all the generations.[45]

A story is told of a priest in whose house a fire broke out and consumed thirty <bolsters>,[46] sixty garments, twenty-four jugs of wine, ten jugs of oil, and other possessions as well. Thereupon the priest came and said to the Sages: "My Masters, there befell a fire in my house which consumed thirty bolsters, sixty garments, twenty-four jugs of wine, ten jugs of oil, and other things I had." At this news, regret and sorrow equal to the priest's seized the Sages. It is said, however, that before they left the place they were in, a man, unversed in Halaḵah, came along, and asked the priest, "Does the law permit a man to use heave offering[47] as fodder for his animal?" The priest answered, "<It is permitted>". The man asked, "You're sure it is not forbidden?" The priest answered, "It is not," and then went on, "I am a priest, and I myself use heave offering as fodder for my animal."

When the Sages heard | what the priest had done, [they came **ER**, *p.* 67
to understand that the fire which had consumed all the priest's possessions was his punishment for having used heave offering improperly],[48]

42. The *ḳĕḏušah.* See Hertz, *APB,* p. 134.

43. Isa. 6:3. Literally, "the declaration that the Name is holy."

44. [The man is depressed because he never had the chance (too busy, too poor, or no competent teachers nearby) to study Scripture and Mishnah. He is worried and unhappy. At last he sees a ray of hope—he can at least earn merit by loudly responding to the *sanctus.* Now he feels at least slightly relieved, slightly easier, slightly less guilty. . . . This leads me to conclude that what is meant is *šwḥ,* "to go down, to sink," from which it is only one step to "to settle, to calm down, to rest." L. N.]

45. Cf. parallels in Num. Rabbah 4:20.

46. "bolsters"—Yalḳuṭ *1, Leḵ lĕḵa,* 76; R: "male [animals]".

47. Heave offering is a portion of the produce (about two percent on the average) which was given to the priests, who alone were permitted to eat it. Cf. Num. 18:8; Lev. 22:10; and Deut. 18:4.

48. Heave offering of produce edible by human beings may not be used as fodder

and then they all said as one: "Blessed be He whose presence is everywhere, blessed be He for whom impartiality is the rule in His judgment of men." [Then they said to the priest]: "If heave offering is not consumed by human beings or consecrated food is not consumed by human beings, <then it must not be consumed by anything other than fire>. Clearly <you have not acted in keeping with the law>." The priest replied: "But is it not stated that 'Heave offering of bitter vetch[49] be given as fodder to domesticated animals and wild animals and to fowl?' (Ter 11:9)." The Sages answered: "Permission for such use of heave offering was given because ordinarily bitter vetch is used as fodder. Since bitter vetch is eaten by human beings only in years of famine, David decreed that in years of famine heave offering of bitter vetch may not be used as fodder.[50] Hence [only during years when there are good crops and only then] may heave offering of bitter vetch be used <as fodder>."[51]

Otherwise, as has been said: He who feeds his animal heave offering—whether heave offering of the Land or heave offering from outside the Land—of such a man Scripture says, *But he that maketh his ways despicable shall die*[52] (Prov. 19:16); and Levites are told, *Ye shall not profane the holy things of Israel, that ye die not* (Num. 18:32); and *He that diggeth a pit shall fall into it, and whoso breaketh through a fence,*[53] *a serpent shall bite him* (Eccles. 10:8).

From the foregoing, it is plain that a man should not give public instruction in Torah unless he has read the Five Books, the Prophets, and the Writings and has studied both Mishnah and Midrash, as is said, *Who can utter the mighty teachings of the Lord? Only he who can utter all His praise*[54] (Ps. 106:2).

[But with knowledge of Torah must go good deeds as well]: Scripture says, *In the day when things are good with thee, be sure to be at good*[55] (Eccles. 7:14). The Holy One says to a man: My son, from the day I placed you upon the earth, I intended you to do good deeds and to study Torah in order to save you from larceny, from [sexual] immorality, and from any vile act. Such is the significance of the verse *In the day when things are good with thee, be sure to be at good.* But *In the day of adversity*

---

for animals. Should such heave offering become unclean, it is to be disposed of only by burning. See Sif Lev., *'Emor,* 5 (ed. Weiss [Vienna, 1962], p. 97b), and Ṭoh 4:5.

49. Since bitter vetch, when tender, may be eaten by human beings (see MSh 2:4), the crop, unlike other plants used as fodder, requires heave offering.

50. During the three-year famine in his days. See 2 Sam. 21:1 and P.Ḥal 4:11, 60b.

51. "fodder"—Friedmann; R: "food for humans." Cf. P.Ḥal 4:4, 60b.

52. JV: *But he that despiseth His ways shall die.*

53. The "fence" which the Sages have erected to protect the Torah. See Aḇ 1:1.

54. JV: *Who can express the mighty acts of the Lord, or make all His praise to be heard?* But see B.Hor 13b, Mak 10a, and MTeh 106:1 (YJS, *13, 2,* 187–88).

55. JV: *In the day of prosperity be joyful.*

consider (ibid.)—that is, consider what you have done to bring chastisement down upon you. Keep in mind that chastisement comes upon a man only to do him good—to purge him of the guilt of all his wrongdoing. Hence in the Mishnah the Sages taught: "Do not despair in the face of adversity" (Aḇ 1:7), for, as it is said, *A thoughtful man considereth adversity* (Prov. 27:12)—he considers the adversity of the wicked who are full of contempt [for Providence] and therefore go down to Gehenna. [Of their fate], it is said, *And when ye see this, your heart shall rejoice . . . as the Lord . . . rages against His enemies* (Ps. 66:14). Hence *In the day of adversity consider.*

[On the other hand, the Lord helps those who cannot contend successfully with their fellows]: Thus Scripture says, *The Lord hath ransomed Jacob . . . from the hand of him that is stronger than he* (Jer. 31:10). For example, when a father and son are in contention and one is stronger than the other, God will punish him if he uses his strength to the disadvantage of the other. Such is the significance of *The Lord hath ransomed Jacob . . . [from the hand of him that is stronger than he]*.

Another example of the application of the words *The Lord hath ransomed Jacob.* When two brothers in a household are in contention and one is stronger than the other, God will punish him if he uses his strength to the disadvantage of the other. Such is the significance of *The Lord hath ransomed Jacob . . . [from the hand of him that is stronger than he]*.

Another example of the application of the words *The Lord hath ransomed Jacob.* When two disciples of the wise living in the same city are in contention and one is stronger than the other, God will punish him if he uses his strength to the disadvantage of the other. Such is the significance of *The Lord hath ransomed Jacob . . . [from the hand of him that is stronger than he]*.

Another comment. When two partners are working in one business, or in one field, or in one craft, and one partner | is stronger **ER, *p.* 68**
than the other, God will punish him if he uses his strength to the disadvantage of the other. Such is the significance of *The Lord hath ransomed [Jacob . . . from the hand of him that is stronger than he]*.

Another example of the application of *The Lord hath ransomed Jacob* [etc.]. If a man has two wives, to one of whom he fulfills the obligation of providing food, clothes, and marital relations, but <does not> provide them to the other, great punishment is in store for him. And he who does not admit that he is at fault in such matters and does not accept words of reproof—of him Scripture says, *He that turneth away his ear from hearing instruction, even his prayer is abomination* (Prov. 28:9). And in the same vein the Sages taught in the Mishnah: "Whosoever profanes the name of Heaven in secret, will suffer the penalty for it in public regardless of whether the heavenly Name be profaned in ignorance or in wilfulness" (Aḇ 4:5).

On the other hand, [of him who endeavors to make peace], you find the Psalmist saying, *Behold, how good and how pleasant is he who seeks to have brethren to dwell together in unity!* (Ps. 133:1). When the Holy One spoke to Moses, father of Sages, father of Prophets, [bidding him to go to Egypt], He did not speak to him in a peremptory manner, [but with affability], with the assurance that he would be greeted with joy, as is said, *When* [*Aaron*] *seeth thee, he will rejoice in his heart* (Exod. 4:14). Now if Moses, wisest among the wise, most notable among the notable, father of Prophets,[56] [resisted God's bidding to go to Egypt,[57] yet went] when God gave him the assurance that he would be greeted with joy, all the more strongly do the words of the Psalmist, *Behold, how good and how pleasant,* etc., apply to Moses' brother, Aaron, who set out to bring peace between Israel and their Father in heaven, between one Israelite and another Israelite, between a commoner and a Sage, between a Sage and his fellow Sage, between a man and his fellow man, and between a husband and his wife.

Another comment on the words *Behold, how good and how pleasant.* Of the life of a man who has done good deeds in his youth and increases his good deeds as he grows older, Scripture says, *Behold, how good and how pleasant for brethren,* [*youth and age*], *to dwell together in unity.*

Another comment <on the words *Behold, how good and how pleasant*>, etc. Of a man who read the Five Books, the Prophets, and the Writings in his youth, and then as he grew older studied Mishnah, Midrash,[58] Halakot, Talmud, and 'Aggadot,[59] and kept on studying with his colleagues, the Psalmist says, *Behold how good and how pleasant it is for brethren to dwell together in unity.*

Another comment on the words *Behold, how good and how pleasant.* Two brothers in one house who read Scripture with each other, who study Mishnah with each other, who eat and drink with each other and rejoice in each other—of such the Psalmist says, *Behold how good,* etc.

Another comment on the words *Behold, how good,* etc. One day the Holy One will sit in His <great> academy, with the righteous of the world sitting before Him. He will say to them: My children, I am He for whose sake you gave yourselves to death, I am He for whose sake you let yourselves be slain by the sword. You are like Me and I am like you: even as I live for ever, live and endure for ever and ever, so you will live and endure for ever and ever and ever, as is said, *Thine eyes shall see the King in His beauty* (Isa. 33:17).[60] In speaking thus of the

---

56. See Lev. 26:46 and Deut. 34:10.
57. See above, ER, 19, and Rashi on Exod. 4:14.
58. See above, ER, chap. 2, n. 16.
59. According to Friedmann (Introduction, p. 60), the word "Talmud" is a scribe's interpolation; hence the entire phrase would read "Midrash of Halakot and 'Aggadot."
60. The words which follow, "Solomon before the Holy One," are, at the suggestion of Leon Nemoy, deleted as a reader's gloss.

Holy One, Isaiah was saying: In me there is not [deceit]. . . . [I promise you] that through words of Torah your eyes will see [the King in His beauty].

They shall behold a land stretching afar (ibid.)—that is, the righteous shall behold the Halakot which the Holy One had in mind nine hundred and seventy-four generations before the world was created[61] and which subsequently He came and told to Israel.

And your eyes shall see (Mal. 1:5) the measure of justice; *and you shall say: The Lord is great (ibid.).* These are the utterances of thanksgiving for instruction by chastisements.[62]

The Holy One spoke thus to Israel: My children, read Scripture, recite Mishnah, and continue to do both until I Myself come and tell you whether a thing is ritually clean or whether it is ritually unclean, and getting, indeed, to its very essence in order to determine whether it is unclean or clean. At that time the unclean will have been determined properly as unclean and the clean determined properly as clean. Continue then, as is said, to *sow to yourselves righteousness,* [*Torah*], and *then* [*in the world-to-come*] *you will reap loving-kindness,* [*knowledge of Torah's secrets*][63] (Hos. 10:12).

---

61. See above, ER, 9.
62. See Ber 9:5.
63. So interpreted by Haida.

CHAPTER (14) 15

Encounter with a man who had Scripture but not Mishnah

Summary

The goodness of life is not to be spurned or belittled, for it gives us a taste of God's bounty in the world-to-come. But only after we have been purified in this world, will we be deemed worthy of the bounty in the world-to-come. This bounty is intended only for the seed of Jacob, who are spoken of as *blind and lame* (Jer. 31:7) because they are blind to temptation and do not run after what is forbidden. They are committed instead to right conduct and/or to study of Torah (ER, 69).

As to study of Torah and its effect upon man's conduct, a dialogue ensues between the author and a man who had learning in Scripture but not in Mishnah. The man asked: Even though Scripture says that God gives food to all flesh, is it not true that a man has to get his food for himself? So it would seem, answers the author, but, in fact, it is not so, for without wisdom or understanding—gifts from God—no man could sustain himself even for a single hour. God's greatest gift, however, is the *Fear of the Lord* (Isa. 33:6) set forth in the Torah.

The questioner then asked: Why does the Holy One love words of Torah more than all His other handiwork (ER, 70)? Because, the author answers, words of Torah teach Israel the performance of commandments and thus guide Israel to life in the world-to-come.

The questioner went on to ask: Which should a man put first—his love for Torah or for Israel? The author answers: Israel, the emissary who communicates God's will to the world.

The questioner asked further: At Israel's first banishment from the Land, God told Israel how long they would stay banished. Why did He not do the same at Israel's second banishment? Because, the author answers, during the days of the First Temple, though Israel were idolaters, right conduct characterized them. Besides, after being banished, they wept and followed the way God had laid out for them. If we did the same, God's mercies would flood in on us as upon them (ER, 71).

Upon the questioner's saying that he scarcely dared put such questions to the author, the author responds by thanking the questioner because he had moved him to weigh matters of Torah which he had not examined before (ER, 72).

Chapter (14) 15

ER, *p.* 69 Whenever a man spurns the good life in this world, it is a bad omen for him. With whom may he be contrasted? With [the servant of] a king who [at the beginning of a festival] was invited by the king for a one-day stay with him, and the servant was grateful; the king then invited him for a two-day stay, and he was even more grateful; for a three-day stay, and he was that much more grateful; for a four-day stay, and he was still more grateful. How much more and more grateful then would the servant have been had the king invited him to stay for all eight days of the festival!

[On the other hand, consider the ingratitude of another servant], to whom his king said, "You are invited to join me at a feast for thirty days."[1] After having tasted the king's bounty for fifteen days, the servant said, "I don't care to stay for the remaining fifteen days—take them back as a gift from me," thus throwing them, so to speak, in the king's face. And so this servant revealed himself as grossly ungrateful before the king. Can such behavior be justified? It certainly is not justifiable. How then are we, the children of Israel, to behave toward our King? We, Jacob's seed, are under obligation to bless, praise, exalt, magnify, and hallow the name of the Holy One at whose word the world came into being, blessed be He, for by the delight He brought us with His presence [at our festivals] in this world, He gave us a foretaste of His bounty in the world-to-come. Thus He says to each one of us: Bide a while until the time for [endless] feasting comes. Why does He keep us waiting in this world? To purge us of our sins, so that we can enter, purified, into the life of the world-to-come. There is, indeed, no other people or kingdom from one end to the other end of the world that the Holy One brought into being, [no people or kingdom] but the seed of Jacob whom He intended to be inheritors of life in the world-to-come. Of them He said: *I will bring them from the north country*—[that is, from places in this world where they have been exiled]—*and with them the blind and the lame* (Jer. 31:7) [that is, those who are blind to temptation and those who do not run after what is forbidden. In other words, *the blind and the lame* are] the unlettered in Torah who conduct themselves uprightly in obedience to the precepts of ethical conduct as well as to all other precepts and who, it goes without saying, keep far away from [sexual] transgression, larceny, and any other kind of offensive behavior. Of such people "R. Simeon said . . . One who desists from transgressing is granted a reward like one who performs a precept" (Mak 3:15).

In another comment, *the blind* are taken to mean the Sages and their disciples [who shut their eyes to every kind of temptation] and devote themselves to Scripture, to Mishnah, and to Midrash of Halakot and 'Aggadot.[2] Of these men the Psalmist says, *Blessed are they who see to it that their way be perfect in order that they may walk in the Lord's Torah* (Ps. 119:1), *For the way of God is most perfect, the word of the Lord most pure* (Ps. 18:31).

There are three kinds of men—all reasonably worthy—who are to

---

1. Cf. ER, 11, and B. Ket 8a.

2. Or: "Midrash, Halakot, and 'Aggadot." But see Rashi on B.Kid 49a, and Sif Deut. 30 (ed. Finkelstein, [Breslau, 1936–39], p. 339).

be pitied: (1) men unlettered in Torah who put into practice precepts of right conduct and obey other <precepts as well>, who keep far from [sexual] transgression, larceny, and from any other kind of offensive behavior, [but are to be pitied because they know no Torah];[3] (2) men who have come to knowledge of Scripture and of Mishnah, but have no heart for either [and so are to be pitied]; and (3) Sages and their disciples who all but give their lives to Scripture, Mishnah, Midrash of Halaḵoṯ and 'Aggaḏoṯ,[4] [and yet are to be pitied because they regret the sacrifices they have made for the sake of Torah].[5] All three are meant by Isaiah in the words *Hear, ye who are deaf* (Isa. 42:18).

[With regard to men illiterate in Torah but sagacious in the give-and-take of trade], one is reminded of the parable of a mortal king who had many children and servants, many of them lame, many mute, many blind. Some had knowledge of Scripture. Some had knowledge of Mishnah. Some had experience in the give-and-take of trade. It goes without saying that the king had to have engagements and business with each of the three. Still, when he had to make an estimate [of a planned undertaking], he went for advice not to those who had Mishnah nor to those who had Scripture; <instead he went to those> who, [to be sure, had neither, but] were sagacious. With regard to such men Isaiah says, *Ye who [now vaunt yourselves on your sagacity, but] are deaf [to Torah's call], come ye to heed it (ibid.).* And with regard to the other two kinds of men mentioned earlier as reasonably worthy who are to be pitied,[6] Isaiah says, *I will lead the blind by a road they knew not* (Isa. 42:16).[7]

In another comment on *the blind and the lame* (Jer. 31:7), these are taken to be men who have come to possess knowledge of Scripture and Mishnah but are marred—[blinded and lamed]—by filthy ways <and indecencies such as one cannot even give a name to>. Yet it is difficult for the Father of mercy to cause even men like these to perish out of the world.[8]

In contrast to these, what clause of the verse in hand describes those Sages of Israel and their disciples who all but give their lives to Scripture, to Mishnah, to Halaḵoṯ and 'Aggaḏoṯ? You ask what clause? It is the one immediately following the words *the lame and the blind,* and
ER, *p.* 70 it reads *The woman with child* | *and her that travaileth with child together (ibid.),* its reference being to disciples of the wise who travel in travail to the four ends of the world—south, north, east, and west—each of

---

3. "but are to be pitied . . . know no Torah"—*YY.*
4. See n. 2.
5. The melancholy of the student. Schick.
6. Literally, "With regard to these and those."
7. Cf. the somewhat similar comment in PR 14:13 (YJS, *18, 1,* 289).
8. Thus when Elisha ben Abuyah, a scholar who led an immoral life, died, he was spared stringent judgment and was left for a while in a kind of limbo until his disciple R. Meir intervened in his behalf. See B.Ḥaḡ 15b.

them hoping for and looking forward to, indeed craving, the discovery of even as little as one door into words of Torah and thereby soothing his spirit.

The verse in Jeremiah that we are considering goes on to say, *A great company shall they return hither (ibid.),* which is to say that men, women, and little ones, young people and old people, all of them, will feel the need both to thank Him and to pour out entreaties for mercy as they seek knowledge from Him,[9] as is said, *The earth shall be full of the knowledge of the Lord, as the waters cover the sea* (Isa. 11:9).

Once while I was traveling from one place to another, I came upon a man who had learning in Scripture but not in Mishnah. The man said, "My master, there is a certain thing I want to say to you, but I am afraid to say it because you may be angry with me." I replied, "If you ask me something pertaining to words of Torah, why should I be angry with you?" Whereupon the man said: "My master, why does Scripture say, *To Him . . . who giveth food to all* [*human*] *flesh* (Ps. 136:25), and then say, *God . . . giveth to the beast his food* (Ps. 147:9), [as though God gave equally to man and beast]? Actually, is it not true that a man has to get his food for himself?" I answered: "My son, is not the way life goes that a man works with his hands [to provide for himself], and the Holy One blesses all the work of his hands, as is said in the verse *That the Lord thy God may bless thee in all the work of thy hands* (Deut. 14:29)? But lest it be thought that God's blessing comes to a man who sits in idleness, the verse ends with the injunction *which thou must do (ibid.).*" Thereupon my questioner said to me, "This reply supports what I implied in my question—it's a logical reply." I told him: "My son, my Father in heaven has deigned to give me the wisdom and understanding, the knowledge and insight with which to answer the question you put to me. Go out and look at a simpleton who is wandering about the marketplace. Once wisdom, understanding, knowledge, and insight were taken from him, could he possibly sustain himself even for a single hour? No, nor could any human being. Should wisdom, understanding, knowledge, and insight be taken from men, they would be like cattle, beasts, fowl, and <other> creatures, which God created with the breath of life in them, on the face of the earth. Therefore, I insist, calling heaven and earth to witness, that the Holy One sits and apportions different kinds of food equally to the earth's inhabitants and to all His handiwork in the world He created—from man to cattle, to creeping things, and to birds of heaven."

[In connection with God's generosity to all His creation is cited]

---

9. The comment anticipates the thought of the next verse, *They shall come with weeping, and with supplications will I lead them as I cause them to walk to rivers of water* (Jer. 31:8)—the water being knowledge of Torah and of the Lord.

the verse *The fear of the Lord which is His treasure* (Isa. 33:6). A parable of a mortal king who had many children and servants will serve to explain the verse. When he wished to admonish them—each one of them in his own person—and when he saw that each refused to accept his admonition, he wrote out all he had to say on a piece of paper and hung it in the outer courtyard as an open letter for all people to read. And the crier went forth from the king's presence and proclaimed, "Whoever comes <and reads> this letter will receive bread and provisions from the king." [The king is the Holy One. His children and servants are all the nations of the world. When each in turn refused to be admonished by Him, He offered His admonition—Torah—to any who would come and read it], and it was the house of Israel that then came to partake of the Divine fare of Torah. Hence, when a man comes to understand Scripture and Mishnah and teaches [himself] out of them fear of Heaven and the practice of doing good, the words of Torah feed, nourish, and sustain him until he goes to his eternal home, as is said, *Faithfulness until thy time [comes] will give thee a hoard of deliverance, wisdom, knowledge, and the fear of the Lord which is His treasure* (Isa. 33:10).

My questioner said to me further, "My master, why are words of Torah more beloved <by the Holy One> than all the world's inhabitants and all His handiwork in the world He created?" I said, "My son,
ER, *p.* 71 it is because | words of Torah cause the balance to tip the scales of merit in Israel's favor, training Israel in the performance of commandments and thus guiding them to life in the world-to-come." [In connection with Torah's guidance of Israel, consider] the parable of a mortal king in whose household with its many children dwells a venerable servant teaching the king's children proper conduct and the performance of good deeds. On each and every day that the children and their teacher come into the king's presence, he puts all other matters aside, and gives voice to his appreciation of the venerable servant in his household, saying, "Were it not for the venerable servant who teaches my children right conduct and the performance of good deeds, what would happen to <my children>?" So words of Torah [serve to teach Israel right conduct and performance of good deeds]. Because words of Torah cause the balance to tip the scales of merit in Israel's favor, teaching Israel obedience to precepts and thus guiding them to life in the world-to-come, therefore words of Torah are more beloved by the Holy One than all earth's inhabitants and all His handiwork in the world He created.

My questioner said to me further: "My master, two things in my heart I love with a very great love—Torah and Israel. But I do not know which of them to put first." I replied: "Generally, people say that Torah is to be put first, in keeping with the verse in which Torah says, *The Lord made me as the beginning of His way* (Prov. 8:22). But I would say, Israel <come first>, in keeping with the verse *Israel is the Lord's hallowed portion, His first fruits of the increase"* (Jer. 2:3). [To show that Israel is to be put first], consider the following parable of a king with wife and children in his household. The king published an edict [but his subjects refused to accept it]. Were it not for the queen and the princes, who with their customary loyalty to the king undertook to present the edict again to the people, it would never have reached them. [That it did become available to them was due to the queen and the princes, who], acting as the king's envoys, [took the edict to the people. In short, Israel as God's "helpmeet" took up the rejected Torah and has ever since been preaching it to the other nations of the world].[10] Hence *Israel is the Lord's hallowed portion.* Torah, to be sure, says, *The Lord made me as the beginning of His way.* Nevertheless, in Israel there is a quality [so appealing to Him] that Israel can claim precedence, saying *From afar the Lord appeared unto me, saying, "Yea, I love thee with an everlasting love"* (Jer. 31:2).

My questioner further said to me: "My master, Israel has been banished twice, once in the days of the First Temple, and once again in the days of the Second Temple. Why was the period of Israel's banishment <after the destruction of the First Temple> specified, but not specified after the destruction of the Second Temple?"[11] I replied: "My son, though those who lived during the days of the First Temple were certainly idolaters, right conduct characterized them. And what was the right conduct which characterized them? Charity and loving-kindness, as is said. . . ."[12]

A parable of a mortal king who had many sons and servants—many lame,[13] many mute, many deaf, many blind: when their deeds became offensive, he vowed that he would leave them. When he did leave them, they wept and followed him. Thereupon he said: "Stop following me. After thirty days I shall return to you." So it was with the King of kings and the children of Israel, [many of whom were marred in different ways]. Some of them possessed no more than Scripture, some no more than Mishnah, some were tradesmen [incapable of discussing either]. When their defects became vexatious to Him, God vowed that He would leave them. When He did leave them, they wept and followed Him. Thereupon He said: "Stop following Me. [After seventy years], I shall return to you."

Now, [after the Second Temple's destruction], what are we to do?

---

10. In R and V, several lacunae make the parable all but unintelligible. Leon Nemoy provided its interpretation.

11. *'Ubb'a 'aḥăron* is a *lapsus calami* for *'ubb'a-'aḥăron.* So Leon Nemoy.

12. Another lacuna. The inference may be that Israel's exercise of charity and loving-kindness will some day bring Israel's present banishment to an end.

In B.Yoma 9b, however, the men of the First Temple are charged not only with idolatry, but with unchastity and bloodshed as well.

13. Read *pisḥin,* "lame," instead of *piḳḥin,* "clever, physically perfect," which seems to be a miswriting.

Pour out pleas for mercy and entreat Him with supplications and prayer and find a doorway[14] into words of Torah among all the doorways that God opened for us through His servants the Prophets. Thus it is written, *Yet even now, saith the Lord, turn ye unto Me with all your heart* (Joel 2:12).[15] Perhaps His many mercies will flood in for our sake, and He will fulfill in our behalf what His lips uttered to us in the words *The breaker is gone up before them . . . and the Lord at the head of them* (Mic. 2:13). Then my questioner said to me, "May your spirit meditate serenely, for you have strongly moved my spirit to meditate serenely
ER, *p.* 72 with benefit to me." I said to him: | "One verse, to be sure, says, *Answer one who is truly a fool on the level of his ignorance, lest* [*by arguing with him*], *he comes to deem himself all the wiser*[16] (Prov. 26:5). But another verse tells us, *Answer one who deems himself a fool* [*because of his ignorance*] *not on the level of his ignorance, lest thou grow to be like him*[17] (Prov. 26:4). For in a Mishnah it is written, 'Be eager to teach[18] Torah. At the same time [know] how to deal with a confirmed heretic' " (Ab̲ 2:14). My questioner replied, "The questions I had in my mind I scarcely dared put to you." I replied: "I swear by the [Temple] service that all the questions you have put to me, no man ever put to me before. And but for you I would not have put my mind to them."

Blessed be He whose presence is everywhere. Blessed be He who chose the Sages and their disciples to teach us the Mishnah: "Go as a voluntary exile to a place where Torah is taught. Do not say that the Torah will seek you out. It is those you study with, and 'not reliance on your understanding alone' (Prov. 3:5), that will help make it your permanent possession" (Ab̲ 4:14).

---

14. "A doorway"—R. Friedmann, erroneously, "another doorway."

15. "The Prophets have assured Israel that when they return to God, He would return to them" (Louis Ginzberg in *OT,* p. 271, n. 57).

16. The word *iwwelet,* "folly," is here equated with "ignorance." JV: *Answer a fool according to his folly, lest he be wise in his own eyes.*

17. The implication: your failure to teach Torah will reduce your own understanding of it. JV: *Answer not a fool according to his folly, lest thou also be like unto him.*

For another way of reconciling the two verses see B.Shab 30b.

18. Usually read "Be eager to study." But, depending on vocalization, *llmd* may mean "to study," or "to teach."

CHAPTER (15) 16

Israel increase their merit by setting out for themselves sundry practices

Summary

The author narrates an encounter with another man who knew Scripture but not Mishnah. The man first asked whence the precept of washing the hands came, since it was not prescribed at Mount Sinai. The author answered: There are many practices, many of grave import, which Scripture did not think it necessary to prescribe, but instead put upon Israel the obligation of prescribing them, saying, Let Israel increase their merit by setting out for themselves the precepts governing such practices. Thus the Sages concluded that obedience to the precept of washing the hands for the sake of holiness was a requirement for all—priests, Levites, and Israelites. In response to further inquiry from the questioner, the author discusses certain details in the ritual slaughter of animals as set forth by the Sages (ER, 72); eating human blood which is prohibited by the Sages' reasoning; eating the fat of an animal which is not an offering, likewise prohibited through the Sages' reasoning; cheating a non-Jew (ER, 73) which is similarly prohibited. The questioner by way of agreement then cites an experience (ER, 74) to illustrate the gravity of such an offense, even if unintentional. Then the questioner inquires about sexual relations with one's daughter which, unlike such relations with one's daughter's daughter, are not specifically prohibited in Scripture. Once again the author demonstrates how inference from relevant texts demonstrates the gravity of sexual relations with one's daughter.

The questioner then asked: Which is the graver offense—sexual intercourse of a woman with a man who has a discharge from his member or sexual intercourse of a man with a woman who is menstruating? Though the latter is not clearly prohibited in Scripture, while the former is, the author demonstrates the greater gravity of the latter act—of sexual intercourse, indeed any kind of intimacy, with a woman who is menstruating (ER, 75). And to prove his point, the author tells the story of a scholar who died in the middle of his years, because he failed to be scrupulous in regard to minor intimacies with his wife during the seven days following her menstruation.

The author then shows how the return for transgression is further transgressions. Thus a man who lies to one person (ER, 76) will ultimately lie to everyone. Rudeness, arrogance, cheating, and miserly denial of gifts to the poor similarly grow like leprous spots in a man. Those who plot evil, who distort the words of others, who smite in secret, who mock people in public and cause strife will be served like Korah and his assembly.

There are also those who are unable to bequeath anything to their children, but if by chance they do have something to bequeath to their children, they cause them to be unable to bequeath anything, in their turn, to their children. Among such are dice throwers, usurers, informers, and hypocrites (ER, 77).

On the other hand, those who suffer insults but do not inflict them, who hear themselves reviled but do not answer back, who act through love and rejoice in Divine chastisement, will ultimately be like *the sun when he goeth forth in his might* (Judg. 5:3). They who have a humble opinion of themselves, who are mindful of their own shortcomings, who overcome their Impulse to evil, will prove to be God's own chosen.

The author then goes back to discuss offenses in sexual life: a man's failure to immerse in a ritual bath after an involuntary emission of semen; a woman's failure to immerse during her period even if her discharge of blood amounts to no more than a mustard seed's bulk at a time.

According to one opinion, the prohibition of sexual intercourse for seven days following a woman's menstruation is to help fulfill the command to be fruitful and multiply: the husband's enforced abstinence will make him yearn all the more for his wife (ER, 79).

The author then discourses on related offenses: gluttony, slander, cheating, and, once again, men's failure to keep apart from their wives during the period of seven days following their menstruation (ER, 80).

Chapter (15) 16

ER, *p.* 72 *cont'd* A friend of the questioner [in the previous chapter] who also knew Scripture but not Mishnah[1] came and sat near him, [then asked me whence came the precept of washing the hands]. I replied, "My son, washing the hands is prescribed by Torah." "But, my master," my questioner persisted, "it was not prescribed to us at Mount Sinai." Thereupon I said: "My son, we have many practices, many of grave import, which Scripture did not think it necessary to prescribe, but instead put upon Israel the obligation of prescribing them, saying, Let Israel increase their merit by setting out for themselves the precepts governing such practices. Proof that Israel did so, you can see for yourself. When Israel were in the wilderness, wandering around in it, the Holy One said to Moses: *Go unto the people and sanctify them today and tomorrow* (Exod. 19:10). By 'sanctify the people,' taught the Sages, was meant 'immerse them in the ritual bath.' Likewise we infer the precept of washing the hands from the Torah, for it was [first] said to Moses and to Aaron and to his sons as well, *Thou shalt make a laver of brass* (Exod. 30:18), which Moses,[2] Aaron, and his sons were to use for washing, as is said, *when they go into the Tent of Meeting* (Exod. 30:20). But with regard to Israelites, where does Scripture command washing the hands? In the verse *Sanctify yourselves*[3] *and be holy* (Lev. 11:44). On

1. Friedmann (n. 1) suggests that the man may have been a Christian. But, according to L. Ginzberg, anti-Pharisaic sectaries never disappeared completely from among the Jews. In the eighth century C.E., one offshoot of these sectaries came to be known as Karaites (*OT,* p. 275, n. 121).

2. During all the forty years in the wilderness, Moses is said to have served as High Priest. Hence, ER assumes that Moses, not referred to by name in Exod. 30:20, was also required to wash his hands. On Moses' serving as High Priest, see PR 14:11 (YJS, *18, 1,* 285).

3. The precept was given at the conclusion of a list of swarming things, the eating or touching of which is deemed detestable.

the basis of this verse Rabban Gamaliel [the elder] observed Levitical precautions of self-purification when he ate everyday food.[4] He was wont to say that obedience to the precept of washing the hands for the sake of holiness was required not only of priests, but of priests, Levites, and Israelites—required of every one of them, as Scripture tells us, *The Lord spoke unto Moses, saying: Speak unto*[5] *the congregation of the children of Israel, and say unto them: Ye shall be holy* (Lev. 19:1–2). Hence it is said, When a man belittles the washing of hands, it is an omen of ill fortune for him. Of such a man Scripture says, *Should it come to pass, when he heareth the words of this curse, that he bless himself in his heart, saying: I shall have peace . . . stuffing my gut though my hands thirst for* [*purifying*] *water*[6] *. . . the anger of the Lord shall be kindled against that man* (Deut. 29:-18–19). This is the verse leading us to conclude that it is an omen of ill fortune for a man to contemn the washing of hands."[7]

My new questioner pressed me further: "My master, there is no precept that prescribes the ritual slaughter of an animal by cutting its throat." I replied: My son, how can you think such a thing? To begin with, is not the very precept of ritual slaughter derived from the Torah?[8] [It was thence our Sages drew the inference that an animal intended to be used as everyday food is to be slaughtered in the very same way as an animal intended to be used as a burnt offering, a sin offering, a guilt offering, or any other kind of offering—in short, like all of them.][9] And the Sages went on to proffer precise requirements for obedience to the precept, a requirement such as the following, for example: "If a man slaughtered a bird by [cutting through] either [the windpipe or the gullet], or slaughtered an animal by cutting through both, the slaughtering is valid; so, too, if [he cut through] the greater part of each" (Ḥul 2:1). On the other hand, if in slaughtering an animal, the slaughterer deliberately "misplaces"[10] his cut

---

4. Or, "common, unhallowed food," that is, food not consecrated for sacrifice or offering.

5. MT: *unto all.* See B.Nid 6b and Ber 53b.

6. JV: *that the watered be swept away with the dry.* But, following Haida, *rawah,* "watered," is taken to mean, "that which is to be sated," hence "gut," and *ṣĕme'ah,* "dry," as "thirsty for moisture"—for water which purifies the hands.

7. He will become poor. See B.Shab 62b.

8. [What the Hebrew says literally is, "Is not *šĕḥiṭah* itself part of the corpus of the Torah?" What does the author mean to say by it? I suppose that the Torah uses *šḥṭ* when speaking of sacrificial slaughtering; since in sacrificial offering the procedure was to cut the animal's throat with a sharp knife, and since slaughtering for food is essentially a private sacrificial act, lawful slaughtering must likewise be accomplished by cutting the throat with a sharp knife. Cf. Gesenius-Brown ("usually terminus technicus for killing sacrifice"). In other words, *šḥṭ* implies "cutting the animal's throat"; hence the procedure is of Scriptural origin, and there was no need for the Torah to say expressly "by way of cutting the animal's throat." L. N.]

9. See Deut. 12:21.

10. "Misplacement" is "the performance of *šĕḥiṭah* upon the upper part of the

ER, *p.* 73 by ever so little, | he betrays himself as a man with a greedy eye.

Blessed be the Preserver [of justice] in the world. Blessed be He before whom no one is favored over another, for a man who invalidates the ritual slaughter by deliberately "misplacing" his cut—that is by making it high on the animal's throat in order to appropriate for himself a greater amount of flesh from its body—will have his possessions seized and given to another, as is said, *He that augmenteth his substance by interest and increase, gathereth it for him that is gracious to the poor* (Prov. 28:8).

My questioner pressed me still further: "According to Torah, the eating of human blood is not prohibited." I asked him, "My son, what makes you think so?" He replied, "My master, Scripture says, *Ye shall eat no manner of blood, whether it be of fowl or of beast* (Lev. 7:26)—no mention of human blood here!" I said: "May not the matter be resolved by inference? If [eating the blood] of cattle, beast, or fowl, all customarily regarded as edible, is forbidden to us, surely the blood of man, who is not customarily regarded as edible, should be forbidden to us. Besides in such statements as *Only be steadfast in not eating the blood* (Deut. 12:23), and *The life of all flesh is the blood thereof* (Lev. 17:15), Scripture implies without any doubt the prohibition against eating human blood. Even more specifically Scripture asserts further, *Ye shall eat the blood of no manner of flesh (ibid.),* be it blood from the flesh of a clean animal or of an unclean animal, *For the life of all flesh is the blood thereof (ibid.).* By the [Temple] service, I swear—even eating the blood of a living creature, whether it is blood that spurts out from a wound and coagulates, or blood that oozes out and is drawn off into a vessel, is likewise forbidden, for the general prohibition in Scripture applies to any kind of blood."

My questioner said further: "My master, I take it that eating the fat[11] of an animal from which an offering is made to the Lord is prohibited, but that the eating of fat from an animal which is not an offering is permitted." I asked, "On what ground do you think so?" He replied, "My master, Scripture says, *Whosoever eateth the fat of the beast, of which men present an offering . . . the soul that eateth* [*its fat*] *shall be cut off from his people* (Lev. 7:25), [but says nothing of the fat of an animal which is not presented as an offering]." To this I answered: "My son, observe the power of Torah, how farsighted it is, how profoundly perceptive are all its utterances! Each and every word in it is expressive of wisdom,

---

windpipe, at a point which is not valid for *šěḥiṭah.*" See Maimonides' Code V, III, iii, 12 (YJS, *16,* 273). "Misplacing" is done so that in selling an upper joint of the animal, very little or no meat is left near or on its head. The purpose is to augment profit, meat from the body of the animal being more profitable than meat from the head.

11. Fat, *ḥeleḇ;* the portion of the fat of a kosher domestic animal which it is forbidden to eat; in sacrifices this fat was burnt upon the altar.

understanding, and prescience. Thus, in order that no man say to himself the eating of fat of an animal from which an offering is brought to the Lord is prohibited, but the eating of fat of an animal from which no offering is brought to the Lord is permitted, Scripture, adverting to the matter in another passage, strongly asserts that as the eating of blood is prohibited, so is the eating of fat: [*Neither fat nor blood* (Lev. 3:17)]. *It shall be a perpetual statute (ibid.)*—from now to the world's end; *throughout your generations (ibid.)*—the practice is to continue for generations [and generations]; *in all your dwellings (ibid.)*—in the Land and outside the Land; *neither fat nor blood (ibid.)*— as eating blood is prohibited, so is eating fat prohibited." "But," asked the questioner, "[if the primary purpose of the words just cited is absolutely to prohibit the eating of fat], why does Scripture here mention blood as well as fat?" "In order," [I replied], "to stress the parallel: the eating of blood is like the eating of fat and the eating of fat is like the eating of blood. Transgression with regard to either is punishable by death through excision—[that is, punishable by death at the age of fifty].[12] Hence Scripture's prohibition *neither fat nor blood.* In connection with this prohibition the Sages taught in a Mishnah: 'If when a man refrains from the eating of blood, an act which his soul naturally rejects, he gains a reward, how much greater then his reward of a gain in merit for himself and his generations and the generations of his generations to the end of all generations, if he refrains from cheating and fornication, acts which a man's soul inclines to and desires' " (Mak 3:15).

My questioner asked further: "My master, is cheating a non-Jew[13] permitted?" I exclaimed, "My son, what makes you think such a thing?" He replied, "Such cheating was not forbidden at Mount Sinai."[14] To this I said: Is not the answer to your question implicit in the principle I set out previously? | That is, there are many precepts **ER,** ***p.*** 74
of conduct, a number of them grave indeed, which Scripture did not think it necessary to state explicitly. Instead, responsibility was given to Israel to discern and set out these precepts for themselves and thereby increase Israel's merit. True, Scripture does say, *Honor thy father and thy*

---

12. The phrase "death and excision" is a hendiadys, "death through excision," which, according to a Baraita in B.MḲ 28a, is death at the age of fifty.

Such punishment for eating fat is mentioned in Lev. 7:25 with regard to animals that are brought as offerings, but it is not mentioned in Lev. 3:17, where the eating of the fat of animals that are not brought as offerings is prohibited. Hence the statement at the end of Lev. 3:17, asserting that both blood and fat are prohibited, is taken to intimate that, like the eating of blood, eating of fat from an animal not brought as an offering also incurs the penalty of excision. In a letter, Professor David Weiss-Halivni helped in interpreting this difficult passage.

13. Reading *'aḥ,* "brother," as a contraction of *'aḥer,* "other," that is, a non-Jew. So *Torah šĕlemah, 16,* 111, and Ginzberg, *OT,* p. 292, n. 8.

14. [That is, the prohibition of cheating is not included in the Ten Commandments; see below. L. N.]

mother. Thou shalt not murder. Thou shalt not commit adultery. Thou shalt not steal. Thou shalt not bear false witness against thy neighbor. Thou shalt not covet (Exod. 20:12–14). The reference to neighbor apparently does not prohibit, according to you, cheating a non-Jew.[15] [But Israel lives not only by the precepts of the Torah (the Written Law), but also by the precepts of Halakah (the Oral Law), precepts which Israel discerned and set out for themselves]. Therefore I would say, Israel is disciplined by Torah's entire range—[both the Written and the Oral Law]—even as Israel's spirit is lifted by Torah's entire range—[both the Written and the Oral Law]—as is said, *In the night I desire Thine* [*Oral Law*], *even as in the morning, my spirit within me seeks*[16] *Thy* [*Written Law*].[17] *For when Thy judgments are wrought on earth, the inhabitants of the world learn righteousness*[18] (Isa. 26:9). From Torah's entire range we come to know therefore that for eight reasons the world may be destroyed and that for four reasons the world may go on in orderly fashion. The eight reasons for which the world may be destroyed are these: (1) miscarriage of justice, (2) idolatry, (3) incest, (4) bloodshed, (5) profanation of God's name, (6) lewd speech, (7) arrogance, and (8) slander. Covetousness is sometimes added to the list.

For these eight reasons, some former generations were rooted out of the world. For these eight reasons the generation of the flood who *said unto God: "Depart from us, for we desire not the knowledge of Thy ways"* (Job 21:14) was rooted out of the world.[19] For these eight reasons the generation of the dispersion of the races of man was rooted out of the world. Since Scripture says that in the beginning *The whole earth was of one language and of one speech* (Gen. 11:1), the inference is that mankind, for these eight reasons, was rooted up from its original settlement and scattered throughout the world.[20] For these same eight reasons, the people of Sodom were rooted out of the world. Since Scripture says,

---

15. See n. 13 above.

16. JV: *seeks Thee earnestly.* But *šḥr*, "seek earnestly," may also mean "seek early in the morning."

17. See above ER, 10, and n. 24.

18. [(a) The point is not that "neighbor" does not include the non-Jew (*'ḥ*[r], "the other, the non-Jew")—the point is that cheating is not mentioned in the Ten Commandments, and the author admits that much to his interrogator: "You are right, there is no mention of cheating of a non-Jew" (I must confess I wonder if the equation *'ḥ*, "brother"=*'ḥr*, "the other, the non-Jew," is a later development, and if the author had really meant *'ḥ* = Israelite). (b) The verse Isa. 26:9 need not be interpreted as referring to the two Torahs, but rather as JV interprets it: "Pursuant to the words of the Torah one is chastised (whether one wrongs an Israelite or a Gentile), and pursuant to them one is healed, as it is said . . . *the inhabitants of the world* (Israelites and Gentiles both); cf. Friedmann's note 14, etc." The author then proceeds to cite examples of people who were uprooted from the world for transgression of several principles, not all of Scriptural formulation. Some of them were not Israelites, showing that these principles apply to all. L. N.]

19. See Ginzberg, *Legends, 1,* 152–54, and PRKM 26:2, pp. 387–88.

20. See Ginzberg, *Legends, 1,* 179–81.

The men of Sodom were wicked and sinners against the Lord exceedingly (Gen. 13:13), the inference is that for these eight reasons they were rooted out of the world.[21] For these eight reasons Pharaoh was likewise rooted out of the world. For in quoting Pharaoh as saying *Who is the Lord that I should hearken unto His voice* (Exod. 5:2), Scripture implies that for [some of] these eight reasons he was rooted out of the world. For these eight reasons Sennacherib, king of Assyria, was also rooted out of the world. For in quoting Sennacherib as saying *Hath any of the gods of the nations ever delivered his land out of the hand of the king of Assyria?* (2 Kings 18:35), Scripture implies that for [some of] these eight reasons Sennacherib was rooted out of the world. For these eight reasons Nebuchadnezzar, king of Babylon, was rooted out of the world. For in saying *Thou saidst in thy heart: I will ascend into heaven, above the stars of God will I exalt my throne* (Isa. 14:13), Scripture implies that for [some of] these eight reasons Nebuchadnezzar was rooted out of the world.

And for four reasons—charity, justice, truth, and harmony—the world may go on in orderly fashion.

My same questioner then said: "Listen, O master, to what happened to me. I sold four *kor*[22] of dates to a non-Jew, having measured them out *kor* by *kor* in a dimly lighted room. <The customer said to me>: 'You and God in heaven know the measure you are giving me.' After I measured out the dates [I realized] that I had given him[23] |
three *sĕ'ah* of dates less [than he had paid for]. I took his money, ER, *p.* 75
however, and with it purchased a jar of oil which I put on the very spot where I had turned over the dates to the non-Jew. The jar split apart, and the oil was all spilled and went to waste."[24] Thereupon I said to my questioner: "My son, Scripture tells us *Thou shalt not take advantage of thy neighbor* (Lev. 19:13), which is to say that your neighbor—[whether Jew or non-Jew]—is to be treated like your kin, and your kin like your neighbor. Thus you ought to know that cheating a non-Jew is considered plain cheating.[25] Indeed, because the Holy One saw men

---

21. See *Ibid.,* pp. 245–50.

22. A *kor* is 30 *sĕ'ah.* One *sĕ'ah* equals the contents of one hundred and forty-four eggs.

23. [*mittoḵ še-mĕdadtiw* does *not* mean "after I measured . . . (I realized)," which creates the *false* impression that the seller made an honest mistake. Far from it—he acted with larceny aforethought, undismayed by the buyer's appeal, "I can't see how you measure, but God can, so for your own sake try not to cheat." Hence the correct translation is "I measured out (the dates) so cleverly that I kept three of the four *sĕ'ah* back." L. N.]

24. [I'd insert here the implied question: ("Tell me, has the loss of the oil expiated my sin of cheating the Gentile, or am I still liable to chastisement for it?"). L. N.]

25. The words "And it goes without saying even that of a kinsman *('aḥ),*" which follow, are omitted as in the parallel in Yalḳuṭ, *3, Ṣaw,* 505. So suggested in *Torah šĕlemah, 16,* 111.

On the prohibition of cheating a non-Jew, see below, ER, 140; B.BḲ 113a–b; Šulḥan 'aruḵ, Ḥošen mišpaṭ, 348:2, 359:1; and *ET, 5,* 487–90, *s.v. "Gezel hag-goy."*

in their iniquitousness take advantage of one another and cheat and rob one another, the Holy One, returning to the matter in post-Mosaic Scripture, made explicit, through the priest Ezekiel the son of Buzi, the fate of the man who takes advantage of others: *As for his father, because he heartlessly took advantage*[26] . . . *behold, he dieth for his iniquity*" (Ezek. 18:18).

Next my questioner asked me, "My master, which is the graver offense—sexual intercourse with a daughter or with a daughter's daughter?" I replied, "My son, intercourse with a daughter is incest and intercourse with a daughter's daughter is incest—in this respect, daughter and daughter's daughter are considered the same." He pressed on: "But in the Torah, my master, [intercourse with a daughter is not expressly forbidden]; it does not say, Do not uncover the nakedness of thy daughter!" I replied: "My son, is it not easy to draw the proper inference? For if intercourse with a son's daughter or a daughter's daughter is forbidden, is not intercourse with one's daughter forbidden all the more so? Thus in saying *Thou shalt not uncover the nakedness of a woman and her daughter* (Lev. 18:17), Scripture implies that such intercourse is forbidden between the daughter of a woman and the woman's husband, between the daughter of a woman by a previous marriage and her present husband, between the daughter of a woman's son and the woman's husband, and between the daughter of a woman's daughter and the woman's husband."[27]

My questioner then asked: "Which is the graver offense—sexual intercourse of a woman with a man who has a discharge from his member or sexual intercourse of a man with a woman who is menstruating?" I replied, "Intercourse with a woman who is menstruating is the more grave offense." He answered, "But how can that be? Do we not infer the requirement that a woman immerse in a ritual bath after she has stopped menstruating from the regulations concerning a man suffering a discharge?"[28]

---

26. The words *committed robbery on his brother* are omitted. See Yalḳuṭ, and *Torah Šělemah, 16,* 111.

27. [Friedmann's note 19 interprets the passage: ". . . such intercourse is forbidden, regardless of whether the daughter is by the mother's present husband or by a former husband. And the same applies to *Thou shalt not take her son's daughter or her daughter's daughter (ibid.),* (regardless of whether the granddaughter's parent is the issue of the grandmother's present husband or of a former husband)." L. N.]

28. Of a woman in her menses, Scripture says, "She shall remain in her impurity seven days" (Lev. 15:19). For one who has had a discharge from his member, Scripture states that upon the cessation of the discharge, immersion is required (Lev. 15:13, 18). No such requirement is set down for a woman at the end of her menses, although such is the law (Maimonides' Code V, I, iv, 3 [YJS, *16,* 26]). The question, according to Friedmann's n. 21, is whether the requirement that a woman at the end of her menses immerse is based on analogy with a man who suffers discharge from his member, or is based on an argument a fortiori.

To this I answered: My son, on the contrary, the inference properly goes the other way. Of a man who is suffering a discharge from his member and therefore is not likely to be able to impregnate a woman,[29] the term "unclean" is used in Scripture ten times to designate him and reference to his immersion in a ritual bath occurs seven times.[30] <All the more rigorously forbidden, therefore, is intercourse with a woman during her period of menstruation, [for her uncleanness is such that if she becomes pregnant, the child she gives birth to is likely to be a leper]>.[31] Accordingly, the man who tells his wife, | his **ER**, *p.* 76 sons, and the people of his household, "Do not hesitate to touch vessels [handled by a woman who is menstruating] and go on with your business as usual since, according to the letter of Scripture, there is no requirement that a woman immerse in a ritual bath at the end of her period," will never have contentment in his lifetime.

A story is told of a man who read much Scripture, recited much Mishnah, yet entered into eternal life in the middle of his years. His wife, all but driven to madness [by grief], went around to the doorways of her husband's friends saying to them: "My masters, my husband read much Scripture, recited much Mishnah—why did he have to go to his eternal life in the middle of his years?" They could say nothing in reply.

One time, as I was going through the marketplace, I walked into the courtyard of her dwelling. She came out, sat down in front of me, and wept. I said to her, "My daughter, why do you weep?" She replied, "My husband read much Scripture, recited much Mishnah—why did he have to go to his eternal life in the middle of his years?" I then said to her, "My daughter, at the time of your period, how did he conduct himself with you?" She replied: "My master, he would say to me, 'All the days of your period that you see blood in your issue push them out [of your mind as days forbidden for intercourse]; furthermore, so as not to have any doubt about your ritual purity, wait for seven days after your period has ended before allowing intercourse.' " I then said to her, "My daughter, he spoke rightly to you. For with regard to both men and women who have discharge from their privy parts, [discharge that eventually ceases], and with regard to women after their period of menstruation has ceased and to women who have given birth, the Sages taught that only after seven days of continence are such considered ritually pure for intercourse with their spouses, as is said, *But if she be cleansed of her issue, then shall she number to herself seven days, and after that*

---

29. See Shab 1:3 and Berținoro *ad loc.*

30. Ten assertions of his uncleanness are found in Lev. 15:1–11; and seven references to the requirement of his immersion are found in the same chapter, verses 5–12.

31. "[for her uncleanness . . . likely to be a leper]"—Lev. Rabbah M, 15:5, pp. 331–32. Cf., however, PRKM 28:4 (PRKS, p. 439).

she shall be clean (Lev. 15:28)." [I then went on to question her further, saying], "What about the seven days you wear the required white [garments][32]—how did your husband conduct himself with you? Perhaps with your hand you anointed him with oil? Or he touched <you> with even no more than his little finger?" She replied, "As you live, I did no more than wash his feet, anoint him with oil, and sleep in bed with him. But he never moved his mind to the other matter."[33] I said: My daughter, blessed be the Preserver of the world in whose presence all are judged impartially.[34] For this is what the Torah commands concerning a woman who is menstruating: *Thou shalt not approach unto a woman to uncover her nakedness, as long as she is impure by her uncleanness* (Lev. 18:19). True, a man might suppose [that during his wife's period], it would be all right to embrace her, kiss her, and joke with her. But Scripture commands, *Thou shalt not approach.* Or he might suppose that it would be all right for her with her clothes on to sleep with him. But Scripture says, *Thou shalt not approach.* Hence a man is not to say: "Yes, even as a woman's flesh is forbidden [during her period], her bed is also forbidden; once her discharge has ceased however, her flesh remains <forbidden, but her bed is not forbidden">.[35] [He is wrong]: for the prohibition *Thou shalt not approach* is made even more explicit in post-Mosaic Scripture, which, returning to the matter in hand, declares in the words of the priest Ezekiel, the son of Buzi: *If a man . . . hath not defiled his neighbor's wife, neither hath approached a woman in her impurity . . . he is just, he shall surely live* (Ezek. 18:6–9)—thus approaching a wife before the full period of her menses has ceased is as grave a transgression as approaching a married woman with a view to adultery. Indeed, Scripture warns against approaching a woman during her period in the same way as it warns against all other capital offenses mentioned in both the Written and the Oral Law.[36]

[Remember, I told the mourning widow], what the Holy One says to Israel, *You only have I known of all the families of the earth* (Amos 3:2)

---

32. When the discharge of a menstruating woman ceased, she put on white garments and examined herself for seven days in succession, which had to pass without any further discharge of blood before she could be considered ritually clean. During this time intercourse with her husband was forbidden.

33. Instead of *daḇar 'aḥer,* "the other matter," the text may have had originally an acronym made up of the letters *daleṯ* and *'alef* to represent *dereḵ 'ereṣ,* "the way of the earth," the usual euphemism for sexual intercourse. Subsequently, a copyist misreading the meaning of the acronym spelled it out as *daḇar 'aḥer.* See Friedmann, Introduction, p. 103.

34. Cf. ARN, chap. 2 (YJS, *10,* 16–17); B.Shab 13a; and Tanḥuma, *3, Mĕṣora'.*

35. But how did a scholar permit himself such liberties with his wife before she immersed herself following the period of menses? Because it was customary for a woman to immerse herself at the conclusion of the seven days of her discharge, and of her own will abstain from intercourse for seven more days. So Naḥmanides and Solomon ben Adreṯ, as quoted in Shabbat, ed. Adin Steinsaltz (Jerusalem, 1968), p. 52, note.

36. Literally, "in Torah."

—that is, I chose you out of the seventy languages of the world [to speak My language]. *Therefore will I visit upon you all your iniquities (ibid.)* —that is, I will visit their iniquities even upon the disciples of the Sages of Israel. [Hence because of his approach to you during your period of menstruation, your husband, even though he was a disciple of the Sages, was taken from you in the middle of his years.]

My daughter, I went on, come and learn what [the Oral] Torah says: "The reward for a good deed is another good deed, but the return for transgression is another transgression" (Aḇ 4:2).

Thus when a man lies, his lying multiplies: from lying to his father, he goes on to lie to his mother, then to his wife and to his children, then to his master who taught him Scripture, then to his master who taught him Mishnah | and comprehension of Mishnah,[37] and ulti- **ER,** ***p.*** **77**
mately he lies to every one. He who acts rudely toward his father or his mother will also act rudely toward his wife and children, then toward his master who taught him Scripture and Mishnah and comprehension of both, and ultimately toward everyone. If a man is insolent toward his father or his mother or toward a person who is better than he, a leprous-like scurf will appear on his body. If he takes hold of himself and repents, he will be healed. If he does not, he will stay as he is until the day of his death. If a man is addicted to cheating and indulges in it at every opportunity,[38] leprous spots will break out in the very warp and woof of his beautiful garments. If he takes hold of himself and repents, he will be healed; if he does not, the garments will be taken from him and burned in his presence. If a poor man comes and stands at the doorway of a householder and says, "Lend me a *ḳaḇ*[39] of wheat, or a *ḳaḇ* of barley, or a *ḳaḇ* of dates," and the householder replies, "By the [Temple] service I swear, I have no wheat, I have no barley <or dates>," but does, in fact, have them, signs of leprosy will show in the walls of his house. Should he take hold of himself and repent, his house will be healed. But if he does not, then his neighbors and the people of his city will come and knock apart the walls of his house until they bring it to the ground. Then, as they carry the man's household goods into the street, they will say: Didn't this sinner say: "I have no wheat" which, in fact, he has; "I have no barley <or dates>" which, in fact, he has?[40] Blessed be the Preserver of the

---

37. Literally, "wisdom." "The rationale for a particular teaching, reconciling apparent inconsistencies, and understanding the reason for prohibition or permission, for obligation or exemption." Rashi on B.BM 33a. Reference provided by Professor Saul Lieberman in a private communication.

38. Or, "If a man loves that which he has acquired dishonestly and keeps it by him everywhere he goes, leprous spots," etc.

39. One-sixth of a *sĕʾah,* or the contents of twenty-four eggs.

40. See Lev. Rabbah M, 17:2, p. 373, and PR 17:7 (YJS, *18, 1,* 373–74).

world, blessed be He, who in the open hallows His great name in the world.

[When the house of such a sinner is demolished, the walls it had in common with neighbors' houses are also demolished.[41] Concerning such a loss by neighbors who are innocent of wrongdoing], a prophet told Jehoshaphat, [a king likewise innocent of wrongdoing]: *Because thou hast joined thyself with Ahaziah, the Lord hath made a breach in thy works* (2 Chron. 20:37).

Of the overbearing,[42] the haughty, the insolent, <the brutal, and the pugnacious>—of such Scripture says, *The arms of the wicked shall be broken; but the Lord upholdeth the righteous* (Ps. 37:17). Of those who plot evil, who distort the words of others, who use words <with a hidden meaning imputing something evil>,[43] who are smooth of tongue—of such Scripture says, *If their way be dark and slippery, the angel of the Lord pursueth them* (Ps. 35:6). Those who smite in secret, who openly profane the Name, mock people in public,[44] and cause strife, will be served like Korah and his assembly, of whom Scripture says, *And the earth closed upon them* (Num. 17:33). Of those who hoard fruit of the earth, who lend money usuriously, who cheat in measure of the ephah, and inflate prices[45]—of such Scripture says, *The Lord swore at the overreaching of Jacob: Surely I will never forget any of the works* [*of those who cheat others*] (Amos 8:7).

The following will not bequeath anything to their children, or if they do bequeath something to their children, they cause their children to be unable to bequeath anything to their own children: dice throwers;[46] usurers; breeders of small cattle [who let them graze in other people's fields]; those whose money is risked in transactions with merchants in distant countries;[47] priests and Levites who borrow in advance

---

41. See Neḡ 12:6.

42. Reading, as suggested in Friedmann's n. 29, *'ymtnyn,* "overbearing," instead of, as in R and V, *'wmnyn,* which commentators take to mean "physicians who bleed their patients." These pray for people to get sick and, neglecting the poor, attend only the rich.

43. "Who use words . . . imputing something evil"—Ginzberg in *OT,* p. 306, n. 281. Instead of *ma'amike śafah,* Friedmann in n. 30 suggests the possibility of *mafṭire śafah,* "they who spurn with their lips."

44. Instead of *bdbrym,* "with words," *brbym,* "in public." Hence, "mock people in public"—Ginzberg in *OT,* p. 305, n. 239.

[According to Jastrow (p. 696) *heliz* means "to turn," as in Kil 9:8; hence *mĕlizin bi-dĕḇarim,* "turn (people against each other) with <their> words," is a perfect parallel to the following *u-mĕṭile mahăloḳeṯ.* Thus it would seem to me that Ginzberg's emendation is unnecessary. Besides, those who mock in public are at least less objectionable than those who mock behind their target's back. L. N.]

45. [The Hebrew is more picturesque: "who measure with a small (illegal) ephah." Also "inflate prices" seems somewhat indefinite—"who corner the market?" (Cf. Jastrow, p. 1210.) L. N.]

46. "Because such winnings are not quite honorable" (*Naḥlaṯ Ya'aḳoḇ* on DER, chap. 2, 56b).

47. The hazards in such transactions require all but continuous Divine interven-

on the portions owed them;[48] heretics, informers, apostates, profaners of God's name, and hypocrites. Of all these Scripture declares, *The crooked cannot be made straight* [*unless they make amends*][49] (Eccles. 1:15). | On the other hand, of those who suffer insults, but do not inflict them; who hear themselves reviled but do not answer back; who act through love and rejoice in Divine chastisement—of them Scripture says, *But they that love Him be as the sun when he goeth forth in his might*[50] (Judg. 5:31). **ER, *p.* 78**

Of those who have a humble opinion of themselves, those who even demean themselves, those who are mindful of their own shortcomings, those who overcome their Impulse to evil—of them Scripture says, *Thus saith the Lord, the Redeemer of Israel, his Holy One, to him who holds himself despised among men . . . the Holy One of Israel hath chosen thee* (Isa. 49:7).[51]

Of trustworthy men, of them who return what has been given as collateral, who restore a lost object to its owner, who keep a secret—of such the Psalmist says, *Mine eyes are upon the faithful of the Land, that they may dwell with Me* (Ps. 101:6).

He who does the dearest wishes of his wife,[52] who leads his children in the right path and has his son wed just before he attains puberty and before he comes within the power of sin—of him Scripture says, *And thou shalt know that thy tent is in peace, and when thou examinest thy habitation thou shalt find no sin therein. Thou shalt know also that thy seed shall be great, and thine offspring as the grass of the earth* (Job 5:24–25).

He who weds his sister's daughter,[53] who loves his neighbors, who displays friendliness toward his fellows, and though he himself is in need, lends a *sela'*[54] to a poor man—of him Scripture says, *Thou shalt call, and the Lord will answer; thou shalt cry, and He will say "Here I am"* (Isa. 58:9).[55]

---

tion. Thus a man's store of merit is greatly depleted. See Rashi on B.Pes 50b, and below, S, 9.

48. Heave offering and tithe, respectively. The priest or Levite who borrowed money from a lay Israelite offered some kind of inducement with the understanding that the loan would be repaid generously by the priest or Levite from the portions due him from the lenders. Such transactions are considered unfair and undignified.

49. Cf. parallel in DER, chap. 2, 56a, Soncino tr., pp. 537–38.

50. Cf. DER, *ibid.;* B.Shab 88b; Giṭ 36b; and Yoma 23a.

51. Cf. DER, *ibid.*

52. Her food, her clothing, and her conjugal rights. See Exod. 27:10 and Mek̲, *3,* 27.

53. Because the affection a man has for his sister will be extended to her daughter, his wife, such a union is deemed meritorious. Cf. below, S, 36.

Zoroastrians regarded such a marriage as laudatory. See Friedmann, Introduction, p. 82.

54. A coin equal to one sacred shekel or two common ones.

55. Isa. 58:7 reads, *When thou seest the naked, that thou cover him; and that thou hide not thyself from thine own flesh.* See DER,. Chap. 2, 56a, and B.Yeb̲ 62b–63a.

When a man has had an involuntary emission of semen, he is required by Torah to immerse himself in a ritual bath.[56] If he says, "Who sees me? It doesn't amount to anything," and proceeds on three occasions to dismiss the matter, he transgresses the precept, *When a man has an emission of semen, he shall immerse his whole body in water* (Lev. 15:16). As a result of his transgression, he will end up with a continual discharge from his member, as is said, *The Lord spoke unto Moses: When a man, any man, has a discharge issuing from his member* (Lev. 15:1). What is intended by the repetition of the word "man"? To suggest a connection between chronic discharge from a man's member with occasional involuntary emission of semen during the night. If such a man bestirs himself and shows his repentance [by immersing himself in a ritual bath], he will be healed, but if he does not, he will stay as he is until the day of his death, as is intimated in the words *Such uncleanness in his issue shall continue* (Lev. 15:3).

ER, *p.* 79 | In this connection it is said further: A woman who sees during her period [a speck of] blood no larger than a mustard seed, but says "Who sees [me]? It doesn't amount to anything," and continues to disregard the recurrence of even three such discharges; or a woman who, [having had sexual intercourse], discharges her husband's semen over a period of five *'onah*s,[57] a period during which she has intercourse again, violates the precept *The woman also with whom a man shall lie carnally, they shall both bathe in water, and be unclean until the even* (Lev. 15:18).[58] [If in either of these circumstances, a woman does not immerse in a ritual bath], instead of having her usual issue of blood from time to time, she will come to have such issue continually.

If either of these women bestirs herself, however, and repents, she will be healed forthwith; otherwise she will stay as she is until the day of her death, as is said, *The woman will have continuous issue of her blood*[59] (Lev. 15:25).

And if a woman have an issue, and her issue in her flesh be blood (Lev. 15:19). What does the use of the phrase *in her flesh* signify? That a

---

56. Cf. Ber 3:5–6. Such immersion, however, ceased to be required. See B.Ber 22a and Maimonides' Code I, II, v, 4.

57. An *'onah* (literally "period") is a day or a night. Discharge of semen during any of the first five *'onah*s following a woman's act of intercourse with her husband imposes upon a woman—so says R. 'Aḳiḇa—the obligation to immerse herself in a ritual bath each time she detects such a discharge. Only after immersion is intercourse permitted. See Miḳ 8:3 and Friedmann's n. 40.

58. Following Friedmann, Lev. 15:18 is substituted for "If a woman lie carnally" which is not in Scripture.

The point is that before having intercourse again she is to make herself ritually clean by immersion and then refrain from intercourse until the next evening.

Such immersion, however, ceased to be required.

59. "If either of these women bestirs herself . . . *of her blood*" is, at the suggestion of Friedmann (n. 44), transposed from ER, 79, lines 10–12, to this paragraph.

menstruating woman contracts uncleanness when the flow is internal as well as when it is external.

This particular passage, R. Ishmael pointed out, differs from <other passages concerned with ritual uncleanness> because it was uttered primarily to teach that daughters of Israel [in their normal menses] are considered as people, [whether men or women], who have an abnormal issue.

But, according to R. Meir, this passage was uttered solely to help fulfill the command to be fruitful and multiply. For when a man can eat every kind of food whenever he wants to and drink every kind of drink whenever he wants to, he finds that he does not enjoy either one at all. Hence Torah declares: [*A woman*] *shall be deemed in her impurity seven days* [*after the termination of her menses*] *(ibid.),*[60] so that the day of her immersion [seven days after the menses' termination] be for her husband like the day she entered her bridal bower.[61]

Blessed be the Preserver of the world, blessed be He who gave words of Torah to Israel so that learning right conduct therefrom, their sins might not be multiplied in the world. For he who transgresses what is written in the Torah will be smitten, as is said, *Who* [*but a transgressor*] *crieth, "Woe?" Who* [*but a transgressor*], *"Alas?"*[62] (Prov. 23:29). Hence it is an evil omen for him who rises early and sits late over wine, for with his own hand he roots himself out [of the world]. Of him Scripture says, *Wine is a treacherous dealer, like a man who is* YAHIR (Hab. 2:5), a word which means "diligent and assiduous," | like the word *mahir* **ER, *p.* 80**
in the verse *Seest thou a man diligent* (MAHIR) *in his business* (Prov. 22:29). (With regard to wine's diligence, the ironical quip has been made that a worker who accepts a task from a householder is under obligation to perform it as the householder wishes him to; and if he does not please the householder, Scripture says of him, *Cursed be he that doeth the work of the Lord with a slack hand* [Jer. 48:10]).

To return to the verse in Habakkuk, we are told that *Wine is like a man who is diligent and abideth not. He enlargeth his desire as the nether world* (Hab. 2:5). Because he eats and drinks as though the world were created only for eating and drinking, he does only what is good in his eyes. *He is as death, and cannot be satisfied (ibid.).* Like the angel of death who is not likely to be satisfied though the entire world—everything

---

60. Cf. B.Nid 31b. See also Louis Ginzberg, *OT,* p. 296, n. 63. Cf. ER, 76.

61. "so that the day of her immersion . . . her bridal bower"—R.
The menses last from five to seven days. Together with the seven clean days during which the wife must be clean of any blood or stain which can be attributed to menstruation, the period of abstention lasts from twelve to fourteen days. See MTeh 2:15 (YJS, *13, 1,* 46), and Norman Lamm, *A Hedge of Roses* (New York, 1966), pp. 33–34.

62. One of the preceding verses declares, *Buy the truth, and sell it not; also wisdom, and instruction, and understanding.* These terms are all taken to refer to Torah, the neglect of which, according to ER, will lead to cries of "Woe."

in it—be given to him, so, too, he who early and late is at wine is not likely to be satisfied. Of such a man Scripture says, "The curse of the Lord is in the house of the wicked" (Prov. 3:23). Habakkuk, in going on to say, *But [he] gathereth unto him all nations, and heapeth unto him all peoples* (Hab. 2:5), does not really refer to any power of his over nations or peoples, but implies that led on by his [gluttonous] eating and drinking, the man sets his eyes on all the transgressions that the peoples of the world do and adds their kinds of transgression to his. Such is the sense of Habakkuk's *He gathereth,* etc. And what is meant by the verse that follows, namely, *Shall not all these take up a parable against him?* (Hab. 2:6). That such a man, in effect, destroys all the handiwork of the Holy One from the day the world was created until this very hour. Hence *For whom [but for such a man should one] cry, "Woe?" For whom [but for such a man should one] cry, "Alas?"* (Prov. 23:29).

Further comment on *For whom [but for such a man should one] cry, "Woe?" For whom [but for him should one] cry, "Alas?" (ibid.):* For a man with flattering lips;[63] for a man whose tongue speaks slander;[64] for those who are insolent and arrogant toward their fellow men;[65] for householders who do not <hold themselves back> from cheating their fellows;[66] and finally for [the man who does not keep scrupulously apart from] his wife during the period of seven days following her menstruation,[67] [as the scholar spoken of above, who died in the middle of his years, because he failed to be scrupulous enough in regard to his wife].

---

63. Which lead to the contentions that Prov. 23:29 goes on to speak of.

64. Literally, "great things" (cf. Ps. 12:4). The kind of talk *(śiaḥ)* referred to in Prov. 23:29, which evokes other people's anxiety; hence "slander." Cf. MTeh 12:2 (YJS, *13, 1,* 170–71).

65. The kind of people who get *wounds uncaused [by illness]* (Prov. 23:29), being beaten for their insolence and arrogance.

66. "They who set their eyes upon another man's purse" (Prov. 23:31). Although the *ḳĕri* (the Masoretic instruction for reading) is *kos,* "cup," the *ḳĕṯiḇ* (the traditional spelling) is *kis,* "purse."

67. "One who follows ways that on his own he deems permissible," as ER reads Prov. 23:31b, which in JV reads *it glideth down smoothly.* Apparently ER associates *mešarim,* "smoothly," with the Aramaic *'šr',* which means "holds, or deems permissible." See Lev. Rabbah M, pp. 243–44, n. 5.

The association of the comments in nn. 63–67 with Prov. 23:29–31 is suggested by Haida.

CHAPTER (16)

Why one is to rejoice because of the advent of death, the Impulse to evil, and sitting in the privy

Summary

It was given to the first generations of mankind to live the longest lives of all the generations. Their longevity served as a test of whether they would be kind to their forebears (ER, 80). As it turned out, only Noah passed the test. As his life on earth was a blessing, so his entrance into eternal life was an occasion of joy, for death released him from the weight of his obligation.

Indeed, the very limits of our mortality should give us all cause to rejoice. Fear of the angel of death, for example, keeps the world from being destroyed by the wickedness of men. Likewise, the Impulse to evil which Israel will conquer will earn them the homage of the nations. Even the necessity of use of the privy can bring us to rejoice, for it serves as a reminder that in time idolatry, like excrement, will be eliminated (ER, 81).

To correspond to the forty-eight cities of the Levites, there were in Israel forty-eight Prophets who like the Levites set forth what is written and what is implied in Torah. Whether Israel absorb much or little of Torah, God is always eager for Israel's voicing it even if they voice no more than the Shĕma'.

Isaiah distinguished himself among the Prophets because he consented to utter in apparent seriousness words which God intended to be sarcastic, so as to bring Israel to repentance (ER, 82). At the same time, even when penitence was slight and words of Torah few, Isaiah prophesied all God's kindnesses and consolations for Israel (ER, 83).

Chapter (16)

One time while I sat in the great academy of Jerusalem, a disciple came to me, and in the manner of a son putting a question to his father, said: My master, why is it that out of all the generations of mankind, it was the first generations, every one of them, who had the most days and lived the longest lives? I replied: My son, they were given long lives in order to test their conduct—in order to see whether they would do deeds of kindness for their immediate forebears. As for proof of what they did, you can see it for yourself when you consider the first ten generations: *Adam, Seth, Enosh; Kenan, Mahalalel, Jared; Enoch, Methuselah, Lamech; Noah* (1 Chron. 1:1).[1] Adam came first into the world. His son Seth came after him, and after Seth came his son Enosh. When Enosh was told, "Serve your father," he fed him, provided for him, and sustained him. But when he was told, "Serve your father's father," he

ER, *p.* 80 *cont'd*

1. Cf. Ab 5:2.

said, "I have no obligation toward him." And he forbore to serve Adam. After Enosh had come into the world, his son Kenan followed him. When Kenan was told, "Serve your father's father," he, too, said, "I have no obligation toward him." And so it was with all of the sons in succession until the coming of Noah. When Noah came and was told, "Serve your father," he fed him, provided for him, and sustained him, and then, when told, "Serve your father's father," he took that service also upon himself. Thus he fed and provided for his father, his father's father, and all his forebears who were still living at that time. Nay, [he served many] more besides, for during all the hundred and twenty years until the flood came he used to go forth and forewarn multitudes. Therefore, for the instruction of generations to come, Scripture pro-
ER, *p.* 81 ceeds | to address him thus: *Thee have I seen righteous before Me in this generation* (Gen. 7:1). Because of such as he, it is said: The good are made agents of blessing, and the wicked are made agents of misfortune.[2] Thus it is with all the families of the earth—with Israel and with the nations alike.

In connection with the same passage Scripture says that [*Man's days shall be a hundred and twenty* (Gen. 6:4), implying that] a man has one hundred and twenty years in which he can serve as a vigorous agent of blessing [such as the care of his forebears]. After this span, as he enters eternal life, his death is an occasion of great joy for him.[3] Indeed, the day that Adam was to die, he asked, it is said, that it be deemed a holiday and celebrated as a day of feasting and rejoicing.

Furthermore, there ought to be joy in the world even because of the following three: the angel of death, the Impulse to evil, and the necessity of sitting in the privy. The disciple asked: My master, why do you rejoice because of the angel of death? I replied: My son, but for [our fear of] the angel of death, what might we not be making our Father in heaven [do to us]? We ought to learn from what befell the first ten generations of mankind upon whom God lavished such goodness as to give them a happy foretaste of the goodness of the world-to-come.[4] [However, when the generations no longer lived in the fear of death, they came to the wickedness that] nearly brought about the destruction of the world [by the flood].

Then the disciple asked: Why do you rejoice over the Impulse to evil? I replied: My son, were it not for Israel's conquest of the Impulse to evil, for what reason in the time-to-come will the peoples of the world, as they go up [during the Feast of Sukkot] for their annual pilgrimage to Jerusalem, pay homage to Israel? That the peoples of the

---

2. Cf. Lieberman, *TKF, 5,* 253, 341; Sem 8:14 (YJS, *17,* 64–65); Sif Num. 133; B.Shab 32b; and BB 119b.

3. See Landau.

4. See Ginzberg, *Legends, 1,* 152–53.

world will indeed go up as pilgrims to Jerusalem is implied in the verse *Three times in the year all thy males shall appear before the Lord thy God* (Exod. 23:17). For [the apparently superfluous word *all* suggests that] even as we <go up to Jerusalem to bow down, so all the peoples of the world> will go up to Jerusalem to bow down before the King who is the King of kings, the Holy One, blessed be He. Indeed Scripture sternly declares: *Whoso of the families of the earth goeth not up unto Jerusalem [during the Feast of Sukkot] to worship the King, the Lord of hosts, upon these shall be no rain* (Zech. 14:16); *and this [lack] shall bring about the plague* (Zech. 14:12). Then, as the nations journey on the way [to Jerusalem], they will say, What gift shall we bring with us? Gold and silver are already His, precious stones and pearls are already His. What gift can we possibly bring with us? Thereupon the nations will go and with great homage bring the children of Israel with them, as is said, *And they shall bring all your brethren out of all the nations for an offering unto the Lord* (Isa. 66:20). If they find one infant, <seven> women will be ready to give him suck. <Should they find two infants>,[5] fourteen women —even the greatest princesses among them—will be ready to give the infants suck, as is said, *They shall bring all your brethren out of all the nations to be an offering unto the Lord* (Isa. 66:20). And as the nations walk on the way, they will throw their arms around the children of Israel, embrace and kiss them, yea, lick the dust under their feet, as is said, *Kings shall be thy fosterfathers, and their queens thy nursing mothers; they shall bow down to thee with their face to the earth; and lick the dust of thy feet* (Isa. 49:23).

At that time [when the nations pay homage to Israel] the righteous will be freed of the Impulse to evil,[6] so that they will come readily to Scripture and Mishnah, to teach right conduct, and to do the will of their Father in heaven.

Then the disciple asked: My master, how can there be joy with regard to the necessity for sitting in a privy?[7] I replied: Ultimately the Holy One will redeem Israel from [where it now sits as in a privy among the idols of][8] the nations and will bring Israel the days of the Messiah and the days of redemption. In those days they will be freed for ever from bondage to the three—[the angel of death, the Impulse to evil, and the fecal idolatry of the nations]. Though these three *now*

---

5. [The correct text is clearly, "<Should they find two infants>, fourteen women," etc.; the scribe mistakenly wrote "ten women," noticed his error, added "fourteen," and forgot both to add another "women" and to indicate by superscribed dots that "ten women" is to be crossed out. A very common scribal error. L. N.]

6. Another way of saying: "In the time-to-come, taught R. Judah, the Holy One will bring the Impulse to evil and slay it in the presence of the righteous and the wicked" (B.Suk 53a).

7. During which a man is reduced, so to speak, to a beast's level.

8. Cf. PRKM 13:2 (PRKS, p. 254).

appear as vexation and bitterness, yet [in the time-to-come], my Beloved will be unto me, [Israel], as One who lieth betwixt my breasts . . . my Beloved will be unto me as One who purges me of all [such vexation and bitterness][9] (Song 1:13, 14). And when we recall that [in the time-to-come], these three will be no more, <we> bless, praise, magnify, and hallow our Father in heaven.

ER, *p.* 82 | The disciple asked me further questions: My master, tell me, how many Prophets prophesied to Israel? I replied: "Forty-eight,[10] my son." "And why was the number forty-eight singled out rather than, say, forty-five or fifty?" To correspond, <I replied>, to the number of the cities of refuge which were given to the Levites [to dwell in], forty-eight in number,[11] as is said, *All the cities which ye shall give to the Levites shall be forty and eight cities* (Num. 35:7). It is said: The Prophets did not subtract from anything that is written in the Torah, nor did they add anything to what is written in the Torah.[12] "For those who understand, [words of the Prophets and the Writings] are all counterparts [of the Five Books of Moses] and therefore should likewise be studied by those who seek knowledge [of Torah]"[13] (Prov. 8:9). What parable illustrates how, in the sight of their heavenly Father, the house of Israel in this world [is instructed in all of Scripture]? The parable of a mortal king who had many sons and servants. He took and built many houses and many palaces with extensive—indeed limitless—open ground. Then an idea struck him. He said: I will test my sons and my servants [to find out] who loves me and stands in awe of me. Whereupon he proceeded to build a courtyard four by four cubits wide. At its entrance he made an opening four by four handbreadths wide, and in it set a wicket facing the open ground where people might come to pay their respects to the king. Then, when his sons and his servants came and stationed themselves either in the courtyard or in the lane leading to

---

9. JV: *My beloved is unto me as a bag of myrrh, that lieth betwixt my breasts, my beloved is unto me as a cluster of henna.* But *ṣĕror,* "bag," ER apparently associates with *ṣrr,* "to show hostility, to vex"; *mor,* "myrrh," with "bitterness"; and *'eškol hak-kofer,* "cluster of henna," ER apparently reads *'iš šehak-kol kofer,* "the One who purges all." So Haida. Cf. Song Rabbah.

10. See SOR, chap. 21, p. 90; and B. Meg̃ 15a and Rashi *(ad loc.)* who lists them by name.

11. The words *They, the Tribe of Levi, shall teach Jacob Thine ordinances* (Deut. 33:10) are said to imply that all teachings of Torah go forth out of the mouths of Levi (Sif Deut. 351 [ed. Finkelstein, Breslau, 1936–39, p. 408]). The Tribe of Levi was also the one to whom Moses gave the flawlessly correct Scroll of the Law. See PRKM, pp. 441–42 (PRKS, p. 450).

Accordingly, the provision of forty-eight cities of Levites meant that each of the twelve Tribes had on its four borders, so to speak, four cities of Levites who were to give instruction in Torah (Deut. 33:10). Such also was the task of the Prophets.

12. See parallel in B. Meg̃ 14a.

13. So, too, what is in the Writings is said to be the counterpart of what is in the Five Books. See B.Ta 9a, where Prov. 19:3 is taken to be the counterpart of Gen. 42:38.

it, the king was able to discern those who loved him and stood in awe of him and those who stood in awe of him but did not love him. He who both loved and stood in awe of the king suffered discomfort as he squeezed his way through the wicket facing the open ground beyond it to pay his respects to the king. And he who merely stood in awe of him but did not love him remained standing in the courtyard or in the lane.

How does the parable apply? The Holy One said to those of Israel [who remained standing in His courtyard and lane]: My children, why though I came to pay My respects to you, do you not come to pay your respects to Me? Even though, *Some of you choose to dwell in courtyards* [*outside the open ground before My palace*], *nevertheless, just as companions* [*who, having made their way into the open ground before Me*], *hearken eagerly for your utterance* [*of regard for Me*], *I, too, would have you make Me hear such utterance*[14] (Song 8:13). [Thus God in speaking of *companions* is referring to those authors who in the Writings and in the Books of the Prophets teach Torah. For example, speaking through Isaiah, God says]: *Let there be brought forth* [*into the open ground before Me*] *people who are blind though they have eyes* (Isa. 43:8)—that is, men unlettered in Torah who are obedient to the precepts of right conduct and to other precepts, and, it goes without saying, stay far away from unchastity and any other kind of indecency. And let also be brought *They who are deaf, though they have ears (ibid.):* these may be even Sages and their disciples who give themselves utterly to Scripture, to Mishnah, to Midrash of Halakot and 'Aggadot, [but still fail to comprehend them]. With regard to blind and deaf such as these, Isaiah quotes God as saying: *I have taken hold of thy hand . . . to open the blind eyes, to bring out . . . them that sit in darkness out of the prison house* (Isa. 42:7)[15]—[out of the confining courtyards into the open *ground* beyond].

The disciple further asked me: What distinguished[16] Isaiah the son of Amoz from all other Prophets who prophesied all kinds of boons and comforts to Israel? I replied: My son, because Isaiah joyfully took upon himself the [decrees of the] kingdom of Heaven, saying [with biting sarcasm]: *I heard the voice of the Lord, saying: "Go, and tell this people: Hear ye indeed, but understand not; and see ye indeed, but perceive not. Make the heart of this people fat, and make their ears heavy, and shut their eyes; lest they . . . return and be healed"* (Isa. 6:8–9). If the idea should enter your mind that the Holy One in having Isaiah say this did not, God forbid, desire

---

14. So Landau. In JV, Song 8:13 reads, *Thou that dwellest in the gardens, the companions hearken for thy voice: Cause me to hear it.* But *gannim,* "gardens," also means "enclosures"; hence "courtyards."

15. Cf. above, ER, 69.

16. He prophesied with a double portion of Divine Power. See Lev. Rabbah M, 10:2, p. 199, and PR 29/30A:5 (YJS, *18, 2,* 577).

the repentance of Israel, consider the parable of a mortal king who had an only son dwelling in a principality, to whom he sent an emissary with instructions to say to the prince: "Why not slaughter many bullocks, many kids of the flock, eat their flesh and drink much wine?" [The apparent purpose of the instructions was] to encourage the prince to drowse and be slothful in working his fields or irrigating the fields that needed water. Of course, the real purpose of the instructions was to make the prince [repent of his slothful life], and with the emissary go forth to work in the field, so that the father would then come and take satisfaction in his son.

Nay more, God, [Father of Israel the prince], was fully aware that
ER, ***p.*** **83** Isaiah, [His emissary], | would not argue with Him then and there, for Isaiah knew well that of Israel's Jerusalem it was to be joyfully prophesied: *Jerusalem shall be inhabited without walls, for the multitude of men and cattle therein. For I, saith the Lord, will be unto her a wall of fire round about* (Zech. 2:8–9) and that it was also to be prophesied, *There shall yet old men and old women sit in the broad places of Jerusalem* (Zech. 8:4). [Therefore, knowing that God wished him to be sarcastic as a means of making Israel aware of the extent of its folly], Isaiah kept silent and said no more than *Lord, how long?* (Isa. 6:11). [He knew that then was not the time to try to pacify God in regard to Israel. Like Isaiah], a man should know before Whom he stands and what word it is proper to utter before One who is greater than he, in keeping with what the Sages taught in a Mishnah: "Do not attempt to pacify your Friend in the hour of His anger" (Ab̲ 4:18).

The disciple concluded his questions by asking: My master, in what year did Isaiah the son of Amoz prophesy all God's kindnesses and consolations for Israel? I replied: My son, in the twenty-ninth year of Hezekiah, king of Judah. The disciple then commented: My master, may we not come to a further conclusion by a logical deduction: Since in Hezekiah's twenty-ninth year,[17] when penitence was slight and words of Torah few, Isaiah prophesied all God's kindnesses and consolations for Israel, surely, then, had Israel truly repented at any time between the destruction of the First Temple until the present hour, God would certainly have taken them into His arms, embraced them, kissed them, and put them in His bosom for ever and ever and ever.

---

17. Hezekiah became king when he was twenty-five (2 Kings 18:2). Thus in the fourth year of his reign, before he was able to mount effectively his religious reforms, and in the year when Shalmaneser laid siege to Samaria, Isaiah began to prophesy his consolations.

CHAPTER 17

Why God loves Israel

Summary

Moses' exemplary conduct won God's blessing for him, a blessing which God generously extended to the people of Israel despite their misdeed (ER, 83). He gave them the blessing of His own presence in the Tabernacle because in the privacy of his tent each man of Israel had repented of the sin of the golden calf.

Accordingly, any kind of good thing a man does he should keep to himself.

A series of meditations contrasting the King of kings and a mortal king follows: The King of kings makes peace in heaven and among all the inhabitants of the earth; He Himself studies Torah, dispenses judgment, sustains all creatures, rules events in history, endows certain men with special gifts of wisdom.

God singled out the people of Israel as His hallowed portion because of their regal bearing, because they had not changed their names or their language when they were in Egypt; because each man of Israel went out into the wilderness with but one loaf of bread; because Israel gladly accepted the kingship of Heaven for themselves; because they did not question His inexplicable command to bring Him costly treasures.

In the days of Joshua also and in the time the judges sat, with love Israel took the rule of Heaven upon themselves. Hence God was patient with them, bestowing upon them the blessing of many children. In the days of Samuel, with awe Israel took the rule of Heaven upon themselves (ER, 84–86). Therefore God stayed with them in the war against the Philistines. In the days of Elijah also, Israel became men in awe of Heaven and were thus led to abandon their idolatry.

Hence, whenever Israel are in distress, God weeps for them privately and publicly. But He weeps primarily for those in Israel who died after having profaned themselves by their wickedness (ER, 87). Of these He says, sighing, "Would that they had children or children's children to bring them to favorable remembrance." Thus God seeks to find merit even in sinners as He found merit in Jeroboam who refused to accept slander of the prophet Amos.

God even grants extraordinary deliverances, destined to take place at the end of time, to those who like Hezekiah's generation occupy themselves with Torah. Indeed, so great is God's love for Israel that He cannot execute the fierceness of His anger against her (ER, 88).

Chapter 17

When the Psalmist speaks of a man *that hath clean hands and a pure heart* (Ps. 24:4), he alludes to Moses, father of wisdom and father of the Prophets. For Moses' hands were so clean of anything taken dishonestly from any others that he was able to say in public, "I have not taken one ass from them" (Num. 16:15). In speaking of *a pure heart,* the Psalmist is also alluding to Moses, father of wisdom and father of Prophets, for ER, *p.* 83 *cont'd* the heart of Moses in his fear of God was pure. In the words *He hath not burdened his soul with falsehood (ibid.),* the Psalmist has God bear witness: The life and breath[1] I put into him—in Moses—took on no burden of anything false, nor anything not in keeping with Torah. In the words *And hath not sworn deceitfully (ibid.)* the Psalmist further alludes to Moses who had not, in fact, sworn deceitfully when he took an oath to stay with Jethro [although he later left Jethro to go to Egypt].[2] For in *way-yo'el Moses to stay*[3] (Exod. 2:21), the word *way-yo-'el* has to do with swearing of an oath,[4] as in *way-yo'el Saul the people* (1 Sam. 14:24) the word *way-yo'el* has to do with swearing an oath. As in the incident that concerned Saul, Saul exacted the oath from the people, so in the incident that concerned Moses, Jethro exacted the oath from Moses.

And what was Moses' reward [for his righteousness]? He won the merit of receiving a blessing from his God, as is said, *He shall receive a blessing from the Lord, and mercy from the God of his salvation* (Ps. 24:5).

My Father in heaven, may Your great name be blessed for ever and ever and ever, and may You have contentment in Israel, Your servants wherever they live. For in spite of all the filthy ways they followed, and the indecencies one cannot even give a name to which Israel committed before Your very face, You did not cherish wrath or vengefulness against them, nor did You summon up Your might against them, nor did You keep words of Torah from them. Rather You remembered in their behalf the good things and not the bad things—the good things they did in Your presence and not the bad things they did in Your presence. You reassured them with words which Your own lips uttered: [*Offenses*] *gone by shall not be remembered, nor even come to mind* (Isa. 65:17). Furthermore, when our fathers stood on Mount Sinai to take upon themselves of their own will the kingship of Heaven, in return the Holy One came down from the upper heaven of heavens, from the place of His glory, of His greatness, of His splendor and His

---

1. Jewish thought distinguishes between spirit as the general essence of life bestowed on all human beings by the Creator, and soul or breath as it exists in an individual. See *Dictionary of the Bible,* ed. James Hastings (New York, 1909), *4,* 166b; and *EB, 5,* 903, 930–31.

2. But Moses did not stay in Egypt without returning to Jethro to be released of his vow (see Rashi on Exod. 4:18). Jethro had exacted the vow from Moses because Jethro did not wish—so he said—to have his daughter taken away from him without his knowledge as Moses' forebear Jacob had taken away Laban's daughters (see Exod. Rabbah 1:33; Tanḥuma, *Šemot,* 12). Or, according to another comment, God Himself released Moses from the vow exacted by Jethro when He told Moses: *Go, and bring forth My people the children of Israel out of Egypt* (Exod. 3:9). See Sif Deut. 27, ed. Finkelstein (Breslau, 1936–39), p. 41. Cf. MTeh 27:7 (YJS, *13, 1,* 341).

3. JV: *And Moses was content to dwell.*

4. [The author derives *yo'el* not from *y'l,* "to be content," but from *'lh,* "to swear an oath, or curse." L. N.]

holiness, and willingly suffered His great name to dwell with our fathers.

Hence Isaiah said, *The Willing One devised counsels of generosity, and He will continue to establish such counsels of generosity*[5] (Isa. 32:8).

| Blessed is the man whose deeds are engendered by his wisdom.[6] ER, *p.* 84
What analogy applies to such a man? That of a foot put in a well-fitting shoe and thereby saved from any sort of ache or pain, as is said, *How beautiful are thy steps in sandals, thou who art moved to go thy way through the warmheartedness* [*of wisdom*][7] (Song 7:2). The verse concludes with the words, *the turnings of thy thighs . . .* (Song 7:2)—that is, as the roundings of a woman's thighs are concealed, so the rounding out of any good thing a man does is his concealment of it. He ought to study Torah in privacy[8] and give charity in secrecy; his generosity to his wife, to his children, and his children's children he ought to keep to himself. And when a man acts thus, he will surely find love in the eyes of his Father in heaven. For the Holy One said to Israel: If in fulfilling Torah['s ritual regulations], your steps ought to be kept private, all the more so are they to be kept private in fulfilling precepts of ethical conduct.[9]

[And if you keep private what you do], what may you expect from Me? Even as My name was pronounced over you a hundred times with the threat of punishment,[10] so shall My name be pronounced over you a thousand thousand times for good, because you wreathe the Torah around your arms and upon your hands,[11] as is said, *Seek intimacy*[12] *with Torah, and she will exalt thee* (Prov. 4:8); *She will give to thy head a chaplet of grace* (Prov. 4:9), and *Length of days is in her right hand* (Prov. 3:16).

[If you keep your deeds private, then God will forgive you for your evil deeds just as He forgave Israel for making the golden calf

---

5. The verse is so read by Landau. JV: *But the liberal deviseth liberal things; and by liberal things shall he stand.*

6. Ab̲ 3:9 reads, "Any one whose deeds exceed his wisdom." But apparently ER construes *mĕrubbin* not as "growth in number," but "grow, grow out of"; hence "engendered."

7. Apparently the Hebrew *bat̲,* "daughter," is taken to mean "one who is of a certain kind," and *nad̲ib̲,* "prince," is taken to mean "that which is princely, generous"; hence *warmheartedness.*

8. "Not in the presence of others to show off." Louis Ginzberg in *OT,* p. 290, n. 414. Cf. B.MḲ 16a–b.

9. Precepts of ethical conduct have been revealed before Torah's other regulations. See ER, 3. Or: "There are times when you possess Torah learning. If you do, then you most certainly are scrupulous in ethical conduct." So Professor Jakob J. Petuchowski in a letter.

10. Actually a hundred less two—the curses uttered in Deut. 28. See Rashi on Deut. 29:12, and Tanḥuma, *Niṣṣab̲im,* 1.

11. Such "wreathing" may be a metaphor for putting on tefillin.

12. JV: *Extol her.* But in Rabbinic literature, *sll,* "extol," also has the sense of "closeness, intimacy." See Julius H. Greenstone, *Proverbs* (Philadelphia, 1950), p. 40, where Tos Soṭ 5:7 and B.Yeb̲ 76a are cited; and B.Shab 65a.

and] gave them the Tabernacle in testimony [of His forgiveness, as is said], *These are the accounts of the Tabernacle, the Tabernacle of testimony* [*that God had forgiven the making of the calf*] (Exod. 38:21).[13] Nay more, out of the love He cherished for them and the joy He had in them, He Himself praised them by allowing them to contemplate, out of all the attributes identified with His great name, [a particular one, the attribute of peace], for He said: *Go forth, O builders* [*of the Tabernacle*] *whose name Zion indicates that you bear a sign (ṣywn)* (Song 3:11),[14] [the sign of circumcision, the sign of hair unshaved upon head and face, and the sign of fringes on the corners of your garments],[15] *and gaze upon King Solomon (Šĕlomoh) (ibid.)*—that is, the King of kings of kings, the Holy One, blessed be He, who is Lord of peace.

Another comment upon *And gaze upon King Solomon (Šĕlomoh) (ibid.):* Gaze upon the King who is King of kings, the Holy One, blessed be He, whose way is to make peace among the four billion nine hundred and sixty million ministering angels[16] who stand before Him every day and continually hallow His great name from sunrise to sunset, saying *Holy, holy, holy* (Isa. 6:3) and from sunset to sunrise saying *Praised be the glory of the Lord wherever His place may be* (Ezek. 3:12),[17] as is said, *He maketh peace among those of His on high* (Job 25:2).

Another comment: *And gaze upon King Solomon (Šĕlomoh)* (Song 3:11)—gaze upon the King who is King of kings, blessed be He, whose way is to make peace among all the inhabitants of the world and among all the handiwork He created in the world.[18]

Another comment: *Gaze* [*upon the difference between*] *King Solomon (Šĕlomoh),* [*King of peace*], and any son of David who sits upon a throne and to whom his servants and the people of his principality bring food and drink—sustenance as well as all kinds of royal luxuries. But the Holy One, the King who is King of kings, blessed be He, may His great name be blessed for ever and ever, does not act like a mortal king. As He sits on His throne of glory, a third of each day He reads Scripture and recites Mishnah, a third of each day He gives over to judgment,[19] and a third of each day He gives charity—He feeds, sustains, and provides for all the inhabitants of the world and all His handiwork He

---

13. See ER, 86, 139; Rashi; and *Torah šĕlemah, 23,* 57.

14. JV: *Go forth, O ye daughters of Zion.* But ER apparently takes *banoṯ,* "daughters," to have the general meaning of "builders" (from *banah,* "build"); hence, *builders* [*of the Tabernacle*]. Cf. PRKM 12:1 (PRKS, p. 226).

15. "[the sign of circumcision . . . the corners of your garments]" added as in parallel in PRKM 1:3 (PRKS, p. 8).

16. Cf. above, chap. (6) 7, n. 3; and below, EZ, chap. 12, n. 1.

17. Cf. PR 20:4 (YJS, *18, 1,* 407).

18. Cf. PRKM 1:3, 5.

19. Of Torah, it is said *All her paths are peace* (Prov. 3:18); and of judgment and justice, R. Simeon ben Gamaliel taught: "The world stands on three things, on justice, on truth, and on peace, the three in fact being one, for when justice is in effect, truth is in effect, and peace is in effect" (P.Ta 4:2, 67a). References cited in Haida.

created in the world, as is said, *He giveth food to all flesh* (Ps. 136:25).

Another comment [on *Gaze on King Solomon*]: *Gaze* [*on the difference between*] *King Solomon (Šělomoh),* [*King of peace*], and any mortal king who as he sits on his throne has the elders of his principality sit before him, and from each of them learns a lesson in wisdom, a lesson in understanding, a lesson in knowledge, or a lesson in insight. But the King who is King of kings, blessed be He, may His great name be blessed for ever and ever and ever, does not act like a mortal king. As He sits on His throne of glory, a third of each day He reads Scripture and recites Mishnah, a third of each day He gives over to judgment, and a third of each day He provides and nourishes the righteous and the disciples of the wise with wisdom, understanding, knowledge, and insight, as is said, *He giveth strength to those who weary themselves* [*in quest of Torah*][20] (Isa. 40:29).

Of God's activities Scripture says further: *He changeth the times and the seasons; He removeth kings, and setteth up kings: He giveth wisdom unto the wise, and knowledge to them that know understanding* (Dan. 2:21). The words *He changeth the times* refer to the times | when such places as Sodom[21] [are overthrown because of their vices]; and [*He will change*] . . . *seasons* refers to the seasons when Jerusalem [was restored and will again be restored]. The words *He removeth kings* mean that the power of such as Jehoiakim, king of Judah, is removed;[22] and *setteth up kings,* such as Nebuchadnezzar; *He giveth wisdom unto the wise*—to such as Moses our teacher, father of wisdom, father of Prophets; *and knowledge to them that know understanding*—to those like Joshua, the son[23] of Nun. **ER, *p.* 85**

In another comment the words *He giveth wisdom unto the wise* are taken to allude to the righteous Joseph, as "Pharaoh said unto Joseph . . . 'There is none so discreet and wise as thou' " (Gen. 41:39). And the words *knowledge to them that know understanding* are taken to allude to Daniel and his companions, to whom it was said, *Then was the secret revealed unto Daniel in a vision of the night* (Dan. 2:19). During the vision God revealed to Daniel *the deep things (ibid.),* the depths of the chariot [from which He looks out all over the world so as to provide for it];[24] and *secret things (ibid.),* the work of creation. *He had him know what is in the darkness (ibid.)*—the smiting in requital of the wicked in Gehenna;

---

20. In quest of His wisdom which, the preceding verse says, cannot be fathomed.

21. Since a statement concerning Sodom's overthrow does not seem to belong in Daniel's prophecy, Baer Ratner suggests that "Chaldees" be substituted (see SOR, p. 75, n. 108). However, Haida proposes a bold solution: Since the root *'dn* may mean "season," or "pleasure," he would read Dan. 2:21: *He changeth because of* [*people's succumbing to*] *pleasures,* the kind of pleasures that led to Sodom['s overthrow].

22. See 2 Kings 24:1–8 and 2 Chron. 36:5–8.

23. The word *binah,* "understanding," is taken to be implied in [*Joshua*] *bin Nun,* which is construed as "Joshua the man of understanding." The usual form of "son" is not *bin* but *ben.*

24. "The chariot" refers to Ezekiel's mystic vision (Ezek. 1), which in Jewish thought is taken to represent God's providence.

and the light that dwelleth with Him (ibid.)—the reward of the righteous in the Garden of Eden. Of what God revealed to such as Daniel, Scripture says, *The Lord giveth wisdom, out of His mouth cometh knowledge and discernment* (Prov. 2:6).

All the aforegoing is implied in *Gaze upon* [*the difference between*] *King Solomon (Šĕlomoh),* [*King of peace*] (Song 3:11) and a mortal king.

Gaze . . . upon the crown wherewith He hath crowned it—[*crowned*] *the people which is His very own*[25] *(ibid.).* Gaze upon the Tabernacle which is distinguished by its colors of blue and purple, [the colors of the offerings God asked of Israel in the making of the Tabernacle].[26]

In another comment the verse is read *Gaze . . . upon the* [*tarnished*] *crown wherewith his mother*—[*his ancestry, that is*]—*hath crowned him (ibid.)* when Israel were in the wilderness. [It should be remembered that while they were in Egypt they had not forgotten from whom they were descended and so] had not changed their names or their language.[27] The ministering angels, however, said sarcastically: Surely Israel have behaved no better than had Abraham, Isaac, and Jacob [on certain occasions]. Therefore, the angels were implying that even as Israel had not changed [their conduct for the better, neither had they changed] their names or their language.

In further comment the verse is read, *Gaze . . . upon the crown wherewith His people hath crowned Him (ibid.).* When Israel, [at God's command], went out of Egypt into the wilderness, they went out—each of them—with but one loaf baked on coals,[28] but they did not criticize[29] His ways and said not a word. Their behavior <on this particular occasion> was blameless: [hence the verse is read, *His people hath crowned Him*].

Indeed, if you wish to study, and desire words of Torah, go and learn from those Israelites. Of them, of those who went out of Egypt, the Holy One said: *I remember . . . how thou wentest after Me in the wilderness in a land that was not sown* (Jer. 2:2). And because Israel followed [unquestioningly] after Him, the Holy One declared them a hallowed portion of His in the world. As with a hallowed portion, he who consumes <it> incurs thereby the penalty of death at the hands of Heaven, and this is the point of the words, *Israel is the Lord's hallowed portion* (Jer. 2:3).

When our fathers stood on Mount Sinai to accept the Torah for themselves, the Holy One kept close watch on the world, saying: It may

---

25. JV: *Gaze . . . upon the crown wherewith his mother hath crowned him.* But ER apparently reads *u-lĕ-'immo,* "his mother," as though written *u-lĕ-'ummo,* "the people which is His very own." Cf. Sif, *Millu'im, Šĕmini* (ed. Weiss [Vienna, 1962]), 15, 44c.

26. See Exod. 25:4.

27. Cf. Meḵ, *1,* 34, and MTeh 114:4 (YJS, *13, 2,* 217).

28. Cf. Meḵ, *1,* 110.

29. Here there is a play on *ḥararah,* "loaf baked on coals," and *hirher,* "criticize, question."

be that as the peoples of the world did not accept My Torah,[30] so Israel will not accept it; if so, the decree of [My] judgment will be sealed against them, and they will perish from this world and from the world-to-come. But when they joyfully accepted the yoke of Heaven for themselves, He came down from the place of His glory and splendor, from the uppermost heaven of heavens, and said: *Thy "I", [thy response to the "I" in "I am the Lord thy God"* (Exod. 20:2)], *I shall not forget*[31] (Isa. 49:15); and He said further: *If I forget thee, O Jerusalem, let My right hand [the hand with which I gave the Torah] forget her cunning, let My tongue cleave to the roof of My mouth* (Ps. 137:5–6). And when Israel did gladly accept the kingship of Heaven for themselves, saying: *All that the Lord hath spoken, we will do, and obey* (Exod. 24:7), at once the Holy One said to Moses: *Speak unto the children of Israel, that they take for Me an offering. And this is the offering: . . . gold, and silver . . . and blue, and purple . . . and rams' skins dyed red . . . and oil for the light,* etc. . . . *onyx stones. . . . And let them make Me the Sanctuary* (Exod. 25:1–8). At that time the Holy One said in His heart: Perhaps the children of Israel will not bring an offering unto Me, saying of Him above: Does He need silver or gold? Are not His all the precious stones and pearls, all the kinds of costly treasures in the world? <Is it not in fact written *Mine is the silver, and Mine is the gold, saith the Lord of hosts?* (Hag. 2:8). Why>, then, should He say to mortal man: "<Bring> Me an offering, and make Me the Sanctuary?" Nevertheless, what He requested they gave | <to Him>, and He did what He said He would. **ER, *p.* 86**

And so when your fathers in the wilderness obeyed My wish, I found contentment in them, for note what Scripture says, *And they came every one whose heart stirred him up. . . . They came, both men and women* (Exod. 35:21, 22). They came as though saying, according to Scripture, [Unready to receive Him], *I sleep, but my heart waketh [to Him]*[32] (Song 5:2).

Thus when I set forth the Torah of Priests—[Leviticus, that is]—and gave commands to your fathers, [they did not question at all] the regulations I set down for them concerning men and women with a continual discharge from their private parts,[33] concerning women during their menses, and concerning women just after they have given

30. Cf. PR 21:2/3 (YJS, *18, 2,* 417).

31. JV: *I never could forget you.* Even though *Can a woman forget her baby* (Isa. 49:15a) is quoted, the reference seems to intend Isa. 49:15b. Cf. PR 31:8 (YJS, *18, 2,* 614).

32. Cf. PR 15:6 (YJS, *18, 1,* 313).

33. At their acceptance of the Torah, Israel became sound in body (PRKM 12:19 [PRKS, p. 242]). Only after they had sinned in making the golden calf, did they come again to have in their midst men and women with a continual discharge from their private parts, and lepers (cf. ER, 78), of whom there were so many that the nations of the earth dubbed them "a nation of lepers." See *YY.*

birth.[34] No, your fathers did not criticize Me, they said not a word: their behavior in regard to this particular matter was blameless. [The nations observing God's affliction of Israel with discharges from their private parts and with leprosy, said],[35] according to Scripture: *You house of Israel and house of Judah*[36] *have become the very symbol of a curse to all the nations* (Zech. 8:13), but thereupon God in reassurance of Israel said to them, [*At the time-to-come*], *I will save you, and you shall again become the symbol of blessing (ibid.).*

O my brothers and my people, listen to me![37] He who has eyes can see, who has a heart can understand, who has reins can discern that between man and beast there is no essential difference. Therefore, for man [to be permitted] to sit with the king in his coach—[to sit, that is, in the very presence of the King of kings]—proves that man is given signal distinction. Let him look, then, into his heart, into his body and his being, and come to be aware of the spirit and the soul which the Holy One planted in mankind from world's end to world's end.

When the generality of mankind return to the dust whence they came, none will come back to life again—none, that is, except Israel. Because of the love God cherishes for them and the joy He has in them, He will have them rise to their feet out of the dust, will seat them between His knees, put His arms around them, embrace them, kiss them, and bring them to life in the world-to-come, as is said, *For as the new heavens and the new earth, which I will make, shall endure before Me, saith the Lord, so shall your seed and your name endure. . . . They shall go out and gaze upon the corpses of the men who rebelled against Me* (Isa. 66:22, 24).

When Israel were in the wilderness, they befouled themselves with their misdeeds, but then they bestirred themselves and repented in privacy, as is said, *Whenever Moses went out to the Tent, all the people would rise and stand, each at the entrance of his tent, and gaze after Moses. And when Moses entered the Tent, the pillar of cloud would descend and stand at the entrance of the Tent. . . . When all the people saw the pillar of cloud poised at the entrance of the Tent, all the people would rise and bow low, each at the entrance of his tent* (Exod. 33:8, 9, 10), thus intimating that they repented, each one in the privacy of his tent. Therefore His compassion flooded up and He gave to them, to their children, and to their children's children to the end of all generations the Day of Atonement as a means of securing His pardon.

In the days of Joshua, the son of Nun, the children of Israel with love took upon themselves the rule of Heaven, for when Joshua asked,

---

34. See ER, 75, 78–79.
35. Literally, "of that time."
36. MT reads: *house of Judah and house of Israel.*
37. See 1 Chron. 28:2.

If it seem evil unto you to serve the Lord, choose you this day whom you will serve . . . the people answered and said: "Far be it from us that we should forsake the Lord to serve other gods" (Josh. 24:15–16). The reward of Israel for having taken the rule of Heaven upon themselves with love was that during the time the judges ruled, the Holy One was patient with Israel for three hundred years, treating them like children at school or like sons at the table of their father. And the proof of His kindness toward Israel, you can see for yourself. You need only consider Gideon son of Joash, Abdon son of Hillel, and Ibzan of Beth-lehem. What is written of Gideon? *Gideon had threescore and ten sons of his body begotten* (Judg. 8:30). What is written of Abdon? <*He had forty sons and thirty sons' sons* (Judg. 12:14). What is written of Ibzan of Beth-lehem>? *He had thirty sons and thirty daughters. He gave his daughters in marriage outside his clan, and brought in thirty brides from outside for his sons*[38] (Judg. 12:9). Hence Israel's reward for having taken the rule of Heaven upon themselves with love was not only that during the time the judges ruled, God was patient with them for three hundred years treating them like children at school and like sons at the table of their father, but that He also bestowed upon them the kind of blessing which was to be their goodly portion for ever, as is said, *So Joshua blessed them, and escorted them, and they went unto their tents* (Josh. 22:6)—[there to beget many children].[39]

In the days of the prophet Samuel, with awe Israel took upon themselves the rule of Heaven, as [when at Mizpah "they poured out in repentance[40] their hearts before the Lord like water, fasted . . . and said: 'We have sinned against the Lord' " (1 Sam. 7:6)], and then went on to ask Samuel: *Cease not to cry unto the Lord our God for us, that He save us out of the hand of the Philistines* (1 Sam. 7:8). And, [as later at Gilgal, when Israel in awe of God asked Samuel to pray for them, here at Mizpah likewise], Samuel had replied: *Moreover, as for me, far be it from me that I should sin against the Lord in ceasing to pray for you* (1 Sam. 12:23). Hence it is said: | He who has the chance to beseech mercy ER, *p.* 87
for his fellow man or for the whole congregation, but does not beseech it, is called a sinner, as indeed Samuel declared by saying *I should sin against the Lord* [*in ceasing to beseech for you*] *(ibid.).* Now, the reward of Israel for having taken upon themselves with awe the rule of Heaven was that God came down from the uppermost heaven on high, from the place of His glory and greatness, of His sovereignty, and of His splendor and holiness, and stayed with them in the war [against the Philistines]. That Samuel had beseeched the Lord in Israel's behalf is intimated in the verse *And Samuel took a sucking lamb*—[not one that was

---

38. So *The Jerusalem Bible,* New York, 1966.
39. Cf. Deut. 5:27 and B.Shab 30a.
40. So Targum Jonathan on the verse. See MTeh 29:2 (YJS, *13, 1,* 382).

seven days old, as required in Lev. 22:27]—*and offered it a burnt offering entire* (1 Sam. 7:9). Since the text specifies a *burnt offering,* what need was there to add *entire?* To indicate that [just when Samuel was bringing his offering, the Philistines were right on top of him so that] he did not even have room to skin the animal,[41] for it is said, *Even as Samuel was offering up the burnt offering, the Philistines drew near to battle against Israel* (1 Sam. 7:10). It was then that God bestowed upon them a blessing which is to be their goodly portion for ever, as is said, *For the Lord will not forsake His people for His great name's sake* (1 Sam. 12:22).

In the days of the prophet Elijah, Israel became, in truth, men in awe of Heaven. The happy reward of Israel was that they became men who stood in awe of Heaven [through their abandonment of idolatry]. At that time on Mount Carmel, Elijah rose up, built an altar and made a trench around it big enough to contain two measures of seed, as is said, *And with the stones he built an altar in the name of the Lord; and he made a trench about the altar, as great as would contain two measures of seed* (1 Kings 18:32). Then he said to his disciples: *"Fill four jars with water, and pour it on the burnt offering and on the wood." And he said: "Do it the second time"; and they did it the second time. And he said: "Do it the third time"; and they did it the third time* (1 Kings 18:34). Can you possibly suppose that from only twelve jars of water the entire trench could have been filled? Nevertheless, it was, for Elijah said to his disciples, "He who has some water left in his jar, let him come and pour it over my hands." And Elisha said, "I have some water left in my jar," to which Elijah replied, "Come <and pour it over my hands." Forthwith Elisha poured it> over Elijah's hands. Whereupon from this water ten springs[42] gushed until the entire trench was filled, as is said, *And it came to pass at the time of the offering of the evening offering, that Elijah . . . came near, and said . . . Hear me, O Lord hear me. . . . Then the fire of the Lord fell, and consumed the burnt offering, and the wood and the stones, and the dust, and licked up the water that was in the trench* (1 Kings 18:36, 37, 38). In that instant, Israel abandoned the idols to which they had clung and became in truth men in awe of Heaven, as is said, *And when all the people saw it, they fell on their faces; and they said: "The Lord, He is God; the Lord, He is God"* (1 Kings 18:39).

Thereafter, in each and every generation, the Holy One <claps> His two hands together, puts them over His heart, then places them upon His arms and weeps for Israel privately as well as publicly.[43] Why does He weep over them privately? Because it is demeaning for Him

---

41. Cf. MTeh 27:6 (YJS, *13, 1,* 373).

42. A spring of water from each of Elijah's fingers.

43. He weeps publicly because of Israel's exile and the destruction of the Temple —*YY.* [Clapping one's hands is the customary gesture indicative of strong emotion (of either grief or joy). See Jastrow, p. 533. L. N.]

whose strength is that of a lion to be weeping in the presence of a fox; it is demeaning for Him whose power is that of a king to be weeping in the presence of His servants; it is demeaning for Him whose wisdom is that of a master to be weeping in the presence of His disciples; and it is demeaning for Him whose possessions are those of a householder to be weeping in the presence of a hired hand who hears Him lament *O that My head were waters, and Mine eyes a fountain of tears that I might weep for the slain of the daughter of My people!* (Jer. 8:23). But does the text really say that God asks to weep for[44] *the slain (ḥalĕle)* of Israel? [Does it not really say that He would weep for those in Israel who were slain in punishment for having profaned themselves *(ḥalĕle)* by their wickedness?] The text thus speaks of the Holy One who divided His world into people given to two kinds of conduct—righteous and wicked. What kind of conduct marks the righteous man? He is one of those who are truly willing to study from the age of <thir>teen and beyond. When he arrives at ability to probe Scripture and Mishnah, he learns from them awe of Heaven and the performance of good deeds. These are part of his life until he enters upon eternal life. When he enters eternal life, the Holy One rejoices in him and comes to meet him, saying, "Would that he has a son or a son's son to fill his place," in keeping with the Psalmist's prayer [*May the righteous*] *whose portion is in life* [*eternal*] . . . *be gratified with* [*righteous*] *children* (Ps. 17:14). What kind of behavior marks the wicked? He begins as one of those who seem willing to study from the age of thirteen and beyond. But when he arrives at ability to probe Scripture and Mishnah, then he strays into ways that are ugly, to deeds that are unutterable. Thereupon the Holy One sighs as He comes to meet him, saying | "Would that **ER, *p.* 88**
he has a son or a son's son to bring him to favorable remembrance," in keeping with the verse *When one of you*[*r children*] *repents, whether you are righteous or wicked, you will be looked upon favorably*[45] (Mal. 3:17–18).

[By way of showing God's concern to find merit even in sinners], consider the verse *For the Lord saw the affliction of Israel that it was very bitter. . . . And the Lord said that He would blot out the name of Israel from under heaven; but He saved them by the hand of Jeroboam the son of Joash* (2 Kings 14:26–27). For what reason was Jeroboam thus singled out from among all the kings of Israel who had ruled before him? Was not

---

44. One would expect the preposition *'al* or *'el,* "for, over," and not *'eṯ,* which would mean "with" or "alongside of."

45. JV: *as a man spareth his own son that serveth him. Then ye shall again discern between the righteous and the wicked.* ER apparently construes *šaḇtem,* "shall again," as "one of you[r children] returns," or "repents"; and he construes *rĕ'iṯem,* "shall discern," in the passive sense, "be looked upon favorably." Hence he takes the verse to imply that children who are righteous can redeem their fathers from the punishment of Gehenna.

Jeroboam an idolater? Yes, yet God chose him to save Israel because he refused to accept slander of the prophet Amos.

[Consider what Scripture tells us of Jeroboam]: *When Amaziah the priest of Beth-el sent to Jeroboam king of Israel, saying: "Amos hath conspired against thee in the midst of the house of Israel. For thus Amos saith: Jeroboam shall die by the sword, and Israel shall surely be led away captive out of his land"* (Amos 7:10–11), Jeroboam at once rebuked the bearer of the message and expelled him with a reprimand, saying: "God forbid! The prophet could not have uttered such a prophecy. But if he did utter it, it would not have been his own prophecy but Heaven's.[46] At that instant the Holy One said: Here is a generation that worships idols, and the head of the generation, [its king], worships idols. Yet *The Land of which I swore unto Abraham, to Isaac, and to Jacob, saying: Unto thy seed will I give it* (Exod. 33:1; Deut. 34:4), I will give into the hand of this king, so that people will say: What the Holy One did not give as a possession to Joshua the son of Nun or as a possession to the previous kings of Israel,[47] he gave as a possession to this one. Why? Because he refused to accept slander of the prophet Amos. Hence Scripture praises Jeroboam, saying, *He restored the border of Israel from the entrance of Hamath unto the sea of Arabah* (2 Kings 14:25). Then after him came Zechariah[48] the son of Jeroboam the son of Joash the son of Jehoahaz the son of Jehu. [As the son of a wicked man], had Zechariah repented and become righteous, nevertheless it would have gone <ill> with him; had he not repented and remained wicked, it would most certainly have gone <ill> with him.[49]

In any event, this measure [of affliction that befalls the son of a wicked man] holds for all the kindred of the earth—both for Israel and for the nations.

In the days of Hezekiah, king of Judah, Israel were occupied with Scripture, Mishnah, Midrash of Halakot and 'Aggadot. The reward of Israel for having been occupied with Scripture, Mishnah, and with Midrash of Halakot and 'Aggadot was that a visitation upon Israel's enemies, a visitation destined to take place at the end of time—namely, *The plague wherewith the Lord will smite all the peoples that have warred against Jerusalem* (Zech. 14:12)—was inflicted upon them for the sake of Hezekiah and his generation. And what was the visitation? *And it came to pass that night,* [Scripture tells us], *that the angel of the Lord went*

---

46. Cf. EZ, 184, and B.Pes 87b.

47. The entire territory promised to the Fathers (see Num. 13:21 and 34:7) had been in the hands of Solomon (see 1 Kings 8:65), but in subsequent years its northern portion was lost, to be restored in the days of Jeroboam.

48. He ruled only six months, and was as wicked as his father. See 2 Kings 15:8–9.

49. Cf. below, EZ, 181, 184, and B.Ber 7a.

forth, and smote in the camp of the Assyrians a hundred fourscore and five thousand (2 Kings 19:35). Moreover, upon Hezekiah and his generation God bestowed the kind of comfort which is the best portion to be had in all the world, as is said, *Comfort ye, comfort ye My people, saith your God. Bid Jerusalem take heart* (Isa. 40:1–2). By what parable can the adjuration to take heart be explained? By the parable of a mortal king who became angry at his wife. But he had by her a son who was now some eighteen months old, and every day the child was brought to him, and he would take him into his arms, embrace him, and kiss him, take hold of him with both hands and seat him in his lap, and then say to him: But for my love of you which is so great, I would have kept your mother out of my house for good. Hence, *O Ephraim, what shall I do on thy account?* (Hos. 6:4). *I will not execute the fierceness of My anger* [*against thy mother Israel*][50] (Hos. 11:9).

---

50. Rabbi Saul Leeman points out that in Hos. 4:5 Israel is spoken of as *thy mother.*

CHAPTER 18

A variety of matters: devotion to Torah likened to devotion to a wife; Torah likened to a life-giving river; God the source of man's wisdom, understanding, knowledge, insight; the value of regular attendance in the synagogue; the power of repentance; the strength of God's blessing, the weakness of His curse; God's chastisement of man for his own good; Israel's ultimate redemption; God's compassion for Israel and His watching over them; suffering as the consequence of transgression; the importance of humility before God and man; obedience to the precepts of Torah and punishment of transgression

Summary

God identifies Himself wholly, in sorrow and in joy alike, with every person in Israel, who, in turn, as David did, ought to express gratitude to Him (ER, 89). They ought especially to do so since the reward that comes from God is multiplied a thousand thousand times in this world and even more in the world-to-come (ER, 90). The greatest expression of gratitude, the best gift from Israel, to God, is their devoting themselves to the study of Torah. The exercise of such study by disciples of the wise is amply rewarded by God who bestows upon them wisdom, understanding, knowledge, and insight.

Not only disciples of the wise, but any man, proselyte and slave as well, who fears Heaven will be happy and will benefit from the labor of his hands. At the same time, however, any table that does not have a disciple of the wise benefit from it is not blessed (ER, 91). Furthermore, a wife who fears the Lord is like a vine that brings forth fruit, and her children, like the fruit of the olive, will be richly and variously endowed.

On the other hand, a wife who is flirtatious, domineering, ill-tempered, and impious will bring physical blemishment upon herself and upon her children as well.

Like a man wed to a good wife whom he never abandons, so should a man be wed to Torah. When a man studies and loves Torah, he has wondrous power in the world. For when Israel practice charity and justice in love of Torah, the Holy One rejoices, and Israel are bid to join God in joys that transcend death (ER, 92).

God regards as first-born those who keep discovering new truths in Torah. Indeed, even Gentiles who allow Jews to renew their devotion to Torah every day, God treats as first-born.

Because all the waters of the river of Torah issue from the Sanctuary, the lightest of commandments is as important as the weightiest and the weightiest no more important than the lightest, and both kinds are a healing to Israel. Besides, even a leaf from "the tree of life," from Torah, opens the mouth of Jews for fluent discourse on it. When Israel practice mercy and justice, God's joy in them is so great as to be a thousand thousand times, doubled and redoubled, greater than their joy in Him.

The four qualities—wisdom, understanding, knowledge, and insight—with which disciples of the wise are endowed come ultimately from the Holy One. His hands reach out in mercy to him who turns wholly to Him. He permits nothing to exist in the world whose significance He would not reveal to Israel. The world in which disciples of the wise will live will have a moderate temperature—will be neither too hot nor too cold (ER, 93).

A man should regularly go to a synagogue or to a house of study where through association with others he learns more Torah than he can learn by himself. He should do so even if he is occupied with the study of such mysteries as God's chariot.

Even if a man falter and stumble into sin, he should be aware of the power of repentance. It is a power so great that David who sinned and then repented had kingship conferred upon him and upon his children and children's children after him.

No enemy can prevail over the work of the truly righteous. Hence Moses' Tabernacle endured (ER, 94) but Solomon's Temple was destroyed because of his lapse from righteousness. The final Temple which God Himself will build, no foe will prevail over.

No riches should induce a man to leave a city where there is Torah for a city where there is no Torah.

Though God may set a curse upon Israel when they do not do His will, still they endure, for His curse, made up of only eight letters of the alphabet, is weak and limited in contrast to His blessing, which is powerful and abundant, made up, as it is, of all twenty-two letters of the alphabet (ER, 95). Still one is to remember that because of wilful neglect of study of Torah, Jerusalem and the Temple were destroyed and Israel was all but destroyed.

For such chastisements also we are to give thanks, because they intend our good, intend to save us from the consequences of what we have done. God desires to harm us no more than a father desires to harm his son. So we are always to sing a song of gladness to Him, for ultimately He will restore Israel's glory (ER, 96).

Because disciples of the wise have reverence in their hearts, precepts of Torah are decreed through them and are carried out on their authority. And so even when they are in distress the Holy One gives them gladness.

But why are we to make ourselves bless God under all circumstances? Because we never know the dangers from which He delivers us.

In an apparent aside, a story told of Elijah, the assurance of ultimate redemption for Israel is set forth (ER, 97).

One is ever to be mindful of the compassion of God who ordains that punishment for iniquity in this world is to be put off for three or four generations (ER, 98).

Since poor men are identified by their children's proficiency in Torah, God gives many children to the poor. And when they do not have many children or when the birth of their children is delayed, it is because God wishes to purify them by suffering and bring them to entreat Him urgently for mercy (ER, 99).

Still, a man is to remember at all times that while only one or two angels guard him when he gives himself to some extent to Torah, God Himself keeps watch over him when he does so wholly. Not only does He keep watch over each man in Israel, but He keeps watch over the people of Israel as a whole to make sure that their lineage be not marred by mixed stock.

Hence any kind of suffering must be considered as the consequence of evildoing (ER, 100), particularly in sexual matters, as shown by illustrations from law and from the instructions given by Moses at the time of the revelation on Sinai and by Joshua at the time of Israel's entrance into the Land (ER, 101).

Indeed, an offense committed in secrecy turned out to be the reason for the calamity at Ai (ER, 102). In the event, Joshua's indignation at God was to prove ill-directed. Still, because of the bluntness of his speech and the wisdom and the understanding he possessed, God threw His arms about Joshua.

Nevertheless, a man should realize before Whom he stands and what he presumes to say to One greater than he. Arrogance of spirit is to be avoided at all times. A man regarding himself in humility, becomes aware that in a little while he is to die and lifts his eyes to heaven and asks, Who created all the works of creation (ER, 103). Thereupon he should thank God for the life and breath which in the evening he gives back to its real Owner and finds it restored to him in the morning.

In entering a house a man should be affable, modest in his choice of the seat he takes, and resourceful in performance of deeds that bespeak his fear of God. A man innocent of transgression, who is lowly and humble, dwells with God. Humility of spirit is deemed equal to all the sacrifices prescribed in the Torah. The humble man will never say to himself, "I committed no transgression."

As water makes grow all the works the hands of the Holy One created, so should a man's heart make every part of his body eager to obey the will of Him by whose word the world came into being (ER, 104).

Even as water is life for the world, so is Torah life for the house of Israel, indeed for the world which could not endure without Torah. As water makes seed grow, so the seed of Israel's wicked, and true proselytes will grow truly into the house of Israel. As water purifies, so words of Torah purify Israel wherever they dwell, if only they repent.

As water flows into a river and is gone forever, so each and every man in Israel who has had a quarrel with his fellow should not harbor anger or vengefulness against him (ER, 105). A man should resort to a hundred acts of dissembling rather than make one cruel disclosure that results in the humiliation of his fellow. Nor should one be a hypocrite—soft-spoken but hard-hearted.

A Sage in Israel who truly possesses words of Torah has in his heart a hundred thoughts about Scripture, a hundred thoughts about Mishnah and about matters in Talmud. The wicked man, however, has in his heart a hundred thoughts of larceny, a hundred thoughts of lustful pleasure, and a hundred thoughts of bloodshed. The former makes peace; the latter causes quarrels (ER, 106)—indeed he quarrels with God Himself, for whoever quarrels with disciples of the wise is as one who quarrels with Him at whose word the world came into being. Notable among such were Dathan and Abiram, Doeg the Edomite, and Ahithophel the Gilonite who set out to slay Moses and David with their tongues, slander being an enormity which leads to the most grievous transgressions in the world. Hence, even though God Himself accorded honor to Doeg and Ahithophel, in the end, even Doeg's secular remarks, never mind his discourse on Torah, ceased to be mentioned (ER, 107).

When destroying angels seize slanderers to throw them into Gehenna,

Gehenna protests, saying, I cannot stand a slanderer. Upon receiving other kinds of transgressors, however, it stops seething and is satisfied.

Even those who transgress with utmost secrecy in a dark place and in a completely hidden area will not be successful in concealing their acts and will go down into Gehenna (ER, 108).

As the Holy One puts up with transgression and overlooks it, so should a man put up with transgression and overlook it. At the same time, if you know the transgressor is not your enemy, you are to rebuke him, but if you know that the transgressor hates you, you are not called upon to rebuke him.

The wicked will have their downfall as may be seen from what happened to Nabal of Carmel. He was given a period of grace, ten days, corresponding to the ten days of repentance between New Year's Day and the Day of Atonement, but not having taken advantage of them he perished. And that is the way things work out in the world (ER, 109).

Chapter 18

Arise, sing even in the night, etc. (Lam. 2:19)

Blessed be the Preserver of the world, blessed be He whose compassion for Israel is great. Even though Israel befoul themselves with their misdeeds and make Him angry at Israel, His mercies keep coming on every day without fail. And so, as is said, *I will sing of the mercies of the Lord for ever* (Ps. 89:2), and as is also said, *We will tell of Thy praise to all generations* (Ps. 79:13). Elsewhere in post-Mosaic Scripture, God's mercies and Israel's praises of Him are made explicit by the prophet Isaiah in verses such as the following: *The people which I formed for Myself, that they might tell of My praise* (Isa. 43:21); *I will make mention of the mercies of the Lord, and the praises of the Lord* (Isa. 63:7); *He said: "Surely they are My people." . . . In all their affliction, He*[1] *is afflicted* (Isa. 63:8, 9). We know from the last verse that He is afflicted when the whole congregation of Israel is afflicted. But the proof of His affliction when only one person is afflicted? The verse *He shall call upon Me, and I will answer him; I will be with him in trouble, I will rescue him, and bring him to honor* (Ps. 91:15).[2] Hence it is said, *In all their affliction* (Isa. 63:9), [*all* referring to each and every person]. The Holy One says, In each and every affliction which befalls Israel, I—if one dare attribute such words to God—am with them. Thus the word *He* in the phrase *He is afflicted (ibid.)* is not to be read *He* but "I," [as in the following verse where speaking in the first person He identifies Himself with Israel]: ER, *p.* 89

---

1. The word is spelled *lw,* "to Him, He" instead of the *kĕṯiḇ, l',* "no." ER cites the *ḳĕri;* "Ancient versions read *So He was their Deliverer. No* (so *kĕṯiḇ*) *angel or messenger, His own presence delivered them*" (Isaiah, NJV, note).
2. Cf. Sif Num. 84.

He said unto me: "Thou art My servant, Israel in whom I will be glorified" (Isa. 49:3).

Hence the verse *Arise, sing [words of Torah] even in the night* (Lam. 2:19) is to be understood as follows: Opposite every disciple of the wise who sits by himself and reads Scripture or recites Mishnah, sits the Holy One face to face with him and reads Scripture and recites Mishnah with him, for the entire verse in Lamentations reads, *Arise, sing [words of Torah] even in the night over against the face of the Lord (ibid.).* A like opposition appears in the verse *They—the children of Israel and the Arameans—encamped one over against the other* (1 Kings 20:29), implying that the two armies were actually face to face—indeed, nose to nose. The verse goes on to say, *And so it was that in the seventh day the battle was joined, [the two armies being in the closest possible proximity] (ibid.).* Were it not written [that God and the disciple of the wise were in such close proximity], it would have been impossible to say such a thing, and he who did say it would incur the penalty of death.

What else does Scripture teach in the words [*Pour out thy heart like water*] *over against the face of the Lord* (Lam. 2:19)? They teach that the mercies of the Lord are poured out in abundance upon Israel, both upon the wicked among them and upon the virtuous among them. And the proof? You can deduce it for yourself from what Scripture tells us of David, king of Israel: [Though David did no more than speak of building a House for the Lord, still] in the love He cherished for him and because of the delight He took in him [for his mere speaking of building such a House], He sent word to him through the prophet Nathan: *It came to pass the same night, that the word of the Lord came unto Nathan, saying: "Go and tell My servant David: Thus saith the Lord: Wilt thou indeed build Me a House for Me to dwell in? The truth is, I have not dwelt in a House since the day that I brought up the children of Israel out of Egypt, even to this day, but have walked in a Tent and in a Tabernacle* (2 Sam. 7:4–6) . . . *thy house and thy kingdom shall therefore be made sure for ever before thee; thy throne shall be established for ever"* (2 Sam. 7:16). Hence it is said: If a man has no more to offer his fellow for sustenance than bread and salt, or a salad leaf to dip, or even no more than dates and dried ones at that, his fellow who is offered such meager sustenance, though he may have a hundred meals every day like the meals of Solomon in the days of his glory,[3] should express his gratitude right to his would-be benefactor's face. It was in this way that the Lord expressed His gratitude to David, saying *I have not dwelt in a House . . . thy house and thy kingdom shall therefore be made sure for ever.*

When David heard God speak thus, he prostrated himself at full

---

3. Before Ashmedai removed him from the throne. See MTeh 78:12 (YJS, *13, 2,* 37).

length on the ground, then rose and seating himself before the Presence, said: My Father in heaven, may Your great name be blessed for ever and ever and ever, and may You have contentment from Israel Your servants wherever they dwell, for that You have elevated us, exalted us, hallowed us, beautified us, and from one end of the world to the other, [wherever we dwell], You bound a crown upon our heads, the crown of words of Torah. The Torah I obeyed, I obeyed only with what is Yours; the deeds of loving-kindness I did I did only with what is Yours. Yet as a reward for the bit of Torah I obeyed in Your presence, You have brought it about that this world is to belong to me all the way into the days of the Messiah and of the world-to-come, as is said, *Then David the king went in and having meditated upon*[4] *the Lord, said: "Who am I, O Lord God, and what is my house that Thou hast brought me hitherto?"* (2 Sam. 7:18). By what parable may the significance of this verse be understood? By the parable of a mortal king who had a servant whom he loved with utter love. | Every day the servant was brought ER, *p.* 90
into his presence, and the king would accord him great honor in the sight of all his other servants. Thereupon the servant having meditated upon the king, said, "My lord king, what work have I done, or what satisfaction have you found in me that in the sight of all your other servants you accord me such honor?" It is of honor such as this that David used the word *hitherto* when he said: *Who am I, O Lord God, and what is my house, that Thou hast brought me hitherto (hălom)?* (2 Sam. 7:18). [By *hălom* he meant his fitness and that of his descendants to wear the crown.][5] And Saul used the same word, saying, [as the chiefs of the people were withdrawing from him], *Come back hitherto (hălom),* [signifying by this word his royal person],[6] *all ye chiefs of the people* (1 Sam. 14:38). On the other hand, God said to Moses: *Draw not nigh hitherto (hălom)* (Exod. 3:5): [royal descendants are not to be yours].[7]

---

4. The simple active of the very *yašab̲,* "he sat," is taken here in the intensive sense *yiššeb̲,* "he meditated." Cf. MTeh 1:1 (YJS, *13, 1,* 4).

5. The word *hălom* is associated with the verb *hlm,* "fit [to wear the crown]." Thus of Adonijah it is said that he attempted to fit the crown on his head but it did not fit him (B.Sanh 21b in comment on 1 Kings 1:5). An 'Aggad̲ah quoted by Rashi *ad loc.* runs as follows: A golden rod passing through the crown from front to back fitted into a cleft or indentation in the skull—a characteristic peculiarity of some in the house of David. Only he whom the crown fitted was deemed worthy to be king.

On the other hand, when Joash son of Ahaziah was six years old, and his claim to the throne had to be established, the crown placed upon his head did fit him. See 2 Kings 11:12, 2 Chron. 23:11, and comment thereon in B.AZ 44a.

6. ER apparently reads 1 Sam. 14:36, "Let us bring the king *(hălom)* near unto God" (JV: *Let us draw near hither unto God).* When Saul received no answer, and saw the chiefs losing confidence in him and drawing away, he said imperiously: "Draw near, to the royal presence, all ye chiefs of the people" (1 Sam. 14:38).

7. The dignity to be conferred upon Moses by God was intended for him personally, not for his descendants who were not to be a royal house, that distinction having been allotted to David. See Gen. Rabbah 55:6; Exod. Rabbah 2:6; B.Zeb̲ 102a; and Ginzberg, *Legends, 2,* 316.

And so what David meant when he used the word *hitherto (hălom)* (2 Sam. 7:18) was <kingship>,[8] [the royal house that God accorded him], as you can see for yourself. Indeed, because of the many good deeds the Holy One found to David's credit, the Holy One will seat him at the right of the Presence, as is said, *The Lord saith unto my lord: Sit thou at My right hand* (Ps. 110:1).

In what way, [O God], is the reward from You accorded? When a man does a bit of Torah for Your sake, You multiply his reward a thousand thousand times and set it aside for his good. And besides, there is coming to him what no creature in this world can know. When a man does a bit of charity and performs a few acts of kindness for Your sake, You multiply his reward a thousand thousand times for good, and no creature can know what that reward is, for David said: *And this was yet a small thing in Thine eyes . . . but Thou hast spoken also . . . of that which is far off* (2 Sam. 7:19), namely, the world-to-come where there is no death ever, not ever and ever. *And this is [the reward] for a man's Torah (ibid.),* the reward for the bit of Torah a man does for Your sake, *O Lord God (ibid.).* And David went on to speak to God some more: < *What more can David say unto Thee? For Thou knowest Thy servant, O Lord God!* (2 Sam. 7:20)>. Happy is he who knows in his heart how he stands with his Father in heaven when all his deeds are performed with trust in his Father in heaven. Happy is he who without display fears Heaven; he depends [upon God for protection] like one who shelters himself behind a person armed with shield and buckler.

Thus, we find, it was with David. Even though chastisements had come upon him, still because of his deeds he depended [upon God for protection] like one who shelters himself behind a person armed with shield and buckler. As David said: *The God who is my rock, in Him I take refuge. . . . Praised, I cry, is the Lord. . . . For the waves of death compassed me. . . . In my distress I called upon the Lord . . . and my cry did enter into His ears* (2 Sam. 22:2–7).

A story is told of a priest who without display feared Heaven. He had ten children by one wife, six boys and four girls. Each and every day, stretching himself out on the ground, he would pray, supplicate, and beg [for God's] mercy, all but licking the dust with his tongue as he implored that not one of his children be lured into transgression or into committing some ugly deed. How did the priest go about [saving his children]? Every day he would bring them into an inner part of the house while he sat in an outer part of the house, guarding them as he prayed, having stretched himself out on the ground and besought mercy, all but licking the dust with his tongue in supplication that not one of his children be lured into transgression or into committing some ugly deed.

---

8. Cf. MTeh 1:1, 108:2 (YJS, *13, 1,* 4, and *2,* 200).

The story tells us further that before the end of that same year,[9] Ezra came and brought Israel up out of Babylonia and brought the priest along with them. The priest did not enter into eternal life for fifty years thereafter.[10] During this time he saw his children and children's children become novice priests and High Priests, and then he entered into eternal life. Of such a one it is said, *Trust in the Lord, and do good . . . and He shall give thee the petitions of thy heart* (Ps. 37:3).

The Holy One spoke thus to Israel: My children, among the follies of the nations—[their idols]—are there any that can give food and drink and provisions to those who worship them in this world, and, it goes without saying, in the world-to-come? Therefore, come to Me [for food, and drink, and provisions], for everything is Mine, and all is the work of My hands. A third of the day I read Scripture and recite Mishnah, a third of the day I give over to judgment, and a third of the day I give over to charity, feeding, providing, and sustaining all the inhabitants of the world, indeed, all My handiwork, as is said, *Trust ye in the Lord for ever and ever* (Isa. 26:4). *For ever and ever,* says the verse, because two worlds are Mine: *In the Lord,* | *even the Lord, rock of worlds* ER, *p.* 91 *(ibid.)*—[rock of this world and the next]. Therefore, [O God], all who trust in Your name will never be brought to shame—a reward You promised us through Your servants the Prophets, as is said, *Blessed is the man who trusteth in the Lord* (Jer. 17:7), *For he shall be as a tree planted by the water,* etc. (Jer. 17:8).

Blessed are the righteous who have such trust, trusting in their Father in heaven who created the world with wisdom, understanding, knowledge, and discernment. Hence it is said, *He,* [*the righteous man*], *shall be as a tree planted by the waters, and that spreadeth out its roots by the river (ibid.).* Elsewhere, another verse goes on to say, *In that time shall a gift be brought to the Lord of hosts* (Isa. 18:7). By what parable may these words be illustrated? By the parable of a mortal king whose servant brought an ephah of wheat as a gift to him. Had the servant ground it but not sifted it, the gift would have been unseemly. Had he sifted it but not ground it, the gift would have been unseemly. Had he sifted it and ground it, but not separated out the fine flour, the gift would have been passable. But if he had sifted the wheat, ground it, and separated out the fine flour, the gift would have been perfect.

The parable applies to disciples of the wise in this world with regard to their knowledge of Torah. When a man reads Scripture but does not recite Mishnah, it is unseemly. When he recites Mishnah but reads no Scripture, it is unseemly. When he reads Scripture and recites Mishnah, but does not put himself under the guidance of disciples of

---

9. Literally, "Before that same year elapsed, before the onset of the next year or of the following year."

10. [That is, he lived on for fifty years, to a far advanced age. L. N.]

the wise,[11] his conduct is passable. But when a man has read the Five Books, the Prophets, and the Writings, recited Mishnah and Midrash of Halakot and 'Aggadot, and put himself under the guidance of disciples of the wise, his conduct is perfect. Hence *In that time shall the gift* [*of his perfect conduct*] *be brought to the Lord of hosts (ibid.),* as pleasing to Israel's Father in heaven as a gift to a king.

Scripture also says, *And by the river upon the bank thereof, on this side and on that side* (Ezek. 47:12). What is there in the river? There is Torah in it: Scripture, Mishnah, Midrash of Halakot and 'Aggadot, good deeds and study of Torah. All these have their source in, and come forth from, the Divine Power, and they flow through Israel whose disciples of the wise are *on this side and on that side* with everything [in Torah] made ready and set before them. By what parable may the point be made? By that of a mortal king whose servants and members of his household were seated before him at table. When he saw that they had eaten the food and that it delighted them, had quaffed the drink and that it delighted them, he took and put before them heaps and heaps [of other provender] without stint. So, too, are the righteous in this world served with regard to Torah. After they read Scripture and recite Mishnah with delight, the Holy One in His mercies gives them wisdom and understanding, knowledge and insight, the capacity to do good deeds and to study more Torah. Hence the verse that begins *And by the river upon the bank thereof, on this side and on that side,* concludes with the words *shall grow every tree for food, whose leaf shall not wither, neither shall the fruit thereof fail,* etc. *(ibid.)*—[that is, disciples of the wise who dwell by the river and absorb its life-giving waters will never fail in their understanding of Torah]. *Happy,* indeed, as the olive tree whose leaves do not fall either during the sunny season or during the rainy season, *is every one that feareth the Lord. . . .* [*If thou art such as fear Him*] *when thou eatest the labor of thy hands . . . thy children,* [*too, shall flourish like*] *sprouts of the olive tree* (Ps. 128:1–3).

It should be said that proselytes and slaves who are fearers of Heaven[12] are also included in the assertion *Happy is every one that feareth the Lord.* <Otherwise> the Psalm would have said: Happy are the Sages, happy their disciples, happy they who teach the disciples. But that the assertion applies to all who fear the Lord may be inferred from the subsequent verse, *When thou eatest the labor of thy hands*—[that is, every person whatsoever who fears the Lord will benefit from the labor of his hands].

---

11. See above, ER, 37, and n. 70.

12. Or the Gentile *metuentes* who reject idolatry and may even be inclined to convert, but who have not yet accepted conversion. See William G. Braude, *Jewish Proselyting* (Providence, R.I., 1940), pp. 136–38; and Bernard J. Bamberger, *Proselytism* (Cincinnati, 1939), pp. 135–38.

I bring heaven and earth to witness that whenever a disciple of the wise eats only of his own provisions, benefits only from his own labor and takes no benefit at all from the labor of the congregation, he is included in the assertion *Happy,* etc. By the same token, however, any table that does not have a disciple of the wise benefit from it is not blessed, as is said, *When at his food there be none of those who have withdrawn,*[13] *his prosperity shall not endure* (Job 20:21), "those who have withdrawn" being disciples of the wise, as in the verse *And among those that have withdrawn*[14] *[from worldly concerns] whom the lord shall call* (Joel 3:5).

| [Further, if your wife fears the Lord, then, as the Psalmist says], *When she stays [chastely] in the innermost parts of thy house thy wife shall be as a fruitful vine* (Ps. 128:3)—your wife shall be like a vine that brings forth fruit and not like a vine that does not bring forth fruit. Not only *shall thy wife be as a fruitful vine,* etc. *(ibid.),* but as long as she stays [chastely] in the innermost parts of your house, your children by her will be like olive plants. What is true of an olive tree? It bears olives to be eaten out of hand, olives for drying, olives for fine oil, olives for preserving, olives for fuel oil to burn in all kinds of lamps. So also, so long as your wife stays [chastely] in the innermost parts of your house, she is like a tree which, never being moved from its place, [can ripen its fruit. And as the fruit of the olive serves in many ways], so your wife's children will serve in many ways—some will be masters of Scripture; some, masters of Mishnah; some, masters of business; some, men of wisdom; some, men of insight; and some, men of practical affairs[15] who know what has to be done at a particular time. Such is the significance of *Thy wife shall be as a fruitful vine.* **ER,** ***p.*** **92**

Another sort of wife, however, one who spins in the marketplace,[16] speaks with any man, and sets her eyes on every man, will bring evil upon herself and be liable for the punishment she brings upon herself and her children as well. Hence it is said: A woman can herself be liable for the physical blemishment she brings upon herself and her children as well. How so? If she lords it over her husband, she herself brings physical blemishment upon herself and her children as well. If she curses his parents in his presence, she brings physical blemishment upon herself and upon her children. If sometimes she [goes] outside the house or on public thoroughfares [with head

13. JV: *There was nothing left that he devoured not.*

14. [*Śarad* (Arabic *sharada*) does not mean "to stay" (as in JV)—rather the opposite, "to run away, to escape." L. N.]; hence "to withdraw." Cf. B.Sanh 92a.

15. The translation is *ad sensum.* ["Practical affairs" is logical but does not fit Friedmann's interpolated *binah* (which is in effect the same as the preceding *nĕḇonim*). Some term like *ma'aśeh* or *dereḵ'ereṣ* seems to be required. L. N.]

16. [Spinning involved baring of the woman's arms, and when done in public was considered unseemly. L. N.] See Maimonides' Code IV, I, xxiv, 12 (YJS, *19,* 154).

uncovered],[17] she brings physical blemishment upon herself and upon her children as well. If she does not set aside the dough offering at a time when she is ritually clean,[18] or if <she makes vows which> she does not keep,[19] she brings physical blemishment upon herself and upon her children as well. Moreover, she will never find contentment in life: because of her offensive conduct, one of her sons will be lame or blind, and another will be an imbecile or a criminal.

In this connection, observe the Holy One's consideration for disciples of the wise. As long as disciples of the wise stay in the innermost parts of a house of study, the Holy One has compassion for them and gives them wisdom and understanding, knowledge and insight, and the capacity to do good deeds and to study more Torah. And the proof of His consideration you can infer for yourself by observing His treatment of a disciple from the time he is a child [until he becomes an adult]. When he is judged, he is judged not by his behavior as an infant, nor by his behavior when he is weaned from his mother's milk, but only by his conduct after he is brought into his teacher's house. Then, after having arrived at the ability to probe Scripture and Mishnah, if he abandons everything and goes his own way, <only then is he judged [and sentence pronounced upon him]>.

[A man wed to Torah, never to abandon it, is like a man wed to a good wife, never to abandon her.] And the proof that Torah is like a good wife? The verse *Yet ye say: "Wherefore?" Because the Lord hath been witness between thee and the wife of thy youth* (Mal. 2:14), and again, *Whoso findeth a wife findeth a great good, and shaketh out favor from the Lord* (Prov. 18:22). When a man studies[20] Torah, he has wondrous power in the world, for he can ask mercy, shake the firmament, and bring rain to the world, as is said, *Whoso findeth a wife findeth a great good,* etc; on the other hand, *The Lord calls thee a wife forsaken and grieved in spirit when the wife of one's youth is rejected* (Isa. 54:6). When Israel [in love of Torah] practice charity and justice, the Holy One rejoices. Indeed, Scripture says that His rejoicing in Israel continues to the end of all generations, as is said, *If thy children keep My covenant . . . then the Lord will have chosen Zion,* [*and declare of it*]: *This is My resting place for ever* (Ps. 132:12–13). Hence the Holy One said to them, to all of Israel: My children, what joy can a man have in this world except only in words of Torah? He who rejoices in silver, in gold, in precious stones or pearls, what is his joy in them after the moment of death? After your joy [in such things], there is death, so what profit of all your joy? Therefore, come and

---

17. See *ibid.* The interpolations were suggested and the reference provided by Leon Nemoy.
18. See Num. 15:20 and Ḥal 3:2.
19. Cf. Keṯ 7:6.
20. The word for "and loves" is not in R.

rejoice [in Torah] with Me in pure joy as I rejoice in you for ever and ever, as is said, *Be ye glad and rejoice for ever in that which I create* (Isa. 65:18).

| *As for those who see it—[Torah]—as ever new*[21] (Ezek. 47:12), who discover new truths in Torah, who every day without fail discover new truths in Torah, *He regards as first-born (ibid.).* One who finds these truths is like a first-born to his father and to his mother, one in whom every one rejoices. How so? When a man has a son in a teacher's house, and there is Torah in his son, joy is renewed every day without fail in his father's heart. Of such a son, Scripture says, *A wise son maketh a glad father* (Prov. 10:1). On the other hand, if the son rebels and lets his wisdom, understanding, knowledge, and insight <stray> into alien fields of study but is spared by his father, Scripture says of such a father, *He that spareth his rod hateth his son; but he that loveth him chasteneth him betimes* (Prov. 13:24). ER, *p.* 93

In another comment, the verse is read, *Those who allow renewal, He treats as first-born* (Ezek. 47:12), and is taken to refer to God's appreciation of those Gentiles who allow Jews to renew their devotion[22] to Torah every day. The explanation of this reading? In a city full of Gentiles where there are only ten families of Jews who go morning and evening to the synagogue and to the house of study, the Gentiles surrounding this small aggregation of Jews honor them and accord them respect for their devotion to Torah, as is said, *For this a cruel nation holds thee, [Israel], in honor, a city of ruthless Gentiles respects thee* (Isa. 25:3).

The verse in Ezekiel continues: *Because the waters thereof—the waters of the river of Torah—issue out of the Sanctuary* (Ezek. 47:12). And because [they all issue from the Sanctuary], the lightest of commandments is equal to the weightiest and the weightiest is equal to the lightest, and both kinds are a healing to Israel in this world, in the days of the Messiah, and in the world-to-come, for, as the verse goes on to say, *The fruit thereof shall be for food, and even the leaf thereof for healing (li-ṯĕrufah) (ibid.).* Besides, *li-ṯĕrufah,* "for healing," may be read *lĕ-hattir peh,* "to open the mouth"—that is, even one leaf from the tree of life opens the mouth of Jews for fluent discourse on Torah.[23] When Israel practice mercy and justice, [according to the commandments], the

---

21. JV: *it shall bring forth new fruit every month.*

22. The equating of *bkr* and *kbd* (the form of *r* and *d* in Hebrew is almost identical) in this comment sustains—so says Professor Saul Lieberman in a private communication—the reading of the Venice edition in B.Zeḇ 115b in the comment on Exod. 29:43. In the Venice edition, the comment asserts: "Do not read *bik-kĕḇoḏi,* 'My honor,' but *bib-bĕḵori* (or *bib-bĕḵoray*), 'My first-born,' "—that is, Nadab and Abihu. See S. Z. Rabbinovicz, *Diḳduḳe Sofĕrim* (Munich and Przemysl, 1868–97 [16 vols.]), Zĕḇaḥim, 232, n. 1; and *Torah šĕlemah, 20,* 244.

23. Cf. Deut. Rabbah 1:1 and MTeh 23:7 (YJS, *13, 1,* 334).

Holy One rejoices in them. Indeed when it comes to bestowal of blessings, His joy in them is so great as to be a thousand thousand times, doubled and redoubled, greater than their joy in Him.

It is said: *I went down into the garden of nuts* (Song 6:11). Even as a certain variety of nut has four segments, so each and every sage in Israel who truly has words of Torah within him comes to have [four qualities of spirit], wisdom, understanding, knowledge, and insight within him. By what parable may this statement be understood? By the one of a mortal king who comes regularly from time to time to inspect his household, and proceeds to examine his servants. He does not examine them, however, concerning [their care of] his silver, or gold, or his precious stones and pearls. Instead he asks, "Does my servant So-and-so read Scripture or recite Mishnah?" They reply, "He reads Scripture, recites Mishnah, and does more of it than his fellow." Then when the king asks concerning another, "Is So-and-so wholly committed to me?" they reply, "He is indeed, and far more than his fellow." Forthwith the king is satisfied [that all his servants are men of high moral worth], and cuts short his inspection.[24] Such is the meaning of God's saying, *I went down into the garden of nuts . . . to see whether the vine budded, and the pomegranates were in flower* (Song 6:11). The budding of the vine and the flowering of the pomegranates refer to a man's good deeds and to his capacity [through wisdom, understanding, knowledge, and insight] to see into the depths of Torah, a capacity which Sages in Torah yearn to achieve.

Whence, originally, do these four qualities come? From the mouth of the Holy One [who displays them in His utterance of Torah]. Hence His hands reach out to him who turns wholly to Him, [acknowledging that] all is His and everything is His handiwork.

[As said earlier, even one leaf from the tree of life opens the mouth of Jews for fluent discourse on Torah], because the Holy One permits nothing to exist in the world whose significance the Holy One does not reveal to Israel, as is said, *The counsel of the Lord is with them that fear Him* (Ps. 25:14); *For the Lord God will do nothing, but He revealeth His counsel unto His servants the Prophets* (Amos 3:7).

And shall not see when heat cometh (Jer. 17:8). He who occupies himself with Torah will never, either in this world or in the days of the Messiah or in the world-to-come, suffer the measure of punishment by heat which must befall [the wicked]. What is to be the temperature of the abode in which dwells the man who occupies himself with Torah? Moderate—neither too hot nor too cold. What season has such a temperature? The season of the Sukkot Festival, of which Scripture says, "I will again make thee dwell in tents [for your abodes], as in the days of the season [of Sukkot]" (Hos. 12:10). And Jeremiah goes on to say

24. Leon Nemoy interpreted the preceding parable.

[of the abode in which dwells the man who occupies himself with Torah], *The foliage [that bedecks his tent] shall be luxuriant* (Jer. 17:8)—[that is, in the shade of Torah] he will be able to find ease in the world.

When Israel do the will of their Father in heaven, how are they spoken of? As *A leafy olive tree, fair with goodly fruit* (Jer. 11:16), of which it is further said, *It shall not see when heat cometh, but its foliage shall be luxuriant; and shall not be anxious in the year of drought, neither shall cease from yielding fruit* (Jer. 17:8). By what parable may the verse be understood? By the parable of ten men who assembled for a banquet. | One brought large fish, another brought small fish; one brought fish ER, *p.* 94
salted and unsalted; one brought boiled cabbage and beets; another brought eggs; another brought cheese; another brought meat of an ox, another brought meat of a ram, and another brought meat of a fowl. All these dishes were brought at the same time to the men's table, and each took his share of all the ten kinds of food and went back to his house.

So, too, when a man goes to a synagogue or a house of study,[25] he may learn from each of the nine men already there a single verse of Torah, a single interpretation, a single Halakah, [and the nine may learn the same from him]. Thus each of the ten men[26] takes away with him ten Halakot, ten verses of Torah, ten interpretations, and goes back to his house.

Therefore I say, even if a man sits and occupies himself privately with the mystery of God's chariot[27] and with all His beneficent ways in the world,[28] occasionally he should put all his own occupation aside and go to a synagogue or to a house of study—indeed to any place where new insights into Torah are discovered. Because of a man's presence in a synagogue or a house of study, joy is renewed for him every day without fail. So it is said explicitly in post-Mosaic Scripture by Isaiah son of Amoz: *The Lord God hath given me the tongue of them that are taught by taking note of the times when men [meet] who languish for God's word.*[29] *Morning by morning He rouses my ear. . . . Thus the Lord God helps*

---

25. In a synagogue one learns Scripture; in a house of study, Halakah. So Louis Ginzberg in *OT,* p. 281, n. 253.

26. [Ten men is the minyan or quorum necessary for conducting Jewish public worship. The ten evidently include the man, since the author proceeds to list ten Halakot, ten verses, etc. (not eleven Halakot, etc.). L. N.]

27. See ER, chap. 17. n. 24.

28. [*Ma'aśeh merkabah* and *middot tobot* can hardly mean, in this context, "Providence and God's beneficience." What the author clearly means is that no matter how advanced one's *private studies* may be—even if they deal with the *mystery of God's chariot* or with the *highest ideals of moral conduct* (which, strictly speaking, do not come under the academic discipline of Torah), he should nevertheless put it all aside and go to the synagogue, etc. L. N.]

29. JV: *that are taught, that I should know how to sustain with words him that is weary.* The word *'wt,* variously read "sustain," "feed," "reply to" (Septuagint) is here understood as a verbal form of *'t,* "time"; hence "taking note of the times." See Rashi *ad loc.*

me (Isa. 50:4–7). In these words the prophet Isaiah was referring specifically to one's presence in the house of study. And Scripture says elsewhere of a man's presence in a house of study and his prospects of coming upon new insights in Torah, *They are new morning after morning; great is Thy faithfulness* (Lam. 3:23).

When transgressors in Israel came to deprive David, king of Israel, of his kingship, hurling at him the well-known reproach,[30] even as they were hurling the reproach, the Presence came, and hovering above him, gave answer to the transgressors in these words It spoke to David: "David, My son, *The Lord hath sworn, and will not repent: Thou art a priest for ever, a rightful king by My decree*[31] (Ps. 110:4). Come and learn from these words how great is the power of repentance such as was David's, for it is capable of conferring kingship upon human beings in the world, setting crowns upon their heads. It is also capable of healing a sick man of his illness, of delivering him from all kinds of distress, sorrow, and grieving, or of delivering him even from judgment in Gehenna. As for Israel, when they do the will of their Father in heaven, what is said of them? *The Lord will take away from thee all sickness* (Deut. 7:15). And when Israel do not do the will of their Father in heaven, what is said of them? *Return, ye backsliding children, I will heal your backslidings* (Jer. 3:2). Blessed is the man who on bended knees, in humility, contrition, and certainty of judgment fears Heaven.

The text resumes its comment on *Arise, sing even in the night* (Lam. 2:19). No song other than the song of Torah is true joy. Thus it is said, *Thou art my hiding place; Thou wilt preserve me from the adversary; with songs of deliverance*[32] *Thou wilt compass me about* (Ps. 32:7); and also *Be glad in the Lord, and rejoice, ye righteous; and sing for joy all ye that are upright in heart* (Ps. 32:11). You may perhaps say that until Jeremiah urged Israel to *Arise, sing,* the righteous had had no other experience of joy. [Of course they had.] We find they had joy in the days of David, joy in the days of Solomon, and joy in the days of the Great Assembly.[33] The proof that they had joy in the days of David? The verse *Then the people rejoiced, for that they offered willingly, because with a whole heart they offered willingly to the Lord* (1 Chron. 29:9).[34] And the proof that they

---

30. Doeg and Ahithophel asked: "Is it possible that he who took the ewe lamb [Bath-sheba], murdered its shepherd [her husband], and caused the people of Israel to die by the sword can ever have help from God?" See MTeh 4:2 (YJS, *13, 1,* 61). But, of course, as indicated in Ps. 51, David repented.

31. So NJV; JV: *a priest for ever, after the manner of Melchizedek.*

32. These songs are identified with Torah, since the next verse quotes God as saying, *I will instruct thee and teach thee in the way which thou shalt go.*

33. "The institution which embodied the spiritual leadership of the Jewish people at the beginning of the Second Temple . . . and constituted the supreme authority in matters of religion and law." *The Standard Jewish Encyclopedia,* ed. Cecil Roth (New York, 1959), p. 790.

34. There is no reference in our text of ER to the rejoicing in the days of Solomon, which is mentioned in 1 Kings 8:66 and 2 Chron. 7:10.

had such joy in the days of the Great Assembly? The verse *And they offered great sacrifices that day, and rejoiced* (Neh. 12:43).

Blessed are the righteous over the work of whose hands no enemy prevails. Thus we find of the Tabernacle which Moses made that no enemy prevailed over it, nor was the table of his authority turned upside down.[35] We find, however, of | <the Temple> Solomon ER, *p.* 95
made, that the foe did prevail over it and that the table of his authority was turned upside down.[36] But the final Temple, which the Holy One will build speedily in a time that nears, no foe will ever prevail over, and the Holy One will dwell in it for ever and ever and ever.[37]

[In regard to Israel's singing], look and take note of the difference between the company of Moses and the company of Solomon. Of the company of Moses, what is said? [That Moses and Aaron the priests went into the Tent: *Moses and Aaron went into the Tent of Meeting*]. . . . *And there came forth fire from before the Lord . . . and when all the people saw it, they sang, and fell on their faces* (Lev. 9:23–24). But of the company of Solomon, what does Scripture say? [That the priests could not enter: *The priests could not enter into the House of the Lord*]. . . . *And all Israel looked on, when the fire came down . . . and they bowed themselves with their faces to the ground* (2 Chron. 7:2–3). Elsewhere, of the time before Solomon, the Psalmist likewise says, *Be glad in the Lord, and rejoice, ye righteous; and sing for joy, all ye that are upright in heart* (Ps. 32:11); and *Let the saints exult in glory, let them sing for joy upon their beds* (Ps. 149:5); and *The voice of singing at deliverance is in the tents of the righteous,* [*for each of them is able to say*], *The Lord hath chastened me sore; but He hath not given me over unto death* (Ps. 118:15, 18). Thus it was at Horeb in the Tent of Meeting of which it is said, *In the* [*days of the*] *Tent, even as a man was dying* [*he kept giving himself to the study of this*] *Torah*[38] (Num. 19:14)—saying of this [unique] Torah, My delight is in her, my delight is in her.[39] Of Torah it is said, *She is more precious than rubies, and all the things thou canst desire are not to be compared unto her* (Prov. 3:15); and *It delights the Lord, for His vindication, that* [*His servant*] *magnify and glorify Torah*[40] (Isa. 42:21).

One time as I was on my way from one city to another—it was during a year of dearth—a magistrate[41] came up to me and asked me: My master, what place are you from? I replied: From Jabneh, my son,

---

35. It was hidden from sight. See B.Soṭ 9a and Yoma 53b, 52b.

36. Unlike Moses who retained his authority until the end, Solomon lost his throne for a while. See B.Giṭ 68a and MTeh 78:12 (YJS, *13, 2,* 35).

37. Cf. ER, 129.

38. JV: *This is the law: when a man dieth in a tent.* But see B.Shab 83b.

39. See Isa. 62:4 and 2 Kings 21:1. The repetition of "delight" may refer to both Torahs, the Written and the Oral.

40. JV: *The Lord was pleased, for His righteousness' sake, to make the teaching great and glorious.*

41. The word *ḳwdyr* is taken to be a form of *ḳwsdwr,* "quaesitor."

a place of Sages and Rabbis. He said: My master, come and stay in the place I will show you, and I will give you wheat and barley, beans, lentils, and all kinds of other legumes. I said: My son, even if you give me a thousand thousand thousands of denar of gold, I shall not leave a place of Torah and go to a place where there is no Torah. He asked: My master, why? I said: Because all the people you see in this world who have a sufficiency of worldly goods prefer to stay in <their> places. But if in such places there are no words of Torah, then, when these people die and go out of this world, [they must go without their worldly goods]: only words of Torah can escort a man to his eternal abode, as is said, [*Thy words of Torah*] *shall be righteousness unto thee before the Lord thy God*[42] (Deut. 24:13); and *Thy righteousness shall go before thee, and the glory of the Lord shall be thy rearward* (Isa. 58:8).

As long as Israel do the will of their Father in heaven, He Himself turns to bestow blessing upon them, as is said, *When* [*Torah's*] *truth springeth from the earth, mercy looketh down from heaven* (Ps. 85:12), looking down being associated here with blessing,[43] as is said, *Look down from Thy holy habitation, from heaven, and bless Thy people Israel* (Deut. 26:15). And as long as Israel do not do the will of their Father in heaven, He Himself turns to set a curse upon them, as is said, *Because of transgression, an* [*enemy*] *host will be set upon that which is to endure* (Dan. 8:12). This is to say that Israel, they who are to endure, will be under a curse *because of transgression,* their transgression of Torah. *When thou didst fling down truth to the ground, it wrought and prospered (ibid.):* <Indeed, O Israel, when you fling> words of Torah down to the ground, whatever the wicked kingdom does, will prosper at once.[44]

Come and take note that the Holy One's standard of conduct is not at all like a mortal's standard. When the Holy One blessed Israel, He blessed them with [all twenty-two letters of the alphabet], as is intimated by the verses whose first word begins with *'alef* [the first letter of the alphabet], and whose last word ends with *taw* [the last letter of the alphabet]—from *If ('im) ye walk in My statutes* to *made you go upright*
ER, *p.* 96 *(ḳomĕmiyyuṭ)*[45] (Lev. 26:3–13). | But he cursed them [only with eight letters], as is intimated by the verses whose first word begins with *waw* [the sixth letter of the alphabet], and whose last word ends with *mem* [the thirteenth letter of the alphabet], from *But if (wĕ-'im) ye will not hearken* to *And their soul (nafšam) abhorred My statutes* (Lev. 26:

---

42. "A man's righteousness goes up to the throne of glory." See Sif Deut. 277 (ed. Finkelstein [Breslau, 1936–39], p. 295).

43. Except in connection with charity for the poor, God's "looking down from heaven" intimates, as is stated elsewhere, that He is about to bestow a curse. See P.MSh 8:8, 56c, and Rashi on Gen. 18:16.

44. Cf. P.RH 3:8, 59a, and PRKM 15:5, p. 255 (PRKS, pp. 279–80).

45. The word *'im,* "if," begins with an *'alef,* and the word *ḳomĕmiyuṭ,* "upright," ends with a *taw.*

14–43)[46]—[with only eight letters, even though] *All Israel have transgressed ('t) Thy law* [*from A to Z*], *having turned aside, so as not to hearken to Thy voice* (Dan. 9:11). How else is the particle *'t* to be understood here except that Israel transgressed the Torah from beginning to end?[47]

Come and take note of how grievous is wilful neglect of [study of] Torah: In time gone by Israel was all but destroyed only because of their wilful neglect [of study] of Torah. Indeed, Jerusalem was destroyed and the Temple was destroyed only because of wilful neglect of Torah, as is said, *For the* [*wilful*] *transgression of all this by Jacob* (Mic. 1:5). The word *this* refers here to Torah, as in the verse "Who is the wise man, that he may understand [what is meant by] 'this?' . . . That the Land perished . . . because they forsook [study of] My Torah"[48] (Jer. 9:11–12).

Blessed be the Preserver of the world, blessed be He, who chose you out of the nations speaking the seventy different languages of the world and gave you such wisdom, understanding, knowledge, and insight as to lead you to trust Him each and every hour.

The text returns again to comment on the verse *Arise, sing out in the night* (Lam. 2:19). "Singing out" here refers to a man's giving of thanks for chastisement. Why should he do so? After all, whatever he did he is done and over with. Yes, but chastisements come upon him for his own good—to save him from the consequences of all he did. Hence at midnight a man should rise up from his bed and, [like David], bless, praise, extol, magnify, and hallow the name of Him, blessed be He, at whose word the world came into being, as David said: *At midnight I rise and confess unto Thee* (Ps. 119:62). But how was David able to determine the exact middle of the night? It is said, by means of a harp hung over his couch. When midnight came, the north wind would blow through its strings, and the harp would play of itself. Hence David could say, *At midnight I rise and confess unto Thee.*[49] In this matter of confession it is said, *He that covereth his transgression shall not prosper; but whoso confesseth and leaveth* [*it for God to proceed in His wisdom*], *shall obtain mercy* (Prov. 28:13). What are the matters a man should leave to the [wisdom of the] Preserver of the world? Because of all a man has done, chastisements come upon him, come upon him for his own good, to save him from the consequences of all he has done. A man should not say, I am righteous, I am upright—why should chastisements come upon me? I am compassionate, I bestow mercy—why should

---

46. Here the word *wĕ'im,* "but if," begins with a *waw,* and *nafšam,* "their soul," ends with a *mem.* See B.BB 88b and Lev. Rabbah M, 35:1, p. 818 and n. 5.

47. Literally, "from *'alef* to *taw.*" These two letters which make up the word *'t* are ordinarily taken to indicate that the noun following is the object.

48. Louis Ginzberg's (*OT,* p. 291, n. 420) interpretation is followed here.

49. Cf. B.Ber 3b and PR 17:3 (YJS, *18, 2,* 363–64).

chastisements come upon me?[50] I feed the hungry, I give the thirsty to drink—why should chastisements come upon me? A man should not chatter where he is not qualified to speak. Nor should he protest in a situation where he is not qualified to speak. Let a man look at himself and acknowledge that in fact the Holy One shows no favor even in matters that directly concern Him, for He says, *Israel is My son, My first-born* (Exod. 4:22), and again *Ye are the children of the Lord your God* (Deut. 14:1) [and chastises them nevertheless]. Accordingly, when God chastises a man of Israel, He chastises him only to bring him to the truth that he should own,[51] as is said, *And thou shalt consider in thy heart, that, as a man chasteneth his son, so the Lord thy God chasteneth thee* (Deut. 8:5). Would anyone in the world desire harm for his own son? Perish the thought! *For the Lord your God, He is God of gods, and Lord of lords, the great God, the mighty, and the awful who regardeth not persons* (Deut. 10:17).

In another comment the verse is read, *Rise and sing, even in the night* [*of exile*] (Lam. 2:19). "Singing" here refers to a song of gladness, as in the verse *Thus saith the Lord: Sing with gladness for Jacob* (Jer. 31:6) and in *Sing and rejoice, O daughter of Zion* (Zech. 2:14). Sing all kinds of song and rejoice in all sorts of gladness. Why? Because *I come, and I dwell in the midst of thee, saith the Lord (ibid.).* And sing because in time *The Lord will take away thy judgments, will cast out thine enemy* (Zeph. 3:15). Indeed, *The Lord showed me four craftsmen* [*who will restore your glory*] (Zech. 2:3): Messiah the son of David, Messiah the son of Joseph, Elijah, and the Righteous Priest.[52]

Blessed be the Preserver of the world, blessed be He who chose the Sages, their disciples, and the disciples of their disciples, and makes it a rule of life for them that as a man measures, it is measured out to
ER, *p.* 97 him. For they sit | in synagogues and in houses of study where on whatever day they are free, they read Scripture for the sake of Heaven and recite Mishnah for the sake of Heaven. And because they have reverence in their hearts, precepts of Torah are decreed through them

---

50. "I am compassionate . . . come upon me?"—R.

51. See another interpretation of "the truth that he should own" in *TSE,* p. 167.

52. The two messiahs are called craftsmen because they will build the Temple; Elijah, because he built the altar on Mount Carmel; the Righteous Priest identified as Melchizedek, another name for Shem (see Lev. Rabbah M, 25:6, p. 580), built the ark with the help of his father Noah. So Rashi on B.Suk 52b.

Or perhaps, the four craftsmen are the ones who in the words of Zech. 2:3 *will come . . . to cast down the horns of the nations.* In that case, the proper order of the four might be Elijah, Messiah son of Joseph, who would lead a war against Israel's enemies of whom Gog and Magog are the symbols. Messiah son of Joseph would be followed by the great redeemer, Messiah son of David, whose war would be led by the Righteous Priest anointed to exhort the armies of Israel. See Friedmann, Introduction, p. 9; PRKM 5:9 (PRKS, p. 109); and Num. Rabbah 14:1 (Soncino tr., p. 558).

and put into effect,[53] [as is said], *When the word is very nigh unto thee, in thy mouth, and in thy heart,* [*then what thou sayest will be regarded as law*], *and will be done*[54] (Deut. 30:14).

<Therefore, since they take upon themselves the yoke of Heaven, [even when they are under duress], the Holy One, as only He can do, gives them gladness against their will, as is said, *Thou hast put gladness in my heart, even when the corn* [*of the wicked*] *and their wine increase* (Ps. 4:8).> By what parable may the verse be illustrated? By the one of a mortal king who had a grove of trees near his house. He manured the grove, making sure that the manuring was done at the right time, he hoed it, and he irrigated it from the ditch. Consequently, each and every tree in the grove became more comely as it aged than it was in its youth. The same is true of each and every sage in Israel who truly has words of Torah within him: the years of his old age become him more than the years of his youth, as is said, *They shall not build, and another inhabit, they shall not plant, and another eat; for as the days of a tree shall be the days of My people. . . . They shall not labor in vain* (Isa. 65:22–23). And it is further said, *They that wait for the Lord shall renew their strength . . . they shall run, and not be weary* (Isa. 40:31). This is the promise of how it will be with them at the end of time and how it is, in part, in this world today.

In another comment on the verse *Rise, sing even in the night* (Lam. 2:19), "sing" is taken as a call to praise [of God]. As long as Israel do the will of their Father in heaven, He comes and through them causes His great name to be praised in their presence. That [even in the midst of grief] one is to praise God is proved by the verse *Sing, O barren, thou that didst not bear . . . for the children of the wife forlorn shall outnumber those of the espoused, saith the Lord* (Isa. 54:1). That [when Israel do their Father's will, He causes His name to be praised through them] is proved by the verse *They shall come and sing in the height of Zion, and shall flow unto the goodness of the Lord . . . and My people shall be satisfied with My goodness, saith the Lord*[55] (Jer. 31:11, 13). Therefore, I would say this: For all things good and bad alike that come to a man, he should bless, praise, extol, magnify, and hallow the name of Him, blessed be He, by whose word the world came into being. Bless Him under any circumstances? Yes. If a lion met a man and did not devour him, the

53. [The context seems to require that *u-mĕḥaḳĕḳin . . . u-mĕḳayyĕmin ʿaleyhen* refer to the Sages, "they engrave the words of Torah upon their mouths and perform them accordingly." I am sorely tempted to suggest that *mĕḥaḳĕḳin* is an Arabism (*ḥaḳḳaka,* to make or declare something true <al-hakk, the True One, is one of the 99 "beautiful names" of Allah>—"they render words of Torah true upon their mouths)." L. N.]

54. JV: *that thou mayest do it.*

55. The section begins with the words *Hear the word of the Lord, O ye nations, and declare it in the isles afar off.*

man should bless, praise, extol, magnify, and hallow Him, blessed be He, by whose word the world came into being. For he may well have been destined to be devoured by the lion, but the Holy One had pity on him, so that the lion did not get to devour him. If a bear or a wolf met him and did not devour him or mutilate him, he should bless, praise, magnify, and extol Him, blessed be He, by whose word the world came into being. For he may well have been destined to be devoured or mutilated by the bear or the wolf, but the Holy One had pity on him, so that neither got to devour him or mutilate him. If a dog met him and did not bite him, he should bless, praise, magnify, and extol Him, blessed be He, by whose word the world came into being. For he may well have been destined to be bitten by the dog, but the Holy One had pity on him, so that the dog did not get to bite him. If a snake or a scorpion met him and did not sting him, he should bless, praise, magnify, extol, and hallow Him, blessed be He, by whose word the world came into being. For he may well have been destined to be bitten by the snake or the scorpion, but they did not get to bite him. If a thorn pricked a man in a fleshy part of the body and not in a part where there are blood vessels or bones, he should bless, praise, and extol Him by whose word the world came into being because the thorn pricked him in a fleshy part of the body and not in a part of the body where there are blood vessels or bones.

If a man, as he prays, utters thanks for escape from lesser dangers <he is as much regarded as the one who utters thanks for escape from greater dangers>. Why? Because the Holy One delivers men from <lesser and> greater dangers alike, as is said, *When a faithful man prays for this*—[*for escape from*] *whatever* [*little thing*] *may befall*—[*he is regarded in Heaven as though he were praying that in some greater danger such as*] *when the great waters overflow, they do not reach him* (Ps. 32:6).

One time our Masters sat and inquired <from whose seed Elijah came>. Some said: From the seed of Rachel. Some said: From the seed of Leah. As they sat discussing the matter, Elijah came and stood before them. He said: My Masters, I come from the seed of Rachel.[56] Is it not,

---

56. Elijah's assertion that he was a descendant of Rachel involves, according to Friedmann (Introduction, p. 6), not merely a genealogical fact. An ancient tradition concerning the ancestry of the Messiah lies behind Elijah's assertion. According to this tradition, Edom, the wicked nation, is to be surrendered not to a descendant of one of Jacob's haughty sons, but to a scion of Jacob's lowly sons, Joseph and Benjamin (see PR 13:2 [YJS, *18, 1,* 246] and Friedmann's n. 54 in his edition of PR in which he cites the relevant parallels). Of course, the Messiah son of Joseph is frequently referred to, but where is the evidence that the other who will wreak deliverance for Israel is to spring from the Tribe of Benjamin, the beloved of the Lord in whose portion the Temples of the past and the Temple of the future are to stand? (See Sif Deut. [ed. Friedmann, p. 352, n. 10].) The evidence is in 1 Chron. 8:27, which identifies Elijah as a descendant of Benjamin.

According to this interpretation, the statement in 1 Kings 17:1 that Elijah was *of the residents of Gilead,* which would make him a Gadite (1 Chron. 5:11, 14), is construed to

indeed, so stated in the genealogy of Benjamin? *Adashah,*[57] *Elijah, and Zichri, were the sons of Jeroham* (1 Chron. 8:27). They asked him: But are you not a priest, [and therefore a descendant of Levi son of Leah]? Did you not ask the widow [of Zarephath for *ḥallah,* the dough offering due to a priest, saying]: *Make me of the dough offering a little cake first,*[58] *and bring it forth unto me, and afterward make* [*a cake*] *for thee and for thy son* (1 Kings 17:13)? Elijah replied: The son [I was referring to] was Messiah | the son of Joseph, and by asking for a little cake first, I was [not asking for a dough offering but] intimating that first, [as the Messiah's forerunner], I would go down to Babylonia [into exile] and that afterward the Messiah would come.[59] ER, *p.* 98

[The Holy One is full of compassion for a poor man, and so it is said], *At the beginning of each of the* [*three*] *watches* [*of the night*] *pour out thy heart like water* (Lam. 2:19). Even the lowliest man in Israel, provided he has <wisdom> [and pours out his heart during each of the three watches][60] is more acceptable to the Holy One than [mighty] Ahab, king of Israel,[61] as is said, *Better is a lowly and wise child than an old and foolish king* (Eccles. 4:13); and *A prayer of a lowly man when he fainteth, and poureth out his plea before the Lord* [*is heeded*] (Ps. 102:1). In the manner of a lowly man when he is faint, David stood in prayer before the Holy One, saying: Master of the universe, had You not written in our behalf that in this world punishment for iniquity is to be put off for three or four generations,[62] no man would remain alive on the face of the earth, and the entire world—all of it—would be destroyed. But in Your wisdom and in Your understanding what did You

---

indicate that he was one of the "residents" of *Gal 'ed,* "a pile and a witness" (see Gen. 31:37). That is, "the Hall of Hewn stones, where the Sanhedrin, the supreme religious court, sat, was the pile whence the testimony—[the witnessing]—of Torah went forth to Israel." See Gen. Rabbah 71:9 (Soncino tr., n. 2).

57. MT: *Jaareshiah.* [The two forms *'dšh* and *y'ršyh*) are very much alike in the Hebrew script. L. N.]

58. Elijah would thus be a descendant of Leah. Cf. Gen. Rabbah TA 71:9, pp. 833–35; B.BM 114b; and PR 4:2 (YJS, *18, 1,* 84).

59. The prophet Jonah, said to have been the son of the widow of Zarephath (see P.Suk 5:1, 55a, and Yalkuṭ Jonah, 550), was also an incarnation of Messiah son of [the Tribe of] Joseph, who was to precede Messiah son of David (see ER, 96). So Haida, citing Yalkuṭ ḥadaš. See also *EJ, 11,* 1410–12.

60. The three periods of prayer during the night (see B.Ber 3a) are here referred to.

61. The reference to Ahab may perhaps be found in the phrase *ro'š 'ašmurot,* usually read "at the beginning of the watches." Here ER seems to read the verse "As for the sovereign *(ro'š)* of Samaria *('ašmurot),* it is better to pour out one's heart like water."

62. If even one of the sinner's descendants over such a span of generations proved to be a righteous man, the sinning ancestor was thereby saved from punishment. See Mišnat R. Eliezer, ed. Enelow (New York, 5694 [1934]), p. 96; and *Torah šělemah, 16,* 42–45, and *22,* 69–70. Exod. 34:7 is thus read: "He holds off punishment of the fathers because of children and children's children for three or four generations."

[I think what the Hebrew says is "that punishment for iniquity was put off for three or four generations, and thus to the end of all generations." L. N.]

do in our behalf? In our behalf, You ordained that, until the very end of time, punishment for iniquity in this world be put off for three or four generations. Assuredly, *The Lord is slow to anger, because He is plenteous in loving-kindness . . . putting off punishment of the fathers because of the children, as long as the third or even the fourth generation* (Num. 14:18). <Why> do You put off punishment? Because You are compassionate, because You are gracious, You are slow to anger and rich in loving-kindness. But You are also just and would judge men, each according to his ways, and would requite men, each and every one according to his deeds, and would carry out judgment of them according to the rule that in the measure a man measures, it is measured out to him. [But if that is Your way], why do You act otherwise? Because You desire good for men and do not desire misery for them. You desire
ER, *p.* 99 to bestow good with joy. | You are not eager to bestow misery, and do so with a sigh, as is said, *Thou art not a God who desires evil, misery cannot abide with Thee* (Ps. 5:5); and *Out of the depths I call Thee, O Lord. . . . If Thou keepest account of sins, O Lord, who will survive?* (Ps. 130:1, 4).

David said another thing to God: Master of the universe, by what means is a poor man known in Your presence? A rich man is known by his possessions—his silver and gold, his precious stones and pearls, and all kinds of costly things [which he shares with the needy]. But how is a poor man known in Your presence? [The answer is that] he is known through his son. How so? When his son stands up in the synagogue and reads the Torah, people ask: "That one, whose son is he?" and are told, "He is a son of So-and-so, a poor man." Thus by way of the son of a poor man, a great many people in the synagogue are led to bless Your great name. Likewise when a poor man's son rises in the academy and raises a question concerning the Oral Law, people ask: "That one, whose son is he?" and are told, "He is a son of So-and-so, a poor man." Thus by way of the son of a poor man, a great many people in the academy are led to bless Your great name.

From what was just said, it follows that the Holy One with forethought gives many children to the poor,[63] as is said, *Rob not the poor* [*of the opportunity to study*]. . . . *Verily, the Lord taketh up their cause: because of those who set upon them, He sets* [*many*] *souls among them*[64] (Prov. 22:22–23).

One time as I was traveling from one place to another, an old man

---

63. See Louis Ginzberg's n. 51 in *TSE,* p. 173, which suggests the interpolation of *'l'* before *bmḥšbh.*

64. JV: *Rob not the poor . . . for the Lord will plead their cause, and despoil the life of those that despoil them.* But ER apparently takes *ḳb',* "despoil," in a dual sense: "set upon" and "set." That here "robbing the poor" means robbing them of the opportunity to study is, according to Haida, intimated in a preceding verse, Prov. 22:20, *In* [*the Books of*] *counsels and knowledge have I not written unto thee things which are to be trusted?* (see PRKM 12:12, p. 213 [PRKS, p. 237]).

accosted me and asked: My master, why is the joy of having children withheld from some householders in Israel? I replied: Because, my son, the Holy One who loves them with an utter love and rejoices in them, purifies them [through suffering] and brings them to entreat Him urgently for mercy. The old man said: No. The answer is that they have only the satisfaction of lust in their hearts, and so God renders the women they wed incapable of bearing children. I replied: [Not so], my son. The fact is that we have many householders who drive asses for a living [and being long absent from home have only infrequent intercourse with their wives].[65] Men such as these are not likely to have children, particularly if they have only one wife. [Hence they urgently entreat God to have pity on them and bless them with children. And God answers their prayers], as you can see for yourself when you consider our father Abraham [and our mother Sarah], who, having been childless for seventy-five years,[66] urgently entreated God for compassion, whereupon Isaac came, and they rejoiced in him. Consider Rebekah, who, having been childless for twenty years,[67] urgently entreated God for compassion, whereupon Jacob came, and she and Isaac rejoiced in him. Consider Rachel, who, having been childless for fourteen years before she had either of her children,[68] urgently entreated God for compassion, whereupon both her children came, and she and Jacob rejoiced in them. Consider Hannah, who, having been childless for nineteen years and six months, urgently entreated God for compassion, whereupon her son Samuel came, and she rejoiced in him.[69] You have no choice therefore but to accept the reply which I gave you immediately at the beginning of our conversation, namely: Because the Holy One loves householders in Israel with an utter love and rejoices in them, He purifies them [through suffering] in order that they should urgently entreat Him for compassion.[70]

In another comment, the phrase *ro'š 'ašmuroṯ* (Lam. 2:19), usually read "the beginning of the watches," is read *ro'š* (superior to) *'ašmuroṯ* (Samaria)—i.e., "superior to Samaria." The point of this reading is that even a small town in Israel [such as Abel] where there was Torah was superior in the eyes of the Holy One to a principality like Samaria where there was no Torah.[71] Hence a woman of Abel could say, *Even*

---

65. See Keṯ 5:6.

66. Since Sarah gave birth when she was ninety years old (Gen. 17:18, 21:5), she must have been fourteen at the time of her marriage.

67. See Gen. 25:20, 26.

68. Jacob said to Laban: *These twenty years have I been in thy house; I served thee fourteen years for thy two daughters, and six years for thy flock* (Gen. 31:41). He began to serve for the flock only after the birth of Joseph (Gen. 30:25–31). Since Rachel wed Jacob after he had served Laban for seven years (Gen. 29:26), ER apparently includes the seven she might have been married as years without children.

69. See PR 43:5 (YJS, *18, 2,* 763) for the reckoning.

70. Cf. B.Yeḇ 64a.

71. Cf. above, ER, 49.

I am able to perfect the faithful ones in Israel[72] (2 Sam. 20:19) [by means of my instruction of them in Torah], so that our town, small as it is in Israel, is more than a town: [*it is a city and a mother in Israel (ibid.)*].

ER, *p.* 100 | In this connection it is said: When a man has only right conduct and [study of] the Five Books to his credit, he is given <one angel> to guard him, as is said, *Behold, I send an angel before thee, to keep thee because of the way* [*of right conduct*][73] (Exod. 23:20). If a man read the Five Books and also the Prophets and the Writings, he is given two angels to guard him, as is said, *He will give His angels charge over thee to keep thee because* [*thou followest Him*] *in all thy ways* (Ps. 91:12). When a man has read the Five Books, the Prophets, and the Writings, recited Mishnah and Midrash of Halakot, and 'Aggadot, and put himself under the guidance of Sages,[74] then the Holy One Himself keeps watch over him. By what parable may the matter be illustrated? By the parable of a mortal king who together with his son was traveling through the wilderness. When the heat of the day became intense, the father stationed himself against the sun and made shade for his son so that he was untouched by the intense heat, as is said, *The Lord is thy keeper; the Lord is thy shade upon thy right hand* (Ps. 121:5).

My Father in heaven, may Your great name be blessed for ever and ever and ever! May You draw contentment from Israel Your servants wherever they live! Had You not written such a thing as *Behold, He that keepeth Israel doth neither slumber nor sleep* (Ps. 121:4), who would have dared write it or even utter it? By what parable may the verse be illustrated? By the parable of a mortal king who was sitting on his throne, in front of him a golden salver on which were figs, grapes, pomegranates, nuts, dates, dried figs, apples, and citrons. Sitting over the fruit, he sorted them, putting the figs apart, the dried figs apart, the citrons apart, and so on. And as he turned away to other matters, the wind came up and mixed all the fruit together again. Thereupon sitting to the task again, he sorted them once more, putting the figs apart, the grapes apart, the pomegranates apart, the nuts apart, the dates

---

72. A woman in Abel, a small town of no particular distinction, uttered these words which in JV read: *We are of them that are peaceable and faithful in Israel.* But *šĕlume*, "peaceable," can mean "those who perfect."

73. The immediately preceding verse, *Thou shalt not seethe a kid in its mother's milk* (Exod. 23:19), is construed elsewhere as God's reminder to the angels that when they visited Abraham they violated the law by mixing milk and meat. The reproach so confounded them that they were unable to continue protesting the giving to Israel of the Ten Commandments, and God proceeded to give them at once, saying to Moses, *Write thou these words* (Exod. 34:27). By *these words*—so says Haida—are meant the Five Books and man's delving into them. See PRKM 10:9, pp. 171–72 (PRKS, p. 196).

Louis Ginzberg suggests emending "right conduct and [study of] the Five Books" to "right conduct and God's precepts." See *OT,* p. 288, n. 387.

74. See ER, 37.

apart, the dried figs apart, and the apples apart. And again as he turned away to other matters, the wind came up and mixed up the different fruits all over again. [Just as the mortal king kept sorting out the fruit, so does the King of Israel see to it that the different classes of His people are kept separate from one another]: "Ten classes of people of different ancestries"—so taught the Sages in a Mishnah—"came up from Babylonia: (1) Priests, (2) Levites, (3) Israelites; in addition, (4) proselytes; (5) offspring of unions forbidden to priests;[75] (6) slaves who had been freed; (7) persons born out of an adulterous or incestuous union; (8) slaves in service to the Temple;[76] (9) persons who did not know who their fathers were;[77] (10) foundlings" (Ḳid 4:1). Had the Holy One let go of Israel for two or three successive generations, the ten different classes would have freely intermarried, and Israel would have become [a mixed stock] like the other peoples of the world.

Thus you are ingrates and children of ingrates. Why do you not thank, praise, and bless <your> Father in heaven who with both hands drew you into His embrace and who takes care that you come not to any blemish of your lineage, as is said: *I am the Lord, that is My name . . . I will not yield My renown to those who are blemished* [*in lineage*][78] (Isa. 42:8). Why then, [asks the Lord], do you follow filthy ways and commit such indecencies as one cannot even give a name to? Why do you spurn the chastisements that come upon you? What am I to do except continue them since I have already made the declaration that you are My children and My servants? Having declared that *Unto Me the children of Israel are servants* (Lev. 25:55), then *Behold, I refine them, and try them* (Jer. 9:6). As is said of My messenger, *He shall sit as a refiner and purifier of silver, and he shall purify the sons of Levi* (Mal. 3:3).

One time while journeying among those in exile in Babylonia, I came into a great city which was entirely Jewish—there were no Gentiles at all in it. I found there a teacher of young men who had before him two hundred students, most of whom were between eighteen and twenty years old.[79] But because these young people were guilty of

---

75. See Lev. 21:1ff.

76. JV: *The Nethinim* (Ezra 2:43). According to Rabbinic tradition, however, they were the Gibeonites whom Joshua "gave" *(ntn),* so to speak, to God, assigning them to be hewers of wood and drawers of water in the Temple (Josh. 9:27).

77. They who are silent *(šĕṯuḳi)* when reproached with spurious descent (B.Keṯ 14b); or "one who knows his mother but not his father" (Ḳid 4:2).

78. NJV: *I will not yield . . . My renown to idols.* But ER apparently reads *pĕsilim,* "idols," as though written *pĕsulim,* "blemished."

79. Friedmann omits the words "Their teacher was not among them, there was only a son of his and a grandson" which follow. Haida interpolates before the sentence quoted the words "The following year I returned and found the same students," and reads the sentence "Their teacher was not among them, only a descendant of his who was a great grandson."

self-abuse, their teacher died, his wife died, his son died, and his grandson died, as did every one of the students most of whom were between ER, *p.* 101 the ages of eighteen | and twenty. Even as I wept and groaned for them, an angel came to me and asked: Why do you weep and groan? I replied: Shall I not weep for those who came to possess knowledge of Scripture and Mishnah and are now gone as if they had never been? The angel said: With good cause you weep and groan. Still, why should these young men have followed filthy ways and committed indecencies such as one dare not record? Why should they have let themselves become so foul as to spill their seed in self-abuse? Should not they themselves have known that death in the guise of pleasure was enticing them into their sinful way?[80]

Since restraint is the right rule of conduct in sexual matters, the following teaching was given to the Sages: "A man must take care not to be secluded with two women" (Ḳid 4:12). If you go on to quote what follows in the Mishnah, namely, that "A woman may let herself be secluded with two men" *(ibid.)*, remember that [this is no more than a dictum]—not the law,[81] for if one of the two men should proceed to have forbidden intercourse with the woman, there will be insufficient testimony against the man and the woman.[82] A woman may let herself be secluded with three men, however, for if one of them proceeds to transgress by having intercourse with her, there will be sufficient testimony [against him and her].

[Aside from the matter of testimony], why should the law make a distinction between a woman's letting herself be secluded with two men or being secluded with three men?[83] However, the teaching that a woman may let herself be secluded with three men applies only if the three are disciples of the wise or great Sages: as for ordinary men, considering their appetites, a woman may not let herself be secluded even with a hundred of them.

Hence, taught the Sages, "An unmarried man may not teach little children [since their mothers come to school to pick them up, with the result that he may become enamored of the mothers]. Similarly, a

---

80. By giving themselves *unto the shameful thing* (Hos. 9:10), presumably the self-abuse associated with the rites of Baal-peor *(ibid.)*, the Tribe of Ephraim may be described as bringing forth their *children to the slayer* (Hos. 9:13)—to death. So Friedmann in note 71, who thus suggests a Scriptural foundation for what happened in Babylonia.

Instead of "that death in the guise . . . their sinful way," Leon Nemoy suggests "that [premature] death will overtake them."

81. See Maimonides' Code V, I, xxii, 8 (YJS, *16,* 142). See also David Halivni *Mĕḳorot u-mĕsorot,* (Tel Aviv, 5729 [1968]), pp. 718–19.

82. Two witnesses are required for valid testimony.

83. After all, just as one man may not find the presence of another embarrassing, just so one of three men may not find the presence of two others embarrassing.

woman may not teach little children, [since the fathers come to school to pick them up with the result that the fathers may find themselves alone with the woman teacher].[84]

R. Eleazar said: Even a man whose wife is absent[85] may not teach little children (Ḳid 4:13). And such a rule is widely observed in Israel.[86]

[And in order to prevent other sexual transgression, it is further taught that] "An unmarried man may not herd cattle, nor may two unmarried men sleep under the same cloak"[87] (Ḳid 4:14). And this rule is also widely observed in Israel.[88]

For the same reason, the following practice prevails among Jews whose business brings them into contact with women—makers of oven grates, painters [of ovens],[89] rougheners [of handmills], web combers, tailors, spice peddlers, barbers, and launderers: all these take care not to be secluded with women.[90]

If you wish to study and take delight in words of Torah, go ahead and draw the right inference from what happened to us from the beginning—that is, from the beginning of our experience [of Torah]. When our fathers stood at Mount Sinai to take Torah upon themselves from Sinai, the Holy One said to Moses no more than: *Go unto the people, and sanctify them today and tomorrow* (Exod. 19:10). However, Moses came and said to them: *Be ready after three days* [*to be sanctified*]: *come not near a woman* (Exod. 19:15).[91] But in asking them to ready themselves to be sanctified, did Moses mean them to refrain only from coming near women? What he actually said was "Refrain from impure thoughts, from larceny, and from every improper act so that you will be pure when you stand at Mount Sinai."

So, too, Joshua came and said to the children of Israel: *Sanctify yourselves; for tomorrow the Lord will do wonders among you* (Josh. 3:5), and also said: *Prepare you victuals*[92] (Josh. 1:11). But were there victuals in the desert that required preparation? Were not the children of Israel

---

84. For lines interpolated see B.Ḳid 82a and Maimonides' Code V, I, xxii, 13 (YJS, *16,* 143–44). The prohibition does not apply to teachers working in a school where other teachers are also employed.

85. Or deceased, or divorced.

86. "An unmarried man . . . widely observed in Israel"—R.

87. Such is not the law, Israelites not being under suspicion of sodomy or bestiality. See Maimonides' Code V, I, xxii, 2 (YJS, *16,* 141). But ER appears to be more stringent.

88. "And this rule . . . in Israel"—R.

89. See Kel 5:2 and 15:2, ed. Albeck (Jerusalem, 1958), *6,* 42, 69.

90. See B.Ḳid 82a.

91. He thus added a third day. See B.Shab 87a.

92. The request is followed by *for within three days ye are to pass over this Jordan, to go in to possess the Land (ibid.).*

eaters of manna which they gathered fresh each and every morning, since what they left until evening got spoiled by evening? What, then, did Joshua mean by *Prepare you victuals?* What he meant was: Prepare to be resolute,[93] for after you enter the Land of your fathers, your sustenance will [no longer come from manna, but] from the Land of Canaan's produce[94] [that you will have to grow for yourselves]. Prepare to be resolute as you enter the Land, as is said, *Because the manna ceased the next day . . . they had to eat of the fruit of the land of Canaan that*
ER, *p.* 102 *year* (Josh. 5:12). | As it turned out, however, after manna ceased, study of Torah likewise ceased.[95] <Thereupon an angel came forth to destroy the entire Jewish people>, as we know from what *The captain of the Lord's host said to Joshua: Put off thy shoe from off thy foot* (Josh. 5:15). <By this the angel meant: What, Joshua, are you continuing to wear shoes and so not observing mourning for Israel! Aren't you aware that when manna ceased, the study of Torah ceased with it? *Put off thy shoe from off thy foot (ibid.)* [as a sign of mourning for those in Israel who are about to be among the dead].>[96]

Therefore I say: Blessed is the man who spends much time sitting [over Torah] and laboring in it, but spends little time at business because every day without fail he sits and meditates upon words of Torah. Such, indeed, was the wish made explicit in post-Mosaic Scripture by David king of Israel: *One thing have I asked of the Lord that I will seek after: that I may sit [and study] in the house of the Lord all my days* (Ps. 27:4).

To return to Joshua: When the children of Israel went out to war against Ai, thirty-six righteous men[97] of their number fell (see Josh. 7:5). Then Joshua and the elders came and fell to the earth upon their faces before the Ark of the Lord (see Josh. 7:7) and *Joshua said: Alas, O Lord God, wherefore hast Thou at all brought this people over the Jordan, to deliver us into the hand of the Amorites to cause us to perish? (ibid.).* And he went on to say, *When the Canaanites and all the inhabitants of the Land hear of it, they will . . . cut off our name from the earth; and what wilt Thou do for Thy great name?* (Josh. 7:8). God replied: Am I not the very One who at the beginning [of the events leading to the exodus] said to your master Moses: *Come now therefore, and I will send thee* (Exod. 3:10)? Thereupon, reluctant to go, Moses replied: *Oh Lord, send, I pray Thee, by the hand of him whom Thou wilt send* (Exod. 4:13), and later on said:

---

93. Literally, "Resolve upon" or "Avow repentance."

94. "Your sustenance . . . Canaan's produce"—R.

95. For Israel were busy securing their livelihood.

96. Friedmann interpolates here from Yalḳuṭ Josh. 1:11, which cites ER as the source.

97. The term *'iš*, "man," is taken to signify a man of distinction. See PR 32:1 (YJS, *18, 2,* 621).

Since I came to Pharaoh to speak in Thy name, he hath dealt ill with this people (Exod. 5:23). [Nevertheless, with assurance of My help of Israel, I sent him to deal with Pharaoh. Likewise now, with assurance of My help, I send you to deal with Israel's enemies in the Land. But first you must cleanse Israel of sin, for if Israel have, (in flight), turned their backs on the enemy, it is because they have sinned.][98]

And the Lord said unto Joshua: Get thee up; wherefore art thou now fallen upon thy face? Israel hath sinned; yea, they have even transgressed My covenant . . . yea, they have even taken of the devoted thing—[*the thing set aside for Me*]; *and have also stolen, and dissembled also, and they have even put it among their own stuff* (Josh. 7:10–11). Thereupon Joshua spoke up: "Master of the universe, tell me the name of the man who has done any such things." God answered: "What, Joshua, am I to be an informer![99] You go and have the Twelve Tribes of Israel assemble and cast lots upon them and bring forth out of Israel the man who has done any such things." Joshua went and had the Twelve Tribes of Israel assemble, cast lots upon them, and brought forth out of Israel the [guilty] man, Achan of the family of Zerah. Thereupon Achan burst into great sobs as he said to himself: "Woe unto me! Even things set aside for God, things such as my companions had some time ago captured from the Midianites and had given to Moses,[100] I did not give up. Therefore great shame and humiliation will come upon me." Nevertheless, Achan spoke up brazenly: "What, Joshua! If you cast lots upon Eleazar and Ithamar, will not the lot fall upon one of the two?"[101] Thereupon Joshua said to Achan: "My son, what are you saying?[102] You should repent | so ER, *p.* 103
that you may enter the world-to-come," as is said, *Joshua said unto Achan: Show concern, I pray thee,* [*for the sake of thy soul*], *the glory*[103] *bestowed by the Lord, the God of Israel, and make confession unto Him. . . . And Achan answered Joshua, and said: Of a truth I have sinned against*

98. The conclusion, missing in ER, is a simplified paraphrase of what Friedmann in n. 85 suggests be read as follows: "But Moses, God went on, did not say, 'Would that we remain in Egypt!' Thereat I said to Moses, *Now shalt thou see what I will do to Pharaoh* (Exod. 6:1) and went on: *I am the Lord; and I appeared unto Abraham, unto Isaac, and unto Jacob, as God Almighty, but by My name* YHWH *I made Me not known unto them* (Exod. 6:2–3). And to you Joshua, I say, If Israel did turn their backs before their enemies, it is because Israel had sinned."

99. See Louis Ginzberg in *OT*, p. 306, n. 276.

100. See Num. 31:50.

101. Achan was saying that choosing by lot (see Josh. 7:16–18) means depending on chance, so that the outcome of the choice is not necessarily right.

[I think what Achan meant was that casting of lots invariably produces a loser, even if all the subjects are in fact innocent of any wrongdoing—hence the process is unreliable. L. N.]

102. Since Joshua knew that the Land was to be divided by lot (Num. 36:35), he wanted no aspersions cast on the efficacy of the lot. See B.Sanh 43b.

103. JV: *My son, give, I pray thee, glory to the Lord, the God of Israel.* But *glory* can be, as in Ps. 57:9, a synonym for "soul."

the Lord. . . . When I saw among the spoil a goodly Shinar mantle, and two hundred shekels of silver, etc., *then I coveted them; and, behold, they are hid in the earth in the midst of my tent* (Josh. 7:19–21). At once Joshua's messengers ran and brought the articles kept by Achan and put them into Joshua's hand. But Joshua flung them to the ground and said: "To think that because of such trash there have fallen out of Israel thirty-six godly men, half the great Sanhedrin!" Thereupon he threw the articles in God's face. Said the Holy One to Joshua: What, Joshua! I said that I would so refine[104] My children and My servants as to make them aware that I know the heart of each and every one of them, [yet you are so unaware of Me] that you throw My own things into My face! My son, you did not act properly. Thereat, Joshua because of his transgression fell to mourning without a stop, and finally he expressed his awareness of his transgression by saying: *Ye cannot serve the Lord; for He is a holy God; He is a jealous God; He will not forgive your transgression nor your sins. If ye forsake the Lord . . . then He will . . . consume you* (Josh. 24:19). To this the Holy One replied: Now you [are so unaware of Me that you] again utter slander about Me. Am I not the One who even before your master Moses thought of interceding in Israel's behalf said to him: *Now, therefore, let Me be* (Exod. 32:10). [Since up to this point, Moses had not interceded for Israel but had let God be, Moses understood His words as a hint to take hold of Him, so to speak, in behalf of Israel.][105] Hence when Moses went ahead with prayer to Me and mentioned the names of the Patriarchs, I listened to his prayer at once. When a great pestilence came upon Israel because of the spies [who had gone into the Land with Joshua],[106] am I not the One who, as soon as Moses said, *Forgive, I pray Thee* (Num. 14:19), responded by saying, *I have forgiven* (Num. 14:20)? Am I not the merciful One who for the reassurance of generations that will come after you, had words such as the following addressed to Me: *Who is a God like unto Thee, that pardoneth the iniquity?* (Mic. 7:18).

And then and there, [despite His reproach of Joshua], the Holy One threw His arms about him and kissed his hands because of the wisdom and understanding [he had shown on previous occasions].[107] Thereupon Joshua said to Israel: This reward is given to me because of my blunt speech to you, for on each and every occasion I speak to you, I speak not only straightforwardly to you but in behalf of you: *A*

---

104. Through the terrifying experience of the death of the thirty-six righteous men.

105. Cf. ER, 17.

106. See Num. 13–14.

107. When he reproached God for the death of the thirty-six righteous men at Ai, he showed love for his people. Then again, when he warned Israel that God would not forgive transgression, he effectively put the fear of God into their hearts, as shown by their immediate response: *Nay; but we will serve the Lord* (Josh. 24:20).

sharp warning entereth deeper into a man of understanding than a hundred stripes into a fool (Prov. 17:10). [Because of Joshua's blunt speech, Israel conducted themselves properly and so were able to heed the counsel], *Let thy foot be seldom in thy Friend's house* [*with guilt offerings and sin offerings*],[108] *lest He come to be sated with thee, and hate thee* (Prov. 25:17).

At the same time, [with all due allowance for Joshua's precipitous reproach of God after the death of the thirty-six men at Ai], a man should realize before Whom he stands and what he presumes to say to One who is greater than he; [even as he should be mindful of what] the Sages taught in a Mishnah: "Do not attempt to pacify your fellow in the hour of his anger"[109] (Ab̲ 4:18).

Entreat mercy of the Holy One on behalf of householders in Israel because of their good conduct, and entreat Him all the more so if they [have children who][110] study Torah. Entreat mercy for those who occupy themselves for Heaven's sake with the business of the congregation. The Holy One requites the modest behavior of such people with reward in this world, but their principal reward will be in the world-to-come. On the other hand, householders in Israel are ousted from their place in the world, indeed lose their possessions because they have become arrogant in spirit as is likely when they eat too much, drink too much, get sated, and then dance with joy in the abundance [of good things they have and believe themselves to deserve]. As Scripture says, *Three things the earth . . . cannot endure . . . a servant who thinks he has the right to reign; a churl* [*who becomes arrogant*] *when he is filled with food; and alien wisdom which should be despised taken in wedlock* (Prov. 30:21–22).[111] Because of those who are arrogant in spirit like the three just mentioned, all kinds of mishaps take place. Hence in the words of Isaiah, *To open eyes blind* (Isa. 42:6) [signifies that when the eyes of the arrogant in spirit are opened to the teachings of Torah, they are like *prisoners who have been brought out of the dungeon (ibid.)* into the light of day].

Listen to me, my brothers and my people,[112] so that you do not come to arrogance of spirit. Let a man look at himself in humility and be aware that in a little while he is to die; let him lift his eyes to heaven and ask, "Who created these—the sun, the moon, the stars, the planets,

---

108. Construed as in B.Ḥaḡ 7a. So Haida.

109. Analogous with R. Johanan's assertion that God said to Moses, *My countenance will go and I will give thee rest* (Exod. 33:14), by which He meant: Wait till My wrathful countenance will go, and then I shall give thee rest. See B.Ber 7a.

110. "have children who"—Louis Ginzberg, *OT,* p. 300, n. 161. Cf. below, ER, chap. (21) 19, n. 15.

111. JV: *For three things the earth . . . cannot endure: for a servant when he reigneth; and a churl when he is filled with food; for an odious woman when she is married.* But ER apparently construes "an odious woman" as representing wisdom that is alien, not being rooted in Torah.

112. See 1 Chron. 28:2.

the four points of heaven and all the works of creation—each and every one of them?" It is because of His wisdom and His understanding with regard to each and every one of His creations that all of them hang on the utterance of His lips, as is said, *By the word of the Lord were the heavens made, and all the host of them by the breath of His mouth* (Ps. 33:b). Let a man once again look at the handiwork of the Holy One in man and beast, in the fowl of heaven, and in the fish of the sea. The food of each and every one is in His hand, and the breath of each and every one is held in His hand, as is said, *The Lord God is He that created the heavens and stretched them forth, He that spread forth the earth and that which cometh out of it, He that giveth breath unto the people upon it, and life to them that walk therein* (Isa. 42:5). Therefore, I say, a man should bless, praise,
ER, ***p.*** **104** extol, magnify, and hallow the name of | Him, blessed be He, at whose word the world came into being, [and thank Him] for the life and breath which in the evening he gives back to its true Owner and in the morning finds it restored to him, as is said, *In whose hand is the soul of every living thing, and the breath of all mankind* (Job 12:10), and *Into Thy hand I commit my life, and then Thou dost release it to me, O Lord God, Thou who art to be relied on* (Ps. 31:6).

A man should always be affable on entering [a house]; be modest in his choice of the seat he takes; resourceful in deeds that bespeak fear of God; be wholly at peace <with his brothers>, with his father and with his mother, with his teacher who taught him Scripture, and with his master who taught him Mishnah—indeed be at peace with every man in the world; he should be ready to acknowledge truth; ready to acknowledge openly what he has committed himself to in his heart;[113] and ready with soft answer to turn away wrath, as is said, *A soft answer turneth away wrath, but a grievous word stirreth up anger* (Prov. 15:1).

Blessed is the man in whom there is no transgression, no iniquity or sin; in whom are good deeds and study of Torah; who is lowly and humble. Such a one, said the Holy One, dwells in the high place with Him, as is said, *Thus saith the High and Lofty One . . . I dwell in the high and lofty place with him that is of a contrite and humble spirit* (Isa. 57:15). "Your own deeds," say the Sages, "will bring you near [to God], and your own deeds will remove you far [from Him]" (Ed 5:7). For example, when a man follows filthy ways and commits such indecencies as one cannot even give a name to, they remove him far from the Presence, as is said, *Your iniquities have separated between you and your God* (Isa. 59:2). When a man does good deeds and engages in study of Torah, they bring him near the Presence, for it is said, *Thus saith the High and Lofty One . . . I dwell . . . with him . . . that is of a contrite and humble spirit* (Isa. 57:15): <note that the latter part of this verse can

113. Cf. ER, 63.

also be read, "he that is of a . . . humble spirit [dwells] with Me" >.[114]

Nor should a man say to himself: Since I have committed no transgression and am guilty of neither iniquity nor sin, I am exalted above other mortals, and I can regard myself as greatly superior to them. Such a man should be told: Do not speak thus, if you would live out your days. He should be told that a lowly spirit and a humble soul are preferable to the offerings in the entire range of sacrifices prescribed in the Torah, as is said, [*True*] *sacrifices to God are a broken spirit* (Ps. 51:19). Hence it is said: When a man brings a burnt offering, to be sure the reward for the burnt offering is his; when he brings a meal offering, to be sure the reward for the meal offering is his; when he brings a sin offering, to be sure the reward for the sin offering is his; when he brings a guilt offering, to be sure the reward for the guilt offering is his; when he brings peace offerings, to be sure the reward for peace offerings is his. But him whose spirit is humble, Scripture regards as though he had brought all the sacrifices prescribed in the Torah, for it is said, *The sacrifices to God are a broken spirit.*[115] Note that the Psalm does not say "The sacrifice to God is a broken spirit," but *The sacrifices to God are a broken spirit.*

Likewise, our father Jacob told his son Joseph: My son, say not, "Since I have committed no transgression and am guilty of no iniquity or sin, I can exalt myself over other mortals and consider myself greatly superior to them." Take heed, Jacob said, and do not speak thus, if you would live out your days. For the Holy One gave wisdom, understanding, knowledge, and insight to man only to have him hallow His great name. Thus it is said of Joseph: *They,* [*his brothers*], *who became men of strife embittered his life; they who were destined to share with him his inheritance hated him. But his prophecy concerning them was fulfilled* [*because he observed the Law in secret*] *and put his trust in the Mighty One, and therefore gold was placed on his arms*[116] (Gen. 49:23–24)—[that is, gold bracelets as a symbol of authority in Egypt were given him to wear on his arms]. <And all of this happened because Joseph heeded *the counsel of mighty Jacob (ibid.)* >.[117]

You mortals have no understanding, for you do not realize that *Except the Lord build the house, they labor in vain that build it; except the Lord keep the city, the watchman waketh but in vain* (Ps. 127:1). Therefore *I have set watchmen*[118] *upon thy walls, O Jerusalem,* [*so that*] *Ye who are the Lord's remembrancers, take no rest, and give no rest to Him* (Isa.

---

114. The addition of a *yoḏ* to the particle *'t* makes this translation possible.
115. Cf. B.Soṭ 5b.
116. ER follows here Targum Onḳelos.
117. JV: *by the hands of the Mighty One of Jacob.* But see Friedmann's n. 100.
118. The Lord's watchmen are teachers of Scripture and teachers of Mishnah. See PRKM 15:5, pp. 253–54 (PRKS, p. 278).

62:6–7), <as you *Rise and sing even in the night* (Lam. 2:19)>.[119]

[To continue comment on the verse *Pour out thy heart like water (ibid.)*]: As water makes grow all the inhabitants of the world and all the works that the hands of the Holy One created, so should a man's heart make every part of his body grow eager to obey the will of Him by whose word the world came into being.

Another comment on *Pour out thy heart like water:* As water |
ER, *p.* 105 gives gratification, summer and winter, to all the inhabitants of the world and to all the works that the hands of the Holy One created in the world, so should a man give gratification, [summer and winter], to Him by whose word the world came into being.

Another comment on *Pour out thy heart like water:* As water is life for all the inhabitants of the world and for all the works that the hands of the Holy One created in the world, so words of Torah are life to the house of Israel—may I serve to atone for them![120]—who, wherever they live, cannot endure except through words of Torah.

Another comment on *Pour out thy heart like water:* As water is life for the world, so words of Torah are life for the world. What is true of water? The world began with water. Things grow in the world only because of water. But for water the world would not endure. So, but for Israel and words of Torah, heaven and earth would not endure, as is said, *If not for My covenant* [*with Israel and for the Torah which is to be studied*] *day and night, I would not sustain the fixed ways of heaven and earth* (Jer. 33:25). [By *My covenant,* God means His covenant with Israel], as in the verse *This is the covenant I will make with the house of Israel* (Jer. 31:32).

Another comment on *Pour out thy heart like water:* What is true of water? A man puts seeds in the ground, then pours water over them, thus causing the sprouting and growth of produce from which live all the inhabitants of the world and all His handiwork which He created in the world. < So in the world-to-come will sprout and grow the young children of Israel's wicked, and those who are true proselytes. > Hence the Holy One Said: *I will pour water upon the thirsty land . . . I will pour My spirit upon thy seed . . . and they shall spring up . . . as willows by the watercourses* (Isa. 44:3). To receive the outpouring of God's spirit, Israel will be divided into four companies: *One* [*company*] *shall say: "I am the Lord's"; and another shall call itself by the name of Jacob; and another shall subscribe with its hand unto the Lord, and surname itself by the house of Israel* (Isa. 44:5). Every one of the completely righteous will say, *I am the Lord's;* every one of the young children of the wicked of Israel *will call*

---

119. See Friedmann's n. 101.

120. May I be the sacrifice making atonement for any punishment that may have to come upon them! See Neḡ 2:1 (Soncino tr., p. 238).

himself by the name of Jacob; every one of the wicked, who having had a change of heart forsook his [evil] ways and resolved upon repentance, will subscribe *with his hand unto the Lord;* and every one of the true proselytes will *surname himself by the house of Israel.*[121]

Another comment on *Pour out thy heart like water:* Water makes a purifying pool for all the inhabitants of the world and for all His handiwork in the creation of the world, as is said, *Every thing that may abide the fire, ye shall make go through the fire, and it shall be clean; nevertheless it shall be purified with the water of sprinkling* (Num. 31:23). So, too, words of Torah are a purifying pool for Israel wherever they dwell. Come and see how great is the power of Torah to purge transgressors in Israel if they no more than reject the idols they are holding in their hands, as is said, *I will sprinkle clean water upon you, and ye shall be clean; from all your uncleannesses, and from all your idols will I cleanse you* (Ezek. 36:25). *Water* here stands for Torah, as is said, "Ho, every one that thirsteth, come ye for water" (Isa. 55:1); and *clean* refers likewise to Torah, as is said, "The words of the Lord are clean words . . . refined seven times seven"[122] (Ps. 12:7).

In another comment, the verse is read, *Pour* [*ill feeling*] *out of thy heart like water:* As water goes into a river and never returns, so each and every man in Israel who has had a quarrel with his fellow should not harbor anger or vengefulness in his heart against him, nor be overweening toward him, [but should let ill feeling drain out of his heart] and not withhold words of Torah from him. Thus he will heed Scripture's admonition: *Go not forth on the morrow to strive* (Prov. 25:8).

[This verse may also be read: *Go not forth to strive . . . when thy Friend hath put thee to shame*[123] *(ibid.).* When you think you have been put to shame], do not get into the habit of hurling challenges against the court above, for if He should deem it necessary to have it out with you, you will be unable to stand up | against His arguments, for Scripture goes ER, *p.* 106
on to say, *Thou canst debate thy cause only with thy* [*mortal*] *neighbor* (Prov. 25:9).

[*And reveal not the secret of another* (Prov. 25:8).] For example? If a man has committed a transgression during the year, when the Day of Atonement comes, he is forgiven for the transgression. Accordingly, do

121. For parallels to the passage on the four companies, cf. ARN, chap. 36 (YJS, *10,* 148); Meḵ, *3,* 141; and Midrash Tehillim, with commentary by Aaron Moses Padua (Warsaw, 1865), p. 51 (YJS, *13, 1,* 225).

122. JV: *refined seven times.* But in the comment, *šḇʿtym,* the dual form of *šḇʿ,* "seven," is understood to mean "forty-nine," that is, seven times seven, and thus refers to the Torah which is interpreted in forty-nine ways. See PR 14:6 (YJS, *18, 1,* 267).

123. JV: *Do not go forth hastily to strive . . . when thy neighbor hath put thee to shame.* But apparently ER reads *mhr,* "hastily," as though written *mḥr,* "on the morrow"; and *reʿaḵa,* "thy neighbor," as "thy Friend [above]." So Louis Ginzberg in *OT,* p. 307, n. 292.

not make any reference to it the following year. For, taught the Sages, a hundred acts of dissembling are to be resorted to rather than one cruel disclosure [that results in a man's humiliation]. Moreover, the Sages taught in a Mishnah: "If a man is a repentant sinner, one should not say to him, 'Call to mind your past misdeeds.' If he is a son of proselytes, one should not say to him, 'Call to mind the [heathenish] deeds of your fathers,' for it is said, *A proselyte shalt thou not wrong, neither shalt thou oppress him* (Exod. 22:20)" (BM 4:10), and it is also said, *Thou shalt not go up and down as a talebearer among thy people*[124] (Lev. 19:16).

In another comment the verse just cited is read, *Thou shalt not go up and down as a rakil among thy people: rakil* is read here as made up of *rak,* "soft," and *kil,* "hard":[125] hence the verse tells us, Do not be a hypocrite, soft-spoken but hardhearted.

Another comment: Even as a seller of spices *(rokel)* carries with him a hundred kinds of spices, so each and every sage in Israel who truly carries words of Torah within has in his heart a hundred thoughts about Scripture, a hundred thoughts about Mishnah, and a hundred matters in Talmud to be debated, as is said, *Who is this that cometh up out of the wilderness, like pillars of smoke, perfumed with myrrh and frankincense, with all powders of a seller of spices?*[126] (Song 3:6)—who but men like Moses and Aaron? In contrast to these, consider the wicked Dathan and Abiram, one of whom deliberately picked a quarrel with the other.[127] In the heart of each were a hundred thoughts of larceny, a hundred lustful thoughts, and a hundred thoughts of bloodshed, as is said, *He that separateth himself [from the Holy One] seeketh his own desire* (Prov. 18:1). And the consequence? They speak with evil tongues on earth and with perverseness against the throne of glory [in heaven]. Thus Scripture says, *They have set their mouths against Heaven, and their tongue walketh through the earth* (Ps. 73:9). Though they know Heaven's authority, they trespass against it.

Another comment on *Thou shalt not go up and down as a talebearer among thy people* (Lev. 19:16): In this verse four exercises in conduct are intimated, namely, (1) the conduct of the righteous in regard to the relationship between God and man and (2) in regard to the relationship between man and his fellows; (3) the conduct of the wicked in regard

---

124. The prohibition against talebearing includes the admonition not to humiliate another person. See Maimonides' Code I, II, vii, 1–2 (Moses Hyamson tr., Jerusalem, 5762/1962, 56a).

The words "blessed be He" which follow in the text are deleted by Friedmann.

125. *Kil* is related to *kilay,* "knavish, crafty, miserly" (Isa. 32:5).

126. All powders of the merchant of spices are said to imply "rare powers." See PR 51:1 (YJS, *18, 2,* 856).

127. In order to create an occasion whereby Moses, as he did with the Egyptian, would intervene and the two would thus be able to denounce him to the Egyptians. See Ginzberg, *Legends, 2,* 281.

to the relationship between God and man and (4) in regard to the relationship between man and his fellows.[128] The conduct of the righteous? You may infer it from [the actions of] Moses and Aaron who deliberately set out to make peace between Israel and their Father in heaven, between Israel and the Sages, between a sage and his fellow, between a man and his companion, and between a husband and his wife. Because of the efforts of these two men a good name was established for them, for their children, and for their children's children until the end of all generations, as is said, *These are that (hu')*[129] *Moses and Aaron* (Exod. 6:27).[130] And the conduct of the wicked? You may infer it from [the actions of] wicked Dathan and Abiram who [by their talebearing] deliberately set out to cause strife between Israel and their Father in heaven, between Israel and <the Sages>, between a sage and his fellow, between a man and his companion, between a husband and his wife. Because of the efforts of these two men an evil name was established for them, for their children, and for their children's children until the end of all generations, as is said, *These are that (hu')*[131] *Dathan and Abiram* (Num. 26:9).

[*Dathan and Abiram*] . . . *the wicked* (Num. 16:25–26). Why does Scripture speak of Dathan and Abiram as wicked men? Because the very same men, Dathan and Abiram, were the two who had said defiantly to Moses in Egypt: *Who made thee a ruler and a judge over us?* (Exod. 2:14). Moreover, you find Scripture saying, *The officers, including them who stood rigid (niṣṣaḇim),*[132] *met Moses and Aaron coming toward them*[133] (Exod. 5:19–20) [and reproached them]. And in Numbers Scripture speaks of men who *came out and stood rigid (niṣṣaḇim) at the door of their tents* [*and defied Moses*] (Num. 16:27), the word "stood rigid" *(niṣṣaḇim)* occurring in both verses. Since the word *niṣṣaḇim* in Numbers refers to the wicked Dathan and Abiram, so | the word *niṣṣaḇim* in Exodus must also refer to the wicked Dathan and Abiram. ER, *p.* 107
Again, you find Scripture saying, *And he went out the second day, and behold, two men of the Hebrews were quarreling together* (Exod. 2:13); and

---

128. Literally, "In this verse four exercises in conduct are intimated—two exercises in the conduct of the righteous and two exercises in the conduct of the wicked."

129. *Hu'* is an emphatic pronoun ("that same"), which is taken to imply that they persisted in their righteousness from beginning to end (see B.Meḡ 11a), persisted in making peace between Israel and God, and among the people of Israel.

130. Unlike R, which reads *These are that Aaron and Moses,* etc. (Exod. 6:26), V cites Exod. 6:27. ER presumably takes the apparently unnecessary repetition of the names of the two brothers to intimate that from beginning to end they persisted in right conduct.

131. Here *hu'* implies that they persisted in their wickedness from beginning to end (see B.Meḡ 11a).

132. The usual word for "stand" is *'omĕdim.*

133. JV: *The officers . . . met Moses and Aaron, who stood in the way.* But "stood" *(niṣṣaḇim)* may be transposed to have the word refer to the officers among whom were Dathan and Abiram.

later in the same Book Scripture says, *Notwithstanding, they hearkened not unto Moses; but some of them left of the manna until morning* (Exod. 16:20). Since the [disobedient] men mentioned in this verse were the wicked Dathan and Abiram,[134] it may be concluded that the quarreling men mentioned in the previous verse were also the wicked Dathan and Abiram. Hence it is said: Whatever wickedness you seek to fix the blame for, fix it on a man who is notorious for his wickedness.[135]

But how can it be said that a man is capable of setting out to quarrel with Him at whose word the world came into being? What Scripture aims to tell you in answer to this question, however, is that whoever quarrels with disciples of the wise is as one who quarrels with Him at whose word the world came into being, as is said, *These are that Dathan and Abiram, the elect of the congregation, who quarreled with Moses and Aaron . . . it was as though they quarreled with the Lord*[136] (Num. 26:9). Although the wicked Dathan and Abiram knew that Moses and Aaron were men of immaculate character and destined for life in the world-to-come, the two set out, nevertheless, to slay them with their tongues. Although Doeg the Edomite and Ahithophel the Gilonite knew that David, king of Israel, was of immaculate character and destined for life in the world-to-come, the two set out, nevertheless, to slay him with their tongues. Hence it is said, *May the Lord cut off all smooth lips, the tongue that speaketh enormous things* (Ps. 12:4), *enormous things* referring to words of slander which are an enormity, leading to the most grievous transgressions in the world.[137]

Blessed be the Preserver of the world, blessed be He before whom no man is favored above another. Even as He accorded honor to Ahithophel the Gilonite, calling him "counselor," as is said, *The counsel of Ahithophel, which he counseled in those days, was as if a man inquired of the word of God* (2 Sam. 16:23), so He accorded honor to Doeg the Edomite, calling him "mighty man," as is said, *Why boastest thou thyself of evil, O mighty man?* (Ps. 52:3). By what parable may the matter be illustrated? By the parable of a mortal king who had a servant whom he loved with a great love. So he provided him with a hundred comely garments, he anointed him with a hundred fragrant oils, and kept putting fresh wreaths upon his head. Even so, God accorded honor to Doeg the Edomite calling him "mighty man," as in the verse already

---

134. So Targum Jonathan and Exod. Rabbah 25:10.

135. [That is, where guilt for certain wicked acts cannot be charged with certainty to a particular individual, it is preferable to suspect a proven evildoer than a person whose known record is clean. L. N.]

136. JV: *when they strove against the Lord.* But apparently ER reads the letter *bet,* meaning "when," as *kaf,* meaning "as though." Cf. B.Sanh 110a.

137. Cf. MTeh 12:2 (YJS, *13, 1,* 171–72).

quoted, *Why boastest thou thyself of evil, O mighty man? . . . Thy tongue deviseth destruction . . . thou lovest evil more than good . . . thou lovest all pernicious words. . . . God will likewise break thee for ever* (Ps. 52:3–7). [In the latter words, despite the honor God accorded to Doeg, is His assertion that because of Doeg's love of evil, He will break him] in this world as well as in the world-to-come. *He will take thee up, and pluck thee out of thy tent (ibid.)*—[He will pluck Doeg out of] the house of study, for according to the Sages, in this world, in the world-to-come, and in the days of the Messiah, even Doeg's secular discourse, [never mind his discourse on Torah], will not be mentioned in the house of study. *And He will root thee out of the land of the living (ibid.)*—out of the world-to-come in which the righteous live and endure for ever and ever and ever.[138]

Blessed be the Preserver of the world, blessed be He, who chose the Sages, their disciples, and the disciples of their disciples, and fulfills for them the words "In the measure that a man measures, it is measured out to him." Whenever they have an opportunity, they sit in synagogues, in academies, indeed in any place available to them, and in these places read Scripture for the sake of Heaven with reverence in their hearts. By their mouths words of Torah are enforced, and through them is fulfilled the verse *It is good for a man that he bear the yoke [of Torah] in his youth* (Lam. 3:27). Even so, should one of them ask—if one dare say such a thing—for the entire world, all of it, at one time, it will be given to him forthwith, as is said, *When I speak with regard to [Torah's] decree . . . God says, Ask of Me, and I will give the nations for thine inheritance* (Ps. 2:7–8). But the wicked have no such promise, for it is said, *Not so the wicked; but they are like chaff which the wind driveth away* (Ps. 1:4).

Blessed be the Preserver of the world, blessed be He in whose presence no man is favored over another. When slander, spread about on earth, mounts up even to the throne of glory, destroying angels descend at the command | of Divine Power and seize the slanderers **ER, *p.* 108**
and throw them into the furnace of Gehenna. Thereupon Gehenna objects, saying: I cannot stand a slanderer, indeed the entire world, every part of it, cannot stand him, for the tongue of a slanderer reaches from the earth up to the firmament. First send Your arrows at him, and then I will receive him, as is said, *Sharp arrows from the Mighty, then coals of broom* (Ps. 120:4). By *the Mighty* is meant the Holy One, may His name be blessed for ever and ever and ever. He is called "the Mighty" elsewhere, as in the verse *The great God, the mighty, and the awful* (Deut. 10:17). Because He is mighty, He does awesome things, for it is also said, *The Lord will go forth as a mighty man* (Isa. 42:13).

---

138. Cf. MTeh 52:2–8 (YJS, *13, 1,* 475–83).

The utterly wicked in Gehenna are like brine or fish stock[139] added to seething liquor in a pot. Even as when the seething liquor in a pot stops seething and becomes still when brine or fish stock is added to it, so Gehenna stops seething and becomes still when Israel's transgressors are added to it. What is the story that goes with this statement? When Gehenna was seething, the Holy One asked: Why are you seething? Gehenna replied: I am seething, quivering with anger, shaking because of the wicked among the peoples of the earth who stand up and say vile things about Israel. Such a one was the king of Babylon to whom Scripture said at his death, *The nether world was seething because of thee* (Isa. 14:9), [but became still when it received thee]. Then it began to seethe again. The Holy One asked: Why are you seething? And Gehenna replied: Master of the universe, now give me those who know Torah, yet transgress it, [and I will be still]. Thereupon the Holy One tried to argue with Gehenna, saying to her: Perhaps you do not have enough room for them. Thereat Gehenna swore an oath declaring that she did have room, as is said, *Therefore, by her soul, said Gehenna, she had room*[140] (Isa. 5:14). *Therefore* in this context intimates the swearing of an oath as *therefore* in a similar context, *Therefore I have sworn unto the house of Eli* (1 Sam. 3:14), also intimates the swearing of an oath.

[The verse from Isaiah beginning *Therefore, by her soul, said Gehenna, she had room* (Isa. 5:14)], continues with the words *and down goeth hăḏarah*[141] *(ibid.).* What is meant by these words? That even those who transgress with utmost secrecy in the innermost chambers *(ḥăḏarim)* of their dwellings, in a place of darkness and in an area completely hidden, saying, Who can see us, who can know of us?—[even those will go down into Gehenna, for the Lord sees them]. *Woe, then, unto them that would hide their plans deep from the Lord! Who do their work in dark places, and say "Who seeth us, who taketh note of us?"* (Isa. 29:15) and keep telling themselves: *"The Lord will not see, neither will the God of Jacob give heed"* (Ps. 94:7), and *"The Lord seeth us not, the Lord hath forsaken the Land"* (Ezek. 8:12).

Blessed be He whose presence is everywhere, blessed be He who judges all men equally. Though those who commit transgression do so with utmost secrecy in the innermost chambers of their dwellings, in a place of darkness and in an area completely hidden, God uncovers them, nevertheless, uncovers them in their innermost chambers no matter how secret, even in a place well hidden by rocks, even in places

---

139. The word *mwryys* is taken to mean "fish fat, salt, oil, and wine" (Lieberman, *TKF, 2,* 57). Hence, "fish stock."

140. The verse, according to ER, goes on to say, *and opened her mouth for those without* [*Torah's*] *law.* JV: *Therefore the nether world hath enlarged her desire, and opened her mouth without measure.*

141. Usual translation: *her glory.*

dug into the ground.[142] As God says: *At that time I will search Jerusalem with lamps; and I will punish the men . . . that say: "The Lord will not do good, neither will He do evil"* (Zeph. 1:12). Scripture goes on to say of the transgressors, *Therefore their wealth shall become a booty, and their houses a desolation* (Zeph. 1:13). Hence [in regard to the punishment of Israel's transgressors] *hăḏarah* (Isa. 5:14) [is to be read *ḥăḏarah,* "that which men do in secrecy"].

Another comment on *hăḏarah:* read not *hăḏarah* but *ḥaḏrah,* "roam about"[143]—that is, those who roam about seeking to commit transgressions and commit them [will go down into Gehenna]. Such is the extended meaning of *ḥaḏrah.*

[In further comment on Isaiah 5:14, the words usually read *their tumult* (in *And down goeth their glory and their tumult*) are read] "its bands"[144] and are taken to refer to those who get together in various bands or gangs of five or ten or fifteen to rob, commit larcenies, and fornicate in one another's presence.[145] They have no shame before any one above or below. They swear to falsehoods and in court they deny all charges against them.

Śĕ'onah[146] in the same verse from Isaiah (5:14) means "being at ease." All of the crimes just mentioned are committed by bandits who, out of boredom with their life of ease, roam about and rob their fellows. Hence Isaiah is saying this: Men such as those who, bored by a life of ease, roam about in gangs will be made to go down into Gehenna which will be glad <and will at once stop seething>.

And you, the world's righteous, who every day obeyed My will in the Torah, come <and behold> the utterly wicked in Israel and the wicked among the nations of the earth going down into Gehenna. Thus Scripture | says, *Thou shalt fan them, and the wind shall carry them away, and the whirlwind shall scatter them, and thou shalt rejoice in the Lord, thou shalt glory in the Holy One of Israel* (Isa. 41:16). ER, *p.* 109

<*Do not hate thy brother in thy heart* (Lev. 19:17).> Blessed be the Preserver of the world, blessed be He in whose presence no man is favored over another. The Holy One, may His great name be blessed for ever and ever and ever, puts up with transgression, overlooks it, and does not harbor hatred or vengefulness toward Israel wherever they live, nor does He withhold words of Torah from them. Likewise, a man

---

142. Cf. Ben Sira 16:17, 17:19f, 23:18f, 42:20; and Wisdom of Solomon 1:6f.

143. [*ḥaḏar* means the opposite of "roam about"—it means "to enclose, to encompass": "who concentrate on committing transgressions." L. N.]

144. *Hamon,* "tumult," can also mean "band, crowd."

145. So, as suggested by Professor E. E. Urbach, is the reading in R. Instead of correctly reading *mznyn,* Friedmann reads it *mwnyn* which might be translated "and then divide their loot with one another."

146. JV: *their uproar.* But *ša'on,* "uproar," is related by ER to *sa'anan,* "at ease, comfortable."

should put up with an affront, overlook it, and not harbor in his heart hatred or vengefulness toward any Israelite wherever he lives, nor withhold words of Torah from him, as is said, *Do not hate thy brother in thy heart.* <What is intimated by *in thy heart?*> The hatred that dwells hidden <in the heart>.[147] Surely, it is not about brothers in a family that Scripture is speaking of here, but rather about "brothers" who recognize their common brotherhood in relation to God. God Himself has no brothers in this world, nor will He have any in the days of the Messiah or in the world-to-come. Nevertheless, God calls "My brothers and My companions" those who are the righteous of the world and who obey His Torah every day without fail. It is these He speaks of as "His brothers and companions," as when He said: *For My brethren and companions' sakes, I speak of that* [*Torah*] *which brings peace within thee*[148] (Ps. 122:8).

Thou shalt surely rebuke one who is close by thee (Lev. 19:18). You may suppose that only when you know that someone is not your enemy, may you rebuke him [if the occasion arises], but that otherwise you are not called upon to rebuke him. Therefore Scripture says, *Thou shalt surely rebuke one who is close by thee.*

In a different comment, the last phrase in the verse just cited is read, *one who is of thy kind.* If he is like you in obedience to commandments, you are to rebuke him [if the occasion arises], but if he is a wicked man who hates you, you are not called upon to rebuke him, for it is said, *He that correcteth a scorner getteth to himself shame* (Prov. 9:7). Moreover, said R. Eleazar ben Mathia:[149] If there is a matter at issue between your neighbor and you, speak to him [privately] so that you do not sin because of him, for it is said, *Thou shalt surely rebuke thy neighbor, and not bear sin because of him* (Lev. 19:17).

Note that Scripture says, *Rejoice not when thine enemy falleth, and let not thy heart be glad when he stumbleth* (Prov. 24:17). But elsewhere Scripture says, *When the wicked perish, there is joy* (Prov. 11:10). How are the two verses to be reconciled? The first verse refers to a disciple of the wise who one day betters you in discussion of Halak̲ah, but another day gets himself into trouble: do not rejoice at his downfall, for the Lord sees your rejoicing and it is displeasing in His sight.[150] On the other hand, if you see a Jew who wishes his fellow evil, he is thoroughly wicked, [and you may rejoice at his downfall].

---

147. But it is permissible to frown at one's fellow and speak in sharp disapproval in order to correct him. Haida.

148. JV: *For my brethren and companions' sake, I will now say: "Peace be within thee"* (Ps. 122:8).

149. A second generation Tanna, contemporary of Ben Azzai. See Yeb̲ 10:3.

150. Perhaps this is what R. Samuel haḳ-Ḳatan meant in his cryptic utterance in Ab̲ 4:19.

As for proof of the downfall of the wicked, you may readily find it in what happened to Nabal the Carmelite. Ten of David's young men had come up [to Nabal's dwelling], and there had seen all sorts of food and drink, but had been churlishly denied any of them. Indeed the young men were told that Nabal intended to slay them. [The Lord, however, smote him instead.]

Blessed be the Preserver of the world, blessed be He, before whom all men are judged equally. Because Nabal sought the death of the young men, his breath failed him after ten days, as is said, *It came to pass about ten days after, that the Lord smote Nabal,* etc. (1 Sam. 25:38). What is signified by *about* in the phrase *about ten days?* If it were a greater number of days, Scripture would have specified "forty days" or "fifty days"; if a lesser number, Scripture would have specified "four days" or "five days." In the phrase *about ten days,* however, the preposition *kĕ,* "about," is to be understood not as meaning "about," but as meaning "like." Hence the ten days are to be considered like the ten days between New Year's Day and the Day of Atonement that the Holy One gave to Israel for resolving upon repentance, so that He could pardon them for all their iniquities. Nabal likewise was given a period of ten days to resolve upon repentance, but he did not repent. Such is the meaning of *It came to pass after a period like the ten days that the Lord smote Nabal.* Then what does Scripture go on to say? *When David heard that Nabal was dead, he said: Blessed be the Lord, that hath pleaded the cause of my reproach from the hand of Nabal* (1 Sam. 25:39). Assuredly, as is said, *The wicked man . . . may prepare raiment, but the just shall put it on* (Job 27:17). And that is the way things work out in the world.

CHAPTER (19)

Israel's preoccupation with Torah

Summary

Even under adverse circumstances, all kinds of Jews engage themselves and their children in the study of Torah. Moreover, in contrast to the heathen, even under chastisement Jews continue to bless and glorify the name of God. They do so because they are aware of God's punishment of wrongdoers, as in the case of the incredibly wicked king Manasseh (ER, 110). Though sinners such as he know they are responsible for the slaying of their young, they persist in their iniquities, saying of them, "What I'm doing isn't really anything." The righteous, on the other hand, are ever aware of the consequences of their wrongdoing saying, "Woe is me! Should one of my sons die because of my iniquities?" (ER, 111). And because such concern is true of most Jews, the author prays that God keep in mind His possessions Israel and Torah, but for whom the world could not continue to exist (ER, 112).

Chapter (19)

ER, ***p.*** **110** [*Pour out thy heart like water*] *before the face of the Lord* (Lam. 2:19). <Our Father> in heaven, behold our affliction and defend our cause. May the humiliation which we suffer each and every hour come to Your notice! Remember how many householders in Israel possess nothing at all, yet occupy themselves with Torah every day without fail. Remember how many are the poor and needy in Israel from whose persons the peoples of the world tear the very flesh [by exaction of taxes], yet these poor and needy occupy themselves with Torah every day without fail. Remember how many blind there are in Israel who do not even have food, yet manage <to pay> for the instruction of their children in Torah. Remember how many youngsters and little ones there are in Israel who do not know their right hand from their left, yet, as little as they know, occupy themselves with Torah every day without fail. Remember how many old men and old women there are in Israel who go to the synagogue and to the academy morning and evening, and every day without fail, hope for, look forward to, indeed yearn for Your deliverance [of Israel]. My Father in heaven, You are just but loving, and so all Your works are done in mercy. May Your compassions flood again and again over Your children! For if, in a small town —"small" as defined by the Sages[1]—among the heathen nations of the

---

1. A town that did not have ten men of leisure and of ample means to devote themselves to the welfare of the community (Meḡ 1:3, 3:1).

world, You were to find ten men and inflict chastisements upon them and bring poverty upon them, would they, if they could manage to survive these afflictions, bless You, praise You, glorify You [as does the smallest congregation in Israel]?

Soon, very soon, may Your name be blessed before all mortals! As for our conduct, [in contrast to the heathen's], nothing need be said.

By the [Temple] service I swear that every day and every time I read a certain verse, the verse in which God is quoted as saying *I will go and return to My place* (Hos. 5:15), my heart breaks within me. For His assertion is a direct repudiation of the resolute valor of my kinsmen of the Tribe of Benjamin [who fought and died in vain for the sake of Ephraim].[2] Nevertheless, I offer you a parable to illustrate God's reason for saying that He would abandon us and return to His place,[3] [a parable that has to do with Manasseh during his fifty-five–year rule[4] of Judah]: Suppose you had in your house a servant whom you had brought up from the day he came into the world until he reached manhood. And suppose that then you gave him a wife and that he begot sons and daughters whom you helped bring up through grief, enslavement, exile, trouble, | distress, and even want of food. Suppose that ER, *p.* 111
on a certain occasion you said to him: [To show your gratitude] tell your sons that [for my sake] you want them to do some work with you in private, and then, [when they went with him, and he had them by themselves], he proceeded [in blackest ingratitude and malice] to slay all of them at one and the same time.[5] Such a servant, how would you regard him? Were it not better altogether if he had not come into the world?

Or suppose that in your household you had a son whom you brought up from the day he came into the world until the day he reached manhood. Suppose that then you gave him a wife, built him a house, filled his house with wheat, barley, beans, and lentils, and all other kinds of legumes. Suppose that on a certain occasion, while you were both seated at the same table, he rose up and came at you from behind, smote you, and laid you low on the ground. How would you

---

2. This crux is explained by Friedmann (n. 10), by means of a special interpretation of Hos. 5:7–14, as follows: When Ephraim was threatened with invasion, the trumpet of alarm was sounded in the territory of the Tribe of Benjamin. Though Benjamin was part of the kingdom of Judah, it nevertheless resolutely sought to help Ephraim only to be also crushed by the invader. Now since Elijah was a descendant of the Tribe of Benjamin (see ER, 97), his heart breaks at the thought of Benjamin's futile act of valor.

3. Literally, "I shall illustrate the reason for the earlier statement." Or, [to explain what is the substance of the matter. L. N.].

4. See 2 Chron. 33:1.

5. The reference is to Hos. 9:13 which, according to Targum Jonathan, asserts that Ephraim offered up their children as sacrifices to idols.

regard him? If he were your son, you would not let him remain in your house for one instant.

Or suppose you had in your household a son in ever-burning haste[6] to commit [sexual] transgressions, yet saying, "What I'm doing isn't really anything"; in ever-burning haste to commit larceny, yet saying, "What I'm doing isn't really anything"; in ever-burning haste to shed blood, yet saying, "What I'm doing isn't really anything." Idling in the academy, idling at acquiring any Torah therein, in the meantime he puts his wife, his children, and his household in jeopardy of Divine punishment. How would you regard such a son? He is the sort who is subject to all of the four penalties of death which a court has the power to impose, and also subject to the other kinds of death penalties spoken of in Scripture.[7]

Such sinners surely realize that their iniquities cause their children's death, as is said, *In thy skirts is found the blood of the souls of the innocent* (Jer. 2:34). On the other hand, *The righteous foreknoweth the soul of his innocent lambkin* (Prov. 12:10). *The righteous foreknoweth.* Just how? Well, if there are words of Torah within a man, he knows from within that he should not commit any transgression or perform any indecent act. If the thought of any wrongdoing does come into his mind, he says, "Woe is me! Should one of my sons die because of my iniquities?" Hence it is said, *The righteous foreknoweth the soul of his innocent lambkin.* As for the wicked, the verse goes on to say: *The wicked are cruel even to their own children*[8] *(ibid.).* Even though they know that their iniquities are cruelly responsible for the death of their young, nevertheless they persist in their iniquities and thus cause the death of their young. This is what is signified by *The wicked are cruel even to their own children.* And in the measure that they measured out, You will measure out to them, as is said, *Behold, the day of the Lord cometh, cruel, and full of wrath and fierce anger . . . to destroy the sinners* (Isa. 13:9). These in ever-burning haste to commit [sexual] transgressions, keep saying, "What I'm doing isn't really anything"; in ever-burning haste to perpetrate larceny, keep saying, "What I'm doing isn't really anything"; in ever-burning haste to shed blood, keep saying, "What I'm doing isn't really anything." Hence it is said, *The wickedness burneth as the fire* (Isa. 9:17). And in the measure that they measured out, You will measure out to them, as is

6. [Neither Jastrow nor Ben-Yehudah record *hib̲'ir* in the sense of "eager to do something"—this must be the author's own neologism (another proof of his mastery of style). L. N.]

7. The court's penalties are stoning, burning, beheading, and strangling (Sanh 7:1). The other penalties are different kinds of excision as decreed by Heaven.

8. JV: *But the tender mercies of the wicked are cruel.* ER, however, seems to construe *raḥăme,* "tender mercies," (literally "womb"), as "the issue of the womb."

said, *Behold, the day [of judgment] cometh, it burneth as a furnace* (Mal. 3:19).

Manasseh, the son of Hezekiah, was only twelve years old when he became king of Judea.[9] It was the Holy One who made him king, brought him up in well-being, increased peace for him, and gave to him more years of rule than to any of the kings before him. Nay, more: God came down with His great name from the upper heaven of heavens and from the place of His glory, greatness, splendor, and holiness to dwell with Manasseh in the Temple. But Manasseh proceeded to do the immeasurably idolatrous things [we know of].[10] Thereupon God said: "I have done right in not continuing to stay in the same place with him." And You were indeed right, for Manasseh scorned the thought of using his extraordinary powers in love of You as You love Israel, or did not joy in You as You rejoice in Israel.

You set apart Israel from among seventy nations, and from among Israel You set apart the Tribe of Levi, and out of the Tribe of Levi You set apart the High Priest who stands up to pray at each and every hour to procure forgiveness for all of Israel. [I pray to You as Aaron did]: Remember how many householders there are in Israel from whose persons the peoples of the world tear the very flesh [by exaction of taxes], yet every day without fail the householders occupy themselves with Torah. My Father in heaven, remember Your covenant | with **ER, *p.* 112** the forefathers, the three righteous men, Abraham, Isaac, and Jacob. Remember how many poor and needy are in Israel who have nothing at all, yet every day without fail occupy themselves with Torah. My Father in heaven, in Your Torah You wrote, *Thou shalt not oppress Thy neighbor nor rob him* (Lev. 19:13), and *If Thy brother be waxen poor, and his means fail with Thee, then Thou shalt uphold him* (Lev. 25:35). Remember how many in Israel are lame and blind and have no food, yet manage to pay tuition so that their children be taught Torah. My Father in heaven, remember what possessions are Yours from of old: [Israel], which was reminded, *Is not He thy father that hath gotten thee?* (Deut. 32:14); and [Torah], which said of itself, *The Lord made me as the beginning of His way* (Prov. 8:22). Remember how many orphans and widows there are in Israel who have nothing at all, yet every day without fail occupy themselves with Torah. My Father in heaven, remember Your compassions which are of old, [as is said], *Remember, O Lord, Thy compassions and Thy mercies* (Ps. 25:6); *The Lord is good to all; and His tender mercies are over all His works* (Ps. 145:9); and *To the Lord*

---

9. See 2 Kings 21:1.

10. Among other things, *he put the graven image of Asherah in the House of which the Lord said . . . "In this House . . . will I put My name for ever"* (2 Kings 21:7).

our God belong compassions and forgivenesses (Dan. 9:9); and *The Lord, the Lord, God, merciful and gracious* (Exod. 34:6). Remember how many old men and old women there are in Israel who morning and evening go to the synagogue and to the academy, and every day without fail hope for, look forward to, indeed yearn for Your deliverance [of Israel]. My Father in heaven, in Your Torah You wrote, *The fathers shall not be put to death for the children, neither shall the children be put to death for the fathers* (Deut. 24:16); and *The son shall not bear the iniquity of the father with him, neither shall the father bear the iniquity of the son with him; the righteousness of the righteous shall be upon him, and the wickedness of the wicked shall be upon him* (Ezek. 19:20). Should Israel, God forbid, perish from the world, Your Torah, too, will perish from the world. And in a Mishnah, our Sages taught: "If there is no Torah, there is no way for the world [to continue]; if there is no way for the world [to continue], there is no Torah" (Ab̲ 3:17). Our Father in heaven, for the sake of Your great name that was uttered over us, for the sake of the Seventh Day, and for the sake of the other commandments, act in our behalf. Remember how many youngsters and little ones there are in Israel who do not know their right hand from their left, yet as little as they know, occupy themselves with Torah every day without fail. Our Father in heaven, to hearten us, You wrote the verse which You gave us through Your servants the Prophets, namely, *Should I not have pity on Nineveh, that great city?* (Jon. 4:11). Would that Your great compassions flood over us, and in our behalf there be fulfilled *For Mine own sake, for Mine own sake, will I do it!* (Isa. 48:11).

CHAPTER (20)

God's condescension and justice

Summary

Prophets summon all Israel, elders and children alike, to assemble in order to learn how to heed Torah's teaching and how to help (ER, 112) the congregation when it is in distress. In such an event a Sage may enter even the most holy place with his supplication of God to spare His people.

A man ought never shut himself off from his fellows in distress nor from study of Torah. God Himself came down from heaven and dwelt among the people of Israel because of their devotion to Torah. This was also King David's devotion. Accordingly, wealthy men are to leave their business affairs from time to time and go into synagogues and academies to study Torah. Furthermore, such men are to welcome into their homes impoverished disciples of the wise who have always proved to be the bearers of blessing.

In the days of the Messiah the nations will bring all kinds of riches—tokens of blessing—to the people of Israel. At that time also God will restore years to compensate them for their years of suffering in this world (ER, 113). For that matter, even in our day God in His endeavor to protect Israel divided His world between two nations, so that by their divided rule Israel's burden of suffering would be eased. Still, in order to hallow God's name, punishment is visited upon Israel. Ultimately, however, each and every man, each and every people is rewarded according to the kind of person or people it is (ER, 114). Such precise reckoning is made evident in Scripture—the Books of counsels and knowledge. Hence God's people may be certain that in the world-to-come they will not be put to shame (ER, 115).

Chapter (20)

From the verse *Lift up thy hands toward Him for the life of thy young children* (Lam. 2:19), it is inferred that a man should so guard himself, his children, and the people of his household that not one of them comes to transgression or to indecent acts. Hence it is said, *Assemble the people, the men and the women, and the little ones . . . that they may observe faithfully every word of this teaching* (Deut. 31:12). ER, *p.* 112 *cont'd*

[Israel, young and old alike, are asked to assemble for still another purpose]: *Gather the people, sanctify the congregation, assemble the elders, gather the children—those that suck the breasts; let the bridegroom go forth from his chamber and the bride out of her pavilion* (Joel 2:16)—[all for the purpose of helping the congregation when it is in distress]. By *elders* is meant disciples of the wise, as in the verse "Gather unto Me seventy men of the elders of Israel" (Num. 11:16). By *children* is meant children at school [who take instruction from Torah], for *breasts* in *those that suck the breasts* refers to Torah, as in the verse "That ye may suck, and be satisfied with the breast of her consolations" (Isa. 66:11). The verse

cited from Joel goes on, *Let the bridegroom go forth from his chamber and the bride out of her pavilion.* Hence it is said: Even a sage in Israel who is [as humble] as our teacher Moses and as loving as his brother Aaron should not say, "Since I am [secure] in my own house, all is well with
ER, *p.* 113 you, my soul," but he should go forth and join with | the congregation when it is in distress.[1] This is what Scripture teaches in the words *Let the bridegroom go forth from his chamber and the bride out of her pavilion.* [Such a sage, clothed in compassion, is permitted to come even to the place] *between the Porch and the Altar*[2] (Joel 2:17), the place where ordinarily only priests [who are unblemished and not in mourning] come with sin offerings, guilt offerings, peace offerings, and with all kinds of other sacrifices. [It is there that the sage may pray, in a time of distress, *Spare Thy people, O Lord (ibid.).*]

Another comment on *Between the Porch and the Altar (ibid.)*: Even as [one goes down from the Porch to the Altar,[3] so] the Holy One, may His great name be blessed for ever and ever, came down from the uppermost heaven of heavens, from the place of His glory, His greatness, His kingship, His splendor, His holiness, and His great name, and dwelt among the people of Israel because of their willingness to obey the precepts of Torah. Hence it is said: Even if a man owns a hundred houses, a hundred vineyards and fields, let him leave all [his business affairs from time to time][4] and go [humbly] into synagogues and academies and to every place where new insights into Torah may be gained. For so conducting himself a man merits all kinds of reward. Thus [in humility] David said: *I will not give sleep to mine eyes nor slumber to mine eyelids, until I find the place for [instruction in the will of] the Lord, the dwelling place of the Mighty One of Jacob*[5] (Ps. 132:4). For having conducted himself in this way, David merited great rewards.[6] Hence it is said: A disciple of the wise whom you are willing to have in your house will come to know your needs,[7] and [his mere presence] will help provide for the members of your household.

---

1. See B.Ta 11a.

2. "In the area between the Porch and the Altar . . . no priest who has a blemish, or whose hair had grown long, or whose clothes were rent [in observance of mourning], might enter therein." See Kel 1:9.

3. Between the Porch on the eastern side of the *hekal,* the Holy Place, and the Altar in the courtyard there were twelve steps. See Mid 3:6.

4. As did R. Eleazar ben Ḥarsom. See B.Yoma 35b.

According to Louis Ginzberg, *yaniaḥ* here does not mean "renounce" but "withdraw" (*OT,* p. 289, n. 399).

5. The Temple served also as a place for study and prayer. See PR 40:6 (YJS, *18, 2,* 713–14).

6. The Psalm goes on to say: *The Lord swore unto David . . . Of the fruit of thy body will I set upon thy throne* (Ps. 132:11).

7. [I find no evidence in Jastrow that *middah* may mean "need." . . . Hence *wywd'* must be a misreading—perhaps read *wywrk bmydwtyk,* "he will instruct you as to your moral conduct and help provide for your family," i.e., he will be beneficial both to yourself and your dependents. L. N.]

Blessing always accompanies the handiwork of a disciple of the wise. So it was with Joseph, for when he entered Potiphar's house, what is said of him? *And it came to pass from the time that* [*Potiphar*] *appointed him overseer in his house . . . that the Lord blessed the Egyptian's house for Joseph's sake* (Gen. 39:5). Hence it is said: There are four occasions in which one action follows immediately upon another: the slaughtering of the sacrificial animal comes immediately after the rite of laying the hands upon its head;[8] the Eighteen Benedictions[9] are said immediately after the Blessing of Redemption;[10] the blessing over the bread is said immediately after the rite of washing the hands;[11] and blessing befalls a man's handiwork immediately [upon the presence] of a disciple of the wise in his household.[12]

[The verse from Joel cited above concludes with a call to prayer]: *And let them say: "Spare Thy people, O Lord"* (Joel 2:17). <O Lord, gracious>, compassionate, indeed, full of many kinds of compassion, You whose lips speak uprightly, whose lips are comely with wisdom, understanding, knowledge, and insight, You who hear prayer at once, [as is said]: *For what great nation is there, that hath God so nigh unto them, as the Lord our God is whensoever we call upon Him* (Deut. 4:7). David also prayed in Israel's behalf: *I beseech Thee, O Lord, save my soul*[13] (Ps. 116:4). But the Holy One gave [Joel an unexpected] response, as is said, *The Lord answered and said unto His people: Behold, I will send you corn, and wine, and oil, and ye shall be satisfied therewith* (Joel 2:19). Why [did God answer Israel's prayer for its soul to be saved with a promise of corn, wine, and oil]? So that Israel would not have to travel out of their communities[14] and go to towns [where heathen dwell] to fetch grain, meat, and provisions to their houses. Such is the point of the verse *Spare Thy people.*

In the days of the Messiah all the nations remaining on earth will go to the Land of Israel and take grain, meat, and provisions to the dwelling of Israelites—indeed they will enrich Jews with great riches, as is said, *All the nations will strengthen you*[15] (Mal. 3:12). And Scripture

---

8. Cf. Maimonides' Code VIII, v, iii, 12 (YJS, *12,* 174).

9. It is also known as *Tĕfillah* or *'Amiḏah.* See *APB,* pp. 44–54.

10. The supplications in the Eighteen Benedictions are properly uttered immediately after the worshiper has proclaimed the miracle of God's redemption in the blessing "Lord, who hast redeemed Israel [from Egypt]" (*APB,* p. 44).

11. Both the blessing at the washing of the hands and the blessing over bread are found in *APB,* p. 78. See MTeh 4:9 (YJS, *13, 1,* 74) and Lieberman, *TKF, 2,* 76 and 92.

12. Cf. B.Ber 42a. In the Babylonian tradition, unlike the Palestinian, the third of the occasions is to be understood: "Grace follows immediately upon the washing of the hands." This second washing at the end of the meal (B.Ber 53b), whether or not the table has been cleared, is the signal that the meal is finished.

13. "All that David said in his book of Psalms applies to himself, and to all Israel." See MTeh 18:1 (YJS, *13, 1,* 230).

14. Literally, "houses."

15. [The author may be referring to the close similarity between *'šr,* "to

says further: *I will restore to you the years that the locust hath eaten, the canker worm, and the caterpillar, and the palmer worm* (Joel 2:24), these vermin standing for the four kingdoms[16] which enslaved Israel. And why the restoration of the years? To make it up to Israel for their affliction by the four kingdoms. By what parable may the matter be understood? By the parable of a mortal king who became angry at his son, seized him by the hand, and brought him to the house of the son's teacher for chastisement. Thereupon with the permission of the father the teacher set to and struck the son some great blows. Toward the end of the day, <the son> came and stretched himself out in supplication before his father, who said, "My son, even though I had you struck some great blows [to teach you a lesson], these in fact are light blows [as you will see when I make them up to you]." Even so, Israel are chastised for their misdeeds with blows which, in fact, must be thought of as light, because they culminate in God's assurance *I will restore to you the years,* etc.

Once, while I was traveling from one place to another, an old man accosted me and asked: My master, why did the Holy One divide His world between two nations, between two kingdoms? I replied: | If the entire world, all of it, were delivered into the hand of one nation, then Sennacherib, king of Assyria, and Nebuchadnezzar, king of Babylon, would have gone ahead and done their will with Israel unhindered. Therefore the Holy One divided the rule of His world between two nations, between two kingdoms, only in order to protect Israel. [As God thus reduces the blows aimed at Israel, so all the other blows He allows the nations to inflict upon Israel are, in fact, light blows meant to protect them.] By what parable may the matter be illustrated? By the parable of some schoolchildren and their teacher who, [resorting to blows now and then, thus] saw to it that they did not go out and drown in the river, that they did not go out and strike one another, that the sun did not smite them. <Even so, God saw to it that eventually those who had come under the yoke[17] of Egypt for a time [would have it lifted from them and then would come under the yoke of Babylon], as is said, *Thus saith the Lord: Behold, waters rise up out of the north,* [*out of Babylon*], *and shall become an overflowing stream, and they shall overflow the Land and all that is therein* (Jer. 47:2).> And why such a punishment at all? In order to hallow God's great name, as is said, *The Lord is our*

ER, *p.* 114

---

strengthen," and *'śr,* "to enrich," and suggesting that the verse may be translated *the nations will enrich you;* particularly as in later Hebrew and in Babylonian Aramaic the phonetic difference between the letters *'alef* and *'ayin* has tended to become obscured. L. N.]

16. Egypt, Babylon, Greece, and Rome.

17. *'Ole,* "they who came up," is emended to *'ol,* "yoke." So *YY.*

Judge, the Lord is our Lawgiver, the Lord is our King; [*having punished us*], *He will save us* (Isa. 33:22). Not only will He save us: He assures us, *And ye shall eat in plenty and be satisfied* (Joel 2:26). Here "to be satisfied" means to be satisfied with words of Torah, as is said, *The righteous eateth to the satisfying of his soul* (Prov. 13:25). And of such satisfaction Joel goes on to say, *Ye shall eat in plenty and be satisfied, and shall praise the name of the Lord your God, that hath dealt with you so that distinctions become evident*[18] (Joel 2:26)—that is, He has enabled you to distinguish between the deeds of the righteous and the deeds of the wicked, between the reward of the righteous in the Garden of Eden and the requital of the wicked by punishment in Gehenna. For each and every man who comes into the world gets his reward according to the kind of person he is. Thus the Holy One put up with the world and even brought Abraham [into it] as a reward for Shem who for four hundred years spoke as a prophet concerning the lands in a world which refused to heed him.[19] The Holy One brought the kingdom of Greece into the world and put up with it only as a reward for Japheth who covered the nakedness of his father.[20] The Holy One brought the kingdom of Rome into the world and put up with it only as a reward for Esau who wept and sighed because Isaac had blessed Jacob.[21] The Holy One brought the kingdom of Media into the world and put up with it only as a reward for Cyrus who wept and sighed when the heathen destroyed the Temple. The Holy One brought Sennacherib into the world and put up with him only as a reward for Asshur, for Asshur, a virtuous man,[22] was the counselor | of our father Abraham. The Holy One **ER, *p.* 115**
<brought Nebuchadnezzar> into the world and put up with him only as a reward for Merodach who accorded honor to our Father in heaven.[23] The Holy One brought Haman into the world and put up with him only as a reward for Agag who wept and sighed when he was confined in prison, saying, "Woe is me! It may be that my seed shall now perish for ever."[24] However, [says God, since none of the nations

18. JV: *That hath dealt wondrously with you.* But *lĕ-hafli'*, "wondrously," may also mean "to specify" hence "to distinguish."

19. Abraham descended from Shem who was born four hundred and three years earlier (see Gen. 11:10–27). Shem was righteous, and yet (ER, 29) it is not recorded of him, as it is of his descendant Abraham, that he converted men to belief in the one God. Hence ER assumes that his pleas for such belief were in vain.

20. See Gen. 9:23.

21. See Gen. 27:38.

22. When men began to plan the tower of Babel, "Asshur said: 'How shall I live among these wicked men?' And he exiled himself." See below, S, 45; MTeh 118:11 (YJS, *13, 2,* 238); and Gen. Rabbah 37:4.

23. See PRKM 2:5, p. 24 (PRKS, pp. 28–29).

24. His concern for having progeny earned him the reward of continuance of his line. See 1 Sam. 15:1–33.

just mentioned shall ever rule alone], *My people will never perish in the world*[25] (Joel 2:27).

In another comment, the verse is read, *My people shall not be ashamed in the world.* Our Father in heaven—our name <is like His name and His name> becomes Him, for all is His and all is the work of His hands. May His great name be blessed for ever and ever and ever! May You have gratification from Your servants Israel wherever they dwell! Had You not written for us [the sacred] Books of counsels and knowledge whose words are to be trusted,[26] You would have been made[27] out to be a cruel Being all of whose ways show Your cruelty. But You, with Your wisdom and understanding, provided for us in the Books of counsels and knowledge words which are to be trusted. You let us know: Such-and-such a generation obeyed Torah in these respects, and thus I bestowed good upon it. Such-and-such a man obeyed Torah in these respects, and thus I bestowed good upon him. Such-and-such a generation did evil in these respects, and thus I brought death to it. Such-and-such a man did evil in these respects, and thus I brought death upon him. Hence *And My people shall not be ashamed in the world, [for My ways are just]* (Joel 2:27).

---

25. JV: *And My people shall never be ashamed.* But *yeḇošu,* "be ashamed," vocalized *yiḇšu,* means "dry out"; hence "perish."

26. See Prov. 22:20 as construed in PRKM 12:12, p. 213 (PRKS, p. 237).

27. Literally, "made me," a euphemism for "made You."

CHAPTER (21) 19

Israel's first concern should be their own and their children's study of Torah

Summary

A man should ask God's compassion for himself and all his household to the end that no one of them be guilty of any transgression. He should see to it, furthermore, that his children receive instruction in Torah, for if they lack such instruction, God grieves. On the other hand, Israel's study of Torah led even Balaam (ER, 115) to utter words of consolation and favor in their behalf. Indeed, because they have Torah, Israel are said to be greater than all the other work of God's hands, greater even than the ministering angels. Israel's immersion in Torah leads them to disdain weapons of war; leads them to revere chastity so much as to die for its sake. And small wonder, for Torah is like a stream whose waters purify those who immerse themselves in it.

Those who first cultivate wisdom, understanding, knowledge, and insight in their hearts, and then teach Torah to the young (ER, 116), teaching them to do the will of their Father in Heaven, are like gardens by the river which flourish by absorption of its waters. Sages, too, and their disciples who in companionship study Torah are likewise deemed gardens. Even prideful men who come to study of Torah absorb its words, and all the more so do humble men.

When Israel in disdain of Torah, however, worshiped the golden calf, God decreed that henceforth they were to study Torah in distress and exile, even in hunger. Still, God, in compassion for their suffering, will one day double and redouble their recompense (ER, 117).

The one hunger a man should ever seek to satisfy is hunger to study Torah with fear and reverence, with trepidation and awe, to learn to know that in a little while he is to die, that God created the stars in the firmament and to each one gave its place and its course, even as He gave beginning and end to each kingdom on the earth. Hence let a man feel awe at all times, acknowledge Torah's truth, and speak its truth in his heart (ER, 118).

Chapter (21) 19

Another comment on *Lift up thy hands toward Him for the life of thy young children* (Lam. 2:19) implies that a man should seek compassion [from Heaven] for himself, for his wife, for his children, and for the members of his household to the end that no one of them go and give himself to transgression or give himself to indecent conduct. In this connection, even if it is a man's father or his mother who says things that should not be said,[1] and the man knows it, he should not remain silent. If he

ER, *p.* 115 *cont'd*

1. Literally, "excessive"; e.g., slander. So *YY.*

does so nevertheless, neither he nor they will live out their days, as is said, *Only take heed to thyself, and keep thy life diligently by not forgetting the things which thine eyes saw* (Deut. 4:9).

[*Give heed,* the verse from Lamentations continues, to] *thy young children, that faint for hunger at the head of every street* (Lam. 2:19). The words *every street* here are taken to allude to academies, as in the verse *Run ye to and fro through the streets of Jerusalem . . . if there be any that seeketh truth*[2] (Jer. 5:1). For whenever children hunger for instruction in Torah, the Holy One lets sorrow and sadness enter His heart even though no mortal is aware of His grief,[3] as is said, *My soul weepeth in secret* (Jer. 13:17).[4]

At the time when Balaam the son of Beor came to Balak the son of Zippor king of Moab, the Holy One let sorrow and sadness enter ER, *p.* 116 His heart, even though no mortal was aware | of His grief, [for it seemed that Balaam meant to ally himself with Balak against the children of Israel]. *But when Balaam went with Balak, they came to Kiriath-huzoth* (Num. 22:39)—[to the "city of streets," which is to say, the city of Torah study][5]—and there Balaam came and found Israel seated in a great many assemblies occupying themselves with Torah. Of them, it might have been said, "The rivalry of scribes increases wisdom."[6] And such rivalry is a good sign for Israel. Later, after Balaam's bones had been broken, one of his eyes put out, and his mouth pressed against the ground,[7] he uttered all his notable words of favor and consolation for Israel, as is said, *He took up his parable, and said: From Aram, Balak bringeth me. . . . How shall I curse whom God hath not cursed?* (Num. 23:7–8). *And Balaam lifted up his eyes, and he saw Israel dwelling Tribe by Tribe . . . and said . . . How goodly are thy tents* [*of Torah*], *O Jacob* (Num. 24:2–3). It is because Israel have Torah that it is said: Israel are greater than the ministering angels in that they are great in words of Torah; they are, in this respect, greater than all the other inhabitants of the world, greater even than all the other work that His hands created in the world.[8] And this greatness is Israel's, the Sages taught in a Mishnah, [because Israel heed the call], "Be fierce as a leopard, swift as an eagle . . . to do the will of your Father who is in heaven" (Ab̲ 5:20).

---

2. *Truth* is identified with Torah. Cf. B.Shab 119b and Ḥag̅ 14a.

3. Weeping as He does in the innermost recesses called "Secret." See B.Ḥag̅ 5b.

4. *YY* suggests the substitution of Jer. 13:17 for *In their streets they gird themselves with sackcloth* (Isa. 15:3), a verse which is difficult to fit into the context.

5. Since it goes without saying that a city has streets, ER associates the redundant *huzoth,* "streets," with *ḥuṣot̲,* "streets," in the phrase *the streets of Jerusalem* (Jer. 5:1) in which, he says, a man may *seek the truth*—Torah.

6. B.BB 21a.

7. In Num. 24:4 Balaam is described as one whose eye had been gouged out (see Rashi), and who had been felled—hence, bones broken and mouth pressed against the ground.

8. See MTeh 78:12 (YJS, *13, 2,* 35).

Who can count the stags of Jacob or reckon the couchings of Israel[9] (Num. 23:10) [in obedience to His will]? How many stags there are in Israel, [young men], who do not make use of weapons and have no desire for them, as is said, *Flee [from warfare], my beloved, be thou like to a gazelle or to a young stag upon the mountains of spices* (Song 8:14)! How many householders there are in Israel who have been occupied with Torah from the day the Holy One chose our father Abraham until this day![10] How many young boys there are in Israel who own the seals [of their virginity] until they come into their wedding chambers! How many young girls there are in Israel who own the seals [of their virginity] until they enter their wedding chambers!

A story of a maiden whose father was very friendly with a heathen. As they ate and drank and made merry, the heathen said to the maiden's father, "Give your daughter to my son for a wife." [Though the father consented], he said nothing to her of the matter until the time of her wedding came. When the time came, [and she was told], she went up to a roof, jumped off, and died. A Divine Voice was heard, saying: Because of such as she, Scripture says, *Who can reckon the [purity of the] couchings of Israel?* (Num. 23:10).

And when Balaam, the son of Beor, prophesied favors and consolations for Israel, he wept inwardly, saying: *Let me die the death of the righteous, and let mine end be like theirs (ibid.).* This is to say that wicked Balaam was yearning for the kind of death that Moses and Aaron were to have. If I die soon on my couch, Balaam said, I shall have died peacefully like Moses and Aaron. If I do not die soon on my couch, then I know I shall not die peacefully like Moses and Aaron.

How goodly are thy tents [of Torah], O Jacob . . . as streams stretched out! (Num. 24:5). What is the point here of speaking of streams in connection with academies of Torah? Because, as men who are defiled go down into streams, immerse themselves, and then come up from the water purified, so are [men who attend] academies of Torah. Men go into them full of iniquities and come out of them purified. Such is the point of the words *How goodly are thy tents [of Torah], O Jacob . . . as streams stretched out!*

The word *gardens* in *as gardens by the riverside* (Num. 24:6) refers to teachers of the young | in Israel, teachers who in their hearts **ER, *p.*** 117
cultivate wisdom, understanding, knowledge, and insight so that they

---

9. JV: *Who hath counted the dust of Jacob, or numbered the stock of Israel.* But *'afar,* "dust," can be construed as *'ofer,* "stag," and *rb',* "stock," as "couching." See B.Nid 31a where *Who* is taken to intimate here that God Himself counts the young men and the "couchings," the sexual couplings, in Israel.

10. ER apparently takes the phrase *from the top of the rocks* (Num. 23:9) as referring to Abraham.

teach children to do the will of their Father in heaven. Hence teachers are spoken of *as gardens by the riverside.*[11]

In another comment, the word *gardens* is taken to mean Israel's Sages and men of understanding who occupy themselves with Torah every day, without fail. Of them Scripture says, *O thou that dwellest in the gardens, the companions hearken to thy voice: Cause Me to hear it* (Song 8:13). Had the text said: "Israel hearken," I would have said, "All Israel have to hearken." But the text says, *the companions hearken,* so that if only two or three companions occupy themselves with Torah every day, without fail, God hearkening to their voices says to them, *"Cause Me to hear it*[12]—[let Me hear your voices in study of Torah]." Thus in the words *as gardens by the riverside* (Num. 24:6) the word *gardens* is taken to allude to Israel's Sages, even as the words that follow, *as tents ('ohălim) set up by the Lord (ibid.),* are taken to refer to academies.

In another comment, the word is read not *'ohălim,* "tents," but *'ăhalim,* "aloes"—[hence *How goodly are thy aloes*]! By what analogy may the reading be understood? By that of a mortal king who prepared a feast [fragrant as aloe wood] for all the notables of the kingdom who came to his palace.[13]

In the phrase *As cedars beside the waters* (Num. 24:6), *cedars* stands for the arrogant in Israel. Even Israel's arrogant men who possess <words of Torah [come to be filled with these words as cedars beside streams draw water into themselves]>. All the more so, then, will they who humble themselves for the sake of Torah come to be possessed of words of Torah, as is said, *As for him who belittles himself, water will flow*[14] *throughout his branches* (Num. 24:7). The next words of the verse, *And his seed shall be in many waters (ibid.),* mean that the offspring of such modest householders in Israel as he will branch out through many generations—through their children[15] and their children's children. Such is the meaning of *And his seed shall be in many waters.*

And his king, the verse goes on, *shall be lifted above Agag (ibid.),* Agag who wept and sobbed at the time he was confined in prison, saying, "Woe unto me! Now my seed will perish from the world."

---

11. "The identification of gardens with schools [and Sages] has its reason in the fact that in Palestine, as well as in Babylonia, the academies were in gardens." Louis Ginzberg in *OT,* p. 281, n. 255.

12. Cf. Aḇ 3:6.

13. On the fragrance of aloes, see *EB, 1,* 128–29. Miriam's well brought fragrant herbs with it (see Ginzberg, *Legends, 3,* 53); and the taste of the manna was in accordance with the needs and capacity of each and every person (see PRKM 12:25, p. 224 [PRKS, p. 249]).

14. JV: *Water shall flow from his branches.* But apparently ER derives *yizzal,* "flow," from *zlzl,* "to belittle."

15. Following Louis Ginzberg's suggestion that the text had the contraction *b''b = bĕne ba'ale battim,* "householders' children," a contraction which, misunderstood, was changed to *ben.* See *OT,* p. 300, n. 161.

[And so it turned out.] As Scripture tells us, *And* [*a descendant of*] *his* [*Israel's*] *king* [*Saul*] *shall be lifted above Agag.* [16]

In another comment, the words are read, *When his own good counsel enters* [*the heart of*] *one of Israel even more wicked than Agag, he will be lifted up.* [17] The allusion here is to a man in Israel who has been utterly wicked during his lifetime, but who, as death draws near, opens his heart to sorrow and sadness because of his misdeeds, then feels a change within, yearns to repent, and dies in a mood of contrition[18]—such as he are heirs of the world-to-come.

[In comment on *Lift up thy hands toward Him for the life of thy young children*] *that faint for hunger at the head of every street* (Lam. 2:19), it is said: When Moses came down from Mount Sinai and perceived the grievous consequences of the misdeeds whereby Israel had befouled themselves, he gazed upon the Tables and saw that the writing on them had vanished. Thereupon he broke them at the foot of the Mount, <at once grew silent>, and felt himself unable to say anything in Israel's behalf. At that time it was decreed for Israel that they study words of Torah in distress, in enslavement, in wandering and uncertainty, suffering for lack of food. However, as compensation for the distress which afflicted them, the Holy One in the days of the Messiah will double and redouble their reward, as is said, *Behold, the Lord God will come as a Mighty One, and His arm will rule for Him; behold, His reward is with Him, and His recompense before Him* (Isa. 40:10). [Indeed, says the Holy One], *Whoever has given Me anything beforehand, him I shall repay* (Job 41:3). As the jingle goes, "In my behalf, I own, my heifer broke her leg bone," for the hole she fell into happened to contain a very substantial treasure.[19] [Likewise, for the afflictions that have befallen me, the Holy One will provide substantial compensation. So it turned out with Aaron, for instance, in the matter of the fire-pans for incense brought by Korah and his fellow rebels to the Tabernacle. Although the Lord had the ground open up and swallow all the rebels, He

---

16. Agag thus foresaw the triumph of Mordecai, scion of Saul who confronted Agag and was seemingly worsted, while Mordecai eventually vanquished Haman, a descendant of Agag. See 1 Sam. 15 and Esther 2:5.

17. ER seems to construe Agag not as a particular person but as the embodiment of wickedness; and *malko,* not as "his king," but as "his own good counsel," which led the Jewish sinner to repent. So Friedmann in n. 22.

18. Cf. above, ER, 22.

19. Abba Yudan, who had been a wealthy and very charitable man, having lost his money was unable to respond to the plea of R. Eliezer, R. ‘Aḳiḇa, and R. Joshua for the support of Sages and so felt very bad. At the suggestion of his wife, however, he sold half of his one remaining field and gave the money to the visiting scholars. Afterwards, as he was plowing, his heifer fell into a hole and broke its leg. When he went into the hole to recover the heifer, he came upon a treasure, and thereupon said, "My heifer broke its leg in my behalf." See Lev. Rabbah M, 5:4, pp. 111–12.

"The hole she fell into . . . substantial treasure" paraphrases the literal "so that my reward may be complete."

commanded Aaron to have the fire-pans hammered out and be made *into beaten plates for the covering of the altar* (Num. 17:3).] Hence Aaron said: Had not Korah risen up against me, would the Lord have covenanted with me that only my seed may burn incense before the Lord? For it is said, *A reminder unto the children of Israel to the end that no common man, that is not of the seed of Aaron, draw near to burn incense before the Lord* (Num. 17:5). Here we have a further illustration of the jingle, "In my behalf, I own, my heifer broke her leg bone"—the Holy One provides substantial compensation for the affliction that befalls me.

ER, *p.* 118 | In another comment on *That faint for hunger* (Lam. 2:19), *hunger* is taken to allude to hunger for words of Torah, as is said, *Behold, the days come, saith the Lord God, that I will send a famine to the land, not a famine of bread . . . but of hearing the words of the Lord* (Amos 8:11). [When he seeks to satisfy his hunger for Torah], a man, it is said, should study Torah with fear and reverence, with trepidation and awe. Let him look at himself and become aware that in a little while he will die. Let him lift his eyes to heaven and say: Who created the stars in the firmament and gave to each one its place, to each one its way and its course? How many towers did the kingdom of Rome build, but Who smote them and toppled them to the ground? How many towers did the kingdom of Media build, but Who smote them and toppled them to the ground? Who kicked at the first tower, [the tower of Babel],[20] so that the top of it landed in one spot and its bulk in another spot with twenty-one miles between the two? Upon such deeds as these, [O Israel], *thy heart shall muse in awe: Where is He that weighed* [*the stars*], *where is He that counted the towers?* (Isa. 33:18). In musing thus, a man will feel awe of Heaven at all times, will acknowledge the truth [of Torah],[21] and will speak its truth in his heart. He will rise early each and every day and say: Sovereign of all worlds! Not because of our righteous acts do we lay our supplications before You, but because of Your abundant mercies, etc.,[22] [for, as You have promised], *At that time I will bring you in, and at that time will I gather you; for I will make you be a name and a praise among all the peoples of the earth, when I turn back your captivity before your eyes, saith the Lord* (Zeph. 3:20).

---

20. See Gen. 11. On a possible significance of "toppled towers," see Isa. 30:25.
21. See n. 2 above.
22. This prayer is part of the daily morning service. See *APB,* pp. 7–9, and Israel Abrahams, *Companion to the Authorised Daily Prayer Book,* rev. ed. [London 5682/1922], pp. xxi–xxiv.

On the possibility that the prayer may have been composed in the second century C.E. during Hadrian's persecution, see Louis Finkelstein, *Pharisaism in the Making* [New York, 1972], pp. 414–21.

CHAPTER (22) 20

God's concern for justice and His reward of the righteous

Summary

Since God promised that He Himself would minister to Israel, why, when He gave them the Torah, did He make use of emissaries? As He provided Israel in the desert with manna, quail, and the water of Miriam's well, so at Sinai He provided emissaries to abate Israel's terror at His presence (ER, 118–19). Having thus won Israel's confidence, God went on to give Israel laws concerning injury to people and property.

One of these laws prescribes that a thief sold into slavery by a court to repay what he has stolen, be liberally provided for when he is freed. Hence, from the prosperity of the wicked in this world, one may learn that the reward of the righteous will be bestowed in the world-to-come. Comparable reward will be bestowed upon Israel in the days of the Messiah. At that time the nations who oppressed Israel will behold Israel's joy, then melt away into dust, never to return (ER, 120). The nations who did not afflict Israel will voluntarily become farmers and vintagers in the service of Israel. As for the world-to-come, which is of the highest degree of sanctity, no uncircumcised person—Jew or heathen—shall dwell therein.

A disciple not thoroughly conversant in Halakah complained that though he yearned to possess Torah, it did not come to him. In reply he was told that to merit Torah one must be ready to surrender himself to labor in it even unto death.

A change of heart and a resolve to repent win pardon for the transgressor and procure for him a special kind of joy (ER, 121).

Chapter (22) 20

Comment on the words *Behold, I send an angel before thee,* etc. (Exod. 23:20) [begins with the blessing]: Blessed be the Preserver of the world, blessed be He who chose Israel out of all the inhabitants of the world and out of all the works He created in the world—not only chose Israel but took | them to be wholly His possession, sons and servants for His name's sake. Come and see what God had Moses say to them: *Wherefore say unto the children of Israel: I am the Lord, and I will bring you out from under the burdens of the Egyptians . . . and I will take you to Me for a people, and I will be to you a God . . . and I will bring you in unto the Land . . . and I will give it to you for a heritage* (Exod. 6:6–8). [Yet later on, despite His promise that He Himself would bring them into the Land], God said, *Behold, I send an angel before thee . . .* [*to help bring thee into the place which I have prepared*] (Exod. 23:20). May it be Your will, I beseech You, my Father in heaven, that You Yourself [will always

ER, *p.* 118 *cont'd*

ER, *p.* 119

minister to us and] never put us into the hands of an emissary. By what parable then may the presence of emissaries at the giving of Torah be understood? By the parable of a mortal king who, preceded by horses and their riders and many troops as well, came into the capital city. When the servants and members of his household [who dwelt in the city] heard [of his arrival with such an array of forerunners], they were shaken and afraid—indeed filled with great dread. [But they need not have been so terrified, for] the king was wise and far-sighted, a man of perception and understanding. So he came and established himself in the city—it was near his own dwelling place—and said: How many householders are there among the dwellers in this city? Give them so much wheat, so much barley, and so much wool to clothe them. How many poor and needy are there among them? How many blind and lame among them? Give them so much wheat, so much barley, and so much wool to clothe them. How many deaf-mutes among them? Give them so much wheat, so much barley, and so much wool to clothe them. How many children and infants among them? Give them so much wheat, so much barley, and so much wool to clothe them. How many old men and old women among them? Give them so much, etc. So, too, when the Holy One was about to give the Torah to His children, He first sent [as emissaries] before Him two hundred and forty-eight [myriads of angels], then another two hundred and forty-eight [myriads], and then still another two hundred and forty-eight [myriads], as is said, *The chariots of God: two myriads and two thousand*[1] *angels* (Ps. 68:18). Furthermore, *After God came from Teman* [*Edom*] *and the Holy One from Mount Paran* [*Ishmael*],[2] *His glory* [*going before Him*] *covered the heavens* [*at Sinai*] . . . *and there His strength* [*Torah*] *which had been hidden* [*was revealed*][3] (Hab. 3:3–4). When the Holy One arrived and rested on Mount Sinai, He saw to it that before each Commandment [was uttered, His emissaries], ministering angels, took each and every man in Israel twenty-four thousand cubits[4] away from the Mount and [after it was uttered] took each and every man twenty-four thousand cubits back to the Mount, a distance of forty-eight thousand cubits altogether. Hence at the time of the giving of Torah, God is described as *An eagle who rouses his nestlings, gliding down to his young* (Deut. 32:11), [even as each angel is described] as *spreading his wings and taking* [*an Israelite*],

---

1. Instead of "two hundred and forty-eight," so Haida and *YY* suggest, the number should be "two hundred and twenty-two," corresponding to the numerical value of the letters of *rkb,* "chariot"; twenty-two thousand is suggested in parallel accounts. See PR 21:7 (YJS, *18, 1,* 425) and PRKM 12:22, pp. 219–20 (PRKS, p. 243).

2. The allusion here is to God's attempts to give the Torah to other nations, each of whom refused to accept it. See PR 21:2/3 (YJS, *18, 1,* 416–17).

3. JV: *And there is the hiding of His power.*

4. Literally, "twelve *mil.*" A *mil* (mile) is 2000 cubits; a cubit is approximately 18 inches.

then bearing him back on his pinions (ibid.).[5] [The angels had to minister thus to Israel because] when our fathers stood at Sinai to accept the Torah for themselves, | they shook with alarm, they trembled and were afraid, were filled indeed with great terror, as is said, *And it came to pass on the third day . . . that there were thunders and lightnings and a thick cloud upon the Mount . . . and the voice of a horn exceeding loud* (Exod. 19:16). *And all the people saw the thunderings, and the lightnings, and the voice of the horn . . . and when the people saw it, they trembled, and stood afar off. And they said unto Moses: Speak thou with us, and we will hear, but let not God speak with us lest we die* (Exod. 20:15–16). [Hence Israel's terror at being in God's very presence was abated by the distance at which they heard the utterance of the Commandments.] When Moses saw that terror at the Holy One's presence was still upon them, he said to them: *Fear not; for God is come to exalt*[6] *you* (Exod. 20:20). Thus, having first won Israel's confidence [by ministering to them with such gifts as manna, quail, and the water of Miriam's well, and later, at Sinai, having abated their terror at His presence by sending emissaries to them], God went on to set before them the laws concerning those who do injury to people or property and concerning other matters calling for the exercise of justice. ER, *p.* 120

Among such matters is the one concerning servants, as is said, *Now these are the ordinances. . . . If thou buy a Hebrew servant.*[7] *. . . Since he comes in destitute, he should rightly go out destitute*[8] (Exod. 21:1–3). Woe unto the wicked such as he, who because of their deeds which are corrupt and their words which one dare not record, bring themselves to low estate and should rightly remain destitute to the day of their death. Nevertheless, Scripture says of such wicked men who have been sold into servitude because of the thefts they committed, that when you let any one of them go free, [after he has repaid his victim], *Thou shalt furnish him liberally out of thy flock. . . . It shall not seem hard unto thee*

---

5. Because the preceding verse is construed as "God compassed Israel about and gave him understanding of Torah"—so Onkelos—the verse cited is taken, according to Haida, to describe God's and the angels' actions during the revelation on Sinai. See also NJV. JV: *As an eagle that stirreth up her nest, hovereth over her young, spreadeth abroad her wings, taketh them, beareth them on her pinions.*

6. *Lĕ-nassot.* "That you may obtain a great name among the nations because He has revealed Himself to you in His glory" is Rashi's interpretation: "to make you as outstanding as a banner or a flag." JV: *God is come that He may prove you.* But since Moses sought to reassure them by saying "Do not fear," ER concludes that here *nassot* means not "prove, try," but "exalt."

7. A Hebrew servant bought from a court which sold him into slavery for theft, as is said, *If the thief have nothing, then he shall be sold for his theft* (Exod. 22:2).

8. [I suspect from the context that the author interprets *bĕ-gappo* not as "by himself" but as "destitute, without any terminal pay to help him to sustain himself as once more a free man." Note that this interpretation is not recorded by Jastrow (p. 262), who cites two other interpretations; showing once more what an original thinker the author was. L. N.]

(Deut. 15:14, 18). All the more then should the utterly righteous men who every day obey God's will without fail be well provided for. By what parable may the matter be understood? By the parable of a mortal king who had a great palace with a barred gate from which a shelf projected with figs, grapes, pomegranates, and all kinds of other fine fruits upon it. Close to it there projected another shelf with silks, combed flax, and all kinds of dyed garments upon it. Also nearby there projected still another shelf with food, drink, victuals, and all kinds of provisions upon it. All the people who happened to be in the area outside the palace were free to go and take their choice of the good things the king's palace offered. And what did passersby say about this? From what comes out of the king's palace, they said, one may learn what is within the palace. By the same token, from the chastisements of the righteous in this world, you may learn the measure of punishment of the wicked in Gehenna. On the other hand, from the prosperity of the wicked in this world you may learn the reward of the righteous in the world-to-come, as is said, *Oh how abundant is Thy goodness, which Thou hast laid up for them that fear Thee* (Ps. 31:20), an abundance *Whereof men from of old have not heard, nor perceived by the ear* (Isa. 64:3).

Once, as I was going from one place to another, I came upon an old man who asked me: My master, will there be separate nations in the days of the Messiah? I replied: My son, all the nations and all the kingdoms who have afflicted Israel and oppressed Israel will come and behold the joy of Israel, then melt into dust and return no more to the world, as is said, *The wicked shall see, and be vexed, he shall gnash with his*
ER, *p.* 121 *teeth, and melt away* | (Ps. 112:10), [leaving only his name as a curse], as is said to the wicked, *Ye shall leave your name for a curse unto Mine elect* (Isa. 65:15). And all kingdoms and all nations who have not afflicted Israel and have not oppressed them will [voluntarily] come and be farmers and vintagers for Israel, as is said, *Strangers shall stand and feed your flocks, and aliens shall be your plowmen and your vinedressers. But ye shall be named the priests of the Lord . . . ye shall eat the wealth of the nations, and in their splendor shall ye revel* (Isa. 61:5–6). It is further said of the days of the Messiah: *Then will I turn to the peoples a pure language, that they may all call upon the name of the Lord, to serve Him with one consent. From beyond the rivers of Ethiopia shall they bring My suppliants* (Zeph. 3:9–10). Then *He shall call His servants by another name* (Isa. 65:15). He will call them all worthy—Jew and heathen alike—in the days of the Messiah. You might suppose that since they will all be included in the days of the Messiah, they will also be included in the days to come. You must, therefore, take some exception to the words I have just spoken and give heed to words of Scripture which are more severe than my previous ones: with regard to the Paschal lamb, Scripture says, *No uncircumcised person,* [*not even a Jew*], *shall eat thereof* (Exod. 12:28). Now if Scripture says of the Paschal lamb which is of minor holiness, *No uncircumcised*

person shall eat thereof, all the more strongly does the injunction apply to the world-to-come. No uncircumcised person shall savor it, for it is of the highest degree of sanctity, and no uncircumcised person—[Jew or heathen]—shall dwell therein.

While I was standing there in discussion, a disciple who was not thoroughly conversant with Halakah came up to me. He said to me: My master, I occupy myself with words of Torah, hoping, waiting, indeed yearning for Torah to come to me, yet Torah does not come to me. I replied: My son, a man does not come to merit words of Torah unless he is ready to surrender himself for the glory of Heaven, ready even to surrender himself unto death, like an ox which is brought under the yoke and which, out of regard for its master, surrenders itself to serve him with its life, as is said, *Much increase is by the strength of the ox* (Prov. 14:4). As farmers say, "It takes the strength of an ox to bring in the crops." Scripture goes on to say, however, *The preparations of the heart are man's, but the answer from the tongue is the Lord's* (Prov. 16:1), and says further, *When those who deem themselves poor* [*in knowledge of Torah*] *and needful* [*of it*], *seek* [*its*] *water, and there seems to be none*[9] . . . *I the Lord will answer them* [*with draughts of Torah*] (Isa. 41:17).

My Father in heaven, may Your great name be blessed for ever and ever and ever, and may You have contentment in Israel Your servants wherever they dwell. You have promised: "I shall receive their transgressors who come in repentance. Even if a man heaps up a hundred transgressions, one above the other, in My compassion I will receive him if he comes in repentance." Even if a man stands up and flings blasphemies toward Him above, but then has a change of heart and resolves upon repentance, the Holy One will pardon all [his transgressions], as is said, *Then shall the lame man leap as a hart* (Isa. 35:6). By *lame man* here is meant one who is defective in knowledge and defective in good deeds. Then, for such a man, as the verse continues, *In the wilderness shall waters* [*of forgiveness*] *break out, and streams in the desert (ibid.).*

---

9. JV: *The poor and needy seek water, and there is none.*

CHAPTER (23) 21

The worth of the generation that came out of Egypt: Its faithfulness to God because of His compassion in the exercise of justice

Summary

The ordinances of Torah concerning the relations between men and women reveal His compassion. For example, if a man has married his maidservant and then casts her off and marries another woman, it is ordained that he must still provide for the former wife: If he did not observe this ordinance, it is likely that she would sell herself to get money for food. Her lack of food would be the consequence of his lack of Torah.

God's compassion in His exercise of justice is further revealed by ordinances concerning those who, overzealous in the administering of punishment, inadvertently kill the persons they are punishing. In such cases, God requires the repentance of the inadvertent transgressors. If they do not repent, however, God's punishment of them ensues by having them commit an offense that will call for a levy upon their property, though in contrast to the offense, the requital will be mild (ER, 121–22).

Moses assured Israel at Sinai of God's compassion toward transgressors who repent and then set before Israel ordinances governing injuries to persons and property. Israel in Egypt had already proved their faithfulness to God, as a number of events during their stay in Egypt attests. Hence, as His care of them in the wilderness shows, He had a special regard for the generation that came out of Egypt (ER, 123–24).

Chapter (23) 21

ER, *p.* 121 *cont'd* Consider the ordinances of Torah [revealing tender concern for the welfare] of women. Suppose, for example, *A man sells his daughter to be a maidservant* (Exod. 21:7). [No matter whether she is subsequently guilty of misdeeds and so deserves to be cast off, or whether she no longer suits the whims of her master and so does not deserve to be cast off, either meaning being implied in the words] *If she please not her master who espoused her to himself, he can allow her to be redeemed* (Exod. 21:8). Blessed is the man all of whose actions are for the sake of Heaven. When he acts, he ought to know whether he is acting on principle or in his own selfish interest.[1] In any event, *If he take him another wife,*

---

1. Literally, "But when he acts, only the heart knows whether he is *'aḳel,* 'weaving,' or *'aḳalḳaloṭ,* 'twisting.' " The contrast suggested by *'aḳel* and *'aḳalḳaloṭ* is that between a straightforward statement and one that is twisting the truth. A play on the sound of the two Hebrew words can be approximated by opposing "honest weaving"

neither the food, nor the raiment, nor the conjugal rights [*of the first wife*] *shall be diminish* (Exod. 21:10), | [that is, he should still provide sufficient maintenance for the first wife].[2] I recall, for example, that once, while I was in the academy in Jerusalem in the presence of Sages, we were engaged in a discussion concerning the laws affecting women. I said, "My Masters, if I had a Canaanite maidservant, I would not say to her, 'Here's some money. Go get me some greens from the market.' " They asked me, "Why not?" I replied, "Because, my Masters, for as little as an immediate meal, a woman [who is desperately hungry], will give herself to fornication, and say, 'In my situation it doesn't matter a bit.' " ER, *p.* 122

For, according to Scripture, women declare *Our skin is as hot* [*with hunger*] *as an oven because of the burning heat of famine* (Lam. 5:10). This verse is followed immediately by the verse *The women in Zion allow themselves to be ravished* (Lam. 5:11). The connection between the two verses? Their conjunction is meant to teach you that when there is a famine—[that is want of Israel's attention to the ordinances of Torah]—in the world, a woman is forced to give herself to fornication, and say, "Under the circumstances it doesn't matter a bit." Such is the consequence implied by the two verses *Our skin is as hot* [*with hunger*] *as an oven because of the burning heat of famine* and *The women in Zion allow themselves to be ravished.*

[In connection with regulations concerning women who for whatever reason need to be provided for], the Sages at the time of the famine in Jerusalem in the days of Jeremiah,[3] set out the following rule of inheritance: "If a man dies, leaving sons and daughters, and the estate is large,[4] the sons inherit and the daughters receive maintenance, but if the estate is small, the daughters receive maintenance and the sons go a-begging. [The rule continued to be enforced], even though Admon[5] commented skeptically, [The son may rightly complain], 'Must I suffer total loss because I am a male?' and Rabban Gamaliel used to say, 'Admon's comment has my approval' " (Keṯ 13:3 and BB 9:1). ▪

In connection with providing for women's needs it is said that in any household where there is a Hebrew maidservant, strife is likely to ensue between the master and the maidservant's father [concerning proper maintenance for her] because she is never satisfied, as is in-

---

to "deceiving," or "being on the level" to "in league with the devil." See parallels in B.Sanh 26a and Lam. Rabbah 1:31.

2. Cf. below, ER, 139.

3. Literally, "At that time."

4. Large enough to provide for the maintenance of both until they reach their majority. See B.BB 139b.

5. Admon was presumably a distinguished judge in Jerusalem, one of the few such identified by name; and the elder Rabban Gamaliel, who lived in the first half of the first century C.E., was president of the Sanhedrin.

dicated by the conjunction of two verses in a passage of Scripture, AND[6] *if men quarrel* (Exod. 21:18), and *If a man sell his daughter to be a maidservant* (Exod. 21:7). What is the purpose of the conjunction? To make you aware that strife and never any peace result in a household with a Hebrew maidservant. The AND in AND *if men quarrel, and one smite the other with a stone* (Exod. 21:18) joins the cause to the result.

Consider further, my Masters, I went on, the following cases: An overzealous[7] officer of the court, in the course of laying on stripes, [inadvertently] slew the man he was punishing—a circumstance obliquely referred to earlier in Exod. 21:13;[8] likewise, an overzealous[9] teacher of young children, [in the course of punishing a mischievous pupil, inadvertently] slew him. The penalty for each such offender is that he be deprived of his job and be put to doing another kind of work. If, however, either overzealous man has a change of heart and resolves to repent, he gets his job back. But if neither repents, each one is likely to commit an offense that will call for a levy upon his property by way of requital, though in contrast to the offense the levy will be mild, as is said, *When men fight, and one of them pushes a pregnant woman and a miscarriage results, but no other misfortune ensues, the one responsible shall be fined* (Exod. 21:22). [Similarly, if unrepentant, a man has committed an offense by striking or killing a person of servile status, eventually he will find himself in the situation described in] the verse *When a man*

6. The copula AND will be construed as linking this verse with another verse in the same passage.

7. The word *meziḏ* [*mzyd*] is usually translated "with evil intent, in full consciousness of doing wrong." However, in Arabic the root *zyd* means "to add, become greater, overdo." Hence here "overzealous." The Arabic parallel was pointed out by Zadok Rubin and confirmed by Benjamin Meir Braude.

[I cannot agree with your interpretation of *meziḏ.* In the first place, Hebrew *zyd* and Arabic *zyd* are only remotely connected semantically (like, e.g., *leḥem* and Arabic *laḥm,* which probably in proto-Semitic meant "food," but branched out into the Hebrew "bread" and the Arabic "meat,"—one cannot argue therefrom that *leḥem* can therefore be used in the sense of "meat".) In the second place, no derivative of the Arabic *zyd* is ever used in the sense of "deliberately, with intent aforethought" (the Arabic terms for the latter are *quaṣdan* or *'amdan*), whereas in Hebrew *bĕ-meziḏ* is the standard legal term for it, and when used in a legal discussion must be presumed to intend just that. In the third place, while homicide *bĕ-meziḏ* is punishable by death, the death penalty is in permanent abeyance, hence the guilty judge or teacher cannot be executed; yet, since he remains alive, he must be given a chance to earn his bread—the solution is to make him revert to some other profession where he can earn a living without becoming a menace to society. . . .

Nor can I agree with your interpretation of what follows. What the Hebrew says is: "If they do not repent, (they should not only be excluded from their professions, but also, since they cannot be put to death for their crimes of homicide), they should be assessed with a monetary fine, even if their crimes are less than homicidal (and are only mayhem or even temporary incapacitation of the victim)." L. N.]

8. In that verse it is said that the slayer must have slain deliberately and with guile, guile which did not motivate the officer of the court or the teacher. See Meḵ, *3,* 36–37.

9. See n. 7.

strikes his slave, male or female, with a rod . . . if the person stricken survive a day or two [*and then die*], *the man,* [*to be sure*], *shall not be punished; for the slave is the man's property* (Exod. 21:20), [and he has suffered financial loss by way of requital, though in contrast to the offense the loss is mild].

Consider this case also, I said to the Sages: My Masters, if an overzealous midwife, in the course of delivering a child, slew the mother or child,[10] then felt a pang of remorse and unmistakably[11] resolved upon repentance, she is exculpated. But if she does not repent, it is likely that she, [like the overzealous officer of the court, or the teacher of young children], will commit an offense that will call for a levy upon her property by way of requital, though in contrast to the offense, the levy will be mild. As Scripture tells us, *When people*[12] *are quarreling, and one of them pushes a pregnant woman and a miscarriage results . . . the one responsible shall be fined . . . on the basis of requital for causing the loss of an eye as much as an eye is worth, or requital for causing a burn as much as the skin is worth* (Exod. 21:22–25).

When Israel, [who were shocked by the apparent harshness of the laws revealed after God's appearance at Mount Sinai], realized that in each of the foregoing regulations the compassion of the Holy One <was abundant>, they said: Would that the Presence never depart from among us!

[Besides, by the time Israel had come to Sinai, they were already of one heart, as will be made clear.] As they were of one heart in Egypt, so when our forebears stood at Mount Sinai to accept the Torah for themselves they were of one heart, for God had already won their confidence [by taking them out of Egypt, dividing the Red Sea for them, bringing down manna for them, bringing up the well for them, causing quail to fly in as provender for them, fighting the battle against Amalek for them].[13] It was then, [because He had their confidence], that He set out laws before them concerning those who do damage to

---

10. "If a woman is in hard travail, the child in her womb is cut up and brought forth member by member, because the woman's life comes before that of [the child]. But if the greater part has proceeded forth one may not touch it, for one may not set aside one person's life for that of another" (Oh 7:6). In this instance, so Haida suggests, after the infant's head emerges, and the rest of it cannot come forth, the midwife, to save the mother, pulls at the infant and thus slays it; or the midwife, putting her hands into the womb to bring out the child, thus slays the mother.

11. Literally "signs of contrition come forth, are evident"; hence "unmistakably."

Unmistakable evidence of remorse is required of a woman, since "by temperament women are said to be unstable" (B.Shab 33b and Ḳid 80b).

12. MT reads *When men,* etc., but the regulation applies to women as well. Hence *people.*

13. For the lines interpolated see Meḳ, *2,* 229–30. Professor Yochanan Muffs of the Jewish Theological Seminary suggested the interpretation of this difficult passage.

persons and property and laws concerning other matters that call for ER, *p.* 123 adjudication.[14] Thereupon Israel said: Blessed be the Lord | God, the God of Israel, the God of hosts who sits over the cherubim.[15] You alone are God over all the kingdoms of the earth. With understanding You made the heavens <and the heaven> of heavens.

In Egypt, [as already stated], the children of Israel taking thought, united—all of them became as one. Thus they came to covenant to act with kindness toward one another and to keep in their hearts the covenant of Abraham, Isaac, and Jacob; they also covenanted not to forsake the language of the house of their father Jacob and not to learn the language of Egypt because use of the language might lead them to idolatry.

Thus in not changing their language, Israel in Egypt continued to serve their Father in heaven though the Egyptians kept asking them: Why are you serving Him? If you were to serve the God of Egypt, he would make your work for him lighter. In reply, Israel said: Perchance, did Abraham, Isaac, and Jacob abandon our God in heaven as an example for their children after them to do so? The Egyptians said: No. Then Israel declared: As they did not abandon Him, so we will not abandon Him.

And Israel in Egypt continued to circumcise their sons. The Egyptians said: If you desist [from this practice], the heavy work may be made lighter for you. Israel replied saying: Perchance, did Abraham, Isaac, and Jacob forget their covenant with our Father in heaven as an example for their children after them to forget it? The Egyptians replied: No. Israel said: As Abraham, Isaac, and Jacob did not forget the covenant with our Father in heaven, neither will their children after them forget it.

Another traditional story of Israel in Egypt who continued to circumcise their sons: The Egyptians said to Israel, Why do you circumcise those whom in no time at all we shall fling into the river? Israel replied: We will circumcise them nevertheless. Then you can do with them as you wish.

Furthermore, Israel in Egypt continued to make [wedding] feasts for their sons and daughters.[16] Said the Egyptians: Why do you make feasts for those whom we shall soon fetch out for oppression and affliction? Israel replied: We shall make the feasts nevertheless. Then you can do with them as you wish. The Egyptians fetched out the grooms sometimes after two days, sometimes after three days, some-

---

14. Such as thieves who, though sold into servitude, are given consideration.

15. In the heaven nearest to the earth. See ER, chap. 1, n. 2.

16. The Egyptians used every device to prevent Israelites from couching with their wives and thus heeding God's command to be fruitful and multiply (see above, ER, 42). Hence Haida suggests that unmarried men were not taken to work.

times after seven days. Some died, some were slain, and others managed to stay alive. In the course of their affliction of the newlyweds, the Egyptians struck them, taunted them, punched them and slapped them, and there was no means of escape for them, as is said, *All the day is my confusion before me, and the shame of my face hath covered me, for the voice of him that taunteth and blasphemeth. . . . All this is come upon us; yet have we not forgotten Thee* (Ps. 44:16–19). Indeed, *Though Thou hast crushed us into a place of crocodiles*[17] (Ps. 44:20)—that is, crushed us by means of Pharaoh king of Egypt and all the Egyptians; *and plunged us into deepest darkness (ibid.)*—that is, plunged us into a life of distress; nevertheless, *if we had forgotten the name of our God . . . would not God search this [transgression] out?* (Ps. 44:21–22). Hence, when Israel do the will of their Father in heaven, < what is said of them? *Behold, He that keepeth Israel doth neither slumber nor sleep* (Ps. 121:3). And when they do not do the will of Him whose presence is everywhere >, what is said of them? *Awake, why sleepest Thou, O Lord? . . . Wherefore hidest Thou Thy face? . . . For our soul is bowed down to the dust. . . . Arise for our help* (Ps. 44:24–27).

One time, when I was going from one place to another, an old man accosted me and asked: My master, recent generations are more worthy than those that came out of Egypt. I asked: My son, what makes you say that recent generations are more worthy than those that came out of Egypt? See with your eyes and hear with your ears! Was not the generation of Moses worthy, since it had the Torah in its midst? See with your eyes and hear with your ears, and apply your intelligence[18] | to all kinds of evidence, and you will discover that both Torah and **ER, *p.* 124** Prophets[19] were in the very midst of that generation. The old man then said: It is not the generations [preceding the First Temple] that I have in mind, but the generations from the day the First Temple was built until the Second Temple was built, [whom I would deem more worthy than the generation which came out of Egypt]. I said: To be sure, did not those later generations have the Five Books, the Prophets, and the Writings, and did they not discuss the dialectics of Torah in regard to them? [Nevertheless, they were not more worthy than those who came out of Egypt.] If you wish to learn and truly desire words of instruction, [I went on], go and consider what God said of those who came out of Egypt: *I remember for thee the affection of thy youth, the love of thine espousals; how thou wentest after Me in the wilderness, in a land that was not sown* (Jer. 2:2). In truth, when Israel went < through the wilderness—and for that

---

17. JV: *jackals.* But *tanim,* "jackals," also means "crocodiles." Egypt is spoken of as *The great crocodile that lieth in the midst of his rivers* (Ezek. 29:3).

18. See Ezek. 44:5 and Prov. 22:17.

19. The Torah which the Patriarchs studied (B.Yoma 28b); Aaron prophesied the redemption (Exod. Rabbah 3:16, 5:11); and Miriam was a prophet (Exod. 15:20).

matter while they were under the yoke of Babylon and of Assyria, too, until the building > [20] of the Second Temple in sorrow—there was not a thing in the world which the Holy One did not reveal to Israel, as is said, *The counsel of the Lord is with them that fear Him* (Ps. 25:14), and also *The Lord God will do nothing but He revealeth His counsel unto His servants the Prophets* [21] (Amos 3:7). I swear by the [Temple] service!—each and every day, each and every hour, [as I recall] all the happenings in Egypt, I fall to the ground and bless, exalt, extol, and hallow the name of Him, blessed be He, at whose word the world came into being. I call heaven and earth to witness that the Holy One who sits and apportions food to all the world's inhabitants and to all the handiwork He created in the world—to man and beast and creeping things and the fowl of heaven, indeed to all the living things He made—[that the Holy One showed His love for the generation that came out of Egypt by providing manna,[22] Miriam's well, and quail for Israel during their forty years in the wilderness].[23]

King David also spoke in praise of those who came out of Egypt. They who came out of Egypt, obedient to one command, multiplied it into a great many commands: [the one command was that] they unite and live so closely together as to become one people; thence they were led to make a covenant that they would act with loving-kindness toward one another, that they would practice circumcision—the covenant of Abraham, Isaac, and Jacob—upon their flesh, and that they would not abandon the language of their father Jacob and proceed to learn the language of Egypt, a language which might bring them to idolatry. Hence it is said, *And who is like Thy people, like Israel, a nation one in the earth, that divine beings went to redeem?* (2 Sam. 7:23); by *divine beings* is meant Moses and Aaron who went *to redeem [Israel] for God's sake (ibid.)*. The verse goes on, *Thy people whom Thou didst redeem to Thee out of Egypt, the nations and their gods (ibid.),* but do not read it thus; read instead, *Thy people, whom Thou didst redeem to Thee out of Egypt, [and didst cause to perish] the nations and their gods.* [24]

---

20. See Friedmann's n. 17.

21. For "at the Red Sea a bondswoman could see what not even Isaiah or Ezekiel . . . ever saw" (Mek, *2,* 24). And to Isaiah and Ezekiel extraordinary visions were vouchsafed. See Isa. 6 and Ezek. 1; and Judah Goldin, *The Song at the Sea* (New Haven and London, 1971), p. 112.

22. Because manna was food completely absorbed by the body, it was possible for Israel to give all their time to study of Torah. They did not have to take time to get food or to eliminate its waste. "Only to those who have manna to eat is it given to study the Torah" (Mek, *2,* 104).

23. "[that the Holy One showed His love . . . in the wilderness]"—a paraphrase by Haida.

24. Cf. MTeh 119:4 (YJS, *13, 2,* 249–50).

CHAPTER (24) 22

Circumcision a mark and a reminder of the Covenant

Summary

The children of Israel who maintained the practice of circumcision also made a covenant that they would act with loving-kindness toward one another (ER, 124) and would not abandon their language and learn Egyptian, which might bring them to idolatry. On the other hand, Esau and his children did not maintain the practice of circumcision, so that before long Esau's one virtue, his filial piety, ceased to mean much because of the enormity of his sins.

Yet even among his seed, it is noted, there were men such as Obadiah who feared God (ER, 125).

Esau's abandonment of circumcision led to the bad upbringing of Amalek, a descendant of Esau, who has sought to destroy the entire Jewish world and who will be punished ultimately by being crucified like the vilest criminal. So great is his wickedness that each time he considers doing a wicked deed, he is condemned as though he had done it. Since the intention of Esau and his seed has always been to cause God's withdrawal from the world, God will extirpate Esau and his seed from the world (ER, 126).

As long ago as the time of Shem, son of Noah, the nations were offered Torah's precepts, but they rejected them even as they spurned God's sovereignty.

When Israel complained to God, saying: Now that the Torah in written form has been given and the nations have ready access to its words, there appears to be no difference between Israel and the nations, God then gave Israel the entire Torah, both the Written Torah and the Oral Torah (ER, 127).

Chapter (24) 22

In connection with the verse *Grant not, O Lord, the desires of the wicked* (Ps. 140:9), come and see the difference between[1] those who went out of Egypt and those who were the seed of wicked Esau. Those who went out of Egypt were aware of but one command, which they multiplied into a great many commands: [in obedience to that one command] they united and lived so closely together as to become one people; thence they were led to make a covenant that they would act with loving-kindness toward one another; that they would practice circumcision, the covenant of Abraham, Isaac, | and Jacob; that they would not abandon the language of the house of Jacob and take to learning the

ER, *p.* 124 *cont'd*

ER, *p.* 125

1. [You do not translate *še-hen,* emended by Friedmann to *koḥan,* "the steadfastness of" (I suppose). Both seem disruptive of the idiom, and I suspect that you are right in ignoring them, and that *še-hen* is an error for the following *šel;* the copyist, as it often happens, added the correct *šel* but neglected to cross out the erroneous *še-hen.* L. N.]

language of Egypt, for it might bring them to idolatry. But the seed of Esau did not continue to heed any of these commands. True, as long as Isaac was alive, they kept up the practice of circumcision of their flesh. But as soon as Isaac died, they brought to an end the practice of circumcision of their flesh. The consequence of their disregarding the commands is alluded to in the verse *The Lord plucks up the house of the proud, but He establishes the border of the widow* (Prov. 15:25). *The Lord plucks up the house of the proud*—the house of Esau; *but He establishes the border of the widow*—the house of Obadiah.[2] By what parable may the matter be illustrated? By the parable of a mortal king who gave his crown to his favorite, saying to him: May it rest on your head and the heads of your descendants for ever! The king's favorite wore the crown on his head until he entered his eternal home. After he entered his eternal home, the king said: <I will go and see> whether the crown rests on the head of my favorite's son. The king went and found the crown lying [on a dung heap, whereupon] he turned and went back [to his palace] in great indignation. Likewise when the Holy One [came to Edom and saw circumcision given up, He] turned in great indignation[3] and went back, as is said, *Lord, when Thou didst go forth out of Seir, when Thou didst march out of the field of Edom . . . the mountains quaked at the presence of the Lord, even yon Sinai* (Judg. 5:4–5).[4]

With whom may we compare the wicked Esau, Eliphaz the Temanite,[5] his son Amalek, Jeroboam son of Nebat, Nebuchadnezzar king of Babylon, and Haman the Agagite? With a man who found a garment on a highway near a city. He picked it up, brought it into the city, and cried his find, saying: To whom does this lost garment belong? To whom does this lost garment belong? All the people of the city came together and hailed him, saying to one another: Have you ever seen a man like him? How righteous he is! How kind! <How noble!> Thereupon they proceeded to make him chief and magistrate of the city. Within a period of three years, he disrupted every province in the whole country. With this man may be compared wicked Esau, Eliphaz the Temanite, his son Amalek, Nebuchadnezzar king of Babylon, Jero-

---

2. In behalf of Obadiah's impoverished widow, Elisha miraculously provided oil for her empty vessels (2 Kings 4:1–7). Obadiah was, according to R. Meir, an Edomite proselyte (B.Sanh 39b).

3. [*Bi-ḳĕṣeh hag-gĕbul,* "at the border's edge," which makes poor sense here, is obviously a misreading of *bĕ-ḳeṣef gaḏol,* "with great indignation" (as in the variants cited in Friedmann's n. 4). L. N.]

4. God offered the Torah to Edom, but Edom rejected it (see PR 15:6 [YJS, *18, 1,* 314, n. 36]), and Amalek, Edom's descendant, added insult to injury by ridiculing circumcision (PRKM 3:6, 11, pp. 44, 49 [PRKS, pp. 48, 52]).

5. Eliphaz, son of Esau, is said to have been brought up in Isaac's lap. See Deut. Rabbah 2:20 and Rashi on Gen. 29:11.

ER identifies Eliphaz son of Esau with the prophet Eliphaz, the friend of Job. See Targum Jonathan on Gen. 36:12 and Ginzberg, *Legends, 1,* 421, and *5,* 322, 384.

boam son of Nebat, and Haman the Agagite. Was it not on account of the two tears Esau shed in his father's presence[6] that he was given Mount Seir from which rains of blessing never cease? Was it not as a reward to Eliphaz the Temanite for according honor to his father that Amalek came into the world as a descendant of his?[7] Was it not as a reward to Jeroboam son of Nebat who spoke properly to the king that the Ten Tribes were given to him?[8] Was it not as a reward for Merodach who accorded honor to our Father in heaven that Nebuchadnezzar came into the world as a descendant of his?[9] Was it not as a reward for Agag who, weeping and grieving for himself when he was confined in prison, said, "Woe is me, my seed may perish from the world!"[10] that wicked Haman came into the world a descendant of his? To all the aforementioned applies the verse *A thief begetteth, and [from him] a gang [worse than he] spreadeth abroad*[11] (Hos. 7:1).

Scripture tells us: [Still, even among the seed of accursed Edom there were men such as Obadiah who feared God, even as among Israel there were reprobates such as Ahab who did not fear God. In this connection] Scripture tells us: [*And the famine was sore in Samaria*]. *And Ahab called [to account] Obadiah who was over the household* (1 Kings 18:3). Why did Ahab call Obadiah to account? He called him to account, asking: Obadiah, can it be that your deeds are not as spotless as the deeds of the faithful? For with Jacob, even the house of Laban, [who was not a Jew], was blessed only because of him, as Laban said to Jacob: *I have learned by divination that the Lord hath blessed me because of thee* (Gen. 30:27); and Jacob said to Laban: *The Lord hath blessed thee because of me* | (Gen. 30:30). So, too, Potiphar's house was blessed only because of ER, *p.* 126
Joseph, as is said, *The Lord blessed the Egyptian's house for Joseph's sake* (Gen. 39:5). [Since I have not been blessed because of you, Obadiah], can it be that your deeds are not like the deeds of Jacob or Joseph? Such is the meaning of *Ahab called [to account] Obadiah who was over the household* (1 Kings 18:3). And what follows in the verse? [A Divine Voice asserting]: *Obadiah feared the Lord greatly (ibid.).* [Hence it is your fault, Ahab, that blessing has been withheld from you.][12]

Eliphaz the Temanite had a son whom he asked: Amalek, my son, who is the one who will inherit both this world and the world-to-come?

---

6. See Gen. 27:34 and Ginzberg, *Legends, 1,* 339.
7. See Gen. 36:10–12.
8. See 1 Kings 12:1–4.
9. See PRKM 2:5, pp. 23–24 (PRKS, pp. 28–29).
10. Since concern for survival of his children was a worthy concern, his prayer was granted.
11. The word *yaḇo',* "entereth in," is, at the suggestion of Leon Nemoy, understood in the sense of *ba' 'al,* "know sexually, beget." JV: *The thief entereth in, and the troop of robbers maketh a raid without.*
12. Cf. B.Sanh 39b.

Eliphaz should have gone on to answer the question himself: Israel will be the inheritors of this world and the world-to-come. So dig wells for them and prepare roads for them. If you do, you will have with Israel the privilege of inheriting a share [in this world] and possessing the world-to-come. But Eliphaz did not say these things. After he had put the matter to Amalek in an oblique way, he said no more. Thereupon Amalek went forth to destroy the entire [Jewish] world, every part of it, as is said, *Then came Amalek, and fought with Israel on account of*[13] *Rephidim* (Exod. 17:8). *Rephidim,* made up of *rfh* meaning "let go" and *ydym* meaning "hands," [is taken here not as a place-name], but as designating Israel's moral lapse in having let go of God's commands [after Sinai].[14] Now, however, the Holy One, who examines the hearts and reins of men, said to Amalek: You cocksure fool! did I not create you only after I had created [the peoples who speak] the seventy languages of the world? Now you [who were created last] will be first of all those who are to go down into Gehenna [for punishment], as is said, *And* [*Balaam*] *looked on Amalek, and took up his parable, and said:* [*For punishment*] *Amalek will be first of the nations; and his fate is to perish for ever* (Num. 24:20). [And elsewhere Scripture tells us that God said to Israel]: *Therefore it shall be, when the Lord thy God hath given thee rest from all thine enemies round about . . . that thou shalt blot out the remembrance of Amalek from under heaven; thou shalt not forget* (Deut. 25:19); and [God promised further], *I will utterly blot out the remembrance of Amalek from under heaven* (Exod. 17:14). [Against Amalek], it is said further, [will be enforced] *the Lord's decree: hand upon a cross* [*of wood*][15] (Exod. 17:16), a verse which brings to mind the popular saying frequently

---

13. JV: *in Rephidim.*

14. According to R. Joshua, Amalek's attack on Israel took place after the revelation on Sinai. See *Měḵilta dě-R. Ishmael,* ed. Friedmann (Vienna, 1870), p. 53a, n. 2.

15. JV: *the hand upon the throne.* But ER seems to take *ks,* "throne," as though it read *ḳys,* "wood, cross." For other examples in which the letters *kaf* and *ḳof* are interchanged, see Kel 16:5 and *Mišnah "im peruš . . . Mošeh ben Maymon, Ḳodošim-Ṭohoroṯ* (Jerusalem, 5732 [1972]), pp. 44–45.

[I can't imagine a master like the author equating *ks* (=*ks'*) with *ḳys.* No sir, he quotes the verse in its obvious sense, *The hand upon the throne of the Lord,* [*to swear that*] *the Lord will have war with Amalek!* . . . Louis Ginzberg, of blessed memory, was fond of bold hypotheses, often too bold for a literal minded pick-and-shovel fellow like your humble servant. The same applies to his next emendation of *bad-din* to *bě-yaḏan,* to drag in an obscure Persian mode of execution. Friedmann, not given to such bold flights of fancy, characteristically confesses, "Its meaning I do not get." And "garbage" (*nefel* is usually "fetus") hardly fits here. Of course the *šbggym* is corrupt. The only way out I see is to regard it as a lapsus calami for *šeb-bě-goyim;* obviously a word before it has dropped out. Conjecturally the sentence read originally something like *'afillu (hat-tam) šeb-bě-goyim,* etc.: "Even the simplest of the heathen is more acceptable (to God) than those (Israelites) who are hanged on wooden gallows by order of the court of law"—in other words, a law-abiding heathen is favored by God over the criminal Israelite—how much more so over a dyed-in-the-wool heathen malefactor like Amalek. Note 16 would then have to be rewritten as simply a summary of Ginzberg's hypothesis. L. N.]

heard: Even garbage is better thought of among the nations than Amalekites who are destined to be hanged with their hands nailed to a cross.[16] Such they deserved and more, for it was wicked Esau's descendants who did away with circumcision of their flesh[17] and who brought to a stop the observance of Sabbath and of all other commandments in the Torah. *And it was they who gave the dead bodies of Thy servants to be food unto the fowls of heaven* (Ps. 79:2). The Holy One who examines the hearts and reins of men said to Amalek: Had there been circumcision of your flesh, each time you considered doing a wicked deed I would not have condemned you as though you had done it.[18] But now that there is no circumcision of your flesh, each time you consider doing a wicked deed I shall condemn you as though you had done it. Thus condemnation applies even to what you consider doing in the future, even if you do not in fact do it. *Therefore, as I live, saith the Lord God, I will prepare thee unto blood, and blood shall pursue thee; surely thou hast hated thine own blood, therefore blood shall pursue thee* (Ezek. 35:6): You hated the blood of circumcision, and so I shall make you into blood for multitudes. *Thou,* [*Esau*], *saidst* [*in thy heart*]: *These two nations and these two countries shall be mine, and we will possess it* (Ezek. 35:10). *But the Lord was there (ibid.).* Who disclosed Esau's secret thoughts? You must reply: the Holy One, for, as the verse declares, *The Lord was there.*

[*O Edom*] . . . *behold, I make thee least among the nations; thou art greatly despised* (Obad. 1:2; Jer. 49:15). *O Edom . . . tflṣtḵ*[19] *hath betrayed thee* (Jer. 49:16): You who are the least *(tfl)* among the nations are, nevertheless, a scorner *(lyṣn).* The blasphemous scorn that you cherish will bring about your removal from the world. Hence, *O Edom . . . thy scorn hath betrayed thee (ibid.).*

O Edom . . . though thou make thy nest as high as the eagle . . . I shall bring thee down from thence (Obad. 1:4). Blessed be the Preserver of the world, blessed be He who will requite the enemies of Israel: Even as Esau's intention had been to cause the Holy One[20] to withdraw from the world, so shall He cause Esau and his seed to be extirpated from the world, as is said, *The house of Jacob shall be a fire, and the house of Joseph a flame . . . and they shall kindle . . . and devour . . . and there shall not be any remaining of the house of Esau* (Obad. 1:18). It is also said, *Whereas Edom saith: "We are beaten down, but we will return and build the waste*

---

16. Amalekites will thus be executed in a way which in Persia was deemed to be the most humiliating. So Louis Ginzberg in *OT,* p. 295, n. 56. The unintelligible first part of the saying *'fylw sbggym,* Ginzberg emends to read *'fylw nfl šbgwym (ibid.).*

17. Apparently ER construes Esau's doing away with circumcision as intended blasphemy. See PRKM 3:11, p. 49 (PRKS, p. 52).

18. See MTeh 30:4 (YJS, *13, 1,* 388–89).

19. JV: *thy terribleness.*

20. [Your translation presupposes the emendation of *šel hḳb"h* into *'al hḳb"h.* L. N.]

places"; Thus saith the Lord of hosts: They shall build, but I will throw down (Mal. 1:4); and it is said further, *For the violence done to thy brother Jacob, shame shall cover thee, and thou shalt be cut off for ever* (Obad. 1:10):[21] For the violence that [your] Impulse to evil did to your brother Jacob, shame will cover you, and you will be cut off for ever. For the violence that the four kingdoms[22] did to your brother Jacob in not permitting a Scroll of Torah to be left in Jacob's hand, shame will cover you, and you will be cut off for ever. What is more, [despite you, the Torah did abide with Jacob]. In this connection, take note that [the dispersion of the nations was] their punishment for not taking upon themselves the **ER, *p.* 127** teachings of the great Shem | who for four hundred years had prophesied to all the nations of the world.[23] He used to say to the nations, "Will you take upon yourselves the Torah?" And they would inquire, "What is written in Your Torah?" He would reply, "You shall not commit murder, you shall not commit adultery, you shall not steal, you shall not bear false witness, you shall not covet." So they said, "All these are beautiful precepts!" Nevertheless,[24] they did not take Your Torah, nor[25] did they take Your sovereignty, Lord, upon themselves. We, however, Your people, children of Your covenant, children of Abraham, Isaac, and Jacob who carried out Your will in the world, [ask that You] provide [us] with contentment in keeping with the promise You made to Your children. May the petition *Arise, O Lord, in Thine anger . . . let the congregation of the peoples compass Thee about, and over them return Thou on high* (Ps. 7:7–8) be granted, so that despite *the peoples* [*that*] *compass Thee about,* that are gathered around You, You will return to be enthroned on high. In this vein David went on to plead: *O Lord, that ministerest judgment to the peoples . . . Let the evil of the wicked come to an end* (Ps. 7:9–10). And he concluded *I look to God to shield me; the deliverer of the upright*[26] (Ps. 7:11).

All Israel and Moses with them assembled, and he spoke up to God: Master of the universe, between us and the peoples of the world there is in fact no difference.[27] *For how would it be known that I have found grace in Thy sight, I and Thy people, unless Thou goest with us that we may be distinguished, I and Thy people, from all the people that are upon the face of the earth?* (Exod. 33:16). Thereupon the Holy One swore by His

---

21. The words "For the violence you did to your brother Jacob, shame will cover you, and you will be cut off for ever" are omitted as dittography.

22. Egypt, Babylon, Greece, Edom [Rome].

23. See ER, 114.

24. [I wonder if *'lw dbrym yfyn hn* is meant as irony—"What fancy words these are!" In other words, "Stuff and nonsense!" The following sentence would then have to read, "And they did not take," etc. L. N.]

25. "they did not take Your Torah, nor"—R.

26. So NJV; JV: *My shield is with God, who saveth the upright in heart.*

27. Like us they have access to the commandments set down in written form.

great name that the entire Torah [both Written and Oral] would be given to them[28]—all of it arrayed in order, set out before Israel like beakers filled with [wine],[29] like cups and tables laden with an abundance of all the delicacies in the world, as is said, *Thy navel is like a round goblet, wherein no mingled wine is wanting* (Song 7:3). And the Holy One went on to swear to His people that He would never exchange them for another nation, never give them up or substitute another people for them. And with regard to Israel alone, God asserted, *I will not execute the fierceness of Mine anger* (Hos. 11:9).

---

28. Cf. PR 5:1 (YJS, *18, 1,* 93).
29. "wine"—V; R: "water."

CHAPTER (25) 23

The rewards of awe of God and of willingness of heart

Summary

God, who took Israel as His permanent possession, speaks to all of them as though he were speaking to each one individually. And so, hearkening to Him, each man should ask himself: When will my deeds match the deeds of Abraham, Isaac, and Jacob, who came to own this world and the world-to-come only because of their good deeds and study of Torah? A man should not say to himself: Because this world is full of chaos and confusion (ER, 127), I will consider only my own comfort—eat, drink, and enjoy myself. No, a man should feel for others and share the distress of the community.

God comes to accept man as His very own through man's love of his fellow man, through his brotherliness, his reverence, his amity, his truth, his peace, his deference, his humility, his sitting at study, his little concern for worldly business, his attendance on Sages, his discussion with disciples, his gladness of heart, his right conduct, his Nay being Nay, his Yea being Yea, and finally through his fear of God, as exemplified in the lives of Abraham, Isaac (ER, 128), and Jacob.

Indeed, as a reward for Israel's awe of their Father in heaven and as a reward for their trust in Him, the Holy One will deliver them from the peoples of the world and bring them the days of the Messiah. At that time the Tabernacle and all its vessels which had been concealed will be brought forth out of their hiding places. For God sees to it that what had been made by the hands of worthy men imbued with willingness of heart, endures (ER, 129).

Chapter (25) 23

ER, *p.* 127 *cont'd* Comment on the verse *And God spoke all these words, saying: I am the Lord thy God,* etc. (Exod. 20:1–2) [begins with the blessing]: Blessed be He whose Presence is everywhere, blessed be He who chose Israel out of all the inhabitants of the world and out of all the work of His hands that He created in the world. Indeed, He took Israel as His permanent possession, sons and servants, for His name's sake. At times He addresses them as one speaking to a multitude, at other times, [as in the verse cited above], He addresses them as though speaking to each of them individually. The fact is that because of the love He cherishes for Israel and because of the joy He has in them, even when He speaks to all of them He does so as if He were speaking <to each one of them individually>. [And because each man is thus directly addressed by Him], every one in Israel should ask himself, When will my deeds match the deeds of Abraham, Isaac, and Jacob, who came to own this world and the world-to-come only because of their good deeds and

study of Torah? As the Sages taught in a Mishnah: "[Because] each and every man in Israel is obligated to say, The world was created for my sake" (Sanh 4:5), he should not say to himself, Because this world is full of chaos and confusion, | I will go, eat and drink, enjoy myself, **ER, *p.* 128**
and then leave the world. If he does as he says, the verse *The fool hath said in his heart: "There is no God,"* etc. (Ps. 14:1) applies to him. And if he happens to be a disciple of the wise, he strips himself of wisdom and understanding, knowledge and insight. If he then turns away to other, [to alien], ideas, the words *The vile person will speak villany,* etc. (Isa. 32:6) apply to him. Moreover, a man who beholds the many in distress ought not say, I will go, eat, and enjoy myself in the world. If he goes ahead and lives according to what is said in the words *Behold, joy and gladness, slaying oxen and killing sheep, eating flesh and drinking wine: "Let us eat, and drink, for tomorrow we shall die"* (Isa. 22:13), let him note what is said in the verse that follows: *The Lord of hosts revealed Himself in mine ears: Surely this iniquity shall not be expiated by you till ye die* (Isa. 22:14). In this connection it is said: Even if there were a Sage in Israel who, like Moses, was an elder in wisdom and father of Prophets, and who was as devout as Moses' brother Aaron, he should not say: "Since I am at ease in my own house, let my soul be at peace." Instead he should leave his house and share the distress of the community. If he does not act in this way, the verse *Come ye, I will fetch wine, and we will fill ourselves with strong drink; and tomorrow shall be as this day; and much more abundant* (Isa. 56:12) applies to him. And the consequence of his selfish indifference to others? It is in the next verse: *The* [*apparently*] *righteous perisheth, and no man layeth it to heart . . . that because of his own evil, the man* [*seemingly*] *righteous was taken away* (Isa. 57:1). But if he helps his fellows in distress? Then, as the following verse says, [he will be told at the end of his life] *Let him come in peace, let him who has walked in his uprightness rest on his couch* [*and await My kingly feast*] (Isa. 57:2).

Hence if it be asked, How does a man earn [the regard of] his Father in heaven, the answer is that he earns it through good deeds as well as study of Torah. Thereafter the Holy One sees to it that he comes to own this world, the world-to-come, and the days of the Messiah. God comes to accept man as His very own through [man's] love, through his brotherliness, through his reverence, through his amity, through his truth, through his peacefulness, through his deference, through his humility, through his sitting [at study], through his little concern for worldly business, through his attendance on Sages,[1] through his discussion with disciples, through his gladness of heart, through his right conduct, through his Nay being Nay, and through his Yea being Yea.

[And through his fear of God]: so we learned from <our father

---

1. See above, ER, chap. (6) 7, nn. 70, 71.

Abraham, [father of such virtuous men]>. It was fear of the Holy One that preceded all his subsequent acts. [Because he feared Him], the Holy One said to him: *Fear not, Abram,* etc. (Gen. 15:1). *Fear not* is said only to a man who genuinely fears Heaven. By what parable may the matter be illustrated? By the parable of a mortal king who said to his son: My son, go out and slay all who are robbers. Should they fall <at your hands>, do not benefit from their possessions, so that people will not be able to say: The prince went out and slew the robbers for no reason other than to get hold of their possessions. Upon the prince's return, his father went out to meet him and said to him: May you be blessed! May you have contentment in the world because you did not benefit at all from their possessions! Now come, and I will give you silver and gold, precious stones and pearls from my own treasury.

[Thus God rewards those who stand in awe of Him, obey Him, and act only out of righteousness], as did Abraham when he went out and slew the marauding kings. Upon his return, the king of Sodom, supposing that Abraham wanted to get the reward due him, went out to meet him. *So the king of Sodom said unto Abram: "Give me thy captives, and take the goods to thyself"* (Gen. 14:21). *And Abram said unto the king of Sodom: "I have lifted up my hand unto the Lord . . . that I will not take a thread nor a shoe-latchet nor aught that is thine"* (Gen. 14:22). You fool, Abraham went on, do I need silver or gold, precious stones or costly treasures? Look, the booty is flung to the ground before me to show that I got no benefit whatever from their possessions, as is said, *I will not take a thread nor a shoe-latchet . . . save only that which the young men have eaten,* etc. (Gen. 14:23–24). Thereupon our father Abraham hallowed the name of the Holy One by proceeding to restore all the goods of Sodom and Gomorrah to them. *After these things* (Gen. 15:1)—after Abraham returned all the goods of Sodom and Gomorrah—*the word of the Lord came unto Abraham in a vision, saying: "Fear not Abram, I am thy shield, thy reward shall be exceeding great" (ibid.).*

From Isaac, too, we learn that from the beginning of his experiences, he feared the Lord. Isaac was seventy-five years old when
ER, *p.* 129 Abraham entered his eternal abode. | Isaac said: Woe is me! Perhaps I do not have the capacity for good deeds that my father had. What will happen to me at the hands of the Holy One? At once the compassion of the Holy One crested like a wave, and He then reassured Isaac, as is said, *The Lord appeared unto him the same night, and said: I am the God of Abraham thy father. Fear not* (Gen. 26:24). From Jacob, also, we learn that it was fear of the Holy One which preceded all his subsequent acts, as is said, *And he was afraid, and said: "How full of awe is this place!"* (Gen. 28:17).

From our earliest forebears we learn that it was fear of the Holy One which preceded all their subsequent acts, as is said, *Israel saw the great work which the Lord did upon the Egyptians, and the people feared the*

Lord (Exod. 14:31). You may conclude, therefore, that as a reward for Israel's awe of their Father in heaven and as a reward for Israel's trust in their Father in heaven, the Holy One will come and deliver Israel from among the peoples of the world and bring them the days of the Messiah and the days of redemption, when God will say, *Be in pain, and labor to bring forth, O daughter of Zion, like a woman in travail; for now shalt thou go forth . . . unto Babylon . . . there shall the Lord redeem thee from the hand of thine enemies* (Mic. 4:10).[2] So, too, Israel left all their sins in Babylon and went up pure to the Land of Israel, as is signified by the verse *Then I came back and*[3] *lifted mine eyes, and saw, and behold, there came forth two women . . . and they lifted up the measure* [*of wickedness*]. . . . *Then said I to the angel that spoke with me: "Whither do these bear the measure?" And he said unto me: "To build for her a house in the land of Shinar"* (Zech. 5:9–10). Why is Babylon called "Shinar?" Because [it was there that] Israel disposed[4] *(mĕna'ereṯ)*—[disposed, that is, of the sins that were] upon Israel. Hence it is said, *To build for her*—[for wickedness, that is] —*a house in the land of Shinar* (Zech. 5:11).

The verse continues, *And when* [*the place for God's dwelling on earth*] *is finally prepared,* [*the Tabernacle*] *shall be set there,* [*in Jerusalem*], *in its own place* (Zech. 5:11). Then the Tabernacle will be restored to where it belongs,[5] and within the Tabernacle will be the Ark and the Tables of the Commandments,[6] the cruse <of the anointing oil,[7] and the jar of manna>,[8] of which *The Lord said to Moses:*[9] *"Take a jar, and put an omerful of manna therein, and lay it up before the Lord, to be kept throughout your generations"* (Exod. 16:33), for "This is the bread that I had [Israel] eat in the wilderness."[10] It is said that the Ark and the Tables of the Commandments will be within the Tabernacle. But how do we know that the Tables of the Commandments were preserved? Because Moses

---

2. Since earlier verses (1–4) in Mic. 4 speak of messianic redemption, ER construes Mic. 4:10 as alluding to a kind of interim redemption.

3. *came back and* is not in MT.

4. "Disposed" *(mĕna'ereṯ)* is construed as coming from the same stem as *n'r* in Shinar. [*ni'er* means "to shake," and the subject of it is Babylon, not Israel: "Because Babylon shook off *(mĕna'ereṯ)* of Israel (their sins). Hence it is said," etc. L. N.]

5. The Tabernacle is said to have been concealed by Solomon. See 1 Kings 8:4 and Tos Soṭ 13:1 (Lieberman, *TKF, Našim, 2,* 229).

6. Presumably the Tables which Moses broke (Exod. 32:19).

7. With this oil Moses anointed the sacred implements. See Lev. 8.

8. Before the exile, the Ark and the Tables of the Commandments, the cruse of the anointing oil, and the jar of manna were concealed, according to one tradition, by king Josiah (Tos Soṭ 13:1 [Lieberman, *TKF, Našim, 2,* 299]); and according to another tradition, the Ark, the altar of incense, and the Tabernacle also were concealed by Jeremiah (2 Macc. 2:4–5 [ed. Zeitlin-Tedesche, Philadelphia, 1954, p. 111]). Upon Israel's return from Babylon, the Tabernacle and all its vessels will be brought forth out of their hiding place. See Ginzberg, *Legends, 6,* 19. But cf. B.Yoma 21b.

9. MT: *Moses said to Aaron.*

10. Cf. Meḵ, *2,* 125–26.

said: *These words the Lord spoke unto all your assembly in the Mount. . . . He wrote them upon two tables of stone* (Deut. 5:19), which is to say, "These are the Ten Commandments that I spoke to you at Sinai."[11] And why is the Tabernacle preserved to this day? Because with willingness of heart worthy men built it,[12] and it is difficult for our Father in heaven to let end all that has been made <by the hands of> worthy men imbued with willingness of heart. And the reward of those who made the Tabernacle with willingness of heart is that the Holy One will come and dwell in it as He did formerly, as is said, *Awake, O north wind; and come, thou south*[13] (Song 4:16). *I am come into My garden, My sister, My bride* (Song 5:1), [both *sister* and *bride*] alluding to the congregation of Israel. *I have gathered My myrrh with My spices (ibid.)*—the Five Books, the Prophets, and the Writings. *I have eaten My honeycomb with My honey (ibid.)*—Midrash of Halak̲ot̲ and 'Aggad̲ot̲. *I have drunk My wine with My milk (ibid.)*—good deeds and the study of Torah which Sages of Torah thirst for. *Drink, yea, drink abundantly, O beloved (ibid.).*

---

11. Since God Himself wrote them, it must be presumed that they were not destroyed but preserved. Cf. ER, 95.

12. See Exod. 35:5.

13. Taken to refer to the time of the exiles' ingathering. See Rashi *ad loc.*

CHAPTER (26) 24

The Ten Commandments all of a piece

Summary

God took Israel to be wholly His own and spoke to them as though He were speaking to each one individually (ER, 129). Hence when He gave Israel the Ten Commandments, He addressed each one to one of the ten individuals who He knew would spurn it. Each Commandment implied the threat of punishment but also contained a promise of reward (ER, 130). Among such men as Abraham, Isaac, Jacob, Boaz, and Hananiah, Mishael, and Azariah, all of whom lived by the Commandments, Joseph in particular was the one who in the face of danger and temptation heeded all ten (ER, 131).

Certain of the Commandments are coupled with others to show that the Ten are all of a piece, and hence that the performance of one Commandment leads to the performance of many others and that disregard of one leads to the disregard of many others. For example, the coupling of *Remember the Sabbath day, to keep it holy* with *Honor thy father and thy mother* indicates that as long as a man honors his father and his mother, he will not be led into profanation of the Sabbath or into any other sin. On the other hand, for a man to disregard the Commandment *Honor thy father and thy mother* means that he is also disregarding the Commandment *Thou shalt not murder,* for in not providing for his parents, it is as if he were murdering souls in the very presence of God.

With reference to the Commandment *Remember the Sabbath day, to keep it holy,* it is said that the Sabbath, the Lord, and Israel are equal in holiness. Hence upon Jews who oppress their own people, there shall come evil (ER, 132–34). But for those who, for example, provide contentment for their parents, God will provide goodly treasures (ER, 135).

Chapter (26) 24

Another comment on *God spoke all these words, saying: I am the Lord thy God* (Exod. 20:1–2). Blessed be He whose Presence is everywhere, blessed be He who chose Israel out of all the peoples of the world, out of all the work of His hands that He created in the world—indeed, took Israel to be wholly His possession, sons and servants for His name's sake. At times He addresses them as though speaking to a multitude, at other times, [as in the verse cited], He addresses them as though speaking to each one individually. | The fact is that because of the love He cherishes for Israel and because of the joy He finds in them, He speaks to them as though He were speaking to < each one individually > . This is what the Holy One said to Israel: My children, I am He who for nine hundred and seventy-four generations before the world[1] was to be created, sat and pondered, analyzed, tested, and refined all

ER, *p.* 129 *cont'd*

ER, *p.* 130

1. See above, ER, chap. 2, n. 22.

the words of Torah. From the day the world was created until the hour [of Torah's revelation], I used to sit on My throne of glory devoting a third of the day to reading Scripture and reciting Mishnah, a third of the day to judging the world, and a third of the day to bestowing mercy while I fed, sustained, and provided for the entire world and for all the work of My hands that I created in the world.[2] I am the One who, before the world was to be created, put to the side nine hundred and seventy-four generations [to whom I had planned to give life] and came and cleaved to you.[3] I am the One who put to the side the nations speaking the seventy languages of the earth and came and cleaved to you. I am the only One who can say, *I am God, and there is none else; I am God and there is none like Me* (Isa. 46:9), and yet, [in My love of you], I called you godlike beings,[4] My children, and My servants. I am He who can say, *Before Me there was no God formed, neither shall any be after Me* (Isa. 43:10), and yet I called you My brothers and My companions.[5] I am He who can say, *A just God yet a savior, there is none beside Me* (Isa. 45:21), and yet I linked your name to Mine.[6] I am He who was before the world was created. I am He who is since the world was created. I am in this world. I am in the world-to-come: *I kill and I make alive* (Deut. 32:39).

Another comment on *I ('nky) am the Lord thy God.* The word *'nky* is to be read as an acronym: "I Myself wrote and gave [the Torah]."[7]

In another comment on *I am the Lord thy God,* the verse is taken as implying that the Holy One looked at the world which He created —all of it, from world's end to world's end—and saw in it ten individuals each of whom would spurn Him [by choosing to transgress one of the Ten Commandments which He introduced by the words *I am the Lord thy God*]. These individuals were Micah (Judg. 17); Jeroboam son of Nebat (1 Kings 12); the half-breed Israelite (Lev. 24:11); the man who gathered sticks upon the Sabbath day (Num. 15:32); Absalom (2 Sam. 15); Joab (1 Kings 2:5); Samson (Judg. 14:3); Achan son of Zerah (Josh. 7); the witnesses against Naboth; and Ahab (1 Kings 21). Micah spurned the Commandment *I am the Lord thy God;* Jeroboam spurned the Commandment *Thou shalt have no other gods before Me* (Exod. 20:2). The half-breed Israelite, [a blasphemer], spurned the Commandment *Thou shalt not take the name of the Lord thy God in vain* (Exod. 20:7); the man who gathered sticks on the Sabbath spurned *Remember the Sabbath*

---

2. See above, ER, 62.
3. See above, ER, 9.
4. See Ps. 82:6.
5. See Ps. 122:8.
6. The name Israel means "prince (or ruler) of divine beings." See Gen. 32:29 and *APB,* p. 9.
7. *'n' nfšy ktbyt yhbyt.* Louis Ginzberg's emendation is followed (*OT,* p. 274, n. 102).

day (Exod. 20:8) and *Keep the Sabbath day* (Deut. 5:12); Absalom spurned *Honor thy father and thy mother* (Exod. 20:12); Joab spurned *Thou shalt not murder* (Exod. 20:13); Samson spurned *Thou shalt not commit adultery (ibid.);* Achan son of Zerah spurned *Thou shalt not steal (ibid.);* the witnesses against Naboth spurned *Thou shalt not bear false witness (ibid.);* and Ahab spurned *Thou shalt not covet* (Exod. 20:14).[8]

I am the Lord thy God. If you live by this Commandment, I, your God, will say, "Ye are godlike beings, and all of you are sons of the Most High" (Ps. 82:6). If you transgress it, "Ye shall die like mortals, and fall even as a prince [must fall]" *(ibid.).*

Thou shalt have no other gods before Me (Exod. 20:2). If you live by this Commandment, "I will have respect unto you, and make you fruitful" (Lev. 26:9). If you transgress it, "I will set My face against you" (Lev. 26:17).

Thou shalt not take the name of the Lord thy God in vain (Exod. 20:7). If you live by this Commandment, "The Lord hath sworn by His right hand and by the arm of His strength: 'Surely I will no more give thy corn to be food for thine enemies' " (Isa. 62:8). If you transgress it, [the outcome will be as on a previous occasion, when it was said], "The Lord's anger was kindled in that day, and He swore saying: 'Surely none of the men . . . shall see the Land' " (Num. 32:10).

Remember the Sabbath day (Exod. 20:8). If you live by this Commandment, "Thou shalt delight thyself in the Lord"[9] (Isa. 58:14). If you transgress it, "Then shall the Land be paid back her Sabbaths, throughout the time that she lies desolate"[10] (Lev. 26:34).

| *Honor thy father and thy mother* (Exod. 20:12). If you live by this ER, *p.* 131
Commandment, "The nations shall see thy triumph, and all kings thy glory"[11] (Isa. 62:2). If you transgress it, "The fathers shall eat the sons in the midst of thee, and the sons shall eat their fathers" (Ezek. 5:10).

Thou shalt not murder (Exod. 20:13). If you live by this Commandment, "The sword shall not go through your Land" (Lev. 26:4). If you transgress it, "I will draw out the sword after you" (Lev. 26:33).

Thou shalt not commit adultery (Exod. 20:13). If you live by this Commandment, "The virgin shall rejoice in the dance" (Jer. 31:12). If you transgress it, "I will not punish your daughters when they commit harlotry" (Hos. 4:14).

Thou shalt not steal (Exod. 20:13). If you live by this Command-

---

8. Cf. PR 21:12, 15 (YJS, *18, 1,* 432, 438–39).

9. The protasis in the preceding verse reads, "If thou turn away thy foot because of the Sabbath, from pursuing thy business on My holy day."

10. When the Land lies desolate—at rest, so to speak—it will be paid back the Sabbaths that Israel took from her by working the Land on Sabbaths.

11. A fulfillment of the promise in Deut. 5:16 that it will go well with him who honors his father and mother. So *YY.*

ER may read *kĕḇodeḵ,* "thy glory," as "thine honoring [of thy father]."

ment, [you will be so strong that] "You will be able to devour all the heathen peoples" (Deut. 7:16). If you transgress it, you will be constrained to cry out "Nebuchadnezzar the king of Babylon hath devoured me, he hath crushed me" (Jer. 51:34).

Thou shalt not bear false witness (Exod. 20:13). If you live by this Commandment, "Ye are My witnesses, saith the Lord, that I am God" (Isa. 43:12). If you transgress it, [Woe unto you]! "What shall I take to witness that could console you in your suffering, with what dire fate shall I, to console you, match the fate that will befall you?"[12] (Lam. 2:13).

Thou shalt not covet (Exod. 20:14). If you live by this Commandment, "No man shall covet thy Land" (Exod. 34:24). If you transgress it, "Others will covet thy fields, and seize them; and houses, and take them away" (Mic. 2:2).

Joseph lived by the Commandment *I am the Lord thy God,* for he said, "Am I in the place of God?" (Gen. 50:19). Jacob lived by the Commandment *Thou shalt have no other gods before Me* (Exod. 20:2), for at his request his sons "gave unto Jacob all the foreign gods that were in their hands . . . and Jacob hid them" (Gen. 35:4). Joseph lived by the Commandment *Thou shalt not take the name of the Lord thy God in vain* (Exod. 20:7), for in swearing an oath, he used the formula "As Pharaoh liveth" (Gen. 42:15), [not "as God liveth"]. Now, if he kept his word when he swore by a mortal king, all the more so would he have kept it had he sworn by the King of kings of kings, the Holy One, blessed be He. And Joseph also lived by the Commandment *Remember the Sabbath day* (Exod. 20:8), for he said to the household, "Slaughter the beasts, and prepare" (Gen. 43:16), the term "prepare" intimating, as in the verse "On the sixth day . . . they shall prepare that which they bring in" (Exod. 16:5), that the preparation was for the Sabbath. In another comment, the words are read *Slaughter the beasts but make sure to prepare* [*before and after*] (Gen. 43:16), which is to say, before slaughtering one must examine the edge of the slaughterer's knife, and after slaughtering one must remove the sciatic nerve. In still another comment, the words read "Slaughter the beasts and prepare the meat" *(ibid.)* are taken to imply that Joseph said to the cook: "Uncover for the sons of Jacob the place on the throat where the cut of the slaughterer is to be made;[13] and prepare the meat by removing the sciatic nerve in the presence of the brothers."[14]

Another comment: Hananiah, Mishael, and Azariah also lived by

---

12. A free paraphrase of the verse which in JV reads: *What shall I take to witness for thee, what shall I liken to thee?*

13. To convince the brothers that the slaughtering was according to ritual.

14. See above, ER, 35; Targum Jonathan *ad loc.,* Gen. Rabbah 92:4; and B.Ḥul 91a.

the Commandment *Remember the Sabbath day* (Exod. 20:8), for, according to Scripture, God said to them: "Concerning the king's officers[15] that keep My Sabbaths . . . unto them will I give in My house and within My walls a monument and a memorial" (Isa. 56:4–5).

And Joseph also lived by the Commandment *Honor thy father* (Exod. 20:12), for when Jacob said to Joseph, "Do not thy brethren feed the flock in Shechem? Come, and I will send thee unto them," he replied, "Here am I" (Gen. 37:13).

Another comment on *Honor thy father* (Exod. 20:12): Isaac lived by this Commandment, for he let himself be thrown down before his father like a lamb to be slaughtered or like a ewe before the shearers.

Joseph lived by the Commandment *Thou shalt not murder* (Exod. 20:13), for he did not listen to the plea of Potiphar's wife that he slay her husband.

Another comment on *Thou shalt not murder:* Judah lived by this Commandment, for he said, "What profit is it that we slay our brother?" (Gen. 37:26).

Thou shalt not commit adultery (Exod. 20:13): Joseph lived by this Commandment, for he said, "How then can I do this great wickedness and commit this sin—by God" (Gen. 39:9). What do the words "by God" imply? That Joseph forswore his Impulse to evil, saying, "By God, I shall not do this thing."

Another comment on *Thou shalt not commit adultery:* Boaz lived by this Commandment, for he said to Ruth, "Tarry this night, and it shall be in the morning that . . . I will do the part of a kinsman to thee"[16] (Ruth 3:13).

Thou shalt not steal (Exod. 20:13): Joseph lived by this Commandment, for it is said, "Joseph gathered up all the money that was found in the land of Egypt . . . and . . . brought the money into Pharaoh's house" (Gen. 47:14).[17]

Another comment on *Thou shalt not steal:* the Tribe Fathers lived by this Commandment, for they said, "How then should we steal out of thy lord's house silver or gold?" (Gen. 44:8).

---

15. JV: *concerning the eunuchs.* But after Hananiah, Mishael, and Azariah had come forth out of the fiery furnace, it is said that they went to the Land of Israel where they took wives and begot sons and daughters (B.Sanh 93a). Hence the three could not have been eunuchs. The assertion that descendants of the Tribe of Judah, presumably such as Hananiah, Mishael, and Azariah, will serve as eunuchs *(sarisim)* in the palace of the king of Babylon (Isa. 39:7) is construed as meaning: they will serve at a time when idolatry will be "castrated," rooted out of Babylon (B.Sanh 93b).

16. Ruth sought out Boaz, a kinsman of her dead husband Chilion, in the hope that by wedding her he would provide an heir for Chilion, Naomi's son. Though she lay all night at his feet, he forbore to touch her, saying that in the morning he would ascertain whether a redeeming kinsman closer than Boaz was ready to wed Ruth; if not, he would wed her. See Ruth 2:20 and 3:1 through 4:11.

17. Cf. Mek̲, *1,* 179–80.

Thou shalt not bear false witness (Exod. 20:13) and *Thou shalt not covet* (Exod. 20:14): Abraham lived by these Commandments, for he said to the king of Sodom, "I will not take a thread nor a shoe-latchet, nor aught that is thine . . . save only that which the young men have eaten" (Gen. 14:23–24).

ER, *p.* 132 | *I am the Lord thy God. . . . Thou shalt have no other gods before Me. . . . Thou shalt not take the name of the Lord thy God in vain* (Exod. 20:2, 3, 7). What was the significance of having these three Commandments next to each other? To teach you that a man who is in the habit of swearing in vain[18] and swearing falsely[19] is, in effect, worshiping an idol, and he who is not in the habit of swearing <in vain and swearing> falsely gratifies Him by whose word the world came into being.

Woe to the wicked who end up disqualifying themselves as witnesses because of their deeds which are corrupt and their utterances which are unfit. [Since people lose faith in such wretches], they stay poor until the day of their death,[20] as is said, *I cause [the punishment for a false oath] to go forth, saith the Lord of hosts, and it shall enter into the house of the thief, and into the house of him that sweareth falsely by My name; and it shall abide in the midst of his house, and shall consume it with the timber and the stones thereof* (Zech. 5:4). *I cause* punishment for a false oath *to go forth* at once,[21] says God. [*Punishment*] *shall enter into the house of the thief*—of him who knows that there is no money owed him by his fellow, but who deceives people[22] into thinking that his fellow does owe him money. [Punishment] *shall* then *enter,* actually enter, *into the house of him that sweareth falsely by My name.* With regard to all other transgressions mentioned in the Torah, a man is punished by levies upon his property, but with regard to a false oath a man is punished both by levies upon his property and a taxing of his person,[23] as is said,

---

18. "Vain oaths are . . . divisible into four types. The first is an oath stating that a known fact is not a fact. For example, one may swear that a man is a woman, or that a woman is a man. . . . The second is an oath stating that a known fact which no man doubts is indeed a fact. For example, one may swear that heaven is heaven . . . or that two are two. . . . The third is an oath not to fulfill a commandment. For example, one may swear . . . not to eat unleavened bread on Passover night, or to fast on Sabbaths and festivals. The fourth is an oath to do something that is not within one's power to do. For example, one may swear not to sleep both night and day for three consecutive days" (Maimonides' Code VI, I, i, 4–7 [YJS, *15,* 5–6]).

19. Swearing "I ate," when in fact he has not eaten, or "I did not eat," when he has eaten; or denial by oath of possessing money belonging to a companion (Maimonides' Code VI, I, i, 3, 8 [YJS, *15,* 5–6]).

20. See Louis Ginzberg in *OT,* p. 297, n. 92.

21. "With regard to all other transgressions in the Torah, if a man has merit, punishment is suspended for two or three generations" (B. Shebu 39a).

22. [Literally, "steals the mind of the people"; a deceiver steals true knowledge from those entitled to possess it, and plants falsehood in its place. He can therefore legitimately be called a thief. L. N.]

23. He is liable to a flogging (Maimonides' Code VI, I, i, 3 [YJS, *15,* 5]).

[*Punishment*] *shall abide in the midst of his house, and shall consume it with the timber and the stones thereof.*[24] Nay more: The Holy One Himself will bear witness against him, as is said, *I will come near to you to judgment; and I will be a swift witness . . . against false swearers* (Mal. 3:5); and *Because they have spoken words in My name falsely . . . I am He that knoweth, and am witness, saith the Lord*[25] (Jer. 29:23).

Thou shalt not take the name of the Lord thy God in vain (Exod. 20:7), and *Remember the Sabbath day* (Exod. 20:8). What is the significance of having these two Commandments next to each other? That a man who is in the habit of swearing in vain <and swearing falsely> does not accept the complete sovereignty of Heaven over himself,[26] but he who is not in the habit of swearing in vain and swearing falsely accepts the complete sovereignty of God over himself. Moreover, a man who is in the habit of swearing in vain and swearing falsely does not come to own life in the world-to-come; but he who is not in the habit of swearing in vain <and swearing falsely> comes to own life in the world-to-come.[27]

A man should not say to himself: "I am willing to love Heaven and fear Heaven," provided I am free to transgress any one[28] of the Commandments of Torah. If this is his stipulation, it is an evil omen for him; an evil portion will be his, and harsh judgments will befall him. Rather should a man say: I am going to love Heaven and fear Heaven and will not transgress any one of the Commandments of Torah. If such is his intention, it is a good omen for him; a good portion will be his, and [such sin as] profanation of the Sabbath[29] will not come his way.

How do you know [that the carrying out of one command leads to the carrying out of many others]? You can find the answer for yourself. When Israel were in the wilderness, what is said of them? *While the children of Israel were in the wilderness, they found a man gathering sticks upon the Sabbath day,* etc. (Num. 15:32). The Holy One asked Moses, "Moses, why does this man profane the Sabbath?" Moses replied, "Master of the universe, I do not know." God said: "On a weekday, there are tefillin on his head and on his arm, so that as he

---

24. See B.Shebu 39a and PR 22:6 (YJS, *18, 1,* 467).

25. "Is there any remedy for a slave whose master brings him near to judge him, and hastens to testify against him?" (B.Ḥag 5a).

26. An affirmation made by the Sabbath, associated as it is with God's creation of the world (Gen. 2:1–3).

27. "Life in the world-to-come is wholly suffused with Sabbath." See above, ER, 7; and 'Otiyyot dĕ-R. 'Aḳiba in *Batte Midrašot,* ed. Abraham Wertheimer (Jerusalem, 5713), *2,* 416.

28. See Louis Ginzberg in *OT,* p. 312, n. 407.

29. Reading not *ḥt,* "sin," but *ḥš,* which is an acronym for *ḥillul šabbat,* "profanation of the Sabbath." Cf. Louis Ginzberg in *OT,* p. 293, n. 34. Leon Nemoy points out that the context deals with *both Sabbath and perjury,* not with Sabbath alone. Hence *ḥt*['] signifies "sin of perjury or profanation of the Sabbath."

beholds them, he scrutinizes his actions.[30] But today [on the Sabbath] he does not put on tefillin, so he profanes the Sabbath [gathering sticks]." Thereupon the Holy One said to Moses: Moses, go out and <state clearly> to Israel that there is a command they should carry out also on festivals and on Sabbaths. And what is the command? The command concerning fringes [which remind them to scrutinize their actions], of which it is said, *Speak unto the children of Israel, and bid them that they make them lĕ-ḏoroṯam (throughout their generations) fringes in the corners of their garments* (Num. 15:38). Here the word *lĕ-ḏoroṯam* is to be read as "that they be a generation *(lĕ-dor)* unblemished *(tam)*"; *tam* alludes to Jacob, of whom it is said, "And Jacob was an unblemished *(tam)* man" (Gen. 25:27), unblemished by dishonest dealing, unblemished by [sexual] transgression.

For this reason, the command *that they put with the fringe of each corner a thread of blue* (Num. 15:38) was taken and placed alongside "Hear, O Israel, the Lord is our God, the Lord alone," the affirmation of God's sovereignty, which is a major precept.[31] Thus you learn that [what appears to be] the least of the commands is as important as a major one, and that a major one is as important as the least one.

ER, *p.* 133 | Another comment on *Remember the Sabbath day, to keep it holy* (Exod. 20:8). How are you to give recognition to it? With reading of Scripture, with reciting of Mishnah, with [appropriate] food and drink, and with rest [of body and spirit]. He who takes delight in the Sabbath is as one who gives delight to Him by whose word the world came into being, as is said, *If thou . . . call the Sabbath a delight, then the Holy One, the Lord, will be honored*[32] (Isa. 58:13). In other words, If you call the Sabbath a delight [and make it so], you honor the Holy One, the Lord.

Though R. 'Aḳiḇa said, "Treat your Sabbath like a weekday rather than be dependent on mortals,"[33] still, [in acknowledgment of the Sabbath], a man should take [some] meat, but not too much wine. For if he takes too much wine, he does not heed Scripture's admonition, *Be not among wine bibbers,* etc. (Prov. 23:20). If a man does not deserve to win the Holy One's compassion so that words of Torah go into his innards, let him entreat the Holy One's compassion that not too much food and drink go into his innards [so that poverty, if not Torah, will purify him], as is said, *Behold, I have refined thee, but not as silver, I have purged thee through the furnace of poverty* (Isa. 48:10). As you can put into a furnace every kind of wood there is in the world, and the furnace will burn them all up and consume them, so you can put into a man's gullet every kind of delicious food in the world, and the gullet will swallow

---

30. See Louis Ginzberg, *TSE,* p. 126, n. 65.
31. See *APB,* pp. 40–42, and B.Men 43b.
32. Cf. PR 22:3, 9 (YJS, *18, 1,* 478, 490).
33. Cf. B.Pes 112a.

and take it all in. [But it is not through his insatiable gullet that a man wins rest in his eternal abode.]

A story of R. Judah [I] the Patriarch. At the time he was dying, he said: It is known and revealed to Him at whose word the world came into being that I have labored with my ten fingers, but ate sparingly with only one.[34] Because I did not maintain that life was no more than vanity,[35] I did not say: I will go, eat, drink, have a good time, and then leave the world. Of the man who lives like R. Judah, the Psalmist says, *All goes well with the man who lends generously, yet but stintingly provides for his own needs*[36] (Ps. 112:5). I used only enough of the things of the world to live on, [said R. Judah], and all my life occupied myself with Torah. Now give me rest in my eternal abode. What reply was given his prayer? *Let him come in peace, let him who has walked in his uprightness rest on his couch [and await My kingly feast]* (Isa. 57:2).

From the foregoing, you can infer that the Lord, the Sabbath, and Israel are all three alike in holiness. Of the holiness of the Holy One, what does Scripture say? *Yet Thou art holy, O Thou that art enthroned upon the praises of Israel. In Thee did our fathers trust,* etc. (Ps. 22:4). Of the holiness of the Sabbath, what does Scripture say? *Ye shall keep the Sabbath therefore, for it is holy unto you* (Exod. 31:14). Of the holiness of Israel, what does Scripture say? *Israel is the Lord's hallowed portion* (Jer. 2:3).

[Because of Israel's holiness], *All that devour [Israel] shall be held guilty, [a bizarre] evil shall overtake them [in Gehenna], saith the Lord (ibid.).* Of this evil, it is said: [In Gehenna], the teeth of those Jews who devour Israel will grow to be twenty-four cubits long, or, according to the Sages, thirty cubits long.[37] Why the difference of opinion as to twenty-four[38] or thirty? [It depends on how you count.] If you count six[39] months, the time that the presence of the infant in the womb is visible, and add the twenty-four months the infant is at the breast, you get thirty. [If you count only the months the infant is at the breast, you

---

34. See parallel in B.Ket 104a.

35. *Ḥibbalti,* "I did not take advantage (?)," is read *hibbalti,* "I did not maintain that life was no more than vanity." So Friedmann, Introduction, p. 53.

[I don't see how "I did not maintain that life was no more than vanity" fits into the context. The motif of the anecdote is moderation, avoidance of excess—hence *wĕ-lo' ḥibbalti* must mean "I did not deviate from the path of moderation." L. N.]

36. NJV: *who conducts his affairs with equity.* But *yĕḵalkel,* "conducts," can also mean "provides"; *dĕḇaraw,* "his affairs," can also mean "his needs"; and *mišpaṭ,* "equity," also means "discrimination"—hence, by extension, "stintingly." So also Rashi *ad loc.* Cf. B.Ḥul 84b and Rashi.

37. The wicked in Gehenna, their teeth inordinately lengthened, will be fed gravel, thus bringing them to both ridicule and pain. See Beṯ ham-Midraš, ed. A. Jellinek (Leipzig, 1853), *1,* 148; and B.Ber 54b.

38. The words "or twenty-five" are deleted.

39. The word "nine" is emended to "six."

get twenty-four.] Should the mother die after these twenty-four months, it is of no concern to the infant, [who will have sucked the mother dry]. Like this infant, are those Jews who devour their own people: they strip the flesh from the poor and devour them. And when the poor die, it is of no concern to such Jews. Consider that even when the nations of the world rise to strip Israel of her possessions, they seize
ER, *p.* 134 only that which is at hand, | as is said, *And so it was, when Israel had sown, that the Midianites came up, and the Amalekites . . . they encamped against* [*Israel*], *and destroyed the produce of the Land,* etc. (Judg. 6:3–4). But those Jews who devour their own people go beyond this. They strip the flesh from the poor and devour it; they break their bones, boil them in a pot until the fat comes swimming up, then eat the fat and throw the bones onto a refuse heap, as is said, [*Hear, O rulers of the house of Israel*] . . . *who eat the flesh of my people, and flay their skin from off them, and break their bones, yea, they chop their pieces, as that which is in the pot* (Mic. 3:3). But what is said immediately after this verse? One day the devourers *shall cry unto the Lord, but He will not answer them* (Mic. 3:4).

Remember the Sabbath day, to keep it holy (Exod. 20:8) and *Honor thy father and thy mother* (Exod. 20:12). What is signified by placing these two Commandments next to each other? That as long as a man honors his father and his mother, neither profanation of the Sabbath,[40] [nor any other sin], will come his way, as is said, *Happy is the man that doeth this*—[*honors his parents*][41] . . . *he will keep the Sabbath and refrain from profaning it (mĕḥallĕlo)* (Isa. 56:2). *Mĕḥallĕlo* may also be read as though it were written *maḥul lo*—[that is, even if he should sin], "he will be forgiven."

When a man does not truly honor his father and his mother, harsh decrees befall him, as may be inferred from the verse *The Lord said: Because this people hath approached* [*Me*] *with its mouth, and honored Me with its lips, but has kept its heart far from Me . . . therefore I shall further shock this people with shock upon shock* (Isa. 29:13–14).[42] Let not a man say to himself: Since my Father in heaven was first to grant life to me, I will go and do the will of my Father in heaven and forego doing the will of my father and mother [on earth]. Hence it is said, *Honor thy father and thy mother* [even to the extent of begging from door to door if you have not the means of providing for them, whereas of honoring

---

40. See above, n. 29.

41. After God had made the woman out of Adam's rib and brought her to him, Adam said: *She* (*zo'ṯ*, literally "this") *shall be called woman, because she was taken out of man* (Gen. 2:23). Hence in Isa. 56:2, the word *zo'ṯ*, "this," whose antecedent is not clear, is taken to refer to parenthood and the honor to be shown to parents. So Haida.

42. So, with slight modification, NJV. A man's relation to his father and mother, Professor Sid Z. Leiman suggests, is analogous to Israel's relation to its Father in heaven: as Israel is punished for not honoring God properly, so is a man punished for not honoring his father and mother properly.

God, you are told no more than] *Honor the Lord with thy substance* (Prov. 3:9).[43] A man should not say to himself: Since the command to honor one's father and mother puts one's father first, I will do my father's will and forego doing my mother's will. Hence it is said elsewhere, *Ye shall fear every man his mother, and his father* (Lev. 19:3), [the command here putting one's mother first. So solemn is this command that it uses the word "fear" in the same sense of profound reverence], as in the command *Thou shalt fear the Lord thy God* (Deut. 6:13).

When a man curses his father or his mother, or strikes them, leaving bruises upon them, the Holy One [in withdrawal from him], draws His feet back, if one dare say such a thing, under the throne of glory declaring: I required that his honoring of his parents be equal to his honoring of Me, the three of us, his parents and I, deserving to be honored equally. Had I been dwelling with the man guilty of such abuse of his parents, he would have done the same thing to Me. I do well in refusing to live in the same house with such a man.

Accordingly, he who would have days and years of life, wealth and goods, and life in this world, and long life in the unending world-to-come, should do both the will of his Father in heaven and the will of his father and mother [on earth] in keeping with the Commandment *Honor thy father and thy mother that thy days may be long upon the Land which the Lord thy God giveth thee* (Exod. 20:12).

Honor thy father and thy mother (ibid.), and *Thou shalt not murder* (Exod. 20:13). What is signified by having these two Commandments next to each other? That if a man has ample provisions in his home, yet refuses to give the benefit of them to his father and his mother in their old age, it is as if all his days he had been committing murder, as if he were murdering souls in the very presence of the Preserver of the world. Hence the Commandment *Honor thy father and thy mother* is followed by *Thou shalt not commit murder.*

| <*Honor thy father and thy mother* (Exod. 20:12)>; *Thou shalt not commit murder* (Exod. 20:13); *Thou shalt not commit adultery (ibid.).* What is intended by placing the fifth Commandment near the seventh? To teach you that if a man weds a woman who eventually refuses to honor his father or his mother in their old age, it is as though all his days he were committing adultery. For this reason *Honor thy father and thy mother* is placed near *Thou shalt not commit adultery.* **ER, *p.* 135**

Honor thy father and thy mother; Thou shalt not steal (ibid.). What is intended by placing the fifth Commandment near the eighth? To teach you this: If a man has sons and daughters in his house and [has not brought them up] to honor his father or his mother in their old age,

---

43. Gleanings, overlooked sheaves, and corners of the field are to be set aside for Him. See PR 23/24:2 (YJS, *18, 1,* 498–99).

it is as if all his days he had been stealing, stealing souls, from the very presence of the Holy One.[44] For this reason *Honor thy father and thy mother* is placed near *Thou shalt not steal.*

Honor thy father and thy mother, and *Thou shalt not bear false witness against thy neighbor* (Exod. 20:13). What is intended by placing the fifth Commandment near the ninth? To teach you this: If a man has ample provisions in his house, yet refuses to give the benefit of them to his father or his mother in their old age, it is as though for all of his days in the very presence of the Preserver of the world, he were testifying falsely that [his father and his mother were not his].

[*Honor thy father and thy mother,* and *Thou shalt not covet* (Exod. 20:14). What is intended by placing the fifth Commandment near the tenth? To teach you this: If a man has ample provisions in his house, yet refuses to give the benefit of them to his father or his mother in their old age, it is as though for all of his days he had been coveting (the possessions of others) in the very presence of the Preserver of the world.][45]

From the foregoing comments it is plain to see what was intended to be taught by placing the Commandments *Honor thy father and thy mother, Thou shalt not murder, Thou shalt not commit adultery, Thou shalt not steal, Thou shalt not bear false witness, Thou shalt not covet,* adjacent to one another.

When a man honors his father and his mother in their old age, with whom may he be compared? With a king who was visited by his favorite's son. When the king asked him, "Where did you come from?" he replied, "From the house of my father and my mother." When the king asked, "How are they?" he replied, "From their contentment in this world they departed to their abode in eternity." The king then said: "My son, may you be blessed! May you have contentment in the world for having provided contentment for your father and mother until they went to their abode in eternity. And now come and see the goodly treasures that I have been keeping by me for you." [Likewise, says the King of kings to a dutiful son]: *If thou wilt diligently hearken to the voice of the Lord thy God . . . and wilt give ear to His commandments . . . I will put none of the diseases upon thee, which I have put upon the Egyptians; for I am the Lord that healeth thee* (Exod. 15:26). [Here *commandments* includes a reference to honoring one's father and mother, as specified in the Commandment alluded to in the words *Honor thy father and thy mother, as the Lord thy God commanded thee*[46] (Deut. 5:16). When a man

44. He thus shows that he has no right to claim these sons and daughters as his own.

45. [*"Honor thy father and thy mother,* and *Thou shalt not covet* . . . Preserver of the world"]—so Samuel Haida, and Louis Ginzberg, *OT,* p. 293, n. 37.

46. *There,* at Marah, it is said, *God made for them . . . an ordinance* (Exod. 15:25),

who has observed this Commandment finally departs from this world, the Holy One says to him: Come and see the goodly treasures I have kept by Me for you], as is said, *If thou shalt keep the commandments of the Lord thy God* (Deut. 28:9), [*commandments* here alluding to the honoring of one's father and mother, then, as Scripture goes on to say, *The Lord will open unto thee His good treasure* (Deut. 28:12)].[47]

Finally, *If thou art to keep the commandments of the Lord thy God, and walk in His ways* (Deut. 28:9), in the ways of Heaven, so, as the ways of Heaven are being merciful and compassionate toward the wicked and accepting them in repentance, you are to be compassionate toward one another. And, as the ways of Heaven are to be gracious, graciously bestowing gifts not only upon those who know Him but also upon those who do not know Him, so you are to bestow gifts upon one another. And, as the ways of Heaven are to be long-suffering, long-suffering with the wicked and then accepting them in repentance, so you are to be long-suffering [with the wicked] for their good and not impatient to impose punishment upon them.[48] For, as the ways of Heaven are abundant in loving-kindness, ever leaning to loving-kindness, so are you ever to lean toward doing kindness to others rather than lean toward doing them harm.

---

a command concerning the honoring of one's father and mother. See Mek, *2,* 94, and PR, YJS, *18, 1,* 313, n. 32.

47. In the preceding paragraph the passages within brackets have been interpolated in keeping with the reconstruction suggested by Louis Ginzberg in *OT,* p. 294, n. 38.

48. Or: "Be long-suffering with each other when such a posture is beneficial; do not be long-suffering with each other when such a posture is destructive." So Professor Sid Z. Leiman.

Agreeing with Sid Leiman, Leon Nemoy suggests: "Be long-suffering with each other for everyone's good and not evil."

CHAPTER (27) 25

Satisfying the hunger for bread made of wheat and the hunger for Torah, bread of the spirit

Summary

The order in which a man is to provide for the needy is as follows: first come his father and his mother, then his nearest kin, then the people of his family, then his immediate neighbors, and finally people throughout Israel (ER, 135).

Such charity, particularly to the poor who are embittered, is to be dispensed with great tact. The man who gives freely brings peace into the world, and may be said to accomplish as much as notables like Aaron, David, and Rabban Johanan ben Zakkai.

In providing for one's father and mother, a man should spend somewhat more than he can afford, for the honor due to father and mother equals the honor due to God. But a son is not to obey his father when the father bids him to disobey God's commands (ER, 136), even though the three—mother, father, and God—are equally responsible for a man's coming into being.

Bread fed to the hungry is not merely wheaten bread; it is also Torah, bread of the spirit. Moreover, when a man feeds others with words of Torah, his own wisdom increases.

A man who has Torah within him learns to live with afflictions, for he resigns himself to what the will of God has decreed for him.

Whether a man studies Torah in a synagogue or in an academy, or studies it in a private and secluded place, he is blessed. Similarly Israel, who have set themselves apart in this world (ER, 137), are allowed to dwell with God in the Eternal House. As for disciples of the wise who in different ways have *bound themselves* (Ps. 68:7), God sets them *free safe and sound (ibid.).* Men unlettered in Torah who bind themselves to live by its precepts likewise experience being set *free safe and sound (ibid.).*

In further comment on Ps. 68:7, the author asserts that the self-denial of Sarah, Rebekah, Rachel, and Leah caused God to be patient with Israel's misdeeds, and ultimately to set Israel *free safe and sound.*

Even as earlier in the chapter the author construes *bread to the hungry* (Isa. 58:7) as instruction in Torah, so "covering the naked" *(ibid.)* he now construes similarly, for a man in whom there are no words of Torah is said to be naked, the *ornament of ornaments* (Ezek. 16:7) being God's commandments—ornaments of the spirit. Indeed only after Israel in Egypt had assumed two obligations to God, one concerning the Paschal lamb and the other concerning circumcision, did God conclude that the time of Israel's redemption promised to Abraham, Isaac, Jacob, and the Tribe Fathers who had proved their love of God, has indeed come. Henceforth Israel are to be known as *'is ra'ah 'el,* "man (ER, 138) who sees God," all of whose actions are therefore directed toward Him.

Further comments on *That thou hide not thyself from thine own flesh* (Isa. 58:7): (1) In sparing yourself from punishment for transgression you will have taken care to *hide not thyself from thine own flesh;* (2) the disciple of the wise and his family are as much a part of you as your own flesh; (3) for the wife you have divorced you are to provide, for she was of *thine own flesh.*

The chapter's peroration sets forth the purpose of man's life (ER, 139).

Chapter 27 (25)

In connection with the Commandment, as just cited, that a man should honor his father and his mother [particularly by providing for them] in their old age, post-Mosaic Scripture in a question put by Isaiah the prophet son of Amoz suggests the order in which a man is to provide for the needy in general: *Is it not to deal thy bread to the hungry . . . and, it goes without saying, that thou hide not thyself from thine own flesh?* (Isa. 58:7). So, if a man has abundant provisions in his house and wishes to set some aside for the sustenance of the needy, what order is he to follow in providing for them? ER, *p.* 135 *cont'd*

First, of course, he should take care of his father and his mother. If he has some provisions left, he should take care of his brother and his sister. If he still has some provisions left, he should take care of the members of his household. If he again has some provisions left, he should take care of the people of his family. Then, if he has some left, he should take care of the people in his immediate neighborhood. Next, if he has some left, he should take care of the people on his street. And finally, [with what remains], he should provide charity freely throughout Israel.[1] | [And he should do so with such tact as not to embarrass] *the poor who are wretched*[2] *(ibid.).* When a man eats what is his own, his spirit is composed, but when poverty makes him eat what he is given by others, his spirit is embittered. Even if a poor man eats what belongs to his son or his daughter, his spirit is embittered, let alone if he has to eat what he is given by strangers. ER, *p.* 136

Happy is the man who has ample provisions in his house, so that his servants and the members of his household come and partake of them with him at his table. Of him Scripture says, *When thou eatest the labor of thy hands, happy shall thou be*[3] (Ps. 128:2). He can become like

---

1. Cf. B.BM 71a and Meḵ, *3,* 148; Maimonides' Code VII, II, vii–x; and Šulḥan 'aruḵ, Yoreh de'ah, 251.

2. JV: *that are cast out.* But *mĕrudim* may also be derived from *rwd,* "to be distraught, to be wretched." [*"Rwd,* according to Gesenius-Brown, means "to be restless, to roam," which no doubt involves distraction and wretchedness but does not signify it. An indigent person must roam in search of sustenance, and has scarcely a home worthy of the name. L. N.]

3. By his willingness to share his gifts with all and sundry, he shows, in the words of the preceding verse, that he *feareth the Lord* and *walketh in His ways.* Such a course makes him a happy and blessed man, one who according to the last verse in Ps. 128 brings peace to Israel, particularly to Israel's households. For, as the saying goes, "When the barley is quite gone from the pitcher, strife comes knocking at the door" (B.BM 59a). Hence the generous man is compared with Aaron who throughout his life sought to bring peace to households in Israel. Furthermore, Isaiah says to the man who deals his bread to the hungry, *Thy righteousness shall go before thee* (Isa. 58:8). Hence the generous man is also compared with David who is described as having *executed justice as well as righteousness unto all his people* (2 Sam. 8:15). *Righteousness* in this context is understood as David's giving assistance out of his own purse to poor men condemned by a court (B.Sanh 6b). Finally, Isaiah says to the generous man, *If thou draw out thy soul to the hungry, thou wilt satisfy the deprived soul* (Isa. 58:10) a verse signifying that the soul which is deprived of

the High Priest Aaron who dedicated himself to making an abundance of peace between Israel and their Father in heaven. He can become like David who dedicated himself to fostering an abundance of loving-kindness between Israel and their Father in heaven. He can become like Rabban Johanan ben Zakkai who dedicated himself to having his pupils rejoice with him in Halakah.

[Sages like Rabban Johanan ben Zakkai, to be sure, rejoice and make others rejoice in Halakah, yet every sage in Israel is in anguish because of the iniquities of his generation. Scripture assures us, however, that] *Out of his anguish he shall see the vindication which the arm of the Lord effects, he shall enjoy it to the full through his devotion*[4] [*to Torah and to Israel*] (Isa. 53:11). The first part of this verse signifies that in every generation disciples of the wise bear by themselves the iniquities of their generation, and no mortal is aware of their anguish, for, as the verse goes on to say of a disciple of the wise, *their iniquities he did bear* [*in silence*] *(ibid.).* And if there be only ten disciples who act thus—and, it goes without saying, if it be the entire congregation [of Israel]—then, because of their uncomplaining devotion, *No weapon that is formed against thee,* [*O Israel*], *shall prosper* (Isa. 54:17).

[In connection with a man's responsibility to his parents and to his fellow man, there is cited from Isaiah another part of the verse, in which the prophet tells us further what a true fast requires], *When thou seest the naked,* [*see*] *that thou cover him* (Isa. 58:7). When the Holy One—may His great name be blessed for ever and ever and ever!—saw Adam naked, He did not delay at all in clothing him, as is said, *The Lord God made for Adam and for his wife garments of skins, and clothed them* (Gen. 3:21). <Likewise>, a man seeing his father or his mother standing in shabby garments should not turn his face away, but should clothe them in comely garments. If he himself wears clothing worth five minas, he should clothe his father and his mother in ten minas' worth; if he wears ten minas' worth, he should clothe his father and his mother in fifteen minas' worth. In short, he should spend somewhat more on his father and his mother than he can afford, so that they will look even better dressed than he.

By what parable may the relation between Israel and their Father in heaven be understood? By the parable of a mortal king one of whose servants ran away from him time and again. But the king kept searching for him through land after land until the servant fell into his hand and was brought back into his presence. When the servant was thus taken

---

Torah is deemed to be afflicted. Thus the generous man is compared with Rabban Johanan ben Zakkai who in freely sharing Torah with his pupils gave them joy. See *YY* and Landau.

4. NJV; JV: *Of the travail of his soul he shall see to the full, even My servant, who by his knowledge,* etc.

and brought into the king's presence, the king took him by the hand, brought him into his palace, showed him silver and gold, precious stones and pearls, and all the other valuables he had in his palace. Later, he took him outdoors and showed him the gardens and orchards and all the other good things he had growing in his fields. Then he showed him his sons, both the older and the younger ones, and his other servants, both the older and the younger ones. After the king had shown the runaway servant everything, he said to him: Do you see now that I have no need of you for anything? Nevertheless, come and do my work alongside my sons and servants, both the older and the younger ones. Accord me honor and show me respect the way other men accord me honor and show me respect.

[Like the runaway servant, Israel keep leaving their King, but He seeks them out nevertheless and brings them back into His presence even though He has no need of them.][5] He expects from them only the honor due Him, honor equal to that due a father and a mother, as is said, *A son honoreth his father, and a servant his master. If then I be a father, where is the honor due Me, and if I be a master, where is the respect due Me?* (Mal. 1:6). By the same token, when Israel bring doves and pigeons and other lesser holy offerings to God, but fail to honor the will of their fathers and mothers, [an act of respect which God esteems as a holy offering to Him, greater than an offering of doves or pigeons], with what words does He at once reproach Israel? *You, O priests, who despise My name*[6] *(ibid.).*

In another comment on [*A son honoreth his father*] . . . *saith the Lord unto you, O priests, who despise My name (ibid.),* these words are read in a different light as admonishing a son to obey his father without question, even if his father is so senile that spittle is running down his beard. Of course, if such a father tells his son to violate Torah's prohibition of acts of sexual transgression, dishonest dealing, and other such grave offenses, the son should not obey. But not to obey his father in regard to these grave offenses does not make it all right for a son—[no matter how much he wants to honor his father]—to obey him if the latter tells him to violate the other commandments of Torah concerning lesser offenses. In regard to these, he is also required not to obey his father [even under such extraordinary circumstances as may endanger his life]. Indeed, it is violations such as these [as well as more serious

5. Cf. above, ER, 34.

6. The honoring of father and mother is equated with offerings, and so the priests, here standing for Israel, who fail to honor father and mother are said, in effect, to despise God's name.

[It seems to me, the point is not that the priests represent Israel. The point is that they too sass their parents. If the commoners sass their fathers and mothers, one might perhaps ascribe it to ignorance. But the priests, charged with the actual offering of the sacrifices, surely know better, and are doubly sinful." L. N.]

violations] that make up the answer to the question *Wherein have we despised Thy name? (ibid.).*[7]

ER, *p.* 137 | [In further discourse on man's responsibility to his father and mother, consider again Isaiah's words]: *Is it not . . . that thou hide not thyself from thine own flesh?* (Isa. 58:7). By what parable are these words to be understood? By the parable of a man who had been confined for nine months in a city far over the sea. Who was responsible for his having been confined? Who sustained him while he was confined? [Who delivered him from confinement?] He who delivered him not only sustained him until he found his place in the world, but also gave him a ship by which he journeyed to safe harbor.

[The parable is to be understood as follows: A man begins life in his mother's womb where he is confined for nine months. His father puts him there, his mother nourishes him there. Then God brings him safely forth, provides him with sustenance and sees to it that he finds his place in the world.]

When the man comes to think of all three of them, he surely does not say, "My father did more for me than my mother, my mother did more for me than my God." Rather he acknowledges his obligation to all three of them equally. [As he is obligated to them for their care of him, so he is obligated to care for them. Hence it is said, *Is it not . . . that thou hide not thyself from thine own flesh* and in so doing hide not yourself from God?]

Further comment on the verse from Isaiah considers the words *Is it not to deal thy bread to the hungry?* (Isa. 58:7). By the word *bread* is meant words of Torah, as is said, *Behold, the days come, saith the Lord, that I will send a famine in the Land . . . a famine . . . of hearing the words of the Lord* (Amos 8:11). In this connection it is said: When a man has words of Torah within him, he is to feed others with them, so that the wisdom he already has will increase, and even more of it will keep on being given him. He who feeds others in this way will not be denied the good that is destined to come to them, to Israel, in the days of the Messiah. Of such a man Scripture says, *To him that ordereth his way aright will I show the salvation of God* (Ps. 50:23). By *way* is meant Torah, as in the verse "Ye shall walk in all the way which the Lord your God hath commanded you" (Deut. 5:30); and by *salvation* are meant the days of the Messiah, as in the verse "My favor is near, My salvation is gone forth, and Mine arms shall judge the peoples" (Isa. 51:5). On the other hand, when a man has words of Torah within him and does not nourish others with them, the result is that the wisdom he has diminishes because it is not being replenished. Of the latter, Scripture says, *He that*

7. Dr. Louis Finkelstein kindly provided the interpretation of the preceding paragraph.

withholdeth corn, the people shall curse him (Prov. 11:26); of the former, Scripture says, *But blessing shall be upon the head of him that dispenseth it (ibid.).*

Is it not that thou art able to put up with wretched afflictions in thy house?[8] (Isa. 58:7). How so? When a man has words of Torah within him, and afflictions befall him, his heart learns to live with them. But if he has no words of Torah within him, and afflictions befall him, his heart grows wretched. On the other hand, what is a man with Torah in him capable of doing [when affliction befalls him]? He resigns himself to what the will of God has decreed for him. Thus, if he is hungry, he is willing, in the words of Scripture, to serve *in hunger* (Deut. 28:48); if he is thirsty, he is willing, in the words of Scripture, to serve *in thirst (ibid.).* If he is naked, he is willing, in the words of Scripture, to serve *in nakedness (ibid.);* if he has no food to eat, he is willing, in the words of Scripture, to serve *in want of all things (ibid.).*

Even when <a ruthless nation> is permitted to endure and live on in the world [after setting upon you] *with the aim of destroying you* [*as a people*] (Deut. 28:51), the man with Torah in him will endure [the attack] and live on, saying, Blessed be the Preserver of the world, blessed be He who has given me life in the world. Thus also David said: Had not words of Torah reconciled me to my lot when affliction came upon me, I would have rooted myself out of the world, as is said: *Unless Thy Torah had been my delight, I should then have perished because of mine affliction* (Ps. 119:92).

Blessed be the Preserver of the world, blessed be He who chooses the Sages, their disciples, and the disciples of their disciples and fulfills for them the rule "In the measure a man measures, it is measured out to him." As they sit in synagogues and academies, indeed wherever a place is available, and with reverence in their hearts read Scripture for the sake of Heaven, recite Mishnah for the sake of Heaven, the words of Torah proceeding from their mouths have the force of decrees and are put into effect, as is said, *When the word is very nigh unto thee, in thy mouth, and in thy heart,* [*then what thou sayest will be regarded as law*] *and will be done*[9] (Deut. 30:14). Blessed also is the man in whom Torah dwells, who sits [not in a synagogue or in an academy, but] reads Scripture and recites Mishnah in a secluded and private place. With whom is such a man permitted to abide? You must answer, "With the Holy One," as is said, *Thou that dwellest in the covert of the Most High, wilt abide in the shadow of the Almighty* (Ps. 91:1).

[As Sages set themselves apart from worldly men], so Israel set themselves apart in this world and do not have with them people who

8. JV: *That thou bring the poor that are cast out to thy house.*
9. JV: *that thou mayest do it.*

are alien to their ways. [As for the Sages in relation to Israel], Scripture
ER, *p.* 138 says, | *He maketh the solitary dwell* [*with Him*] *in the* [*Eternal*] *House, those who bound themselves He sets free safe and sound*[10] (Ps. 68:7). By *those who bound themselves* are meant disciples of the wise who willingly bind and give themselves to study of Scripture, of Mishnah, and of Midrash of Halakot and 'Aggadot.

[In another comment on *Those who bound themselves He sets free safe and sound,* the verse is related to *Thus saith the Lord . . . I have answered thee*], *saying to those who bound themselves, "Go free"* (Isa. 49:9). Here the words *Those who bound themselves* refer to those men who are unlettered in Torah but who have bound themselves, nevertheless, to live by its precepts: their conduct is chaste, for they keep far from sexual immorality and from dishonest dealing and heed the commandments concerning all other transgressions. As for disciples of the wise who live in places not suitable for such men as they—that is, *to them that are in darkness (ibid.)*—God says, *"Free yourselves"*[11] *(ibid.),* [from the neighborhood of ignorant men and live with your equals in learning].

[In still another comment the verse is read *Because of the persons who were brought to dwell in (Jacob's) house, He set free safe and sound those who were bound* (Ps. 68:7), and the latter part of the verse is taken to refer to the people of Israel.] The Holy One was patient with them, [and, despite their misdeeds],[12] at length set them free from Egypt, but did so only as a reward for the conduct of Sarah, Rebekah, Rachel, and Leah; as a reward for Sarah's taking Hagar and bringing her to Abraham's couch;[13] as a reward for Rebekah who, when asked, *Wilt thou go with this man?"* said, *"I will go"* (Gen. 24:58), thus putting her trust in her Father in heaven; as a reward for Rachel because she took Bilhah and brought her to Jacob's couch;[14] as a reward for Leah because she took Zilpah and brought her to Jacob's couch.[15] It was because of such conduct on the part of Sarah, Rebekah, Rachel, and Leah, that the Holy One was patient with the people of Israel and took them out of Egypt. Hence it is said, *Because of the persons who were brought to dwell in* [*Jacob's*] *house, He set free safe and sound those who were bound* (Ps. 68:7).

When thou seest the naked, [*see*] *that thou cover him* (Isa. 58:7). For example? If you see a man who has no Torah within him, bring him into your house and teach him the Shĕm'a and the *Tĕfillah.* Teach him one verse of Scripture or one Halakah and spur him to the carrying out

---

10. So NJV.
11. JV: *show yourselves.* But *higgalu,* "show," may also mean "banish yourselves [into freedom]."
12. See above, ER, 34.
13. See Gen. 16:2.
14. See Gen. 30:3–8.
15. See Gen. 30:9–12.

of precepts. Remember that in Israel a man in whom there are no words of Torah is the same as naked.

You find much the same thing said in [the writings of] the Great Assembly,[16] where God says to Israel, *I caused thee to increase as the growth of the field. And thou didst increase and grow up, and thou didst acquire the ornament of ornaments*[17] (Ezek. 16:7). Understand *ornament of ornaments* not as referring to acquisition of ornaments of the body, but rather to acquisition of God's commandments which are ornaments of the spirit. For there was a time, O Israel, when you [were unadorned with commandments and] had but two obligations to meet, one concerning the Paschal lamb, the other concerning circumcision, [and both calling for the shedding of blood], as is said, *When I passed by thee, and saw thee stained in the blood*[18] [*thou wast obliged to shed*], *I said unto thee: In thy blood, live; yea, I said unto thee: In thy blood, live* (Ezek. 16:6). One might suppose that in this verse God was saying to Israel: If only because of your meeting the two obligations that call for the shedding of blood, you have earned the right to live for ever. Hence, God went on to say to Israel, *Now when I passed by thee, and looked upon thee, and, behold, thy time was the time of love* [*such as was promised to those who loved Me* (Ezek. 16:8)—that is, when you met the two obligations I had imposed on you, I knew the time was ripe for your deliverance from Egypt, promised to those who proved their love of Me]. Thus when I said to Abraham your father, *Get thee out of thy country, and from thy kindred, and from thy father's house, unto the Land that I will show thee* (Gen. 12:1), he hearkened to My words at once. Hence *Behold, thy time was the time of love* [*such as was promised to those who proved their love of Me*].[19]

Another comment on *Behold, thy time was the time of love:* When I told your father Abraham, Circumcise your flesh with a sword, he hearkened at once. Hence *Behold, thy time was the time of love* [*such as was promised to those who proved their love of Me*].

Another comment on *Behold, thy time was the time of love:* When I said to your father Abraham, Raise your son upon the altar, he hearkened at once to My message. Hence *Behold, thy time was the time of love* [*such as was promised to those who proved their love of Me*].

Another comment on *Behold, thy time was the time,* etc.: When [Abraham was about to sacrifice Isaac], Isaac, who at the time was thirty-seven years of age,[20] young and in the prime of life, said to his

---

16. A legislative body of one hundred and twenty men said to have functioned just prior to, during, and after the Persian period in Jewish history, about 500–300 B.C.E. Among its first members was Ezekiel. See Ezek. 2:2–3 and B.BB 15a.

17. JV: *thou camest to excellent beauty.* But literally *'ady 'adayyim* means "ornament of ornaments."

18. JV: *wallowing in thy blood.*

19. Cf. Mek, *1,* 33–34.

20. See Rashi on Gen. 25:20.

father: "Father, bind me securely before you put me on the pile of wood, otherwise I might struggle and kick you or even strike you and thus incur two penalties of death from Heaven."[21] Hence *Behold, thy time was the time of love* [*such as was promised to those who proved their love of Me*].

Another comment on *Behold, thy time was the time,* etc.: When I found your father Jacob declaring what is true, [that I am God], and acknowledging this truth in his own heart, [I revealed Myself to him at once], as is said, *God appeared to him even as he was coming from Paddan-aram, and blessed him* (Gen. 35:9).[22] Hence *Behold, thy time was the time of love* [*such as was promised to those who proved their love of Me*].

Another comment on *Behold, thy time was the time,* etc.: When I found that the Tribe Fathers were willing to obey the wish of their father Jacob,[23] I said of them *Like grapes in the wilderness I find* [*the sons of*] *Israel* (Hos. 9:10). Here Israel is to be read *'Iš ra'ah 'El,* "a man

ER, *p.* 139 | who sees God," meaning men all of whose actions are therefore directed to Him. Hence *Behold, thy time was the time of love* [*such as was promised to those who proved their love of Me*].

Speaking through Ezekiel, God went on to say: *I spread My skirt* —by which He meant the Torah—*over thee, and covered thy nakedness* (Ezek. 16:8), by which He meant the Tabernacle.[24] *Yea, I swore to thee (ibid.)* [that I would provide for you][25] during your forty years' dwelling in the wilderness; *and entered into a covenant with thee . . . and thou becamest Mine (ibid.).* Thus He spoke when, [after the incident of the spies],[26] He returned to dwell in the Tabernacle.

[Further comment on the verse] *That thou hide not thyself from thine own flesh* (Isa. 58:7): The Holy One spoke thus to every man: My son, in the days I have given you on earth, engage in good deeds and in

---

21. One, for not honoring his father, and the other, for invalidating a burnt offering.

22. God said to Jacob: *Go up to Beth-el and make there an altar unto God who appeared unto thee when thou didst flee from the face of Esau thy brother* (Gen. 35:1). But Jacob, going beyond God's specific instructions, said: *I will build . . . an altar to the God who answered me when I was in distress and who has been with me wherever I have gone* (Gen. 35:4). For this God rewarded him by revealing Himself to Jacob at once. So Friedmann in n. 27.

23. Jacob asked his sons to hearken to the God of Israel, Israel who was their father, and they responded by saying to him, *Hear, O Israel* [*our Father*], *the Lord is our God, the Lord alone* (Deut. 6:4). See Gen. Rabbah 98:3.

24. The phrase *malkuṭ šamayim,* "kingdom of heaven," is—so Louis Ginzberg says—a scribe's erroneous expansion of the letters *mš* meant to be an abbreviation of *mškn,* "Tabernacle." "The erection of the Tabernacle did away with the shame, 'the nakedness' of the golden calf" (*OT,* p. 287, n. 368). [I prefer the text as it stands—God clothes the naked synagogue with the kingdom of heaven, by causing her to become worthy of it; *malkuṭ šamayim* is surely a suitable parallel to Torah, whereas *mškn,* sacred though it is, is not. L. N.]

25. With manna, quail, and Miriam's well.

26. "after the incident of the spies" (Num. 13–14)—Louis Ginzberg in *OT,* p. 287, n. 368.

study of Torah, gird yourself against [sexual] transgression and unseemly behavior. [In sparing yourself from punishment for transgression, you will have taken care to] *hide not thyself from thine own flesh* [that is to say, do not subject your own self to the unbearable burden of transgression of God's precepts].

Another comment on *That thou hide not thyself from thine own flesh:* This refers to a householder who has a disciple of the wise living in his home and, knowing that he reads Scripture for the sake of Heaven and recites Mishnah for the sake of Heaven, feeds, sustains, and provides for him. In thus maintaining the disciple, his wife and his children, and all the rest of his family who are with him, the householder is treating them as though they were members of his own family. Hence one is adjured, [*See to it*] *that thou hide not thyself from thine own flesh.*

Another comment on the verse: If a man, having wed, finds cause to divorce his wife and she presently becomes poor, he must continue to provide for her as much as he can. Hence, [*See to it*] *that thou hide not thyself from* [*her who had been*] *thine own flesh*[27]

Another comment: Let a man look at himself and realize that soon death is to come to him. Let him lift up his eyes to heaven and say: Who created these—sun and moon, stars and planets, the four points of the compass, and all the work of creation, every single one of them morning and evening obeying the will of their creator? With such a thought in mind, in order to do His will as voiced in His Torah, you are to be at words of Torah morning and evening every day without fail. You will then be like the sun which gives light to many and like the moon which gives light to many—as Isaiah says, *Then shall thy light break forth as the morning* (Isa. 58:8)—as the light of morning dispels the greatest dark, so your light will illumine for others the most difficult words of Torah.[28]

If every day without fail you do My will as voiced in My Torah, *then thy healing shall spring forth speedily (ibid.):* When you open your mouth to expound Torah, I will cause you to do so with such precision that no man will be able to contradict you; you will see yourself so strong in your precise interpretation of Torah that besides there being no man able to contradict you, your bones will grow in strength

---

27. R. Jose the Galilean found himself compelled to divorce his most unmanageable wife, who then remarried. When she and her new husband were reduced to begging in the streets, R. Jose provided for her and her husband living quarters and maintenance (Gen. Rabbah 17:3 and Lev. Rabbah M 34:14, pp. 802–6). Apparently ER would have every husband who divorced his wife follow R. Jose's example of extraordinary generosity. Cf. ER, 121.

28. A paraphrase of Louis Ginzberg's interpretation, which reads *ḳallah šeb-bah ka-ḥămurah šeb-bah bĕ-yaḏḵa,* "You will master the light as well as the difficult part thereof" (*OT,* p. 290, n. 210). Friedmann (in his n. 32) suggests: "The least of your insights will be as illuminating to others as is the greatest insight of your colleague's."

through your performance of Torah's commandments, as is said, *The Lord will guide thee continually, and satisfy thy soul in drought, and make strong thy bones* (Isa. 58:11). You will be like a spring which flows forth in a garden, watering figs and grapes and all other kinds of fruit, every one of them, as is said, *Thou shalt be like a watered garden, and like a spring of water, whose waters fail not (ibid.).*

Even as you gave delight to your father and your mother in their old age, so will you have delight from Him at whose word the world came into being, as is said, *Then shalt thou delight thyself in the Lord, and I will make thee to ride upon the high places of the earth, and I will feed thee with the heritage of Jacob thy father: for the mouth of the Lord hath spoken it* (Isa. 58:14).

CHAPTER (28) 26

True love of God

Summary

Even as God loves Israel (ER, 139), Israel is to love God—indeed, as in the Shĕma‘, we declare this love loud and clear. Another way of declaring one's love for God is to be loving in the give-and-take of everyday life. Indeed, Torah teaches us to glorify God's great name by honest dealing with both Jew and Gentile (ER, 140).

A man who merely fears God will receive his reward in this world; but he who both loves and fears Him is assured of the reward of life in the world-to-come.

To show their love of God, Israel practice circumcision, read Scripture, and recite Mishnah. In short, they give of themselves to enter the covenant. Accordingly, if the nations of the earth offer their gold and silver for the crown of the house of Aaron and the crown of the house of David—even if they offer to build a Temple surpassing the one which the Jews built—God will refuse to give them one word of Torah as their prize.

For true love does not depend on a material cause (ER, 141). Such dependence was exemplified in the life of Balaam son of Beor. He was a prophet sent by God to the nations who complained that had He given them a prophet like Moses, they would have accepted His Torah. So God sent Balaam who surpassed Moses in native intelligence, but morally was so inferior that for God to reveal Himself to Balaam was an experience of uncleanness.

Balaam came to Balak king of Moab with no intention other than to curse Israel, but he should have realized that God would not destroy the people of Israel who were beloved descendants of the beloved Abraham, Isaac, and Jacob. He should have dissuaded Balak from his evil plan, but Balaam calculated instead that by multiplying sacrifices to God, He would induce him to curse Israel (ER, 142). He should have known, finally, that God's love of Israel does not depend on such material things as sacrifices of bullocks and rams to Him.

But if so, why did God institute sacrifices such as the offering of two lambs, one in the morning and one in the evening? In order that Israel thereby bring into His presence remembrance of them and remembrance of their Fathers, who, like Isaac, were willing to have themselves bound as an offering on the altar of Mount Moriah. What God truly wants of Israel, however, is that they show their love of Him by loving one another, by honoring one another, and by respecting one another (ER, 143).

Chapter (28) 26

Whence the proof that God loves Israel and that Israel should love God?[1] To begin with, the Holy One, blessed be He, may His great **ER, *p.* 139** ***cont'd***

---

1. See ER, 127–28.

name be blessed for ever and ever and ever, loves all the children of Israel wherever they dwell, and especially loves disciples of the wise,
ER, *p.* 140 as is said, *I have loved you, saith the Lord,* | *but I loved Jacob* [*particularly*] (Mal. 1:2), [he being first among those who dwell in tents of Torah].[2] With such love, likewise, should a man love Israel wherever they dwell and should particularly love disciples of the wise. [Another proof of God's love for Israel] is expressed in the verse *The Lord did not set His love upon you . . . because ye were more in number . . . but because the Lord loved you* (Deut. 7:7–8). But what is the text that proves to us we should love God? It is a weighty commandment, the most weighty of the Torah, the command to love God, *Thou shalt love the Lord thy God* (Deut. 6:5) being conjoined with the verse which affirms His sovereignty, *Hear, O Israel: the Lord is our God, the Lord alone* (Deut. 6:4).

In this connection, it is said: A man who says the Shĕma' loud enough so that his ears can hear what he is saying is to be praised. On the other hand, a man who says the *Tĕfillah* loud enough so that he hears himself, [is praying as though God were hard of hearing, and hence] is bearing false witness against Him; or, as some say, is lacking in faith [because he is praying as though God pays no attention to silent prayer].[3]

In another comment on *Thou shalt love the Lord thy God* (Deut. 6:5), [*wĕ-'ahabta,* "thou shalt love," is read *wĕ-he'ĕhabta,* "thou shalt cause to be loved],"[4]—that is, you are to cause the name of Heaven to be loved by mankind. Hence you are to be loving in the give-and-take of everyday life—in your going about in the marketplace and in your dealing with men. For when a man is loving in the give-and-take of daily life—in his going about in the marketplace and in his dealing with men—and besides reads Scripture and recites Mishnah, people seeing him say: "Blessed is So-and-so who studied Torah! Alas for my father who did not teach me Torah! See how comely are the deeds, how beautiful are the ways of this one who studied Torah. By the [Temple] service! Let us study Torah and teach our children Torah." Thus, through such a man, is the name of Heaven hallowed.

On the other hand, when a man is not loving in the give-and-take of his daily life—in his going about in the marketplace and in his dealing with men—even if he reads Scripture and recites Mishnah, people, seeing him say: "Alas for So-and-so who has studied Torah! Blessed be my father who did not teach me Torah! So-and-so has studied Torah, yet see how evil are his deeds, how corrupt his ways! By the [Temple] service! Let us not study Torah, nor teach Torah to

---

2. See Gen. 25:27 and Rashi *ad loc.*
3. See B. Ber 15a, 31a, and 24b.
4. Cf. MTeh 18:7 (YJS, *13, 1,* 235).

our children." Thus, through such a man, is the name of Heaven profaned.[5]

Torah was given only to hallow God's great name, as is said, *God said unto me: "Thou art My servant, Israel, through whom I will be glorified"* (Isa. 49:3). [By your deeds you will glorify Me among all men.] Hence the Sages said a man should keep away from dishonesty in dealing, whether with Jew or Gentile, indeed with any one in the marketplace. Besides, he who steals from a Gentile will in the end steal from a Jew; and he who cheats a Gentile will in the end cheat a Jew; he who swears [falsely] to a Gentile will in the end swear [falsely] to a Jew; he who acts deceitfully toward a Gentile will in the end act deceitfully toward a Jew; he who sheds the blood of a Gentile will in the end shed the blood of a Jew.

That the Torah was given only to hallow God's great name [in all the world] is shown by the verse *I will work a sign among* [*all the nations and tongues*], *and send from them survivors . . . to the distant coasts* (Isa. 66:19). And what then? What is declared at the end of the verse: These survivors *shall declare My glory among the nations.*

To answer the question of what the difference is between love and awe, consider a parable by which the difference may be understood, the parable of a mortal king who had to go away to a city far across the sea.[6] He had two servants: one both loved the king and was in awe of him; the other was in awe of him but did not love him. He who loved the king and was in awe of him went and planted gardens and orchards of all kinds of fruit, every variety of each. But he who was only in awe of him did nothing at all.[7] Presently a letter [announcing the king's return] arrived by messenger, and soon afterward | the king came **ER, *p.* 141**
back. When he entered the first servant's house and beheld the figs and grapes and all kinds of other fruit—heaped up together—he made a careful arrangement of all the provisions set out before him, [thereby showing his appreciation] of the kindly forethought of the servant who loved him. And when the servant who loved the king appeared and saw [the king gazing at] all the varieties of fruit—all heaped up—there was satisfaction in his heart at sight of the king's pleasure. But the servant who was only in awe of the king had provided scarcely anything at all for him, so that when the king entered the second servant's house and saw nothing at all but dried-up stuff set out, he arranged it before him, all the dried-up stuff, in such a way [as to make plain his displeasure]! [When the second servant entered], he trembled as he realized the consequences of the king's displeasure. For, in accordance with the

5. Cf. B.Yoma 86a.
6. The lines enclosed within parentheses in ER are omitted in keeping with the suggestion in Friedmann's n. 5.
7. Cf. similar parables in B.Shab 152b and 153a.

measure of justice, of such a man as he, it is said, *God tears away his portion*[8] [*in the world-to-come*] (Ps. 111:5).

[The following], *He will ever be mindful of His covenant (ibid.),* means [the granting of the] *world-to-come* to him who has Torah [and loves as well as fears the Lord]. The preceding, *He hath made a memorial . . . full of compassion*[9] (Ps. 111:4), means [the granting of] *this world* to him who has Torah [but merely fears the Lord]. Thus *He hath made a memorial* indicates the reward of him who merely fears the Lord. But whence the range of reward for him who [both] loves [and fears] the Lord? The verse *Thou shalt have no other gods before Me . . . who showeth mercy unto the thousandth generation of them that love Me* (Exod. 20:3–6).[10] Thus you learn that two portions are the reward given to one who loves [and fears] God, whereas only a single portion is the reward given to one who only fears Him. Accordingly, the peoples of the earth have the merit of enjoying only this world, whereas Israel have the merit of enjoying two worlds—this world and the world-to-come.

[As Israel loves God and keeps the covenant with Him, so He loves them.] But, as the Sages taught in a Mishnah: "He who profanes things sacred . . . <who makes void the covenant of Abraham our father, and makes the Torah bear a meaning other than the right one> . . . has no portion in the world-to-come" (Ab̲ 3:11). "May I make atonement for Israel (Neḡ 2:1) wherever they dwell! For they practice circumcision, read Scripture, recite Mishnah, and thus enter the covenant only out of love for their Father in heaven. Therefore the Holy One said: Even if the nations of the earth should rise up and give Me their silver and their gold and all the precious things they delight in, and say, "Give us in return the crown of the house of Aaron and the

---

8. JV: *The Lord giveth food.* But *ṭeref,* "food," can also mean "tearing, rending"; hence "tears away his portion." The point of the comment on the verse would seem to be that a man who only fears God is incapable of giving Him the love that would be expected of him in the world-to-come.

9. For "He remembers His covenant with the world, *He will ever be mindful of His covenant* (Ps. 111:5)," Leon Nemoy suggests *He hath made a memorial* (Ps. 111:4).

10. Leon Nemoy provided the interpretation of the passage beginning "For, in accordance with the measure of justice," and ending *"of them that love Me* (Exod. 20: 3–6)." In a private communication he added: "I conjecture that the author read Ps. 111:5: *'God tears away their portion* [*in the world-to-come*] *from those who* [*merely*] *fear Him, but He will ever be mindful of His covenant* [*with those who love Him*].' He based his argument on the fact that *naṯan* and *'aśah* (in verse 4) are in the past tense referring to those who merely fear Him, whereas *yizkor,* 'He will remember,' referring to those who love Him, is in the future tense. From which he concludes that the Lord's favor to those who merely fear Him will have to cease with their earthly death, while His favor to those who love Him will endure into the world-to-come."

"The reference to Exod. 20:3–6 does not seem to me," Leon Nemoy writes, "really pertinent, and I wonder if the quotation was originally only the initial word, or even an acronym, and the copyist extended it into the wrong verse."

crown of the house of David," I will not give them even one word of the precious treasure of Torah, as is said, *Many waters*—[that is, all the precious things proffered by the nations]—*cannot quench* [*God's*] *love* [*of Israel*] (Song 8:7). At that time the Holy One also said: Even if the nations of the world should rise and build for Me a Temple surpassing yours, saying, "Give us the crown of the house of Aaron and the crown of the house of David," I would not give them even a single word of the precious treasure of Torah. Hence *Many waters,* etc.[11]

Concerning the nature of love, the Sages taught in a Mishnah: "Whenever love depends upon some material cause, with the passing away of that cause, love, too, passes away" (Aḇ 5:16). "Which was the love that depended upon a material cause?" *(ibid.)*—the love between Balaam son of Beor,[12] and Balak son of Zippor king of Moab. "And that which is not dependent upon such a cause will not pass away for ever" *(ibid.)*—such as the love of Abraham, Isaac, and Jacob for one another, for their children, and for the children of their children until the end of all generations. After Noah came into the world, the Holy One said to Shem: Shem, had My Torah—[the six commandments given to Adam][13]—been kept at all among the first ten generations, do you suppose that I would have considered destroying My world on account of them and their transgressions? Now prophesy to them in the hope that they will take My Torah upon themselves. | So for four **ER, *p.* 142** hundred years Shem prophesied to all the nations of the world, but they were not willing to heed him. After him, [uttering prophecy, came] Eliphaz the Temanite, Zophar the Naamathite, Bildad the Shuhite, Elihu son of Barachel the Buzite, Job of the land of Uz, and the last of all of them, Balaam son of Beor.[14] There was not a thing in the world that the Holy One did not reveal to Balaam. Why? Because otherwise all the nations of the earth would have spoken up to Him and said: Master of the universe, had You given us [as well as Israel] a prophet like Moses, we would have accepted <Your> Torah. Therefore the Holy One gave them Balaam son of Beor who in his native intelligence surpassed Moses. [Nevertheless, Balaam was morally inferior to Moses, as shown by the fact that] in His revelation to Moses God made use of the letter[15] *'alef,* the very letter which in revealing Himself to Balaam He omitted. Thus Scripture says, *The Lord called* [*wyḳr'* with the *'alef* at the end] *unto Moses* (Lev. 1:1). But of Balaam, how does Scripture put it? *God called* [*wyḳr* without the *'alef*] *unto Balaam* (Num.

---

11. Cf. MTeh 15:4 (YJS, *13, 1,* 191–92), and Song Rabbah 8:7.
12. Balaam was charged with love of lucre. See Num. 22:2ff.
13. See above, ER, chap. 1, n. 7.
14. See Ginzberg, *Legends, 6,* 125.
15. The word *daḇar,* "word," is taken to stand for "letter," as suggested by *YY.*

23:4). [Since in this verse *wyḳr* lacks the final *'alef,* it is to be taken as derived from *miḳreh* in the phrase "That which has been rendered unclean by nocturnal emission" *(miḳreh)* (Deut. 23:11).[16] Hence God's having to reveal Himself to Balaam was an experience for Him of something unclean]. And so Moses was told, *As for thee, stand thou here by Me* (Deut. 5:35), whereas Balaam in God's presence is described as *Fallen down, yet with eyes open* (Num. 24:4). [In native intelligence, however, as already stated, Balaam exceeded Moses, for] Moses had to plead with God, *Show me now Thy glory* (Exod. 33:18); whereas Balaam [did not have to ask to share God's knowledge, for] his speech is referred to in Scripture as *The saying of him . . . who knoweth the knowledge of the Most High* (Num. 24:15).

O my people, Balaam son of Beor came to Balak son of Zippor with no intention other than to curse Israel. And the proof of his intention? You can see for yourself what his intention was when you consider what happened at the very beginning when Balak sent messengers to Balaam. *He sent messengers,* Scripture tells us, *unto Balaam son of Beor . . . saying . . . "Come now therefore, I pray thee, curse me this people"* (Num. 22:56). <Balaam should have said to the messengers that he would not go.> But he did not say so. Instead he rejoiced so greatly [at what Balak had asked of him] that sleep did not come to him, as is intimated by the words *And God came unto Balaam at night,* etc. (Num. 22:20). Balaam should then have declared: "Master of the universe, You are not a man that You would lie, or a son of man that You would undo the work of Your own hands. These—[the people of Israel]—are beloved sons of beloved men, descendants of Abraham, Isaac, and Jacob who ever obeyed Your will. [And therefore I will not curse Your people.]" But instead of saying this, he rejoiced greatly and rose up early in the morning to go to Balak at once, as is said, *And Balaam rose up in the morning, and saddled his ass, and went with the princes of Moab. And God's anger was kindled because he went,* etc. (Num. 22:21–22). The Holy One said: Look at this person who knows that I see into the heart of each and every man, yet is going to curse Israel nevertheless. Hence *God's anger was kindled because he went (ibid.).*

When Balaam came to Balak, he should have said, "Why do you engage in such schemes as will bring great afflictions to you and in the end will cause you to perish from the world?" But Balaam asked no such question. Instead he said to Balak: "For four hundred years Shem prophesied to all the nations of the world, but they did not heed him. After him, [uttering prophecy, came] Eliphaz the Temanite, Bildad the

---

16. See R. Ḥama bar Ḥanina's utterance in Lev. Rabbah M 1:13, p. 28, and Soncino tr., p. 15; and EZ, 191.

Shuhite, Zophar the Naamathite, Elihu son of Barachel the Buzite, and Job of the land of Uz. Now I, the last of all of them, will tell you what the ancestor of these people did. He went and built an altar, and three times a year offered twenty-one bullocks and twenty-one rams upon it.[17] As for you, Balak, I will now tell you what to do: *Build me here seven altars, and prepare me here seven bullocks and seven rams*" (Num. 23:1).

Thereupon the Holy One laughed at Balaam [for thinking that by multiplying his sacrifices to the Holy One, the Holy One would allow him to curse Israel. As it was, when Balaam sought to curse Israel, the Holy One *put a word in his mouth* (Num. 23:5), so that all that came out of it was blessing and praise of Israel. Hence it is said, *Wherewith shall I come before the Lord? . . . Shall I come before Him with burnt offerings? . . . Will the Lord be pleased with thousands of rams? Or*] *shall I give my* | *first-born for my transgression?* (Mic. 6:6–7). [We are to remember, the **ER, *p.* 143** Holy One admonishes us, the story of Balak and Balaam]: *O My people, remember now what Balak, king of Moab, devised, and what Balaam son of Beor answered him* (Mic. 6:5). [And what more are we to remember? That God's love of Israel does not depend on such material things as sacrifices of bullocks and rams to Him.]

But if so, why did the Holy One institute sacrifices, as in the words *The one lamb, shalt thou offer in the morning* (Num. 28:4)? After all, the greatness of the Holy One is such that if He wanted food or drink, no one could provide enough for Him. And besides, is there in His nature such a thing as hunger? Does He not say, *If I were hungry, I would not tell thee* (Ps. 50:12)? *I know all the birds of the mountains; and the wild beasts of the field are Mine* (Ps. 50:11). *Do I eat the flesh of bulls, or drink the blood of goats?* (Ps. 50:13). Why, then, did the Holy One institute the offering of two lambs, one in the morning and one in the evening? That thereby Israel bring into His presence remembrance of them and remembrance of their Fathers.[18]

The Holy One spoke thus to Israel: My children, do I ask that you suffer material loss on My account?[19] What do I ask of you? Only that you [show your love of Me by] loving one another, by honoring one another, by respecting one another; that there be found among you no [sexual] transgression, no dishonest dealing, no unseemly conduct, so that unbesmirched you will never be disqualified [from bearing witness], as is said, *It hath been told thee, O man, what is good, and what the Lord doth require of thee: only to do justly, and to love mercy, and to walk*

---

17. A number based presumably on the account in Job 42:8.

18. See above, ER, 36.

19. So also Louis Ginzberg (*OT,* p. 306, n. 269). But Solomon Schechter translates the line, "Do I lack anything at all [that I should have to turn] to you?" (*Some Aspects of Rabbinic Theology* [New York, 1923], p. 92, n. 1).

humbly with thy God (Mic. 6:8). Do not read *walk humbly with ('im) thy God,* but read also "walk humbly and thy God will be with thee." As long as you walk humbly performing without display the good deeds He commands[20] He will descend and humbly walk with you. Such is the additional meaning of *walk humbly with thy God.*

20. The words "walk humbly performing . . . deeds He commands" paraphrase "walk humbly with Him."

CHAPTER (29) 27

God's compassion an example for Israel

Summary

It is her own people who bring Israel to grief by their transgressions. But God is slow to anger and full of compassion for Israel wherever they dwell (ER, 143). His compassion goes out in particular to the poor and needy, orphans and widows. A man should strive to show the same compassion—should not only give charity but give it with joy.

God's compassion goes out not only to those in need but even to those who transgress His commands. He would not even have killed the spies who brought back a false report about the Land had they not set upon Moses and Aaron to slay them. Indeed, He even spared the lives of Canaanites as a reward for the kindly way that the Canaanite giants, Sheshai and Talmai, treated the spies who came to the Land. Furthermore, though Israel in the wilderness were under a ban for forty years (ER, 144–45), God told Moses to reassure Israel—they would yet come into the Land and bring offerings to Him. Even converts who joined Israel out of unworthy motives and subsequently backslid, are not to be given up out of hand: whatever the motives of such converts, Israel must do all she can to draw them to her, and hold them.

In connection with the spies' false testimony concerning the Land, Israel are admonished to make certain that no false or prejudiced testimony be admitted in litigation. For example, a judge should not listen to one litigant unless the other litigant is also present. Litigants are cautioned against any kind of conniving (ER, 146) in the presentation of testimony that might favor them. Men guilty of breach of trust or dishonest dealing are deemed unfit as witnesses. One may not witness against another known to be his enemy. It goes without saying that judges who are enemies or kin of the litigants are disqualified from presiding in cases affecting such litigants.

Finally, it is proved from Scripture that capital cases require a panel of twenty-three judges (ER, 147).

Chapter (29) 27

Scripture says, *Look not upon me that I am swarthy, that the sun hath tanned me, my mother's sons sought to bring me to grief*[1] (Song 1:6). [Consider this verse in the light of what] the congregation of Israel declared to the Holy One: "Master of the universe, no person within my ranks came to sin except through me." You can see for yourself the truth of this statement: a tree is uprooted only by a [tool that is made in] part of the ER, *p.* 143 *cont'd*

1. JV: *my mother's sons were incensed against me.* But *niḥăru,* "incensed against me," may also mean "sought to bring me to grief."

tree's own substance;[2] flesh makes its own stink.[3] To illustrate the point, R. Ishmael used to tell the parable of a king's daughter whose kin sought to bring her to grief by putting her out in the open field to glean among the sheaves.[4] The sun bore down upon her, and her face became black as the bottom of a pot. Thereupon her companions laughed at her, saying, "Is this the king's daughter of whom it has been said, 'She is comely and beautiful' "? She replied: "My kin sought to bring me to grief and put me out into the open field to glean among the sheaves.[5] The sun bore down upon me, and my face became black as the bottom of a pot." [Likewise, the congregation of Israel declared]: Master of the universe, who brought me to such a measure of grief? My own people brought me to it, for though it is said, *My mother's sons sought to bring me to grief (ibid.),* read not *My mother's ('immi) sons* but "My people's (*'immati*)[6] sons."[7]

[To spare Israel grief, a man should act] with compassion. Specifically, how? Like the Holy One, may His great name be blessed for ever and ever and ever, who is compassionate toward Israel wherever they dwell—compassionate toward the poor and the needy, toward those who languish and are in want, toward orphans when they require help, and toward widows at all times. Likewise, a mortal should be compassionate toward Israel wherever they dwell, compassionate toward |
ER, ***p.*** **144** the poor and the needy, toward those who languish and are in want, toward orphans when they require help, and toward widows at all times, so that his own wife be not widowed and his own children be not orphaned, as is said, *Ye shall not afflict any widow, or fatherless child. If thou afflict them in any wise . . . My wrath shall wax hot and your wives shall be widows, and your children fatherless* (Exod. 22:21–23). Of a man's compassion, it is further said: Let a man give his charity[8] with joy, and it will be credited to him as righteousness; let a man set aside with joy the heave offering that is due the priests from him, and it will be credited to him as righteousness; let a man give his tithes with joy, and it will be credited to him as righteousness, as Scripture tells us, *I have*

---

2. "When iron was created the trees began to tremble. Said God to them: 'Why do you tremble? Let none of your wood enter it, and not one of you shall be harmed' " (Gen. Rabbah 5:7).

3. "The joint putrefies from within" (B.Sanh 39b).

4. Leon Nemoy suggests: "whose brothers waxed angry at her and [sought to ruin her good looks by] driving her out into the field," etc.

5. See n. 4.

6. For a similar play on the word, cf. below, ER, 149, and PRKM 1:3, p. 7 (PRKS, p. 11).

7. Wicked kings, such as Jeroboam and Ahab; and false prophets, such as Zedekiah son of Chenaanah (1 Kings 22:11). See Targum Jonathan *ad loc.* and ER, 149.

8. Literally, "Let a man do his Torah." The substitution is suggested by Louis Ginzberg who writes: "The three forms of charity are thus enumerated: gift to the poor . . . gift to the priest, and . . . gift to the Levite" (*OT,* p. 292, n. 15).

said, "The world is maintained through loving-kindness"[9] (Ps. 89:3), and it is given stability only through righteousness, as is said, *In righteousness shalt thou be established* (Isa. 54:14). Hence, when David prayed, he addressed the Lord [as gracious, righteous, and compassionate, saying]: *I beseech Thee, O Lord, deliver my soul. Gracious is the Lord, and righteous, yea, our God is compassionate* (Ps. 116:4–5); and also *The Lord thy God is a merciful God* (Deut. 4:31).

[In further regard to the Lord's compassion, consider the conversation between Him and Moses just before Israel's spies went into the Land.] Speaking up boldly, the righteous Moses asked the Holy One: Master of all universes, wherewith do You judge all the world's inhabitants and all Your handiwork in the world You created? With slowness to anger, God answered. But, said Moses, do not people eat and drink well and generally enjoy themselves, yet rebel in the midst of [Your] bounty? In reply the Holy One kept silent and said not a word to Moses. But presently, when the shocking incident of the spies befell Israel, the Holy One said to Moses: *How long will this people despise Me? . . . I will smite them with pestilence and destroy them* (Num. 14:11–12). At once Moses spoke up again to the Holy One: Master of the universe, *When the Egyptians shall hear . . . they will say to the inhabitants of this Land . . . Because the Lord was not able to bring this people into the Land . . . He hath slain them in the wilderness* (Num. 14:13–16). Thereupon the Holy One said: Moses, you now appear to require in Me the qualities [of compassion and mercy] which previously you would have had Me reject. Indeed, I do require them, Moses admitted: *Now, I pray Thee, let the power of the Lord God be great, according as Thou hast spoken, saying: The Lord is slow to anger, and plenteous in loving-kindness. . . . Pardon, I pray Thee, the iniquity of this people according unto the greatness of Thy loving-kindness. . . . And the Lord said: I have pardoned according to thy word* (Num. 14:17–20). Nevertheless, though God forgave [Israel for their conduct], He allowed His decree against them to stand. Hence it is said that anyone who is aware of what the Torah decrees and yet causes its commandments to be transgressed is utterly wicked. Israel should have said to the princes [who served as spies]: "We will not heed you. The Lord brought us up out of Egypt in peace. He slew all their first-born, and we are at peace. He gave us the Egyptians' silver and gold and all precious things they delighted in, and we are at peace." But Israel did not say this. Instead, no sooner had they come up from the Red Sea than they began to press petitions upon Moses, saying to Him: *Let us send men before us, that they may search the Land for us* (Deut. 1:22). Now Moses stood in awe of the Holy One and feared that He might not be pleased with such a venture. Had He not said, "I Myself go with them"

9. JV: *For I have said: "For ever is mercy built."*

—*The Lord went before them by day in a pillar of cloud, to lead them the way* (Exod. 13:21)—something which, if not set down in Scripture, would have been impossible to credit? [Hence Moses would have put the Israelites off, but instead he told them], *Ye came near unto me every one of you* (Deut. 1:22)—every single one of you, not just some of you; and *every one of you,* adults and children alike, said, *"Let us send men before us, that they may search the Land for us" (ibid.).* Thereupon the Holy One said to Moses: *Send thou men, that they may spy out the Land* (Num. 13:2) —*send thou,* He said, but on your say-so, not on Mine. *Send thou,* He said, [this time addressing Israel], because you think you need such a mission—I do not need it; you think the Land needs spying out—I do not need such spying. Nevertheless, He let them *spy out the Land.*

So Moses sent ten princes and sent Joshua and Caleb with them, instructing them: Do not enter the Land as thieves. If you are asked, "What did you come for?" reply, "Only for five figs, five pomegranates, and a cluster of grapes." Say "No," if you are asked, "Perhaps you intend to cut down the trees that are our idols, or destroy the wooden standards we hold sacred?" So the spies were to enter [the Land] pretending to be emissaries and come forth pretending they were peddlers [selling fruit] off their donkeys' backs.[10] Upon reaching Hebron, they took thence five figs, five pomegranates, and a cluster
ER, *p.* 145 | of grapes. When Sheshai and Talmai, [sons of the giant Anak], heard of the spies, they came to confront them. Sheshai let out one shout, and all of them fell [senseless] to the earth. Thereupon Sheshai and Talmai proceeded to breathe their own breath into the spies' faces and rub their noses, and they kept breathing into their faces and rubbing their noses until they came to. After the spies came to, Sheshai and Talmai asked them, "Have you perhaps come to cut down the trees that are our idols, or to destroy the wooden standards we hold sacred?" The spies said, "No." And Sheshai and Talmai did not slay them: they were allowed to go forth in peace. As a reward for the giants' not slaying them and for sending them away in peace, the Holy One preserved some of the Canaanites until the destruction of the Second Temple < and Israel's subsequent exile—some say >, preserved them, besides the Gibeonites,[11] until this very day.

When Moses heard that the spies had returned, he entered his great academy and sat down in it with all Israel seated about him—twelve miles to the north, twelve miles to the south, twelve miles to the east, and twelve miles to the west. <Moses> then rose to his feet and addressed them; and all Israel for twelve miles roundabout heard his

---

10. Reading *ḥammarin,* "ass-drivers," as in Yalḳuṭ, ed. Saloniki, *ad loc.,* and not *'mwryn,* "Amorites," as in V and R. The Canaanites would have little reason to fear such petty traders whose donkeys can carry only tiny loads.

11. See Josh. 9:3–27.

voice. When the spies came in, a space was cleared for them, and they sat down among the children of Israel who asked them, "Why are you sitting down? Tell us what you have to say." The spies replied: *The Land whither thou sentest us . . . surely . . . floweth with milk and honey. . . . Howbeit the people that dwell therein are fierce. . . . And there we saw the Nephilim* [*the giants*]; *and we were in our own sight as grasshoppers* (Num. 13:27–28, 30). Thereupon *All the congregation lifted up their voice, and wept* (Num. 14:1).

Blessed be the Preserver of the world, blessed be He in whose presence no one is favored more than another. Because of the weeping Israel did on that day[12] without any real reason for weeping, the observance of the same day was set aside for weeping throughout the generations, beginning with the <thirty-eight> years they spent in the wilderness.[13]

I call heaven and earth to witness that it was not God's intention to slay [the spies], the ten princes of Israel. [Nevertheless He had them killed by a plague,[14] because with evil intent they][15] pursued Moses and Aaron who had to be protected by being drawn in under the clouds of God's glory. Scripture tells us what happened beforehand: *Moses and Aaron fell on their faces before all the assembly of the congregation of the children of Israel. And Joshua the son of Nun and Caleb the son of Jephunneh, who were of them that spied out the Land, rent their clothes. And they spoke to all the congregation. . . . The Land . . . is an exceeding good Land. . . . If the Lord delight in us, then He will bring us into this Land. . . . Only rebel not against the Lord* (Num. 14:5–9). But the princes began to fling stones at Moses and Aaron, as is said, *But the entire band* [*of the spies*][16] *bade stone them with stones, when the glory of the Lord appeared* (Num. 14:10). Take note of how Israel acted then: saying just the opposite of what they had said before, they declared, *Lo, we will go up to the place which the Lord hath promised* (Num. 14:40), even though Moses had warned them, *There the Amalekite and the Canaanite are before you* (Num. 14:43), and even

---

12. The day was the ninth of Ab, the day on which both Temples were to be destroyed. See B.Ta 29a and Soṭ 35a.

13. See MTeh 78:7 (YJS, *13, 2,* 27).

14. "Their tongues stretched to so great a length that they touched the navel; and worms crawled out of their tongues, and pierced the navel." See Num. 14:37; B.Soṭ 35a; and Ginzberg, *Legends, 6,* 98–99, n. 552.

15. So Haida. [All the Hebrew says is, "because Moses and Aaron had to flee (from the wrath of the disappointed Israelites) and were drawn under the clouds of," etc. The spies were struck down for the consequences of their lies—the mutiny of the mass of the people against Moses—not for their pursuit of Moses (why should they pursue him? Their report accomplished what they wished to accomplish, at least for the moment.). L. N.]

Accordingly, Leon Nemoy would translate Num. 14:10, quoted just below: *But the entire congregation bade stone them,* etc.

16. ER may take *kl,* "all, entire," to mean "they who had all the power"; hence "the princes who had served as spies." So Haida.

though they had been so terrified earlier by the spies' report that they sat down to mourn: *The people mourned greatly* (Num. 14:39).

[They had cause to mourn greatly for another reason besides their supposed danger from the Canaanites.] For if a man is under a ban in this world for one day, the ban is lifted at the end of the day, but in heaven the ban is not lifted for three days. If a man is under a ban for three days in this world, the ban is lifted at the end of the three days, ER, *p.* 146 | but in heaven the ban is not lifted for seven days. If a man is under a ban for seven days in this world, the ban is lifted at the end of the seven days, but in heaven the ban is not lifted for thirty days. If a man is under a ban for thirty days in this world, the ban is lifted at the end of the thirty days, but in heaven the ban is not lifted until his life has ended in this world.[17] Hence, because of the lifelong ban upon them, *The people mourned greatly*[18] *(ibid.).*

While they were mourning, the Holy One said to Moses: Moses, go and reassure those wretched people whose heart has all but left them. Moses asked: Master of the universe, how shall I reassure them? God replied: Go and reassure them with words of Torah: *When ye are come into the Land of your habitations . . . and will make an offering by fire unto the Lord . . . then shall he that bringeth his offering present a meal offering unto the Lord* (Num. 15:3). At that moment a quarrel arose in regard to the offering between Israelites and converts.[19] The Holy One asked Moses: Moses, why are they quarreling with each other? Moses replied: Master of the universe, You know—[they are quarreling as to whether converts who are not *home-born* (Num. 15:13) are privileged to bring

---

17. Literally, "for ever and ever and ever."

18. According to one account, Israel in the wilderness had been under a ban for thirty-eight years, beginning with the dispatch of the spies during the second year following the exodus—hence during the remainder of that generation's lifespan. At the end of this period, when all the men who at the time of the sending of the spies had been twenty years and over were dead, Moses was able to say again, *God spoke to me* (Deut. 2:16). See Sif Lev., *Nĕdaḇah,* 2:13 (ed. Weiss [Vienna, 1962], p. 4b).

"In the meantime, while they were in excommunication before God, so that He did not speak even to Moses during all that period, He in His mercy told Moses to teach them the words of the Torah which had already been revealed to him.

"The author was evidently trying to explain the difficulty which worried commentators on the Sifra. The question is how could one deny that God spoke to Moses during the thirty-eight years when the people were excommunicated, since many commandments are cited in the Book of Numbers after the incident of the spies. The author replies that while God did not speak to Moses during all that time, that is, did not give him any commands, He had already given him the whole Torah on Mount Sinai. The commandments recorded in the Bible thereafter were simply taught by Moses to the people at that time, for while they were still under Divine excommunication, they were no longer excommunicated in human law, and Moses could talk to them." Dr. Louis Finkelstein in a private communication.

19. Num. 15:13 reads *All that are home-born shall do these things after this manner, in presenting an offering made by fire.* Israelites, according to ER, contended that the term "home-born" applied only to them, while converts insisted that the term included them as well.

offerings]. Thereupon God declared: Did I not say to you, *As for the congregation, there shall be one statute both for you and for the convert that sojourneth with you . . . as ye are, so shall the convert be before the Lord. One law and one ordinance shall be both for you, and for the convert that sojourneth with you* (Num. 15:15–16). [In connection with the three references to converts in Exod. 12:48, Lev. 19:33, and Num. 9:14], it has been said that there are three kinds of converts: a convert like our father Abraham; a convert like Hamor;[20] and a convert who is still in every respect a heathen. How so? A convert of this third kind has in his house flesh of carrion, of diseased animals, and of abominable and creeping creatures, [all forbidden to Jews]. To be sure, he did say, "Isn't it time that I become converted and be among Jews whose food is wholesome, who have [delicacies at their] festivals and Sabbaths, so that I shall have no more vile food in my house? I will make myself become a convert." After a while, if this man returns to his habit of eating refuse, the chastisements that come upon him will be for his own good—to preserve what [merit] he had gained. Concerning even such a man the Holy One says: Even as he was drawn to you, so you are to draw him to you, as is said, *Love ye therefore the convert* (Deut. 10:19).

Another kind of convert is like Hamor. How so? If he seeks to wed a Jewish maiden and is told [by her kinsmen], we will not give her to you as a wife until you consent to be converted, <the Gentile replies>: "I will make myself become a convert." After a while, if he returns to his habit of eating refuse, the chastisements that come upon him will be for his own good—to preserve what [merit] he had gained. The Holy One says: As this one sought the security [of your congregation from you], so you give security to him, as is said, *A convert shalt thou not wrong, neither shalt thou oppress him* (Exod. 22:20).

Finally, the third kind of convert is, in his own way, like our father Abraham. How so? He went about making inquiries among all the peoples, and when he heard them all speak of the excellence of Israel, he said, "Isn't it time that I become a convert, <be one of Israel>, and enter under the wings of the Presence?" Of such a man it is said: *Neither let the alien, that hath joined himself to the Lord, speak, saying: "The Lord will keep me apart from His people." . . . For thus saith the Lord concerning . . . [those] that hold fast by My covenant: I will give them in My House and within My walls a monument and a name* (Isa. 56:3–5).

[In connection with the spies' false testimony concerning the Land, Scripture's admonition] *Thou shalt not take up a false report* (Exod. 23:1) [is pertinent]. This is an injunction against those who listen to and accept malicious gossip.

---

20. Hamor, the father of Shechem who seduced Dinah the daughter of Jacob and Leah. See Gen. 34.

This injunction also applies to a judge who should not listen to one litigant unless the other litigant is also present, as is said, *The cause of both parties shall come before the judges* (Exod. 22:8).

Moreover, the injunction applies as well to one litigant, who should not set forth his case to the judge unless the other litigant is present, for it is said, *Then both the men, between whom the controversy is, shall stand before the judges* (Deut. 19:17).

[There is also an injunction against collusion.] Suppose a man should say to his fellow: So-and-so owes me two hundred [zuz],[21] but I have only one witness. Come now and join him in testifying in my behalf; then, [when I collect], you will get one mina and I shall get the other mina. His fellow responds: You know that even if a man should here and now give me the entire world, I would not lie. As it happens,
ER, ***p.*** **147** however, So-and-so | does owe me a mina, and I, too, have only one witness. Come now and join him in testifying in my behalf, [and I will do the same for you. It is with regard to such an agreement that Scripture says, *Put not thy hand with the wicked* (Exod. 23:1)].[22]

In regard to this injunction, note that men of Jerusalem were exceedingly cautious in their association with others: thus not one of them would ever go to a banquet unless he knew who would be there with him; not one of them would sign a matrimonial document unless he knew who would sign with him.

R. Nathan differed with this interpretation of the injunction, saying, Does not the verse refer to [someone other than] a witness who gives false testimony and is therefore clearly wicked? What Scripture is really saying in *Put not thy hand with the wicked* is that men guilty of breach of trust or dishonest dealing are to be deemed unfit as witnesses. Scripture is referring to such men in the verse *When a witness given to expropriating the property of others by chicanery rises up against any man to bear perverted witness against him . . . then shall ye do unto him, as he had purposed to do unto his brother* (Deut. 19:16–19).[23]

Likewise, in saying *If he was not his enemy, nor sought him harm*[24] (Num. 35:23), Scripture implies that a man may bear witness against another man only if the former be not the latter's enemy; that a man may sit in judgment over another man only if the former seek to do no harm to the latter. . . . *Only then may the congregation—*[*the court*]*—judge* (Num. 35:24), which is to say that a man's enemies are disqualified to sit in judgment upon him. We thus have sanction for the disqualification

21. One hundred zuz make a mina.

22. The bracketed passage is interpolated as in a parallel in Meḵ, *2,* 161.

23. The passage is interpreted in keeping with the parallel in Mĕḵilta dĕ-Rabbi Ishmael, ed. Horovitz-Rabin (Frankfurt am Main, 5691/1931), p. 322, n. 12.

24. In the comment that follows, Num. 35:23b is construed not as the conclusion of the preceding verse, but as an introduction to the verse that follows.

of enemies as witnesses. Whence the sanction that kinsmen are likewise disqualified? Because the verse goes on to limit the personnel of a court in the words *whether the smiter*—[*that is, an enemy*]—*or the avenger of blood* —[*that is, a kinsman*] *(ibid.).* We thus have sanction from Scripture that disqualifies both enemies and kinsmen as judges. Whence the proof that they are likewise disqualified as witnesses? By inference. According to the Torah, we may sentence [an accused person] to death only by the testimony of two witnesses; we may put [an accused person] to death only by the order of judges. As judges are to be disqualified, if there be among them enemies or kinsmen [of an accused person], so witnesses are likewise to be disqualified if there be among them enemies or kinsmen [of an accused person]. Besides, the matter may be argued a fortiori: If enemies and kinsmen of the accused are disqualified as judges, even though legal procedure does not permit them to testify, all the more so should the accused's enemies and kinsmen be disqualified as witnesses on the basis of whose testimony sentence might be pronounced.

Thus from the context we have proof that such regulations apply if the accused be charged with murder. Whence the proof that these regulations apply to proceedings against those accused of other offenses which incur the death penalty? Because the verse goes on to say, *according to these ordinances (ibid.).* We thus have proof that the regulations apply to proceedings against "home-born" Jews. Whence the proof that they apply also to converts? Again from the words *according to these ordinances.*[25]

We thus have proof that these regulations apply to capital cases. Whence the proof that they apply also to civil cases? Because in the words *according to these ordinances,* [the plural *ordinances* implies all kinds of cases].[26]

You may argue that since capital cases require a panel of twenty-three judges, civil cases should also require a panel of twenty-three judges. But Scripture in saying *these* suggests that only particular cases, [those in which the death penalty is possible], require a panel of twenty-three judges, but that civil cases do not require a panel of twenty-three judges.

Now in all charges of trespass or misappropriation, *the case of both parties shall come before* [*a panel of three*] *judges* (Exod. 22:8); but what evidence is there from Scripture that in capital cases the panel be made up of twenty-three judges? To begin with, in saying the *congregation may condemn* (Num. 35:24), Scripture implies that in such a panel there

---

25. Ordinances which, according to an earlier verse in the chapter, verse 15, refer and apply to both convert and settler. See David Pardo, Sifre dĕbe Rab (Saloniki, 5559 [1799]), p. 167c.

26. See *ibid.*

must be ten who may choose to condemn [for ten is the minimum number of a congregation]; and in going on to say, *the congregation may acquit* (Num. 35:25), Scripture implies that in such a panel there must be ten who may choose to acquit. Thus you have a requirement of at least twenty judges. But whence the proof that twenty-three are required? By inference: The Torah says that we may sentence [an accused] to death only on the testimony of two witnesses and that we may put [an accuser] to death only by the order of judges. Now, even as there must be two witnesses, so there must be [a majority of] two judges [who rule against the accused].[27] And since a court may not be made up of an even number of judges, one more judge is added. Thus you have a panel of twenty-three [judges in capital cases].

Those who go to undue lengths[28] used to say: The words *the congregation*—[*at least, ten*]—*may condemn* (Num. 35:24), *the congregation* —[*at least, ten*]—*may acquit* (Num. 35:25), and *the congregation*—[*at least, ten*]—*may restore (ibid.)* imply that capital cases require a panel of thirty judges.[29]

---

27. See Exod. 23:2 and Rashi *ad loc.*

28. The phrase *'anše mĕšuḥoṯ* is here related not to *mašoḇoṯ,* "measurers, surveyors" (as in Er 4:11), but to *'ĕnošin dĕ-mišḥon,* "men of great size" (Targum Onḳelos on Num. 13:32). Hence "those who go to undue lengths." Cf. *mafriz 'al ham-middoṯ,* "who breaks through beyond measures" (B.Nid 4b). Professor Ch. Z. Dimitrovsky, in a private communication, suggested the interpretation of the crux.

29. See parallel in Sif Num. 160 (ed. Horovitz [Frankfurt am Main, 1917], pp. 219–20).

CHAPTER (30) 28

During the exiles' long night God weeps

Summary

Knowing that God Himself dwelt in Israel's Holy Place and remembering His judgments upon Egypt, the nations He called upon to invade Jerusalem were at first frightened, believing that He would not permit such action against Jerusalem. But since He is One in whom justice is perfect, He did permit the bodies of His *servants to be food unto the fowls of the heaven* (Ps. 79:1–2). Indeed, He permitted His dwelling in Shiloh as well as in Jerusalem to be invaded, academies of learning to be set on fire, and the disciples of the wise within them to be slain. But for Rachel's entreaty in Israel's behalf, they might never have been restored to their own place (ER, 147–48).

Still, not God but Israel are to be blamed for what befell them because they followed the counsel of false prophets. Secretly, however, God laments the fate of Jerusalem in whose ultimate restoration Israel are to have faith. Indeed, at the Temple's one wall which was not destroyed, God is there weeping because the Levites, singers of His glory, had been despoiled by the foe. But in this instance also the Levites themselves were to blame for their fate because they had failed in their duty to sing to the glory of God. Yet as soon as the Levites cried out, *How shall we sing the Lord's song in a foreign land?* (Ps. 137:4), the Lord swore that He would make it up to Jerusalem measure for measure (ER, 149).

When the Temple was destroyed, God was about to destroy the entire world, even turn the throne of glory upside down. After all, did not God build the Temple with His own hands? Moreover, Nebuchadnezzar, its destroyer, the instrument of God's punishment of Israel, had overstepped the bounds of His commission.

Psalm 79, the Psalm which speaks of the heathen's coming into God's inheritance, is significantly not captioned "Weeping of Asaph" or "Dirge of Asaph" but *Psalm of Asaph* (ER, 150), for Asaph understood that God's intention was to preserve Jerusalem and ultimately raise her up again.

God grieved sorely for those of Israel who were victims of the heathen in Alexandria and Bethar, grieved for the martyr's death of Miriam's sons and of R. Ishmael and Rabban Simeon ben Gamaliel (ER, 151–53).

Even though some of the victims had been idol worshipers, no sooner did they resolve upon repentance, than He wept for them. It is to be remembered that no one feels such compassion for Israel as does God, who from the beginning intended His world for them. And so He weeps for them during the exiles' long night (ER, 154). Indeed, year after year, He cries like a father who had driven his family away, or like a mother hen clucking for her lost chicks. Hence, when Israel were going into exile in silence, without weeping, God asked them not to remain silent, but to weep and thus stir Him to mercy.

During both nights of exile—the one following the destruction of the First Temple and the one following the destruction of the Second—God weeps as He repeatedly looks for the man who truly has words of Torah within him. Indeed, if a man obeys but two or three commandments, he is given an angel to watch over him. As for the Jew who has immersed himself in the entire Torah and has also ministered to the Sages, God Himself watches over him (ER, 155).

Finally, God assures Israel: The morning of your redemption is certain to come. In the meantime, remember that understanding of Torah is given only to one who suffers distress for its sake—the kind of distress that you are made to experience in living among the uncircumcised whose lands are deemed spiritual deserts (ER, 156).

Chapter (30) 28

ER, *p.* 147 *cont'd* *A Psalm of Asaph. O God, the heathen are come into Thine inheritance. They have given the dead bodies of Thy servants to be food unto the fowls of the heaven* (Ps. 79:1–2). [Nevertheless, our faith in You does not falter.] Blessed be the Preserver of the world, blessed be He who remembers Jerusalem each and every hour, for in His nature there is no defect, no lapse of memory, and no favoring of one nation over another. The matter is made explicit in post-Mosaic Scripture by David, king of Israel: *O*
ER, *p.* 148 *God, awesome art Thou because of Thy holy places* (Ps. 68:36). | What is implied by these words? That when Moses set up the Tabernacle, all the peoples of the world, shaken and stricken with awe by the presence of the Holy One, said, "For these [children of Israel], 'Wondrous deeds were done in Egypt, in the land of Ham, awesome deeds at the Red Sea' (Ps. 106:22). In behalf of His children, God executed judgment upon Egypt and upon their first-born, and hence is all the more likely to act against any one who as much as touches His children now," as is said, *Surely he that toucheth you, toucheth the apple of His eye* (Zech. 2:12). By this verse is meant that to the Holy One, Israel—if one dare say such a thing—is God's eye, [all the more precious to Him because it is] His only eye. Hence *Surely he that toucheth you toucheth the apple of His eye.* Nevertheless, God is quoted elsewhere in post-Mosaic Scripture by the prophet Jeremiah as saying: *My Tent is spoiled, and all My cords are broken, My children are gone forth of Me, and they are not* (Jer. 10:20). In the words *My Tent is spoiled,* God seems to be saying—if one dare assert He would say such a thing—that "certain spoilers came and plundered My city, My House, and My Temple." And who were the spoilers of whom God speaks? The princes of the king of Babylon, as referred to in the verses *When Jerusalem was taken . . . all the princes of the king of Babylon came in, and sat in the middle gate* (Jer. 39:1–3).

In another interpretation of *My Tent is spoiled, Tent* is taken as referring to [the Tent of Shiloh],[1] the seat of the Presence, identical with the one spoken of in the verse "Moses used to take the Tent and to pitch it without the camp . . . and he called it the Tent of Meeting" (Exod. 33:7).

Or, in the words *My Tent is spoiled,* by *Tent* is meant the Temple

---

1. "the Tent of Shiloh"—so *YY.*

Sanctuary, the one referred to in the verse "And let them make Me the Sanctuary, that I may dwell among them"[2] (Exod. 25:5).

Or, as in "Suddenly are My tents [of study] spoiled" (Jer. 4:20), *tent* in *My tent is spoiled* refers to academies: for example, in the verse "Nebuchadnezzar . . . burnt the house of the Lord and the king's house; and all the houses of Jerusalem, even every house where [the word] is magnified,[3] burnt he with fire" (2 Kings 25:9; Jer. 52:13).

Another comment on *My tent is spoiled* (Jer. 10:20): As a tent cannot stand without pegs and without cords, so Israel cannot stand without disciples of the wise, for, as intimated in the next words of the verse, *and all my cords (metaray) are broken (ibid.),* we are to read not *metaray,* "cords," but *mattiray* in reference to the Sages in Israel, who in determining what is allowed *(mattirin)* and determining what is prohibited, serve Israel like tent cords that endure. Hence *All my cords are broken* [alludes to the means by which Israel used to be sustained].[4]

[Still, by way of consolation], the conclusion of the verse from Jeremiah, *My children have gone forth of Me, and yet they have not* (Jer. 10:20), may be taken as saying: Even though Israel are exiled among the nations of the world, yet, because they are occupied with Torah, it is as though they have not gone forth into exile.

In another comment, the words are read, *My children have gone forth of Me, and they might not have been.* As Israel were about to be exiled among the peoples of the world, it was not the Holy One's intention to restore them to their own place until Rachel stood up in entreaty before the Holy One, saying to Him: Master of the universe, let it be remembered to my credit that I did not mind the wife who was my rival. Nay more! Let it be remembered for my sake that though my husband worked for seven years to wed me, yet when I was about to enter the bridal chamber, my sister Leah took my place. I refrained then from saying anything to Jacob, so that he would not be able to tell my voice from my sister's voice. Now to the point: If I, who am mortal, did not mind the wife who was my rival, will You mind the rival who is no more than an idol? Of such as it, Scripture declares, *Eyes have they, but they see not; they have ears, but they hear not* (Ps. 115:5–6). At once the Holy One's compassion crested like a wave, and He swore to Rachel that He would restore Israel to their place, as is said, *Thus saith the Lord: A voice is heard in Ramah, lamentation, and bitter weeping, Rachel weeping*

2. The first part of the word *šakanti* (I may dwell) is construed as *škn,* "the Dwelling [that was to stand]," and the concluding part of the word, *ti,* is construed as "four hundred and ten years," the numerical value of the two letters; hence "the Temple that was to stand for four hundred and ten years." So *Ba'al haṭ-ṭurim* on Exod. 25:8.

3. "Places of assembly where Torah and prayer are cultivated." So Rashi *ad loc.* JV: *all the houses of Jerusalem, even every great man's house.* See also Louis Ginzberg in *OT,* p. 281, n. 257.

4. Cf. PR 28:1 (YJS, *18, 2,* 552–53).

for her children, etc. (Jer. 31:14); read not, however, *Rachel weeping for her children,* but rather "It was she who caused the spirit of God *(Ruaḥ 'El)* to weep for her children."[5] *When she refused to be comforted for her children, because they were not (ibid.),* the Lord said: *Refrain thy voice from weeping . . . they shall come back from the land of the enemy, and there is hope for thy future—*[*they will be restored to their own place*], *saith the Lord* (Jer. 31:15).

ER, *p.* 149 | In another comment on *My children are gone forth of Me, and they are not,* the words *they are not* are taken to mean that the festivals are not observed in the right way.[6] The congregation of Israel declared to the Holy One: Master of the universe, when I was on my own soil, I used to observe each festival on the designated day, as was the proper way to observe it. Now I observe it on a second day as well, and not on only one day as is proper. Master of the universe, who brought it about that I should come to such a state? The answer is in the verse usually read *My mother's sons caused me this grief* (Song 1:6). Do not read "My mother's *('immi)* sons caused me this grief"; read rather "My own people's *('ummati)* sons caused me this grief"—my own people's sons, such as Hananiah the son of Azzur,[7] Ahab the son of Kolaiah, and Zedekiah the son of Maaseiah,[8] all of whom spoke false prophecies to me. Such is the implication of the words *My mother's sons caused me this grief.*[9]

On the occasion when Rabbi Zadok entered the Temple area and saw the destroyed Temple, he said: My Father in heaven, You destroyed Your city and burned Your Temple, yet now You sit by tranquilly, untroubled. Presently R. Zadok dozed off, and it was then that he saw the Holy One standing there in lamentation, the ministering angels lamenting with Him. Thereupon he exclaimed: Hail to thee, Jerusalem, in whose restoration we are to have faith! [as is said, *The city in whose redemption one is to have faith* (Isa. 1:26–27)].[10]

On another occasion, R. Nathan entered the Temple area and found the Temple destroyed but for one wall still standing.[11] He asked: What does it signify that this wall is still standing? Someone replied: I

---

5. [I would say, "the spirit of God (thus appealed to by Rachel) joined (her) in weeping for her children." L. N.]

6. Since the phases of the moon had to be ascertained from visual observation by the Sanhedrin in Israel, exile meant uncertainty as to the exact day the new month began; consequently, each festival had to be observed for two days. In the comment that follows, Jer. 10:20 is construed: "My [heavenly] tent is made to appear in disarray."

7. Jer. 28:1.

8. Jer. 29:23 and PRKM 24:15, pp. 373–74 (PRKS, p. 381).

9. Cf. above, ER, 143, and PR 28:2 (YJS, *18, 2,* 554).

10. JV: *The faithful city . . . shall be redeemed.* But *n'ĕemanah,* "faithful," may also mean "one in which faith is to be put."

11. The western wall of the Temple which will never be destroyed. See PR 15:10 (YJS, *18, 1,* 320–21).

will show you. Then taking a ring, he pressed it against the wall. Thereupon R. Nathan realized that the wall was trembling, trembling because of the presence of the Holy One,[12] for in the same moment he saw Him [at the wall] bow down and straighten up and weep as He stood up, bow down and straighten up and weep as He stood up, as is said, *Běroš is wailing,* [13] *for the cedar is fallen* (Zech. 11:2). Read not *běroš,* "cypress," but *bě-roš* "in the Head," "Head" signifying the Holy One—may the name of the Holy One, blessed be He, be blessed for ever and ever. He is called "Head," as in the verse *Their king is passed on before them, and the Lord as the Head (Roš) of them* (Mic. 2:13).

The verse from Zechariah quoted above continues, *Because the singers of glory are spoiled* (Zech. 11:2)—that is, the Holy One was also weeping at the wall because the singers of His glory, [the Levites], had been despoiled by the foe. It was these singers who declared: *By the rivers of Babylon, there we sat down, again we wept,* [*when we remembered Zion*] (Ps. 137:1). They did not say, "There we sat down and wept," but said, *there we sat down, again we wept,* thus intimating that they wept, ceased weeping, and then resumed weeping. For what is meant by *when we remembered Zion* but that whenever the Levites recalled Zion, they wept, fell silent, and then wept again.

Upon the willows in the midst thereof we hanged up our harps, for there they that led us captive asked of us words of song, and they that laid us on heaps[14] *asked of us mirth* (Ps. 137:2). The words *they . . . laid us on heaps* intimate that the Chaldeans piled up heaps and heaps of slain Israelites and then had the gall to say to the Levites, *Sing us one of the songs of Zion (ibid.).* The Levites replied: You are the greatest fools in the world! Had we sung the songs [we were supposed to sing to the glory of God], we would not have been carried away captive from our Land. [How can you expect us to sing now?] Consider the preceding dialogue in the light of the parable of a king's son who having married a princess, said to her, "Mix me a cup of wine,[15] else I will divorce you." She refused to mix the cup and he divorced her. After he divorced her, she went and married a man stricken with boils. And he, too, said to her, "Mix me a cup of wine." Thereupon she said: "You are the greatest fool in the world! I was divorced [by the king's son] because I refused to mix a cup for him; yet you who don't amount to any more than one of the servants of my servants dare say to me, 'Mix me a cup!' "

---

12. A paraphrase of "the ring kept moving hither and thither."

13. JV: *Wail, O cypress tree.* The entire verse is construed as referring to the destruction of the Temple, here metaphorically referred to as "the cedar." See ARN, chap. 4 (YJS, *10,* 37).

14. So AV, margin. JV: *And our tormentors asked of us mirth.*

15. [A service usually performed by a maidservant for a wealthy person or by a wife for an indigent person, but certainly not by a wife who is a royal princess. L. N.]

When, [at the time of the Temple's destruction], the Chaldeans asked Israel to sing the songs of Zion, the Levites gave them the same reply: You are the greatest fools in the world! *How shall we sing the Lord's song in a foreign land,* etc.? (Ps. 137:4). Thereupon God declared to them: *Can a woman forget her sucking child, that she should not have compassion on the son of her womb? Yea, these may forget, yet will not I forget thee* (Isa. 49:15); and *If I forget thee, O Jerusalem, let My right hand wither* (Ps. 137:5), the very hand with which I gave the Torah, as is said, "At His right hand was a fiery law unto them" (Deut. 33:2). *Let My tongue cleave to the roof of My mouth* (Ps. 137:6), God went on to say, [if I do not make it up to Israel] measure for measure, [for the destruction of the Temple by their foes]. As it is said, *The tongue of the sucking child cleaveth to the roof of his mouth for thirst* (Lam. 4:4), so God said: *Let My tongue cleave to the roof of My mouth* [if I do not satisfy My thirst to avenge Israel and Jerusalem]!

ER, *p.* 150 At that | moment, the Holy One was about to destroy the entire world, all of it; and not merely the earth: at that moment He was about to turn even the throne of glory upside down, as intimated in the plea *Do not contemn [us], for Thy name's sake, do not dishonor the throne of Thy glory* (Jer. 14:21): For Your name's sake, do not bring Yourself to show contempt [for Your world]! Do not dishonor Your throne!

But the Holy One immediately replied: I will bring heaven and earth together, smiting one against the other, and thus destroy the entire world, all of it, as is said, *I will also smite My hands together, and I will satisfy My fury* (Ezek. 21:22) and be comforted.

[God spoke thus because] by that time Nebuchadnezzar had thought things over and said to himself: I know that this people Israel is inclined to repentance and that the hand of their God is stretched out to one who resolves upon repentance. Should they resolve upon repentance, He will receive them and thus proceed to humiliate me. Right away, therefore, Nebuchadnezzar had his guards track down Israel even at night, as Israel said, *Our pursuers were swifter than the eagles of heaven; they chased us upon the mountains, they lay in wait for us in the wilderness*[16] (Lam. 4:19).

[To account further for God's weeping, it is noted that His own hands wrought the Temple, for the *My* of] *My Tent is spoiled* intimates strongly that the Temple had been built not by men's hands, but—if one dare say such a thing—by the hands of God Himself,[17] as is said, *The Sanctuary, O Lord, which Thy hands have established* (Exod. 15:17),

16. Solitary places where Israel might have been moved to thoughts of repentance. For the entire passage concerning Nebuchadnezzar, cf. MTeh 137:3–5 (YJS, *13, 2,* 331–35) and PR 28:2–3, 31:4–5 (YJS, *18, 2,* 554–59, 606–09).

17. Each stone in the Temple is said to have come flying and settled in its proper place, so that the building got built of itself. See PR 6:7 (YJS, *18, 1,* 127).

and as is said further, *Awesome is God out of Thy holy places* (Ps. 68:36).

[Consider by way of the following parable how Nebuchadnezzar, whom God intended to be the instrument of His punishment of Israel for their transgressions, overstepped the bounds of his commission, as indicated by Scripture in the Psalm of Asaph previously quoted]: *O God, the heathen are come into Thine inheritance. They have given the dead bodies of Thy servants to be food unto the fowls of the heaven* (Ps. 79:1–2). The parable, as told by R. Jose the Galilean, concerned a mortal king who had to set out for a city far across the sea. As he was about to entrust his son to the care of a wicked guardian, his friends and servants said to him: My lord king, do not entrust your son to this wicked guardian. Nevertheless the king, ignoring the counsel of his friends and servants, entrusted his son to the wicked guardian. What did the guardian do? He proceeded to destroy the king's city, have his house consumed by fire, and slay his son with the sword. After a while the king returned. When he saw his city destroyed and desolate, his house consumed by fire, his son slain with the sword, he pulled out the hair of his head and his beard and broke out into wild weeping, saying: Woe is me! How <foolish> I have been, how senselessly I acted in this kingdom of mine in entrusting my son to a wicked guardian!

Likewise, the Holy One. The Prophets had pleaded with Him: Master of the universe, do not turn over Your inheritance and Your people to the heathen, do not turn over Your children to the wicked Nebuchadnezzar who hates the Holy One. But God ignored the counsel of Asaph and the Prophets and entrusted His children to the wicked Nebuchadnezzar. What did Nebuchadnezzar do? He proceeded to burn Jerusalem, destroy the Temple, and banish Israel to Babylon. Thereupon the Holy One said: I commanded that wicked man to do no more than subjugate My children to words of Torah, but he went beyond the bounds of justice [which, as a means of making trial of Israel, I had set for him and the kings of other nations],[18] as is said, *These are the nations which the Lord left, to prove Israel by them* (Judg. 3:1). [When Nebuchadnezzar overstepped his bounds, however, God exclaimed]: *Now, therefore, what do I here, saith the Lord, seeing that My people is taken away for naught?* (Isa. 52:5).

Another comment on *A Psalm of Asaph* (Ps. 79:1). Should not the Psalm have been titled "Weeping of Asaph," or "Lamentation of Asaph," or "Dirge of Asaph"? Why "Psalm of Asaph"? To show that Asaph and those Prophets, [who were descendants of Korah],[19] found reason to rejoice at the destruction of the Temple. By what parable may

---

18. See ER, chap. 1, n. 33.

19. Korah whom the earth had swallowed. See Num. 16:1–35 and Ginzberg, *Legends, 6,* 105; also MTeh 79:3 (YJS, *13, 2,* 44–45).

the matter be understood? By the parable of the daughter of a poor ER, *p.* 151 family who went to draw water from a well. | Her clay bucket came loose, and [the bucket] tumbled into the well. The daughter of the poor family fell to weeping and moaning. Then the king's daughter came to draw water from the well, and her golden bucket came loose, and [that bucket too] fell into the well. Thereupon the daughter of the poor family jumped for joy. When she was asked, "You have just been weeping and moaning—how is it that you are now jumping for joy?" she replied, "He who brings up the golden bucket will also bring up the clay bucket."

Likewise, when Asaph and those Prophets [who were descendants of Korah] understood that Scripture's saying *Her gates are sunk in the ground* (Lam. 2:9) implies that they were to be lifted up and restored, Asaph and the Prophets rejoiced at the assurance, and Asaph said at once: He who restores Jerusalem will also bring up my father's father from the depths of the earth.

The elder R. Eliezer, quoting *A Psalm of Asaph. O God, the heathen have come* (Ps. 79:1), said: Hadrian Caesar came and seized Alexandria of Egypt where there were one hundred and twenty myriads of Jews. He misled them by having them advised as follows: Go forth and take your stand in the valley of Yadaim, and this [Egyptian] people will be unable to prevail over you. The Jews did as he advised. Thereupon at their rear, Hadrian stationed fifty thousand of his men armed with swords who kept killing the Jews until not one of them remained, as is said, *They shed their blood like water* (Ps. 79:3)—indeed, three rivers of blood, so say the Sages, flowed out of the valley of Yadaim and into the Great [Mediterranean] Sea. The Sages tested the waters of the Great Sea and found three parts of it to be blood and only one part water. Some say: For seven years the nations of the world fertilized[20] their vineyards with the blood of Israel.[21]

R. Eliezer, quoting *A Psalm of Asaph* (Ps. 79:1), said: Rome came and slew all of Bethar.[22] At that time the Romans slew four myriads of Jews, so that the blood ran out of doorways and water pipes—indeed the flow was such that Bethar seemed then to be in the rainy season. It is said further that [after the slaughter] there were found in Bethar three hundred baskets of tefillin, each basket containing three *sĕ'ah* for a total of nine hundred *sĕ'ah* of tefillin.[23]

---

20. Literally, "gathered their vintage from."

21. The incident referred to may have been the Roman devastation of the Jewish quarter in Alexandria in the days of Alexander Tiberius (first century C.E.). The attribution to Hadrian is thus an error. The valley of Yadaim, "Hands," where the Jews assembled, was the Delta of the Nile. See S. J. L. Rapoport, *'Ereḳ millin* (Prague, 5612 [1852]), p. 96. Cf. B.Giṭ 57a.

22. In southern Palestine, the center of the revolt of Bar Kokhba.

23. The equivalent of 28,000 dry quarts. Cf. B.Giṭ 58a.

And the Sages, quoting *A Psalm of Asaph (ibid.),* further report the following: Hadrian Caesar came and seized a widow, named Miriam daughter of Tanḥum, and her seven sons. When he asked her, "Who are you?" she replied, "I am a widow." "And these young children standing with you—whose are they?" She replied, "They are mine." Hadrian took them and imprisoned them separately. He then had the oldest of the children brought to him and said, "Bow down to this divinity as your brothers have done." The lad replied: "God forbid that my brothers should have so bowed down. I, likewise, will not bow down to the work of man's hands, for thus it is written: *Know this day, and lay it to thy heart, that the Lord, He is God in heaven above and upon the earth beneath; there is none else"* (Deut. 4:39). At once his guards took a sword and cut off his head. Hadrian then had the second son brought and said to him, "Bow down to this divinity as your brothers have done." The boy replied: "God forbid that my brothers should have so bowed down! I, likewise, will not bow down, for thus it is written in the Torah: *The Lord your God, He is God of gods, and Lord of lords"* (Deut. 10:17). At once his guards took a sword and cut off his head. Hadrian then had the third boy brought and said to him, "Bow down to this divinity just as the others have done." The boy replied: "God forbid! I will not bow down to the work | of man's hands, for thus it is **ER, *p.* 152** written in the Torah: *Thou shalt have no other gods before Me"* (Exod. 20:3). At once the guards took a sword and cut off his head. Hadrian then had the fourth boy brought, to whom he said, "Come, bow down to this." The boy replied: "God forbid! I will not bow down to the work of man's hands, for thus it is written in the Torah: *Thou shalt bow down to no other god"* (Exod. 34:14). At once the guards took a sword and cut off his head. Hadrian then had the fifth boy brought and said to him, "Come, bow down to this." The boy replied: "God forbid! I will not bow down to the work of man's hands, for thus it is written in the Torah: *He that sacrificeth unto the gods . . . shall be utterly destroyed"* (Exod. 22:19). At once the guards took a sword and cut off his head. Hadrian then had the sixth boy brought, to whom he said, "Come, bow down to this." The boy replied: "God forbid! I will not bow down to the work of man's hands, for thus it is written in the Torah: *The Lord shall reign for ever and ever"* (Exod. 15:18). At once the guards took a sword and cut off his head.[24] Hadrian then had the seventh son, the youngest of them, brought, and said to him, "Come, bow down to this." The child replied: "God forbid! I will not bow down to the work of man's hands, for we Jews swore an oath to the Holy One that we would not worship any other god, and in return, the Holy One swore to us that He would not exchange us for another people, as is said, *Thou*

---

24. "At once . . . his head"—R.

hast avouched the Lord this day to be thy God . . . and the Lord hath avouched thee this day to be His own treasure" (Deut. 26:17–18). Thereupon the king said: "If you will not bow down, then I will throw this ring before the divinity, so that when you [bend over] <to pick up the ring>, [it will seem that you are bowing down], and the onlookers will say: Look, he listened to Caesar's command and bowed down to the divinity." The boy replied: "Shame on you, Caesar, for what you have just asked me to do! Why should you, a being of flesh-and-blood like me, not know better than to try such a cheap trick [for the sake of pleasing an idol]? I, for one, know better than to try such trickery on my King, [the King of kings]." Hadrian then asked, "Is there a [one and only] God in the world?" The lad replied, "Do you think the world has no owner?" Hadrian asked, "Does your God have a head?" The lad replied, "It has already been said, *His head is as the most fine gold*" (Song 5:11). Hadrian asked, "Does your God have ears?" The lad replied, "It has already been said, *The Lord hearkened, and heard*" (Mal. 3:16). Hadrian asked, "Does your God also have eyes?" The lad replied, "Has it not already been said, *The eyes of the Lord run to and fro . . . through the whole earth*" (Zech. 4:10)? Hadrian asked, "Does your God have a nose?" The lad replied, "Has it not already been said, *The Lord smelled the sweet savor*" (Gen. 8:21)? Hadrian asked, "Does your God have a mouth?" The lad replied, "Has it not already been said, *The host of the* [*heavens were made*] *by the breath of His mouth*" (Ps. 33:6)? Hadrian asked, "Does your God have a palate?" The lad replied, "Has it not already been said, *His palate is sweet, yea, He is altogether lovely*" (Song 5:15)? Hadrian asked, "Does your God have hands?" The lad replied, "Has it not already been said, *Yea, My hand hath laid the foundation of the earth, and My right hand hath spread out the heavens*" (Isa. 48:13)? Hadrian asked, "Does your God have feet?" The lad replied, "Has it not already been said, *And His feet shall stand in that day upon the Mount of Olives*" (Zech. 14:4)? Hadrian then asked, "But does your God have power?" The lad replied, "Has it not already been said, *Behold, the Lord's hand is not shortened, that it cannot save*" (Isa. 59:1)? Hadrian asked further, "Well, then, since your God has power, and His eyes see and His ears hearken, why did He not disclose Himself and save you from my hands?" The lad replied: "You are the biggest fool in the world! You are not worthy of having miracles performed on your account. And, besides, we mortals are already marked for death. If you do not slay us, He whose presence is everywhere has many slayers besides you. He whose presence is everywhere has many bears, for example. He whose presence is everywhere has many leopards, many serpents, many scorpions, many lions who might have attacked us." Immediately Hadrian ordered the boy to be put to death.

At that instant the mother of the boys said to Hadrian: "By your life, Caesar! By your life, Caesar! Give me my son for me to kiss." They

gave him to her. She embraced him, hugged him, and kissed him. Then she took hold of her nipples and put them in his mouth, and honey and milk overflowed from his mouth and fell to the ground, thus fulfilling
| the words *Honey and milk are under thy tongue* (Song 4:11). Then she ER, *p.* 153
said further: "By your life, Caesar! By your life, Caesar! Put the sword <at the same moment> to my neck and the neck of my son." Caesar replied: "God forbid! I cannot do such a thing, for it is written thus in the Torah: *Whether it be cow or ewe, ye shall not kill it and its young both in one day* (Lev. 22:28)." At this the child said to him: "You are the biggest fool in the world! Do you think that in fulfilling this one verse, you are fulfilling all the rest of Torah?" At once the executioners took a sword and cut off his head.

The Sages calculated the age of the child, and he was found to have been two years, six months, and seven and a half hours old.

At the moment of his death the peoples of the world tore the hair out of their heads and their beards and wept in great sobs, asking: What has the Father of these children done that they are so willing to be slain for His sake? The question asked by the peoples of the world is intimated in the words of Scripture *Wherein is thy Beloved more than another beloved, O thou fairest among women?* (Song 5:9).

As her last son died, the mother of the seven children said, "My children, go and say to your father Abraham: Do not be proud because you are able to say, 'I built an altar and offered up my son upon it'—Behold! I built seven altars and offered my seven sons upon them."

The mother said further: "My children, happy are you in that you did the will of your Father in heaven. You were in the world only in order that His great name be hallowed <through you> ; as is said, *Through them that are nigh unto Me I will be hallowed"* (Lev. 10:3). Thereupon she dropped to the floor in prayer, then went up to the roof, threw herself off, and died. A Divine Voice proclaimed: Of you the Psalmist said, *The mother of such children causeth rejoicing* (Ps. 113:9).[25]

When Rabban Simeon and R. Ishmael were taken out to be slain, Rabban Simeon wept as he asked: Why are we to be slain like idolaters,[26] like violators of the Sabbath? Why should our death be like the death of those [who eat] carrion or the flesh of animals dead of disease, or [eat] the flesh of reptiles and creeping things? R. Ishmael replied: My master, may I argue the matter in your presence? Maybe [we deserve to be slain], for at times, as we sat to pass judgment, perhaps we did not judge properly, because false witnesses came and testified before us, so that the accused men were [unjustly] condemned to death. Or maybe we went to the bathhouse and got engaged in eating and

---

25. Cf. B.Giṭ 57b; 2 Macc. 7; and PR 43:4 (YJS, *18, 2,* 761).
26. "idolators"—R. Friedmann misread "transgressors."

drinking, so that when orphans and widows came to ask for sustenance, the attendant told them that it was not the right time [to see us]. Come and see how great is the punishment for such an offense, for it is said, *Ye shall not afflict any widow or fatherless child. If thou afflict them in any wise . . . My wrath shall wax hot, and I will kill you with the sword* (Exod. 22:21–23).

At the time the two Rabbis were to be slain they sought to honor each other, the one saying: "I am more renowned and more distinguished than my colleague. Slay me first so that I shall not have to look upon the death of my colleague." And the other likewise said: "I am more renowned than my colleague. Slay me first so that I shall not have to look upon the death of my colleague."

So lots were cast, and the lot fell upon Rabban Simeon ben Gamaliel [so that he was beheaded first]. Thereupon R. Ishmael took R. Simeon['s severed head],[27] clasped it to his bosom, embraced it, hugged it, and kissed it, as he spoke to it: How is it that you are to be laid in the dust? How is it that your tongue is to be filled with dust and ash like [the tongues of] idolaters,[28] violators of the Sabbath, [eaters] of carrion, of animals dead of disease, [eaters] of reptiles and creeping things? R. Ishmael had not finished what he was saying when a sword was taken up and he, too, was beheaded.

At once the Holy One said: On account of these two, I will take heaven and earth and smite them one against the other, and thus destroy My world, as is said, *I will also smite My hands together, and I will satisfy My fury* (Ezek. 21:22).[29]

ER, *p.* 154 | And God grieved not only for this—[that is, for Israel's martyred notables, but also for the inhabitants of all the towns who had been provoking Him]. By the time Nebuchadnezzar king of Babylon came and surrounded Jerusalem, the inhabitants of the towns in the territories of the Tribes of Judah and Benjamin had already gathered in many companies within it. *Why do we sit still here?* they had asked, *Assemble yourselves, and let us enter into the fortified cities* (Jer. 8:14). Rise and let us go up to the House of our God. [But there they were taken captive by Nebuchadnezzar and led into exile.]

Then, when they got to the waters of the Euphrates and drank of them [to assuage their thirst], the tainted waters slew more of them than the Chaldees had slain,[30] [so that the survivors], as they were plodding

---

27. [The *Vorlage* probably read *nṭlw 't r šl r yšʿm'l,* and the copyist thought that *r šl* were to be crossed out (the author's readers knew all his material inside out, and if the copyist had stopped to think he would no doubt have remembered that the first *r* stands for *r'šw,* but copyists were paid by the quire, and time was money to them, much to our disadvantage). L. N.]
28. See n. 26.
29. Cf. ARN, chap. 38 (YJS, *10,* 159–60) and Sem, chap. 8 (YJS, *17,* 59–60).
30. Cf. PR 28:2 (YJS, *18, 2,* 555).

along the road, cried out: *Withhold not Thy peace, O God* (Ps. 83:2), Withhold not Thy peace, O God!

In reply, the holy spirit said to them: You are the world's greatest fools! When you worshiped idols on mountains and on hills, you did not ask, Who [is truly the God that] dwells[31] in the world? Now you say *Withhold not Thy peace, O God.* [Despite His reproach of them], the mercies of the Holy One then overflowed, and He chose for them [the peace of painless] death through cold—they enfolded themselves in their garments and died.

Nay more! For their sake, He came down from the upper heaven of heavens, from the place of His glory, greatness, kingship, splendor, holiness, and His holy name, and gave voice to a dirge for them, as is said, *The burden concerning the Valley of Vision. . . . Thou that hadst been full of uproar, a tumultuous city, a joyous town. . . . Now all thy rulers are fled together. . . . Therefore said I: "Look away from Me, I will weep bitterly"* (Isa. 22:1–4).

Accordingly, come and see how plentiful always are the mercies of the Holy One in behalf of Israel, for [off and on] all their days they had been idol worshipers, but no sooner did they resolve upon repentance, slight as it was, than He wept for them.

Incidentally, from His weeping over such as these you may infer that in any generation you will find righteous, faithful, and worthy men [for whom the Holy One grieves]. He strikes both hands together, clasps them over His heart, then folds His arms as He weeps over the righteous sometimes secretly, sometimes openly. Why does He weep over them secretly? Because it is unseemly for a lion to weep before a fox, unseemly for a Sage to weep before his disciple, unseemly for a king to weep before the least of his servants, unseemly for a householder to weep before a hired man,[32] as is said, *So that ye will not hear it, My soul shall weep in secret for your pride* (Jer. 13:17). What is implied by the phrase *for your pride?* That all the angels who stand before Him in heaven should not pride themselves, saying: What benefit to the Holy One that He gave the Torah to creatures of flesh-and-blood rather than to us? Such is the point of the words *for your pride.*

Another comment on the phrase: It implies that the peoples speaking the earth's seventy languages should not gloat, saying as God weeps: What benefit to the Holy One in that He gave Israel the Torah, etc.[33]

---

31. Leon Nemoy suggests that the author might have been thinking of the Arabic *dāra* (root *dwr*), "to encompass, to encircle."

32. Cf. ER, 87.

33. The angels wanted to have the Torah given to them, and the nations to whom it had been offered rejected it. See MTeh 8:2 (YJS, *13, 1,* 122–23) and PR 21:3 and 30:4 (YJS, *18, 1,* 417–18, and *2,* 597).

Another comment: The verse in hand, *My soul shall weep in secret (ibid.),* goes on to say, *Mine eye shall weep sore, and run down with tears because the Lord's flock is carried away captive.* But Scripture says elsewhere, *Let them make haste and take up a wailing for us, that our eyes may run down with tears, and our eyelids gush out with waters* (Jer. 9:17). Why *mine eye* in the former verse and *our eyes* in the latter? The answer—if one dare say such a thing—is that in comparison with other beings, no one feels such compassion for Israel as does the Holy One, who from the beginning intended His world for them, as is indicated by His saying *Let us make man in Our image, after Our likeness* (Gen. 1:26). [By *man* He meant Israel, for Israel in their worship of Him, their Creator, and not of His creation, alone deserved the designation of "man".][34] Hence *Mine eye* [alone, says the Holy One], *shall weep sore, and run down with tears because the Lord's flock is carried away captive* (Jer. 13:17).

In still another passage in Scripture, the Holy One is described as weeping for Israel and so set the example of weeping for Israel's generations [in the night: The Presence] *will continue to weep in the night, and her tears continue on her cheeks* (Lam. 1:2). But is it only in the night that Israel weep? Do they not also weep during the day? [By *night,* however, is meant the long night of exile which set in with R. 'Aḳiḇa's death, a death which appeared to mark the crushing of all hope for the restoration of the kingdom of Israel.][35] From the time when the decree was issued against R. 'Aḳiḇa and his companions, Israel's green branches were utterly broken,[36] [and hence God *will continue to weep*
ER, *p.* 155 *during the night*]. | By what parable may the point be made? By the parable of a mortal king whose children and wife had so offended him that he proceeded to set his hand against them and drove them out of his house. Then, year after year, he would go to the place whence he had driven them out, stretch out his full length on the ground, [and weep for them]. Were it not so set down in Scripture, it would have been illicit to say [of God that He acted] like a father [who, having driven his family away], cries out in longing, "My sons, my sons," or like a mother hen that clucks for her lost young, as is said, *For it is a day of trouble, and of treading down, and of perplexity by the Lord God of hosts in the Valley of Vision breaking down the walls (mĕḳarḳer ḳir) and crying at the mountains* (Isa. 22:5), [*mĕḳarḳer ḳir* being understood here as a form of *ḳrḳr,* "clucking like a hen"].

---

34. Since Jews worship God, they are told: You are called "men." See Ezek. 34:31. So Friedmann in n. 35.

35. The Babylonian exile in 586 B.C.E. lasted only seventy years, and Jerusalem, burned by Titus in 70 C.E., appeared to be free again in 132 C.E. under Bar Kokhba, one of whose strongest backers was R. 'Aḳiḇa.

36. See Friedmann's n. 36.

As Israel went into [the night] of exile, they went, every one of them, in silence,[37] [without weeping], as if unaware of [the cause of their exile]—their offense against God. But God came to them and said: My children, why do you remain silent? Why do you not weep? Is it not for the merit of the two tears that Esau wept before his father that I have come to show the graciousness of My sovereignty in Seir [a land where the rains of blessing never cease]?[38] Hence [*Throw off*] *the burden of silence* [*and weep*]. *My God calls me to remember Seir*[39] (Isa. 21:11).

Watchman, what of the night? Watchman, what of the night? (ibid.). Having said *Watchman, what of the night* once, why does the text repeat it? Because as Israel's well-being is associated with the day, so Israel's adversity is associated with the night. And since [the present exile] as well as the seventy years between the First Temple and the Second Temple are both referred to as night, the text says twice *What of the night.*[40]

Another comment: Having said *Watchman, what of the night* once, why does the text repeat it? <Because, [during the night of exile], the Holy One repeatedly looks for the man who truly has words of Torah within him, a man such as Hananiah, as Mishael, or Azariah, [through whose merit Israel were delivered from exile in Babylon].[41] Hence the words *Watchman, what of the night* are repeated.>

In this connection it is said: When a man obeys two or three commandments, he is given an angel to watch over him, as is said, *Behold, I send an angel before thee to keep thee because* [*thou hast kept to some*] *of the way* (Exod. 23:20). When a man has read the Five Books, the Prophets, and the Writings, he is given two angels to watch over him, as is said, *He will give His angels charge over thee, to keep thee because of all the ways thou hast kept* (Ps. 91:11). But when a man has read the Five Books, the Prophets, and the Writings, has recited Mishnah as well as Midrash of Hala<u>k</u>o<u>t</u> and 'Agga<u>d</u>o<u>t</u>, and has also put himself under the guidance of the Sages, the Holy One Himself watches over him. By what parable may the matter be illustrated? By the one of a mortal king who together with his son took the road into the wilderness. When they encountered intense heat, the father stationed himself against the sun

---

37. Reading not *nit̲'almu,* "vanished," but *nit̲'almu,* "were silent."

38. See above, ER, 125.

39. JV: *The burden of Dumah. One calleth unto me out of Seir.* But ER seems to take *Dumah* to mean "silence," and reads *'elay,* "unto me," as *'eli,* "my God."

40. [I suspect that the author interprets the two forms, the longer *lylh* and the shorter *lyl,* as referring to the shorter (Babylonian) exile and the longer (Roman) exile. L. N.]

41. The three were saved from the fiery furnace into which Nebuchadnezzar had cast them. See Dan. 3 and Schick.

and made shade for his son so that he would be protected from the torrid heat, as is said, *The Lord is thy keeper; the Lord is thy shade upon thy right hand* (Ps. 121:5).[42]

The Watchman said: "The morning cometh" (Isa. 21:12). The Holy One reassured Israel, saying: My children, did I not tell you beforehand
ER, *p.* 156 that even though you will build the Second Temple in distress | it will have to be destroyed because of your iniquities. Nevertheless, come and rejoice with Me in utter joy as I rejoice in you for ever and ever and ever, as is said, [Your experiences in exile are like the miraculous events in Egypt] *when fire kindled the hail as it melted*[43] (Isa. 64:1ff); [likewise, miraculously, the morning of your redemption is certain to come].[44]

And also the night (Isa. 21:12), namely, the years that you dwell in exile among the peoples of the world; the verse goes on to counsel, *If you would inquire* [*into Torah*], *keep inquiring: return, come (ibid.).* The fact is that understanding of the Torah is given only to one who has undergone distress for its sake, as the text goes on: *The pronouncement concerning Arab. In the thickets (ya'ar) in Arab* (Isa. 21:13). The word *Arab,* literally "desert land," stands here for those [among whom we are forced to live] who are uncircumcised *('Arel);*[45] and *ya'ar* signifies the distress *(ṣa'ar)*[46] we undergo. Hence *The pronouncement concerning* [*uncircumcised*] *Arab. . . . Unto him, distressed in such exile*[47] *. . . bring ye water* (Isa. 21:13–14)—[the water of Torah].

In relation to Israel's Father in heaven, with whom are they to be compared in this world? With one of the two servants of a mortal king to each of whom he gave two sticks of wood, saying to them: "Go get these sticks lighted and bring them back so that we can have a fire to cook by and to warm us." The one who was willing to suffer distress

---

42. Cf. above, ER, 100.

43. The seventh plague is described in the words *There was hail, and fire flashing continually amidst the hail* (Exod. 9:24). See PRKM 1:3, p. 6 (PRKS, pp. 9–10). JV: *When fire kindleth the brush-wood.*

44. Taken to be intimated in the next verse, which speaks of God's coming down and doing *tremendous things . . . whereof from of old men have not heard, nor perceived by the ear* (Isa. 64:2–3).

45. Here by a cipher (in which the *'alef,* first in its group of ten letters, is read as *kaf,* the next first in its group of ten letters, and so forth) the *beṯ* is read as *lameḏ,* so that *'rb* is taken as *'rl,* "uncircumcised." Being, as it were, uncircumcised, the land is deemed a desert where growth of spirit is difficult if not impossible.

46. The cipher (known as the Aṭbaḥ of R. Ḥiyya) in which the letters of the alphabet are arranged in groups of two, each group having the numerical value of ten, e.g., *'alef* (1) + *ṭeṯ* (9) = 10; *beṯ* (2) + *ḥeṯ* (8) = 10, etc.; or having the numerical value of one hundred, e.g., as here, *yoḏ* (10) + *ṣaḏe* (90) = 100. In this instance, *yoḏ,* the first letter of *ya'ar,* is by Aṭbaḥ changed into *ṣa'ar,* "distress." See B.Suk 52b, Soncino tr., p. 249, n. 12. ER presumably regards "thickets" in a desert as unlikely. Hence he resorts to the reading by cipher.

47. JV: *Unto him that is thirsty.* But cf. Ezek. 19:13, where "a dry and thirsty ground" is a metaphor for life in exile.

for the sake of the king brought the fire for him. The one who was not willing to suffer distress for the sake of the king did not bring the fire for him.[48]

In another comment on the relation between Israel and their King, a parable is told of a mortal king who sat on his throne with his servant ministering to him. When the king saw that the servant was in fear of him, he rose from his throne, took hold of him by the hand, and seated him in his presence.

[So also Israel plead: If we are Your children, have mercy upon us as a father has mercy (Ps. 103:13); if we are Your servants, our eyes are the eyes of servants unto their master (Ps. 123:2).] Thereupon the Holy One replies to Israel: My children, do the will of your children and your servants as eagerly as I do the will of My children and My servants, as is said, *Who is among you that feareth the Lord, let him heed the voice of his servant,* [*as I heed Mine*]. *Should a man believe himself to be walking in darkness, it is because he has no light* [*of Torah*]. *Let him trust in the name of the Lord, and rely upon his God* (Isa. 50:10).[49]

---

48. [In the wilderness this would involve a long and thirsty walk to find a human habitation. L. N.]

49. The interpolation at the beginning of the paragraph and the interpretation of Isa. 50:10 follow *MṢ.* JV: *Who is among you that feareth the Lord, that obeyeth the voice of His servant? Though he walketh in darkness, and hath no light, let him trust in the name of the Lord, and stay upon his God.*

CHAPTER (31) 29

God's punishment of the arrogant and His blessing of the humble through the six eras of the world's history

Summary

To earn the favor of God a man is to emulate Him in His quest for peace (ER, 156). Aaron was preeminently such a man, but he was also a humble one. In contrast to him, Ahithophel the Gilonite, though a Sage, had so much pride that because of it he was rooted out of the world. For choking back in hurt pride his utterance of the Halakah concerning the proper procedure for conveying the Ark, he was to die by being choked to death (ER, 157).

Others like him who were shameless, brazen, and proud were rooted out of the world: the generation of the flood, the men of the Tower of Babel, the people of Sodom, Sennacherib, Nebuchadnezzar (ER, 158), the people of the generation of the wilderness, and Saul, king of Israel. Because of its brazenness, the house of Israel itself was banished from its Land. Still, though Israel's bones be broken, their eyes plucked out, and blood run from their mouths to the ground, Israel, for ever faithful to God, will continue to proclaim His kingship over themselves.

Both idolatry and arrogance are spoken of in Scripture as "abomination." Humility in man is proper acknowledgment of God's power as Creator (ER, 159).

In His creation of the world, God took counsel of the Torah, and unlike mortal kings when they build palaces for themselves, He brought heaven and earth into being all at once.

The gradations of the two levels in God's "palace" are six: (1) the dwelling of the cherubim, (2) the dwelling of the *'ofannim,* (3) the dwelling of the ministering angels, (4) the place of the throne of glory, (5) the floor of sapphire, and (6) the dwelling of God in the uppermost heaven.

To correspond to the six gradations of the two levels of God's palace, six eras in the history of the world are reckoned: (1) the era of the creation of Torah, Gehenna, the Garden of Eden, the throne of glory, the name of the Messiah, the Temple, and the physical world, including man; (2) the era from Noah to the coming of Manasseh; (3) the era from the end of Manasseh's generation until the building of the Second Temple; (4) the era from the building of the Second Temple until its destruction and the years beyond; (5) the era of the days of the Messiah; and (6) the time-to-come (ER, 160).

It was Adam's sin in the first era that led to the expulsion from God's presence of the four principal creatures: man, wild animals, domestic animals, and fowl. When these four began to weep at their expulsion, God, to make it up to them, had their faces represented upon His heavenly chariot (ER, 161). Nevertheless, despite God's expulsion of man from the Garden of Eden, the inhabitants of the world kept provoking Him until He brought the flood upon them. When He did, He ceased from all work and went into mourning, asking Noah to do likewise.

During the second era, from the flood until the generation of Manasseh, God sent Prophets to admonish each generation for its wickedness (ER, 162) so that in the days of Manasseh the Prophets persuaded Manasseh the king and his people to throw away their idols and vow never to raise them again.

The third era from the end of the generation of Manasseh to the building of the Second Temple lasted until the year 3408 after the creation of the physical world. The fourth era began with the building of the Second Temple, the Temple which was to endure 420 years.

And now, more anxiously than a father who waits for his son, God waits for Israel to resolve upon repentance and then find among them men learned in all of Torah, thus making it possible for the Messiah to come in the fifth era of history.

Though God is so remote that neither mortals nor ministering angels can see Him—not even the creatures that carry His throne can see His glory—yet again and again during Israel's history, He has embraced Israel; again and again His hand has been stretched out over them against every foe. So, no matter what our capacity, we would still be unable to thank God enough and express sufficiently our gratitude to Him (ER, 163).

In the days of the Messiah, the righteous will be restored to the grace from which they were banished, and they will again enjoy the companionship of God and His hosts as did mankind in the first era before Adam's disobedience.

In the meantime God continues to act, as He has always acted, in mercy. Thus, though Adam was at first condemned to subsist like an animal on thorns and thistles, when he showed contrition, God relented and allowed him to eat bread. God went still further in His mercy by promising Adam resurrection after death.

His mercy is plainly evident in Torah's account of the world's creation, which begins not with the *'alef,* the alphabet's first letter, but with its second letter, the *beṯ,* which is the initial letter of *bĕraḵah,* "blessing." Indeed, to commemorate God's beginning of the world with *beṯ,* sign of God's mercy and blessing, a child learning the alphabet is taught to start with the letter *beṯ* followed by the letter *'alef,* the first letter of the word *'arur,* "cursed."

Ultimately, however, whether blessing or curse is to prevail in a man's life is determined by his deeds.

At some time in or after the days of the Messiah, in the sixth era, all those who rise to life again will go to the Land of Israel and never again return to the dust they came from (ER, 164). In the Land, the Holy One Himself will receive the righteous who will come before Him like children coming into the presence of their father, and like disciples coming into the presence of their teacher (ER, 165).

Chapter (31) 29

How does a man come to earn the favor of his Creator? By continually seeking to make peace in emulation of the Holy One, blessed be He, may His great name be blessed for ever and ever and ever, who seeks to make peace among the four hundred and ninety-six thousand myriads[1] of ministering angels who, standing before Him, say, *Holy, holy, holy* (Isa. 6:3) every day without fail from sunrise to sunset, and from sunset to sunrise say, *Blessed be the glory of the Lord wherever His place may* ER, *p.* 156 *cont'd*

1. Cf. above, ER, 34.

be (Ezek. 3:12).[2] He continually seeks to make peace among the nations speaking the seventy languages of the world; He continually seeks to
ER, *p.* 157 make peace among all the world's inhabitants | and among all His handiwork in the world He created, as is said, *In His heights*[3] *He makes peace* (Job 25:2). In emulation of Him, Aaron sought to make peace between Israel and their Father in heaven, between Israel and the Sages, between a sage and his fellow sage, between a man and his fellow man, between a husband and his wife. To Aaron, [as to God], apply the words *Say ye of the Righteous One that He is good* (Isa. 3:10), for He says, *Keep ye justice, and bring about reconciliation; My salvation will then come soon, and My deliverance be revealed* (Isa. 56:1). The Holy One, who examines the hearts and reins of men, said to Aaron: You continually sought to make peace between Israel and My great name.[4] Therefore, I will bring sons out of you, sons who will make atonement for the children of Israel each and every year and will invoke peace for them each and every day, by saying, *May the Lord bless thee,* etc. (Num. 6:24).

In this connection, it should be said that the man who seeks to make peace must also be a humble man, not an arrogant one such as was Ahithophel the Gilonite, a sage with Torah in him, who was nevertheless rooted out of the world because of his overweening pride.[5] To him apply the words *Woe unto the wicked! it shall be ill with him; for the work of his hands shall be done to him* (Isa. 3:11). In what way did his overweening pride first show itself? In his not speaking up to remind all Israel and David, when they were assembled *to bring up . . . the Ark of God* (2 Sam. 6:2; 1 Chron. 13:6) [to the house of David], that they had forgotten a Halakah requiring the Ark to be brought up on the shoulders of the sons of Kohath. Instead, all of them agreed that since the Ark had originally come up in a wagon from the field of the Philistines, so, too, it should come up in a wagon to the house of David, king of Israel. By His great name the Holy One had sworn, however, on the day in Egypt when for the sake of heaven, Amram [of the sons of Kohath] wed Jochebed his aunt [again],[6] that the Ark and the Torah

---

2. See PR 20:4 (YJS, *18, 1,* 407).

3. JV: *He maketh peace in His high places.* [How did the author get the equation: high places, heights = creatures? The only answer I can think of is that he equated *marom* with *tĕrumah,* as a derivative of *herim (hif'il* of *rwm),* "something held up high" out of something else = something manufactured (in the original sense *manu factus,* handmade) out of shapeless original materials. L. N.]

4. Cf. above, ER, 63.

5. His pride was hurt by his being passed over when David, shortly after ascending the throne, appointed on a single day no less than ninety thousand functionaries (P.Sanh 10:2, p. 29a). Because David chose only pious men, he passed over Ahithophel who was learned but not pious (Ginzberg, *Legends, 4,* 95, and *6,* 257–58).

6. He did so with great display in order that Israel should see what he was doing and bring back their own wives (PR 43:4 [YJS, *18, 2,* 760]). The implication: the law that only sons of Kohath are to bear the Ark on their shoulders became as widely known as Amram's remarriage.

with it would be taken up by Amram, indeed entrusted to his arm, as is said, *But unto the sons of Kohath he gave nothing,*[7] *because the service of the holy things belonged unto them; they bore them upon their shoulders* (Num. 7:9). Hence, when Israel, [unaware of their transgression of the Halak̲ah], took the Ark and loaded it upon a wagon, the Ark [lifted itself above the wagon and] suspended itself between earth and heaven, neither rising nor falling. [Fearful of its falling, however], Uzzah, who was standing nearby, put forth his hand and took hold of the Ark.

In that instant the transgressors in Israel said: Had not Uzzah put forth his hand and taken hold of the Ark, it could have fallen to the ground. But when Uzzah instantly died [because of his presumption in touching the Ark], and his hand was pulled away from it, the transgression of the Halak̲ah came to be recognized by all Israel, for the Ark still remained suspended between earth and heaven, neither rising nor falling.

Blessed be the Preserver of the world, blessed be He in whose presence no one is favored more than another. Since Ahithophel the Gilonite choked back the Halak̲ah in his throat and did not utter it to the multitude, eventually he was to die by being choked to death, which is one of the four kinds of death penalty left to the discretion of the court, as is said, *When Ahithophel saw that his plot* [*against David*] *had not been carried out . . . he got him home . . . he instructed his household, and was strangled*[8] (2 Sam. 17:23). What instructions did he give his household? According to some, he said: Never engage in civil strife. According to others: Rebel not against the dynasty of David.[9]

When David heard of these events, he came [and humbling himself before the Presence] prostrated himself to his full length on the ground and said: My Father in heaven, may Your great name be blessed for ever and ever and ever! May You have contentment in Israel wherever they dwell! For You magnified us, hallowed us, praised us, exalted us, and from world's end to world's end bound us with a <[great] knot> to words of Torah,[10] as is said, *Thou, O Lord God didst magnify*[11] *us* (2 Sam. 7:22). [Yet despite the favor You have shown us, we still do] such things as were done by Doeg the Edomite[12] and

---

7. No wagons in which to carry the Ark, the conveying of which was to be, as stated, the charge of the sons of Kohath.

8. He who in urgent cases keeps vital knowledge to himself and does not impart it to others is punished by strangulation. See V. Aptowitzer, "Observations on the Criminal Law of the Jews," *JQR, 15* (1924–25), 65–68.

9. See Ginzberg, *Legends, 4,* 94–97.

10. The word *Yśr'l,* "Israel," may be taken as an acronym for *yeš šiššim ribbo' o'tiyyot̲ lat-Torah,* "The Torah has six hundred thousand letters." Accordingly, each of the six hundred thousand in Israel was bound to one of Torah's six hundred thousand letters. So *YY.*

11. JV: *Thou art great, O Lord God.*

12. Doeg had been president of the Sanhedrin and the greatest scholar of his age. See Ginzberg, *Legends, 4,* 74–77.

ER, *p.* 158 Ahithophel the Gilonite, things that are not right in Your eyes. | And it is certain that what befell these two because of their actions will befall[13] any one at all who displays an overweening pride in his actions —he will be rooted out of the world.

Rooted out of the world were the men of the generation of the flood because shamelessness dwelt within them. *They said unto God: Depart from us; for we desire not the knowledge of Thy ways* (Job 21:14). What did they use to do? They would remove their garments, discard them upon the ground, and walk about naked in the marketplace, as is said, *They go about naked without clothing*[14] (Job 24:10). Hence, the Holy One had them float like hollow gourds over the face of the waters,[15] as is said, *He will be light upon the face of the waters* (Job 24:18). Such men as these are adjured, *Be ye afraid of the sword, for wrathful are the punishments of the sword, that ye may know that there is punishment (šaddun)* (Job 19:29). Read here not *šaddun* but *šed-din,* "that there is judgment" from above.

Rooted out of the world were the men of the Tower of Babel because shamelessness dwelt within them. Of them Scripture says, *The whole earth was of one language . . . and they said: Come . . . let us build us a tower, with its top in heaven* (Gen. 11:1, 4).[16]

[In giving all mankind one and the same language], God had extended great kindness to them.[17] Consider, for example, a man who travels from country to country. If he hears someone speaking the same language, he gains reassurance and self-assurance. [From such self-assurance, however, grew the arrogance of] the generation of the Tower of Babel who finally said: *Come, let us build us a city, and a tower, with its top in heaven* (Gen. 11:4), their intention being rebellion against the Holy One. As they said *Come . . . let us build* [*up*], the Holy One responded with *Come,*[18] [*let us go down*] (Gen. 11:7). As they said *Come; let us build us a city,* etc. (Gen. 11:4), so did the Holy One come down from the upper heaven of heavens and scattered them in confusion to the four corners of the earth. *Let us go down,* He said, *and . . . confound their language. . . . So the Lord scattered them abroad. Therefore was the name of the city called Babel; because the Lord did there confound (balal) the language of all the earth* (Gen. 11:7–9).

---

13. Literally, " 'And not only this'—it is said—'but will befall,' " etc.

14. *A vile nation* (Deut. 32:21) is one whose people "go naked in the streets, there being nothing more objectionable or abominable to Him who is present everywhere" (B.Yeb 63b).

15. Cf. Sif Deut. 311 (ed. Finkelstein [Breslau, 1936–39], p. 351) and B.Sanh 108a.

16. The generation of the Tower of Babel said, "He has no right to choose the celestial spheres for Himself and assign the terrestrial world to us!" (Gen. Rabbah 38:6).

17. So interpreted in *Torah šělemah, 2,* 508.

18. A deliberate put-down of brazen rebels.

Rooted out of the world were the people of Sodom because shamelessness dwelt within them, as is said, *Now the men of Sodom were wicked and sinners against the Lord exceedingly* (Gen. 13:13):[19] they were *wicked* in larceny; *sinners* in unchastity; <*against the Lord*> as profaners of His name; *exceedingly,* in that they sinned deliberately. Thus, when Lot offered them natural sexual intercourse with his own daughters [in order to divert them from unnatural intercourse with his male visitors], they said, *Stand back*[20] (Gen. 19:9); but when he argued with them against such unnatural intercourse with his visitors, they mocked him saying, *This one fellow came in to sojourn, and he will needs play the judge (ibid.).*[21]

Rooted out of the world was Sennacherib because brazenness dwelt within him: *Who are they,* he said, *among all the gods of the countries, that have delivered their country out of my hand, that the Lord should deliver Jerusalem out of my hand?* (2 Kings 18:35). But what does Scripture say befell him and his host? *And it came to pass that night, that the angel of the Lord went forth, and smote in the camp of the Assyrians a hundred fourscore and five thousand* (2 Kings 19:3), all of them kings who wore crowns upon their heads.[22]

Rooted out of the world was Nebuchadnezzar because brazenness dwelt within him. *Thou saidst in thy heart,* he was told, *"I will ascend unto heaven, above the stars of God will I exalt my throne"* (Isa. 14:13). But what did Scripture tell him his fate was to be? *Thou shalt be brought down to the nether world* (Isa. 14:15). Incidentally, it is said of the wicked Nebuchadnezzar that he was exceedingly short of stature,[23] so that as he went from province to province the people in each city, who gathered and went out to meet him, laughed among themselves, saying: Is this [dwarf] to rule from world's end to world's end? *They who behold you, stare . . .* [*and ask*], *"Is this the man who shook the earth?"* (Isa. 14:16).

Rooted out of the world was Pharaoh because brazenness dwelt in him, for he said, *Who is the Lord that I should hearken unto His voice?* (Exod. 5:2).

| Because brazenness dwelt within the people of the generation in the wilderness, they died before they could come into the Land. For **ER, *p.* 159**

19. The words "Another comment," which follow, are omitted, as in V.

20. [The author accentuates the negative—the Sodomites initially asked only for Lot's guests, bad enough, but only one count in their indictment. When Lot self-sacrificingly offered them his own daughters, they grinned wolfishly and said, "Goody, goody, produce the [women]; but we'll have your guests also just the same!" thus doubling the counts in the indictment. . . . Hence I think the author interpreted *gĕš hal'ah* not as *stand back!* but as *Lead (them = [Lot's daughters] out to us)!* In other words, he equated the *qal nāgăš* with the *hif'il higgîš,* so that *gĕš* = *haggĕš.* L. N.]

21. See Louis Ginzberg in *OT,* p. 298, n. 125.

22. Cf. above, ER, 44–45.

23. He is described as *the lowest of men* (Dan. 4:14). See PR 31:4 (YJS, *18, 2,* 607).

of them it is said, *The people spoke against God, and against Moses,* etc. (Num. 21:5) and indeed had spoken in the same rebellious way on four and five preceding occasions.[24]

Because brazenness dwelt in Saul, king of Israel, he was slain and his royal line was extirpated. When Samuel asked, *What meaneth then this bleating of the sheep in mine ears, and the lowing of the oxen which I hear?* Saul replied, *"They have brought them from the Amalekites; for the people spared the best of the sheep and of the oxen, to sacrifice unto the Lord thy God"* (1 Sam. 15:14–15). By what parable may the matter be illustrated? By the parable of a mortal king who said to his son: "Fence in this field. Hoe this field. Water this field." The son fenced in part of the field, but did not fence in all of it. He hoed part of it, but did not hoe all of it. He watered part of it, but did not water all of it. When the father came, he asked his son, "My son, did you do all I commanded you to do?" The son replied, "If I did not accomplish all you commanded, you should have anticipated that I might not, and therefore should not have asked so much of me." Just as this son tried to brazen out his failure to his father, so *Saul said* [*brazenly*] *unto Samuel: "Yea, I have hearkened to the voice of the Lord, and have gone the way which the Lord sent me"* (1 Sam. 15:20). [But, in fact, in sparing the sheep and the oxen of the Amalekites, Saul had gone against the express command of the King of kings to *utterly destroy all that they have, and spare them not* (1 Sam. 15:3).]

Nay, Saul was all the more at fault! For thereafter in his heart, he cherished hostility and vengefulness against Israel wherever they dwelt.[25] What he had been commanded to do, he did not do, as when he was told, *Now go and smite Amalek, and utterly destroy all that they have (ibid.).* What he had not been commanded to do, he did for he slew [all the people and all the animals of] Nob, the city of priests (1 Sam. 21–22). Moreover, he disregarded the regulations concerning marriage, for *he had given Michal his daughter, David's wife, to Palti the son of Laish* (1 Sam. 25:44). He practiced divination through ghosts and familiar spirits (1 Sam. 28:7) and was guilty of many other great abominations in Israel. Therefore he was slain and his royal line was extirpated.

Because brazenness dwelt within "the house of Israel—may I make atonement for them" (Neg̱ 2:1) wherever they dwell!—they were banished from their Land.

---

24. ER apparently refers here to the ten trials whereby the children of Israel tried God; this one, particularly offensive in its brazenness, meant to be a kind of climax (see Num. 14:22 and Aḇ 5:4; so Haida). Cf. above, ER 18, 19, and 33.

Why "four and five" instead of "nine" is not clear.

25. He charged that even the people of Benjamin—his own Tribe—were all conspiring against him (1 Sam. 22:7–8). For a different view of Saul, see MTeh 7:2 (YJS, *13, 1,* 101–3).

Ezekiel the son of Buzi was asked, "If a priest buys a slave, may the slave eat of heave offering received by his master?" Ezekiel replied, "He may eat of it."[26] "If his master sells him to others, may he eat of such produce?" Ezekiel replied, "He may not eat of it." Then his questioners said: "We once lived in the Lord's own Holy city and we worshiped Him in His [Holy] place. Now that we are exiled among the peoples of the earth [and are slaves to others], *Let us be as the nations, as the families of heathen countries, to serve idols of wood and stone* [*and not Him*]" (Ezek. 20:32). Ezekiel replied: "Even when your bones are broken, your eyes plucked out, your blood running down from your mouth to the ground, you will continue to proclaim His kingship over you, for you have accepted Him from the beginning, saying, *All that the Lord hath spoken, we will do and obey* (Exod. 24:7); and He will continue to proclaim His kingship over you, as is said, *The Lord hath avouched thee this day to be His treasure*" (Deut. 26:18).

[Not you, but He alone knows your future], for, as Scripture says, *That which cometh into your minds will be, will not be*[27] (Ezek. 20:32). Blessed be the Preserver of the world, blessed be He in whose presence no one is favored more than another. If the verse says *will be,* why does it go on to say *will not be?* And if it says *will not be,* why does it begin by saying *will be?* It implies that when Israel say, "We will be like the nations, as the families of heathen countries," what they say *will not be.*[28] But when Israel said, "Nebuchadnezzar will not come to the Land," it was Scripture's prediction, *will be,* [that turned out to be true].

The sum of the matter is that as the term "abomination" is used of idolatry, so the term "abomination" is also used of arrogance. The term "abomination" is used of idolatry in the verse *Thou shalt not bring an abomination into thy house* (Deut. 7:27); and the term "abomination" is used of arrogance in the verse *Every one that is proud of heart is an abomination to the Lord* (Prov. 16:5). Indeed, the Holy One, to whom everything belongs, everything being the work of His hands, cannot endure the arrogant, as is said, *Whoso is haughty of eye and proud of heart, him will I not suffer* (Ps. 101:5).[29]

| Scripture says, *With whom took He counsel, and who instructed Him,* etc? (Isa. 40:14). When He created the world, whence did He take counsel? He took counsel only of the Torah, for the Torah says, *Then I was by Him as a nursling ('amon)* (Prov. 8:30). Read not *'amon,* but *'uman,* meaning "overall design"—I was in His mind like the overall design of a craftsman, a craftsman who is capable of realizing his design [all at once. In contrast to the unique craftsmanship of the King of **ER,** ***p.*** **160**

---

26. See Lev. 22:10–11 and Rashi *ad loc.*
27. JV: *And that which cometh into your mind shall not be at all.* But the commentator construes *hayo lo' tihyeh* literally "will be, will not be."
28. Cf. Sif Num. 115 (ed. Horovitz [Frankfurt am Main, 1917], p. 128).
29. Cf. B.Soṭ 4b.

kings], consider how a king of flesh-and-blood builds a palace worthy of his name. He has to bring foremen[30] and have the beams put up. Then he has to bring a scroll and ink and <have designed> a throne room worthy of his name, an upper sleeping chamber worthy of his name, as well as a privy worthy of his name, and only then does he build. But the [palace of the King of kings, the] work of heaven and earth, was built all at once, as is said, *When I call unto them, they stand up together* (Isa. 48:13).

And what was the plan by which the Holy One brought His palace into existence? He brought it into existence on two levels: on the first level were two thousand myriads of cherubim, two thousand myriads of *'ofannim,*[31] and two thousand myriads of ministering angels; above these, [on the second level], was the throne of glory, above it was stone, all of sapphire, and above them all reigned the Holy One, dwelling in the uppermost heaven. Were not such a thing written in Scripture, it would have been improper to say it, but we are told: *Above the firmament that was over their heads was the likeness of a throne, as the appearance of a sapphire stone; and upon the likeness of the throne was a likeness as the appearance of a man upon it above* (Ezek. 1:26).

[As the gradations of the two levels in God's palace are six, so there are six eras in the history of the world. In the first era], early in creation, He made six special things—the Torah, Gehenna, the Garden of Eden, the throne of glory, the name of the Messiah, and the Temple —[before proceeding to His creation of the physical world and all the work of His hands in it, including man; this era ended with the flood. The second era began with Noah and ended with the coming of Manasseh and his generation; the third extended from the end of Manasseh's generation to the building of the Second Temple; the fourth began with the building of the Second Temple and lasted until its destruction and the days since; the fifth will be composed of the days of the Messiah; and the sixth of the time-to-come].[32]

The proof that Torah was created at the beginning? Torah's saying *The Lord made me as the beginning of His way*[33] (Prov. 8:22). And Gehenna? *Tophet was ordained at a time before [the creation of the physical world]*[34] (Isa. 30:33). By *Tophet* is meant Gehenna whose bastion was

---

30. *Parašin* from the Greek *ephoros.* See B.Shab 154a. [*'Ephoros* is tempting, but an ephor in ancient Greece was an "overseer" (not a foreman) as a magistrate, not as a supervisor *(episkopos)* of craftsmen. I think *ḳarašin,* "carpenters, makers of wooden boards," suits the context much better. Again the word may be a scribal corruption. L. N.]

31. Literally, "wheels, orbs." Hence possibly "angels in charge of the spheres."

32. Louis Ginzberg who suggests seven eras likewise divides the last into two periods—the days of the Messiah and the time-to-come (*TSE,* p. 103, n. 130).

33. The speaker in this verse is wisdom—Torah.

34. JV: *of old;* but figuratively *'eṯmol* means "formerly." Hence *before,* etc.

established before God made all other things [in the physical world including man. Only on the sixth day of creation following Adam's offense] did the Holy One make [fire and ice dwell in] Gehenna,[35] and therefore proceeded to praise all the work of His hands, as is said, "And God saw everything that He had made, and behold, it was very good"[36] (Gen. 1:31). Of Tophet, Isaiah goes on to say, *Yea, for the king it is prepared* (Isa. 30:33), *the king* standing here for the Impulse to evil, as in the verse "Better is a poor and wise child than an old and foolish king" (Eccles. 4:13), where "child" stands for the Impulse to good and "king" stands for the Impulse to evil.[37]

(An incidental comment: <"Better is a poor and wise child">, such as was R. 'Aḳiḇa, [poor in misdeeds like a child], in contrast to "an old and foolish king," such as wicked Rufus, [a veteran in wickedness and vanity]).[38]

Tophet, as Isaiah goes on to describe it, is *deep and large* (Isa. 30:33), deep enough and wide enough to accommodate the full measure of the angel of death. *The pile [of Gehenna] being fire and much wood, the breath of the Lord, like a stream of brimstone will kindle it (ibid.)* [and eventually consume the angel of death].

[Of God's other special creations, what does Scripture say?] The Garden of Eden: *Of yore,* [39] *the Lord God planted a Garden of Eden* (Gen. 2:8). The throne of glory: *Thy throne is established of old* (Ps. 93:2). The name of the Messiah: *His name was made to sprout before the sun*[40] (Ps. 72:17). The Sanctuary: *A glorious high throne from the beginning is the place of our Sanctuary* (Jer. 17:12).[41]

| [After these special creations], simultaneously God made both ER, *p.* 161
heaven and earth in their entirety and then gave them permanent form by shaping them. He gave them their finishing touch by hammering them out; thereby He made the earth fit to dwell in while He stretched out the sky above it. Where is the proof that He gave them their permanent form by shaping them? The verse *The heaven and the earth got their permanent shaping*[42] (Gen. 2:1). And the proof that He gave them their finishing touch by hammering them out? The verse *Yea, My hand hath laid the foundation of the earth, and My right hand hath hammered*

---

35. See above, ER, 3.

36. Out of fear of Gehenna, mankind will obey the commandments and thus preserve the world. So Haida. Or: The wicked, purged in Gehenna, will remain in life and receive reward for the good deeds they did. So Landau.

37. "Why is the Impulse to evil called 'king?' Because all parts of the body heed it." Cf. MTeh 9:5 (YJS, *13, 1,* 135).

38. In an argument R. 'Aḳiḇa worsted Tineius Rufus, then governor of Judea. See PR 23:8 (YJS, *18, 1,* 486–89).

39. *Miḳḳeḏem;* JV: *eastward.*

40. Cf. B.Sanh 98b.

41. Cf. Gen. Rabbah 1:4; B.Neḏ 49b; and other parallels.

42. JV: *The heaven and the earth were finished.*

out the heavens (Isa. 48:13). And the proof that He made the earth fit to dwell in while He stretched out the sky above it? The verse *It is He . . . that stretched out the heavens as a curtain, and spread them out as a tent to dwell in* (Isa. 40:22).[43]

As for the angelic presences, [the myriads of cherubim, *'ofannim,* and ministering angels],[44] they were like those who eat and <drink>, and thus sated, greatly rejoice. It follows logically then that if they who stand outside [the throne of glory] and do no more than behold the Presence within, rejoice as though they had eaten and drunk and thus sated greatly rejoice, how much more and more joy awaits those who enter into [the very radiance of] His throne of glory![45]

After the Holy One created the world, [and Adam had sinned], He proceeded to press [against the four chief creatures of His making] until He put them out of His immediate presence. Thereupon they cried, wailed, and howled, weeping sorely, and said to Him: Master of the universe, why did You put us out of the good estate [You made for us]? Why did You put us out of the contentment of our estate?

Whereat the Holy One set in His throne of glory a representation of each of the four principal kinds of creatures in His world: the sons of man were represented by the face of a man; the beasts were represented by the face of a lion; the cattle were represented by the face of an ox; the fowl were represented by the face of an eagle. "By figuring the faces of these creatures on My chariot, I will have made compensation to them [for My expulsion of them]," said God. "At the same time I will have made compensation to the world which I created,[46] for the face of a man figured on the heavenly chariot, [as described in Ezek. 1:10], is My compensation to all human beings on earth [for their being excluded from sight of My throne of glory]; <the face of the lion figured on the heavenly chariot [is My compensation] to all the beasts of the earth>; the face of the ox figured on the heavenly chariot [is My compensation] to all cattle on the earth; the face of the eagle figured

---

43. In a private communication, Professor Jonas C. Greenfield of the Hebrew University elucidated the preceding paragraph.

44. See above, ER, 160.

45. "Perhaps another way of describing entrance into the seventh *hekal,* 'heavenly palace,' where the throne of glory stands." A private communication from Professor Gershom Scholem of the Hebrew University.

46. [What disquiets me is that *naṭalti śĕk̲ari* is past (*not:* future) tense and means "I have (*not:* will) TAKEN (*not:* MADE) compensation." To the best of my judgment the entire phrase *tĕnu śĕk̲aran lĕ-ḥayyot̲ 'imraṭi, naṭalti śĕk̲ari bĕ-'olami šeb-bar'aṭi* is incongruous in its context and disturbs the logic of the narrative—it should be taken out as possibly a reader's marginal gloss. Once this is done, the thread of thought makes sense: ". . . the face of an eagle. The face of a man figured on the heavenly chariot . . . is My compensation to all human beings," etc. Having their coats of arms on the *merkab̲ah* is a signal honor, conditioned on each species minding its p's and q's—if they misbehave, their arms are removed. By the way, the interpolation is a rhymed couplet, which adds to its probability of being an extraneous insertion. L. N.]

on the heavenly chariot [is My compensation] to all fowl on the earth." This arrangement for compensation God wrote down and sealed [in secrecy until its details were disclosed by Ezekiel]. After Israel had sinned in the matter of the golden calf, however, He went and replaced the ox with a cherub, as is said, *And every one had four faces: the first face was the face of the cherub, and the second face was the face of a man, and the third the face of a lion, and the fourth the face of an eagle* (Ezek. 10:14).[47] And *Over the heads of these living creatures there was the likeness of a firmament, like the color of the terrible ice,* etc. (Ezek. 1:22)—like the ice upon the mighty mountains, [with the firmament] *stretched forth over their heads above (ibid.).*

| [In connection with the imparting of the secret lore of the chariot], the Sages taught: If you see a man whose eyelids[48] are fair and whose eyes are light, know that he is wicked and sinful before our God, [and therefore the secrets of the chariot are not to be imparted to him].[49] **ER,** ***p.*** **162**

[After the creation of God's palace, there came during the first era in the history of the world, the creation of the six special things, the creation of the physical world—including man—and all it contained.] From the time it was created until the flood, there were one thousand six hundred and fifty-six years, and during this time all the inhabitants of the world kept provoking God until He brought the flood upon them.[50] Once He brought the flood upon them, He ceased reading Scripture, reciting Mishnah, and doing any kind of work. But had He been doing any work from the time He created the world until the hour He brought the flood upon it? Yes, He used to sit on His throne of glory, and a third of the day read Scripture and recite Mishnah, a third of the day would pass judgment, and a third of the day would accord mercy, feeding, sustaining, and providing for the entire world and for all the work of His hands in the world He created.[51] But when He brought the flood to the world, He stopped reading Scripture, reciting Mishnah, and doing any kind of work. And that time of cessation from all His work was the measure of His mourning. When Noah came into the world, [and, unlike his fellow men, was obedient to God's will], the Holy One was to say to him, *Come thou and all thy house into the ark*

---

47. Earlier in Ezek. 1:10 the faces are given as man, lion, ox, and eagle. Cf. B. Ḥaḡ 13b.

48. Emending *dĕ-šaḇiṭ,* "shooting star" or "planet shebit," to *dškynw,* "eyelids," as in V. So Professor Saul Lieberman, *JQR, 36* (1946), 323–24. The reference was provided by Professor Gershom Scholem in a private communication.

49. See Ḥaḡ 2:1. In a private communication Chancellor Louis Finkelstein elucidated the relevance of this passage.

50. During this era God had been patient for a long time, but finally concluded that mankind had to be destroyed.

51. See above, ER, 130.

(Gen. 7:1), but *thou and thy sons* (Gen. 6:18) by yourselves, and *thy wife and thy sons' wives (ibid.)* by themselves, [thus restraining them from marital intercourse]. When Noah was about to leave the ark, the Holy One said to him, "Go forth from the ark," thus permitting them to resume marital intercourse, for Scripture says, *Go forth from the ark, thou, and thy wife, and thy sons, and thy sons' wives* WITH THEE[52] (Gen. 8:16).

[As the flood was coming to its end], the ministering angels [again, as at the creation of Adam], took counsel and banded together in a protest right to the face of the Holy One. [As they had done], when He created Adam, they again asked: Master of the universe, *What is man, that thou art mindful of him . . . that Thou shouldst make him have dominion over . . . the beasts of the field, the fowl of the air, and the fish of the sea?* (Ps. 8:5–9). And now again the Holy One replied to the ministering angels: Set your eyes upon the chariot and let the sight of it be enough for you. Even if mankind displays to Me only one of the four qualities which I had represented by the four faces figured on My throne of glory, I have already decreed in mankind's behalf that they shall have the use of this world.

The second era lasted from the flood until the generation of Manasseh. [In this era God sent Prophets to Israel to warn each generation of its wickedness, in the hope of bringing its people to right conduct.] Concerning the generation of Manasseh, the following parable is told: A king summoned all the servants in his household, provided each of them with a shield, and then went out at the head of them to a field. As they all went along, they came upon a man hiding in a cleft in a rock.[53] They took him by the feet and pulled him out of the rock. His face was as pale as though he had been overcome by the heat of the sun or by a blow from a sword.[54] So they blew into his face and rubbed his nose to bring him to. But once he came to, he began to
ER, *p.* 163 rebuke them | and kept on rebuking them until they threw to the ground the shields they had been holding, saying, "From the place these shields fell, they shall never be lifted up again."[55]

---

52. Mourners are prohibited to indulge in sexual intercourse. See Šulḥan ʿaruḵ, Yoreh deʿah, 383.

53. Cf. Exod. 33:21–22; B.Meḡ 19a; and PR 4:2 (YJS, *18, 1,* 80).

54. In keeping with Friedmann's suggestion (n. 47) *yḥrw,* "were kindled, grew hot" is read *yḥwwrw,* "wax pale"; and *ḥwrbwṯ* is construed in a dual sense, "heat of the sun" as well as "blow by a sword."

55. [I cannot agree with the translation of what precedes. . . . The meaning is that they kept on blowing "until the matter became too long for them (for any hope of reviving him). When it did so become, they threw down their shields and said, From the place where such as he had fallen, they cannot rise, as is said, *And men shall go into the caves of the rocks, and into the holes of the earth,* etc., *(therefore) cease ye from (trying to resuscitate) man,* etc. (Isa. 2:19–22)."

The next two paragraphs should be crossed out, as they are not in the Hebrew. The author's purpose was to elucidate the passage in Isaiah, in the sense that on the day of

The parable turns on the following verses from Isaiah: *Men shall go into the caves of the rocks and into the holes of the earth from before the terror of the Lord, and from the glory of His majesty when He ariseth to shake mightily the earth. In that day a man shall cast away his idols of silver, and his idols of gold* (Isa. 2:19–20).

[In the light of these verses, the parable is to be understood as follows: Manasseh the king provided the people of his generation with idols of silver and gold to shield them, as he thought, in their iniquity, as is said, *Manasseh king of Judah hath done these abominations . . . and hath made Judah also to sin with his idols* (2 Kings 21:11). On one occasion, however, there was discovered to Manasseh and his people a man hiding in a cleft in a rock, a prophet of the Lord so stricken with awe of Him that he was in a swoon. Brought back to his senses, he saw that Manasseh and his people trusted in idols of silver and gold to shield them in their iniquity and he began to rebuke them and continued rebuking them, until in fear of the earthshaking wrath of the Lord, they threw down their idols vowing never to raise them up again.]

The third era extended from the end of the generation of Manasseh to the building of the Second Temple, three thousand four hundred and eight years having elapsed since the creation of the physical world.[56]

[The fourth era began with the destruction of the Second Temple]; from the time it was built until it was destroyed four hundred and twenty years have elapsed,[57] and from the time it was destroyed until the present day, nine hundred years have elapsed.[58]

My Father in heaven, may Your name be blessed, etc., for You sit and wait until the days of the Messiah come to Israel when You will find among them men learned in Scripture, men learned in Mishnah, men well-versed in the give-and-take [of discussion of Torah]. And You will then be able to say to the angels who stand with You on high: At the beginning of the world did you not say to Me: *How little is man to be accounted?* (Isa. 2:22). Behold now among Israel men learned in Scripture, men learned in Mishnah, men well-versed in the give-and-take [of discussion of Torah]. I ask heaven and earth to witness in My behalf that I sit and wait more anxiously than a father for his son, than a woman for her daughter, for Israel to resolve upon repentance and for My words to be fulfilled.

The two ranks [of angels] that stand before Him, every day con-

---

wrath, the *dies irae,* even hiding in rock-holes won't save the sinner. This he has done. L. N.]

56. The common era equivalent of A.M. 3408 is 515 B.C.E.

57. The First Temple stood 410 years. See above, ER, chap. 4, n. 28.

58. A.M. 3408 + 420 + 900 = A.M. 4728 = 968 C.E. Cf. above, ER, chap. 1, n. 1.

tinually hallowing His great name from sunrise to sunset, say, *Holy, holy, holy,* and from sunset to sunrise, say, *Praised be the glory of the Lord wherever His place may be* (Ezek. 3:12). The repetition of *Holy* three times implies that mortals cannot see Him, that ministering angels cannot see Him, and that even the creatures that carry His throne cannot see His glory.

"The house of Israel—may I make atonement for them" (Neḡ 2:1) wherever they dwell! During the forty years from the time Israel left Egypt until Israel came into the Land, how many times did the Holy One take them into His arms, hold them close, and kiss them! During the next four hundred and forty years before the First Temple was built, His hand was stretched out over them against every adversary and foe. During the following four hundred and ten years from the time the First Temple was built until it was destroyed, how many times did He take them into His arms, hold them close, and kiss them! During the seventy years after the First Temple was destroyed and before the Second Temple built, His hand was stretched out over them against every adversary and foe. During the four hundred and twenty years from the time the Second Temple was built until it was destroyed, His hand was stretched out over them against every adversary and foe. During the final nine hundred years from the time the Second Temple was destroyed until the present moment how many times did He take them into His arms, hold them close, and kiss them!

So, if from the present moment on, we and our sons and daughters were to rise up and were our mouths as deep as the sea and our tongues able to roar like its waves and our lips as wide as the firmament, we would be unable to thank You enough and to express our gratitude to You, O Lord our God.

ER, ***p.*** **164** | In the time-to-come, [the fifth era of history], what semblance of joy will the Holy One bestow upon the persons of the righteous? [It will resemble the joy of the angels in His companionship when at the beginning of time He brought them into existence] on the first level of God's palace.[59] By what parable may the comparison be understood? By the parable of a mortal king who was accompanied by [pack] horses, by soldiers on foot, and soldiers on horseback, <so that he would be rightly attended among those he came to live with>. When his servants and the members of his household learned [what the king's regimen was to be], they, too, came with numerous [pack] horses, with soldiers both on foot and on horseback in the hope that the king would also have them dwell with him and his retinue.

[But enjoyment of the companionship of God and His retinue, the hosts of angels, was denied to mankind, His servants, when, because

---

59. See above, ER, 160.

of Adam's sin],[60] *He drove out the man* (Gen. 3:24). [Only in the time-to-come will such enjoyment as He originally intended be bestowed upon man.]

Why does not Scripture tell us, "He drove out the cattle, He drove out the beasts, He drove out the fowl?" I take heaven and earth to witness that cattle, beasts, and fowl are not called upon to practice circumcision, to read Scripture, and to recite Mishnah. It was up to mankind alone to act in obedience to God's will. [And when mankind failed], *He drove out the man.* Because of man's disobedience, Scripture says in an earlier verse, *Thorns and thistles shall it* [*the ground*] *bring forth to thee* [*for food*] (Gen. 3:18). When the Holy One said this to Adam, all of Adam's limbs trembled.[61] Thereupon God said out of pity for him: Because your limbs trembled at My verdict, I will allow you to eat bread, as is said, *Because of the trembling of your countenance you will eat bread*[62] (Gen. 3:19).

[God went even further in His mercy, for] the passage goes on to quote Him as saying to Adam: *Dust thou art, and to dust shalt thou return (ibid.).* Note that He did not say "go" but *return.* Thus there is in Torah a hint <of the resurrection of the dead>, for the verse just quoted is to be read *Dust thou art and in dust* [*wilt lie, yet*] *shalt thou return.*

In what respect is the letter *beṯ,* [another sign of God's mercy], distinguished from the other twenty-two letters of the alphabet? Because it is the first letter of the first word in Torah's account of the Holy One's creation of the world: *Bĕr'ešiṯ (Beginning) His handiwork, God created,* etc. (Gen. 1:1). In normal word order would not the verse have read *God created the world in the beginning (bĕr'ešiṯ),* [instead of *Beginning His handiwork, God created,* etc.]? Hence, in order to commemorate God's beginning of the world with *beṯ*, a child beginning to learn the alphabet is taught to start with the letter *beṯ* followed by the letter *'alef* and only afterward is taught to say *'alef, beṯ.*[63] What further illustration do we have of the *beṯ*'s distinction over the other letters of the alphabet? The fact that the order of blessings and curses in the Book of Deuteronomy[64] also begins with the letter *beṯ* just as [the account of God's mercy in] creating the world begins with the letter *beṯ: Bĕr'ešiṯ (Beginning) His handiwork, God created,* etc.

---

60. After intense examination of the preceding parable and its application, Professor H. Z. Dimitrovsky made helpful suggestions but wrote in a letter that the passage still remained obscure.

61. His fear that he would be reduced to the level of a grazing animal bespoke contrition.

62. Not fodder like an animal, but bread, food artfully prepared. Cf. ARN, chap. 1, (YJS, *10,* 14). JV: *In the sweat of thy face shalt thou eat bread.* But *ze'ah,* "sweat," may also mean "trembling."

63. Such, according to Friedmann's n. 63, was the practice.

64. See Deut. 28:3–20.

[Let it be remembered, however, that God's mercy is not indicated by the letter *beṯ* alone.] For, as blessing [*bĕraḵah*] is identified with the letter *beṯ*, so blessing is also identified with the letter *'alef.* Blessing is signified by the word *baruḵ*, "blessed," but blessing as signified by the word *'nky*—[the special form of the first pronoun by which God identifies Himself to Israel]—also begins with an *'alef: I ('nky) am the Lord thy God* (Exod. 20:2).

[Ultimately, however, whether blessing or curse is to prevail in man's life is determined by man's deeds.] For "curse" also may be linked with the *beṯ*, even as it is linked with the *'alef.* "Curse" is linked with the *beṯ* in *baḵoh* ("weeping"), *she weeps sore in the night* (Lam. 1:2), and "curse" is linked with the *'alef* in the word *'arur*, "cursed" (Deut. 27:15–26).

At some time in the days of the Messiah, [in the sixth era], all those who rise to life again will go to the Land of Israel and never again return to the dust they came from, as is said, *And it shall come to pass, that he that is left in Zion, and he that remaineth in Jerusalem, shall be called holy,*[65] *even every one that is written unto life in Jerusalem* (Isa. 4:3). [And when they come into the Land], whither will they go? In the time-to-
ER, *p.* 165 come, when | the Holy One receives the righteous, they will come before Him like children coming into the presence of their father, like servants coming into the presence of their master, and like disciples coming into the presence of their teacher, as is said, *And ye,* [*the men of Gog and Magog who attempt three final assaults upon Jerusalem*],[66] *shall flee to the valley of the mountains . . . and the Lord my God shall come, and all the holy ones for thy sake,* [*O Jerusalem*] (Zech. 14:5).

---

65. "Even as that which is holy exists for ever, so will the righteous exist for ever." Thus reads the parallel of this passage as quoted in B.Sanh 92a.

66. See MTeh 119:2 (YJS, *13, 2,* 247).

ELIYYAHU ZUṬA

CHAPTER 1

Resourcefulness in the fear of God enhanced by study of Torah; merit gained by the exercise of charity

Summary

A man should be resourceful in his fear of God and strive to be well-regarded by his fellows. He should, like Moses, endeavor to share the trouble of his community.

To learn such conduct, a man must labor mightily in study of words of Torah and in the giving of charity. Thereby he brings about the surrender of his Evil Impulse to him (EZ, 167). On the other hand, neglect of the study of Torah can lead to the destruction of the Jewish world or to sexual transgression.

The man of compassion will exercise charity as did the great worthies in Israel's past (EZ, 168–70). Charity lengthens a man's years and brings him to life in the world-to-come. The exercise of charity is taken to be equal to the study of Torah, and the man who exercises it will ultimately be seated over against God's throne of glory. Of the virtue of charity Scripture speaks again and again (EZ, 171).

Chapter 1

In the name of the School of Elijah the prophet it is said: A man should EZ, *p.* 167
always be resourceful[1] in exercising his fear of God; *giving the soft answer that turns away wrath* (Prov. 15:1), he should strive to be on the best of terms with his father, with his mother, with his master, with his fellow Jew in the street, even with a heathen. Thus he will be loved on high and be well regarded here below; his company will be welcomed by his fellows,[2] and his days will be filled with good.

[In his compassion, he will not endure that] *The righteous perisheth, and no man layeth it to heart* (Isa. 57:1). Of the compassionate man, it is said: He who shares the trouble of his community will live to see the community's deliverance. When we are told, *Moses' hands were heavy; and they took a stone, and put it under him, and he sat thereon* (Exod. 17:12), we ask: But did not Moses have a bolster or a seat to sit on? The point, however, is that Moses would not sit in comfort, saying: While the community is deep in trouble, I shall share the trouble with them. Hence, blessed is the man who shares the trouble of the community. He does not look upon the many who are in deep distress, then go to

---

1. Literally, "cunning," "to endeavor to seek out new ways to fear God." Rashi on B.Ber 17a.

2. Cf. above, ER, 63, and B.Ber 17a.

his home, eat and drink, and say, "As for me, let my life remain untroubled." If he acts in this way [and gives himself over to] *rejoicing and merriment, killing of cattle and slaughtering of sheep, to eating of meat and drinking of wine,* [*saying*] *"Eat and drink, for tomorrow we die"* (Isa. 22:13), then, as Isaiah goes on at once to say, *This iniquity shall never be forgiven you until you die, said my Lord God of hosts* (Isa. 22:14). And if this iniquity is not to be forgiven ordinary self-indulgent people, what is to befall the truly wicked people who say, *Come, I'll buy some wine; let us swill liquor. And tomorrow we'll do just the same, or even more of it!* (Isa. 56:12)?[3]

[For a man to learn right conduct], it is said in the name of the School of Elijah the prophet, he should with the stubbornness of an ox under the yoke, an ass under its burden, cattle plowing in the furrow —with just such stubbornness should he occupy himself in words of Torah, as is said, *Blessed are ye who, like the ox and the ass, sow eagerly beside all waters, for thus you rein in the foot*[*'s Impulse to go astray*][4] (Isa. 32:20). Blessed are Israel when they occupy themselves with Torah and with loving-kindness: their Impulse [to evil] is then made to surrender to them, not they to the Impulse. By *sow* in the verse cited above is meant the giving of charity, as is said, *Sow for yourselves by means of charity* (Hos. 10:12). And by *water* is meant Torah, as in the verse *Ho, every one that thirsteth, come ye for water* (Isa. 55:1).[5] Upon a man who has read the Five Books, the Prophets, the Writings, recited Halaḵot, recited Mishnah, recited Midrash, recited Haggaḏot, recited Talmud, and engaged in dialectics—upon such a man the holy spirit comes to rest at once, as is said, *The spirit of the Lord spoke by me, and His word was upon my tongue* (2 Sam. 23:2).

Once, as I was traveling from city to city, a magistrate[6] who did not know me accosted me, and after greeting me asked: My master, EZ, *p.* 168 from what place are you? I replied: | I am from great Jabneh, a city of Sages and Rabbis. He said: My master, come and dwell in the place I will show you, and I will supply you with wheat, barley, beans, lentils, and all kinds of pulse. I said to him: My son, if you were to give me a thousand thousands of thousands of gold denar, I would not leave a place where there is Torah and dwell in a place where there is no Torah. He asked: Why not? I replied: My son, the [Jewish] world was destroyed only because of wilful neglect [of study] of Torah. The Land

---

3. Cf. above, ER, 112, 128, and B.Ta 11a.

4. JV: *Happy are ye that sow beside all waters, that send forth freely the feet of the ox and the ass.* But the word *reḡel* (singular), "foot," is taken either as *reḡel,* "habit," or as the "foot['s Impulse to evil]," the most notorious of rovers. See B.AZ 5b and Rashi *ad loc.*

As for the phrase *the ox and the ass,* it is taken to be qualifying those who are determined to "sow beside all waters," that is, to give charity and to study Torah.

5. Cf. above, ER, 8, 105.

6. Literally, "quaesitor."

of Israel was destroyed only because of wilful neglect [of study] of Torah. Indeed, all the troubles that befall Israel <come from wilful neglect of study of Torah>. A great and grievous transgression in the eyes of the Holy One is neglect [of study] of Torah. Such neglect is equal to the sum of all the transgressions in the world, as is said, *For the* [*wilful*] *transgression of Jacob is all this* (Mic. 1:5). Here the word *this* refers to Torah, as in the verse "Who is the wise man, that he may understand [that it is because of neglect of] this . . . the Land perished. . . . Because they have forsaken [study of] My Torah" (Jer. 9:11–12).[7] Thereupon the magistrate said: My master, blessed be the Lord who chose your nation out of the seventy nations that speak the seventy languages of the world, and gave you the Torah, for you trust Him no matter what befalls you.

In the days of R. Dosa ben Orkinas, [word came to the academy, presumably in his name, of] a ruling that if a man who had two wives died, then his brother who was the father of the one widow was permitted to marry the other widow.[8] The ruling was very disturbing to the Sages[9] because R. Dosa was a great sage [who had previously supported the rule which forbade such marriages]. But now, because he was advanced in years and his eyesight was failing, he was unable to come to the academy. Hence a discussion took place as to who should go and tell him [that his recent ruling would be disregarded]. R. Joshua ben Hananiah said: "I will go." "And who will go along to back him up?" "R. Eleazar ben Azariah." "And who will back up R. Eleazar?" "R. 'Aḳiḇa." The three of them went and sat down at the entrance of R. Dosa's house. His maidservant entered the house and told R. Dosa: "Master, the Sages of Israel are come to you." He said: "Let them come in." When they came in, he took hold of R. Joshua ben Hananiah and had him sit on a golden couch. The latter said to R. Dosa, "My master, will you ask another disciple to sit?" R. Dosa asked, "Who is he?" R. Joshua replied, "R. Eleazar ben Azariah." R. Dosa asked, "Does our colleague Azariah have a son?" [He was told "Yes"] and thereupon applied to Azariah the verse *I have been young and now I am old, and* [now that I know Azariah is blessed with a son, I say again that I] *have not seen the righteous forsaken* (Ps. 37:25). Then R. Joshua said, "Will you

7. Cf. PRKM 15:5 (PRKS, pp. 278–79).

8. The other widow as co-wife of a relative whom it is forbidden to marry is herself deemed such a relative, and is therefore, according to law, exempt from both *ḥăliṣah* and levirate marriage (Yeḇ 1:1–2; and Maimonides' Code IV, III, vi, 14–15 [YJS, *19,* 307–8]). Still, because of neglect of the study of Torah, the prohibition of such marriages—imposed, as will be presently stated, in the days of Haggai (fourth century B.C.E.)—came to be lifted, purportedly in the name of Dosa ben Orkinas, the highest legal authority in the Land.

9. They were reluctant to act against his decision without having consulted him first.

ask another disciple of yours to sit?" R. Dosa asked, "Who is he?" R. Joshua replied, "R. 'Aḳiḇa." R. Dosa said, "Are you really 'Aḳiḇa, the interpreter of Scripture whose name has gone forth throughout every part of the entire world? Sit, my son, sit. May there be many like you in Israel!" And he applied to him the verse *The young lions do lack, and suffer hunger; but they that seek the Lord want not any good thing*[10] (Ps.
EZ, *p.* 169 34:11). Thereupon the Rabbis began to put to R. Dosa | all sorts of questions on legal matters[11] until they reached the subject of the special case mentioned above. When they reached it, they asked him, "What is the ruling that applies when a man with two wives dies and his brother who is the father of one of the widows wishes to marry the other widow?" "This," he answered, "is a question in dispute between the School of Shammai and the School of Hillel." "And what is the final ruling?" "The ruling is in keeping with the opinion of the School of Hillel [that such a marriage is forbidden]."[12] "But it has been said in your name that such a marriage is permitted." Dosa asked, "Did you hear Dosa quoted or the son of Horkinas quoted?" "By the life of our master," they replied, "we heard no mention of a son's name." "I have a younger brother," Dosa then said, "who is a 'limb of Satan,'[13] first [in stubborn debate], and his name is Jonathan, one of the disciples of the School of Shammai. Take care that he does not overwhelm you on questions of established practice and say to you that the sort of marriage we are discussing is permitted. But I call heaven and earth to witness that upon this mortar-shaped seat sat the prophet Haggai[14] and delivered the following three rulings: that marriage between one widow of a man and his brother who is the father of the man's other widow is forbidden; that in the lands of Ammon and Moab the tithe of the poor is to be given in the seventh year;[15] and that proselytes may be accepted from the Carduenes[16] and the Palmyrenes."[17]

---

10. Though R. 'Aḳiḇa had many pupils, he was able to provide for all of them.

11. Literally, "surrounded him with Halaḵoṯ."

12. According to this school, one widow may not marry her deceased husband's brother if he is the father of the other widow.

13. Literally, "the first-born of Satan." R. Dosa seems to be playing upon the rhyme *'aḥ ḳaṭan, bĕḵor śaṭan,* and *Yonaṯan* ("younger brother," "first-born of Satan," "Jonathan").

14. "This means that he had an incontrovertible tradition on the matter" (Meiri, as quoted in B.Yeḇ 16a, Soncino tr.).

15. Of the seven-year cycle. "The countries of Ammon and Moab, though conquered by Moses and included in the boundary of the Land of Israel, were in the days of the Second Temple excluded. The laws of the seventh or Sabbatical year which apply to the Land of Israel were consequently inapplicable to the lands of Ammon and Moab. Any Jews living in those countries, it was ordained by the Rabbis, were to be allowed to cultivate their fields in this year, but besides the first tithe which is due in all other years, they were to give the tithe of the poor also" (B.Yeḇ 16a, Soncino tr.).

16. Literally, "Cardamians."

17. Despite the opinion of some Rabbis that the peoples referred to were of

When the Tannaim came, they had all entered through one door, but when they left, they left through three different doors [to avoid Jonathan].[18] But Jonathan accosted R. 'Aḳiḇa and asked him: "Are you 'Aḳiḇa ben Joseph whose name has gone throughout every part of the entire world? By the [Temple] service, [judging by your rulings], you are not even the equal of one of the cattle herdsmen." R. 'Aḳiḇa replied [with the sort of soft answer that turns away wrath], "I beg your pardon, not even the equal of one of the shepherds."[19] [In the matter of proselytes], however, take note that because the Ten Tribes had been absorbed by the heathen Cutheans,[20] proselytes will not be accepted from the Cutheans until Elijah and the Messiah come and clear up their ancestry,[21] as is said, *Behold, I will send you Elijah the prophet before the coming of the great and terrible day of the Lord. And he shall turn the heart of the fathers to the children, and the heart of the children to their fathers* (Mal. 3:24–25).

In the name of the School of Elijah the prophet it is taught: Great is charity, for from the day the world was created until the present, he who gives it is especially favored and spares himself punishment in Gehenna, as is said, *Happy is he that considereth the poor; the Lord will deliver him in the day of evil* (Ps. 41:2). *The day of evil* can only mean the day of punishment in Gehenna, as implied in the verse *Therefore remove from thy heart that which causes God vexation,*[22] *and thus put away evil from thy flesh* (Eccles. 11:10), for *Happy are they that keep justice, that do charity at all times* (Ps. 106:3).

How did our early forebears come to gain merit for themselves not only in this world, but also in the days of the Messiah and in the world-to-come? By conducting themselves in exercise of charity. Abraham, Isaac, and Jacob, Moses and Aaron, David and his son Solomon were singled out for praise by reference to their exercise of charity. <Abraham was singled out for praise | by reference to his **EZ, *p.* 170**
exercise of charity>, as God said, *For I have singled him out, to the end*

---

bastard stock. See William G. Braude, *Jewish Proselyting in the First Five Centuries of the Common Era* (Providence, 1940), pp. 66–71.

18. Or, on the contrary, in the hope that at least one of them might meet him.

19. Or: Jonathan reproached R. 'Aḳiḇa: You cite Haggai one of the last Prophets, but not one of the earlier ones such as Amos the herdsman (Amos 1:1). Indeed not, replied R. 'Aḳiḇa, my authority goes all the way back to the "shepherd," to Moses.

R. 'Aḳiḇa makes such a claim because marriage between one widow of a man and the brother who is the father of the man's other widow is actually forbidden on the basis of *gĕzerah šawah,* the similarity of one word occurring in two passages (see B.Yeḇ 3b); however, the *gĕzerah šawah,* one of the norms by which practices not specifically sanctioned in Torah are authorized, may be used only if sanctioned by a tradition going back all the way to the "shepherd," Moses at Sinai. So Samuel Edels on B.Yeḇ 16b.

20. The child who is the offspring of a daughter of Israel and a heathen is a bastard, according to one opinion (B.Yeḇ 46a).

21. Cf. Ed 8:7 and Ben Sira 48:10.

22. JV: *Therefore remove vexation from thy heart.* But see Rashi *ad loc.*

that he may instruct his children . . . to do charity and justice (Gen. 18:19). <Isaac was singled out for praise by reference to his exercise of charity, as is said, *Isaac sowed in that land* (Gen. 26:12), sowing here referring to the bestowal of charity>,[23] as in the verse "Sow for yourselves in charity" (Hos. 10:2). Jacob singled himself out for praise by reference to his own exercise of charity, for he said: *Because of all my acts of loving-kindness, I have reduced my possessions to little*[24] (Gen. 32:11)—that is, because [of my generosity in] acts of loving-kindness, I own only a little now [in contrast to what I would otherwise own]. But *It is good to be [reduced to a] little by dispensing charity [generously]*[25] (Prov. 16:8). Moses was singled out for praise by reference to his exercise of charity, as is said, *He executed the charity of the Lord* (Deut. 33:21). Aaron was singled out for praise by reference to his exercise of charity, as is said, *The law of truth was in his mouth* (Mal. 2:6), *truth* standing here for charity, as intimated in the verse "When truth springeth out of the earth, charity looks down from heaven" (Ps. 85:12). David was singled out for praise by reference to his practice of charity, as is said, <"And David executed justice as well as charity" (2 Sam. 8:15). And Solomon was singled out for praise by reference to his exercise of charity, as is said, "Give Thy mercy . . . unto king [David]'s son" (Ps. 72:1)>. Even the Holy One is singled out for praise with reference to His exercise of charity, as is said, *The Lord of hosts is exalted through justice, but God the Holy One is sanctified through charity* (Isa. 5:16). The throne of glory also is singled out especially for praise because of its Occupant's exercise of charity, as is said,[26] *Charity and then justice are the foundation of His throne* (Ps. 97:2).

Great is charity because it saves men from the way of death. Great is charity because it lengthens a man's days and years. Great is charity because it brings man to life in the world-to-come. Great is charity because its exercise is comparable to study of Torah. Great is charity because Torah is compared with it. Great is charity because it brings more speedily the days of the Messiah and the days of redemption. Great is charity because it lifts up and seats him who exercises it over against the throne of glory.

And the proof that charity saves men from the way of death? The verse *Riches profit not in the day of wrath; but charity delivereth from death* (Prov. 11:4). Come and see that as a man measures, so it is measured

---

23. Since Isaac had been told to do no more than sojourn in the land of Gerar (Gen. 26:3), he would not have been sowing grain. Hence the conclusion that what he sowed was deeds of charity. So David Luria, in PRE, chap. 33.

24. JV: *I am not worthy of all the mercies.*

25. JV: *Better is a little with righteousness.*

26. The words *Clouds and darkness are round Him* are deleted because they appear to be irrelevant to the comment.

out to him. When a man gives charity to his fellow in this world, seeing to it that he lives, not dies, the Holy One likewise sees to it that the giver lives, not dies. And the proof that he who has the means to exercise charity yet does not exercise it in order to sustain lives, and that he who has the means to maintain lives yet does not so maintain them, brings death upon himself? The verse *Nabal answered David's servants, and said: Who is David? . . . Shall I then take my bread, and my water, and my flesh that I have killed for my shearers, and give it unto men of whom I know not whence they are?* (1 Sam. 25:10–11). At once sentence of death was passed on him, as is said, *And it came to pass about ten days later, that the Lord smote Nabal, so that he died* (1 Sam. 25:38). And the proof that the exercise of charity prolongs a man's days and years? The verses *Choose . . . to cleave unto Him; for that is thy life, and the length of thy days* (Deut. 30:19–20), and *Wisdom . . . is a tree of life to them that lay hold upon her, and happy is every one that holdeth her fast* (Prov. 3:18). [In the light of these words] consider what is said of obedience to a lesser commandment in the Torah:[27] *That it may be well with thee, and that thou mayest prolong thy days* (Deut. 22:7). All the more certain is the prolongation of our days as the happy consequence of the exercise of charity to which a far graver command in the Torah calls us. And the proof that the exercise of charity brings a man to life in the world-to-come? | The verse *Blessed is the man that hath not walked in the counsel* EZ, *p.* 171
of the wicked. . . . But his delight is in the law of the Lord. . . . He shall be like a tree planted by streams of water (Ps. 1:1–3), and *Blessed are they that keep justice, that do charity at all times* (Ps. 106:3). The word *Blessed* is used with regard to Torah and is used also with regard to charity. As *Blessed* said with regard to Torah implies that the man obedient to Torah will be an inheritor of the world-to-come, so *Blessed* said with regard to charity implies that the man who exercises it will be an inheritor of the world-to-come. And the proof that exercise of charity is held equal to obedience to Torah? The verse *If ye walk in My statutes, and keep My commandments, then I will give your rains in their season* (Lev. 26:3), and *The Lord made me,* says Torah, *as the beginning of His way,*[28] *the first of His works of old* (Prov. 8:22). Furthermore, [when Torah is observed], *I will give peace in the Land* (Lev. 26:6), says Scripture, and says likewise of charity: *The work of charity shall be peace, and the effect of charity quietness and confidence for ever* (Isa. 32:17). And the proof that obedience to Torah is held equal to exercise of charity? There is nothing the Holy One created in His world that measures up to the greatness of Torah, as is said, *Extol her, and she will exalt thee; she will bring*

---

27. Letting the mother of newborn birds go and taking only the young.

28. A preceding verse, verse 20, reads *I walk in the way of charity;* hence the commentator draws the conclusion that since *way* is used of both charity and Torah, the first is held equal to the second. So Haida.

thee to honor, when thou dost embrace her (Prov. 4:8), and "She will seat thee among princes" (Ben Sira 11:1). Nevertheless, [great as she is], Torah herself is referred to as charity, as is said, *And it shall be deemed as [the doing of] charity unto us, if we observe to do all this commandment before the Lord our God, as He hath commanded us* (Deut. 6:25). And the proof that charity brings speedily the days of the Messiah and the days of redemption? The verse *Keep ye justice, and do charity; then will My salvation be near to come, and My favor to be revealed* (Isa. 56:1). And the proof that charity lifts up him who gives it and seats him over against the throne of glory? The verses *He that walketh in charity, and speaketh uprightly . . . he shall dwell on high. . . . Thine eyes shall see the King in His beauty* (Isa. 33:15–17).

CHAPTER 2

Refutation of a skeptic's argument concerning the source of Mishnah, and patterns of reward and punishment; Israel's distinguished role is delineated

Summary

A skeptic asserts that Mishnah was not given from Mount Sinai as Torah was. The assertion is refuted by a parable (EZ, 171) pointing out that as fine flour is derived from wheat and fine linen from flax, so Mishnah is derived from Torah. In the same way certain liturgical practices not specified in Scripture are nevertheless derived from it. Thus both, Mishnah and such practices, were given from Sinai. The norms by which such derivation is validated are identified.

To the skeptic's inquiry concerning God's patterns of reward and requital, it is replied that in this world a man receives his reward and his portion. In addition, whenever he endures affliction because of his commitment to Torah, a further reward is given him in this world, but the principal reward is kept for him in the world-to-come (EZ, 172). God did not find such men until the Jews came, men who were willing to suffer affliction, even anguish, for the sake of Torah and its commandments. Hence God chose Israel out of all the nations, chose the Tribe of Levi to serve in the Tabernacle, and chose Aaron to be His priest and stand before Him year after year to make expiation for Israel. This people Israel, God brought to the Land set apart from all other lands; the Tribe of Levi He brought to Jerusalem, the heave offering of the Land; and Aaron's sons He brought to the Temple set apart from Jerusalem. It is said: In the place whence Adam's dust was taken, there, in Jerusalem, the Temple's altar was built, the altar which made expiation for Israel's sins as long as the Temple stood. Nowadays, Sages and their disciples make expiation for such sins. Accordingly, when a man responds to the needs of Sages and their disciples, Scripture regards him as though he had brought first fruits to the Temple (EZ, 173).

When the skeptic asks why it is that the peoples of the world are permitted to have so much joy in this world, he is told that it is because Israel came out of their midst. The questioner probes further, saying that they who carry out God's commands and they who commit transgressions seem to be all treated alike. No, is the reply, and then by a series of examples drawn from Scripture, it is demonstrated that in the matter of reward and punishment God exercises precise discrimination (EZ, 174–75).

Chapter 2

One time, as I was walking along a road, a man accosted me. He came at me aggressively with the sort of argument that leads to heresy. It turned out that the man had Scripture but no Mishnah. He asserted: Scripture was given us from Mount Sinai. Mishnah was not given us EZ, *p.* 171 *cont'd* from Mount Sinai. I replied: My son, were not both Scripture and Mishnah given by the Almighty? Does the fact that they are different from each other mean that both cannot have been given by Him?[1] By what parable may the question be answered? By the one of a mortal king who had two servants whom he loved with utter love. To one he gave a measure of wheat and to the other he gave a measure of wheat, to one a bundle of flax and to the other a bundle of flax. What did the clever one of the two do? He took the flax and wove it into a tablecloth. He took the wheat and made it into fine flour by sifting the grain first and grinding it. Then he kneaded the dough and baked it, set the loaf upon the table, spread the tablecloth over it, and kept it to await the coming of the king.

But the foolish one of the two did not do anything at all.

After a while the king came into his house and said to the two servants: My sons, bring me what I gave you. One brought out the table with <the loaf baked of> fine flour on it, and with the tablecloth spread over it. And the other brought out his wheat in a basket with the bundle of flax over the wheat grains.

What a shame! What a disgrace! Need it be asked which of the two servants was the more beloved? He, of course, who laid out the table with <the loaf baked of> fine flour upon it.

EZ, *p.* 172 | [At the conclusion of my parable] I said, "My son, if I were to lead you freely through the Mishnah of the Sages [and show you how it can be said to have its origin in Sinai], would you concede that what you said about its not being of Divine origin was a mistake?" He replied, "Yes, but—." I said, "My son, when you are standing[2] before the reader's desk[3] on the Sabbath, tell me, how many blessings [of the *Tĕfillah*] do you recite?" He replied, "Seven."[4] "And on other days?" "The entire *Tĕfillah*."[5] "How many men read Scripture on the Sabbath?" "Seven." "On Sabbath afternoon, on the second, and on the fifth day of the week, how many?" He replied, "On each occasion, three." "And how many blessings are recited when we eat one of the

---

1. Instead of "Does the fact . . . given by Him," Parma MS 2785 reads, "The only difference between Scripture and Mishnah is that the former is text, and the latter is exposition."

2. Literally, "when you are down," down because the reader's desk was at the lower end of the synagogue floor which sloped down, thus enabling the reader to say, *Out of the depths, I call Thee, O Lord* (Ps. 130:1).

3. [Jastrow defines *tbh* as the chest in which the Holy Scrolls were kept. It is certainly not a desk in the modern sense. L. N.]

4. Like the festival *Tĕfillah,* the Sabbath *Tĕfillah* consists of seven blessings (B.Ber 29a); of these the first three and the last three are constant in all forms of the *Tĕfillah* —weekday, Sabbath, or Festival. The blessing uttered between the two groups is peculiar to the special occasion and varies in all four services of the Sabbath. See *Companion* to *APB,* p. cxxx.

5. The Eighteen Benedictions of *'Amiḏah.* See *ibid,* pp. lv–lix.

seven staples of the Land of Israel?"[6] "Two—a blessing before and a blessing afterwards." "And if we eat of foods other than the seven?" "One blessing before." "And how many blessings are there in the Grace after Meals?" "Three,[7] and with the blessing 'He who is good and bestows good,' a total of four." I then asked: My son, was the observance of the practices just mentioned commanded from Mount Sinai? Do they not, in fact, come out of the Mishnah of the Sages? The truth is that when the Holy One gave the Torah to Israel, He gave it to them as wheat out of which the fine flour of Mishnah was to be produced and as flax out of which the fine linen cloth of Mishnah was to be produced.

[The way in which the "fine flour" and "fine linen cloth" of Mishnah are produced is set forth in the definite norms for interpretation of Scripture.] Thus, (1) if a general statement is followed by a particular, then the general statement applies only to the particular. (2) If a particular is followed by a general statement, then what is stated in the general statement applies to the particular. (3) If a general statement is followed by a particular which, in turn, is followed by a repetition of the general statement, then one must be guided by what the particular states. [For illustration of the last norm, consider what Scripture says of the second tithe which is required to be eaten in Jerusalem]: If the tithe be of such produce as to make it too difficult to carry to Jerusalem, it may be converted into money. Then Scripture proceeds to make a general statement concerning the money's use, *Thou mayest spend the money on anything thy soul desireth* (Deut. 14:25), goes on to specify the particulars the money may be spent for, *for oxen, or for sheep, or for wine, or for strong drink*[8] *(ibid.),* and then restates the generalization, *whatsoever thy soul asketh of thee (ibid.).*

And there is a fourth norm for interpretation of Scripture: When for the sake of clarity, a general statement must be supported by a particular even as the particular must be supported by a general statement, [then the first two norms as given above do not hold].[9]

My questioner said to me further: My master, [has it been true] from the time the world was created until the present hour that when

---

6. Wheat and barley, grapes, figs, and pomegranates, olive oil and date honey. See Deut. 8:8 and B.Ber 37a–b.

7. One blessing for the food, one for the Land, and one for Jerusalem. See *APB,* pp. 280–83, and B.Ber 48b.

8. Hence, it is concluded, the only food that may be purchased with second tithe money is food directly produced by the earth or made from produce deriving its nourishment from the earth, thus excluding brine, water, salt, and, according to some, fish (B.Er 27b).

9. For illustrations of the way in which these four norms are applied, see Sif Lev., ed. Weiss (Vienna, 1962), p. la; and Philip Birnbaum, *Daily Prayer Book* (New York, 1949), pp. 41–43.

a man carries out a command of Torah, he is given the reward he deserves, and when he commits a transgression he is given the requital he deserves? I replied: My son, had not Scripture been so clear on this point, one would not dare say what I am about to say: Consider, to begin with, that the Holy One is King from one end of the world to the other, and the entire world—every part of it—is His, as is said, *Behold, unto the Lord thy God belongeth the heaven, and the heaven of heavens, the earth with all that therein is* (Deut. 10:14): He has only to *Look down from heaven, and see* [*His creation*] (Isa. 63:15). Not only the heaven, but the heavens and the heaven of heavens, all seven of them, as well as the world, all of it, is His: the throne of glory is His. Therefore, [in the lifetime] of both the just and the unjust, each receives his deserts from God in the world that He created. But it must be made clear to mortals that whenever a man endures affliction because of his study of Torah and endures affliction because of his carrying out the commandments, a reward for his exemplary behavior in this world is indeed given to him, but the principal reward is kept for him [in the world-to-come].

The Holy One did not find among mankind a people such as would be willing to endure affliction in their commitment to Torah, endure affliction in carrying out the commandments, endure affliction
EZ, *p.* 173 in building the Second Temple,[10] endure affliction | for the sake of Torah and its commandments—[did not find such a people] until the coming of the Jews. Because they endured affliction in their commitment to Torah and commandments, endured affliction in carrying out the Torah and commandments, endured affliction in building the Second Temple,[11] therefore the Holy One gave them Mishnah—[a double reward, a reward in this world and a reward in the world-to-come]—gave it to them and to their children and their children's children until the end of all generations.

And the proof that the Holy One receives His reward in His world, the world He created? The verse *The Lord's portion is His people* (Deut. 32:9), and also the verse *When the lot fell upon me to be Your portion, it was a lot most pleasant*[12] (Ps. 16:6). By what parable may the matter be understood? By the one of a mortal king who built a palace and decorated it and then, because of the joy he took in it, finally decided to make it his own dwelling. Such is the reward given the Land of Israel, [the palace of the King of kings], in the midst of which the Holy One stood and created all the lands, every one of them;[13] out of all the peoples He selected Israel as a heave offering; out of Israel He selected the Tribe of Levi [to serve in the Tabernacle]; and out of the

---

10. See Neh. 4:9–17.
11. "endured affliction in building the Second Temple"—Parma MS 2785.
12. JV: *The lines are fallen unto me in pleasant places.*
13. For parallels, see above, ER, 21, and Sif Deut. 37 (ed. Finkelstein [Breslau, 1936–39], p. 70).

Tribe of Levi He selected Aaron to be His priest. He sanctified him, anointed him, and adorned him with the garments of priesthood, with the diadem on the mitre, with the Urim and Thummim—all this for Aaron who stands before God and year after year makes expiation for Israel.[14] Then the Holy One brought Israel, the heave offering out of all the peoples [of the world], to the Land of Israel which is set apart from all Lands; brought the Tribe of Levi, which He set apart out of Israel, to Jerusalem, the heave offering out of the Land of Israel; brought Aaron's sons, whom He set apart out of the Tribe of Levi, to the Temple that He set apart out of Jerusalem, [the Temple where they were] to stand and do His will with a whole heart. Hence it is said, *He stood, and measured the Land*[15] (Hab. 3:6)—[that is, God assigned the aforementioned to their places in the Land].

[On the other hand, where the heathen nations are concerned, it is said]: *With His glance He made the nations quake, decreed that they be dispersed, and that what they thought were their everlasting mountains be shattered, their enduring hills be sunk into the earth (ibid.).* [As for Israel, however, the verse goes on to say], *But the goings (hălikot), the world, his.*[16] These words, say the Sages, signify that he who studies what Israel's "ways" *(hălikot)* ought to be, his is the world-to-come [as well as this world].

Some say: In the place whence Adam's dust was taken, there [in Jerusalem], the altar was built, for it is said, *Then the Lord God formed man of the dust of that earth*[17] (Gen. 2:7), and *An altar of* [*that*] *earth thou shalt make Me* (Exod. 20:24). Hence it is said: As long as the Temple stood, the altar within it made expiation for Israel's sins everywhere Israel dwelt. And outside the Land, Sages and disciples of the Sages make expiation for Israel's sins everywhere Israel dwells. Thus, as it is said, expiation is to be had *If thou bring a meal offering of first fruits unto the Lord* (Lev. 2:14). [In connection with such an offering Scripture tells us of a man who brought it as an act of expiation]: *There came a man*

---

14. For parallel, see above, ER, 111.

15. JV: *He standeth and shaketh the earth.* But the root *mdd,* "shake," may also mean "measure"; and *'rṣ,* "earth," is frequently taken to mean "the Land [of Israel]."

16. In the Hebrew text the quotation ends with *dispersed,* and is followed by the abbreviation for "and so on." The "and so on" is understood to imply the entire verse which in JV reads: *He beholdeth, and maketh the nations to tremble; and the everlasting mountains are dashed in pieces, the ancient hills do bow; His goings are as of old.* The last clause is translated variously, transposed, or not translated at all. In the comment that follows, "his" is taken to refer not to God but to man, specifically to the man who studies Torah's oral laws which set forth what a man's "ways" *(haliḵoṯ)* ought to be; and *'olam,* "of old," is taken in its other meaning of "world." Cf. B.Meḡ 28b.

In the comment the physical act of going *(haliḵoṯ)* is thus equated with *Halaḵoṯ,* the rules of conduct and worship.

17. The definite article identifying the earth from which the dust to make Adam was taken is construed as intimating that it is the best known or the best part of the earth, that part underneath the altar in Jerusalem where sins are expiated. Cf. Gen. Rabbah 14:8 and Maimonides' Code VIII, I, ii, 2 (YJS, *12,* 10).

from Baal-shalishah, and brought [*to Elisha*], *the man of God, bread of the first fruits* (2 Kings 4:42). But was Elisha a priest? No. Besides, [where he was], there was no Temple, no altar, and no High Priest. Elisha was a prophet, however, and disciples of the wise sat before him at Dothan or at Samaria.[18] Hence it is said: If a man responds to the needs of Sages and their disciples, Scripture regards him as though he had brought first fruits [to the Temple] and thus did the will of his Father in heaven.[19]

EZ, *p.* 174 | My questioner then asked me: Why are the peoples of the world treated differently [from Israel] in being permitted to have so much joy in this world? I replied: My son, it is because the Holy One selected Israel from their midst that they are permitted to enjoy this world—such is their reward. By what parable may the matter be understood? By the parable of a mortal king who found in a numerous family only one who did his will. Thereupon, because of the one who did his will, the king sent many gifts to all the rest of the family. So it is with the nations of the world. Because the Holy One selected Israel from among them, reward is theirs and they are permitted to enjoy this world.

My questioner said further to me: My master, if what you say is so, then he who carries out a command is given the reward he deserves, and he who commits a transgression is likewise given a reward as though he deserves it. I replied: Not so, my son; can you consider the requital of the ancient serpent who proceeded to corrupt the whole world a reward? Can you consider the requital of Adam and Eve who disobeyed the command a reward? Can you consider the requital of Cain who slew his brother Abel a reward? Consider what, on the other hand, was the reward of Lamech who mourned the death of his father's father.[20] Consider what was the reward of Shem who honored his father as compared with the requital of Ham who did not honor his father.[21] And consider also what was the reward of Noah who proceeded to upbraid multitudes of men for all of one hundred and twenty years, so that the punishment that had been decreed for them would not befall them. Wherefore Scripture said in praise of him, praise announced to all the generations after him: *Thee have I seen righteous before Me in this generation* (Gen. 7:1). Consider, too, what was the reward of the great Shem who for four hundred years prophesied to

18. See 2 Kings 6:13, 32.

19. "One who brings a gift to a scholar is deemed as though he had offered first fruits." B.Keṯ 105b.

20. R reads "brother." The emendation is suggested by Louis Ginzberg who says: "Cain is meant who was mourned by his grandson (i.e., descendant) Lamech (comp. *Legends, 1,* 116–17); and Lamech's reward was that his daughter Naamah became the mother of mankind by her marriage to Noah; comp. *Legends, 5,* 147, n. 45" (*TSE,* p. 188, n. 115).

Or, according to *MṢ,* Lamech mourned for his grandfather Enoch who died at the then youthful age of 365. For such mourning Lamech's reward was his fathering of Noah.

21. Gen. 9:21–25.

all the peoples of the world who would not, however, heed him.[22] Consider what was the reward of Abraham who rose up and demolished all the idols in his world. Nevertheless, because he said something improper to God, his children had to go down into [slavery] in Egypt. What he said was, *O Lord God, whereby shall I know that I can take possession of the Land?* (Gen. 15:8), and on account of the doubt implied in his question, his children had to go down into Egypt. Consider, also, what was the reward of Ishmael who went and buried his father.[23] Consider what was the reward of Isaac who said to his father: Bind me well and only then lay me upon the altar lest I, who am only thirty-seven,[24] young and full of strength, kick you or strike you and thus incur a double death penalty from Heaven.[25] Consider what was the reward even of Esau who because he shed two tears before his father was given Mount Seir upon which rains of blessing never cease.[26] And because the sons of Seir had received the sons of Esau affably,[27] they, too, were given their reward. In this connection it is said: | Even if a man have EZ, *p.* 175
neither Scripture nor Mishnah, yet all day meditates on the verse *Lotan's sister was Timna*[28] (Gen. 36:22), the reward for study of Torah will be his. Consider what was the reward of Jacob who, for all of his life, declared the truth [that the Lord is God] and in his heart also acknowledged that truth. Consider what was the reward of the Twelve Tribe-fathers who carried out the will of their father Jacob.[29] Of them it is said, *I found Israel like grapes in the wilderness, I saw your fathers as the first-ripe in the fig tree at her first season* (Hos. 9:10). Consider finally what was the reward of Abraham, Isaac, and Jacob, men of the one nation out of the nations that speak the seventy languages of the world, who instilled fear of God in themselves, in their children, and in their children's children to the end of all generations.

---

22. Cf. above, ER, 114.

23. Even though toward the end of his days Abraham sent Ishmael's brothers far away to the land of the East, an act which no doubt grieved Ishmael. See Gen. 25:1–8.
In the comment Keturah is thus identified as Hagar, Ishmael's mother. See Ginzberg, *Legends, 5,* 265.

24. Sarah was ninety at the time she gave birth to Isaac; shortly after Abraham prepared to sacrifice him, she died at the age of 127. See Ginzberg, *Legends, 1,* 273.

25. For striking his father and for invalidating a sacrifice. See above, ER, 138, and Gen. Rabbah 56:8.

26. Cf. above, ER, 65, 125, 155; Tanḥuma B, *1,* 144; and MTeh 80:4 (YJS, *13, 2,* 50).

27. The Seirites intermarried freely with the descendants of Esau. Thus Timna, sister of Lotan a Seirite, was willing to become Eliphaz' concubine only because Eliphaz was Esau's son. See Gen. 36:22, 12.

28. On the great significance of even this verse which apparently says so little, see Sif Deut. 336 (ed. Finkelstein, pp. 385–86), and B.Sanh 99b.

29. Instead of "their father Jacob," Parma MS 2785 reads "their Father in Heaven."

CHAPTER [3]

God's creation of everything in the world except falsehood and iniquity

Summary

Had not mankind been marked for death because of their sins, no man would die in distress. Because of man's sinful ways, fruits and vegetables rot, even as for the same reason men's eyes grow dim, their bodies are defiled with leprous spots, and women's bodies are defiled through issue of menstrual blood. Yet God's intention in creating man had been for him to dwell happily in the world He made (EZ, 175).

There are three occasions when a man ought to meditate upon sin and its consequences: when he makes use of a privy, when he is bled, and when he sees a corpse. Yet despite such reminders of his mortality, man fails to repent of his sins and turn to right conduct. When he does act rightly, however, he is assigned an angel who helps him on the way he has chosen. By the same token, when he acts wickedly, he is assigned an angel who leads him on to further wickedness. In short, good comes to the good, and evil to the evil (EZ, 176). For proof, consider that the kinds of children men beget differ according to their motives in marrying. When a man marries only for the sake of satisfying his lust, the outcome will be a rebellious son. When he marries only for the sake of money, the outcome will be his dependence on others. When a man marries only for the sake of social status, the outcome will be that the members of the family he weds into will make nothing of the children he fathers. On the other hand, when a man marries for the sake of bringing children into the world, the outcome will be such children as will save Israel in a time of trouble. As for those men who marry out of Israel, no children at all will be left of them (ER, 177). Finally, for proof of what happens to the children of men who marry for the sake of Heaven—to have children—consider Boaz: from him came David and Solomon who caused study of Torah and observance of commandments to flourish in Israel (EZ, 178).

Chapter [3]

EZ, ***p.*** **175** *cont'd* The Holy One created everything in His world, but He did not create the stuff of falsehood and He did not create the stuff of iniquity,[1] for, as Scripture says, *The Rock, His work is perfect; for all His ways are justice; a God of faithfulness and without iniquity, just and right is He* (Deut. 32:4); and *The Lord who is righteous is in the midst of her, He doth not make unrighteousness, but every morning bringeth His right to light; it faileth not* (Zeph. 3:5); and *Far be it from God, that He should make wickedness; and from the Almighty, that He should bring iniquity into being—in truth, man's*

---

1. Cf. PR 24:3 (YJS, *18, 1,* 509).

own work requiteth him, causeth every man to find [*requital*] *according to his ways* (Job 34:10–11).

I call heaven and earth to witness that had not mankind been marked for death [because of Adam's sinful ways], no mortal would die in distress; instead, only after he had eaten and drunk and rejoiced—he and his wife with his sons and the members of his household—only then would he [painlessly] depart to his eternal abode.[2] Only on account of mankind's sinful ways do fruits and vegetables end up rotten. Mankind come to shame only because of their own [sinful] ways. After half a lifetime the eyes of mankind grow dim only because of their own [sinful] ways. <Mankind come to be defiled with leprous spots only because of their own [sinful] ways.> Women come to be defiled through issue of menstrual blood only because of their own [sinful] ways, as is said, *For thus saith the Lord that created the heavens. He is God; that formed the earth and made it, He established it, He created it not a waste, He formed it to be inhabited: I am the Lord, and there is none else* (Isa. 45:18) —[that is, He created the earth not to be wasted, not to be defiled, but to be dwelt in happily]. Go and draw this conclusion for yourself from your own observation of the world. Does a man build himself a house for any purpose other than to bring food into it, to bring furnishings into it, to bring valuables into it? | Or does he build it to use it for EZ, *p.* 176
firewood?

If mankind [do not live happily in this world, it is their own fault]. They are being punished because of their [sinful] ways and their [neglect of] right conduct in order to save them from the Day of Judgment that is to come upon them, as is said, *Woe unto them! for they have strayed from Me. Destruction unto them! for they have strayed against Me* (Hos. 7:13).

There are three occasions that a man ought to meditate upon every day: when he makes use of a privy, when he is bled, when he stands over a corpse. When he makes use of a privy, he is being told, Behold, your ways are the same as the ways of an animal. When he is being bled, he is being told, Behold, you are flesh-and-blood. And when he stands over a dead body, he is being told, Behold what your end is to be. Despite such admonitions, he does not return in penitence [to right conduct]. On the contrary, he keeps saying things that are uncalled for, of which Scripture says, *The foolishness of man perverteth his way; and his heart fretteth against the Lord* (Prov. 19:3); he tells lies in disregard of the injunction *Keep thee far from a false matter; and the innocent and righteous slay thou not, for I will not justify the wicked* (Exod. 23:7); he is the sort of man who schemes evil against his neighbor in disregard of the admonition *Let none of you devise evil in your hearts against his neighbor;*

---

2. Death would be death by a kiss—pleasant and easy.

and love no false oath; for all these are things that I hate, saith the Lord (Zech. 8:17). On the other hand, what happens when a man makes himself act like a righteous man and speaks the truth? He is assigned an angel who goes along with him in the way of the righteous and helps him to speak the truth. When a man makes himself act like a saint, being willing to suffer all, he is assigned an angel who goes along with him in the way of saints and helps the man to accept all suffering. If, on the other hand, a man makes himself act like a wicked man, deceiving and lying, he is assigned an angel who goes along with him in the way of the wicked and leads him on to deceit and lying. And if a man makes himself follow a middle way, he is assigned an angel who goes along with him in the middle way. So we are told by the Holy One Himself: *I the Lord search the heart, I try the reins, even to give every man* [*an angel*] *according to his ways, according to the fruit of his doings* (Jer. 17:10). And David, addressing himself to God, says likewise: *With the merciful Thou dost show Thyself merciful, with the upright man Thou dost show Thyself upright; with the pure Thou dost show Thyself pure; and with the crooked Thou dost show Thyself astute* (Ps. 18:26–27).

Scripture praises His evenhandedness further, saying, *The poor people Thou dost save; but Thine eyes are upon the haughty, that Thou mayest humble them* (2 Sam. 22:28). *The poor people Thou dost save,* the people [of Israel] whom poverty becomes;[3] *Thine eyes are upon the haughty that Thou mayest humble them—the haughty* being the [heathen] nations of the world.

It is said further of God: *Is it not at the word of the Most High that evil and good befall?* (Lam. 3:38). <How can one say such a thing? Do not only measures of good come from Him? You must therefore conclude>: Good does not come to him who does evil, and evil does not come to him who does good, but good comes to the good, and evil to
EZ, *p.* 177 the evil. And the proof | you can see for yourself. Generally men marry for one of four reasons: A man may marry for the sake of satisfying his lust, he may marry for the sake of money, he may marry for social status, or he may marry for the sake of Heaven.[4] When a man marries for the sake of satisfying his lust, a stubborn and rebellious son will spring from him. When a man marries for the sake of money, in the end he will be dependent on others. When a man marries for the sake of social status, in the end the men who are members of the family into which he weds will make nothing of the children he fathers.[5] But

3. Cf. PRKM 14:3 (PRKS, p. 268); B.Shab 104a; Ḥag̅ 9b; and Mak 10b.
4. To have children, in obedience to the commandment to be fruitful and multiply.
5. Leon Nemoy suggests: "in the end his issue belonging to that aristocratic family will be scant indeed."

when a man marries for the sake of Heaven, he will have sons who will deliver Israel in time of trouble.[6]

And the proof that the man who marries for the sake of satisfying his lust will have a stubborn and rebellious son? He is the man whom Scripture addresses in the verse *When thou . . . seest among the captives a woman of goodly form* (Deut. 21:11). After he has taken such a woman to wife, people begin to criticize him [for having married her only for the sake of satisfying his lust]. And because of the criticism people direct at him, he goes and weds another wife, as is intimated in the next passage in Deuteronomy, *If a man have two wives,* etc. (Deut. 21:15). Because he weds another, he comes to love one and hate the other, as Scripture goes on to say, *the one beloved, and the other hated (ibid.),* and because he loves one and hates the other, there will issue from him [by the hated wife] a stubborn and rebellious son.

And the proof that he who marries for the sake of money in the end will be dependent on others? So it was with the sons of Eli the priest who married wives not suitable for them.[7] In the end Eli's sons had to depend on other kinsmen. As Eli was told: *It shall come to pass, that every one that is left in thy house shall come and bow down to* [*the faithful priest*] *for a piece of silver and a loaf of bread, and shall say: Put me, I pray thee, into one of the priests' offices, that I may eat a morsel of bread* (1 Sam. 2:36).

And the proof that when a man marries for the sake of social status in the end the men who are members of the family into which he weds will make nothing of the children he fathers?[8] So it was with Jehoshaphat king of Judah, who upon seeing that Ahab king of Israel had seventy sons, said: Isn't this person sure to inherit the world? Thereupon Jehoshaphat went and arranged to have his son [Joram][9] wed Ahab's daughter [Athaliah], as is said, *Jehoshaphat made a complete union*[10] *with the king of Israel* (1 Kings 22:45). And the proof that the [surviving] children who sprang from Joram, Jehoshaphat's son, were made nothing of?[11] The verse *Now when Athaliah*—[of Ahab's prestigious family into which Jehoshaphat had his son wed]—*the mother*

6. For parallels which discuss such marriages, see B.Ḳid 70a and DEZ, chap. 10.

7. If the sons of Eli were so greedy that they helped themselves to portions of offerings which did not belong to them (1 Sam. 2:13–17), then surely like greed motivated them in their choice of wives. So Haida.

MṢ offers another explanation for EZ's assertion. EZ, according to *MṢ*, renders *ṣobĕ'ot,* "that did service" (1 Sam. 2:22), as "that laid siege to," and hence surmises that the sons of Eli wed women who, "armed" with rich dowries, "laid siege" to the Tent of Meeting where they sought to get themselves well-placed husbands.

8. See n. 5.

9. Joram, Jehoshaphat's son, was married to Athaliah, granddaughter of Omri and daughter of Ahab. See 2 Kings 8:26.

10. JV: *made peace.* But the root *šlm,* "make peace," can also mean "become complete, unite."

11. Leon Nemoy suggests "were very few."

of Ahaziah saw that her son was dead, she arose and destroyed all the seed royal. But Jehosheba, the daughter of king Joram . . . took Joash the son of Ahaziah, and stole him away from the king's sons that were to be slain (2 Kings 11:1–2). Indeed, but for the covenant the Holy One made with David, Joash too would have been slain at that time, and the line of David would have ceased to be.

And what else is the [sorry] requital of these—of the man who marries for the sake of satisfying his lust, the one who marries for the sake of money, or who marries for the sake of social status? Go and find the answer to the question by considering two men, one poor and one rich, both from the same Tribe, both from the same neighborhood, and both from the same family. The rich man should have engaged in friendly give-and-take with the poor man, [such as arranging marriages between their children]. But he did not do so, even though Scripture says, *Have we not all one father? Hath not one God created us? Why do we deal treacherously every man against his brother, profaning the covenant of our fathers?* (Mal. 2:10). [So much for weddings entered into for improper motives.] But Malachi, going on [to speak of intermarriage], says, *Judah hath dealt treacherously, and an abomination is committed in Israel and in Jerusalem; for Judah hath profaned the holy wedlock of the Lord which He loveth, and hath married the daughter of a strange god* (Mal. 2:11). Their requital, therefore, was that no offspring at all were left of them. [Indeed not only Israel but Judah as well] forsook the seed the Holy One proved out of the nations that speak the seventy languages of the world and went and cleaved to those whom it was not fitting for them to marry, as is said, *The Lord will cut off to the man him that waketh ('er) and him that answereth, out of the tents of Jacob, and him that offereth an offering unto the Lord of hosts* (Mal. 2:12). This means [that if a Jew marries a non-Jew], he will have no offspring wakeful among the Sages and none responding among the disciples: none wakeful among the Sages—none, that is, who in the academy inquires to the point about a matter of Halakah; and none who answers properly among the disciples. And if the Jew is a priest, he will have no son bringing an offering unto the Lord of hosts.[12]

On the other hand, what is the proof that when a man marries for the sake of Heaven he will have children who deliver Israel in time of distress? Go and draw the right inference <from the example of Amram who married for the sake of Heaven:[13] from him there issued Moses, Aaron, and Miriam who caused Torah and commandments to
EZ, *p.* 178 flourish in Israel. Go | and draw the right inference> from the example of Boaz son of Salmon, son of Nahshon, son of Amminadab,

12. For parallel see B.Shab 55b.
13. Cf. above, ER, 157.

who married for the sake of Heaven: from him in the end there issued David and Solomon his son who caused Torah and commandments to flourish in Israel. Of them, of the likes of them, of those who resemble them, and of those who pattern their deeds after them, Scripture says, *For as the new heavens and the new earth, which I will make, shall remain before Me, saith the Lord, so shall your seed and your name remain* (Isa. 66:22).

CHAPTER [4]

Forbearance, God's and man's

Summary

God's forbearance toward Israel is of the kind that men should endeavor to practice toward one another. Thus, even though Israel as God's affianced had committed adultery, so to speak, in worshiping the golden calf, still God was so forbearing toward His people that in describing their infamy He resorted to euphemism (EZ, 178).

He did, however, take away the crowns of radiance and immortality which He had had angels set upon each and every one in Israel. These crowns in the days of the Messiah and in the time-to-come will be restored, for the gift of the Torah at Sinai implies freedom from death, freedom from fear of the angel of death (EZ, 179).

In connection with Aaron's part in the making of the golden calf, it should be noted that he intended to delay Israel's worship of it until Moses came down from the Mount and then destroy it, even as Jacob upon his return to the Land had destroyed his children's idols.

When Moses came down from the Mount he saw that the writing upon the Tables had flown away. Thereupon he broke them. At the same moment God decreed that it would be Israel's destiny to study Torah in distress, in bondage, in oppression, and in hunger. Nevertheless, in the days of the Messiah Israel will be compensated with immortality for the distress they will have suffered.

During the forty days which followed the breaking of the Tables, Moses used to take the Tent and pitch it outside the camp of Israel by way of indicating that they were excommunicated. But God finally showed Moses a doorway of mercy open to Israel, so that the ban might be lifted and the Tent be brought back into the camp.

During the forty days when Moses went up a second time to Mount Sinai to fetch the Torah (EZ, 180), the people of Israel set aside the daytime hours of each day for fasting and affliction. On the last of the forty days, they again decreed self-affliction and in this way also spent the night preceding the fortieth day. In the morning, they rose early and went up before Mount Sinai. They were weeping as they met Moses, and Moses was weeping as he met them, and at length the weeping rose up on high.

In that instant God said in His compassion: This weeping will be a joyous weeping for you because this day will be one of pardon, atonement, and forgiveness—Yom Kippur—for you (EZ, 181).

Chapter [4]

EZ, *p.* 178 *cont'd* The Sages taught: Be forbearing toward every man, and more so, in particular, toward the members of your household than toward all others. The reason you can see for yourself: you need only follow the example of the Holy One who was forbearing toward His people not only on one occasion but on two and even three occasions. He did not act toward them as they acted toward Him, nor did He punish them according to their iniquities, but simply showed forbearance. And the proof of His forbearance you can see for yourself from what happened during the one hundred and twenty days from the day the perfect Torah was given to Israel until the Day of Atonement.

Were it not for God's forbearance toward Israel during the first forty days that Moses was up on Mount Sinai to bring the Torah to his people, the Torah would not have been given to Israel. By what parable may the matter be illustrated? By the parable of a mortal king who wed a woman he loved with utter love. Having sent for a man whom he would have act as go-between between him and his future queen, he showed the emissary all his nuptial chambers, his halls of state, and his private living quarters. The king then said to the go-between: Go and say on my behalf to the lady, "I do not require anything from you. You need make for me only a small nuptial chamber where I can come and dwell with you, so that my servants and the members of my household will know that I love you with utter love." Yet even while the king was concerning himself with the measurements of the nuptial chamber [she was to make for him] and while he was ordering a messenger to convey many, many gifts to the lady, people came and told him: "Your future wife has committed adultery with another man." At once the king put aside all the plans he had in hand. The go-between was expelled and withdrew confounded from the king's presence, as is said, *While the King was thinking* [*about the measurements*] *of His nuptial chamber, my spikenard let go* [*and lost*] *its fragrance*[1] (Song 1:14).

| [In the foregoing parable, the king is God; the future wife is Israel; the go-between, Moses; the bride's nuptial chamber, the Tabernacle; the adultery, Israel's worship of the golden calf. Yet, despite Israel's sin, God was forbearing toward them.] EZ, *p.* 179

Blessed be He at whose word the world came into being, blessed be He, blessed be He who says and does [what He says], blessed be He who decrees and carries out, blessed be the Author of creation, blessed be He who remembered [Israel's] earlier good deeds and had pass out of His mind their later evil deeds. Had He not remembered the former and had not pass out of His mind the latter, Scripture would have said, "my spikenard gave forth its stench." However, because Israel accepted the Holy One's sovereignty when they said, *All that the*

1. A euphemism for "I, Israel, gave forth a fetid odor [of sin]." Cf. Targum and Song Rabbah *ad loc.;* B.Shab 88b; and Giṭ 36b. Spikenard produced a rare and fragrant unguent. See John 12:3.

JV: *While the king sat at his table, my spikenard sent forth its fragrance.* But the word *mĕsibbo,* "his table," can also mean "that which is round about him"—hence "the measurements of His [God's] nuptial chamber."

Lord hath spoken we will do, and we will obey (Exod. 24:7), Scripture quotes Israel as saying [ambiguously], *my spikenard let go* [*and lost*] *its fragrance* (Song 1:2), and not "my spikenard gave forth its stench."

R. Ishmael ben Eleazar said: When Israel accepted the Holy One's sovereignty and said, *All that the Lord hath spoken we will do, and we will obey,* sixty myriads of ministering angels came down and set two crowns upon the head of each and every one in Israel[2]—one for Israel's saying *we will do,* and one for their saying *we will obey*—two crowns like Adam's crown,[3] as is said, *Ye shall be unto Me a kingdom of priests, and a holy nation*[4] (Exod. 19:6). But when Israel acted abominably in making the calf, one hundred and twenty myriads of angels of destruction[5] came down and took away the crowns from Israel, as is said, *And the children of Israel were stripped of their ornaments* [*set upon the head of each one in Israel*] *at Horeb* (Exod. 33:6). Lest you might think they were taken away for ever, it is also said, *The ransomed of the Lord shall return, and come with singing unto Zion, because the joy of long ago shall be upon their heads* (Isa. 35:10)—not "the joy of long ago in their hearts," but *upon their heads.* We are thus taught that the Holy One will restore all of Israel's crowns in the days of the Messiah and in the time-to-come: hence *the joy of long ago . . . upon their heads.*

And what thought had been in the Holy One's mind [from the beginning]? It was this: that each and every nation and kingdom would come and accept the Torah, and so would live and endure for ever and ever and ever, as is said, *The tables were the work of God, and the writing was the writing of God, graven (ḥaruṯ) upon the tables* (Exod. 32:16). Read

---

2. Cf. PR 33:10 (YJS, *18, 2,* 648) and PRKM 16:3 (PRKS, p. 290).

3. A crown of radiance and a crown of immortality. See PRKM 12:1 (PRKS, p. 228).

After these crowns were taken away, it is said that *Moses took the radiance* (Exod. 33:7) (the word *'hl,* "tent," being associated with *hll,* "shine, be radiant"; see B.Shab 88a). EZ apparently understands such radiance to be of two kinds: the radiance which enabled Adam (Ginzberg, *Legends, 1,* 61) and Moses (EZ, 183; see Exod. 34:30) to read the future; and the radiance of "immortality," death without suffering, "by a kiss." Such was the death of Moses whose eyes were undimmed and whose vigor unabated at the age of 120 when he died (Deut. 34:7).

4. The word for "kingdom" may be *mlkwt* with only one letter *mem.* Hence in the form *mmlkt* in the verse, a form which has two *mems*, EZ—so says Haida—finds the intimation that two crowns, two kingships so to speak, were set upon each one in Israel. The nature of the crowns is intimated in the next word, *priests* whose urim and thummim gave them a vision of the future; and in the phrase *holy nation,* a nation made holy by its possession of the crown of Torah which is deathless. See Targum Jonathan *ad loc.* and B.Shab 88a.

5. Why 120 myriads and not 60 myriads as before? Because God finds it easier to give than to take (see Tosafoṯ on B.Shab 88a). Or, because at the giving of Torah the body and soul of each Israelite merged; after the making of the calf, body and soul were separated so that in a manner of speaking there were 120 myriads of Israelites. Since no angel is assigned two tasks, 120 myriads were sent by God to remove the 120,000 crowns. So Landau.

not, however, *ḥaruṯ,* "graven," but *ḥeruṯ,* "freedom"[6]—freedom from death, that is, for no man is truly free unless the angel of death has no power over him. Hence, we are to read the verse *From Mattanah to Nahaliel; and from Nahaliel to Bamoth* (Num. 21:19) as follows: After the giving *(mattan)* of Torah, Israel possessed themselves of a false god [*Nahaliel* being read here as though written *naḥălu 'el*],[7] and because they worshiped a false god, the angel of death came upon them [*Bamoth* being read here as though written *ba' maweṯ*].[8] Thus, at first God said [to Israel], *Ye are godlike beings* [*and will live for ever*] (Ps. 82:6), but after their deeds became corrupt, God went on to say, *Surely, ye shall die like men*[9] (Ps. 82:7).

| Now, concerning Aaron's part in the making of the golden calf, **EZ, *p.* 180**
what is written and said in Scripture? *The law of truth was in his mouth, and unrighteousness was not found in his lips* (Mal. 2:6). Would the thought then enter your mind that Aaron worshiped an idol? The fact is that Aaron was deliberately endeavoring to delay [its making] until Moses came down from the Mount.[10] Some say [he intended to do] as our father Jacob did. For our father Jacob obeyed the Torah's command [*Thou shalt have no other gods before Me* (Exod. 20:3)] even before it was given <to his descendants>, as is said, *And they gave unto Jacob all the foreign gods which were in their hand . . . and Jacob hid them under the terebinth which was by Shechem* (Gen. 35:4). What was Jacob's reward for obeying that command? That when *they*—[*he and his household*]—*journeyed, a terror of God was upon the cities that were round about them* (Gen. 35:5). What Jacob did, Aaron had also intended—[the idol's destruction].[11] Nevertheless, although Aaron meant to obey Torah's command even before the Torah was given to Israel, Scripture regards him as having worshiped the idol [because he did make it at the people's behest], as is said, *The Lord smote the people, because they made the calf, which Aaron made* (Exod. 32:35).

It is said: When Moses came down from Mount Sinai and saw the abomination which Israel had committed in making the calf, he looked at the Tables and saw that the writing upon them had flown away. Thereupon he broke them at the foot of the Mount and at once fell silent, being unable to say anything in Israel's behalf.[12] In the same moment it was decreed against Israel that they study Torah in distress, in bondage, in exile, in banishment, in oppression, and in hunger.

---

6. For a somewhat different version, cf. Aḇ 6:2.
7. *Naḥălu 'el,* "they acquired a god."
8. *Bamoth,* "the angel of death came out." Cf. MTeh 5:1 (YJS, *13, 1,* 80).
9. For parallels cf. Meḵ, *2,* 272 and PR 14:10 (YJS, *18, 1,* 282).
10. For parallel see Exod. Rabbah 37:2.
11. Cf. above, ER, 35 and 131.
12. For parallel accounts see above, ER, 17, and ARN, chap. 2 (YJS, *10,* 20–21).

However, as a recompense for the distress they suffer, the Holy One will give them their recompense in the days of the Messiah and in the world-to-come, as is said, *Behold, the Lord God will come as a Mighty One, and His arm will rule for Him; behold, His reward is with Him, and His recompense before Him* (Isa. 40:10); and in post-Mosaic Scripture, [with Israel's suffering in mind, God declares]: *Who hath given Me anything beforehand, him I shall repay* (Job 41:3). As the jingle goes, "In my behalf, I own, my heifer broke her leg bone"—that is, the Holy One will make up for my suffering with substantial compensation.[13]

During the next forty days, in the middle of the period, Moses took up the Tent and pitched it outside the camp, as is said, *Now Moses used to take the Tent and to pitch it without the camp; and he called it the Tent of Meeting* (Exod. 33:7). In the meantime, during all these days, Israel observed mourning for themselves until the King of kings of kings, the Holy One, may His great name be blessed for ever and ever and ever, revealed Himself to Moses and showed him a doorway of mercy open for Israel. The Holy One said to Moses: What shall these wretched people do? They are excommunicated by the Master and excommunicated by the disciple; they have been excommunicated by Me and excommunicated by you. Get back, go into the camp. Thus it is said, *The Lord spoke unto Moses concerning Face and face*[14] (Exod. 33:11). I would not have known that this verse [refers to the anger on God's Face and the anger on Moses' face, but] in going on to say *Moses returned to the camp (ibid.),* Scripture is telling us that God freed Moses from his vow [to absent himself from Israel],[15] so that he could bring the Tent back to the camp. By what parable may the matter be illustrated? By the parable of a mortal king who on a certain occasion became angry at his son. As it happened, one of the notables of the kingdom was sitting with the king, so the king said to his son: You good-for-nothing, had not So-and-so who is my friend been sitting with me, I would have struck you heavy blows. Moses at that hour [of Israel's distress] was like the king's friend, [for he could say to himself: What will befall Israel depends on me]. Thereupon *Moses besought the Lord his God, and said: Lord, why doth Thy wrath wax hot against Thy people? . . . Wherefore should the Egyptians speak, saying: For evil did He bring them forth. . . . Remember*

---

13. Literally, "so that my reward may be complete." Cf. ER, 117, n. 17 and Friedmann's n. 24.

14. JV: *The Lord spoke unto Moses face to face.* EZ, possibly troubled, however, by the anthropomorphic implication of the phrase *face to face,* takes the phrase to refer to the anger of both God and Moses. Cf. MTeh 25:6 (YJS, *13, 1,* 351).

15. Since Moses had been away from the camp for forty days, his continued absence, says Haida, came to be regarded as due to a vow.

PRE, chap. 46, also has Moses spend on earth the middle of the period of 120 days. According to others, Moses spent the middle of the period on Mount Sinai—thus three times on Mount Sinai, each time forty days. See PRE, p. 360, n. 7.

Abraham, Isaac, and Jacob Thy servants, to whom Thou didst swear: I will multiply your seed as the stars of heaven (Exod. 32:11–13). At once God was forbearing toward Israel, as is said, *The Lord repented of the evil which He said He would do unto His people* (Exod. 32:14).

During the last forty days when Moses went up a second time to Mount Sinai to fetch the Torah, Israel decreed for themselves that the daytime hours of each day be set aside for fasting and self-affliction. The last day of the entire period, | the last of the forty, they again decreed EZ, *p.* 181
self-affliction and spent the night also in such self-affliction as would not allow the Inclination to evil to have any power over them. In the morning they rose early and went up before Mount Sinai. They were weeping as they met Moses, and Moses was weeping as he met them, and at length that weeping rose up on high. At once the compassion of the Holy One welled up in their behalf, and the holy spirit gave them good tidings and great consolation, as He said to them: My children, I swear by My great name that this weeping will be a joyous weeping for you because this day will be a day of pardon, atonement, and forgiveness[16] for you—for you, for your children, and for your children's children until the end of all generations.

---

16. The Day of Atonement.

CHAPTER [5]

The poor—pillars of the Lord

Summary

The presence of poor people gives us an opportunity to exercise charity in behalf of God's children, and subsequently He rewards us for doing so.

Men are poor either because of their own wickedness or because of the wickedness of their forebears. But even if they were virtuous for generation after generation, poverty is to be regarded as a gift because it teaches men to fear God. The poor, who are often the righteous, are thus the pillars of the Lord (EZ, 181–82).

Chapter [5]

EZ, *p.* 181 *cont'd* The term *dal* means "one so poor that he has no roof over his head." By what parable may his situation be explained? By the parable of a mortal king who commanded his son not to come to his table any longer though the king knew that his son was hungry and thirsty. Nevertheless the king said: Blessed be the man who brings my son into his house, gives him a morsel of bread, and has him both eat and drink. Since my son will some day inherit all that is mine, [he will repay his benefactor], of whom it is said, *He that is gracious to one so poor that he has no roof over his head, lendeth unto the Lord,*[1] *and his good deed God will repay him* (Prov. 19:17).[2]

It is said: If a man sprung from a father so poor as never to have had a roof over his head, and himself so poor that he longs for everything he has never had—if such a man resolves to repent of his misdeeds, he is accounted a righteous man afflicted with adversity. If he does not resolve to repent, then he is accounted a wicked man afflicted with adversity.

If an average poor man, sprung from a father so poor that he longed for everything he never had, the father himself the son of a man so poor that he did not even have a roof over his head—if such a man resolves to repent of his misdeeds, he is accounted a righteous man afflicted with adversity. If he does not resolve to repent, then he is accounted a wicked man afflicted with adversity.

If a man who has been deprived of his possessions, a man sprung

---

1. See *MṢ.* JV: *He that is gracious unto the poor lendeth unto the Lord.* But *dal,* "poor," may also mean "one so deprived that he does not even have a roof over his head."
2. Cf. B.BB 10a.

from a father whose poverty was average, <himself the son of one so poor that he yearned for everything he had never had>, the yearner in turn, son of one so poor that he had not even had a roof over his head—if such a man resolves to repent of his misdeeds, he is accounted a righteous man afflicted with adversity. If he does not resolve to repent, then he is accounted a wicked man afflicted with adversity.[3]

But if the four different kinds of poor men mentioned above are virtuous, how can one justify their condition, as described in the verse *The poor and needy seek water and there is none, and their tongue faileth for thirst* (Isa. 41:17)? Note that Scripture supplies answers to the question: *The humble . . . shall increase their joy in the Lord, and the neediest among men shall exult in the Holy One of Israel* (Isa. 29:19); and *Behold, I have refined thee, but not as silver; I have purified thee in the furnace of poverty* (Isa. 48:10). The last two verses show that the Holy One, in casting about among all the most desirable conditions in the world, found no condition more beneficial for Israel than poverty, for through poverty they come to fear the Lord.[4] If they have no bread to eat, no clothes to wear, no oil for anointing, then they seek the Lord of mercy and find Him. Thus it is through poverty that they come to fear the Lord. For they who act out of love come to it only through poverty; they who bestow many kinds of charity come to it only through poverty. And they who fear Heaven come to it only through poverty, as is said, *He raiseth up the poor out of the dust* (1 Sam. 2:8): note that Scripture does not say, "He raiseth up the rich out of his bed." *For the distressed (měṣuḳe)*[5] *of the earth are the Lord's* [*pillars*] *(ibid.)*, "the distressed" being disciples of the wise [who lack worldly goods], as in the verse *Every one that was in distress ('is maṣoḳ) . . . gathered themselves unto* [*David*][6] (1 Sam. 22:2).

| From the Holy One's presence each and every day angels of destruction come down intending to destroy the entire world and every one in it. Indeed, were it not for synagogues and academies in which Jews sit and occupy themselves with Torah, these angels would have at once destroyed [the world and all its people], as is intimated in the EZ, *p.* 182

---

3. There are seven kinds of poor people: (1) *'ani,* "the ordinary poor"; (2) *'eḇyon,* "those so poor that they long for everything they have never had"; (3) *misken,* "those held in disdain"; (4) *roš,* "those deprived of possessions"; (5) *dal,* "those deprived of a roof over their heads"; (6) *daḳ,* "so depressed that they can neither eat nor drink"; (7) *maḳ,* "those as low as a threshold upon which all tread." See Lev. Rabbah M, 34:6, p. 782.

4. "Poverty," said R. 'Aḳiḇa, "is as becoming to the daughter of Jacob as a red ribbon on the neck of a white horse" (PRKM, 14:3 [PRKS, p. 268]).

5. JV: *pillars.*

6. It is assumed that David's retinue was made up of scholars who were both "pillars" and men "in distress." Any one whose name was recorded in the rolls of the king's army was permitted to marry into priestly stock and did not need to trace his descent to qualify (so R. Ḥananiah ben Antigonus in Ḳid 4:5).

verse *Wherefore when I came was there no man? When I called, was there none to answer?*[7] (Isa. 50:2).

Go out and observe the way of the world. Does a man plant a vineyard for any purpose other than to eat grapes from it or drink wine from it, or does he plant it to have it overgrown with weeds? If it is overgrown with weeds, he will say to his people, "Go and set fire to it." But then, if a hundred vines or two hundred vines survive in the vineyard [despite the weeds], he will say to his people, "Manure it, hoe it, prune it, and irrigate it because of the vines in it." So it is [with the world when] the righteous are in it. When they arrive and stand upright in the world, they are like the pillars of a house, and the entire world is sustained by them. Such is the meaning of *The pillars of the earth are the Lord's, and He hath set the world upon them* (1 Sam. 2:8).

---

7. In the same verse, Isaiah goes on to quote God as saying, *Behold, at My rebuke I dry up the sea, I make the rivers a wilderness.*

CHAPTER [6]

Instructing Israel in God's plan for the world

Summary

God, who is compassionate, provides for the inhabitants of the world. Why, then, does He ask of us that we give charity to the four kinds of men who are poverty-stricken? He asks only with regard to men who did not conduct themselves rightly and therefore had adversity decreed for them and their descendants for as many as four generations. Bound by His decree, God cannot act toward such men with His wonted compassion (EZ, 182). So that Israel should not, however, be baffled by His apparent lack of compassion, He has provided for each generation-to-come its Sages, its Prophets, its interpreters of Scripture, the leaders of its communities, and its saints to make clear His good intentions toward Israel.

Still, although God explained some of His actions to Moses, the plan itself whereby the world is directed God left unexplained, other than to say that His way is one of loving-kindness and compassion (EZ, 183).

Chapter [6]

Judging from the list of God's attributes,[1] one must conclude that His compassion for the world is abundant. If so, then why does He tell us to give charity [to all four classes of those who are poverty-stricken]: to the average poor; to the poor who long for everything they have never had; to the poor who have no roof over their heads; and to the poor who are utterly wanting in possessions? Does He not Himself feed, sustain, and provide for all the inhabitants of the world, and for all the work of His hands in the world He created? Yes, but just the same He tells us to give charity to the average poor, to the poor who long for everything they have never had, to the poor who have no roof over their heads, and to the poor who are utterly wanting in possessions. The poor whom He has in mind, however, are those who did something that was not right and therefore had adversity imposed upon them [and their descendants] for as many as four generations. It is the descendant of such a man we mean when we speak of "a righteous man afflicted with adversity." In regard to the fate of such a man our teacher Moses concluded that Israel might be unwilling to attempt to fathom the intricate ways of Him whose presence is everywhere, and hence the decree of punishment, God forbid, would surely be sealed against them and they would be smitten each and every hour. By what parable may EZ, *p.* 182 *cont'd*

---

1. His thirteen attributes of mercy specified in Exod. 34:6–7.

the matter be understood? By the one of a mortal king who took a wife and traveled with her from province to province. Whenever she displeased him, he had her whipped with the lash. At length the king's father-in-law sent a messenger to the king asking: Tell me exactly what you desire from a wife, and I will instruct my daughter to provide what you ask. Thereupon the king sent five kinds of fruit to his father-in-law, each fruit accompanied by a letter indicating that the fruit stood for a particular thing the king wanted his wife to serve him. When the fruits and the letters reached the king's father-in-law, he read the first of the letters in which the king had written, "This is the kind of fruit that a wife of the right kind would serve me." He read the second letter in which was written, "This is the kind of fruit that a wife of the right kind would serve me"; the third in which was written, "This is the kind of fruit that a wife of the right kind would serve me"; the fourth in which was written, "This is the kind of fruit that a wife of the right kind would serve me." When the father-in-law reached the last letter in which the king indicated what he wanted his wife to serve him, the king's father-in-law notified his daughter, saying to her: The king [wants you to serve him what he loves: he] loves truth, loves peace, loves justice and charity.[2]

EZ, *p.* 183 | [Like the father-in-law in the parable], Moses asked: *Now, therefore, I pray Thee, if I have found favor in Thy sight, show me now Thy ways, that I may know Thee* (Exod. 33:13), [for Moses was fearful that the people of Israel, baffled by what appeared to be God's arbitrary ways and thus tempted to disregard His commands, would be punished by Him. For Israel's sake Moses asked the Holy One what means of explaining His ways to them He would provide]. Thereupon, the Holy One showed him each generation-to-come with its Sages, with its Prophets, with its interpreters of Scripture, with the leaders of its communities, with its saints in whose behalf miracles occur. Through such men, [the "letters" spoken of in the parable], God promised Moses that His plan for this world and for the world-to-come would be made clear to Israel.

Thereupon Moses spoke up to God saying: Master of the universe, You have shown me Your plan of [instruction, the Torah, for] the world. Now show me the plan whereby the world is directed. Lo, I see the righteous man who enjoys prosperity and the righteous man who

---

2. The intent of the parable: God accompanies Israel His spouse from country to country. Whenever Israel displeases Him, He has her whipped (afflicted by the nations). At length, Moses, Israel's "father" and God's "father-in-law," asks God just how He wants Israel to conduct herself. God's reply in His letters—i.e., His instruction of Israel in right conduct by way of Torah as communicated by the Sages, Prophets, interpreters of Scripture, etc.—requires Israel to serve Him with the fruit of understanding of Torah, the fruits being truth, peace, justice, and charity in service of Him and mankind.

is afflicted with adversity, the wicked man who enjoys prosperity and the wicked man who is afflicted with adversity, the rich man with whom things go well and the rich man with whom things go ill, the poor man with whom things go well and the poor man with whom things go ill: *Show me, I pray Thee, Thy glory* (Exod. 33:18). The Holy One replied: Moses, you cannot fathom My ways. But I will show you some of My ways. For example, I see men from whom there is no expectation of merit—neither from their deeds nor from the deeds of their fathers. Still, because they rise up to bless, beseech, and supplicate Me with prayers, I respond to them and double the provisions I intended for them, as is said, *He will regard the prayer of the man who raises a cry*[3] [*for mercy*] (Ps. 102:18)—[that is, the cry of the average man who has no particular merit, but cries mercy]. And God went on: *I will make all My goodness* [*bestowed alike upon the righteous and the wicked*] *pass before thee* (Exod. 33:19)—*"My goodness,"* as specified by its thirteen attributes: *The Lord, the Lord, God, merciful and gracious, long-suffering, and abundant in goodness and truth; keeping mercy unto the thousandth generation, forgiving iniquity, and having pass out of mind transgression and sin, clearing* [*those who repent*][4] (Exod. 34:6–7). Had God said, "My goodness," and not *all My goodness,* I might have supposed that the days of the Messiah were not included, [days during which recompense is to be given to the righteous who in this world did not supplicate for the happiness which God's mercy bestows]. But since He said, *all My goodness,* He meant to include the days of the Messiah.[5] And God went on to say, *I will proclaim the name of the Lord* [*of mercy*] *before thee (ibid.).* Then, as Scripture says, *The Lord descended in the cloud and proclaimed that the name Lord* [*implies mercy*], *for He has* [*all Israel's evil*] *pass away from before Him, so that he is able to proclaim Himself the Lord* [*of mercy*],[6] etc. (Exod. 34:5–6). When Moses saw God's way to be one of loving-kindness and of compassion, he enfolded himself [in a prayer shawl] and stood up in prayer before the Holy One, as is said, *If now I have found grace in Thy sight, O Lord, let the Lord, I pray Thee, go in the midst of us* (Exod. 34:8).

---

3. Rashi on the verse and on Isa. 15:5 associates *'r'r* (in Ps. 102:18, JV, "destitute") with *yĕʿoʿeru,* "raise." See above, ER, 20.

4. JV: *forgiving iniquity and transgression and sin, and that will by no means clear.* But here the latter phrase is rendered literally "clearing [those who repent], but not clearing [those who do not]." See Rashi *ad loc.* and PR 16:1 (YJS, *18, 1,* 343–44).

5. In two private communications, Professor Louis Finkelstein interpreted the preceding parable as well as the passage that follows it.

6. JV: *proclaimed the name of the Lord: And the Lord passed by before him, and proclaimed: "The Lord,"* etc. But see above, ER, 3.

CHAPTER [7]

Through the agency of good men, good things are brought about even to the fourth generation

Summary

Jehu was a God-fearing man, but after he had achieved eminence his deeds became corrupt. Nevertheless, well-being was bestowed upon his descendants through four generations. For example, to his great grandson, Jeroboam, who accorded honor to Prophets, God gave territory in the Land which had not been turned over to Joshua (EZ, 184).

Chapter [7]

EZ, *p.* 184 Come and see the measure of well-being [a man can enjoy]. When a man has done a good deed, well-being is bestowed upon him [and his descendants] through four generations. So it was with Jehu son of Nimshi, as is said, *And the Lord said unto Jehu: Because thou hast done well in executing that which is right in Mine eyes . . . thy sons of the fourth generation shall sit on the throne of Israel* (2 Kings 10:30). Of Jehu son of Nimshi it is said that he was a God-fearing man to begin with and was not drawn to the worship of the golden calves that Jeroboam son of Nebat had made. Once Jehu reached eminence, however, and entered upon his reign, his deeds became corrupt. Had his son Jehoahaz come and vowed repentance [for his own sins], he would have been in the class of righteous men upon whom well-being is bestowed; had he not vowed repentance, he would have been in the class of wicked men upon whom well-being is bestowed. When Joash son of Jehoahaz, son of Jehu, came to the throne after him, had he vowed repentance [for his own sins], he too would have been in the class of righteous men upon whom well-being is bestowed; had he not vowed repentance, he would have been in the class of wicked men upon whom well-being is bestowed. When Jeroboam son of Joash, son of Jehoahaz, son of Jehu came to the throne,[1] had he vowed repentance [for his own sins], he would likewise have been in the class of righteous men upon whom well-being is bestowed; had he not vowed repentance, he would have been in the class of wicked men upon whom well-being is bestowed.

Of Jeroboam son of Joash it is said that he was a man who accorded honor to Prophets. Hence what territory the Holy One did not turn

---

1. On the succession—Jehu, Jehoahaz, Joash, Jeroboam—see 2 Kings 10:30 through 14:29.

over to Joshua son of Nun and to David, king of Israel, he turned over to Jeroboam, as is said, *He restored the border of Israel from the entrance of Hamath unto the sea of the Arabah, according to the word of the Lord . . . which He spoke by the hand of His servant Jonah the son of Amittai* (2 Kings 14:25). Of Jeroboam, Scripture says further, *For the Lord saw the affliction of Israel, that it was very bitter. . . . And the Lord said not that He would blot out the name of Israel from under heaven; but He saved them by the hand of Jeroboam the son of Joash* (2 Kings 14:26–27). But why such special regard for Jeroboam? Was not Jeroboam an idol-worshiper? Yes, but he refused to accept Amaziah's slander of the prophet Amos, as is said, *Amaziah the priest of Beth-El sent to Jeroboam king of Israel, saying: Amos hath conspired against thee. . . . For thus Amos saith: Jeroboam shall die by the sword,* etc. (Amos 7:10–11). At once Jeroboam rebuked Amaziah and sent him away with a reprimand, for he said: God forbid! The prophet could not have uttered such a prophecy. If he did utter it, however, it would not have been his own prophecy but Heaven's.[2]

Thereupon the Holy One said: Here is a generation that worships idols! The head of the generation worships idols! Nevertheless, [because Jeroboam was a descendant of him upon whom God had bestowed well-being unto the fourth generation, God went on to say]: The Land which I promised—*The Land of which I swore unto Abraham, to Isaac, and to Jacob, saying: Unto thy seed will I give it* (Exod. 33:1)—I shall give into the hand of this very person. Then, as Scripture tells us, [*Jeroboam*] *restored the border of Israel from the entrance of Hamath unto the sea of Arabah* (2 Kings 14:25). Hence it is said: Through the agency of good men, good things are brought about [even to the fourth generation], and through the agency of evil men, evil things are brought about [even to the fourth generation].

This rule applies to all the families of the earth—whether the family of Israel or the families of the nations.

---

2. Cf. above, ER, 88.

CHAPTER [8]

Though Israel's years of sin cause God continuing anguish, He remains merciful

Summary

God resembles a man who was content before he wed, but then, having wed and fathered children who did not behave properly, had sorrow enter his heart. Even so the children of Israel grieve God, thus "diminishing," so to speak, His soul. Such "diminishing" has gone on for three hundred and ninety years out of the four hundred and ten that the First Temple stood. Again and again, Israel —kings and people alike—rejected Prophets who came to admonish Israel (EZ, 185). Nevertheless, though Elijah was right in feeling provoked by Israel, God was displeased that he did not entreat mercy for Israel and said to him: What you have in mind for Me to do, namely, destroy Israel, I cannot do (EZ, 186).

Chapter [*8*]

EZ, *p.* 185 In keeping with His nature as previously discussed, the Holy One rejoices at encountering a man who does good and is saddened at encountering one who does evil. And the truth of this statement you can see for yourself by going out and taking note of how things go in the world. Before a man weds and has children, his disposition is cheerful; in his heart there is neither sorrow nor regret, and in his household there is contentment. Once he weds, and having observed the command to increase and multiply comes to father sons who do not behave properly, he is no longer cheerful, there is sorrow and regret in his heart and no contentment in his household.

Even so, have we, [His sons], brought grief to the Light of our eyes. Until He created man upon the earth, His disposition was cheerful. After He created man upon the earth, we provoked Him like sons who vex the spirit of their father by their ways and their deeds. Thus the Holy One, if one dare say such a thing, allowed sorrow and sighing to enter <His heart>, and finds no contentment in the entire world —nowhere at all. And the proof you can see for yourself. For three hundred years[1] during the time the judges ruled, Israel worshiped idols. Therefore, in the reign of Cushan-rishathaim, [king of Aram-naharaim], God gave them over into this king's hand, so Israel turned about, vowed repentance, and He freed them from Cushan's grasp.[2]

---

1. The same number of years is mentioned above, in ER, 86.
2. Judg. 3:7–11.

But in the days of Eglon, king of Moab, Israel again worshiped idols, and when God gave them over into this king's hand, they turned about, vowed repentance, and He freed them from his grasp.[3] Once again, in the days of Jabin, king of Canaan, when they worshiped idols, God gave them over into this king's hand, they turned about, vowed repentance, and He freed them from his grasp.[4] Both in the Land and outside the Land, Israel worshiped idols. Generation after generation they continued to do so, as is said, *The children of Israel continued to do that which was evil in the sight of the Lord. . . . And the anger of the Lord was kindled against Israel, and He gave them over into the hand of the Philistines, and into the hand of the children of Ammon* (Judg. 10:6–7). So then Israel once more turned about, vowed repentance, and God received them because of their repentance. *And they put away the strange gods from among them, and served the Lord* (Judg. 10:16). Prior to that, the verse goes on to say, *and*— were it not that the verse is so clear, it is scarcely conceivable that one would dare say such a thing—*His soul was diminished because of the grievous mischief of Israel* (Judg. 10:16). And the proof that we wearied Him, vexed Him, and contemned Him? The plain fact that of the four hundred and ten years God dwelt in the First Temple,[5] for all but twenty years of its existence was He alone worshiped there: during the remaining three hundred and ninety[6] years the kings of Israel and the kings of Judah worshiped idols.

From each and every prophet who spoke to Israel, they did not take the boon that he proffered. Instead they said: We do not want your prophecy. As for the proof of their rejection, you can see it for yourself in the argument between Ahab king of Israel and Elijah the Tishbite. Ahab began by saying, It is written in the Torah, *Take heed to yourselves, lest your heart be deceived, and ye turn aside, and serve other gods, and worship them; and the anger of the Lord be kindled against you, and He shut up the heaven, so that there shall be no rain* (Deut. 11:16–17). Yet to me, who worship all the idols in the world, just see how many boons have come in my lifetime! Thus, as Scripture says, *In* [*Ahab's*] *days did Hiel the Beth-elite rebuild Jericho; with Abiram his first-born he laid the foundation thereof, and with his youngest son Segub he set up the gates thereof; according to the word of the Lord which He spoke by the hand of Joshua the son of Nun*

---

3. Judg. 3:12–30.
4. Judg. 4–5.
5. Cf. above, ER, 19.
6. A number intimated in the number of days God told Ezekiel to lie on his left side (Ezek. 4:4–5). Apparently, only during the first twenty years after the Temple was built, was there no worship of idols. But then the wives whom Solomon wed introduced various cults of idolatry (1 Kings 11:1–10) which continued in Judah or in Israel or in both countries until the Temple was destroyed. So Haida. See also SOR, chap. 26.

But, according to Louis Ginzberg, "these twenty years probably represent the reign of Josiah; although he reigned for thirty-one years, he began the work of purification only in the twelfth year of his kingship; (2 Chron. 34:3)." See *An Unknown Jewish Sect* (New York, 5736/1976), p. 259, n. 7.

(1 Kings 16:34). [Now Ahab doubted that the death of Hiel's sons was indeed the result of Joshua's curse that Jericho be not rebuilt, arguing: If the words of Moses concerning rain remain unfulfilled, for in spite of my idolatry, there is so much rain that the roads are impassable, is it likely that the words of Joshua have come true]?[7] At once, Elijah [who was then with Ahab in Hiel's home] was filled with great wrath at Ahab, and said to him: You good-for-nothing wretch! You spurned Him who created the entire world, every bit of it, for His glory—spurned Him who gave us the words of Torah for His glory. As you live, I shall impose punishment upon you according to your very own words. Hence, as is said in the very next verse, *Elijah the Tishbite, who was of the settlers of Gilead, replied to Ahab: As the Lord the God of Israel liveth . . . there shall not be dew nor rain these years, but according to my word* (1
EZ, *p.* 186 Kings 17:1). Then Elijah took | the key to rain and went away. And [because there was neither dew nor rain] in the entire world, in any part of it, there was a great famine until the Preserver of the world said to Elijah: *Go, show thyself unto Ahab* [*so that he may repent*], *and I will send rain upon the Land* (1 Kings 18:1). Nay more! The Holy One proceeded to force Elijah to go to a place where his forebears were wont to entreat mercy for His children, as is said, [*In Beer-sheba*], *he lay down and slept under a broom-tree. . . . And he arose, and did eat and drink, and went in the strength of that meal forty days and forty nights unto Horeb the Mount of God*[8] (1 Kings 19:5, 8). Then the Holy One asked Elijah: *What doest thou here, Elijah?* (1 Kings 19:9). Elijah should have responded with an entreaty for mercy, saying: Master of the universe, Israel are Your children, the children of those who have been tested by You, the children of Abraham, Isaac, and Jacob who have done Your will in the world. But this was not what Elijah said. Instead he dared to say to God: *I have been very jealous for the Lord, the God of hosts; for the children of Israel have forsaken Thy covenant, thrown down Thine altars, and slain Thy Prophets with the sword; and I, even I, only am left* (1 Kings 19:10). The Holy One then began to utter words meant to placate Elijah, saying to him: When I revealed Myself to give Torah to Israel on Mount Sinai, only ministering angels who desire Israel's good revealed themselves with Me.[9] The Holy One went on to say: *"Go forth, and stand upon the Mount before the Lord* [*of mercy*]*." And, behold, the Lord* [*of mercy*] *passed by, and a great and strong wind rent the mountains . . . but the Lord* [*of mercy*] *was not in the wind; and after the wind an earthquake . . . and after the earthquake a fire; but the Lord* [*of mercy*] *was not in the*

7. For the interpolated passage, see B.Sanh 113a. In Parma MS 2785 a similar passage is set forth in Hebrew.

8. At Beer-sheba, the Patriarchs entreated God; and at Horeb, Moses entreated Him.

9. They bestowed crowns upon each and every one in Israel. See above, EZ, 179.

fire; and after the fire a sound of gentle stillness (1 Kings 19:11–12). For three hours the Holy One waited for Elijah [to come and entreat mercy for Israel]. But Elijah persisted in the words he had uttered previously: *I have been very jealous for the Lord, the God of hosts* (1 Kings 19:14). Thereupon the holy spirit said to Elijah: *"Go, return on the way to the wilderness of Damascus . . . and Jehu the son of Nimshi shalt thou anoint to be king over Israel; and Elisha the son of Shaphat of Abel-meholah shalt thou anoint to be prophet in thy room"*[10] (1 Kings 19:15–16). For what you have in mind for Me to do, [namely, to destroy Israel], I cannot do.

---

10. Jehu was to destroy the worshipers of Baal, and Elisha was to be more forgiving than Elijah.

CHAPTER 9

God's ways of dealing with sinners

Summary

When God said to Hosea, "See what Israel are up to" (EZ, 186), Hosea told Him, "Put another people in their place." In reply, God told him to wed a woman of ill-fame and have children by her. But when He asked Hosea to leave his wife, Hosea said, "I cannot, I have children by her." Whereupon God said: You wed a whorish wife, your children are children of whoredom, yet you say, "I cannot divorce her." How then do you expect Me to give up Israel who are My beloved, children of My beloved Abraham, Isaac, and Jacob—expect Me to give up Israel who are one of the five masterpieces I own in the world?

After Hosea, there prophesied Isaiah who also lived in the reign of Uzziah, king of Judah. Uzziah was followed by Ahaz who wickedly decreed that Israel were not to occupy themselves with Torah (EZ, 187) and by Manasseh who wickedly sought to make it impossible for any one to pray to God.

Nevertheless, it was in the reign of Hoshea that the Ten Tribes were exiled. They were exiled then because until he came, the transgression of idolatry was linked with an individual, each successive king. But when Hoshea came, he abolished the border posts which had kept the people of the northern kingdom from going up to Jerusalem. Instead of going up, however, the people continued in their idolatry. Hoshea should have compelled them to go up to Jerusalem.

Still later, when the Tribe of Judah was about to be exiled, thus marking the exile of the entire people, God wished to go into exile with them (EZ, 188). The angels, seeking to comfort Him, said: But you still have the seventy nations of the world. God replied: I know that in the end the nations will not worship Me and that Israel will repent.

Then God ordered the ministering angels to go down from His presence and lift the burdens from the shoulders of Israel going into exile.

God spared Manasseh, wicked though he was, because He knew that righteous men were to issue from him. Even so He spares Israel, knowing that ultimately righteous men will issue from them (EZ, 189).

Chapter 9

EZ, *p.* 186 *cont'd* In the reign of Uzziah, king of Judah, there were four Prophets[1] who prophesied—Hosea, Isaiah, Amos, and Micah[2]—and Hosea the son of Beeri was the oldest of them. As the Holy One was scrutinizing each one of them to see which would entreat mercy in behalf of His children, the Holy One said to Hosea, "Hosea, do you see[3] Israel and what they

1. "Prophets"—Parma MS 2785; R: "elders."
2. "Hosea, Isaiah, Amos, and Micah"—R. Cf. B.Pes 87a.
3. "do you see"—Parma MS 2785; R: "I see."

are up to?" Hosea should have responded, "[Have mercy on them], Master of the universe, they are Your children, children of those who were tested by You, children of Abraham, Isaac, and Jacob who did Your will." But Hosea did not say this. Instead he dared to say to God: "Master of the universe, | all the world, every part of it, is Yours [to do with as you like]. Put another people in their place." **EZ, *p.* 187**

In saying *When the Lord spoke first by Hosea* (Hos. 1:2), [is Scripture intimating that Hosea was the first of the Prophets]? Were there not, in fact, many Prophets before him? What Scripture means, however, is that among the four older [Prophets] of Uzziah's time, the Lord chose to speak to Hosea first.

When [Hosea told Him to replace Israel with another people], the Holy One said: What shall I do with this creature of flesh-and-blood? I shall tell him: "Take yourself a wife," and he will take a wife and have children. Then I shall tell him: "Leave her." Thereupon if he sends her away and divorces her, I, likewise, will send Israel from My presence. As Scripture tells us, *The Lord said unto Hosea: "Go, take unto thee a wife of harlotry and children of harlotry; for the Land doth commit great harlotry departing from the Lord." So he went and took Gomer the daughter of Diblaim* (Hos. 1:2–3), a woman of ill-fame and the daughter of a woman of ill-fame.[4] *And she conceived, and bore him a son. And the Lord said unto him: Call his name Jezreel, for yet a little while, and I will visit the blood of Jezreel upon the house of Jehu* (Hos. 1:3–4).

Then a daughter was born to Hosea, and God said: *Call her name Lo-ruhamah,* "She that hath not obtained compassion" (Hos. 1:6). Then a third child was born to Hosea, *and God said: Call his name Lo-ammi, for ye, [Israel], are not My people* (Hos. 1:9). Thus three children were born to Hosea, and with them were issued three decrees against Israel:[5] [that they were to be dispersed, that they were to be rejected, that they were not to be regarded with pity].

Next, the Holy One said to Hosea: "Why did you not learn from your master Moses? For as soon as I spoke to him about separating from his wife, he did so.[6] You—why do you continue to live with your wife? Leave her." Hosea replied, "I cannot send her away or divorce her—I have children by her." Then the Holy One said: "You who are mere flesh-and-blood, who wed a whorish wife and whose children are children of whoredom, you who do not know whether the children are yours or another's, still say, 'I cannot divorce her or even put her out,

---

4. [*Diblaim,* seemingly a dual form of *dĕḇelah,* "pressed fig-cake" (possibly used as a euphemism for "harlot"), suggests to the author the similarly sounding dual *dibbaṭayim,* "double ill-fame." L.N.]

5. *Jezreel,* whose stem *zr',* "sow," suggests that God would "sow" or scatter Israel among the nations; *lo-ammi,* "not My people," and *Lo-ruhamah,* "one not evoking pity."

6. See Exod. 18:2.

because I have children by her.' As for Me, Israel are My beloved, children of My beloved, children of Abraham, Isaac, and Jacob. They are one of the five masterpieces I own in My world: Torah is a masterpiece, heaven and earth are a masterpiece, Abraham is a masterpiece, Israel is a masterpiece, the Temple is a masterpiece. How, then, can I put My children out of My presence?" [At God's reproach of him], Hosea began entreating mercy for himself. The Holy One replied: "Hosea, Hosea, because of you, three decrees of punishment were issued against Israel. Go back and heal them of their wounds." At once Hosea said: *The number of the children of Israel shall be as the sand of the sea, which cannot be measured nor numbered* (Hos. 2:1). *And I will sow her unto Me in the Land; and I will have compassion upon her that hath not obtained compassion; and I will say to them that were not My people: "thou art My people"; and they shall say: "Thou art my God"* (Hos. 2:25).[7]

In the reign of Ahaz king of Judah, words of Torah were so accessible that they were like living teachers. Hence, [intending to wage war against God and beginning with war against Torah], Ahaz set to and sealed up the Torah, having decreed that Israel were not to occupy themselves with it,[8] as Isaiah intimates in the verse *Bind up the Testimony, seal up the instruction from among My disciples* (Isa. 8:15). Thereupon, the Holy One said to him, to Isaiah: Isaiah, Isaiah, go say to Ahaz, that creature of mere flesh-and-blood: *Ask thee a sign of* [*the*
EZ, *p.* 188 *omniscience of*] | *the Lord thy God: ask it either in the depth, or in the height above* (Isa. 7:10). [Thus you will get to the heart of Ahaz's intentions. Ahaz, pretending innocence, replied, *"I will not ask, I never meant to test the Lord*]*." "Listen,* [*Ahaz of the*] *house of David,"* [*Isaiah*] *retorted: "Is it not enough for thee that thou treatest men as easily taken in, wouldst thou also treat my God as easily taken in?* (Isa. 7:12–13). [He knows well your enmity to Him.][9]

During the reign of Manasseh the son of Hezekiah king of Judah, it was he who went and made an image with four faces[10] and set it up in the Holy Place, his purpose being to make it impossible for any one to pray therein to the Holy One. Then the Holy One said to Isaiah: Isaiah, Isaiah, go say to that creature of mere flesh-and-blood, *Thus saith the Lord of hosts: The heaven is My throne, and the earth is My footstool* (Isa. 66:1). And not only am I enthroned above the [visible] heaven, but I am also enthroned above all the other, [invisible], heavens variously

---

7. Cf. B.Pes 87a–b.

8. Ahaz is said to have shut up the doors of synagogues and schools to prevent the study of Torah. See 2 Chron. 28:24; MTeh 2:10 (YJS, *13, 1,* 42); and Gen. Rabbah 42:2.

9. Professor Sid Z. Leiman provided the interpretation of this difficult paragraph.

10. Perhaps in imitation of the four faces on the chariot described by Ezekiel. So Schick. Cf. above, ER, 161, and B.Sanh 103b.

described as "curtain," "expanse," "firmament," "habitation," "dwelling," "residence," and "skies." *Where, then, is the house that ye may build unto Me? And where is the place that may be My resting-place? (ibid.).* [Do you suppose, Manasseh, that by the image you set up in the Holy Place, you can convince men that I am only there, in that one place?] When Manasseh's punishment befell him—[he was boiled in a copper kettle][11]—at once he prayed for mercy, as is said, *And he prayed unto Him, and He was entreated of him, and heard his supplication, and brought him back to Jerusalem into his kingdom. Then Manasseh knew that the Lord He was God* (2 Chron. 33:13). [God heeded his prayer, even though] of Manasseh, of those like him, of those who resemble him, and of those who perform deeds like his, what does Scripture say? *Ye have wearied the Lord with your words. Yet ye say: "Wherein have we wearied Him?" In that ye say: "Every one that doeth evil is good in the sight of the Lord, and He delighteth in them; or where is the God of justice?"* (Mal. 2:17).

In the reign of Hoshea son of Elah, the Land was taken, and in his reign the Ten Tribes were exiled. Was Hoshea son of Elah any different from all the kings of Israel who had come before him in that the Land was taken during his reign and the Ten Tribes were exiled during his reign? He was different because from the time Jeroboam son of Nebat ruled until Hoshea son of Elah came to the throne, the transgression of idolatry was identified with an individual, [each successive king], and it was difficult for the Father of mercy to exile the congregation [of Israel] because of the iniquity of an individual. But when Hoshea son of Elah came along, he abolished all the border posts, every one of them, and said in a proclamation: Whoever wishes to go up to Jerusalem, let him go up. [But the people, instead of going up, continued in their idolatry].[12] Of him Scripture says, *And he did that which was evil in the sight of the Lord, yet not as the kings of Israel that were before him. Still because of him*[13] *came up Shalmaneser king of Assyria . . . and carried Israel away unto Assyria* (2 Kings 17:2–3, 6). For what Hoshea did was remove the [iron] collar from his own neck and hang it on the neck of the many [by not compelling them to go up to Jerusalem]. Hence it is said: He who begins doing a command but does not carry it out to the end makes himself, and all that are his, liable to the death penalty —indeed, in the end it is likely that he will bury his wife and his two children.[14]

---

11. Manasseh was put into a copper kettle shaped like a jackass, and a slow fire was started under the kettle. See PRKM 24:11, 27:3 (PRKS, pp. 375–76, 415–16).

12. See B.Ta 30b; Giṭ 88a; and Ginzberg, *Legends, 4,* 265.

13. JV: *against him.*

14. An allusion to Judah, who, having failed to complete the effort he initiated to save Joseph, lost his wife and his two sons. See Gen. 38:12, 7, 9; B.Soṭ 13b; and Gen. Rabbah 85:3.

In the reign of Zedekiah king of Judah, the prophet Jeremiah prophesied [dire things] concerning Israel in the hope that they would resolve to repent and return to the way of goodness. Thereat Israel got ready to slay him and threw him into a pit. Later they had him brought up from the pit and put him in the court of the guardhouse. Many times, Israel prepared to slay him, until he was driven finally to curse them again and again. And each and every time Jeremiah cursed Israel, the Holy One sighed as He came to him and said: *If when thou runnest with footmen, they exhaust thee, then how canst thou contend with horses?*[15] (Jer. 12:5).

When the Ten Tribes went into exile, Jerusalem went into exile with them.[16] When the Tribes of Judah and of Benjamin went into exile and Jerusalem went into exile with them, the Holy One wished to
EZ, *p.* 189 accompany them. | Thereupon the ministering angels gathered in His presence to soothe Him and comfort Him, saying to Him: Master of the universe, [though the Ten Tribes are now in exile with Judah about to join them], You still have seventy peoples in the world. Besides we are here, so many of us that there is no possibility of guessing at our number, never mind counting us. The Holy One replied: Am I flesh-and-blood that I require comforting? Do I not know the beginning of all things and do I not know the end of them? Yes, I know the beginning and I know the end—[I know that in the end the nations will not worship Me and that Israel will repent]—as is said, *Even to old age I am the same, and even to hoar hairs will I carry; I have made, and I will bear; yea, I will carry, and will deliver* (Isa. 46:4). *Therefore said I: Look away from Me, I will weep bitterly; labor not to comfort Me* (Isa. 22:4). Why does not Scripture say, "Gather not to comfort Me," "Assemble not to comfort Me," "Come not to comfort Me," "Continue not to comfort Me?" Instead Scripture says, *Labor not to comfort Me.* By the unusual word *labor* God meant to say: The words of comfort that you would console Me with are like blasphemies.[17] Go down from My presence and look at My people Israel who are going into exile with burdens on their shoulders. Precipitously, the ministering angels went down from His presence and lifted the burdens from the shoulders of Israel. In this connection Scripture says, *Thus saith the Lord, your Re-*

15. A great reward, four kings as descendants, was bestowed upon Merodach-baladan because he took three steps—a pedestrian act—in deference to God (see PRKM 2:5, p. 24 [PRKS, pp. 28–29]). How much greater, then, is the reward coming to Israel whose pace in good deeds may be compared to that of swift steeds! How, then, do you, Jeremiah, expect your curses to take effect? See B.Sanh 96a.

16. Perhaps because there had been many pilgrims from the kingdom of Israel. And so their exile was deemed like the exile of Jerusalem.

17. Rendering *ta'iṣu,* "labor," as if it read *tĕna'ăṣu* "blaspheme": "Do not blaspheme by way of comforting Me."

deemer, the Holy One of Israel: For your sake I had Myself go[18] *to Babylon* (Isa. 43:14).

If you say that when a man commits a transgression, he should die at once, then it follows that the entire world, all of it, should be destroyed [because no mortal is free of transgression]. And the proof of this statement? Go infer it from the example of Manasseh, the son of Hezekiah, king of Judah, who left no idol in the world which he did not worship. Yet the Holy One spared him and did not slay him. Why? Because righteous men were to issue from him. Hence it is said: Even if a man should brazenly commit a hundred transgressions, each and every one more grievous than the one preceding, but then should turn about and resolve upon repentance, < the Holy One will say, I am with him in compassion and will receive him in repentance. Or if a man should proceed to blaspheme against the One above, but then turn about and resolve upon repentance, the Holy One will say >, I forgive him all his iniquities, as is said, *Have I any pleasure at all that the wicked shall die? saith the Lord God; and not rather that he should return from his ways, and live?* (Ezek. 18:23). *For I have no pleasure in the death of him that dieth, saith the Lord God; wherefore turn yourselves, and live* (Ezek. 33:11); and *Then shall ye again discern between the righteous and the wicked, between him that serveth God and him that serveth Him not* (Mal. 3:18).

The Holy One said further to Israel: My children, come and enter deep into Torah and see what I wrote therein for you to do so as to enable Me to bear your transgressions, to put away your iniquities, and to have your sins pass out of My sight. Now come at Me with words of Torah, and you will find yourselves face to face with Me as close as a man confronting his fellow in battle,[19] as is said, *Return, O Israel, close unto the Lord thy God. . . . Take with you words* [*of Torah*] (Hos. 14:2–3).

---

18. This rendering is required by the comment which interprets the word *šillaḥti,* "I sent," as though it read *šullaḥti,* "I was sent," that is, "I had Myself go." See Meḵ, *1,* 115, and PR 28:2 (YJS, *18, 2,* 556–57).

19. Cf. above, ER, 89.

CHAPTER [10]

The rightness of God's ways

Summary

A man should not mutter about the ways of God. After all, nine hundred and seventy-four generations before the world was to be created, God analyzed, refined, and tested all the words of Torah two hundred and forty-eight times with the same care He gave to putting together the two hundred and forty-eight parts of the human body (EZ, 189). With like care He set down every word in His Torah. Hence, to move even one word of Torah ever so little from its place is to bring about the destruction of the entire world, every bit of it. Thus, when He changed His mind and decided to give the power of speech to the serpent, the serpent forthwith corrupted the world, all of it. When He changed His mind and decided not to visit the iniquity of the fathers upon the children, the ten generations between Adam and Noah sank into violence, robbery, lewdness, and bloodshed. When He changed His mind and decided that all mankind was to speak one language, they immediately sought to destroy the world, every bit of it. When He changed His mind and decided to take away the High Priesthood from Phinehas and give it to the descendants of Ithamar, they proceeded to abuse it with their iniquities (EZ, 190). So, too, His changing His mind and His decision to give Torah to Balaam as well as to Israel resulted in an experience for God of something unclean.

It was then God swore that thereafter He would not exchange Israel for another people, nor have them dwell in a city other than Jerusalem (EZ, 191).

Chapter [10]

EZ, *p.* 189 *cont'd* You thus learn that a man should not fall to muttering when he sees that of two men, the righteous one suffers <adversity>, and the wicked one enjoys prosperity. If he falls to muttering, he is liable to incur the penalty of death, as is said, *Suffer not thy mouth to bring thy flesh into guilt* (Eccles. 5:5).

The Sages taught: Nine hundred and seventy-four generations before the world was to be created,[1] the Holy One sat and inquired into, analyzed, refined, and tested all words of Torah two hundred and forty-eight times with the same painstaking care He gave to selecting and putting together the two hundred and forty-eight parts of the
EZ, *p.* 190 human body.[2] Then | the Holy One took up the words and set them in His Torah, His very own. Take note again that each and every word

---

1. On the number of generations, see above, ER, chap. 2, n. 22.

2. On the number of parts in the human body, see *Masseket 'Ohălot,* ed. Abraham Goldberg (Jerusalem, 5715/1955), p. 9, in comment on Oh 1:9.

that the Holy One took up and set in His Torah, <He did not set in His Torah> until He had inquired into, analyzed, refined, and tested it two hundred and forty-eight times with the same painstaking care He gave to selecting and putting together the two hundred and forty-eight parts of the human body, as is said, *The words of the Lord are pure words, as silver tried in a crucible on the earth, refined seven times seven*[3] (Ps. 12:7). Only after [such intensive study] did the Holy One take up each word and set it in His Torah. Accordingly, to move any one word of Torah ever so little from its set place is to bring about the destruction of the entire world, every bit of it.

It had been the intention of the Holy One not to give the power of speech to animals, but when He changed His mind and gave the power of speech to the serpent, the serpent corrupted the world, all of it.[4]

In regard to the ten generations from Adam to Noah, it had been the Holy One's intention to visit at once the iniquity of the fathers upon the children. <But He changed His mind>, and instead made each and every man sovereign over his wife, his children, and the members of his household. As a result men had no <fear> of government, nor of the possibility of punishment, nor of the possibility of Divine justice, as is said, *Their houses are safe without fear, neither is there the rod of God upon them*[5] (Job 21:9). <So they ate, and drank, and were sated, and being full of beans became insolent>: *They said unto God: Depart from us; for we desire not the knowledge of Thy ways* (Job 21:14). They sank into violence and robbery, as is said, *The earth was filled with violence* (Gen. 6:11). They sank into lewdness, as is said, *All flesh had corrupted their way upon the earth* (Exod. 6:12). They sank into bloodshed, as is said, *And God saw the earth, and behold, it was being destroyed* [*by murder*][6] *(ibid.).* Nay more! They discarded their raiment upon the ground and, without their garments, walked naked in public, as is said, *They go about naked without clothing* (Job 24:10).

In regard to the ten generations from Noah to Abraham, it had been the intention of the Holy One <to give each of the seventy peoples of the world its own language. But He changed His mind> and instead had them all speak one language, with the result that they

---

3. JV: *seven times.* But in the preceding comment, *šb'tym,* the dual form of *šb',* "seven," is understood to signify seven times seven, therefore suggesting God's exacting refinement of words of Torah.

4. "People might find fault with God for not having given speech to the animal world—He permitted an exception in enabling the serpent to speak, and the evil brought upon the world by his speech is the best justification for God's limiting speech to man" (Louis Ginzberg, *TSE,* p. 111, n. 12).

5. "as is said, . . . *rod of God upon them*"—Parma MS 2785.

6. JV: *and behold, it was corrupt.*

immediately sought to destroy the whole world, every bit of it, as is said, *And when the whole earth was of one language, they united against the One of the world*[7] (Gen. 11:1).

It had been the intention of the Holy One to give the [High] Priesthood to Phinehas—to him and to his seed for ever. But when, instead, the priesthood was given to the descendants of Ithamar, they proceeded to abuse it with their iniquities.[8]

It had been the Holy One's intention to give kingship to David —to him and to his seed for ever. But when it was given to the kings of Israel, they abused it with their iniquities.

EZ, *p.* 191 | It had been the intention of the Holy One to give Torah and holiness to the peoples of the earth.[9] But when the Torah was given to Balaam the son of Beor, he abused it at once. Yet there was not a thing in the world which the Holy One had left unrevealed to him, to Balaam son of Beor. Why? Because otherwise the nations of the world would have spoken up to the Holy One and said: "Master of the universe, had You given us a prophet like Moses, we would have accepted Your Torah." Therefore the Holy One gave them Balaam son of Beor, who in his native intelligence surpassed Moses. [Still, Balaam was morally inferior to Moses, as shown by the fact that] in His revelation to Moses God made use of the letter[10] *'alef,* the very letter which in revealing Himself to Balaam He omitted. Thus Scripture says, *The Lord called* [*wyḳr',* with the *'alef* at the end] *unto Moses* (Lev. 1:1). But of Balaam, how does Scripture put it? *God called* [*wyḳr* without the *'alef*] *unto Balaam* (Num. 23:4). [Since in this verse *wyḳr* lacks the final *'alef,* it is to be taken as derived from *miḳreh* in the phrase "That which has been rendered unclean by a nocturnal emission" *(miḳreh)* (Deut. 23:11).[11] Hence God's having to reveal Himself to Balaam was an experience for Him of something unclean. In native intelligence, however, as already stated, Balaam exceeded Moses], for Moses had to plead with God, *Show me now Thy glory* (Exod. 33:18);[12] whereas Balaam [did not have to ask to share God's knowledge, for] his speech is referred to in Scripture as *The saying of him . . . who knoweth the knowledge of the Most High* (Num. 24:16).[13] But despite Balaam's knowl-

---

7. To make war against Him. See MTeh 1:13 (YJS, *13, 1,* 17). Leon Nemoy suggests: *"language, and of unanimous intention* [*to defy God*]." JV: *And the whole earth was of one language and of one speech.*

8. Eli, who succeeded Phinehas son of Eleazar, was a descendant of Ithamar, Eleazar's brother. Eli's sons committed iniquitous deeds (see above, ER, 57, and Ginzberg, *Legends, 4,* 61, and *6,* 220).

9. "It had been . . . the peoples of the earth"—Parma MS 2785. R reads: "It had been the intention of the Holy One to give Torah to Israel who are a holy people."

10. The word *daḇar,* "word," is taken to stand for "letter."

11. See R. Ḥama bar Ḥanina's utterance in Lev. Rabbah M, 1:13, p. 28.

12. V and R cite Exod. 33:13, but Exod. 33:18 seems to be more apt.

13. See above, ER, 142.

edge, there was no sincerity in him, nor did any act of mercy come to the world through him. All he came for was to slander [Israel],[14] seeking thereby to destroy the whole world, every bit of it.

Thereupon the Holy One swore to His people that thereafter He would not exchange them for another people, nor give them up for another people, nor have them dwell in any city [other than Jerusalem], as is said, *I will not execute the fierceness of Mine anger, I will not return to destroy Ephraim, for I am . . . the Holy One* [*ever*] *in the midst of thee* (Hos. 11:9).

---

14. He spoke of the calf that the children of Israel had made in the wilderness. See Rashi on Num. 24:1.

CHAPTER [11]

Chastisements of Israel come only for their benefit and only out of God's love for them

Summary

Chastisements of love come to disciples of the wise. If their children die young, they atone for their fathers' sins in this world, and themselves go sinless into the world-to-come.

Hence for the righteous in their earlier years, discord; in their later years, concord. For the wicked, on the other hand, in their earlier years, concord; in their later years, discord (EZ, 191).

The wicked, such as Pharoah, Sennacherib, and Nebuchadnezzar, deserve the punishment allotted to them because God had warned them through a succession of Prophets what their fate was to be. Hence the wicked among the heathen receive the punishment they deserve (EZ, 192).

Chapter [*11*]

EZ, *p.* 191 *cont'd* Chastisements come to Israel only for their own benefit. Chastisements come to Israel only out of God's love for them. By what parable may these statements be illustrated? By the parable of a mortal king, one of whose servants got a wound on his foot [as a result of the king's having him chastised]. The king thereupon summoned a physician to treat the servant and upon his recovery, brought him back into his presence. Thus it is said, *My son, despise not the chastening of the Lord* (Prov. 3:11); and *Whom the Lord loveth He chasteneth, even as a father the son in whom he delighteth* (Prov. 3:12). And what are the chastisements of love? Such as those that come to disciples of the wise <whose children>, if they die young, thereby atone for their fathers' sins in this world, while the children themselves go sinless into the world-to-come. Though Scripture reproaches [those who have thus lost their children], saying, [*Because of thy sins*]—*In thy skirts is found the blood of the souls of innocent* [*children*] (Jer. 2:34), nevertheless Scripture, reversing itself, consoles disciples of the wise by saying, *Whom the Lord loveth He chasteneth, even as a father the son in whom he delighteth* (Prov. 3:11). Hence it is said: For the righteous—in their earlier years, discord; in their later years, concord.[1] For the wicked, on the other hand, in their earlier years, concord; in their later years, discord. Thus Pharaoh had concord in his earlier years, but discord in his later years. What, according to Scripture, did he say in his earlier years? *Who is the Lord, that I should hearken*

1. Because through punishment they have been chastened. Cf. B.Ber 5a–b.

unto His voice to let Israel go? (Exod. 5:2). But what does Scripture say of his later years? *Pharaoh's chariots and his host hath He cast into the sea* (Exod. 15:4). Sennacherib, <king of Assyria>, had concord in his earlier years but discord in his later years. What, according to Scripture, did he say in his earlier years? *Who are they among all the gods of the countries, that have delivered their country out of my hand, that the Lord should deliver Jerusalem out of my hand?* (2 Kings 18:35). But of his later years, | what does Scripture say? *The angel of the Lord went forth, and smote in the camp of the Assyrians . . . and . . . early in the morning, behold, they* EZ, *p.* 192 *were all dead corpses* (2 Kings 19:35). Nebuchadnezzar king of Babylon had concord in his earlier years but discord in his later years. What, according to Scripture, did he say in his earlier years? *I will ascend above the heights of the clouds; I will be like the Most High* (Isa. 14:14). But what was he told in his old age? *Thou shalt be brought down to [the fires of] the nether world, to the uttermost parts of the pit* (Isa. 14:14). And the proof that the wicked have received proper warning and thus deserve the fate which is theirs? Go and reason it out for yourself: From the day the world was created until Israel went out of Egypt, the Holy One went around offering the Torah to each and every nation and tongue, but they all refused to accept it. Moreover, in each and every generation, came witnesses who served warning to the heathen nations [of the fate of the wicked], witnesses such as Eliphaz the Temanite, Bildad the Shuhite, Zophar the Naamathite, Elihu son of Barachel the Buzite, Job from the land of Uz, and the last [and greatest] of all of them, Balaam son of Beor.[2]

Could the Torah possibly have been written with other than God's right hand, or given with other than His right hand? No, for Scripture declares, [*At His right hand was a fiery law unto them* (Deut. 33:2). Hence, let the verse be read], "At His right hand was fire because of the law [which had been offered] unto them." The verse then implies that [the nations' refusal of the Torah led to their wickedness and therefore] from the same hand of God [which bestows mercy] will go forth the fire of His wrath upon the [wicked among the] nations of the world: *The wicked shall be turned into [the fires of] the nether world, all the nations that forget God* (Ps. 9:18). Had Scripture said *The wicked shall be turned into [the fires of] the nether world* and ended the verse with this statement, I would have said that it included both the wicked of Israel and the wicked of the nations of the world. But in going on to say, *all the nations that forget God,* the words "they who forget God" can only mean the wicked among the nations of the world.[3]

And the proof that for the righteous there will be discord in their

---

2. See above, ER, 142, and EZ, 191.

3. Cf. R. Joshua's opinion in Tos Sanh 13:2; and MTeh 9:15 (YJS, *13, 1,* 147). Friedmann erroneously omitted the phrase "wicked among" which is in R.

earlier years and concord in their later years? Abraham had discord in his earlier years and concord in his later years. Of his earlier years, what does Scripture say? *And there was a strife between the herdmen of Abram's cattle and the herdmen of Lot's cattle* (Gen. 13:6). But of his later years, Abraham's servant bore witness, saying, *The Lord hath blessed my master greatly* (Gen. 24:34). Isaac had discord in his earlier years and concord in his later years. Of his earlier years, what does Scripture say? *The herdmen of Gerar strove with Isaac's herdmen* (Gen. 26:20). And of his later years, what does Scripture say? *And he made them a feast* (Gen. 26:30). Jacob had discord in his earlier years and concord in his later years. Of his earlier years, what does Scripture quote him as saying? *Yea, Thou wast angry with me* (Isa. 12:1). And in his later years, what is he quoted as saying? *I will bear the indignation of the Lord . . . until He execute judgment for me . . . and I . . . behold His mercy* (Mic. 7:9); and *Behold, God is my salvation; I will trust, and will not be afraid; for God the Lord is my strength and song, and He is become my salvation* (Isa. 12:2).[4]

---

4. In the three preceding verses, the people of Israel are identified with the experiences of their forebear Jacob who came to be called Israel.

CHAPTER 12

God's reward of the righteous men

Summary

Although God has no need of them, He has many myriads of ministering angels who hallow His name daily. Why, then, does He turn to man, who like an animal eats and defecates? Because by their very nature angels have nothing to overcome in order to prove their love of Him, whereas mortals must struggle hard to serve God. Hence God allows man a crown as radiant as His own (EZ, 193). The degree of radiance on each man's countenance will depend on the righteousness of his ways in his lifetime.

In the world-to-come, in addition to radiance of countenance the righteous will have attendants. These will be ordinary men, unlettered but morally upright (EZ, 194).

Chapter 12

Why, you ask, did the Holy One create man with his Impulse to evil? **EZ, *p.* 193**
Has He not nine hundred and ninety-nine thousand myriads[1] of ministering angels who every day without fail hallow His great name from sunrise to sunset saying, *Holy, holy, holy* (Isa. 6:3), and from sunset to sunrise, saying, *Praised be the glory of the Lord wherever His place be* (Ezek. 3:12)?[2] Does the Holy One have to turn to flesh-and-blood to serve Him, to flesh-and-blood who like an animal eats and defecates? [Indeed, does He even need the service of angels?] When the Holy One appeared on Mount Sinai to give the Torah to His people, He appeared accompanied by only one angel, [the angel closest to His presence],[3] out of the two hundred and forty-eight angels in His immediate entourage, even though the ministering angels and the angels of His entourage, numbering in the thousands as indicated by the verse *The chariots of God are myriads, even thousands upon thousands* (Ps. 68:18), were ready to serve Him. [None of these, however, have anything to overcome in order to show their love of Him by their service.] Consider, on the other hand, a parable of the struggle of mortals to serve Him. A king

---

1. The number (Friedmann, n. 1) may have been derived from a combination of the twenty-two letters of the alphabet forming the words with which God created heaven and earth: nine letters represent numbers under ten; nine letters represent units of ten; and four letters, units of a hundred. To the total of these units, 499, are added the five final letters for a total of 999, a number raised to thousands and myriads. The number 999, not 996, as given above in ER, 84, is correct.

2. Cf. above, ER, 32, 84, and 163.

3. "[the angel closest to His presence]"—so Friedmann (n. 3), who cites *The angel of His presence saved them* (Isa. 63:9).

of flesh-and-blood had servants who dwelt beyond an iron wall, and the king made this proclamation: "Let him who loves me climb up over the iron wall and come to me. For he who comes over the iron wall reveres the king; he who comes over the iron wall loves the king." Accordingly, who may be said to love Him—the ones who came over the wall, [that is, overcame the Impulse to evil], or the ones who did not? Of course, those who came over it are [the ones who loved him and are] the beloved. What is the reward of the angels who minister to Him? *The glory of the Lord reflected from them was like devouring fire*[4] (Exod. 24:17), [but their glory comes not from within them, but from Him]. And the reward of righteous men who serve Him? *They that love Him are as the sun when he goeth forth waxing in his might* (Judg. 5:31)—[their glory comes from within and is their own]. Hence it may be said of God that He is like a householder whose marvelous generosity is such that he allows his servant to win a crown as radiant as his own.[5]

As for the reward of the righteous in the world-to-come, do you suppose that the radiance in the face of the man who read much Scripture and recited much Mishnah and of the man who read little Scripture and recited little Mishnah will be equal? [In this world], no man is favored more than another before God. And the proof you can see for yourself. You need only consider that Moses, Aaron, Nadab and Abihu, and the seventy elders of Israel, all of whom were together at a certain period, originally had equal radiance of countenance. But after Moses went up on high where he read Scripture and recited Mishnah, he grew in his understanding of words of Torah much more than the others did, as is said, *One righteous man is more excellent than his friend* (Prov. 12:26). [In the world-to-come, then, is the radiance of Moses' countenance to be greater than that of any of the others mentioned above?] The prophet Habakkuk sought the answer to this very
EZ, *p.* 194 question | from the Holy One. And because he went ahead and persisted in his questions, the Holy One showed him all the norms that had been disclosed to Moses, father of wisdom and father of Prophets. He showed him [that there was no "harshness in (Divine) judgment" (Lev. 19:35)], that the balances were mercy; the weights, mercy; the measure of an ephah, mercy; and the measure of a hin, mercy.[6] Habakkuk came right to the point: Master of the universe, in regard to the man who read much Scripture and recited much Mishnah and the man

---

4. JV: *The appearance of the glory of the Lord was like devouring fire.* But *mar'eh,* "appearance," may mean "reflection"; hence "reflected from them."

5. God is spoken of as *a sun and a shield* (Ps. 84:12); hence the comparison of the righteous with Him.

Leon Nemoy suggests: "like a householder of fine qualities whose servants wear a crown—that is, a reputation—as fine as his own."

6. Cf. Lev. 19:36.

who read little Scripture and recited little Mishnah, will the radiance in the countenances of the two men be equal in the radiance of countenance bestowed in the time-to-come? God replied: No—the degree of radiance in each man's countenance will depend on the way he conducted himself in his lifetime.

Then, concluded Habakkuk, *In wrath Thou rememberest compassion* (Hab. 3:2)—even when You are in wrath, You remember [and reward with radiance of countenance] the man who has shown compassion to others in his lifetime.

Whence do we know that in the world-to-come the righteous [in addition to radiance of countenance] will have servitors? The [heathen] nations of the earth will then have ceased to be, as is said, *They* [*Israel*] *shall go forth, and look upon the carcasses of the men that have rebelled against Me* (Isa. 66:24). But if the nations no longer exist, whence will the servitors of the righteous come <in the world-to-come>[7]? In reply, you must say: Men unlettered in Torah who did not read Scripture and did not recite Mishnah, but who were not guilty of idolatry, were not guilty of violence or larceny, were not guilty of unchastity, and were not guilty of bloodshed—them the Holy One will fetch and make them servitors of the righteous <in the world-to-come>,[8] as intimated in the verse *In that day shall Israel be šělišiyyah with Egypt and with Assyria* (Isa. 19:24).[9] At first reading I had no idea what *šělišiyyah* meant in this verse, but the next verse made the meaning clear, for it speaks of *My people* [*in*] *Egypt* (Isa. 19:25), a reference to the people of Israel who at one time had come out of Egypt, then goes on to speak of *the work of My hands* [*in*] *Assyria (ibid.),* also a reference to the people of Israel who had been banished to Assyria; and finally speaks of *Israel Mine inheritance (ibid.),* [these being *the poorest of the Land* (2 Kings 25:12) —poorest in their knowledge of Torah—whom the Babylonians did not lead into exile]. Hence the verse[10] *In that day shall Israel be šělišiyyah with Egypt and with Assyria* [means that the Jews unlettered in Torah who were never exiled will make up the *šělišiyyah,* the corps of servitors[11] to those who had been banished to Egypt or to Assyria]. And of those men unlettered in Torah, who will be delivered from such shame, such ignominy? You must conclude that it will be the man who, though

---

7. R: "in the days of the Messiah."

8. See n. 7.

9. The "and so on" at the end of the clause *In that day shall there be a highway out of Egypt* (Isa. 19:23) is taken to refer to the next verse, verse 24, on which EZ's comment is based.

10. See n. 9.

11. The word *šělišiyyah,* usually taken to mean "the third," may be associated with *šališ,* "adjudant, servitor"; hence "a corps of servitors."

Professor Sid Z. Leiman suggested the meaning of *šělišiyyah* in this comment and unraveled the sense of the passage.

unlettered in Torah, had his son read and recite Torah. Indeed, such a son can deliver even a [sinful] father from the punishment of Gehenna. [That a son can deliver a father is shown by Jacob's deliverance of Isaac who begot Esau], as is said, *Therefore thus saith the Lord to the house of Jacob who redeemed Abraham: Jacob shall not now be ashamed, neither shall his face now wax pale* (Isa. 29:22), as did his [father's face or his] grandfather's face.[12]

---

12. In contrast to Abraham's and Isaac's children, all of Jacob's children were whole. See B.Sanh 19b and Gen. Rabbah 63:2.

CHAPTER 13

God's love for those who continually study and obey Torah

Summary

Confirmed transgressors in Israel who have abandoned Torah will stay banished from the Land and never be brought back to it. On the other hand, those who were banished from the Land but persisted in study of Torah will be treated by God with great love (EZ, 194).

Let not a man say to himself: I read and studied today, I do not have to do so again tomorrow. I acted charitably today, I do not have to do so again tomorrow. No, early and late every day without fail, a man is to be at words of Torah in order to learn to do the will of God. Words of Torah are compared with water and bread so as to teach us that as it is impossible for a man to be without bread and water for one day, so it is impossible for a man to be without words of Torah for even an hour. Words of Torah are compared with wine and milk, because like wine and milk, words of Torah give contentment to him who savors them, restoring his spirit and lighting up his eyes (EZ, 195).

Chapter 13

EZ, *p.* 194 *cont'd*

Transgressors in Israel—what is to be their fate on the Day of Judgment?[1] Because they commit transgressions and thus make the feet of the Presence move away from them, the Presence of which it is said, *The whole earth is full of His glory* (Isa. 6:3)—because they transgress, seeking the destruction of the world, they will be banished from their homes to a land where they will no more than sojourn and will not be brought back [to the Land of Israel]. Instead, they will be led forth to a place of execution, as is said, *I will purge out from among you the rebels, and them that transgress against Me; I will bring them forth out of the land where they sojourn, but they shall not enter into the Land of Israel* (Ezek. 20:38). [Such is the fate of those who have not lived by the teachings of Torah.]

What is the difference between one who is engaged in [study of] Scripture and Mishnah [and one who is not]? By what parable may the question be answered? By the parable of a mortal king who had sons and servants whom he loved with utter devotion. He sent them to [study] Scripture and Mishnah, and to learn a useful occupation. Then he waited and yearned for their return, saying: When will they return

1. Literally, "at that time." [In Arabic *sā'ah* means the Day of Resurrection when judgment will be passed. L. N.]

that I may see them? But when he saw that they were not coming, he got up and went to them and found them reading [Scripture], reciting [Mishnah], and engaged in a useful activity. Thereupon he seated them
EZ, *p.* 195 on his lap, took them into his arms, | held them close, and kissed them. Some [were gathered] against his shoulders, some in his arms, some in front of him, some behind him, as is said, *As a shepherd that feedeth his flock, that gathereth the lambs in his arm, and carrieth them in his bosom, and gently leadeth those that give suck* (Isa. 40:11). You might suppose that since God humbles Himself in acting like a shepherd, He is to be considered as ordinary as any other person. But does not the very next verse say of Him that *He hath measured the waters in the hollow of His hand, and meted out heaven with a span,* etc. (Isa. 40:12)? You must therefore admit that He acts like a shepherd only because His compassion for the world is abundant.

And the proof that He will find His children reading Scripture, find them reciting Mishnah, find them engaging in a useful occupation? The verse *They shall walk after the Lord, who shall roar like a lion; for He shall roar, and the children shall come trembling from the sea*[2] (Hos. 11:10), *sea* signifying words of Torah, as in the verse "All the rivers run into the sea [of Torah]" (Eccles. 1:7),[3] Hosea also describes the coming of the children of Israel to the Lord: *They shall come trembling as a bird out of Egypt, and as a dove out of the land of Assyria; and I will make them to dwell in their houses, saith the Lord* (Hos. 11:8).

Let not a man say to himself: I read and studied [Torah] today, I do not have to do so again tomorrow. I acted charitably today, I do not have to do so again tomorrow. I did acts of loving-kindness today, I do not have to do so again tomorrow. Rather let a mortal look at himself and realize that after a short time death comes. Let him lift his eyes to heaven and say: Who created these on high? Heaven and earth, sun and moon, stars and planets, early and late, do the will of their Creator. Even so, early and late, every day without fail, you are to be at words of Torah in order to do the will of your Creator, as is said, *Let us know, eagerly strive to know the Lord, as surely as the going forth of the morning* (Hos. 6:3).

Let a man think it over and realize that words of Torah are like water and like bread. What is the point of comparing Torah with bread and water? To teach you that as it is impossible for a man to be without bread and water for even one day, so it is impossible for him to be without words of Torah for even one hour, as is said, *This book of the law shall not depart out of thy mouth, but thou shalt meditate therein day and*

---

2. JV: *west.* But literally *yam,* "west," stands for the Mediterranean Sea.

3. "All the Torah which a man studies is only in his heart; *yet the sea is not full* (Eccles. 1:7)—yet the heart is not full nor the appetite ever satisfied" (Eccles. Rabbah).

night (Josh. 1:8). Arguing a fortiori we can conclude the following: If even Joshua son of Nun who occupied himself from youth to old age with Torah was told, *This book of the law shall not depart out of thy mouth,* then all the more so should the rest of mankind be aware of the necessity of occupying themselves with Torah.

Let a man think it over and realize that words of Torah are like wine and milk, as is said, *Wine for one made white by the years is better than milk for one whose eyes sparkle*[4] (Gen. 49:12). It is said: Wine is better for an old man than milk for an infant. As milk makes an infant grow, so wine gives delight to a man well on in years; it restores his spirit and lights up his eyes. Words of Torah likewise give contentment to him who labors in them, restoring his spirit and lighting up his eyes, as is said, *The law of the Lord is perfect, restoring the soul. . . . The precepts of the Lord are right, rejoicing the heart, the commandment of the Lord is pure, enlightening the eyes* (Ps. 19:8–9).

---

4. JV: *His eyes shall be red with wine, and his teeth white with milk.* But *ḥaḵlili,* "red," may also mean "sparkle"; and *šinnaim,* "teeth," is read *šanim,* "years."

CHAPTER 14

Amity in Israel; Torah and increase of Israel's number essential to redemption

Summary

To all men, learned and unlearned alike, God gives understanding and knowledge. But no matter what differences there may be among men in degrees of learning, all are to live in amity, abstaining from spending much time at eating and drinking. Reward therefore is given in this world, and even greater reward in the world-to-come, where the supreme boon will be the savoring of a double portion of Torah (EZ, 196).

Israel's immersion in Torah is the key to their redemption which is certain to come, because when ten of Israel's people sit together, and one is endeavoring to read to his fellow, the sound of the others' voices raised in the recitation of Scripture and Mishnah is so great that his voice cannot be heard. The other requirement for redemption is that Israel increase and multiply (EZ, 197).

Chapter 14

EZ, ***p.*** **195** *cont'd* One time as I was going from one city to another, a man who was a scorner and a mocker came at me. I asked him: My son, what will you say to your Father in heaven on the Day of Judgment? He replied: I have answers which I will give to my Father in heaven on the Day of **EZ,** ***p.*** **196** | Judgment. I will say to Him: Understanding and knowledge were not given me from Heaven, [so how can You bring me to judgment]? I said: My son, what is your work? He replied: I am a fisherman. I asked: My son, who told you to bring linen cord, weave it into nets, cast them into the sea, and bring fish up from the depths? He replied: My master, with regard to my work, understanding and knowledge were given me from Heaven. I said: My son, if understanding and knowledge were given you to cast nets and bring fish up from the sea, were not understanding and knowledge of words of Torah also given to you, words of which it is said, *The word is very nigh unto thee* (Deut. 30:14)?

Thereupon he sighed, raised his voice, and wept. I said: My son, do not feel downcast. You are like other men who give a similar reply in this matter while the work of their hands testifies against them.

Of such a man, of those like him, of those who resemble him, and act like him, what does Scripture say? *Moreover they that work in combed flax, and they that weave cotton, shall be ashamed* (Isa. 19:9).

In the end, what it all comes down to is fear of Heaven and doing of good deeds. A man who reads Scripture and recites Mishnah should not spurn a man who is greater [in learning] than he. Nor should a man who reads Scripture and recites Mishnah have no fear of Heaven, for it is said, *The fear of the Lord is the beginning of wisdom,* etc. (Ps. 111:10); and *The end of the matter, all having been heard: Fear God, and keep His commandments* (Eccles. 12:13).

Among those who read Scripture and recite Mishnah, who impoverishes himself? He who spends much time at eating, drinking, <and sleeping>, as is said, *The drunkard and the glutton shall come to poverty; and drowsiness shall clothe a man with rags* (Prov. 23:21); and as is said, *Love not sleep, lest thou come to poverty; open thine eyes, and thou shalt have bread in plenty* (Prov. 20:13). By *bread* here is meant Torah, as in the verse where wisdom says, *Come, eat of my bread* (Prov. 9:5). And [of the teaching and study of Torah it is said], *The Lord God hath given me the tongue of those who know how to teach, of those who know to set fixed times for them who weary themselves for the word*[1] (Isa. 50:4)—that is, words of Torah are absorbed only by one who [regularly occupies himself with them and] wearies himself for their sake.

To such disciples of the wise the holy spirit gave news of good things to come, saying to them: My sons, though I have given you a good Torah in this world, I need not say what Torah will be in the world-to-come. Though great reward is doubled for you in this world, I need not say what your reward will be in the world-to-come. Do not make little of Torah and abstain from spending much time at eating and drinking, as is said, *Return to abstention,*[2] *ye prisoners of hope; even today I declare that I will render double unto thee* (Zech. 9:12); moreover, *I will restore to you the years that the locust hath eaten . . . and ye shall eat in plenty and be satisfied . . . and My people shall never be ashamed* (Joel 2:25–26); and, in addition, *For your shame which was double, and for that they rejoiced: "Confusion is their portion"; therefore in their Land they shall possess double, everlasting joy shall be unto them* (Isa. 61:7). In short, in the days of the Messiah you will savor a double portion [of Torah].

Even if only a single individual of the people of Israel were dwelling at the end of the world with a thousand rivers flowing in front of him, the Holy One would divide <them all for his sake> and bring him to Himself, as is said, *Therefore, behold, the days come, saith the Lord, that it shall no more be said: "As the Lord liveth, that brought us up*[3] *out of the land of Egypt"* (Jer. 16:14, 23:7); instead it will be said, *As the Lord liveth, that brought up and that led the seed of the house of Israel out of the north country, and from all the countries whither I had driven them* (Jer. 23:8).

---

1. JV: *The Lord God hath given me the tongue of them that are taught, that I should know how to sustain with words him that is weary.* But Rashi *ad loc.* associates *'wṯ,* "sustain," with *'eṯ,* "a fixed time."

2. JV: *to the stronghold.* But here *biṣṣaron* appears to be associated with *bṣr,* "deprive oneself, abstain." So *YY.*

3. MT: *that brought up the children of Israel.*

And the proof [that the Holy One will keep the promise in this verse] you can see for yourself: Israel will be redeemed not[4] by reason of their suffering, not by reason of their bondage, not by reason of their continual expulsion, not by reason of their enforced wandering, |
EZ, *p.* 197 not by reason of need, not by reason of hunger, but for this reason: when ten of Israel's people sit together, and one is endeavoring to read to his fellow, [the sound of the others' voices raised in the recitation of Scripture and Mishnah will be so great that] his voice will not be heard, as is said, *Because the Mount (Zion) is distinguished [by reason of resounding study of Torah within its gates]*,[5] *it is holy, and therefore there shall be an escape [from the retribution that will befall the nations]* (Ob. 1:17).

Be it noted that just as our ancestors were redeemed from Egypt only after they had achieved prosperity, [so our present prosperity heralds the coming of the Messiah and his redemption].[6] And as our ancestors came to the hour within forty days[7] [when Torah was given to them, so presently the hour will come when we shall be given our redemption].

[A reproachful aside]:[8] While Israel was resoundingly engaged with Torah all their days, God did not say, "I heard the [studious] murmurings of the voices of the children of Israel." But when, for a short time, they fell to complaining, He said: *I have heard the children of Israel murmuring [in complaint]* (Exod. 16:12).

And the proof that, [as in Egypt, Israel were redeemed only after they had achieved prosperity, so] now Israel will not be redeemed until they increase, multiply, and come to be a substantial part of the world's people? So Scripture tells us in the verse *When thou shalt spread abroad on the right hand and on the left, thou shalt make the desolate cities to be inhabited* (Isa. 54:3).

---

4. At the suggestion of Dr. Louis Finkelstein the word *'l'*, "but," is emended to *l'*, "not."

5. Cf. B.Ber 8a.

6. See Exod. 12:36 and Friedmann's n. 10. In a private communication Louis Finkelstein comments: "At the time of the writer . . . the Jews . . . enjoyed a respite from the previous persecutions. The author assured them that this prosperity itself was a prelude to the Messianic age, provided intensive study of Torah continued."

7. Actually, more than forty days. Israel left Egypt on the fifteenth of Nisan and were given the Torah on the sixth of Sivan, forty-nine days later.

8. [Is this really reproachful, and would the author dare reproach God for noticing Israel's faults but not their merits? This leads me to conclude that the meaning is rather—when Israel behave well, God knows it without telling them, "What good boys you are!" It is only when they misbehave that God tells them, "I am not unmindful of your misbehavior—take care!" L. N.]

CHAPTER 15

Intense study of Torah leads to happiness and radiance of countenance; Elijah's Benjamite ancestry assures success in combat with Esau

Summary

A disciple of the wise, says Elijah, who studies Scripture and Mishnah for the sake of Heaven, and eats what he himself has earned, and benefits only from what is his own and not from what the community owns, is truly happy. If such a man is humble toward all whom he lives and deals with, he will be beloved above and cherished here below (EZ, 197).

When a man has Torah and good deeds to his credit, all who know him revere him. He is the kind of man who never separates himself from the community when its members are in distress. For sharing the distress of the community he will be given ample reward from Heaven. On the other hand, the man who separates himself from the community will not see consolation come to the community.

The man who in his study of Torah makes himself submit like an ox to the yoke is blessed. His countenance in the world-to-come will have the radiance of morning, indeed he will share with God Himself this world, the world-to-come, the Temple, and the days of the Messiah (EZ, 198).

Elijah, as a descendant of Benjamin son of Rachel, was certain to succeed in the give-and-take of combat with the descendants of Esau. Since all the other Tribes except Benjamin had taken part in the sale of Joseph, their own hands were not clean enough for them to deal with the descendants of Esau.

Even the emperor of Rome, as a story affirms, is aware that ultimately all are to bow down to Israel (EZ, 199).

Chapter 15

The teacher Elijah, ever remembered on good occasions and ever remembered for blessing, said: I call heaven and earth to witness that any disciple of the wise who reads Scripture for the sake of Heaven and recites Mishnah for the sake of Heaven, eats what he himself has earned, and benefits only from what is his own and not from what the community owns—of such as he the Psalmist says, *When thou eatest the labor of thy hands, happy shalt thou be* (Ps. 128:2). As the Song of Songs says, *How fair and how pleasant art thou, O love, for delights* (Song 7:7) [when you are delighted with what you have and seek not what others own].[1] EZ, *p.* 197 *cont'd*

Furthermore, both with regard to [the precepts of] Torah and to

1. Cf. above, ER, 26, 91.

[the performance of] good deeds, a man should always be humble with his father, with his mother, with his teacher, his wife, his children, the members of his household, his neighbors, both kin and not kin, even with a heathen he encounters in the marketplace. He will then be beloved above and cherished here below.[2]

EZ, *p.* 198 | When a man has both Torah and good deeds to his credit, his wife reveres him, his children revere him, the members of his household revere him, his neighbors revere him, his kin revere him—even the nations of the world revere him, as is said, *All the peoples of the earth shall see that the name of the Lord is called upon thee; and they shall revere thee* (Deut. 28:10).

[To be revered], a man who sees a great many deep in distress is not to say, "I'll go hence, eat and drink, and take it easy." Should he act thus, [he is disregarding God's call to bewail and lament the distress of our fellows by turning to] *rejoicing and merriment, killing of cattle, and slaughtering of sheep, eating of meat and drinking of wine* (Isa. 22:13). What is said in the very next verse, however, concerning such iniquity? *Then the Lord of hosts revealed Himself to my ears: "This iniquity shall never be forgiven you until you die," said my Lord of hosts* (Isa. 22:14). So read the verses describing the behavior of the average sensual man [and God's subsequent judgment of him]. And in a later passage what does Isaiah quote utterly wicked people as saying? *"Come, I'll buy some wine; let's swill liquor. And tomorrow we'll do just the same, only more of it!"*[3] (Isa. 56:12). [Aside from its rebuke of such wicked people], what does Scripture go on to say [of the man who deems himself better than the average, yet is equally indifferent to the distress of the many]? *The [self]-righteous man perisheth, and no one layeth it to heart that the [self]-righteous man is taken away because of his own evil* (Isa. 57:1). When a great many are deep in distress, and a man separates himself from them, two angels of destruction accompany him from the synagogue to his home and say to him: He who separates himself from the community will not see consolation come to the community. Come and see and learn from the ways of Moses our teacher, of whom it is said, *Moses' hands were heavy; and they took a stone, and put it under him, and he sat thereon* (Exod. 12:12). But did not Moses have even a bolster or cushion or saddle to sit on? That is not the point. Moses had said to himself: Since Israel is deep in distress, I shall suffer distress with them.

Hence it is said: Blessed is the man who shares the distress of the community; he is given ample reward from Heaven.[4]

Blessed, too, is the man who, [in his study of Torah], makes

---

2. Cf. above, ER, 62 and EZ, 167.

3. So NJV. JV: *Come ye, I will fetch wine, and we will fill ourselves with strong drink and tomorrow shall be as this day, and much more abundant.*

4. Cf. above, ER, 112, 128; EZ, 167; and B.Ta 11a.

himself submit like an ox submitting to the yoke, like an ass to the burden, like a heifer to the plow in a field. [Of such a man] it is said, *Blessed are ye that sow beside all waters* (Isa. 32:20), *all waters* signifying all the different elements [of Torah]. Hence,[5] if a man has read the Five Books, he is to read the Prophets; if he has read the Prophets, he is to read the Writings; if he has read the Writings, he is to study Halakot; if he has studied Halakot, he is worthy of the world-to-come, as is said, *The righteous shall be . . . as a morning without clouds* (2 Sam. 23:4)—[like the radiance of morning in the world-to-come].[6]

Blessed is the man who makes himself submit [in his study of Torah] like an ox submitting to the yoke, like an ass to the burden, like a heifer to the plow in a field. [Of such a man it is said], *Blessed are ye that sow beside all waters* (Isa. 32:20), *all waters* signifying all the different elements [of Torah]. Hence,[7] if a man has read the Five Books, he is to read the Prophets; [if he has read] the Prophets, he is to read the Writings; [if] the Writings, he is to study Halakot; [if] Halakot, he is to study Midrash of the Five Books. Besides, he is to attend to the business of the academy and show less concern for the business of the marketplace. Then the Holy One will say to him: My son, this world and the world-to-come will be Mine and yours together. The Temple will be Mine and yours together. The days of the Messiah will be Mine and yours together.[8]

| *The God of Israel said, the Rock of Israel spoke to me* (2 Sam. 23:3). EZ, *p.* 199
[In thus giving God His full titles], king David meant to intimate: I will call attention to the kingship, to the greatness and the might of the Holy One. [Through Him] every day a man is conceived, every day a man is born; every day a man continues in life, every day a man departs from it; every day a man's spirit is taken from him [in sleep] and deposited with the spirit's true Owner; every day, according to his deeds, such sustenance is given him as was given him at his mother's breast.[9]

[Men in the academy who make themselves submit in study of Torah like an ox submitting to the yoke may be vouchsafed a vision of Elijah, as indeed happened][10] on one occasion when our Masters sat and discussed this question: From whose seed did Elijah come? Some said: From the seed of Leah; others, from the seed of Rachel. As they

---

5. The unintelligible *mnyn* is changed to *mikkan,* "hence." So Louis Ginzberg, *OT,* p. 287, n. 379.

6. Instead of 2 Sam. 23:2, as in EZ, Louis Ginzberg suggests substituting 2 Sam. 23:4 (Ginzberg, *OT,* p. 287, n. 379).

[I don't see why 2 Sam. 23:2 is not equally suitable—*The spirit of the Lord shall speak* (JV: *spoke*) *by me* (or perhaps rather *in my presence*—in the world-to-come). L. N.]

7. See n. 5.

8. "Your life will be guided by God Himself." So Landau.

9. Cf. above, ER, 8–9.

10. So Ḥayyim Isaiah hak-Kohen, *Ṭuḇe ḥayyim* (Lublin, 1896).

sat thus engaged, Elijah, ever remembered on good occasions, came and stood before them. He said: My Masters, why are you at odds? I come from the seed of <Rachel>.[11]

[When Israel have both Torah and good deeds to their credit, even under circumstances humiliating for Israel, the nations of the world will still revere Israel, as is evident from what][12] R. Jose said: Once I was walking in the great city of Rome where I saw the emperor riding a horse, and with him were all the notables of Rome. The emperor happened to see a Jewish infant girl, smitten with boils, who had been cast on a dung heap. As soon as the emperor saw her, he got off his horse and prostrated himself before her. All the notables of Rome were vexed with him. They said: So despised, so abhorrent—yet you prostrate yourself before her! He replied: Do not be vexed. All the kings of the nations of the earth will yet bow down to Israel, as is said, *Thus saith the Lord, the Redeemer of Israel, his Holy One, to him who is despised of men, to him who is abhorred of nations, to a servant of rulers: Kings shall see and arise, princes, and they shall prostrate themselves, because of the Lord that loveth thee,* [13] *even the Holy One of Israel that hath chosen thee* (Isa. 49:7)—[I repeat], the Holy One of Israel who has chosen Israel. It is said further of Israel, *Their seed shall be known among the nations, and their offspring among the peoples; all that see them shall acknowledge them, that they are the seed which the Lord hath blessed* (Isa. 61:9).[14]

---

11. EZ: "Leah." But the parallel above in ER, 97, reads "Rachel." The implication: The other Tribes, sons of Leah, had taken part in the sale of Joseph, and so could not join battle with the descendants of Esau. But Elijah, as a descendant of Rachel, could engage the descendants of Esau in combat. Cf. PR 12:5 (YJS, *18, 1,* 228).

12. So Haida.

13. MT: *the Lord that is faithful.*

14. In his final comment (EZ,199), Friedmann argues that EZ proper ends on p. 196 with the quotation from Eccles. 12:13.

PIRḲE DEREḴ 'EREṢ

CHAPTER 1 (EZ, CHAPTER 16)

A miscellany of counsel: moral, practical, personal, and communal, together with observations on the coming of the Messiah and sundry other matters

Summary

The ten masters against which a man must fortify himself with Torah are his two ears, his two hands, his two feet, his mouth, and his male member. With Torah a man finds relief also from all kinds of other preoccupations (S, 1–2), such as the demands of heathen enemies and the distress of poverty.

Happiness is having a handsome wife, good living quarters and utensils, and even shoes on one's feet (S, 3).

The favor of one's Father in heaven is acquired through Torah and good deeds, and God comes to treasure the man who has reverence, humility, meekness, compassion, and close attachment to scholars whose Nay is Nay and whose Yea is Yea. But His favor is earned primarily through labor in Torah and at right conduct.

A disciple of the wise takes precedence over a king, for if a king dies, any man in Israel is deserving of the succession to his throne, whereas if a disciple of the wise dies, no one can take his place (S, 4).

It is a pity that the unlettered harbor hatred for disciples of the wise (S, 5).

All men, learned and unlearned alike, should judge one another charitably. A man should get himself a companion with whom he is to share all manner of things.

He who judges charitably will himself be judged charitably, as is illustrated by a story of a householder who appeared to act harshly toward a man who worked for him, and by another concerning R. Joshua who acted suspiciously (S, 6–7).

Since the Temple was destroyed, people have diminished in learning, and ignoramuses have grown in numbers.

A man may study Torah for ten years and within two years forget it if he neglects for ten months to review what he has learned.

A disciple of the wise who does not act with integrity in his business may bring destruction to the world. So, too, may certain kinds of Tannaim who recite Mishnah by rote without attendant reasoning (S, 8).

People in certain unpleasant occupations are not considered worthy of the office of king, Patriarch, or High Priest—indeed, are not considered worthy of any kind of public office. From among them, guardians of orphans are not appointed, nor are they deemed fit to be witnesses. Wages for certain kinds of employment lack a sign of blessing.

Marriage for the sake of money, of satisfaction of lust, or of social status leads to suffering and frustration; but marriage for the sake of bringing children into the world results in blessing and in children who will deliver Israel in the time of their distress (S, 9).

The longer nights of the year should be used for study of Torah. Trees for the altar are not to be felled during the winter when the logs are not likely to dry sufficiently. The significance of eclipses of the sun and the moon is pointed out (S, 10). Further observations follow on signs and events which portend the coming of the Messiah, on life in villages, on aging, and on personal conduct (S, 11–12). Counsel is offered on what to look for when settling in a city (S, 13). The prediction is made that ignorance of Torah will increase because of repression by the government, and the obligation of communities to provide escort for travelers is stressed (S, 14–15).

*Chapter 1 (EZ, Chapter 16)**

1

S, *p.* 1 R. Simeon [ben Yoḥai][1] said: *Wisdom strengtheneth* [*the heart*] *of a wise man more than ten rulers which are in the city* (Eccles. 7:19). Does a city have ten rulers? Does it not, in fact, have only one ruler? What then does Scripture mean by *ten rulers?* When a disciple of the wise reads Scripture, recites Mishnah, occupies himself with Torah, and resolves on repentance and good deeds, he is delivered from ten harsh masters, namely, his two eyes, his two ears, his two hands, his two feet, his mouth, and his male member: from his two eyes with which he looks upon money that is not his, for, as the Sages taught in a Mishnah, Do not set your eyes longingly upon money which is not yours, for like the sun which [gazes all day upon the world but can never possess it and then] sinks down into darkness behind the gates of heaven, you will go
S, *p.* 2 blind;[2] from his two ears with which he hears | idle words, for, as the Sages taught in a Mishnah, Do not let your ears listen to idle words, since ears catch fire, so to speak, [from evil] before all other organs;[3] from his two hands with which he steals from, robs, and assaults people, for as the Sages taught in a Mishnah, < Let there not be found with you some evil thing [such as a weapon] or something stolen, because your very hands will testify against you; from his two feet with which he runs to [sexual] transgression, for, as the Sages taught in a Mishnah, Let not your feet bring you to commit [sexual] transgression lest the angel of death come to meet you; and from the mouth with which he speaks slander, for, as the Sages taught in a Mishnah, Let not your mouth speak slander, since the mouth is first [of the body's organs] to be brought to judgment. Even[4] > if a man reads Scripture, recites Mishnah, gives all kinds of charity during all his days, feeding the hungry, giving drink

---

* The translators have divided this chapter into sections.

1. "[ben Yoḥai]"—Haida.

2. Leon Nemoy suggests: "Do not set your eyes longingly upon money which is not yours lest they should reach up as far as the gates of heaven."

3. Hearing unworthy or idle talk, a man may proceed to speak unworthy or idle words and then do unworthy or idle things. See DEZ, Soncino tr., p. 579, n. 18.

4. "Let there not be found with you some evil thing . . . to judgment. Even"—Friedmann's reading, n. 8, on the basis of parallels in DEZ, chap. 4.

to the thirsty, clothing the naked, redeeming the captives, his deeds of charity will not for one moment make up for the noxious breath [of slander] which comes out of his mouth, as is said, *All mischief of man has to do with his mouth*[5] (Eccles. 6:7). Finally, [in occupying himself with Torah], he is delivered from the male member's mastery of him, the member with which he sins to excess.

R. Simeon ben Yoḥai said still another thing: He who takes words of Torah to heart is relieved of anxiety about his transgression, anxiety about a war's threat to his life, anxiety about [oppression from] government, anxiety about foolish things, anxiety about the Impulse to evil, anxiety about unchaste things, anxiety about an evil wife,[6] anxiety about idolatry, anxiety about the burden of mortality, anxiety about idle matters. . . . In regard to such preoccupations you are told, *Because*
| *thou didst not serve the Lord thy God with joyfulness, and with gladness of* S, *p.* 3
heart by reason of the abundance of all things; therefore shalt thou serve thine enemy whom the Lord shall send against thee, in hunger, and in thirst, and in nakedness, and in want of all things (Deut. 28:47–48). Inasmuch as you have not served Me with love, you will serve Me in the midst of hostility. Inasmuch as you have not served Me with joy in the midst of abundance of everything, you will serve Me in hunger, in thirst, in nakedness, and in want of all things. [*Thou shalt serve thine enemy*] . . . *in hunger:* for example, <at a time when you crave food and cannot find even coarse bread, the heathen enemy will demand white bread and choice meat from you. [*Thou shalt serve thine enemy*] . . . *in thirst:* for example>,[7] at a time when you long for a drop of bitters or a drop of vinegar <and cannot find it>, the heathen enemy will demand the finest wine in the provinces from you. *In nakedness:* for example, at a time when you are eager to wear a garment even of coarse wool or flax [and cannot find it], the heathen enemy will demand choice silks of you. In short, [*Thou shalt serve*] . . . *in want of all things:* without a pin or a lamp.[8] . . . Hence the words "He who has neither vinegar or salt in his house" have come to be a curse that people utter against others. . . .

---

5. JV: *All the labor of man is for his mouth.*

6. Dr. Louis Finkelstein suggests that instead of *r'h,* "evil," the correct reading is *r',* "friend"; hence "a friend's wife." See his *Maḇo' li-mĕseḵtoṯ 'Aḇoṯ wĕ-'Aḇoṯ dĕ-R. Nathan* (New York, 5711/1950), p. 124.

7. The words "at a time when you crave food . . . *in thirst:* for example" are added from ARN, chap. 20 (YJS, *10,* 95–96), where the entire passage is paralleled.

8. The kind of poverty which prevailed in Palestine in the fourth century. See Saul Lieberman, *JQR, 36,* 344–45.

2

My soul is removed far off from peace (Lam. 3:17), words which to me, says R. Eliezer ben Jacob, mean lack of even enough means to kindle a lamp. *I had forgotten what happiness was (ibid.)*—meaning to me, says R. Joshua, a bath; a handsome wife, handsome living quarters, and handsome utensils, says R. Aḳiḇa; fine bread and the opportunity to wash at the end of the Sabbath [in water from Miriam's well],[9] says R. Nehemiah; and, says R. Juda, <shoes on a man's feet>[10]—an essential need.

S, *p.* 4 Rabbi [Judah the Prince] said: | He who refuses to wash the feet of a scholar will wash the feet of horses; he who refuses to participate in the digging of a well for a public fountain will dig a latrine for scholars instead.[11]

3

How does a man acquire [the favor of] his Father in heaven? R. Eliezer ben Jacob said: He acquires it through study of Torah and good deeds. In return, the Holy One has him acquire this world and the world-to-come. How does the Holy One come to treasure a man? Through [man's] love [of Him]; through his reverence, through humility, through meekness, through compassion, through peace, through diligent study in the academy, through close attachment to scholars, through discussion with disciples, through his Nay being Nay and

---

9. There is a tradition that on Saturday night Miriam's well, which has creative power, moves from well to well throughout the world. Hence water drawn from a well on Saturday night is deemed to have restorative power. So Friedmann (n. 16), who quotes Isserles' gloss in Šulḥan 'aruḵ, 'Oraḥ ḥayyim, 299:10.

10. Friedmann (n. 16), who quotes B.Ber 60b.

11. The unintelligible text is emended to read as follows: *Rby 'mr m'n dl' mšy rgly rb' mšy rgly swsy' wm'n dl' mšmš klpy kry' mšmš klpy rbwth.* On the word *kry,* "digging [a well]," see B.BB 8a. The conclusion, literally "will serve scholars instead," is construed as meaning "will serve scholars in some demeaning capacity"; hence "will dig a latrine for scholars instead."

The emendation of the text was suggested by Dr. Sid Z. Leiman.

Leon Nemoy writes: "I have two objections to Mr. Leiman's emendation: (a) it's too fancy for my simple mind; (b) digging a latrine for the use of scholars is an honorable and laudable service—scholars are human and need one; hence the parallelism is not apt.

"Do I hear you ask: can I do better? I can try. *Rbwth* may, I suppose, be taken as the same as *rĕḇuṭah* or *rabbuta'* (Jastrow, p. 1440b), 'superiority' = Gentile officialdom, and the sentence may be emended to read *wm'n dl' mšmš klpy rb' mšmš klpy rbwth* (the *lpzkrw* is an obvious corruption), 'he who would not serve a scholar will end up as a serf to the [Gentile] officialdom' (which is a reasonable parallel to the preceding).

"The use of 'superiority' for officialdom is well-attested—cf. German *Obrigkeit,* Russian *nachalstvo.*"

through his Yea being Yea;[12] in short, through labor in Torah and labor at right conduct.[13]

4

As between a disciple of the wise and a king, the disciple of the wise takes precedence. For if a king dies, any man in Israel is deserving of the succession to his throne, all Israel being sons of kings, as R. Simeon says; whereas if a disciple of the wise dies and leaves no one who is his equal to take his place, it is fitting to keep sighing for him to the end of time. Hence it is said: If you see a disciple of the wise, gird him about your loins even <if he be a serpent>; as for an unlettered man, even a devout one, do not occupy the same dwelling with him.[14]

| In connection with the verse *Hear the word of the Lord, ye that tremble at His word* (Isa. 66:5), it is said: The hatred that men who are not only unlettered but immoral harbor for disciples of the wise is greater than the hatred that [heathen] nations of the world harbor for us.[15] When Isaiah said, *Hear the word of the Lord, ye that tremble at His word,* take note that he did not say "ye that despise His word," but *ye that tremble at His word* [by which he meant disciples of the wise driven to bitter complaint because they are held in great disdain by certain kinds of their fellow Jews whom] Isaiah speaks of as *Your "brethren," that hate you, that would cast you out (ibid.).* By *your "brethren"* he meant those who possess knowledge of Scripture but hate them who possess knowledge of Mishnah. By <*that hate you*> he meant those who possess knowledge of Mishnah.[16] but hate them who possess knowledge of Talmud. And by *those that would cast you out,* Isaiah meant [unworthy] teachers of young children, teachers who read Scripture but do not teach Mishnah, or if they do read Scripture and recite Mishnah, have no understanding of either of them. It is forbidden to honor such teachers, for, [as Isaiah goes on to say, only *they who are truly concerned for My name's sake will the Lord honor*], but he who does honor such, [teachers that would cast you out],[17] inherits Gehenna—[in Isaiah's words, will *be put to shame (ibid.)*]. S, *p.* 5

---

12. Cf. above, ER, 128.
13. "through labor in Torah and labor at right conduct"—Friedmann's emendation (n. 18). Parma reads: "out of labor, out of ethical conduct."
14. Cf. B.Shab 63a.
15. [The antipathy between disciples of the wise . . . rarely, if ever, led to physical violence, much less to homicide, and much more less mass warfare. L. N.]
16. Apparently *śon'ekem,* "they who hate you," is read *šonekem,* "those of you who study or possess [knowledge of] Mishnah."
17. Friedmann (n. 21) suggests that the teachers referred to are without qualifications, or have unworthy motives. Cf. ARN, chap. 40 (YJS, *10,* 166) and B.BM 33b.

In a private communication, Professor Chaim Zalman Dimitrovsky helped elucidate the preceding paragraph.

5

S, *p.* 6 Always try to judge a man charitably rather than uncharitably. If you have learned two or three chapters [of Torah] from him, revere him as a man reveres Heaven. A man should always get himself a comrade to eat with him, <drink with him>, recite Mishnah with him, read Scripture with him, reveal to him all the arcane things of the Torah[18] and the secrets of worldly things.[19] Thus *The Lord told Moses: Take thee Joshua the son of Nun, a man in whom is spirit* (Num. 27:18): take a comrade for yourself who is brave [enough to stand up to God] and yet humble like you [toward men]. The term *take* implies that a comrade is acquired only through his being "bought" [by one's good qualities]—"bought" that is, as if by [formal contract and] payment of money.[20]

He who judges charitably will himself be judged charitably. By way of illustration, the story of a man who came down from Upper Galilee to do work in the South: It was said of this man that though he had not read Scripture nor recited Mishnah, he was a man of saintly deeds. The man went to work for a householder and worked for him throughout the year until the Day of Atonement came. As the Day of Atonement approached, the man said to the householder, "Give me my wages, so that I may go home and provide for my family." The householder replied, "I have no money to give you," [even though the man saw money in his hand]. Noticing the produce in the householder's house, the man then said, "Then pay me in produce." The householder replied, "I have no produce either." When the man saw an animal in the householder's house, it was the same thing all over again. What did the workman do? He took his gear, slung it on his back, and went home with no payment at all. After the Day of Atonement and the eight days of the Feast [of Sukkot] had gone by, the householder rose up and loaded three asses, one with food, one with
S, *p.* 7 drink, and one with produce, | and went around and about until he reached the workman's house. There he put the food and drink before the man's family, and they ate and drank. Then, as the householder took the man's wages and put them in the man's hand, he asked, "I beg you, tell me, when you asked for your wages, and saw money in my hand, but I replied, 'I have no money,' what did you think?" "I thought," the man replied, "that fields and vineyards may have turned up [for sale], and you had to use the money in your possession to buy

---

18. The principles and methods of logical deduction and reasoning, or, perhaps, mystic lore.

19. For parallel see ARN, chap. 8 (YJS, *10,* 50).

20. [The Hebrew verb *lḳḥ,* "to take," later acquired the technical legal meaning "to purchase." Hence a close friendship must be "paid for" by equal friendship expressed in terms of loyalty, generosity, sharing of knowledge and worldly goods, etc. L. N.]

them." "And when you asked me for an animal, and I replied, 'I have no animal,' and you saw I did have an animal in my house, what did you think?" "I thought that your animals might not as yet have been tithed."[21] "And when you asked me for produce, and I replied, 'I have none,' what did you think?" The man replied, "I supposed that all your possessions had been devoted to Heaven." The householder replied: By the [Temple] service! That's just what happened! For I vowed all my possessions to the Temple, so that my son Hyrcanus would occupy himself [entirely] with Torah,[22] until such time as I would go to the Sages to be released of my vow. [But I delayed carrying out my vow], and when a man delays thus, the Sages—so taught R. Eleazar—delay releasing him for as long a time as he had chosen to act as though he had not made the vow at all.[23] The Sages' delay, it should be added—so taught R. Jose—is put into effect only when the vow was intended to be in force for an extended period. If the vow was to be in force for a brief period, however, a delay of thirty days was considered by the Sages to be sufficient.[24]

A story of R. Joshua: While walking in the marketplace of the Babylonian [merchants in Pĕḳi'in][25] with his disciples behind him, he saw a Roman lady. Thereupon[26] he removed his tefillin, handed them to his pupils, went into the lady's house, and shut the door in their faces. When he came out, he washed up [in a ritual bath] and put on his tefillin again. Then he asked his disciples, "My sons, [having removed my tefillin], and then followed this lady, what did you think?" They replied, "We thought: our master believes that words of Torah [such as are enclosed in tefillin] should not enter a place of defilement." "And when I shut the door in your faces, what did you think?" "We thought that there might be a disciple among us who in our master's eyes was so unknowing as not to respect your seeming wish for privacy." "And when I came out and washed my hands, what did you think?" They replied, "We thought that maybe spittle had spurted from the woman's mouth and fallen upon the master's garments."[27] "By the [Temple]

---

21. [Such animals may not be disposed of until the tithe out of them is set aside first. L. N.]

22. [Since Hyrcanus now had no prospect of inheriting property, he would no longer be tempted to neglect his studies. L. N.]

23. As it happened, the Day of Atonement fell during the period when the Sages felt that Hyrcanus' father should not yet be released from his vow.

24. See Tos Neḏ 1:10 (Lieberman, *TKF, 10,* 409–11) and B.Shab 127b.

25. A city between Lydda and Jabneh in southern Palestine where R. Joshua lived. See B.Sanh 32b and Friedmann, n. 31.

26. Perhaps in order to find out whether they would judge charitably.

27. Because heathen worshiped idols, they, according to one opinion, were at all times deemed to be ritually unclean as one who suffers a flux. (On differing opinions as to the reason for and the degree of uncleanness of heathen or pagans, see Gĕḏalyahu Alon, *Meḥkarim bĕ-tolĕḏot Yiśra'el* [Tel Aviv, 5717/1957], *1,* 121–47.) Hence a fluid such as spittle which emanated from the Roman lady conveyed uncleanness (see Lev. 15:8, Kel 1:3, and Ṭoh 5:8) to R. Joshua—uncleanness which by washing he removed.

service, that's just what happened!" R. Joshua exclaimed. "And as you judged me charitably, so may the Holy One judge you charitably."[28]

6

S, *p.* 8 R. Eliezer ben Jacob said: <From the day the Temple was destroyed>, the Sages became more like schoolteachers [than Sages]; the schoolteachers became more like caretakers of synagogues [than schoolteachers]; caretakers of synagogues[29] became more like pupils [than caretakers]; the pupils became more like ordinary ignorant people, and ordinary ignorant people became more like the people of the [heathen] nations, and the numbers of ignoramuses and heathen keep growing greater and greater.[30]

7

R. Ishmael ben Elisha used to say: One may study [Torah] for ten years and forget it [all] within two years. How so? If, for ten months, a man neglects to review [what he has learned], he is apt to say of the ritually clean, "It is unclean," and of the ritually unclean, "It is clean." If he does not review for twelve months, he is liable to confuse the quoted Sages with one another.[31] If he does not review for eighteen months, he forgets the chapter headings. If he does not review for twenty-four months, he forgets the treatise headings. And after saying of the ritually clean, "It is unclean," and of the ritually unclean, "It is clean," after confusing the quoted Sages with one another, after forgetting the chapter headings <and the treatise headings, finally he can do no more than sit in silence>. Of such as he Solomon said: *I went by the field of the slothful, and by the vineyard of the man void of understanding; and lo, it was all grown over with thistles; the face thereof was covered with nettles, and the stone wall thereof was broken down* (Prov. 24:30–31). The phrase *the*

For parallel accounts of the incident, see ARN (Version B), chap. 19, p. 21b (Anthony J. Saldarini tr. [Leiden, 1975], p. 126).

28. It is likely, since R. Joshua interceded frequently with the Roman authorities in behalf of Jews, that on this occasion, seeing a Roman lady who might have political influence, he took advantage of the opportunity in order to confer with her and test his disciples' judgment.

For parallels of the two preceding stories, see B.Shab 127b.

29. "like caretakers of synagogues [than schoolteachers]; caretakers of synagogues"—as in parallel in Soṭ 9:15. V reads, "like expounders, expounders."

30. For a parallel, cf. Soṭ 9:15.

31. Such confusion is deemed a transgression of a negative command (Deut. 19:14). See Sif Deut. 188 (ed. Finkelstein [Breslau, 1936–39], p. 227).

vineyard of the man void of understanding refers to a man who priding himself on his knowledge of Mishnah neglected to keep reviewing it. The words *and lo, it was all grown over with thistles* imply that when he finally reaches for understanding of something in the Mishnah he is engaged with, he will be unable to clear up [its prickly problems]. The phrase *the face thereof was covered with nettles* implies that he will finally be put to shame [by his inability to take hold of any part of Mishnah]; and the words *the stone wall thereof was broken down* mean that he will never again gather a crop of understanding [from the vineyard of Mishnah].

8

Concerning a disciple of the wise who reads Scripture, recites Mishnah, and is in the give-and-take of business <but does not give and take> with integrity, concerning him, R. Joshua used to cite the Mishnah: "A foolish pietist, <a cunning> rogue, a female Pharisee, certain kinds of Pharisees"[32] (Soṭ 3:4), and certain kinds of Tannaim [who recite by rote][33] bring destruction to the world. But are not Tannaim men <who give stability to> the world? Yes, but he who teaches Halakah [without attendant reasoning] from the Mishnah he is reciting, is among those who bring destruction to the world.

9

The bloodletter, the bathhouse keeper, and the tanner[34]—no one of these should ever be appointed king, Patriarch, or High Priest. Indeed, they should not be given any kind of public office. From among them, guardians of orphans should not be appointed. According to R. Jose, they are deemed unfit to act as witnesses. R. Simeon ben Gamaliel says, Women from their families may not marry into the priesthood. S, *p.* 9

10

Four kinds of money lack a sign of blessing: the wages of scribes, the wages of interpreters, money that comes from overseas, and the money sought by him who marries a woman for the sake of her dowry.[35]

---

32. Seven objectionable kinds are enumerated in B.Soṭ 22b.
33. They report teachings without giving their sources or reasoning.
34. Perhaps because the tanner uses dog urine or dog excrement in the process.
35. Literally, "four *pĕruṭoṭ*," the smallest copper coins. Presumably the term is used because the wage received by scribes and interpreters is meager, and the in-

11

Some men marry for the sake of money, some marry for the satisfaction of lust, some marry for social status, and some marry for the sake of Heaven—[that is, to bring children into the world]. As for him who marries for money, to him apply the words *They have dealt treacherously against the Lord, and they have begotten perverse children; now shall the new moon devour their portions* (Hos. 5:7)—a moon comes, and another moon goes, and lo, their portions, their moneys are devoured. As for a man who marries for the satisfaction of lust, to him apply the words *They shall eat, and not have enough, they shall commit harlotry, and shall not increase* (Hos. 4:10). As for him who marries to advance socially, eventually out of the family into which he weds there will be brought up men who will make naught of the seed that springs from him. As for him who marries for the sake of Heaven, to him apply the words *Blessed shalt thou be when thou comest into [the marriage chamber], and blessed shalt thou be when thou goest out* (Deut. 28:6), for *Thou wilt be blessed in the fruitfulness of thy wife and thou wilt be blessed in [the restoration of] the city [of Jerusalem]*[36] (Deut. 28:3). From such a marriage will come greater and greater blessing: sons who will increase [the knowledge of] Torah and [obedience to] commandments in Israel and will deliver Israel in the time of their distress.[37]

12

S, *p.* 10 R. Eliezer said: From the fifteenth of Ab on, the strength of the sun diminishes, and no more trees are felled for wood for the altar because the logs do not dry out sufficiently.[38] [From this day onward, the nights

---

come from overseas trade and from a marriage for the sake of the dowry uncertain.

If scribes were to become wealthy, they would stop copying Scrolls and mezuzahs.

"Interpreters" refers to officials who repeated loudly and clearly the Sabbath lecture of the Rabbi or of the head of the academy, which he whispered to them, and also the translators into Aramaic of the Sabbath lessons of the Torah. Because the wages of these officials appeared to be wages for work on the Sabbath, there was no blessing in them.

Danger attended the conveyance of wares on the high seas. See above, ER, 77; DEZ, chap. 10; and B.Pes 50b.

36. JV: *Blessed shalt thou be in the city, and blessed shalt thou be in the field.* But here the author apparently contrues *field* as "a wife's fruitfulness," and *the city* as "the city of Jerusalem." Because of the sequence in the comments, the two parts of the verse are transposed.

37. Cf. above, EZ, 177.

38. "Undried wood harbors woodworms, and [so] makes the wood unfit for the altar. After the fifteenth of Ab the rays of the sun are not sufficiently strong to dry the fresh-cut logs, and therefore the felling of trees for the altar was discontinued as from this date. Cf. Mid 2:5" (J. Rabbinowitz in B.Ta 31a, Soncino tr., p. 163, n. 8).

grow longer.] He who [uses the longer nights] to enlarge his knowledge of Torah, will have his life prolonged and gain merit. He who does not do so, his mother will bury him.[39]

13

R. Eliezer said: When the sun is eclipsed, it is a bad omen for the nations of the earth, and when the moon is eclipsed, it is a bad sign—may such things befall Israel's enemies!—for Israel, who reckon time by the moon while the nations of the earth reckon time by the sun. [If the sun is eclipsed in the east, it is a bad omen for dwellers in the east];[40] if in the west, it is a bad omen for dwellers in the west. If in the middle of the sky, it is a bad omen for the whole world. If its face looks red as blood, the sword will come to the world. If it looks like sackcloth,[41] famine will come to the world. If it looks like both blood and sackcloth, arrows of the sword and arrows of famine will be dispatched [against the world]. If the eclipse is at sunset, calamity will tarry in its coming; if at sunrise, calamity will hasten on its way. But some say the omens are to be reversed. And there is no nation which is smitten but that its gods are smitten together with it, as is said, *Against all the gods of Egypt will I execute judgments* (Exod. 12:12). As for Israel, when they do the will of Him whose presence is everywhere, they need have no fear [of omens], as is said, *Thus saith the Lord: Learn not the way of the nations, and be not dismayed at the signs of heaven; for the nations are dismayed at them* (Jer. 10:2)—the nations are dismayed, but Israel need not be dismayed.[42]

14

R. Eleazar, ben Pĕraṭa said something more about eclipses: If the sun is eclipsed in the middle of the month, fish multiply and increase in the sea, and fruit trees repeat their blossoming. If the moon is eclipsed in the middle of the month of Marheshvan, sword and pestilence will come to the world. Furthermore, agony will be added to agony as harsh decrees are renewed. S, *p.* 11

39. He will die prematurely. See parallel in B.Ta 30a.
40. "If the sun . . . in the east"—parallel in Meḳ, *1,* 19.
41. Dark and overcast.
42. See parallel in Tos Suk 2:6 and B.Suk 29a.

15

In regard to the particular seven-year period at the end of which [the Messiah] son of David will appear,[43] [the following things will happen]: In the first year, says God, *I will cause it to rain upon one city and cause it not to rain upon another city* (Amos 4:7). In the second year, arrows of famine will be dispatched [against Israel]. In the third year, there will be a general famine; during the year, men, women, and little children, the devout and the saintly, will die, and [hunger will cause] the Torah to be forgotten among Jews. During the fourth year, there will be a scarcity of one commodity and a surplus of another.[44] During the fifth, there will be great plenty, and knowledge of the Torah will return to those who study it.[45] During the sixth, there will be rumors [of war];[46] and during the seventh, wars. And with the departure of the seventh year, the son of David will appear.

R. Judah said: In the generation during which the son of David comes, the chamber where scholars were wont to meet for study will be used for harlotry, the Gaulan region[47] will be laid waste; the men of Gaulan will go about [begging] from town to town and find no pity. The wisdom of the Scribes will be deemed a stench, and men who fear sin will be despised. The leaders of the generation will be dog-faced [brutes]. Truth will be wanting, as is said, *Truth shall be in fragments*[48] (Isa. 59:15). What is meant by being *in fragments?* According to R. Yannai, truth will fall to pieces and will disappear.[49] *And he that departeth from evil maketh himself an easy mark (mištolel)*—that is, he who departs from evil will be dubbed a fool *(mištolel).*[50]

R. Johanan said: In the generation in which the son of David comes, disciples of the wise will grow few; and as for those who remain

---

43. According to Yĕhudah 'Eben Shĕmu'el, the idea of a seven-year period at the end of which the Messiah was to come is linked with the calculation that at the end of eighty-five Jubilee periods—that is, after Anno Mundi 4250—the Messiah was to be expected. A.M. 4250 corresponded to 447 C.E., a year which many believed would mark the downfall of Rome. As a matter of fact, in 433 C.E., Attila the Hun made himself ruler of Rome. Accordingly, in one of the seven-year periods, in the eighty-sixth Jubilee, the Messiah was expected to appear. See Yĕhudah 'Eben Shĕmu'el, *Midrĕše gĕ'ulah,* 2d ed. (Jerusalem–Tel Aviv, 5714/1954), p. 45. See also PR 1:7 (YJS, *18,* 46–47, n. 51).

44. Literally, "plenty and no plenty."

45. Joseph Klausner *(The Messianic Idea in Israel* [New York, 1955], pp. 449–50) suggests that the temporary disappearance of the Torah from Israel will be among the pangs suffered by Israel during the time preceding the Messiah's coming.

46. Cf. Mark 13:7 and Matt. 24:26. Or "[of thunderings]" or "rumors [that the Messiah is on his way]." So Rashi on B.Sanh 97a.

47. East of the Sea of Galilee and of the upper Jordan. See I. Epstein's note in the Soncino tr., B.Sanh 97a.

48. JV: *Truth is lacking.* In this comment, *'dr,* "lack," is taken in its other sense of "flock" or "band"; hence "fragment, piece."

49. There will be many conflicting opinions as to what the truth is.

50. Cf. Job 12:17.

alive, their eyes will be worn out [with weeping] in sorrow and lamentation. Furthermore, agony will be added to agony as harsh decrees are renewed—indeed, while one decree is still in force, another will be quickly added to it.

R. Nehorai said: In the generation in which the son of David comes, the young will insult | their elders, old men and women alike S, *p.* 12
who will be made to wait upon the young:[51] "The daughter will rise up against her mother, the daughter-in-law against her mother-in-law" (Mic. 6:7).[52] And a son will feel no shame before his father.[53]

R. Nehemiah said: In the generation in which the son of David comes, there will be much poverty; the swindler will have prestige;[54] the vine will yield its fruit, yet wine will be costly; all the kingdoms will be converted to heresy with none to restrain them.[55]

R. Johanan said: The son of David will come only in a generation that is either altogether righteous or altogether wicked. The proof of his coming "in a generation altogether righteous"? *When thy people will be all righteous, they shall inherit the Land for ever* (Isa. 60:21). The proof "in a generation that is altogether wicked"? *And He saw that there was no man, and was astonished that there was no intercessor; therefore His own arm brought salvation unto Him* (Isa. 59:16).[56]

16

R. Eliezer ben Jacob said: They who dwell in villages are like those who dwell in graves[57]—their lives are mere existence, their money [is not safe], and to their daughters applies the verse *Accursed is the one that is forced to lie with any brutish man* (Deut. 28:21).[58]

---

51. [Literally, "youths will cause old men to go pale (with shame), and old women will rise in deference before the young." L. N.]

52. See Matt. 10:35–36 and Luke 12:53.

53. Cf. Amos 2:7.

54. So, citing his teacher, Rashi on B.Sanh 97a. Jastrow (p. 571b) suggests: "high prices will be offensive."

55. R. Nehemiah (ca. 150 C.E.) thus seems to forecast that the Roman Empire would be converted to Christianity, which he terms a [Jewish] heresy, as indeed was to happen under Constantine the Great in 323.

56. For parallels to the preceding passages on the coming of the Messiah, see Soṭ 9:15; B.Sanh 97a, 98a; DEZ, chap. 10; PRKM 5:9, pp. 97–98 (PRKS, pp. 109–10); and PR 15:14/15 (YJS, *1,* 327–28).

57. Note the play on *kĕfarim,* "villages," and *ḳĕḇarim,* "graves."

58. Since their wives are not safe from attack, their daughters may well be bastards. JV: *Cursed be he that lieth with any manner of beast.* See B.Er 55b; Pes 49b; and DEZ, chap. 10.

17

R. Jose ben Ḳisma said: Two are better than three,[59] and alas for one's youth which goes, not to return.[60]

18

Samuel "the Little" was in the habit of quoting the verse *Rejoice not when thine enemy falleth, and let not thy heart be glad when he stumbleth* (Prov. 24:17). He also used to say: Fear one who has no fear; weep not readily with one who weeps; seek not with any one who seeks; do not shame yourself by bowing down with one who keeps bowing down,[61] for he may be a fool and will bring you to folly.

19

S, *p.* 13 Johanan ben Phinehas[62] said: Ḥăḇil Yamma[63] is the glory of Babylonia.[64] Shunya Sharṣunya, Ekah-salla, and Shiṣarya are the glory of Ḥăḇil Yamma. So also, according to R. 'Aḳiḇa, is Aḳruḳia.[65] [Nevertheless, one is not to live in those cities.][66]

20

Disciples of the wise should not live in a city which does not contain the following ten things: a synagogue, a privy, a bathhouse, a school for young children, a court of justice that imposes flagellation and also decrees other penalties, a fund for charity, a fund for spices,[67] a fund

---

59. The two legs in youth are better than the three—that is, two legs and a cane—in old age.

60. See B.Shab 152a and DEZ, chap. 10.

61. ["Do not disgrace yourself with one who disgraces himself, do not be subservient with one who is subservient." L. N.]

62. He is mentioned elsewhere as an officer of the Temple who was in charge of the seals. See Sheḳ 5:1.

63. V's *hb' ymrw* is emended by Friedmann (n. 52) to read "Ḥăḇil Yamma," literally "district of the sea" (cf. Zeph. 2:6). The phrase is used to describe the part of Babylonia which, crisscrossed by rivers and canals, made the land fertile. See Jacob Obermeyer, *Die Landschaft Babylonien* (Frankfurt am Main, 1929), p. 118ff.

64. "The finest and most fertile district" (Friedmann, n. 6).

65. Tentatively identified by Friedmann (n. 52) as Fort (aḳra) Tulbaḳene on the upper reaches of the Euphrates, which was still considered part of Babylonia (B.Ḳid 71b).

66. The words in brackets are interpolated at the suggestion of Professor Chaim Zalman Dimitrovsky.

Thus the utterance may be understood as discouraging the settlement of Jews in Babylonia.

67. The fund for spices was provided to keep away spice peddlers who usually sold their goods to women and were known as seducers. So Friedmann (n. 53), who

for dispensing provisions to the poor every Friday, and, R. 'Aḳiḇa added, all kinds of fruits because [the sight of] all kinds of fruits lights up the eyes.[68]

21

When our Masters entered the vineyard in Jabneh,[69] they said: The day S, *p.* 14
will soon come when a word of Scripture will be sought here and not found, when people will run back and forth from city to city for an explanation of a commandment <and not find it, as is said, *They shall run to and fro to seek*> *the word of the Lord, and shall not find it* (Amos 8:12). They will have to ride all the way up [to Galilee] with regard to getting an answer to such questions as whether a loaf of bread touched by a reptile is ritually unclean. They will be seeking the word of the Lord and will not find it. Hence, R. Simeon ben Yoḥai said: God forbid that Torah should ever be completely forgotten in Israel: indeed, it is said, *It shall not be forgotten out of the mouths of their seed* (Deut. 31:21). What could happen, however, is that So-and-so may say of something <"It is unclean"> but So-and-so may say "It is clean," or that <So-and-so may prohibit> while So-and-so may permit, with the result that there is no clear guidance, no clear teaching.[70]

R. Eliezer said: Communities may be compelled to provide escort for travelers because the reward for such escort is limitless, [as is shown by the following account: *The* [*Israelite*] *scouts saw a man come forth out of the city, and they said unto him: Show us, we pray thee, the entrance into the city, and we will deal kindly with thee.* [*And he showed them the entrance to the city* (Judg. 1:24–25)]. What was the kindness they did for him? *They smote the city with the edge of the sword; but they let the man go and all his family (ibid.).* And what reward did he receive? *The man went into the land of the Hittites, and built a city, and called the name thereof Luz, which is the name thereof unto this day* (Judg. 1:26). This is the Luz in which the
fringes [of the prayer shawl] (Num. 15:38) are dyed blue | for all S, *p.* 15
Israel. Nay more! When Sennacherib came up against the Land, he did not disturb Luz. And Nebuchadnezzar did not destroy it. Even the

---

cites B.Ḳid 52a and Yeḇ 63b concerning the spice peddler's tendency to chase after women.

68. For the understanding of Torah. So Haida.

69. Jabneh was in Judaea, which the Romans renamed Palestine. Following the destruction of Bethar, notes M. Avi-Yonah, " 'of the seventy-five Jewish settlements in Judaea recorded in ancient sources not one has preserved vestiges of Jewish life.' The center of gravity . . . shifted to Galilee, which now doubtless embraced the majority of the Jewish population in the country" (Salo Baron, *A Social and Religious History of the Jews* [Philadelphia, 1952], *2,* 123). For parallels to the account of the gathering in Jabneh, see Tos Eḏ 1:1 and B.Shab 138b.

70. In any of the places they go to (B.Shab 138a–b and Samuel Edels *ad loc.*).

angel of death has no permission to enter it. When old men and old women within it grow weary of life, they are taken outside the wall [of the city] and there they die.

Now may not the matter of providing escort be strongly argued on the basis of the foregoing events? Here was a man—[in fact, a Canaanite]—who did not walk a step or utter a word, but merely pointed with his finger to guide the scouts and yet thereby brought about deliverance for himself and for all his family to the end of all generations. How much greater, then, is the reward a man will receive from the Holy One for escorting—walking along and talking—a disciple of the wise from town to town, from city to city, from province to province.

R. Joshua ben Levi said: When a man is on a journey and has no escort, let him occupy [his mind] with Torah[71] as is said, *They* [*words of Torah*] *shall be an escort*[72] *of grace unto thy head, and chains about thy neck*[73] (Prov. 1:9).

---

71. As a means of protection.
72. JV: *chaplet.* But *liwyaṭ,* "chaplet," may also mean "escort."
73. See parallel in B.Er 54a and Soṭ 46a.

CHAPTER 2 (EZ, CHAPTER 17)

The discipline, glory, and reward of Torah study

Summary

Many are the distinctions of a man who occupies himself with Torah for its own sake. No man can be considered truly free unless he occupies himself with Torah. He who learns from his fellow even a single letter ought to treat him with respect (S, 15–16).

The way of Torah: a morsel of bread with salt to eat; a ration of water to drink; a sleep on the ground; and a life of hardship toiling in study of Torah.

Seek not greatness for yourself and crave not honor. Practice goodness more than learn precepts. Occupation with Torah is greater than priesthood or royalty, for while royalty enjoys thirty prerogatives, and priesthood twenty-four, Torah demands forty-eight attributes of him who toils in it, and God rewards him accordingly.

To those who obey it and maintain it, Torah gives life in this world, in the world-to-come, and in the days of the Messiah. It bestows all kinds of blessing upon those who occupy themselves with it (S, 17–19).

Torah, heaven and earth, Abraham, Israel, and the Temple are the five treasures God cherishes in His world. In regard to Torah, Johanan ben Bag-Bag declared that one is to peruse it again and again, for there is no better rule of life (S, 20).

Even a single chapter in Torah, as shown by the story of a Jewish child captive in a Roman emperor's palace, can demonstrate the glory of God (S, 21). People whose faith is pure and strong, as shown by a story of an old woman and another of a maiden, are capable of instructing even a man as learned in Torah as R. Johanan.

A child who has learned to say, "Bless ye the Lord, who is to be blessed," can thereby free his father from Gehenna where he is being punished for his sins (S, 22).

Chapter 2 (EZ, Chapter 17)

R. Eliezer said: Whosoever occupies himself with Torah for its own S, *p.* 15
sake merits many things—not only merits them, but puts the whole *cont'd*
world in debt to him. He is called beloved [of God], friend and lover
| of Him who is present everywhere. He is called a lover of mankind, S, *p.* 16
one who gives joy to Him who is present everywhere, one who gives
joy to mankind. Torah clothes man | with humility and reverence; it S, *p.* 17
prepares him to become pious, upright, and faithful; it keeps him far from sin and brings him near to virtue; through him, men enjoy counsel and sound knowledge, understanding and strength; it gives him kingly rule and authority and insight into justice; to him, the secrets of heaven and Torah are revealed; he becomes like a fountain that ever gathers force, a never-failing stream, a river that flows on with ever-sustained

vigor. He is[1] modest and patient, overlooking personal offense, for the Torah enlarges his spirit and raises him above all material concern.

[Of those who do not take up the study of Torah] R. Joshua ben Levi said: Each and every day a Divine Voice comes forth from Mount Horeb[2] to proclaim these words: "Woe unto [you], mankind, because of the humiliation Torah suffers [from your neglect]." He who does not occupy himself with Torah is said to be under Divine censure *(nazuf),* as is said, *As a ring of gold in a swine's snout (nezem zahaḇ bĕ-'af),*[3] *so is a fair woman who turneth aside from discretion*[4] (Prov. 11:22). [As for the man who studies Torah, R. Joshua quoted the following verse concerning him]: *The tables were the work of God, and the writing was the writing of God, ḥaruṯ (incised) upon the tables* (Exod. 32:16). Read not *ḥaruṯ,* "incised," but *ḥeruṯ,* "freedom," for there is no man truly free but the man who occupies himself with the study of Torah.[5] He who occupies himself with the study of Torah is lifted to the heights, as is suggested by the names in a verse from the Book of Numbers: *From Mattanah (the gift of the Torah) to Nahaliel (the bequest from God) and from Nahaliel to Bamoth (to the heights)* (Num. 21:19).

He who learns from his fellow a single chapter [of Torah], a single Halaḵah, a single verse, even a single letter, ought to treat him with
S, *p.* 18 respect. So we find with David, king of Israel, who learned | only two things[6] from Ahithophel, yet in a Psalm called him "master"—his guide and his teacher: *Thee, my guide and my teacher, though a commoner, I deem my equal* (Ps. 55:14).[7] And is there not in this matter an inference from the lesser to the greater? If David, king of Israel, who learned only two things from Ahithophel, called him "master"—his guide and his teacher, how much more ought one pay honor to his fellow from whom he has learned a single chapter, a single

---

1. Reading the obscure *hwy* as *hwh,* "he is."

2. That is, Mount Sinai, the place of the revelation of the Torah.

3. The proof text is used to produce a *noṭariḳon*—three letters selected to form a hidden word. The initial letters of *nezem zahaḇ* are combined with the last letter of *bĕ-'af* to form the word *nazuf,* meaning "under censure."

4. *A fair woman who turneth aside from discretion* metaphorically designates here the man who has an aptitude for Torah but makes no use of it.

5. Cf. EZ, 179.

6. The two things are (1) study in association with others, and (2) to go to a house of prayer not alone and leisurely, but in company and eagerly. These two things are derived from Ps. 55:15, which is preceded by a verse in which David is understood as calling Ahithophel "my guide." Psalm 55:15 reads: "We took sweet counsel (i.e., studied Torah) *together;* to the house of God we walked with the throng *(regeš).*" The word *regeš* means "throng," as well as "eagerness, enthusiasm." See Ka Rabbati, chap. 7 (*The Minor Tractates of the Talmud,* Soncino [London, 1965], *2,* 504–5), and Aḇ 6:3, Soncino tr. (London, 1935), p. 81, n. 6.

7. JV: *It was thou, a man mine equal, my companion, and my familiar friend.* But *'ĕnoš,* "man," often means "ordinary man," hence "commoner"; *'aluf,* "companion," is here derived from the verb *'lf,* "to train, to direct," hence "my guide"; and, by a slight change in vocalization, *mĕyudda'i,* "my familair friend," is read *mĕyaddĕ'i,* "one who conveys knowledge to me," hence "my teacher."

Halakah, as is said, *The wise* [*deservedly*] *inherit honor!* (Prov. 3:35).

The way of Torah is this: a morsel of bread with salt to eat; a ration of water to drink; a sleep on the ground; and a life of hardship toiling in the Torah. If you live thus, *Happy shalt thou be, and it shall be well with thee* (Ps. 128:2)—you will be happy in this world, and it will be well with you in the world-to-come.

Seek not greatness and covet not honor. Go beyond what your study [of precepts] prescribes. Yearn not for the table of kings, for your table is greater than theirs, your crown is nobler than theirs, and your Employer is faithful in paying you the wages of your work.

Occupation with Torah is greater than priesthood or royalty, for while royalty enjoys thirty prerogatives, and priesthood twenty-four,[8] Torah demands forty-eight attributes [from its students], namely: study aloud, attentive listening, distinct pronunciation, sensitivity to nuances of inflection in tone, alertness of mind, intuitive insight, awe [of one's master], reverence [for God], humility, cheerfulness, attendance on Sages, close association with colleagues, persistence in the study of Torah and Mishnah, right conduct, moderation in sleep, moderation in pleasure, moderation in worldly interests, moderation in business, patience, a good heart, faith in and deference to the Sages, acceptance of affliction, knowing one's place, contentment with one's lot, restraint upon one's words, refraining from claiming merit for oneself, loving Him who is present everywhere, loving mankind, loving reproof, loving rectitude, shunning honor and—it goes without saying—not seeking honor, avoiding pride in one's learning, | taking no delight in S, *p.* 19
laying down the law, bearing the yoke with one's fellow, judging him charitably, guiding him to truth and peace, showing composure in one's study, asking and answering, learning in order to teach, learning in order to practice [rightly], making his teacher wiser [by his questions to him], noting with precision what one is hearing, and giving credit for a comment to the one who made it. (Indeed, from these words, *And Esther told the king in the name of Mordecai* [Esther 2:22], we learn that whoever cites a comment in the name of the one who made it brings deliverance to the world.)

To those who obey it and maintain it, Torah gives life in this world, in the world-to-come, and in the days of the Messiah, as is said, *They* [*the precepts of Torah*] *are life to those who find them* (Prov. 4:22); and *It shall be health to thy navel, and marrow to thy bones* (Prov. 3:8); *She is a tree of life to them that lay hold upon her; and happy is every one that holdeth her fast* (Prov. 3:18). And it is further said, *Length of days is in her right hand* (Prov. 3:16); and *They* [*her precepts*] *shall be a chaplet of grace unto*

8. In his commentary on 'Abot, Elijah of Wilno lists the royal prerogatives as set forth in 1 Sam. 8 and in Sanh 2, and the priestly prerogatives as set forth in Num. 18 and in various Rabbinic utterances.

thy head (Prov. 1:9). And Torah's wisdom itself says, *By me thy days shall be multiplied* (Prov. 9:11); *Length of days, and years of life . . . will they* [*my precepts*] *add to thee* (Prov. 3:2).

R. Simeon ben Judah said in the name of R. Simeon: Beauty, strength, riches, wisdom, glory, a hoary head, and children are comely [raiment] for the righteous who thereby serve to make the world comely.[9] [That the righteous indeed have such comely raiment is] attested by the verse *The hoary head is a crown of glory, it will be found in the way of righteousness* (Prov. 16:31), and *Children's children are the crown of men who acquired wisdom*[10] (Prov. 17:6), and *The glory of young men is their strength;* [*and the beauty of men who acquired wisdom*[11] *is the hoary head*] (Prov. 20:29), and *Before those of His who acquired wisdom*
S, *p.* 20 *shall be glory*[12] (Isa. 24:23). R. Simeon | ben Mĕnasya said: These seven qualities which the Sages enumerated as becoming to the righteous were all realized in Rabbi [Judah I the Patriarch] and his sons.

There are <five> treasures that the Holy One [cherished most] in His world [and] took for His own, namely, the Torah, heaven and earth, Abraham, Israel, and the Temple. And the proof in regard to Torah? Torah's saying *The Lord possessed me as the beginning of His way* (Prov. 8:22). In regard to heaven and earth? The verse *Thus saith the Lord, the heaven is My throne, and the earth is My footstool* (Isa. 66:1). In regard to Abraham? The verse *Blessed be Abram whom God the Most High took for His own as He had heaven and earth*[13] (Gen. 14:19). In regard to Israel? The verse *Till Thy people pass over, O Lord, till the people pass over that Thou possessest* (Exod. 15:16), and *As for the holy that are in the Land, they are the excellent in whom is all My delight* (Ps. 16:3). And in regard to the Temple? The verse *The Sanctuary, O Lord, which Thy hands have established* (Exod. 15:17), and *He brought them to His holy mountain,*[14] *to the mountain which His right hand had possessed* (Ps. 78:54).

And all these treasures He created only for His own glory, as is said, *Everything that is called by My name, it is for My glory I created it, I have formed it, yea, I have made it* (Isa. 43:7); and [these five], *The Lord shall hold as His cherished treasures*[15] *ever and ever* (Exod. 15:18).[16]

"Johanan ben Bag-Bag used to say of the Torah: Turn it[s pages]

---

9. Literally, "and comely for the world." But see *Tif'ereṯ Yiśra'el* on Aḇ 6:8.

10. JV: *Children's children are the crown of old men.* But here *zḳn,* "old man," is apparently read *zeh šeḳ-ḳanah ḥoḵmah,* "he who has acquired wisdom."

11. JV: *the beauty of old men.* See preceding note.

12. JV: *And before His elders shall be glory.* See preceding note.

13. JV: *Blessed be Abram of God Most High, Maker of heaven and earth.*

14. MT: *His holy border.*

15. At the suggestion of Leon Nemoy, the Hebrew *mlḵ,* "reign," is construed as the Arabic *mlk (malaka),* "to possess anything, to become the owner of"; hence "hold as His cherished possessions."

16. The preceding, from the beginning of the chapter, is paralleled in *Ḳinyan Torah* (Aḇ 6) and Ka Rabbati, chap. 8.

again and again, for all [wisdom] is in it. Pore over it, [grow old and weary in perusal of it], and stir not from it, for you have no better rule than it.

Ben He-He used to say: According to the effort is the reward (Ab̲ 5:22–23). | R. Ḥanina ben Aḳašya <used to say>: The Holy One, wishing to render Israel the more worthy of Him, enlarged the Torah and its commandments for them, as is said, *Ye shall keep My commandments, and,* [*though they be numerous*], *obey them, for I am the Lord* (Lev. 22:31), [who will reward you for each and every command you are able to obey],[17] a promise that is attested in the words of Isaiah, *The Lord was pleased for the sake of His righteousness to magnify the Torah and thus glorify it* (Isa. 42:21). S, *p.* 21

R. Eleazar ben Azariah said in the name of R. Ḥanina: Disciples of the wise increase peace in the world, for it is said, *When all thy children are taught by the Lord, peace shall be increased by thy children* (Isa. 54:13). Read not *banayik̲,* "thy children," but *bonaik̲,* "thy builders," [by which is meant thy learned men].

Consider the story of a young child whose father taught him the Book of Genesis. One day a Roman emperor invaded the province [where the child dwelt], and the child was captured together with his Scroll [of Genesis]. He was first put in prison together with his Scroll, but then his Scroll was placed in the emperor's archives. On one occasion the emperor's mind became troubled [about some matter], and he said: Bring me a book of chronicles [and read me to sleep]. His servants went and found the Book of Genesis. All the notables of the kingdom came, but they could not read it. Finally they said: This is a Scroll of the Scrolls of Israel. As it happens, one of their children is kept in your prison. They went and had the child summoned. When he saw his Scroll, he embraced it and kissed it, and then he read it and commented on it as far as the verse *And the heaven and the earth were finished* (Gen. 2:1). When the emperor heard of the glory of the Holy One—how He created His world—he rose up from his throne and kissed the child's head, saying: I know that the Holy One troubled my mind only for your sake, in order to have you released from prison. | Thereupon the emperor gave the child silver and gold and gems of purest ray and pearls, menservants and maidservants, and sent him with great honor to his father. Is there not here an inference from the lesser to the S, *p.* 22

---

17. The words "who will reward . . . able to obey" are interpolated in keeping with Maimonides' comment which follows: "When a man properly and wholeheartedly fulfills even one command of the 613, in no way mixing it with any worldly motive, he merits life in the world-to-come. Accordingly, since God's commands are numerous it is all but impossible for a man during a lifetime not to obey perfectly at least one command. Through such obedience, the man merits immortality for his soul" (on Mak 3:16).

greater? If such reward came to him who studied only the Book of Genesis, how much greater and greater the reward to one who has studied the entire Torah!

R. Simeon ben Laḳish said: Around the man who goes to great trouble in this world to occupy himself with Torah during the night, the Holy One draws a cordon of grace during the day, as is said, *By day the Lord doth command His grace, because by night His song is with me* (Ps. 42:9).[18] Moreover, the Torah shields him [not only all the years of his life, but even] after he is laid to rest in the dust, as is said, *When thou walkest, it shall lead thee* (Prov. 6:22), in this world; *when thou liest down, it shall watch over thee (ibid.),* at death; and *when thou awakest, it shall talk with thee (ibid.),* in the world-to-come.

R. Johanan said: I studied the entire Torah, all of it, yet not until recently did I learn two lessons: from an old woman [I learned] faith in the bestowal of reward, and from a maiden [I learned] true fear of sin. How [did I learn] from an old woman faith in the bestowal of reward? Once in the synagogue I found an old woman who used to go from [her] city to [my] city to pray. I asked, "My daughter, is there no synagogue [for you to attend] in your own city?" She replied, "Yes, master, but I put myself to the trouble of going from one city to another city in order to pray and thus earn a reward for doing so, and yet you reproach me." Thus from an old woman we learned faith in the bestowal of reward. How [did I learn] true fear of sin from a maiden? Once I walked into a synagogue and found there a maiden standing in prayer and saying: "Gehenna, I am superior to you: If it were my wish to have ten men come to me, dine and drink with me, and then commit an act of lewdness with me, they and I would be [fit inmates of you] and would have to enter you. But I am superior to you, for I make the Inclination to evil bend low before me and thus I save myself from you."[19] Thus from a maiden we learned true fear of sin.

R. Johanan ben Zakkai said: Once, as I was walking along a road, I came upon a man who was gathering fagots. When I spoke to him, he did not reply, but then he came over to me and said, "I am not alive —I am dead." When I asked, "If you are dead, what need have you
S, *p.* 23 of fagots?" | he replied: "Master, listen to me while I tell you my story. When I was alive, my friend and <I> engaged in sodomy,[20] so when we were sentenced to come here [to Gehenna], a penalty of

---

18. See parallel in B.Ḥaḡ 12b.

19. For parallels of the preceding two stories, see B.Soṭ 22a.

20. At the suggestion of Leon Nemoy, *plṭry* is taken to represent the Greek *philetaeria,* "love of [adult] friends," a euphemism for adult homosexuality.

Louis Ginzberg suggests that *plṭry* should be read *pdrsṭy,* "pederasty" (*Genizah Studies,* [New York, 5688/1928], *1,* 236). Max Kadushin accepts the emendation (*TSE,* p. 3, n. 3d).

punishment by burning was handed down against both of us. And now when I gather fagots, they are used to burn my friend, and when he gathers fagots, they are used to burn me."[21] I asked, "How long is your sentence to last?" He replied: "When I came here, I left my wife pregnant, and I know that the child she bears will be a male. And so I beg you, please watch over him from the time of his birth until he reaches the age of five. Then take him to the house of a teacher to learn to read Scripture. For when he learns to say, "Bless ye the Lord, who is to be blessed,"[22] I shall be brought up from the punishment of Gehenna.

---

21. [The man is dead, and the punishment is *now* being executed upon him, in that he suffers the torment of burning *without being consumed, over and over again,* since it is his spiritual person that is being burned, not his consumable earthly one. L. N.]

22. "This invocation to prayer, introducing the main part of the service (the Shĕma' with its benedictions and the *Tĕfillah*), is Biblical (Neh. 9:5)." See *APB,* p. 37, and *Companion to . . . the Daily Prayer Book,* pp. xli–xliii. For parallels of the story, see Ka Rabbati, chap. 2; Moses Gaster, *The Exempla of the Rabbis* (New York, 1968), pp. 92–93; and Louis Ginzberg, *Genizah Studies, 1,* 234–40.

The saying of the Kaddish is a later development in the practice of intercessory prayer alluded to here.

CHAPTER 3 (EZ, CHAPTER 18)

Blessed is the student of Torah

S, *p.* 24 R. Johanan said: I call heaven and earth to witness for me that any disciple of the wise who reads Scripture for the sake of Heaven, recites Mishnah for the sake of Heaven, and eats only what he himself has earned—of such as he the Psalmist says, *Blessed shalt thou be, and it shall be well with thee* (Ps. 128:2): *blessed shalt thou be* in this world, *and it shall be well with thee* in the world-to-come. To this man it is said: *How fair and how pleasant art thou* [*with such blessing*]*!* (Song 7:7). Nay more! His
S, *p.* 25 wife and his children revere him, the nations of the earth | revere him, the ministering angels inquire about his well-being, [and above all], the Holy One loves him with utter love, as is said, *All the peoples of the earth shall see that the name of the Lord is called upon thee; and they shall be afraid of thee. . . . The Lord will open unto thee His good treasure* (Deut. 28:10, 12).[1]

---

1. Cf. above, ER, 26, 91; and EZ, 197.

PIRḲE R. ELIEZER

CHAPTER 1 (EZ, CHAPTER 19)

God and Edom

Summary

God Himself will wreak vengeance upon iniquitous Edom, descendant of Esau who took this world as his portion, even as Jacob took the world-to-come as his portion (S, 26). When Esau saw how great were Jacob's possessions in this world, he proposed a partnership: each would share alike both in this world and in the world-to-come, an offer which Jacob rejected, saying: My children's frailty in observance of God's commandments, together with the burden of Edom's iniquities, would make my children's chastisements in Gehenna unendurable (S, 27).

When God wreaks vengeance upon Edom, it will seem to the ministering angels as though He had vanished. They will turn to the Red Sea, to Sinai, to Zion, inquiring in vain as to His whereabouts (S, 28). Finally they will be told by Isaiah that He had just left Edom, upon whom He had wreaked vengeance not only for its own iniquities but Israel's as well. In deference to Esau's protest at his heavy burden, God took Israel's sins and placed them on His own garments, thus crimsoning them, but then washing them white as snow (S, 29).

In the meantime, however, Israel complains of the favor shown to Edom in this world, whereunto God responds: In the time-to-come, Esau's sons and notables will be given over into Israel's power (S, 30).

Chapter 1 (EZ, Chapter 19)

His disciples addressed R. Eliezer, asking him: What is the proof that S, *p.* 26
the Holy One Himself will wreak vengeance upon Edom? Without hesitation R. Eliezer began his answer by citing *Who is this that cometh from Edom?* (Isa. 63:1). The answer to this question is to be considered in the light of what David, king of Israel, was inspired by the holy spirit to say: *Moab is my washpot, upon Edom do I cast my shoe* (Pss. 60:10, 108:10). <Who is the "I" speaking in this verse? It is no other than> the Holy One, who in His own person comes after wreaking vengeance upon Edom. By what parable may the matter be understood? By the parable of a king who built four palaces in four different provinces. He entered the first palace where he ate and drank but did not first remove his shoes. He did likewise in the second and third palaces. When he entered the fourth, he ate and drank but first removed his shoes, saying to his servants: Go forth and fetch the notables of this province that they may set the repast before me. His servants asked: Why, when you entered the first, the second, and the third palaces did you eat and drink but not first remove your shoes? He replied: When I entered the first and the second and the third, I was preoccupied, for I kept saying to myself each time: When shall I behold

the hour I yearn for? Now that I have beheld that hour, my mind is at ease.

<It may be said figuratively that> the Holy One [did not remove His shoes—that is], in His war against the kingdoms of Pharaoh, Amalek, Sisera, Sennacherib, and Nebuchadnezzar, His mind was not at ease until He Himself had wreaked vengeance upon Edom.

It is said that when Jacob and Esau were in their mother's womb, Jacob said to Esau: Esau, my brother, our father has two of us, even as two worlds—this world and the world-to-come—are before us. In this world there is eating, drinking, the give-and-take of business, marriage, and the begetting of children. But with regard to all these activities, the world-to-come is quite different. If you so prefer, take this world, and I will take the world-to-come. And the proof that Jacob spoke thus in
S, *p.* 27 the womb? Jacob's saying, *Yield me | thy birthright "that day"*[1] (Gen. 25:31) in reference to their agreement that day in the womb. <Thereupon, in reply to Jacob, Esau denied the resurrection of the dead, saying: If the living, who have spirit and breath, die, how is one to suppose that they who have died will come alive?> Thus it came about that Esau took this world as his portion, and Jacob <took> the world-to-come <as his portion>.

Now when Jacob came from Laban's house, and Esau saw that Jacob had menservants and maidservants, Esau said to Jacob: My brother, did you not say to me that you would take the world-to-come [for your portion]? How, then, did you come to all this wealth? Apparently you, like me, are making use of this world. Jacob replied: My possessions are what the Holy One gave me for my use in this world, as Jacob said: *The possessions*[2] *which God hath graciously given thy servant* (Gen. 33:5). In that instant, weighing the matter in his mind, Esau said to himself: If the Holy One gave him <as his reward> so much of this world which is not his portion, how much more and more will He give him of the world-to-come which is his portion! Thereupon Esau said to Jacob: Jacob, my brother, come, let us enter into partnership, you and I—you take one half of this world and one half of the world-to-come, and I will take the other half of this world and the other half of the world-to-come; as Esau said: *Let us start on our further journey, and I will proceed at thy side*[3] (Gen. 33:12). Jacob replied to Esau: *My lord knoweth that the children [of Israel] are frail [with regard to observance of command-*

---

1. Thus there was no sale—Esau yielded what he had already given up. JV: *Sell me first thy birthright.* But see Rashi.

2. JV: *The children.* But apparently here *yĕladim,* "children," is taken in the secondary sense, "that which one comes to possess." Or, as Leon Nemoy suggests, the author read *hay-yĕladim* as *hay-yĕlodim.*

3. Haida and *YY* suggest the substitution of Gen. 33:12 for Gen. 33:15, which is in the text.

ments] (Gen. 33:13). [Hence, if you share this world and the world-to-come with me, the burden of Israel's iniquities will be such as to make the children of Israel] unable to endure the chastisement [of Gehenna] . . . *and if they are driven hard on the Day* [*of Judgment*], *the entire flock* [*of Israel*] *will die (ibid.).*

| According <to the Rabbis> of the Land of Israel, however, R. S, *p.* 28
Eliezer [did not begin his answer with the verse *Who is this that cometh from Edom?* but] with a different verse,[4] namely, *Their love, their hate, their rancor have long since perished* (Eccles. 9:6). In this verse whom did Solomon[5] have in mind? He had Jacob and Esau in mind. By what parable may the verse be understood? By the parable of two men, one whom a king hated and the other whom a general hated. Said he whom the king hated to him whom the general hated: You are fortunate that when you go to another region, there is hope for you [because the general has no authority there]. But I[6] have no hope! Wherever I go, the authority of the king is still over me. So it is with Esau—the Holy One Himself hates him: *But Esau I hate* (Mal. 1:3).

When the Holy One wreaks vengeance upon Edom, the ministering angels will look for the Holy One in order to sing their song in His presence, but they will not find Him. So they will go to the sea and ask it: When did He *who maketh a way in the sea* (Isa. 43:16) last appear to you? The sea will reply: Since the day that He had me dry up and led His children through me, I have not seen Him. They will then go to Mount Sinai and ask it: When did He of whom it is said, *The Lord came from Sinai* | (Deut. 33:2), the Holy One, last appear to you? Mount S, *p.* 29
Sinai will reply: Since the day that He appeared upon me and gave the Torah to His people with Himself as groom, Moses as the bridegroom's friend, and the Torah as the bride, I have not seen Him. They will go to Zion, and ask: Has He, the Holy One, of whom it is said, *The Lord hath chosen Zion* (Ps. 132:13), appeared to you? Zion will reply: Since the day He removed His presence from my midst, destroyed His house, and burned His Temple, I have not seen Him. Then Isaiah will ask the ministering angels: Whom are you seeking? They will reply: The Holy One. Isaiah will say: He has just now gone forth out of Edom, as is intimated in the verse *Who is this that cometh from Edom, with crimsoned garments?* (Isa. 63:1). At once the angels [knowing it to be the Holy One] will go and find Him, and beholding His garments crimson <as cloth of crimson, they will ask: Master of the universe, why are Your garments crimsoned>: *Wherefore is Thine apparel crimson?* (Isa. 63:2). He will say: I had <a small winepress> and trod it Myself: *I*

4. Cf. a similar rhetorical structure in PR 5:11, at the beginning (YJS, *18, 1,* 113).
5. Solomon was considered the author of Ecclesiastes.
6. Literally, "such-and-such a man," a euphemism for "I."

have trodden the winepress alone (ibid.). That is, the Holy One has taken <all> the sins of Israel and charged <them> against wicked Esau [whose cruel decrees led Israel to sin], as is said, *And Seir shall bear upon him all their iniquities*[7] (Lev. 16:22). But when Esau spoke up to the Holy One, saying, "Master of the universe, is my strength such that I can bear all of Jacob's iniquities that You load upon me?" The Holy One took all of Jacob's sins and put them on His own garments, so that their crimson became an intense scarlet. He will wash the garments, however, until they are made white as snow, as is said, *His raiment was as white snow* (Dan. 7:9). All the foregoing discourse was initiated by the question *Who is this that cometh from Edom?* (Isa. 63:1).

<Another comment on *Who is this that cometh from Edom?*: By what parable> may the question be answered? By the parable of a king who had a wife but wed another who was hateful and ugly and whose sons kept on provoking him. So his first wife asked him: Why did you wed a wife who is hateful and ugly and whose sons keep provoking you? He replied: I did not enter her house to stay; I had no intention <of
S, *p.* 30 dallying> with her. His wife said: Yes, I myself | saw you leave her house. So likewise when the Holy One endeavors to comfort Zion, the congregation of Israel will ask Him directly: Master of the universe, why did You go into the dwelling of the wicked one who was both hateful and ugly and whose sons kept provoking You? He will reply: I did not go into her dwelling to stay: I had no intention <of dallying> with her. When Israel says: Yes, I saw You leave it, He will answer: And now here are her sons, [the sons of Edom], and her notables as well, given over to the power of Israel [who will consume them], as is said, *The house of Jacob shall be a fire, and the house of Joseph a flame, and the house of Esau for stubble* (Ob. 1:18).

---

7. JV: *And the goat shall bear upon him all their iniquities.* But here the commentator seems to construe *seir,* "goat," as the designation of Edom whose home is Seir.

CHAPTER 2 (EZ, CHAPTER 20)

God's requital of Israel's enemies on the Day of Judgment, His renewal of heaven and earth, and His reward of Israel's righteous

Summary

Any nation which distresses Israel, God's "hallowed portion," God Himself requites, as He did the nations of Pharaoh and Nebuchadnezzar.

At the time God is to sit in judgment over Edom, He will reproach heaven and earth, the sun and the moon (S, 30), the stars and the planets, the ministering angels, the Fathers of the world, and even the throne of judgment itself for not having interceded earlier in behalf of Israel. None will thus escape Divine judgment.

He will then nullify the present order of the world: He will renew heaven and earth, and bring the dead back to life (S, 31). He will then hear the testimony of earth against the sinful nations, and they will be flung into Gehenna. Gehenna will ask to be filled by Israel's transgressors as well, and God will grant its wish.

God will then invite the righteous to enter the Garden of Eden, where Gabriel will bring two thrones, one for God and one for David. Following the feast, Abraham, Isaac, Jacob, Moses, and Joshua will disqualify themselves from leading in the saying of Grace. David will then say it (S, 32).

As God will discourse on Torah and David will recite 'Aggaḏah, out of Gehenna Israel's transgressors will respond with Amen. Whereupon God will tell the ministering angels to open the Garden of Eden and let the transgressors come and sing in His very presence (S, 33).

Chapter 2 (EZ, Chapter 20)

His disciples asked R. Eliezer: <Our master>, tell us, what is to be our lot at the end? He replied: <I will tell you what it is to be>. No part of the creation will be spared on the Day of Judgment, as is said, *Then the moon shall be confounded, and the sun ashamed* (Isa. 24:23). This verse is to be considered in the light of what the prophet Jeremiah was inspired by the holy spirit to say: *Israel is the Lord's hallowed portion, His first fruits of the increase* (Jer. 2:3). When Jeremiah said <this>, whom did he have in mind? He said it only with the congregation of Israel in mind. For if any nation distresses Israel, [His "hallowed portion"], the Holy One is not content until He Himself requites it. Thus the wicked Pharaoh commanded, *Every son that is born ye shall cast into the river* (Exod. 1:22), and the Holy One Himself requited him, as is said, *The Lord looked down upon the host of the Egyptians through the pillar of fire and of cloud, and discomfited the host of the Egyptians* (Exod. 14:24). Nebu-

S, *p.* 30 *cont'd*

chadnezzar, <the wicked [king] who went up and> destroyed the Temple, the Holy One Himself requited, as is said, *and I will punish Bel in Babel* (Jer. 51:44). The Holy One said to Israel: My children, make certain that you are holy <in My presence>, and you will need not fear the Day of Judgment, as is said, *Ye shall be holy unto Me*[1] (Lev. 20:26). Then, in further exposition [of R. Eliezer's answer to the question his disciples had asked him], thus spoke <our master: In the time-to-come>, the Holy One will bring forth the throne of judgment and sit thereon. At first, He will summon heaven and earth and say to them: In the beginning of everything I created you, as is said, *In the beginning God created the heaven and the earth* (Gen. 1:1). How, then, could you look on at My presence removing itself, My Temple being destroyed, My children being banished among the nations of the world, and not entreat mercy in their behalf? Thereupon He will reprimand heaven and earth and have them stand off to one side. Next, He will summon the sun and the moon and say to them: I created you as the two great lights [of the world], <as is said, *And God made the two great lights* (Gen. 1:16)>. How could you look on at My presence removing itself, My Temple being destroyed, My children being banished, and not entreat mercy in their behalf? Nay more! [the Holy One continued]: Kings from the east and from the west used to come, put their crowns upon their heads, and prostrate themselves before you. Yet you did not say, "We are merely shiny shards like potsherds. Do not bow
S, *p.* 31 down to us." And the proof | that they will be thus summoned [by the Holy One]? *Who commandeth the sherd,*[2] *and it riseth not?* (Job 9:7). Thereupon, having thus reprimanded the sun and moon, He will have them stand off to one side. He will then summon the stars and the planets and say to them: I made your radiance bright from one end of the world to the other, having created you only for the sake of Israel, as is said, *If not for My covenant* [*with Israel, and for the Torah which is to be studied*] *day and night, I would not sustain the fixed ways of heaven and earth* (Jer. 33:25).[3] How, then, could you look on at My presence removing itself, My Temple being destroyed, My children being banished, and not entreat for mercy in their behalf? Thereupon, having

1. In the preceding chapter the children of Israel had already been told *Ye shall be holy* (Lev. 19:2). And so PRE resolves the apparent repetition as follows: Lev. 20:26 comes at the end of a chapter which speaks of certain sexual relations and of the flesh of certain animals as defiling. Since "holy" food, such as heave offering, upon being defiled must be burned, so, too, Israel, a holy people, if it defiles itself, is liable to burning on the Day of Judgment. Hence in Lev. 20:26 God bids His people to remain holy so as to escape the penalty of burning on the Day of Judgment.

2. JV: *Who commanded the sun, and it riseth not.* But *ḥeres,* "sun," also means "sherd," and here the commentator plays on both meanings.

3. Cf. parallel comment in PR 21:21 (YJS, *18, 1,* 450), where God asserts that He created the world for the sake of Torah.

reprimanded the stars and planets, God will have them stand off to one side. And likewise He will reprimand the ministering angels. He will summon Metatron [whom He had delegated to lead Israel to the Land][4] and say to him: I gave you a name [indicating your power] to be equal to Mine, as is said, *for My name is in him* (Exod. 23:21).[5] <How, then, could you look on at> My presence removing itself, My Temple being destroyed, My children being banished, and not ask for mercy in their behalf? <Having thus reprimanded him, God will have him stand off to one side. Next, He will summon the Fathers of the world, to whom He will say: I had issued harsh decrees against your children, yet you asked no mercy in their behalf>. Should you say, "We did not know [of the decrees]," I made it plain to you from the very beginning that your children were to be banished. To Abraham, as Scripture reports, [I said]: *Know of a surety that thy seed shall be a stranger in a land that is not theirs* (Gen. 15:13).[6] With regard to Isaac, Scripture told you, *And it shall come to pass that thou, [Esau], wilt become master when thou seest him break off his yoke*[7] (Gen. 27:40). To Jacob, as Scripture reports, [I said]: *Thou wilt come to have princes who will be spoken of as gods and men*[8] (Gen. 23:49), signifying to Jacob that two "princes" would issue from him, the Exilarch in Babylonia and the Patriarch in the Land of Israel,[9] and thus intimating to Jacob the exile [that was to be decreed against Israel. So God reproached the Fathers of the world]: How could you look on at My presence removing itself, My Temple being destroyed, My children being banished, and not ask for mercy in their behalf? Next, He will summon the throne of judgment and say to it, I made you before all else, as is said, *Thou throne of glory, on high from the beginning* (Jer. 17:12). How, then, could you look on at My presence removing itself, My Temple being destroyed, My children being banished, yet ask no mercy in their behalf? <Having thus repri-

---

4. [Here Metatron (usually interpreted as derived from the Greek *metathronios,* "he who serves behind [God's] throne") is derived from the Latin *metator,* the officer sent out in advance of moving troops to lay out a camp for them. L. N.]

5. [What the Hebrew says is "I gave you a name the same as (*or:* like) Mine." The Karaites were horrified by this statement; see *HUCA,* VII, 355; Soncino Talmud, Sanh 38b (p. 245), n. 12—the numerical values of *mṭṭrwn* and *shaddai* are the same, 314. L. N.]

6. Cf. Gen. Rabbah 44:17, where Abraham foresees Israel's oppression under Babylon, Media, Greece, and Edom [Rome].

7. JV: *And it shall come to pass when thou shalt break loose, that thou shalt shake his yoke from off thy neck.* But see Gen. Rabbah 66:7, where R. Jose ben R. Ḥalfuta interprets these words, "If you see your brother Jacob throw off the yoke of Torah from his neck, then decree his destruction, and you will become his master."

8. JV: *Thou hast striven with gods and with men.* But *śariṭa,* "thou hast striven," here associated with *śar,* "prince," is taken to mean "thou wilt come to have princes."

9. "The heads of Jewry in Babylonia and Palestine, the latter being designated as 'gods,' for they were ordained as judges and leaders, the former as men." See B. Ḥul 92a, Soncino tr., p. 514, n. 9.

manded the throne of judgment, He will have it stand> off to one side.[10] [From all that has been said above], you learn that no part of creation can be exempt from Divine judgment. [After the Holy One has passed judgment], He will abolish the present order of the world, as is said, *The Lord alone shall be exalted in that day* (Isa. 2:11, 17), and then He will renew the heaven and the earth, as is said, *The new heavens and the new earth, which I will make* (Isa. 66:22). [On that day] the Holy One will bring the dead back to life: He will take dust of the earth and dust of the dead <and knead them> together, one with the other, and out of the two kinds of dust He will draw bones and sinews. Then the Holy One will give the word to the ministering angels who are in
S, *p.* 32 charge of the treasuries of souls, | and out <of the treasuries> they will take every single soul, thrust each one into a body, and instantly have all mankind stand up. Then <the earth>, as if it were human, will open its mouth and address the Holy One, saying to Him: Master of the universe, So-and-so committed a [sexual] transgression in such-and-such a place. So-and-so cheated So-and-so in such-and-such a place. So-and-so swore falsely in Your name in such-and-such a place. [Hearing this], the Holy One will fling all the nations of the world into the midst of Gehenna. Gehenna will open its mouth at once and say to the Holy One: Master of the universe, cram me full of Israel's transgressors also. God will respond: I have already filled you with the nations of the earth, and there is no more room in you. Gehenna will reply right away: Master of the universe, did You not promise that Gehenna would be increased in height by so many parasangs [in order to accommodate all transgressors]? <In that instant Gehenna will be expanded by so many parasangs>, and into it the Holy One will fling Israel's transgressors, as is said, *Therefore, by her soul,* [*swears*] *Gehenna, she has room*[11] (Isa. 5:14). The Holy One will then go up and sit with His household, and to Zerubbabel son of Shealtiel standing close to Him as one whose office it is to interpret in Aramaic for the pupils the sense of what the Teacher imparts, to him will He disclose the sound reasoning of Torah.

The Holy One will proceed to say to the righteous: Come, enter the Garden of Eden, which I created only for the sake of the righteous. And David will extend an invitation to the Holy One: Master of the universe, <if You please>, come and feast with us in the Garden of Eden, as is said, *Let my Beloved come into His Garden* (Song 4:16). And He will hearken to David and will go with the righteous into the Garden, as is said, *Let him call unto Me, and I will answer him* (Ps. 91:15). Thereupon Gabriel will bring two thrones,[12] one for the Holy One and

---

10. At the beginning, it had been God's intention to create the world with the measure of justice (PR 40:2 [YJS, *18, 2,* 703]), here identified with the throne of glory.

11. JV: *Therefore the nether world hath enlarged her desire.* But see ER, 108.

12. The idea of two thrones may—so Friedmann (n. 41) suggests—be based on the verse *The Lord saith unto my lord: "Sit thou at My right hand"* (Ps. 110:2).

one for David: *His throne as the sun before Me* (Ps. 89:37), as David said. They will all eat, and drink three cups [during the feast].[13] When it is asked: Who is to lead in saying Grace? Abraham will be bidden, "Take the cup and say Grace, for you are the Patriarch of the world." He will reply: I cannot say Grace, for out of me came seed that provoked the Holy One.[14] When Isaac will be bidden, "Take the cup and say Grace," he will reply: I cannot say Grace, for out of me came seed that destroyed the Holy One's Temple.[15] When Jacob will be bidden, "Take the cup and say Grace," he will reply: I cannot say Grace, for I wed two [who were] sisters,[16] and in the Torah it is written, *Thou shalt not take a woman to her sister* (Lev. 18:18). When Moses will be bidden, "Take the cup and say Grace," he will reply: I cannot say Grace since neither in life nor in death did I merit entering the Land of Israel. When Joshua will be bidden, "Take the cup and say Grace," he will reply: I cannot say Grace since I did not merit the bringing of children into the world.[17] When David will be bidden, "Take the cup and say Grace," he will reply: I shall say Grace. It is proper for me to say it, for I declared: *I will lift up the cup of salvation, and call upon the name of the Lord* (Ps. 116:13).[18]

| After the Holy One and the company will have eaten and drunk S, *p.* 33
and said Grace, the Holy One will bring the Torah, place it in His bosom, and occupy Himself with the Torah in discourse on ritual uncleanness and ritual cleanness, on what is prohibited and what is permitted, and on other Halakot. Then, as David recites 'Aggadah in the presence of the Holy One, the righteous in the Garden of Eden will respond:[19] "May His great name be blessed for ever and ever," and from Gehenna Israel's transgressors will call out, Amen. The Holy One will ask the ministering angels: Who are these answering Amen out of Gehenna? And the angels will reply: Master of the universe, these transgressors in Israel, even though they are in Gehenna, suffering great distress, make a special effort and say Amen before you. Whereupon the Holy One will say to the ministering angels: Open the Garden

---

13. One cup before the meal, another during the meal, and a third after it.

14. Ishmael.

15. Esau.

16. Leah and Rachel.

17. *Nun his son, Joshua his son* (1 Chron. 7:27), but the text does not indicate that Joshua himself had sons.

18. Cf. parallel in B.Pes 119b.

19. They will be responding to Zerubbabel who will interpret in Aramaic to the pupils what the Teacher has imparted in Hebrew. In Rabbinic times, such interpretation was needed during assemblies in Palestine and Babylonia where many of those gathered had only limited knowledge of Hebrew. Somewhat anachronistically the author transfers his own experience to the Messianic days to come.

At the conclusion of the period of study, Zerubbabel will begin with the *Yitgadal* of the Kaddish customarily recited on such occasions. So Friedmann (n. 48) on the basis of parallels.

of Eden to them and let them come and sing in My very presence, for in the verse *Open ye the gates, that the righteous nation,* [*as well as they*] *who keep faithfulnesses ('ĕmunim) may enter in* (Isa. 26:2), *'ĕmunim* is not to be read "they who keep faithfulnesses," but "they who say Amen."[20]

---

20. Note the play on *'ĕmunim,* "faithfulnesses (the plural of *'emun*)," and *'ămenim,* "amens." The plural intimates here the saying of many Amens. Cf. parallel in B.Shab 119b.

CHAPTER 3 (EZ, CHAPTER 21)

The consolation and radiance that are to be Israel's

Summary

God's own light, the light of Torah, is the light promised for the time-to-come (S, 33). When this time comes, the light God had created on the first day, the light which was used for the three days before the sun and the moon were created, and then had hidden because the nations were unworthy of it, will be taken out of hiding. Even that light, perfect as it is, will then say: I look forward only to Your shedding Your light upon me. And Zion, though told by God, *Arise, shine, for thy light is come,* (Isa. 60:1) will reply: You rise and go first, and I after You.

God will thereupon bring Elijah and the Messiah who will gather all Israel into the valley of Jehoshaphat. There nations together with their idols, while crossing a bridge over Gehenna, will fall from the bridge into Gehenna.

At the sight Israel, frightened, will ask God whether the same thing will happen to them. He will tell them to identify themselves. They will say they are God's inheritance (S, 34), and then will ask Abraham, Isaac, and Jacob to bear witness to their identity. Thereupon God will make the radiance of Israel shine from world's end to world's end.

Gehenna will then open its mouth, and the worshipers of idols will come out. Seeing Israel's well-being, they will salute Israel, even as God tells the nations that the difference between them and Israel was that Israel trusted Him and hallowed His name twice daily. Put to shame, the nations will return to Gehenna.

When Israel ask God how it is that He is now reconciled with them after having made them a rejected vessel, He will tell them: From the day I destroyed My house below, I have not gone up and dwelt in My house above, but have sat grieving here in dew and in rain. Now accept from Me the cup of consolation: because Zion acknowledged Me at the Red Sea, I will redouble her with strength (S, 35–36).

Chapter 3 (EZ Chapter 21)

His disciples asked R. Eliezer: Our master, tell us in what light shall we rejoice—in the light of the Holy One or in the light of Jerusalem? R. Eliezer replied: In the light of the Holy One, as is said, *The Lord is God, and will give us light* (Ps. 118:27). The disciples challenged him, saying, But is not Jerusalem told: *Arise, shine, for thy light is come* (Isa. 60:1)? <Thereupon R. Eliezer began his discourse by saying>: The verse is to be considered in regard to what David, king of Israel, was inspired by the holy spirit to say: *For with Thee is the fountain of life; in Thy light shall we see light* (Ps. 36:10). To whom was David attributing these words? To none other than the congregation of Israel, which still says to God: Master of the universe, because of this fountain which was with S, *p.* 33 *cont'd*

You before all the work of creation, I shall shine with Your light in the time-to-come! By *the fountain of life* is meant the Torah, of which it is said, *She is a tree of life to them that lay hold upon her* (Prov. 3:18).[1]

In Thy light shall we see light (Ps. 36:10). What this statement means is that the light which the Holy One created on the first day was used for the three days before the sun and the moon were created. After these luminaries were created, as is said, *And God made the two great lights* (Gen. 1:15), the Holy One took and hid the light [He had created
S, *p.* 34 on the first day]. Why did the Holy One hide it? | Because the nations of the world were destined to provoke Him [and so were judged unworthy of it].[2] Let not those wicked ones make use of that pristine light, He said, let them use instead the light of the sun and of the moon which one day will cease to be <even as the nations will cease to be>. But that first light is to endure for ever and ever: let the righteous come and make use of it, as is said, *And God saw the light that it was [for the] good* (Gen. 1:4). By *the good* are meant the righteous, as is said, *Say ye of the righteous that he is good* (Isa. 3:10). When the light became aware that God had hid it, it rejoiced exceedingly, as is said, *The light for the righteous rejoiceth* (Prov. 13:9). The light proceeded to say to the Holy One: Master of the universe, though I have been withheld from virtuous Israelites in this world, [in the world-to-come, I will shed my light upon them. Nevertheless,][3] what I look forward to even more is Your light which You will shed upon me. At that time the Holy One will say to Zion, *Arise, shine, for thy light is come* (Isa. 60:12), and Zion will reply: Master of the universe, You rise and go first, and I after You. Then God will say: You have spoken well, as is said, *Now I will arise, saith the Lord* (Ps. 12:6). And in what will God rejoice? In the joyous gathering of Zion's children within her, as is said, *Lift up thine eyes round about, and behold: All these gather themselves together and come to thee* (Isa. 49:18). At the moment [they gather], the Holy One will bring Elijah and the Messiah with a flask of oil in their hands <and their staves in their hands>[4], and they will gather all Israel before them—the Presence will be at the head of Israel, the Prophets at their rear, the Torah at their right, the ministering angels at their left —and they will lead Israel to the valley of king Jehoshaphat, where all the nations will be gathered [for judgment], as is said, *I will gather all nations, and will bring them down into the valley of Jehoshaphat; and I will enter into judgment with them . . . because they have cast lots for My people* (Joel 4:2–3). Next, the Holy One will take their idols, and having put spirit and breath into them, will say, Let each and every nation, together

---

1. For parallel, cf. PR 36:1 (YJS, *18, 2,* 677).
2. For parallel, cf. B.Ḥag̅ 12a.
3. "in the world-to-come . . . Nevertheless"—Haida.
4. The flask of oil is to anoint the Messiah, and the staves symbolize authority.

with its carved idols, walk across the bridge over Gehenna. Thereupon they will start passing over the bridge, but when they reach the middle, the bridge will seem to them to have shrunk to the thinness of a thread, and they will fall from it into Gehenna. When they land there—they and their carved idols—and Israel sees the nations of the earth together with their idols lying there, Israel will bluntly ask: Master of the universe, will You do with us as You have done with these? The Holy One will ask: Who are you? Israel will reply: We are Israel, Your people and Your inheritance. | The Holy One will ask: Who will bear witness S, *p.* 35
for you? Israel will reply: Abraham. The Holy One will summon Abraham and ask him: Will you bear witness that they are My people and I their God? Abraham will reply: Yes, and did You not say to me, *Also that nation whom they shall serve, I shall judge* (Gen. 15:14)? Then He will ask further: Who else will bear witness? Israel will reply: Isaac. The Holy One will summon Isaac and ask him: Will you bear witness that they are My people and I their God? Isaac will reply: Master of the universe, did You not say to me, *Unto thee, and unto thy seed, I will give all these lands* (Gen. 26:3)? <The Holy One will ask: Who else will bear witness? Israel will reply: Jacob>. The Holy One will summon Jacob and ask him: Will you bear witness that they are My people and that I am their God? Jacob will reply: Master of the universe, did You not say <to the children of Israel>, *Thou shalt have no other gods before Me* (Exod. 20:3), and did they not say to You, *Hear, O Israel, the Lord is our God, the Lord alone* (Deut. 6:2)? In that instant, the Holy One will pass on before the children of Israel, and they behind Him, as is said, *Their King is passed on before them, the Lord at the head of them* (Mic. 2:13). Taking up the Torah, the Holy One will put it in His bosom and make the radiance of Israel shine from world's end to world's end.

Thereupon Gabriel will say to the Holy One: Master of the universe, let all the worshipers of idols come and see Israel's well-being. And the Holy One will reply: They are not to come <and are not to see, as is said, *Lord, Thy hand was lifted up, yet they see not* (Isa. 26:11). But the Messiah will say to the Holy One>: Master of the universe, let them come and see and be put to shame, as is said, *They shall see with shame Thy zeal for the people; yea, fire shall devour Thine adversaries (ibid.).* And the congregation of Israel will also say: Let them come, see, and be put to shame, as is said, *Then mine enemy shall see it, and shame shall cover her* (Mic. 7:10).

Forthwith Gehenna will open its mouth, and all the worshipers of idols will come out, and seeing Israel's well-being, will fall on their faces and say <in the presence of Israel and in the presence of the Holy One>: How comely is this <Lord>! How comely is this people whom He loves exceedingly, as is said, *Blessed is the people that is in such a case* (Ps. 144:15). The nations will then ask: Master of the universe, wherein is this people different [from us] that You love them so much?

He will reply: You are the greatest fools in the world! You knew Me,
S, *p.* 36 yet you left Me and bowed down to your idols, | <and you trusted in them> but you did not trust in Me. Israel, on the other hand, in hallowing My name twice daily [in the Shĕma‘], showed their trust in Me, and so I shall give them ample reward. Put thus to shame, the nations will return to Gehenna, as is said, *The wicked shall return to the nether world, even all the nations that forget God* (Ps. 9:18). And the Holy One will be seated in the Garden of Eden with the righteous who will bow down <there>. The Holy One seated at the head of the righteous will fetch the light He had hid for the righteous, increasing its radiance three hundred and forty-five times.[5]

Israel will then say to Him: Master of the world, we have been yearning to behold this light, as is said, *My soul thirsteth for God, for the living God: When shall I come and appear before God?* (Ps. 42:3). He will reply: [In this light] you now behold My face. They will say: Master of the universe, since You shine for us with this light of Yours, for whom is that darkness? Thereupon He will reply: [It is] for the children of Esau and the children of Ishmael, as is said, *For, behold, darkness shall cover the earth, and gross darkness the peoples; but upon thee the Lord will arise, and His glory shall be seen upon thee* (Isa. 60:2). And the Holy One will go on to say to Israel: My children, now accept from Me the cup of consolation. Israel will answer: Master of the universe, You were angry at us, You put us out of Your house, You banished us among the nations of the earth, <so that among the nations of the earth we became a rejected vessel>: how is it that now You come to be reconciled with us? He will reply: I will tell you a parable by way of explanation. A man who married his niece became angry at her and put her out of his house. After a while he came to be reconciled with her. She reproached him, saying: You were angry at me and put me out of your house, and now you come to be reconciled with me. He replied: You are still my [beloved] niece. From the day you left my house, do you suppose that <any other woman has entered it? As you live>, I, too, did not enter my house [after you left it]. Similarly the Holy One said to Israel: My children, from the day I destroyed My house below, I have not gone up and dwelt in My house above, but have sat here <in dew and in rain>. And if you do not believe Me, put your hands on My head <and feel the dew on it. Were this not clearly stated in Scripture, it would be impossible to believe that He said such a thing> as *My head*

---

5. The number 345 is derived from Isa. 30:26, which is read "The light of the moon shall be like the light of the sun, and the light of the sun will be seven times seven the light of the seven days [of creation]." Taking the light of the sun and the light of the moon as two units and adding 343, (7 x 7 x 7), the sum of "the seven times seven of the light of the seven days [of creation]" makes a total of 345. So Friedman (n. 31) who quotes Rashi *ad loc,* and on B.Pes 68a.

is filled with dew, My locks with the drops of the night (Song 5:2).[6] Finally the Holy One, in reward for Israel's saying at the Red Sea, *My strength and my song is the Lord's* (Exod. 15:2), will reclothe Zion with her strength. <And the proof that the Lord will reclothe Zion with strength?> The verse *Awake, awake, put on thy strength, O Zion* (Isa. 52:1).

---

6. For parallel, cf. PR 36:2 (YJS, *18, 2,* 680).

CHAPTER 4 (EZ, CHAPTER 22)

The power of repentance

Summary

God's hands are stretched out to receive penitents, but each and every day that Israel do not repent, the measure of justice, waxing stronger and stronger, hurls charges that Israel are guilty of swearing falsely, coveting their neighbors' wives, and slandering their fellows. God responds by speaking in praise of those in Israel who rise early to go to synagogues and academies and live in full obedience to precepts of Torah. So, He concludes, there is ample reason for His favoring Israel.

Repentance is even greater than prayer and greater than charity. Moses' prayers did not help him enter the Land, but God accepted the harlot Rahab because of her repentance (S, 37).

The respite from judgment during the ten days between New Year's Day and the Day of Atonement is given to Israel, so that they can resolve upon repentance.

The summons *Lift up thy voice like a horn* (Isa. 58:1) is meant as commendatory, for the horn was created solely for the purpose of conveying good news, as evident from the horn sounded at the giving of Torah and at the fall of the walls of Jericho, and will be evident from the horn to be sounded at the gathering of the dispersed of Israel (S, 38).

The disciples of the wise who are the teachers of Israel are exhorted to forswear transgression lest they be punished in Gehenna, and Israel are exhorted to avoid sin. By way of example, a story is told of one of R. ‘Aḳiḇa’s most prominent disciples who fell in love with a harlot. She, however, conscience-stricken, refused to yield herself to him and prevailed on him to desist. Both, according to a Divine Voice, were destined for life in the world-to-come (S, 39–40).

Chapter 4 (EZ, Chapter 22)

S, *p.* 37 R. Eliezer asked his disciples: Are you able to accept reasoned reprimands? They replied: Please explain < what you are getting at >. I will, he said: I shall *Cry aloud, spare not* (Isa. 58:1). He then went on: These words of the prophet are to be considered in the light of what he was earlier inspired by the holy spirit to say: *Come now, and let us reason together, saith the Lord* (Isa. 1:18). Whom did Isaiah suppose God to be addressing in this verse? Penitents, none other. For the hands of the Holy One are stretched out to receive penitents as He asks, When will they yearn for repentance so as to be received into My presence as though they came in actual repentance? As the verse *They had the hands of the Man under their wings* (Ezek. 1:8) intimates, the Holy One sits on His throne of glory, the wings of the chariot's creatures[1] [shielding all of Him from view except for] His hands which are extended from under the wings toward <those who yearn for repentance>, as He asks, When will Israel resolve upon <actual> repentance <before Me>? Each and every day, the measure of justice, waxing stronger and stronger, stands before the Holy One and says in His presence: Master of the universe, in the Torah it is written, *Ye shall not swear by My name falsely* (Lev. 19:12). Yet Israel rise early and go to marketplaces where they swear falsely; moreover, they covet their neighbors' wives and slander their fellowmen. [Since You do not exercise the measure of justice against them], is it conceivable that there is bias on Your part in favor of Israel? [The Holy One responds]: But there are other Jews who rise early <from their beds and without fail twice every day hallow My name [with the Shĕma‘], there are disciples of the wise who rise early> to go to synagogues and academies, <men unlettered in Torah who go to synagogues>, and young children who go to schools. All these are circumcised <and live in full obedience to precepts [of Torah]>. Nay more! I created in them the capacity to repent, a blessing which is equal to that of the Torah. [They do these good things of their own free will], yet you say that there is bias on My part in favor of Israel!

In further comment, [R. Eliezer said]: Repentance is even greater than prayer. God was unwilling to accept all the prayers our teacher Moses uttered for permission to enter the Land of Israel, but through her repentance the harlot Rahab was received. Indeed, she was called Rahab—so R. Eliezer ben Jacob suggested—because her merit in repentance was so substantial *(rĕḥoḇah)*. <Because of the repentance she resolved upon, her merit was such, in fact, as to have> seven kings and eight Prophets <issue> from her.[2]

In further comment, [R. Eliezer said]: Repentance is greater than
charity. Charity | requires expenditure of money, but repentance S, *p.* 38
requires no such expenditure: still the Holy One asks no more from Israel than repentance by way of words,[3] as when He says: *Take with you words, and return unto the Lord* (Hos. 14:3).

---

1. Literally, "living creatures"—the angels that bore the chariot. See Ezek. 1 and B.Pes 119a.

2. The eight kings, "who were also priests," may have ruled during the Second Temple. So Friedmann (n. 12). In Sif Num. 78 (ed. Horovitz [Frankfurt am Main, 1917]), eight priests who were Prophets are mentioned, but no kings. See also PR 40:3/4 (YJS, *18, 2,* 706) and PRKM 13:4, pp. 227–28 (PRKS, p. 255), where Jeremiah, a priest and a prophet, is listed as one of Rahab's descendants.

3. An alternative translation of "Charity . . . by way of words": "The giving of charity may be flawed [in that it requires exercise of only one virtue, that of mercy], but repentance is not flawed, [for it calls upon all of men's virtues]. Hence the Holy One asks from Israel nothing other than repentance by means of words," etc.

In still further comment, [R. Eliezer said]: Great is repentance, for it heals Israel of their iniquities, as is said, *Because of their penitence*[4] *I will heal them, and love them freely* (Hos. 14:5).

[In regard to repentance], R. Nehorai put the question: Why was Israel given a respite [from judgment] during the ten days between New Year's Day and the Day of Atonement? To correspond, he answered, to the ten trials whereby [the faith of] our father Abraham was tested and was found perfect in all of them;[5] and also to correspond to the Ten Commandments which Israel took upon themselves at Sinai. <Hence the Holy One gave Israel ten days between New Year's Day and the Day of Atonement>, so that if Israel resolve upon repentance [during these days], He will receive them as though their repentance were a fact.

All the foregoing is implied in the words *Come now, and let us reason together, saith the Lord* [*with the result that though your sins be as scarlet, they shall be as white as snow*] (Isa. 1:18).

Cry with the throat, . . . lift up thy voice like a ram's horn (Isa. 58:1). R. Simeon ben Ḥalafta said: The expression "to cry with the throat" may signify either to praise or to blame: praise, as in *Let the high praises of God be in their throat* (Ps. 149:6), referring to the righteous who praise [God] with their throats; blame, as in the verse *Their throat is an open sepulchre, their tongue slippery* (Ps. 5:10), in reference to the wicked who work mischief with their speech. What Isaiah meant in the verse cited above is that when you speak to the righteous, you need make yourself heard only with the throat [as in ordinary speech], but when you speak to the wicked you must *lift up thy voice like a ram's horn.*

R. Joshua ben Ḳorḥah however interpreted the verse: The ram's horn was created solely for the purpose of conveying good news, for <at Sinai> the Torah was given to Israel to the sounding of a ram's horn, as is said, *When the voice of the horn waxed louder and louder, Moses spoke, and God answered him by a voice* (Exod. 19:19). The wall of Jericho fell to the sounding of a ram's horn, as is said, *When the people heard the sound of the ram's horn . . . the wall fell down flat* (Josh. 6:20). The Holy One will sound a ram's horn when He discloses the Messiah, as is said, [*Behold, thy king cometh unto thee*] . . . *the Lord God will blow the ram's horn* (Zech. 9:9, 14). And the Holy One will sound a ram's horn when He gathers together the dispersed of Israel into their proper place, as is said, *It shall come to pass in that day that a great ram's horn shall be blown in that day . . . and they that were dispersed . . . shall worship the Lord in*

4. JV: *their backsliding.* But the commentator appears to associate *mĕšuḇah,* "backsliding," with *šuḇ,* "return, repent."

5. For a list of the ten trials, see MTeh 18:25 (YJS, *13, 1,* 255–56).

the holy mountain at Jerusalem (Isa. 27:13). Accordingly, *Lift up thy voice like a ram's horn* (Isa. 58:1) [refers to an occasion for rejoicing].

Isaiah goes on to say, *Declare unto My people their transgression (ibid.).*
| By *My people* he meant disciples of the wise, to whom the Holy S, *p.* 39
One said: "I created you solely to guide My children aright on the paths of life. Why, then, do you contrive covert schemes in your hearts?" When you see a generation in which disciples of the wise are at strife with one another, you are seeing people whose hearts contrive covert schemes. What is more, if the business of these people is Torah but they do not keep the Torah, their punishment is to be Gehenna. Hence, *Declare unto My people their transgression, and to the house of Jacob their sins (ibid.)* Who are meant by *the house of Jacob?* The common people of Israel.

A story is told of one of R. 'Aḳiḇa's disciples who ranked first among[6] twenty-four thousand disciples. Once he went into the Street of the Harlots where he saw a harlot with whom he fell in love, and so he had a messenger go back and forth between him and her until evening. In the evening she went up to the roof and saw him seated like a commander of hosts at the head of the disciples with Gabriel standing at his side. She said to herself: Woe unto this woman to whom all kinds of Gehenna's punishments are bound to affix themselves! And he—such a distinguished man who looks like a king!—shall this woman respond to his desire and, as a result, when she dies and ceases to exist in this world, inherit Gehenna? If, however, he is willing to accept her refusal [of him], she will save him and herself from the punishment of Gehenna.

So when he came to her, she said to him, My son, why are you willing to lose life in the world-to-come for the sake of one hour in this world? But his passion was not diminished until she said to him, My son, the part which you desire is the most soiled and sullied of all the parts of the body, <a skin bottle filled with ordure and refuse>, the odor whereof no creature is able to endure. Still his passion was not
diminished until she took hold of his nose and put it at | [her cleft S, *p.* 40
whence there came an odor as of] the grave. When he smelled the odor, the female organ became so repulsive to him that he never married.

Thereupon a Divine Voice was heard, declaring, Such-and-such a woman and Such-and-such a man are destined for life in the world-to-come.

Hence in the words *And to the house of Jacob their sins,* the phrase *the house of Jacob* refers to the common people [and their avoidance of

6. Or: "was in charge of twenty-four," etc.

sin]. Concerning them, the Holy One said to Isaiah: Go, tell Israel, there is no better mode of conduct than repentance which heals Israel of all their iniquities, as is said, *Because of their penitence*[7] *I will heal them, I will love them freely* (Hos. 14:5). And Hosea goes on to say, *They that dwell under His shadow shall again make corn to grow, and shall blossom as the vine* (Hos. 14:8).

---

7. See n. 4.

CHAPTER 5 (EZ, CHAPTER 23)

Why God favors Israel and provides them with the order of prayers for forgiveness

Summary

God stretches out His hand to receive Israel as though Israel were completely penitent. When the measure of justice protests that there is profanation of the Name because God appears to be indulgent of Israel, He replies: Have no misgivings—all the work of creation was done only for Israel's sake. Even the Torah was given only for the sake of Israel, but for whom there would be no one to teach it to (S, 40). You, the measure of justice, say I indulge them. The fact is that long ago Israel and their forebears favored Me in declaring every kind of idol meaningless and thus hallowed My name in the world. Besides, long ago at Sinai, Israel, unlike the nations of the earth, did not come to Me with reservations but with wholeheartedness.

Thereupon the measure of justice agrees.

Like the measure of justice, a Roman emperor asks a Tanna for the evidence of God's justice in instances where infants are born deaf, mute, blind, and lame. The Tanna replies that God, knowing these infants when grown up will be inclined to evil, thus curbs their capacity to do greater evil, and the Tanna proceeds to demonstrate the truth of his assertion (S, 41).

In His love of Israel, God revealed to Moses the order of prayers for forgiveness, saying to him: When troubles come upon Israel, let them stand before Me as one band and utter in My presence the prayers for forgiveness, and I shall answer them (S, 42).

Chapter 5 (EZ, Chapter 23)

His disciples asked R. Eliezer: <Our master>, tell us how to resolve S, *p.* 40 *cont'd*
on repentance so that we may live? He began his reply at once with the verse *The Lord will answer thee in the day of inner distress* [*at thy deeds*] (Ps. 20:2). This verse is to be considered in the light of what Solomon <son of David> king of <Israel> was inspired by the holy spirit to say: *My Beloved put in His hand by the hole of the door, when my heart was moved for Him* (Song 5:4). Whom did Solomon have in mind in this verse? None other than the congregation of Israel, which said to the Holy One: Master of the universe, but for Your many acts of compassion and mercy whereby You show pity for us, and but for Your hand stretched out from under the wings of the creatures[1] [represented upon Your throne, Your hand stretched out] to receive me as though in full

---

1. These shield all of Him from view except for God's hand which is stretched out to receive the penitent. See above, S, 37, and n. 1.

repentance, I would have no strength to stand up before the measure of justice. <Indeed the measure of justice> waxes stronger and stronger as it stands before the Holy One and says to Him, Master of the universe, in the Torah it is written *God, the great, the mighty, the awful* (Deut. 10:17): *the great*— <Your greatness> is shown by all the work of creation; *the mighty*—You wax in might to requite those who transgress Your will; and *the awful*—all are in awe of Your judgment which is true. Hence, if [out of pity] You show favor to Israel, will there not be profanation of the Name because of it? God replied: Have no misgivings where the congregation of Israel is concerned, for all the work of creation was done only for their sake, as is said, *If not for My covenant, day and night, I would not have appointed the ordinances of heaven and earth* (Jer. 33:25). *Covenant* here refers to circumcision because circumcision obtains for Israel [day and night],[2] as is said, *My covenant shall be in your flesh for an everlasting covenant* (Gen. 17:13). The measure of justice said bluntly to God: But the first verse in Scripture speaks [not of Israel but] of Torah as the reason for God's having created "the ordinances of heaven and earth."[3] God replied: But Torah, too, was given only for the sake of Israel, as is said, *Whom shall one teach knowledge? And whom shall one make understand the message? Them that are taken from the milk, them that are drawn from the breasts* (Isa. 28:9). To whom is one to teach Torah's knowledge? Who shall be made to understand God's message? Those that are taken from the milk of their mothers' breasts [and are circumcised]. Hence Israel have merit which encom-
S, *p.* 41 passes them as the sand encompasses the sea. | Yet you say I favor them! The fact is that long ago Israel and their forebears favored Me in declaring every kind of idol absolutely worthless and thus hallowing My name in the world.

Besides, how can you say *I* favor *them?* Long ago, at Sinai, *they* favored *Me* when they accepted the Torah with a whole heart. Unlike the nations of the earth, Israel did not come to Me with any reservations but with wholeheartedness.[4] Yet you say I favor them!

Long ago they favored Me. When they came out of Egypt, they loaded unleavened bread on their shoulders[5] and gathered in a great many groups which occupied themselves with Torah. Moreover, they

---

2. "Which covenant," R. Simon of Teman asks, "obtains by day and by night? You can find none but the covenant of circumcision" (Meḳ, *1,* 218).

3. Gen. 1:1 is read "On account of 'the beginning' did God create heaven and earth," and "The beginning of God's way" (Prov. 8:23) is taken to be Torah. See Rashi on Gen. 1:1.

4. The nations asked what was in the Torah, and when they heard the details, they rejected the Torah. But Israel said: We will do and hearken (see PR 21:3 [YJS, *18, 1,* 417], and below, S, 55).

5. Though they had beasts of burden. See Exod. 12:34 and Meḳ, *1,* 104: "Israel cherished their religious duties."

paid fees to have their children taught Torah.[6] And yet you say that because of [My love of] Israel there is profanation of My name!

Thereupon the measure of justice agreed [with the Holy One], saying, Rightly does Scripture say, *God . . . regardeth not persons, nor taketh reward* (Deut. 10:17) and *All His ways are justice* (Deut. 32:4).

With regard to God's justice, a Roman emperor put the following question to R. Joshua ben Ḳorḥah: Of your God it is written *All His ways are justice.*[7] But where is your God's justice? Even before they have done anything in the world, whether good or evil, there come forth from their mothers' wombs the deaf, the mute, the blind, the lame—is this the justice of your God? R. Joshua ben Korḥaḥ replied: When a man's being created enters God's mind, his deeds in this world, whether good or evil, are already known to God, as is said, *He revealeth the deep and secret things, He knoweth what is in the darkness* (Dan. 2:22). [Hence the man who is born with an affliction is being hindered from doing all the wicked deeds he would otherwise be guilty of in his lifetime]. The emperor asked: But should not repentance be possible for such a man, [born blind, for example]? If he resolves upon repentance [during his lifetime], should not God open his eyes? R. Joshua ben Ḳorḥah replied: Do you wish me to show you <how things turn out in> such a case? Give me a thousand denar and two witnesses you deem reliable. The emperor gave him a thousand denar and two witnesses he deemed reliable. Then R. Joshua went to a blind man who had come forth blind out of his mother's womb, and said to him: The emperor has decreed that I be put to death, and so I am leaving these thousand denar with you. If he does have me put to death, then he will have put me to death; if not, I shall depend on [the return of] these thousand denar. The blind man said: Very well. R. Joshua let three months pass by. Then he came to the blind man and said: Give me the denar. The blind man asked: What denar? R. Joshua said: The denar I left with you. The blind man replied: Such a thing never happened. Thereupon R. Joshua had the blind man brought before the emperor and had the reliable witnesses take the stand and testify [to what had happened] right to the face of the blind man who kept insisting, however, that such a thing had never happened. <But then a certain man came>, and speaking privately to the blind man, said: Alas for this man! I saw his wife dallying with a certain person to whom she said: The blind man will soon be put to death, and you and I shall enjoy the denar. At once the blind man produced the denar and laid them before the emperor who said: You good-for-nothing! Had I not eyewitnesses to this effect you would have gotten away with stealing the thousand denar. [Hence, concluded R. Joshua ben Ḳorḥah, God who made him

---

6. Cf. ER, 123–24.
7. Friedmann substitutes Deut. 32:4 for Deut. 10:17.

blind from his mother's womb is indeed to be trusted, yet you complain about Him.] What is written about Him, namely, that *all His ways are justice,* is therefore true.

Thereupon the emperor bestowed upon R. Joshua a great many
S, *p.* 42 gems of purest ray and said, Blessed be your God | and blessed be His people, and blessed be he who merits the dust of the soles of your feet.

All of the foregoing discourse is derived from the words *My Beloved put in His hand by the hole in the door, when my heart was moved by Him* (Song 5:4).[8]

<Another comment> [made by R. Eliezer] on *The Lord will answer thee in the day of trouble* (Ps. 20:2): David, knowing that because of Israel's iniquities the Temple was to be destroyed and that offerings were to cease, was distressed for Israel and asked: When troubles [in the wake of sin] come upon Israel, <who will atone for them? The Holy One replied: David, do not be distressed. Long ago I disclosed to Moses the order of prayers for forgiveness,[9] saying to him: When troubles come upon Israel>, let them stand before Me as one band and utter in My presence the prayers for forgiveness, and I shall answer them. Where did He reveal this order of prayers? [At Sinai], *When the Lord enfolded His face, and proclaimed* [*the thirteen attributes of His mercy*][10] (Exod. 34:6). This verse proves, so says R. Johanan, that the Holy One came down out of His thick cloud like an emissary of the congregation who enfolds himself in his prayer shawl as he takes his place before the ark, and disclosed to Moses the order of prayers for forgiveness. God also said to Moses: If there be a disciple of the wise who has the ability to relieve Israel of its burden of guilt, let him not disdain them; let him keep Me in mind who had no partner in the work of creation; yet I did not disdain to come down and reveal the order of prayer<s> for forgiveness. <From Me> let all the inhabitants of the world learn. And to him who has the ability to relieve Israel of their burden of guilt I shall give ample reward.

[And the Holy One continued]: Whenever Israel gather in My presence and stand before Me as one band, crying out in My presence the order of prayer<s> for forgiveness, I shall answer them when they say, *Save, Lord; let the King answer us in the day we cry out* (Ps. 20:10).

---

8. God seeks every opportunity to save a man, comes in his heart at the smallest sign of repentance. But the reprobate in the story was adamant in his wickedness, his heart not moved at all.

9. Since the Talmudic phrase *sidre tĕfillah* (B.RH 17b) is believed to be patterned after *sidre sĕliḥah,* "the order of prayers for forgiveness," we have here the oldest reference to *sĕliḥoṭ.* See Daniel Goldschmidt, *Seder has-sĕliḥoṭ kĕ-minhag Liṭa,* etc. (Jerusalem, 5725/1965), p. 5.

10. The thirteen attributes of mercy follow in the same verse. JV: *The Lord passed by before him, and proclaimed.* See B.RH 17b.

CHAPTER 6 (EZ, CHAPTER 24)

Man's mortality and the limits of his glory as compared with God's

Summary

In some ways man appears to be inferior to an animal. Thus, to cite an example, touching an animal's carcass makes one ritually unclean for one day, but touching a human corpse makes one ritually unclean (S, 42) for seven days. Besides, whether it be a feeble day-old infant or potent Og—when either dies, vermin are all over them.

Nevertheless, unlike animals, man says Grace after he eats and drinks, says a blessing when he goes to sleep and when he wakes up. Moreover, when an animal dies, it has rest, but a man, after he dies, must come to judgment (S, 43).

Still, no man, not even Moses, is to glory in his wisdom; no man, not even Samson, is to glory in his might; no man, not even Ahab, is to glory in his riches. The only Being who may glory is the Holy One, for all wealth (S, 44), might, and wisdom are His. In this world all that a man may glory in is the crown of Torah which gives him the kind of strength that never ceases to be, that enriches him, and gives him life in this world and in the world-to-come (S, 45).

Chapter 6 (EZ, Chapter 24)

R. Eliezer said to his disciples: My sons, trust <neither> in wealth, <nor in wisdom>, nor in power, as is said, *Thus saith the Lord: Let not the wise man glory in his wisdom, neither let the mighty man glory in his might, let not the rich man glory in his riches,* etc. (Jer. 9:22). This verse is to be considered in the light of what Solomon son of David was inspired by the holy spirit to say: *For that which befalleth the sons of men, befalleth beasts; even one thing befalleth them* (Eccles. 3:19). In these words what did Solomon have in mind? Nothing other than man's mortality. <Mortal man>—his beginning, the worm, and his end, the worm, so that in this respect a man is not at all superior to an animal. Inferior, rather! Touching an animal's carcass makes one ritually unclean for one day;[1] but touching a human corpse makes one ritually unclean | for seven days.[2] Moreover, an animal carcass does not make the dwelling ritually unclean, but a human corpse makes the dwelling ritually unclean.[3] Furthermore, although touching an animal's carcass makes one ritually

S, *p.* 42 *cont'd*

S, *p.* 43

---

1. See Lev. 11:24–28.
2. See Num. 19:11.
3. See Num. 19:14.

unclean, [touching others thereafter] does not make the others unclean; on the other hand, after touching a human corpse, one becomes unclean and makes others unclean [by touching them].[4] <Of [man's mortality], Solomon also said>: *A living dog is better than a dead lion* (Eccles. 9:4). For a feeble day-old infant for whose survival one is justifiably apprehensive is better than [potent] Og, <king of Bashan>,[5] who ejaculated his semen a distance of forty parasangs—when either dies, vermin are all over him. Now, of Solomon, it is said that *he was wiser than all men* (1 Kings 5:11). Still, if, indeed, he was wiser <than all> men, <how> could he have declared, *Man hath no preeminence above a beast* (Eccles. 3:19)? How indeed? Consider that after a man eats, he says Grace; after he drinks, he says Grace; when he goes to sleep, he says a blessing; and when he wakes up, he says a blessing. How then is he to be thought of as though he were no better than an animal—[an animal] which is incapable of such refinements? What Solomon was referring to by his statement, however, was the disposition made of man at the time of his death. For when a man's time to die has come, the disposing of his body is discussed in much the same way as the disposing of a dying animal is discussed. It was for this reason that Solomon said, *Man hath no preeminence above a beast; for all is vanity (ibid.).* Consider further that when an animal dies, it has final rest. But a man, <even though> he has had <taxing experiences> to endure in his lifetime, still, after he dies, is made to stand trial: all his deeds <are shown> to him, and he is judged accordingly. For this reason, at the time he was about to die, R. Johanan was weeping. His disciples asked him: Our master, if you are weeping [for your misdeeds], what is to befall us [when our time comes]? R. Johanan replied: My children, shall I not weep? I shall be made to stand trial, my deeds will <be shown> to me, and I shall be judged accordingly. Nay more! I shall be asked: Why was[6] your conduct such as to cause the death of your children during your lifetime? It was my fault that I did not gain the merit of maintaining the life of the world.[7]

So, as though it were not enough to have one's children die during one's lifetime, a man is held accountable for their death. Thus in the Book of Psalms David said, *Cast me not off in time of old age* (Ps. 71:9). <By this plea he meant: Master of the universe>, let not my grip on Torah and the commandments grow weak *through failure of my strength,*

---

4. See Num. 19:22.

5. Cf. Tos Shab 17:19 (Lieberman, *TKF, 4,* 84) and MTeh 136:12 (YJS, *13, 2,* 329–30).

6. The obscure *mpny* is taken to be followed by *mh.* Hence "Why was," etc.

7. According to Friedmann (n. 16), R. Johanan ben Zakkai is referred to here. He lost his only grown son (ARN, chap. 14 [YJS, *10,* 76]), and presumably others of his children. The death of young children is construed as evidence that the bereaved father deserves Gehenna. See Rashi on Gen. 37:35.

[the death of my children]; and *forsake me not (ibid.),* do not let my teeth become worn-down and loose on account of the loss of my children. From David's plea you learn that | when a man's children die during S, *p.* 44
his lifetime, his strength fails—his teeth become worn-down and loose, and his eyes grow dim.

All the foregoing discourse is derived from the words *All is vanity* (Eccles. 3:19).

Another comment on *Let not the wise man glory in his wisdom* (Jer. 9:22) even if he be like our teacher Moses, <for even our teacher Moses was not let glory in his wisdom>. Though he went up on high where he received the Torah, he was not relieved of his mortality. It is said of our teacher Moses that when the Holy One told him, "Go up and die on the mountain," he replied: Master of the universe, You wrote in Your Torah, *In the same day thou shalt give him his hire* (Deut. 24:15). Under Your eye I have been a faithful laborer for forty years; now give me my hire. The Holy One then asked Moses: Do you wish to receive your hire in this world? [As] I have given their hire in the world-to-come to Abraham, Isaac, and Jacob who, <as though they were horses>, ran to perform commandments in My sight, so I shall give you your hire in the world-to-come.

The only Being who may glory [in His wisdom] is the Holy One, for all wisdom is His—He created all the work of creation, and yet there was no weariness in Him, as is said, *The Creator of the ends of the earth fainteth not, neither is weary* (Isa. 40:28).

Neither let the mighty man glory in his might (Jer. 9:22), even if he is like Samson. <Samson the son of Manoah was not let glory in his might. It was said of Samson the son of Manoah> that from his crotch to his shoulders there was a span of sixty cubits. But when he died, his strength vanished as he left the world.

The only Being who may glory [in His might] is the Holy One, blessed be His name, for all might is His, as is said, *Thine, O Lord, is the greatness and the power* (1 Chron. 29:11).

Let not the rich man glory in his riches (Jer. 9:22), even if he is as rich as Ahab king of Israel. <Ahab son of Omri, king of Israel, was not let glory in his riches>. It was said of Ahab king of Israel that he had seventy sons and that for each one he built <seventy palaces> of ivory.[8] But when he died, his kingship vanished and his wealth vanished.

The only Being who may glory [in His riches] is the Holy One, for all wealth | is His, as is said, *Mine is the silver, and Mine the gold,* S, *p.* 45
saith the Lord of hosts (Hag. 2:8).

Wherein, then, may a man glory in this world? <He may glory>

---

8. See 2 Kings 10:1; 1 Kings 22:39; Amos 3:15; and Eccles. Rabbah 6:3.

in the crown of Torah,[9] <which enriches him> and gives him life in this world <and in the world-to-come>, as is said, *Length of days is in her right hand; in her left hand are riches and honor* (Prov. 3:16). What is the wealth Torah gives a man? He is given the kind of strength which never ceases to be, as is said, *They that wait for the Lord, shall renew their strength: they shall mount up with wings as eagles . . . they shall walk, and not faint* (Isa. 40:31).

---

9. Based on the verse *But let him that glorieth glory in this* (Jer. 9:23), the verse that follows *Let not the wise man glory,* etc. (Jer. 9:22). The word *this* is often taken as a reference to Torah. See B.AZ 2b, which cites *This is the Torah* (Deut. 4:44) as the proof text.

CHAPTER 7 (EZ, CHAPTER 25)

Abraham's distinctiveness accounts for Israel's distinction

Summary

Though Asshur knew the name of God, he did not proclaim Him. Abraham, however, not only knew His name but also proclaimed Him (S, 45). By taking responsibility for the practice of circumcision, it was he who saved Israel from the punishment of Gehenna.

Hence, God prayed: May it be that all who issue from your loins, O Abraham, be like you! (S, 46).

So great is God's love of Israel, Abraham's progeny, that He does not allow the ministering angels above to sing praise of Him until Israel have sung below. When the ministering angels protest such seeming bias, God replies: I show Israel favor because of their father Abraham. When the angels ask: For what particular deeds of Abraham do You show them such favor? God answers: Abraham was a smasher of idols. He knew them to be absolutely worthless and did not hesitate to say so even to Nimrod, a worshiper of idols (S, 47).

Therefore, upon Nimrod's sentencing him to death (S, 48), God Himself came down at once to deliver him. To the angels' protest that man was unworthy of His deliverance, God replied: Man is a being in whom the Impulse to evil is strong. But if, like Abraham, a man manages to achieve righteousness, I rejoice in him and will deliver him. Although the Impulse to evil does not rule you angels, still when beings of your kind went down to earth, they lusted after the daughters of men, led them to sin, and taught them witchcraft. Abraham, however, hallowed, and will continue to hallow, My name in the world (S, 49).

Chapter 7 (EZ, Chapter 25)

R. Eliezer asked his disciples: My sons, are you aware of the kind of excellence Abraham possessed? They answered: Please tell us. Whereupon R. Eliezer began his discourse with the verse *Thou hast given faithfulness to Jacob, mercy to Abraham* (Mic. 7:20), words to be considered in the light of what David king of Israel was inspired by the holy spirit to say, *He shall be like a tree planted by streams of water* (Ps. 1:3). Of whom did David say these words? Of none other than our father Abraham. <For none of the generations created before Abraham was born> knew the name of the Holy One. True, Asshur knew it, but he did not protest against the scheme of the generation that was dispersed. And the proof that Asshur knew the name of the Holy One? The verse *Out of that land went forth Asshur* (Gen. 10:11).[1] Read not *out of that land* S, *p.* 45 *cont'd*

---

1. Cf. MTeh 118:11 (YJS, *13,2,* 238).

('ereṣ) but "out of that counsel" *('eṣah)*—[that is, out of the counsel of the sinful generation]. And why did not Asshur protest against the scheme of the generation that was dispersed? Because Asshur knew that <a descendant of his>, Sennacherib, would blaspheme and revile Him above. Had Asshur intervened, people would have said of him: [Who is he to protest?] After all, a descendant of his will provoke the Holy One.[2] On the other hand, when Abraham was born, he made known the name of the Holy One and proclaimed Him possessor of heaven and earth, as is said, *Abram said to the king of Sodom: I have lifted my hand unto the Lord God Most High, Possessor of heaven and earth* (Gen. 14:22). Thereupon in joy the Holy One kissed both His hands, saying: Up to this moment no man <in My world> has called Me Lord and Most High, but <now in My world I have been called Lord and Most High>, for Abraham has just said, *I have lifted my hand unto the Lord God Most High, Possessor of heaven and earth.* As a matter of fact, as soon as Abraham was born, <the Holy One> came to be blessed in the
S, *p.* 46 mouths of all mortals, for Melchizedek said, | *Blessed be God the Most High*[3] (Gen. 14:20). But after Abraham was born, the mercies of the Holy One crested like a wave, and the Holy One came to be known as <*Merciful and gracious* (Exod. 34:6)>.[4] After Abraham was born, from then on <the Holy One> was held in awe by all His creatures, as is said, *It is because of the mercies of the Lord that we have not been consumed*[5] (Lam. 3:22). And after Abraham was born and took responsibility for the practice of circumcision, the Holy One swore an oath to Abraham that by virtue of the merit of circumcision He would save Israel from Gehenna,[6] as is said, *As for thee also, because of the blood of thy covenant I send forth thy prisoners out of the pit* (Zech. 9:11), the word *pit* here referring to no place other than Gehenna, as in the verse "that go down to the pavement of the pit" (Isa. 14:19).

The foregoing discourse [concerning Abraham] is derived from the words *And he shall be like a tree planted by streams of water* (Ps. 1:3).

In another comment on *He shall be like a tree planted by streams of*

---

2. In Midrashic literature, particularly in PRE, the early generations, even heathen ones, are said to have had the capacity to read the future. Thus in the days of Moses the magicians who told Pharaoh, *This is the finger of God* (Exod. 8:14), foresaw this very finger, so to speak, inflicting punishment upon Sennacherib (B.Sanh 95b). The comment and the reference were provided by Professor Chaim Zalman Dimitrovsky of the Jewish Theological Seminary.

3. Cf. Sif Deut. 32 (ed. Finkelstein [Breslau, 1936–39], p. 54).

4. Before the coming of Abraham, God used to impose cruel and severe punishment such as the flood and the destruction of Sodom and Gomorrah; but after the coming of Abraham, punishment was less severe, as was the famine in Canaan (Gen. 12:1) which forced Abraham to go to Egypt. See Sif Deut. 311 (ed. Finkelstein, p. 351).

5. So AV; JV: *Surely the Lord's mercies are not consumed.*

6. For parallels, see B.Ber 19a and MTeh 6:1 (YJS, *13, 1,* 94).

water, R. Jose[7] expounded the verse as follows: I will give you a parable by which the verse may be understood. A man was walking in a valley in a barren land where there was no water, and his spirit grew faint from thirst. Then he found a tree with a spring <of water beneath it>, with sweet fruits and with pleasant shade. He drank of the tree's water, sat in its shade, ate the fruit, and his spirit was restored. As he was about to leave, he said: O tree, O tree, how shall I bless you? Shall I wish for you that there be a flow of water beneath you? There is already such a flow beneath you. That your fruit be sweet? Your fruit is already sweet. That your shade be pleasant? Your shade is already pleasant. Therefore, all I can say in blessing is this: May it be the will of God that all shoots taken from you grow up to be like you![8]

Likewise, the Holy One said to Abraham: Abraham, how shall I bless you? Shall I say, Make Me known? You have already made Me known. Proclaim Me King? You have already proclaimed Me King. Therefore I say, May it be [My] will that all who issue from your loins be like you! Such is the meaning of *And he shall be like a tree planted by streams of water, that bringeth forth its fruit in its season* (Ps. 1:3)—that is, among your progeny, Abraham, may there be many disciples of the wise; *whose leaf doth not wither (ibid.)*—that is, among your progeny may trustworthy men never cease. *And in whatsoever he doeth he shall prosper (ibid.), he* referring to our father Abraham whom God caused to prevail over all kings of the east and of the west, as is said, | *Who hath raised* S, *p.* 47
up one from the east, at whose steps victory attendeth? He giveth nations before him, and maketh him rule over kings (Isa. 41:2).[9]

All the foregoing discourse is derived from the verse *He shall be like a tree planted by streams of water* (Ps. 1:3).

Thou showest faithfulness to Jacob, mercy to Abraham (Mic. 7:20). R. Eliezer, the son of R. Jose the Galilean, said: Blessed be His great name, for He cherishes Israel <more than> He does the ministering angels. The ministering angels are not allowed to utter song above until Israel utter it below, as is indicated in Scripture where the words *When the morning stars*[10] *sang together* (Job 38:7) precede the words *All the sons of God shouted for joy (ibid.).*

When New Year's Day comes, the ministering angels ask the Holy One: Master of the universe, why do You show mercy to this people like a man who shows mercy to his comrade? God replies: I show Israel

---

7. Parma MS 1240 reads "Jose ben Yasyan" who was a Tanna and is mentioned in Tos Men 1:15 and B.AZ 42a.

8. For parallel, cf. B.Ta 5a.

9. The verse is frequently interpreted as referring to Abraham. See, e.g., MTeh 110:1–3 (YJS, *13, 2,* 204–5).

10. *"The morning stars* are Israel, who in the verse 'I will multiply thy seed as the stars of heaven' (Gen. 22:18) are likened to stars." See Sif Deut. 306 (ed. Finkelstein, p. 343); B.Ḥul 91b; Gen. Rabbah 65:21; and Ginzberg, *Legends, 5,* 24, n. 6.

favor because of their father Abraham. They then ask: For what particular deeds of Abraham do You show them such favor? God answers: When Abraham's father gave him [images of] divinities and told him to go <sell them> in the marketplace, Abraham went and smashed them; for he considered absolutely worthless all the kinds of idols that were in the marketplace, indeed in the world, and thus he hallowed My name in My world.

It is said of our father Abraham that after his father ordered him to sell [idols] in the marketplace, a man came <and asked>: Have you a divinity to sell? Abraham asked: What divinity do you desire? The man replied: I am a mighty man. Give me a divinity as mighty as I. <Abraham said: I have no divinity as mighty as you>. But then he took an idol who was set on a higher shelf than all the others and said: Take this one. The man replied: You good-for-nothing! Is this divinity as mighty as I?[11] Abraham said: [None of these are], so what do you expect of them? But if you are fool enough [to believe in them, you may well believe that] if this one were not <greater> than the others, he would not be sitting <above all the others>. He will say nothing to you, however, until you give me the money [for him].

After Abraham had taken the money and as the man was about to leave, Abraham asked: How old are you? The man replied: Seventy years old. Abraham asked: This divinity, do you bow down to it, or
S, *p.* 48 | does it bow down to you? The man replied: I bow down to it. Abraham said: You, who are older than your divinity by seventy years, bow down to this thing which <only yesterday my father> made with a mallet!

Thereupon the man returned the idol to its shelf, took back his money, and went thence.

Then came a widow and said [to Abraham]: Give me a divinity as poor as I. Abraham took one which was on a lower shelf than all the others and said: To suit your poverty, take this one. She said: He looks voracious to me, and I am not sure I can afford to maintain him. Abraham said: You are a complete fool! If he were not less demanding than all the others, he would not be sitting below all the others. In any event, he will not budge [from here] until you pay the money. So she gave him the money and was about to leave when he asked her: How old are you? She replied: Quite old. <Abraham said>: May the soul of such a woman as you be blasted! [To think] that you who came into being many years ago should bow down to this thing which my father made with a mallet only yesterday!

---

11. "Is this divinity as mighty as I" is an attempt to make sense of the Hebrew "I have not yet been a divinity."

Thereupon the widow returned the idol to its shelf, took back her money, and went thence.

Then Abraham took the divinities and went back to his father Terah. So Terah's other sons said to their father: This one cannot sell divinities. Come, let us make him their attendant. <Abraham asked>: What is an attendant's work? They replied: He sweeps up around the idols, sprinkles water around them, and gives them food and drink. Abraham said: I will be an attendant. So he swept up around the idols, sprinkled water around them, and placed food and drink before them. Then he said to them: <If you please>, take and eat, take and drink, <and may you be as kind> to me as <you are> to other human beings. But there was not one among the divinities who took anything. He then proceeded to say: *They have mouths, but cannot speak, eyes but cannot see; they have ears, but cannot hear, noses but cannot smell; they have hands, but cannot touch, feet but cannot walk; they can make no sound in their throats. Those who fashion them, all who trust in them, shall become like them* (Ps. 115:5–8). What did Abraham do then? He took a club, smashed all of the idols, threw them into the fire, and sat down nearby.

When Nimrod came and found him there, he asked: Are you Abraham the son of Terah? Abraham replied: Yes. Nimrod asked: Do you not know that I am lord of all things? Sun and moon, stars and planets, and human beings go forth only at my command. And now you have destroyed my divinity, the only thing that I revere.

At that moment the Holy One gave insight to Abraham, and he said to Nimrod: My lord king, I did not know just what your wish was. <Now> let me suggest something which will redound to your greatness <and your fame>. Nimrod said: Suggest it. Abraham said: From the day the world was created until the present time, it is a fact of nature that the sun rises in the east and sets in the west. Tomorrow, command it to rise in the west and set in the east. If it does, I will bear witness that you are lord of all that goes on in the world. Moreover, if you are lord, hidden things are revealed to you; what then is in my mind and what do I mean to do?

Thereupon the wicked man put his hand to his beard and found himself greatly puzzled. Abraham said to him: Do not be so puzzled. You are not Lord. You are a son of the late Cush.[12] If you are indeed Lord, why did you not save him from death? As you were unable to save your father, so you will be unable to save yourself.

Then Nimrod summoned Terah, Abraham's father, and said: You know what is to be the sentence of this one who has burned my divinities? His sentence must be death by fire. At once | Nimrod S, *p.* 49
seized Abraham and put him in prison. <Then his servants spent ten

12. See Gen. 10:8.

years building the furnace in which Abraham was to be burned and hauling and bringing wood for the furnace.> When they finally took him out to burn him in the fiery furnace, at once the Holy One came down to deliver him.

[In connection with God's deliverance of Abraham], the ministering angels spoke up to the Holy One saying: <Master of the universe>, what did You find in Adam that led You to bring Yourself down to his level and make a bower for him in the Garden of Eden <and then come down to dwell with him in the Garden of Eden>? For, as it turned out, he transgressed all Your commandments. God replied: The answer to you stands at your side—[a man such as Abraham]. What do you expect Me to do to a mortal being who lives in [the world below], a place of uncleanness, a being whom the Impulse to evil rules? [For My part, if he manages, like Abraham, to achieve righteousness, I rejoice in him and will deliver him.] In contrast to him, you dwell in a place of cleanness; the Impulse to evil has no power over you. Yet what did beings of your kind, Uzza, Uzzi, and Uzzael do? When they came down to the earth, they lusted after the daughters of man, led them to sin, taught them witchcraft whereby they could have brought down the sun and the moon,[13] <the work of My hands—indeed, they even turned such secret knowledge over to mankind>. But Abraham hallowed My name in his world and will continue to hallow My name in <My> world. Hence, at once the Holy One, <in all His glory>, came down and delivered Abraham.[14]

---

13. See Ginzberg, *Legends, 1,* 124–27.

14. Neh. 9:7 is read: *Thou didst choose Abraham, and broughtest him forth out of the fire ('ur) of the Chaldees.* The word *'ur* may mean "city of Ur," or "fire."

PIRḲE HAY-YĔRIḎOṮ

CHAPTER 1

God as Israel's escort to and from Egypt; Joseph's character and experiences there

Summary

God's first descent into the world was into the Garden of Eden, His second descent to the generation of the Tower of Babel, His third to deliver Abraham, and His fourth to accompany Jacob and his kindred into Egypt in order to make the total company seventy. And later on, when Israel left Egypt, He joined them again, bringing the total to 600,000.

Of Joseph's life in Egypt we are told why ten years were deducted from his life and also told of his deference to Jacob, of his conquest of lustful imaginings, of his knowledge of languages (S, 50–51), of the modesty of his demeanor, and of his skill in keeping prices from rising and in building storehouses.

Accompanied by forty-five thousand Egyptians, Joseph went up to bury his father in the Cave of Machpelah. There Esau was present to assert that the Cave was his. Naphtali, swift of foot, fetched the deed, and Hushim the son of Dan cut off Esau's head which rolled down into the Cave, and Esau's body was sent to Seir (S, 52–53).

Chapter 1[1]

The fourth of God's descents[2] was God's going down to Egypt, saying,[3] S, *p.* 50
[*Jacob*], *I will go down with thee into Egypt* (Gen. 46:4). For when Jacob heard of Joseph that he was alive, he wondered what to do, asking himself: Shall I leave the land of my fathers, the land of my birth, the land in whose midst the Presence dwells, and go to an unclean land among the uncircumcised children of Ham who have no fear of God over them?[4] It was then that the Holy One said to him: *Fear not . . . I will go down with thee into Egypt* (Gen. 46:3–4). And when Jacob heard this assurance, he took his sons and all the people of his household and went down to Egypt, *his sons, and his sons' sons with him, his daughters* (Gen. 46:7), as is said. Though another verse speaks only of *his daughter*

---

1. The three chapters that follow parallel chapters 39, 40, and 41 in PRE.

2. The preceding chapter dealt with God's descent to deliver Abraham. His previous descents were into the Garden of Eden (Gen. 3:8) and to the generation of the Tower of Babel (Gen. 11:5).

3. The unusual acronym *mem, nun,* may represent the two words *me'i ne'ĕmar* = *me-heḳan ne'ĕmar,* "where is it said?" (see Meir Friedmann, *Nispaḥim lĕ-seder Eliyyahu Zuṭa* [Vienna, 1902], Introduction, p. 20). Possibly also *Min-nayin? Ne'ĕmar,* "The proof? The verse."

4. Cf. Exod. 9:30.

Dinah (Gen. 46:15), yet here Scripture says *his daughters.* [Why?] To inform you that all of Jacob's sons wed their sisters,[5] so that Jacob's sons should not marry into the families of the nations of the earth. Hence, they were called a "true seed," as is said, *I had planted thee a noble vine,*
S, *p.* 51 | *wholly a true seed* (Jer. 2:21). When Jacob came to the border of Egypt, all the males [of his household] to the number of sixty-six were entered in the genealogical lists, as is said, *All the souls belonging to Jacob that came into Egypt, . . . all the souls were threescore and six* (Gen. 46:26). These, together with Joseph and his two sons, made threescore and nine, and yet it is written, *Thy fathers went down into Egypt with threescore and ten persons* (Deut. 10:22).[6] What had the Holy One to do with this sum? He entered into their number so that the sum became seventy, thus fulfilling His pledge, *I will go down with thee into Egypt* (Gen. 46:4). And when our forebears were redeemed from Egypt, all the males entered upon the rolls were six hundred thousand less one, as is said, *about six hundred thousand men* (Exod. 12:37). What did the Holy One do? He had Himself entered in the number so that the sum became six hundred thousand, thus fulfilling His pledge, *I will bring thee up, and* [*I too will*] *go up*[7] (Gen. 46:4).

R. Ishmael said: Ten times[8] did the sons of Jacob speak of him to Joseph as "thy servant our father." Though Joseph heard the epithet "servant," he remained silent, his silence implying his consent to it. On this account, ten years were deducted from his life.[9]

When Joseph heard that Jacob had arrived at the border of Egypt, he took the soldiers who were his escort and he went out to meet his father because all the people go forth to meet a king, but a king does not go forth to meet the people. The point is that a man is to regard his father as a king.

R. Menahem said: The holy spirit rested on Joseph from his youth[10] and led him in all matters of wisdom like a shepherd who leads his flock, as is said, *Give ear, O Shepherd of Israel, Thou that leadest Joseph like a flock* (Ps. 80:2). Despite all his wisdom, a woman turned his head,

---

5. The tradition is that besides their sister Dinah, every Tribe Father had a twin sister. See Gen. Rabbah 42:8.

6. Deut. 10:22 and not Gen. 46:27 is cited because Deut. 10:22 contains the words *went down,* echoing God's promise, *I will go down.* Besides, since Jochebed is said to have been born just before the household of Jacob entered Egypt, she—and not God—would have made the seventieth person. So David Luria, PRE, chap. 39, n. 9. See also Ginzberg, *Legends, 5,* 359.

7. JV: *I will also surely bring thee up again.* But the absolute *'lh,* represented in JV by *surely,* is taken to denote a separate act—God's going up.

8. Actually, it was only five times, but since Joseph employed an interpreter the expression was repeated.

9. Joseph died at one hundred and ten (Gen. 50:26). The full life of man is one hundred and twenty years.

10. Cf. Wisd. of Sol. 10:13–14.

but when he sought an occasion to couple with her, the image of his father <came to mind> and pushed him back, so that his lust vanished.

Because of Him who made them in His image, three people conquered their lustful imaginings: Joseph, Boaz, and Palti the son of Laish.[11] It had been anticipated that twelve Tribe Fathers would arise from Joseph. [He was so excited by the advances of Potiphar's wife, however], that from the tips of his ten fingers issued the seed that was to have generated the ten Tribe Fathers, so that there remained within him, then, only the seed that was to generate two Tribe Fathers, Manasseh and Ephraim, as is said, *His male member became detumescent again, after the seed was ejaculated from his fingers* (Gen. 49:24).[12] Then the woman, [Potiphar's wife, who had sought to seduce him], brought grave charges against him so as to undo him, and he was confined to prison for ten[13] years. There he interpreted the dreams of Pharaoh's servants, as was said by one of them: *And it came to pass, as he interpreted to us, so it was* (Gen. 41:13).

It is also said of Joseph that when he went forth into the marketplace and saw all kinds of peoples gathering themselves into many separate crowds and many separate groups, each and every people speaking in its own tongue, he knew what they all were saying, as is said, *God had provided for Jehoseph evidence* [*of his wisdom*] *so that whenever he went forth into the land of Egypt,* [*he found himself saying*]: | *I under-* S, *p.* 52
stand languages which I had never heard[14] (Ps. 81:6).

Furthermore, when he was riding in his chariot and passing through the land of Egypt, Egyptian girls for the sake of a sight of him used to climb walls and throw golden rings down to him, yet he would not look up to gaze upon their beauty—indeed, no mortal eye caught him looking, [such was his modesty]. As Scripture says of him, *Joseph was an elegant son, a son whose gracefulness attracted the eyes, so that maidens climbed walls to gaze* [*upon his beauty*][15] (Gen. 49:22).

When a man asked his fellow as to what price [should be set on

---

11. See Ruth 3:9–15; 1 Sam. 25:44; and Ginzberg, *Legends, 6,* 273, n. 133.

12. JV: *But his bow abode firm, and the arms of his hands were made supple.* But *bĕ-'eṭan,* "firm," is taken to mean "first," or "original form"—hence "detumescent again"; *zĕro'e,* "arms," is read *zar'e,* "seed"; and *way-yofozu,* "were made supple," is read *way-yofuṣu,* "was scattered." See Targum Jonathan *ad loc.* and *Torah šĕlemah, 7,* 1844.

13. Or, more accurately (as in SOR, p. 62) twelve years: one year he served Potiphar; two years later, Pharaoh's chief baker and butler were thrown into prison; ten years later Pharaoh had his prophetic dreams, for *on the day that Joseph stood before Pharaoh he was thirty years old* (Gen. 40:11).

14. After Joseph assumed his high office, "Gabriel came and tried to teach Joseph the seventy languages, but he could not learn them. Thereupon Gabriel added to Joseph's name a letter from the name of the Holy One [hence, *Jehoseph*], and he mastered the languages" (B.Soṭ 36b).

15. JV: *Joseph is a fruitful vine, a fruitful vine by a fountain, its branches run over the wall.* But see Rashi *ad loc.*

a commodity] in the market, what was agreed upon between them, set the market price. Then, when people would come to Joseph [to confirm the price], he would say to them, "The price you heard quoted is firm." Thus by preventing fear of scarcity, he kept prices from rising.[16] You may conclude, then, from Joseph's example that he who brings on a fear of scarcity will never see a sign of blessing.[17]

R. Tanḥuma said: Joseph commanded [what should be done], and the Egyptians built storehouses for food in every city, and all the produce of the land he gathered into the storehouses. The Egyptians talked him down, saying: Now worms will consume Joseph's stores. But no worm had any power over them; neither did the stores diminish until the day of his death.[18] And since he provided for the land in the days of famine, he is called Calcol,[19] "Sustainer," for, as is said, *Joseph sustained his father and his brethren,* etc. (Gen. 47:12).

R. Eliezer said: Just before the time of Jacob's decease he summoned his son Joseph and said to him: My son, swear by the covenant of circumcision that you will take me up to the burial place of my fathers, the Cave of Machpelah, as is said, *Put, I pray thee, thy hand under my thigh. . . . When I sleep with my fathers, . . . bury me in their burying place* (Gen. 47:29–30). Before the Torah was given, former generations used to swear by the covenant of circumcision, and thus did Joseph *swear unto him. And Israel bowed down upon the bed's head* (Gen. 47:31).

When Joseph went up to bury his father, all the notables of the kingdom went up with him to show loving-kindness toward his father Jacob, as is said, *Joseph went up to bury his father; and with him went up all the servants of Pharaoh, the elders of his house, and all the elders of the land of Egypt* (Gen. 50:7). Accordingly, the camp of Joseph contained forty-five thousand men, for *there went up with him both chariots and horsemen;* [*and it was a very (mĕ'od)*[20] *great company*] (Gen. 50:9). Furthermore, on account of the famine [in Egypt, the people of Canaan] brought food to Joseph's camp. [Because of their good will], the Holy One said to the Egyptians: You showed loving-kindness to My servant Jacob, and so

---

16. The Hebrew for "Thus by preventing . . . prices from rising" is interpreted by David Luria in PRE, chap. 39, n. 45.

[This is not what the Hebrew says—it says the opposite: "In order not to let the sale price go down." The idea, I suppose, is that Joseph being the economic czar, could have issued a forecast of falling prices and bought up all supplies of food at less than a fair price, but he did not do so and paid the full current price for corn. L. N.]

17. See B.Ta 10a, Meg 17b, and BB 90b.

18. When Jacob arrived in Egypt at the end of the second year of famine, the famine is said to have ceased and did not resume again until his death. See Sif Deut. 38 (ed. Finkelstein [Breslau, 1936–39], pp. 75–76), and Naḥmanides on Gen. 47:18.

19. See 1 Kings 5:11 and PR 14:9 (YJS, *18, 1,* 273–74).

20. The number "forty-five thousand" may be derived from the numerical value of the letters *mem* (40), *'alef* (1), and *dalet* (4). So Rabbi Alvin Kaunfer. Cf. *Torah šĕlemah, 8,* 1869.

I will give the reward due you to your children's children. Hence, later when the Egyptians were drowned [in the Red Sea], they were not left to float in the water,[21] but were deemed worthy of burial in the earth, as is said, *Thou stretchedst out Thy right hand—the earth swallowed them* (Exod. 15:12).

When Joseph arrived at the Cave of Machpelah, however, the wicked Esau came from Mount Seir to stir up strife, asserting: The Cave of Machpelah is mine. What did Joseph do? He sent Naphtali, who was so swift of foot that he could overtake the planets,[22] to fetch the deed to the cave, for though it is said, *Naphtali is a hind let loose, he giveth goodly words* (Gen. 49:21), read not *goodly (šfr)* words, but "the words of the deed *(sfr).*" Hushim the son of Dan had defective hearing and speech,[23] and so he asked: What's | goin' on here? He was told: The S, *p.* 53 cause of the argument is that man who will not let us show loving-kindness to our father Jacob. What did Hushim do? He took his sword and cut off Esau's head, [which rolled] down into the Cave of Machpelah, and they sent his body to Esau's rightful property, Seir.

Then what did Isaac do? He took Esau's head, brought it before the Holy One, and said in His presence: Master of the universe, shall favor be shown to this wicked one who would not learn righteousness, would not learn any of Torah's commandments, as is said in Scripture, *Shall favor be shown to the wicked who would not learn righteousness* (Isa. 26:10)? [Shall favor be shown to this wicked one] who spoke wrongfully of the Land and of the Cave of Machpelah, as is said, *In the Land of uprightness he would deal wrongfully*[24] *(ibid.)?* The Holy One replied to Isaac, saying: By My life, Esau *will not behold the majesty of the Lord* (Isa. 26:10).

---

21. [*Ng'w bmym* puzzles me, and "left to float in the water" seems no more than a guess. I suppose the root is not *ng',* "to touch, to have contact with," for the Egyptians certainly "touched" the water, since they drowned in it. Nor can it be nifal of *g'h,* which makes no sense in the context. Perhaps it is a nifal of *gw',* "to expire, to perish" = to dissolve: "their corpses did not dissolve in the water, but were (swept by the tide to be) interred on land." Of course, *ng'w* may easily be a corruption of some other more appropriate verb. L. N.]

22. [*Kbs* does not mean "overtake," but rather "press down, conquer." The solution, I suppose, lies in Luria's interpretation (quoted in Friedmann's n. 20) *lĕ-ḥappeś bĕ-mazzaloṯ*—the assumption being that no one knew the location of the deed, and Naphtali had to cast a horoscope (or whatever astrologers cast in such a case) to find it. A copyist reading his *Vorlage* aloud could easily miswrite *li-ḵĕbos* for *lĕ-ḥappeś.* Hence the quotation from Gen. 49:21 should be translated *Naphtali is a hind dispatched to produce the text of the deed.* L. N.]

23. The author may construe Hushim as "troubled," hence defective "in several ways." So Rabbi Saul Leeman. Cf. Targum Jonathan on Gen. 46:23.

24. [The Hebrew text is obviously corrupt here—it must have read something like *hăyuḥan raša' zeh . . . ṣeḏeḳ 'ăšer 'al ha'areṣ—'al mĕ'araṯ ham-maḵpelah—bĕ-'awel hayah mĕdabber ba-'areṣ nĕḵoḥoṯ yĕ'awwel,* etc. L. N.]

CHAPTER 2

God's descent into the thorn bush and the miracles He performed for Moses

Summary

God's fifth descent to earth was when He came down into the thorn bush which was full of thorns and prickles. His descent into it thus fulfilled the words of Scripture, *In all their affliction He was afflicted.*

Details follow concerning the wonder-wreaking rod which was created at twilight on the eve of the first Sabbath. The rod was successively in the possession of Adam, Enoch, Shem, Abraham, Isaac, Jacob, Joseph, Pharaoh's palace, Jethro, and Moses. With the aid of the rod Moses kept Jethro's sheep for forty years, so that no beast bereaved them of their young, and the flock increased greatly.

At the sight of the burning bush, Moses drew near (S, 53), and God told him: Here I shall give the Torah to Israel. He went on to tell Moses to go to Egypt and reassured him about his capacity to speak and the incapacity of his enemies to do him mischief. He also showed him how to work signs and wonders with the rod.

God went on to say to Moses that the fire in the thorn bush was Israel and that its thorns and prickles were the nations. In this world, He said, Israel will not consume the nations, nor will the nations extinguish the flame of Israel. But in the days-to-come, the fire of Israel will consume all (S, 54) the nations.

Finally, from the thorn bush, God turned over to Moses the secret of His Name (S, 55).

Chapter 2

S, *p.* 53 *cont'd* God's fifth descent to earth was when He came down into the thorn bush. *I am come down to deliver them out of the hand of the Egyptians* (Exod. 3:8), <He said>, and He left Mount [Sinai] entirely and dwelt in the thorn bush, as it is said, <*And God called unto him out of the midst of the bush* (Exod. 3:4)>. The thorn bush, full of thorns and prickles, causing pain and distress, thus fulfilled the words of the verse *In all their affliction He was afflicted* (Isa. 63:9);[1] why did God dwell in such trouble and distress? Because He saw Israel dwelling amidst trouble and distress.

R. Levi said: The rod[2] that was created at twilight [on the eve of the Sabbath] was given to Adam in the Garden of Eden.[3] Adam turned it over to Enoch, Enoch turned it over to Noah, Noah turned it over

1. Cf. B.Ta 16a.

2. Wherewith Moses performed God's miracles in Egypt (Exod. 4:17). See Aḇ 5:9.

3. When he was driven out of Eden, Adam took the rod and tilled the soil with it. See Yalḳuṭ, *2, Šĕmoṯ,* 168.

to Shem, Shem turned it over to Abraham, Abraham turned it over to Isaac, Isaac to Jacob.[4] Jacob brought it to Egypt and turned it over to his son Joseph.[5] When Joseph died, his entire property, including the rod, was confiscated [and taken] to Pharaoh's palace. Now Jethro was one of the magicians of Egypt, and when he saw the rod, he read the signs upon it and put forth his hand and took it. <Then when Moses came to Jethro's house, he, too, saw the rod and read the signs on it. When Jethro saw him>,[6] he said: This is he who will deliver Israel from Egypt. Therefore he gave his daughter to Moses for a wife, as is said, *Moses consented to dwell with the man, for he gave Moses Zipporah his daughter* (Exod. 2:21).

With the aid of the rod, Moses kept Jethro's sheep for forty years,[7] and no beast of the field bereaved them [of their young], and they were fruitful and increased greatly: Scripture speaks of them *As the flock of holy things*[8] (Ezek. 36:38). And Moses led the flock until he came to Horeb, as is said, *And he led the flock to the farthest end of the wilderness . . . and came unto Horeb* (Exod. 3:1). There God appeared to him, as is said, *The angel of the Lord appeared unto him in a flame of fire* (Exod. 3:2). Moses saw the fire within the bush. Yet the fire did not consume the bush, for the abundance of water in the ground around the bush, water without which the bush could not have grown there, kept the fire from taking hold. And Moses, with wonder in his heart, drew near to see the prodigies, as is said, *I will turn aside* | *now, and see this great sight* S, *p.* 54
(Exod. 3:3). Stand where you are, said the Holy One, for here I shall give the Torah to Israel; *draw not nigh hither* (Exod. 3:5).

The Holy One went on to say: *Come and I will send thee unto Pharaoh* (Exod. 3:10). Moses replied: Master of the universe, have I not told You[9] three or four times that I have not the capacity [to address him], for I have a poor tongue: *I am slow of speech, and of a slow tongue* (Exod. 4:10). The Holy One reassured him: Who provided man with a mouth, etc.? as is said, *Who hath provided man with a mouth,* etc.? (Exod. 4:11). Then Moses asked: Do You wish to deliver me into the power of my enemies who seek my life? Was it not for this reason that I fled from them? The Holy One replied: Be not afraid. By now they are dead: *All the men are dead that sought thy life* (Exod. 4:19). And who were the men? Dathan and Abiram. But had they died? Were not Dathan and Abiram still alive? Yes, as a sage pointed out, whenever Scripture

---

4. Jacob received it when he fled to Paddan-Aram, saying, *For with my rod I passed over this Jordan* (Gen. 32:10). With the rod Jacob divided the Jordan as Moses later was to divide the Red Sea with it. See Yalḳuṭ, *4, Ḥuḳḳaṭ,* 763.

5. Cf. "the stick of Joseph" (Ezek. 37:19).

6. "Then when . . . saw him"—Friedmann's n. 2.

7. See Sif Deut. 357 (ed. Finkelstein [Breslau, 1936–39], p. 429).

8. The verse is applied to Jethro's sheep because Moses led them to graze near Horeb, the Mount of God.

9. Parma MS 1240 reads: "Have You not said to me."

speaks of men "standing rigid," Dathan and Abiram are meant.[10] Hence the previous reference to dead men signifies that it was not Dathan and Abiram but their fortunes that had withered.

Moses next said to God: Give me a sign. And God replied: Cast your rod to the ground. Moses cast his rod to the ground, and it became a fiery serpent. Why did the Holy One turn it into a fiery serpent and not into something else? Because just as a serpent strikes and kills mankind, so did the Egyptians strike and kill. Then the rod became a dry stick of wood again, as is said, *Put forth thy hand, and take it by the tail . . . and it became a dry stick in his hand* (Exod. 4:4); and God said: So Pharaoh and Egypt will become like this dry stick.

Moses then said to God: Show me a miracle. And God replied: *Put now thy hand into thy bosom . . . and when he took it out, behold, his hand was leprous, as white as snow* (Exod. 4:6). Why did the Holy One perform [a miracle] for Moses by means of something unclean and not by means of something clean? Because just as a leper is himself unclean and causes others to become unclean, so Pharaoh and the Egyptians were unclean and caused Israel and their wives with them to become unclean.[11] Then Moses became clean again, as is said, *Put thy hand back into thy bosom . . . and when he took it out of his bosom, behold, it was turned again as his other flesh* (Exod. 4:7). God said: So, too, I shall cleanse Israel of the uncleanness of Egypt.

Why did the Holy One show Moses a fire in the midst of the thorn bush? To indicate to him that the fire is Israel who in Scripture are likened to fire: *The house of Israel shall be a fire* (Ob. 1:18). The thorn bush is the nations of the earth who are like thorns and prickles. God went on to say to Moses: In this world Israel will be like the thorn bush you see. The fire of Israel will not consume any of the nations, nor will the peoples of the earth extinguish the flame of Israel, which is words of Torah. In the days to come, however, the fire of Israel will indeed
S, *p.* 55 consume all | the nations.

Then Moses replied to the Holy One: Master of the universe, make known to me Your great and holy name that I may call You by Your name, and You will answer us. Whereupon God made it known to him.[12]

When those on high saw that the Holy One had turned over the secret of the Name to Moses, they said: Blessed be the Name, gracious Giver of knowledge.[13]

---

10. See Exod. 5:20; Num. 16:27; and above, ER, 106.

11. By means of the small idols they kept in their bosoms and took out to instruct Israelites in idolatry. So David Luria, PRE, chap. 40, n. 40.

12. Cf. MTeh 91:1, 8 (YJS, *13, 2,* 101, 107).

13. The fourth benediction of the *'Amiḏah* (Hertz, *APB,* p. 137) with the origin of which Moses is thus associated, even as Jacob is associated with the third benediction. See PRE, chap. 35 end (Pirkê de-Rabbi Eliezer, Gerald Friedlander tr. [New York, 1965], p. 267).

CHAPTER 3

God's descent to Mount Sinai and Israel's unity there; God's promise of their deliverance and their praise of Him

Summary

God's sixth descent to earth was when He came down upon Mount Sinai. He had first revealed Himself to the children of Esau, then to the children of Ishmael, indeed to all the peoples of the earth, each of whom successively spurned Him. Only then did He turn and reveal Himself to the children of Israel, holding in His right hand the Torah as a sign of love and of oath-taking (S, 55).

Before Sinai, when Israel camped, they wrangled with one another, but at Sinai all of them encamped with one heart and one counsel.

In response to Israel's prayer to save them from the revilings and taunts of the nations, God assures them: I prepare the world-to-come for you and will have you rule over all the world's inhabitants, who will lick the soles of your feet.

In the meantime, because Israel manage to restrain the Impulse to evil though it rules in their very midst, and because daily they affirm God's uniqueness and sovereignty and look forward to His kingship and to seeing His house rebuilt, the ministering angels on high are not allowed to utter their song in praise of God until Israel below give voice to theirs (S, 56).

Chapter 3

God's sixth descent was His coming down upon Sinai, as is said, *The Lord came down upon Mount Sinai* (Exod. 19:20). When the Holy One revealed Himself over it on the sixth of Sivan, the Mount lifted itself from its place, the heavens opened up, the top of the Mount penetrated into heaven, and thick darkness covered the Mount, as is said, *He bowed the heavens also, and came down; and thick darkness was under His feet* (Ps. 18:1).[1] S, *p.* 55 *cont'd*

After having first revealed Himself unto the children of Esau, the Holy One shone forth as He came to Sinai, as is said, *The Lord came unto Sinai: after having [first] risen at Seir unto the people thereof, then having shined forth at Mount Paran, He came unto the myriads holy, at His right hand a fiery law for them*[2] (Deut. 33:2). That the children of Esau are meant

---

1. Cf. B.Suk 52.

2. JV: *The Lord came from Sinai, and rose from Seir unto them, He shined forth from Mount Paran, and He came from the myriads holy, at His right hand was a fiery law unto them.* Here the commentator attempts to explain God's journeying at the time He was to give the Torah to Israel. To clarify the statement that God came *from* Sinai, whereas in fact

by *Seir* is shown by the verse "So Esau returned that day on his way unto Seir" (Gen. 33:16). When God asked them, Will you accept the Torah for yourselves? they replied: What is written in it? He said: *Thou shalt not murder* (Exod. 20:13). They answered: We cannot give up the blessing Isaac bestowed upon our father Esau when he said, *By thy sword shalt thou live* (Gen. 27:40). If we do not murder, whence the blessing?

Then God turned and revealed Himself to the children of Ishmael: *He shined forth at Mount Paran* (Deut. 33:2). That *Paran* refers to the children of Ishmael is shown by the verse "Ishmael . . . dwelt in the wilderness of Paran" (Gen. 21:21). He asked them: Will you accept the Torah for yourselves? They asked: What is written in it? He replied: *Thou shalt not steal* (Exod. 20:13). They answered: We cannot abandon the custom observed by our fathers, who stole Joseph and brought him to Egypt. For it was to their fathers that Joseph also referred when he said, *I have been stolen once and again*[3] *out of the land of the Hebrews* (Gen. 40:15).[4] Then, from Paran, God sent messengers to all the peoples of the earth, asking them: Will you accept the Torah for yourselves? They asked: What is written in it? He replied: *Thou shalt have no other gods before Me* (Exod. 20:3). They said: We do not want Your Torah. Give Your Torah to Your people: *Let the Lord give strength* [*Torah*] *to His people* (Ps. 29:11). Whereupon He turned and revealed Himself unto the children of Israel, as is said, *He came unto the myriads holy* (Deut. 33:2). By *myriads holy* the children of Israel are meant, as in the verse "And when it rested, he said: Return, O Lord, unto the myriads of the families of Israel" (Num. 10:36). And with Him were thousands, yea, myriads of angelic hosts, as is said, *The chariots of God are myriads, yea, thousands of angelic hosts* (Ps. 68:18). In His right hand He held the Torah, as is said, *At His right hand a fiery Law for them* (Deut. 33:2). Why in His right hand? It was a sign of His love and an act of oath-taking: a sign of His love, as in the verse *Let His left hand be under my head, and His right hand embrace me* (Song 2:6); an act of oath-taking, as in the verse *The Lord hath sworn by His right hand, and by the arm of His strength* (Isa. 62:8).

R. Eliezer said: From the day Israel left Egypt, as they journeyed

---

He came *to* Sinai, the commentator takes the preposition *mi* (usually rendered "from") as meaning rather "the place or region in or at which a thing is" (see Gesenius-Brown, p. 584; cf. Gen. 12:8). The *myriads holy* are the myriads of Israel.

3. As elsewhere in Rabbinic exegesis, the absolute infinitive, *gunnoḇ,* is taken to indicate a separate action (cf. PRKM 10:4, pp. 165–66 [PRKS, p. 191]). Hence Joseph is understood as saying that he was stolen twice, once by his brothers and once again by the Ishmaelites. So, too, *Midraš 'Aggadah,* ed. Buber (Vienna, 5654/1894), p. 94. JV: *For indeed I was stolen away.*

4. Cf. PR 21:2–3 (YJS, *18, 1,* 417).

| and camped, they wrangled with one another, [their lack of unity S, *p.* 56
being intimated by "they" in the verses] *"They* took their journey, *they* encamped" (Exod. 13:20), *"they* came" (Exod. 19:1), <but when they came> to Mount Sinai, all of them encamped over against the Mount with one heart and one counsel, as is said, "And Israel—there *it* encamped before the Mount"[5] (Exod. 19:2). The Holy One asked them: Will you accept the Torah for yourselves? They replied: Even before hearing the Torah, we have kept all the commandments of the Torah, as is said, *All that the Lord hath spoken we will do, for* [*what He is about to speak*] *has already been heeded* [*by the Patriarchs*][6] (Exod. 24:7).

R. Eleazar the Modiite said. . . .[7]

R. Bana'ah expounded the words *O Lord, in the morning hear my voice* (Ps. 5:4). The congregation of Israel said to the Holy One: In response to my prayer, hear my voice and save me from the nations of the earth who humiliate me, revile and curse me each and every day, saying to me: "He has abandoned you to our power, and all your praying to Him is in vain. Lo, ever so many generations have passed, and yet He has not rescued you from our midst!" May it be Your will, then, that You will again have compassion for me and rescue me from their midst and deliver me from their power. For I declare You "King" and affirm Your uniqueness, but they vex You and worship the sun.

Then the Holy One will reply: My daughter, I prepare the world-to-come for you and will have you rule over all the world's inhabitants. All the kings of the world will wait upon you as servants, and their princesses will serve you as nursing mothers. They will for ever lick the dust of the soles of your feet, as is said, *Kings shall be thy foster fathers, and their queens thy nursing mothers; they shall bow down to thee . . . and lick the dust of thy feet* (Isa. 49:23). And I shall make your radiance bright as the radiance of the sun.

Of the congregation of Israel, Solomon said: *Who is she that looketh forth as the dawn, fair as the moon, clear as the sun* (Song 6:10)—who is like the congregation of Israel who looks forth to the dawn, saying: When will the dawn come that I may hallow the Holy One in synagogues and academies and proclaim every day His sovereignty over His handiwork; *fair as the moon*—who is like the congregation of Israel who looks forward to the coming of the moon, saying: When will the new moon come, that I may look upon it new, then declare in the court that the New Moon is sanctified, and utter praises and thanksgivings even as the Holy One makes the radiance of the congregation of Israel bright as the radiance of the moon; *clear as the sun*—who are like the

---

5. Cf. PRKM 12:14, 214–15 (PRKS, pp. 238–39).
6. Cf. above, ER, 35. JV: *All that the Lord hath spoken, we will do and obey.*
7. Here there is a lacuna.

righteous in Israel, who meditate upon words of Torah in this world and whose radiance [in the world-to-come] the Holy One will make as bright as the sun's own radiance?

R. Judah son of R. Il'a'i expounded the verse *After the morning stars sang together,*[8] *all the angels shouted for joy* (Job 38:4) as follows: The ministering angels spoke up to the Holy One, asking, Master of the universe, why are we on high not allowed to utter our song until Israel below utter theirs? The Holy One replied: How can you expect to be allowed to utter your song before Israel—before Israel who, though they dwell on earth and are born of woman, yet manage to restrain the Impulse to evil though it rules in their very midst, daily affirm My uniqueness and proclaim My sovereignty, look forward to My kingship and to seeing My house rebuilt, saying every day: May He who will rebuild Jerusalem gather the dispersed of Israel![9] Amen, soon in our own days.

---

8. "The seed of Jacob are likened to stars, for of Jacob's seed it is said, *They that turn many to righteousness,* [*shall shine*] *as the stars* (Dan. 12:3)" (see Gen. Rabbah 65:21).

9. Cf. Ps. 147:2.

ABBREVIATIONS*

Ab̲	'Ab̲ot̲
Ar	'Ărak̲in
AZ	'Ăb̲od̲ah Zarah
BB	Bab̲a Bat̲ra
Bek̲	Bĕk̲orot̲
Ber	Bĕrak̲ot̲
Beṣ	Beṣah
Bik	Bikkurim
BḲ	Bab̲a Ḳamma
BM	Bab̲a Mĕṣi'a
DER	Derek̲ 'Ereṣ Rabbah
DEZ	Derek̲ 'Ereṣ Zuṭa
Ed̲	'Ed̲uyyot̲
Er	'Erub̲in
Ger	Gerim
Giṭ	Giṭṭin
Ḥag̲	Ḥăg̲ig̲ah
Ḥal	Ḥallah
Hor	Horayot̲
Ḥul	Ḥullin
Ka	Kallah
Kel	Kelim
Ker	Kĕrit̲ot̲
Ket̲	Kĕt̲ubbot̲
Ḳid	Ḳiddušin
Kil	Kil'ayim
Mak	Makkot̲
Meg̲	Mĕg̲illah
Men	Mĕnaḥot̲
Mid	Middot̲
Miḳ	Miḳwa'ot̲
MḲ	Mo'ed̲ Ḳaṭan
MSh	Ma'ăśer Šeni
Naz	Nazir
Ned̲	Nĕd̲arim
Neg̲	Nĕg̲a'im
Nid	Niddah
Oh	'Ŏhalot̲
Or	'Orlah
Par	Parah
Pes	Pĕsaḥim
RH	Roš haš-Šanah
Sanh	Ṣanhed̲rin
Sem	Sĕmaḥot̲
Shab	Šabbat̲
Sheb	Šĕb̲i'it̲
Sheb̲u	Šĕb̲u'ot̲
Sheḳ	Šĕḳalim
Sof	Sofĕrim
Soṭ	Soṭah
Suk	Sukkah
Ta	Ta'ănit̲
Tam	Tamid̲
Tef	Tĕfillin
Tem	Tĕmurah
Ter	Tĕrumot̲
Ṭoh	Ṭoharot̲
Uḳṣ	'Uḳṣin
Yad̲	Yad̲ayim
Yeb̲	Yĕb̲amot̲
Zeb̲	Zĕb̲aḥim

B. prefixed to the name of a tractate indicates a reference to the Babylonian Talmud; P. indicates a reference to the Palestinian (Jerusalemite) Talmud; and Tos a reference to the Tosefta (ed. Zuckermandel, Pasewalk, 1880; 2d ed., Jerusalem, 1937). Otherwise the reference is to tractates of the Mishnah.

Unless another edition is specified, the Midrash Rabbah used—on the Pentateuch as well as on the Five Scrolls—is the Wilno, 1878, edition.

*The titles of works cited frequently are abbreviated, and full bibliographical information for them is given herein. For works not cited frequently, bibliographical information is provided in the notes.

Other Sources and Commentaries

APB	*The Authorized Daily Prayer Book of the United Hebrew Congregations of the British Empire,* with a translation by Simeon Singer [1848–1906], 13th ed., London, 1925
ARN	'Aḇoṯ dĕ-R. Nathan, ed. Solomon Schechter [1847–1915], Vienna, 5647/1887; translated by Judah Goldin [1914–], New Haven, 1955 (YJS, *10*)
'Aruḵ	Nathan ben Jeḥiel of Rome [11th century], *Aruch Completum,* ed. Alexander Kohut [1842–94], facsimile reprint, 8 vols., Vienna, 1926
AV	The Authorized version of the English Bible, first published in 1611
B (appended to a title-abbreviation)	ed. Solomon Buber
B.	Babylonian Talmud
b.	*ben* (Hebrew) or *bar* (Aramaic), "son of"
Ben Yeḥiel	'Aḵiḇa Joseph ben Yeḥiel Schlesinger [1837–1922], *Tosafoṯ ben Yeḥiel,* Commentary on ER, Jerusalem, [5]666 [1906]
Berṭinoro	Obadiah ben Abraham of Berṭinoro [d. ca. 1500], Commentary on the Mishnah
chap.	chapter
EB	*Encyclopedia Biblica,* 7 vols. (in progress), Jerusalem, 1965–76
Edds	Editions of Tanna dĕḇe Eliyyahu other than Meir Friedmann's
EJ	*Encyclopaedia Judaica,* 16 vols., Jerusalem, 1973
'En Ya'ăḵoḇ	by Jacob ben Solomon ibn Ḥabiḇ [ca. 1460–1516], compilation of the haggadic passages in the Babylonian Talmud and in the orders Zĕra'im and Mo'eḏ of the Palestinian Talmud, 4 vols., New York, 1955
ER	Seder Eliyyahu Rabbah
'Eṣ Yosef	by Chanoch Zundel ben Joseph [d. 1867], Commentaries on Tanḥuma (ed. Warsaw, after World War I) and on Midrash Rabbah on the Pentateuch (Wilno, 1897)
ET	*Talmudic Encyclopedia,* 15 vols. (in progress), Jerusalem 5715–36/1955–76
EV	English versions of Scripture (as distinguished from special interpretations made by a Rabbinic commentator)
EZ	Seder Eliyyahu Zuta
Friedmann	Meir Friedmann [1831–1908], in his edition of Tanna dĕḇe Eliyyahu, titled Seder Eliahu Rabba und Seder Eliahu Zuta, Vienna, 1902; and Pseudo-Seder Eliahu Zuta, Vienna, 1904
Friedmann, Introduction	Introduction to his edition of TE (*see* Friedmann)

Gen. Rabbah TA	Genesis Rabbah, ed. Julius Theodor [1849–1923] and Chanoch Albeck [1890–1972], Berlin, 1912–31
Gesenius-Brown	Wilhelm Gesenius, *A Hebrew and English Lexicon of the Old Testament,* translated by Edward Robinson, ed. Francis Brown, S. R. Driver, and Charles A. Briggs, Oxford, 1907
Ginzberg, *Legends*	Louis Ginzberg [1873–1953], *Legends of the Jews,* 7 vols. Philadelphia, 1908–38
Haida	Samuel ben Moses Haida [1626–85], *Sifra' Ziḳḳuḳin dĕ-nur'a u-bi'urin dĕ-'ešša',* * Commentary on TE, Prague, 1676; Warsaw, 1880
Hertz, *APB*	*The Authorized Daily Prayer Book,* rev. ed., by Joseph Herman Hertz [1872–1946], New York, 5714/1954
HUCA	*Hebrew Union College Annual*
Ibn Ezra	Abraham ibn Ezra [1092–1167], Commentary on the Bible
Jastrow	Marcus Jastrow [1829–1903], *A Dictionary of the Targumim, the Talmud Babli and Yerushalmi, and the Midrashic Literature,* 2 vols., London and New York, 1903
JE	*The Jewish Encyclopedia*
JQR	*The Jewish Quarterly Review*
JV (Jewish Version)	*The Holy Scriptures according to the Masoretic Text,* Philadelphia, The Jewish Publication Society of America, 5677/1917
Kĕli paz	by Samuel Laniado [16th century], Commentary on Isaiah, Venice, 1657
Ḳimḥi	David Ḳimḥi [ca. 1160–1235], Commentary on the Bible
Ḳorban ha-'eḏah	by David Fränkel [ca. 1704–64], Commentary on the orders Mo'eḏ, Našim, and Nĕziḳin of the Palestinian Talmud (ed. Wilno, 1922)
Krauss, *Lehnwörter*	Samuel Krauss [1866–1948], *Griechische und lateinische Lehnwörter,* 2 vols., Berlin, 1898–99
Landau	Isaac Elijah ben Samuel Landau [1801–76], *Ma'ăneh Eliyyahu* and *Śiaḥ Yiṣḥaḳ,* Commentaries on TE, Wilno, 1839
Leḳaḥ Ṭoḇ	Tobiah ben Eliezer [11th century], Midrash Leḳaḥ Ṭoḇ, ed. Buber, Wilno, 1880
Lev. Rabbah M	Leviticus Rabbah, ed. Mordecai Margulies [1910–68], 5 vols., Jerusalem, 1953–60
Levy, *Wörterbuch*	Jacob Levy [1819–92], *Neuhebräisches und chaldäisches Wörterbuch über die Talmudim und Midraschim,* 4 vols., Leipzig, 1867–89
Lieberman, *TKF*	Saul Lieberman [1898–], *Tosefta ki-fĕšuṭah,* 12 vols. (in progress), New York, 1955–73
L. N.	Leon Nemoy [1901–]

*"Sparks of fire and tongues of flame." See B.BM 85b.

Mah	by Zĕʼeḇ Wolf Einhorn [d. 1862], Commentary on Midrash Rabbah, Wilno, 1878
Mann, "Date and Place"	Jacob Mann [1888–1940], "Date and Place of Redaction of Seder Eliahu Rabba and Zutta," *HUCA, 4,* 302–10
Mattĕnoṯ kĕhunnah	by Issachar Ber ben Naphtali hak-Kohen [16th century], Comments on the Midrash Rabbah (in the Wilno, 1878, ed. of that Midrash)
Meḵ	Mĕḵilta dĕ-Rabbi Ishmael, ed. Jacob Zallel Lauterbach [1873–1942], 3 vols., Philadelphia, 1933
MGWJ	*Monatsschrift für Geschichte und Wissenschaft des Judentums*
MhG Exod.	Midraš hag-Gaḏol on Exodus, ed. Mordecai Margulies, Jerusalem, 1956
MhG Num.	Midraš hag-Gaḏol on Numbers, ed. Solomon Fisch [1898–], 2 vols., London, 1957–63
Minḥaṯ šay	by Jedidiah Norzi [ca. 1560–1626], Masoretic commentary on the Bible (printed as a supplement in Rabbinic Bibles)
Mishnah (ed. Albeck)	*The Mishnah,* ed. Chanoch Albeck, 6 vols., Jerusalem, 1952–58; and introductory volume, Jerusalem, 1959
Montefiore, *RA*	Claude Goldsmid Montefiore [1859–1939] and Herbert Loewe [1882–1940], *Rabbinic Anthology,* London, 1938
MṢ	Jacob Meir Schechter, *Mišpaṭ u-Ṣĕḏaḳah,* Commentary on ER and EZ, 2 vols., Jerusalem, 5719–22 [1959–62]
MT	Masoretic text of Scripture
MTeh	Midrash Tĕhillim, ed. Solomon Buber, Wilno, 1891; translated by William G. Braude [1907–], New Haven, 1959 (YJS, *13*)
Moore, *Judaism*	George Foot Moore [1851–1931], *Judaism in the First Centuries of the Christian Era: The Age of the Tannaim,* 3 vols., Cambridge, Mass., 1927–30
Naḥmanides	Moses ben Naḥman [1194–ca. 1270], Commentary on the Pentateuch (printed in Rabbinic Bibles)
NJV	*A New Translation of the Holy Scriptures,* Philadelphia, 1962
Onkelos	*see* Targum
OT	Max Kadushin [1895–], *Organic Thinking, A Study in Rabbinic Thought,* New York, 1938
P.	Palestinian Talmud
Parma MS 1240	Parma MS de Rossi 1240 which Friedmann collated with V to edit the Pirḳe R. Eliezer and Pirḳe hay-Yĕriḏoṯ parts of EZ
Parma MS 2785	Parma MS 2785 de Rossi 327, no. 35, which has a different recension of EZ
Pĕne Mošeh	by Moses Margaliṯ [18th century], Commentary on the orders Našim, Zĕraʻim, and Moʻeḏ of

	the Palestinian Talmud, ed. Wilno, after World War I
PH	The Pentateuch and Haftarahs, ed. Joseph Herman Hertz, London, 1956
PR	Pĕsiḳta Rabbaṯi, ed. Meir Friedmann, Vienna, 1880; translated by William G. Braude [1907–], New Haven, 1968 (YJS, *18*)
PRE	Pirḳe dĕ-Rabbi Eliezer, Warsaw, 1852; translated by Gerald Friedlander [1871–1923], London, 1916; reprint, New York, 1965
PRK	Pĕsiḳta dĕ-Raḇ Kahăna
PRKM	Pĕsiḳta dĕ-Raḇ Kahăna, ed. Bernard Mandelbaum [1922–], 2 vols., New York, 1962
PRKS	Pĕsikta dĕ-Raḇ Kahăna, translated by William G. Braude [1907–] and Israel J. Kapstein [1904–], Philadelphia, 1975
Rashi	R. Solomon ben Isaac of Troyes [1040–1105], author of commentaries on the Hebrew Bible and on the Babylonian Talmud
R	Vatican MS 31 (containing ER and EZ [chap. 1–15]) of the year 1073 on which Friedmann's edition of TE is based
RV	Revised version of the English Old Testament (first published in 1885)
S (followed by a numeral)	Supplements, designating Friedmann's Pseudo-Seder Eliahu Zuta, made up of Pirḳe Dereḵ 'Ereṣ, Pirḳe R. Eliezer, and Pirḳe hay-Yĕriḏoṯ, Vienna, 1904
Samuel Edels	Samuel Eliezer ben Judah Edels [1555–1631], Novellae on the Babylonian Talmud (in the Wilno, 1880, ed.)
Schick	Abraham ben Aryeh Yehudah Loeb Schick [19th century], *Mĕ'ore 'eš,* Commentary on TE, Lemberg, 5624/1864
Sif	Sifre, Sifra
Soncino tr.	The English translations of the Babylonian Talmud (1935–52), the Midrash Rabbah (1939), and the Zohar (1931–34), issued by the Soncino Press in London
SOR	Seder 'Olam Rabbah, ed. Ber Ratner [1852–1916], Wilno, 1894
Tanḥuma	ed. Warsaw, after World War I
Tanḥuma B	ed. Solomon Buber, Wilno, 1885
Targum	Ancient translations or paraphrases of the Bible into Aramaic. The most important of these is the translation of the Pentateuch that is ascribed to Onḳelos the Proselyte, a Mishnaic teacher of the first century. The Targum Jonathan is a freer paraphrase of the Bible, ascribed to Jonathan ben Uzziel, a pupil of Hillel.

TE	Tanna dĕḇe Eliyyahu
TSE	Max Kadushin, *The Theology of Seder Eliahu,* New York, 1932
Torah šĕlemah	by Menahem Kasher [1895–], compilation of Rabbinic comments on the Pentateuch and commentary thereon, 29 vols. (in progress), Jerusalem, 1927–78
Tos	Tosefta, ed. Zuckermandel, Pasewalk, 1880; 2nd ed., Jerusalem, 1937
Tosafoṯ	Critical and explanatory glosses on the Talmud by the successors of Rashi
tr.	transmitter
V	Tanna dĕḇe Eliyyahu, Venice, 1598
Yalḳuṭ	The compilation or catena on Scripture known as Yalḳuṭ Šimĕʻoni
Yĕfeh to'ar	by Samuel ben Isaac Jaffe [16th century], comments on Midrash Rabbah (in the Wilno, 1878, ed. of that Midrash)
YJS	Yale Judaica Series
YY	Jacob ben Naphtali Hirtz of Brody [18th century], *Yĕšuʻoṯ Yaʻăḳoḇ,* Commentary on ER and EZ
Zunz, *had-Dĕrašoṯ*	Yom Ṭoḇ Lippmann Zunz [1794–1886], *had-Dĕrašoṯ bĕ-Yiśra'el,* translated by Chanoch Albeck, Jerusalem, 5707/1947
[ ]	Interpolation made for the sake of clarity or based on a parallel reading in another source
< >	Insertion made by Friedmann in his edition of TE
. . .	In the text proper (not in a quotation from Scripture) of ER, EZ, or S indicates a lacuna in the MSS

GLOSSARY

Ab *see* Months

Adar *see* Months

Afternoon Prayer (Minḥah) recited from half an hour after midday until sunset, corresponding to the time set for the daily burnt offering of the afternoon

'Aggadah (pl. *'Aggadot*) that part of Talmudic (and of later Rabbinic) literature which does not deal with legal matters

Altar unless otherwise specified, refers to the Outer Altar, also known as the Altar of Burnt Offering (Exod. 25:6), situated in the courtyard of the Tabernacle or the Temple Court; upon it were burned all sacrifices except the incense, and were offered all sprinklings of blood except those of certain sin offerings

Amalek a people totally evil—hence *the* symbol of evil

'Ămidah (literally "standing") *see Tĕfillah*

Amoraim literally "expounders, expositors"; Talmudic authorities who flourished about 200–500 C.E., and whose discussions are embodied in the Gemara

Analogy the use of a similar expression occurring elsewhere in Scripture in order to apply to one subject a rule, characteristic, or concept already known to apply to another

Atbash ('tbš) a method of interchanging the first letter of the Hebrew alphabet, *'alef,* with the last letter, *taw;* the second, *bet,* with the next to the last, *šin;* and so on

Baraita an extraneous Mishnah, containing a Tannaitic tradition not incorporated in the Mishnah as collected by Rabbi Judah I the Patriarch (ca. 200 C.E.), but cited in the Gemara, the Midrash, or the Tosefta

Bible the Hebrew Bible consists of three main groups: (1) the Law, i.e., the five books of the Pentateuch; (2) the Prophets, subdivided into Prior Prophets (Joshua through Kings) and Latter Prophets (Isaiah through Malachi); and the Writings (Psalms through Chronicles); *see also* Oral Law

Blessing, seasonal benediction ending with the words "who has kept us alive, and preserved us, and enabled us to reach this season"; see Maimonides' Code III, X, i, 3 (YJS, *14,* 454–55) for the full text

Burnt offering offered for sinful desire, for evil thoughts that come into one's mind; cf. Lev. Rabbah 7:3

Clean and unclean animals cf. Lev. 11

Daily burnt offerings two he-lambs were offered daily in the Temple, one in the morning and one in the afternoon, at dusk; cf. Num. 28:1–8

Day and night in the Jewish system of time reckoning, the day begins with the preceding night; the night is counted from dusk to dawn, and the day from dawn to dusk or sunrise to sunset; a daylight hour means a twelfth part of the day as thus defined

Denar a silver coin, which is worth a quarter of a *sela',* approximately 25 cents, or 1/24 of the gold denar

Diverse kinds of seeds or plants, may not be sown together; of garment stuffs, may not be worn together; of cattle, may not be bred to each other; cf. Lev. 19:19 and Deut. 22:9–11

Dough offering (Ḥallah) the portion of dough which belongs to a priest (see Num. 15:20ff); in the Diaspora this is not given to the priest but burned

Edom a Rabbinic designation of Rome

Eighteen Benedictions (Šĕmoneh 'eśreh) *see Tĕfillah*

Elul *see* Months

Ephah standard Biblical dry measure, equal to 10 *'omer* (Exod. 16:36) or 3 *sĕ'ah,* approximately the contents of 432 eggs—1 bushel

'Erub literally "intermingling, blending"; specifically, a symbolic act of "blending" several domains or limits together, for the purpose of making it lawful on the Sabbath to walk or transport things from one to the other

Esau a Rabbinic designation of Rome

Ethrog a species of citron *(Citrus medica L.)* used with the festive cluster on the Feast of Sukkot; *see also* Lulab

Festal peace offering (ḥăgigah) brought on each of the pilgrimage festivals; cf. Deut. 16:16; Exod. 23:14–17; Hag 1:1–2; Pes 6:3–4; and YJS, *4,* 43–44, 49

First fruits a portion of the first ripe fruits brought by the owner of the field to the Temple in thanksgiving, and then consumed by the priests; see Num. 18:17, 18

Firstling the first-born male of cattle and sheep, brought by the owner to the Temple as a hallowed offering consumed by the priests; see Num. 18:17, 18

Four Kingdoms Babylonia, Media and Persia, Greece, and Rome, which kept Israel in subjection; cf. Dan. 7

Gemara that part of the Talmud which contains the comments of the Amoraim on the Mishnah

Habdalah the Benediction of "Separation," recited at the close of the Sabbath or holy day

Haftarah the selection from the Prophets read in the synagogue service after the lesson from the Pentateuch

Halakah (pl. *Halakot)* that part of Talmudic (and of later Rabbinic) literature which deals with legal matters; also a section of a chapter in the Mishnah

Hallel Psalms 113–18, as used for liturgical recitation

Hanukkah minor Jewish festival of eight days, beginning on the 25th day of Kislev, commemorating the rededication of the Temple by the Maccabees in 165 B.C.E.

Heave offering a portion of the produce (about two percent on the average) which was given to the priests, who alone were permitted to eat it; cf. Num. 18:8; Lev. 22:10; and Deut. 18:4

Heave offering of the tithe out of the tithe which he received, the Levite was obliged to give a tenth part to the priest; in other words, one-hundredth of the original produce harvested by the Israelite; cf. Num. 18:25–32

Heshvan *see* Months

Holy spirit the quickening of man's natural faculties by divine inspiration—a level of inspiration below that of prophecy, whereby a prophet receives divine communications in a supranatural manner; see Maimonides, *Guide* (ed. Pines [Chicago, 1973]), 2:45

Homer 11 bushels

Hours, Daylight *see* Day and night

Immersion pool must contain 40 *sĕ'ah* (approximately 60 gallons or 270 liters) of water, which may not be drawn, but must be taken directly from a river or spring, or must consist of rain water led straight into the bath (YJS, *8,* 509–10)

Iyar *see* Months

Jubilee year the year concluding a series of seven Sabbatical cycles comprising 49 years; cf. Lev. 25:8–16

Ḳab 4 pints

Ḳĕri the Masoretic instruction for reading, as opposed to the *kĕṯiḇ,* the traditional spelling of Biblical words

Kĕṯiḇ the traditional spelling of Biblical words, as opposed to the *Ḳĕri,* the Masoretic instruction for reading

Kiddush the ceremony of drinking wine after a blessing in the synagogue or home, by which the advent of the Sabbath or festivals is sanctified

Kislev *see* Months

Kor 11 bushels

Law, the *see* Bible

Levite (a) a descendant of the Tribe of Levi (see Num. 3:5ff.); (b) as contrasted to "priest" and "[lay] Israelite"

Loḡ a liquid measure said to be equal to the displacement of six eggs (cf. B.Er 83a)—1 pint

Lulab the palm branch carried with the festive cluster during the Festival of Sukkot—cf. Lev. 23:40; or, more generally, the cluster of palm branch, myrtle, and willow used with the ethrog on that festival

Mezuzah literally "doorpost" (Deut. 6:9); a piece of parchment bearing the verses Deut. 6:4–9, 11:13–21, enclosed in a cylinder and fastened to the right-hand doorpost

Midrash exposition or exegesis of Scripture

Mishnah (literally "teaching") the collection of legal decisions of the Sages of the first two centuries C.E. (the Tannaim), edited and arranged into six orders by Rabbi Judah I the Patriarch (ca. 200 C.E.); the Mishnah provides the text to which the Gemara is the commentary, the two together constituting the Talmud

Months the Hebrew names of the months are as follows: Nisan, Iyar, Sivan, Tammuz, Ab, Elul, Tishri, Heshvan (Marheshvan), Kislev, Tebet, Shebat, Adar; in an intercalated year a thirteenth month, called 2nd Adar, is added

Musaf (Additional Offering) special offering for the Sabbaths, New Moons, and festivals brought in addition to the regular daily offerings—cf. Num. 28:9–31; after the destruction of the Temple, replaced by the Additional Prayer

Nazirite one who vows to dedicate himself to the service of God; his vow implies (a) abstention from all products of the grapevine; (b) letting his hair grow; (c) avoidance of contact with a dead body (see Num. 6:2–8)

Nisan *see* Months

Noachide Commandments seven universal precepts held to be incumbent not only upon Israelites but also upon all the "sons of Noah," i.e., upon the whole human race; cf. Maimonides' Code XIV, V, ix, 1 (YJS, *3,* 230–31), and MTeh (YJS, *13, 2,* 417–18)

'Omer the sheaf of barley, also called the sheaf of waving, brought as an offering on the 16th day of Nisan; cf. Lev. 23:9–14

Oral Law unlike the written Torah which Moses received at Sinai, the Oral Law or Torah, its authoritative exposition, was never meant to be, but eventually was, committed to writing

Parasang a distance of 8,000 cubits, or 4 miles

Peace offering sacrifice betokening nearness and communion between God and man

Priestly watch the priests and Levites were divided into 24 guards or watches, each one of which was on duty for one week every half year; cf. 1 Chron. 24:4; Ta 4:2

Prophets *see* Bible

Purim the Feast of Lots, observed on the 14th day of Adar in commemoration of the salvation of the Jews in Persia; its full story is recorded in the Book of Esther

Rabbi literally "my master"; a term of respect used in direct address by a disciple to his teacher, and generally by the public to a scholar known for his learning. It was only much later that the term assumed its present meaning of the spiritual leader of a Jewish community.

Ram's horn *see* Shofar

Representatives of the family relatives designated to represent a groom or bride in negotiating betrothal or other matters pertaining to the well-being of either

Ritual bath *see* Immersion pool

Sabbath limit one may not walk on the Sabbath beyond the distance of 2,000 cubits from the city or place where one resides

Sages *see* Scribes

Sanhedrin council, high court; the Great Sanhedrin, the Supreme Court consisting of 71 members; a Small Sanhedrin, a high court consisting of 23 members

Sĕ'ah a peck and a half, or 12 quarts

Scribes or Sages; the post-Biblical scholars dating back to Ezra the Scribe (ca. 440 B.C.); the term, however, is loosely used to apply to the Rabbis of the subsequent period who preserved and transmitted the Oral Law

Scripture *see* Bible

Sheaf of barley *see* *'Omer*

Shebat *see* Months

Shekinah "the Presence" [of God], as a circumlocution when Scripture speaks of God's dwelling in a place, or removing from one, and the like

Shĕma' the name and the first word ("Hear, [O Israel]!") of a group of passages from Scripture (Deut. 6:4–9, 11:13–21; Num. 15:37–41), which must be recited daily in the morning and in the evening

Shofar ram's horn sounded on New Year's Day and on other occasions—cf. Num. 29:1; Lev. 25:9; the notes produced by it were the following: sustained note *(tĕḳi'ah),* tremolo *(tĕru'ah),* and broken note *(šĕḇarim)*

Sivan *see* Months

Sukkah the booth used in observance of the Festival of Sukkot

Talmud the two collections of Rabbinic law and lore comprising Mishnah and Gemara; one, the Palestinian, also known as Jerusalemite Talmud, redacted by the disciples of R. Johanan, ca. 300 C.E.; the other, the Babylonian, redacted by R. Ashi and Rabina, ca. 450 C.E.

Tammuz *see* Months

Tannaim authorities who are cited in the Mishnah and the Baraita and who flourished up to about the year 200 C.E.

Tebet *see* Months

Tĕfillah the name of one of the principal prayers in the daily services, consisting on weekdays of 19 (originally 18) benedictions. Hence called also "Eighteen Benedictions" *(Šĕmoneh 'eśreh),* and, since it is usually recited while standing, *'Ămiḏah* ("Standing [Prayer]")

Tefillin (phylacteries) small leather cases, one worn on the arm and the other on the head during the recital of weekday prayers. Each case contains parchment strips upon which are written four passages from Scripture: Exod. 13:1–10, 11–16; Deut. 6:4–9, 11:13–21.

Tĕḳi'ah *see* Shofar

Tĕru'ah *see* Shofar

Tishri *see* Months

Tithes (ma'aśer) were of three kinds; the first tithe was given to the Levite in each of the first six years of the Sabbatical cycle; the second tithe was separated in the first, second, fourth, and fifth years of the cycle and was consumed by the owner in Jerusalem; the poor man's tithe was given to the poor in the third and sixth year of the cycle

Torah *see* Bible

Tosefta a collection of those legal decisions of the Tannaim which were not included in the Mishnah; redacted by R. Ḥiyya, disciple of Rabbi Judah I the Patriarch

Urim and Thummim the twelve precious stones set in the "breastplate of judgment," upon which were engraved the names of the Twelve Tribes of Israel (Exod. 28:15–30); the letters served as an oracle

Writings *see* Bible

PASSAGES CITED OR REFERRED TO

Scripture

GENESIS

1:1	ER 164; S 30
1:4	S 34
1:15	S 33
1:16	S 30
1:26	ER 154
1:31	ER 160
2:1	ER 161; S 21
2:7	EZ 173
2:8	ER 160
2:18	ER 51
3:18	ER 164
3:19	ER 164
3:21	ER 136
3:24	ER 3, 164
6:4	ER 81
6:11	EZ 190
6:18	ER 162
7:1	ER 81, 162; EZ 174
8:16	ER 162
8:20	ER 35
8:21	ER 152
10:11	S 45
11:1	ER 74, 158; EZ 190
11:4	ER 158
11:7	ER 158
11:8	ER 158
11:9	ER 158
11:31	ER 28
12:1	ER 138
12:5	ER 28
13:6	EZ 192
13:13	ER 74, 158
14:14	ER 28
14:15	ER 28
14:19	ER 29; S 20
14:20	S 46
14:21	ER 128
14:22	ER 128; S 45
14:23	ER 128, 131
14:24	ER 128, 131
15:1	ER 128
15:7	ER 27
15:8	ER 65; EZ 174
15:13	S 31
15:14	S 35
15:16	ER 45
17:13	S 40
18:1	ER 28
18:3	ER 59
18:8	ER 59
18:19	EZ 170
19:9	ER 158
21:12	ER 45
21:21	S 55
21:27	ER 45
22:1	ER 45
22:2	ER 45
22:10	ER 45
23:6	ER 28
23:49	S 31
24:1	ER 29
24:20	ER 54
24:34	EZ 192
24:58	ER 138
25:27	ER 29, 32, 132
25:31	S 26–27
26:3	S 35
26:5	ER 35
26:12	EZ 170
26:20	EZ 192
26:24	ER 129
26:30	EZ 192
27:40	S 31, 55
28:17	ER 129
30:27	ER 125
30:30	ER 125–26
32:11	EZ 170
33:5	S 27
33:12	S 27
33:13	S 27
33:16	S 55
35:4	ER 35, 131; EZ 180
35:5	EZ 180
35:9	ER 138
36:22	EZ 175
37:13	ER 131
37:26	ER 131
37:35	ER 29
38:8	ER 35
39:5	ER 113, 126

1 KINGS *(cont'd)*

18:39 ER 87
19:5 EZ 186
19:8 EZ 186
19:9 EZ 186
19:10 EZ 186
19:11 EZ 186
19:12 EZ 186
19:14 EZ 186
19:15 ER 22, 23; EZ 186
19:16 ER 22, 23; EZ 186
19:17 ER 22, 23
19:18 ER 22, 23
19:19 ER 22, 23
19:20 ER 23
19:21 ER 23
20:13 ER 49
20:14 ER 49
20:15 ER 49
20:29 ER 89
21:25 ER 49
22:45 EZ 177

2 KINGS

2:11 ER 23
3:4 ER 49–50
3:27 ER 50
4:42 EZ 173
6:21 ER 39
6:22 ER 39
10:30 EZ 184
11:1 EZ 177
11:2 EZ 177
14:25 ER 88; EZ 184
14:26 ER 88; EZ 184
14:27 ER 88; EZ 184
17:1 EZ 188
17:2 EZ 188
17:3 EZ 188
17:6 EZ 188
18:35 ER 74, 158; EZ 191
19:3 ER 158
19:24 ER 45
19:35 ER 44, 88; EZ 192
19:37 ER 45
20:4 ER 47
20:5 ER 47
20:8 ER 47
20:9 ER 47
20:10 ER 47
20:11 ER 47
20:17 ER 47
25:9 ER 148

ISAIAH

1:18 S 37, 38
2:11 S 31
2:17 S 31
2:19 ER 163
3:10 ER 157; S 34
3:11 ER 157
4:3 ER 164
5:7 ER 43
5:14 ER 108; S 32
5:16 EZ 170
5:25 ER 65
6:3 ER 34, 84; EZ 193, 194
6:8 ER 82
6:9 ER 82
6:11 ER 83
7:10 EZ 188
7:11 EZ 188
7:12 EZ 188
7:13 EZ 188
7:14 EZ 188
8:15 EZ 187
9:16 ER 64
9:17 ER 111
9:19 ER 61
9:20 ER 61
10:2 ER 53
10:14 ER 44
11:9 ER 70
12:1 EZ 192
12:2 EZ 192
12:3 ER 54
13:9 ER 111
14:9 ER 108
14:13 ER 74, 158
14:14 EZ 192
14:15 ER 74, 158
14:16 ER 158
14:19 ER 24; S 46
18:7 ER 91
19:1 ER 40
19:9 EZ 196
19:11 ER 40
19:14 ER 40
19:25 EZ 194
21:11 ER 155
21:12 ER 155, 156
21:13 ER 156
21:14 ER 156
22:1 ER 154
22:2 ER 154
22:3 ER 154

ISAIAH *(cont'd)*

JEREMIAH

JEREMIAH *(cont'd)*

7:21	ER 38
8:14	ER 154
8:23	ER 87
9:6	ER 100
9:11	ER 96; EZ 168
9:12	ER 96; EZ 168
9:17	ER 154
9:22	S 42, 44
10:2	S 10
10:10	ER 39
10:20	ER 148, 149
11:16	ER 93
12:5	EZ 188
12:8	ER 57
13:16	ER 12
13:17	ER 115, 154
14:21	ER 150
16:14	EZ 196
17:7	ER 91
17:8	ER 91, 93
17:10	EZ 176
17:12	ER 160; S 31
21:12	ER 53
22:10	ER 18
23:7	EZ 196
23:8	EZ 196
23:28	ER 59
23:29	ER 23
29:23	ER 132
31:2	ER 71
31:3	ER 31
31:6	ER 96
31:7	ER 69–70, 70
31:10	ER 67
31:11	ER 97
31:12	ER 131
31:13	ER 97
31:14	ER 148
31:15	ER 148
31:18	ER 37
31:32	ER 105
31:35	ER 52
31:36	ER 52
32:19	ER 40, 44
33:25	ER 105; S 31, 40
39:1	ER 148
39:2	ER 148
39:3	ER 148
47:2	ER 114
48:10	ER 79
49:15	ER 126
49:16	ER 126
50:12	ER 5
51:34	ER 131
51:44	S 30
52:13	ER 148

EZEKIEL

1:1	ER 34
1:2	ER 34
1:3	ER 34
1:4	ER 34
1:5	ER 34
1:8	S 37
1:22	ER 161
1:26	ER 160
2:1	ER 34
3:2	ER 34
3:12	ER 34, 84, 156, 163; EZ 193
5:10	ER 131
8:10	ER 24
8:12	ER 108
10:14	ER 161
16:6	ER 138
16:8	ER 138, 139
18:6	ER 76
18:7	ER 76
18:8	ER 76
18:9	ER 76
18:18	ER 75
18:23	EZ 189
19:20	ER 112
20:14	ER 34
20:32	ER 159
20:38	EZ 194
21:22	ER 150, 153
21:30	ER 28
22:2	ER 23
23:2	ER 49
23:4	ER 49
33:7	ER 56
33:8	ER 56
33:9	ER 56
33:11	EZ 189
33:32	ER 23
35:6	ER 126
35:10	ER 126
36:25	ER 105
36:26	ER 19
36:38	S 53
37:1	ER 24
37:2	ER 24
37:4	ER 24
37:9	ER 24

PSALMS *(cont'd)*

AUTHORITIES CITED OR REFERRED TO

The Rabbis and scholars whose comments and activities are occasionally mentioned or referred to in *Tanna dĕḇe Eliyyahu* are known as Tannaim. The Tannaitic period, from the death of Hillel and Shammai to that of R. Judah I the Patriarch, corresponds approximately to the first two centuries of the Common Era. The Tannaim quoted or referred to in *Tanna dĕḇe Eliyyahu* are identified in this index by the letter T and the numbers 1 through 5, corresponding to the five generations of Tannaim:

First Generation (T1)—ca. 10–ca. 80 C.E.
Second Generation (T2)—ca. 80–ca. 120 C.E.
Third Generation (T3)—ca.120–ca. 140 C.E.
Fourth Generation (T4)—ca. 140–ca. 165 C.E.
Fifth Generation (T5)—ca. 165–ca. 200 C.E.

Only Palestinian Amoraim—and they infrequently—are mentioned in *Tanna dĕḇe Eliyyahu.* The period during which Amoraim flourished ran approximately from the third century C.E. through the fourth. The Amoraim are designated by the letter P (Palestinian) and the numbers 1 through 5 as follows:

First Generation (1)—approximately the first half of the third century C.E.

Second Generation (2)—approximately the second half of the third century C.E. (e.g., Johanan b. Nappaḥa, d. 279; Simeon b. Laḳish, d. 275)

Third Generation (3)—approximately the first half of the fourth century C.E.

Fourth Generation (4)—approximately the third quarter of the fourth century C.E.

Fifth Generation (5)—approximately the fourth quarter of the fourth century C.E.

When the dating of a Tanna or an Amora is uncertain, the letter T or P is followed by a question mark.

The letter "b" occurring in a Rabbi's name stands for *ben* or *bar,* meaning "son of."

Authorities cited

Admon (pre-Tannaitic), ER 122
R. 'Aḳiḇa (T3), ER 41, 61, 133; EZ 168, 169; S 3, 13, 39–40
Ben He-He (pre-Tannaitic), S 20
R. Bana'ah (P1), S 56
R. Dosa b. Orkinas (Horkinas) (T2), EZ 168, 169
R. Eleazar (T4), S 7
R. Eleazar b. Azariah (T2), EZ 168; S 21 (tr.)
R. Eleazar b. Pĕraṭa (T3), S 11
R. Eleazar b. Mathia (T3), ER 109
R. Eleazar the Modiite (T3), ER 41; S 57
R. Eliezer (T4?), S 10, 14, 15, 26, 28, 30, 33, 37, 40, 42, 45, 52, 56
R. Eliezer the elder (T2), ER 43, 151
R. Eliezer b. Jacob (T4), S 3, 4, 8, 12, 37
R. Eliezer (son of R. Jose the Galilean) (T4), S 47
Rabban Gamaliel (pre-Tannaitic), ER 72, 122
R. Ḥanina b. 'Aḳašya (T4), S 21
R. Ḥanina [b. Dosa?] (T1), S 21
Hillel, School of (T1), EZ 169

SUBJECTS AND NAMES*

*In this index all note numbers refer to the notes in this translation.

Adversity, why righteous afflicted with, EZ 181
Agag: feared his seed would perish from world, ER 117, 125; embodiment of wickedness, ER 117, n. 17
Ahab: no man as rich as, ER 49; doubted that death of Hiel's sons resulted from Joshua's curse, EZ 185; in days of, Moses' threat that rain would cease as a result of idolatry remained unfulfilled, EZ 185; famine in days of, EZ 185; charged Obadiah with not being as righteous as he appeared to be, ER 125; hostages held by, became "God-fearers," ER 49; hostages fought against Aram, and left after death of, ER 49–50; has no portion in the world-to-come, ER 16
Ahasuerus, banquets of, attended by Jews in Persia, who shared attendant immorality, ER 4, n. 17
Ahaz: Torah's words were like living teachers in days of, EZ 187; not condemned until he filled world with transgressions, ER 11; began with war against Torah but intended to wage war against God, EZ 188; has no portion in the world-to-come, ER 16
Ahithophel: taught only two things to David, who called him master, S 18; was slanderer, ER 107; pride of, was hurt when he was passed over for office by David, ER 157; rooted out because of pride, ER 157; instructions of, to household, ER 157
Ai, half of Sanhedrin fell at, ER 103
'Aḳiḇa, R., EZ 168; as child, poor in misdeeds, ER 160; was one of Bar Kokhba's strongest supporters, ER 154, n. 35; with death of, Israel's long night of exile set in, ER 154
'Alef, letter, sign of blessing, also sign of curse, ER 164
Alexandria: seized by Hadrian, ER 151; massacre of Jews in, ER 151; Jewish quarter of, devastated in days of Alexander Tiberius, ER 151, n. 22
Altar in Jerusalem, built in place whence Adam's dust was taken, EZ 174
And, meaning of use of, at beginning of regulations concerning certain offerings, ER 38
Angel: ate Gideon's food, ER 60; did not eat Manoah's food, ER 60; helps righteous man to greater righteousness, and wicked man to greater wickedness, EZ 176
Angel of death: existence of, cause for joy, ER 81; sight of, sapped David's strength, ER 39
Angels: at flood's end protested repopulation of world, ER 162; made themselves enjoy Abraham's meal, ER 59; while visiting Abraham, violated the law by mixing milk and meat, ER 100, n. 73; caused God to test Abraham's loyalty with command to bind Isaac, ER 45; lifted children of Israelites thrown by Egyptians into river, ER 43; were sarcastic about Israel's not changing names or language, ER 85; God's purpose in sending of, at giving of Torah, ER 119; remonstrated at giving of Torah, ER 21; wanted Torah given to them, ER 154, n. 33; set crowns upon Israel at giving of Torah, EZ 179; of destruction, took away Israel's crowns after making of golden calf, EZ 179; at Jerusalem's exile God comforted by, EZ 189; will be weeping inwardly in time-to-come, ER 20; disparagement of, S 49; ministering, number of, ER 32, 34; hallow God's name daily, ER 163, 193; radiance of, does not come from within them, EZ 193; not allowed to sing above until Israel sing below, S 47; why not allowed to utter song until Israel below utter theirs, S 56
Anger, God's slowness to, discussed by God and Moses, ER 144
Animal, when slaughtered, must have gullet and windpipe severed, ER 72
Animals, why not granted speech, EZ 191, n. 4

then set before them at Mount Sinai laws concerning injury and exercise of justice, ER 122; provided Israel with Sabbath in order to put out of His mind their offenses against Him, ER 4; hinted to Moses that he intercede in Israel's behalf, ER 17; disclosed to Moses order of prayers for forgiveness, S 41; is forbearing toward Israel from sixth of Sivan to Day of Atonement, EZ 178; asked mountains to sing on Day of Atonement, ER 4; derives great joy from Day of Atonement, ER 4; His revelation to Balaam was experience in uncleanness, ER 142; waited for Elijah for three hours to come and entreat mercy for Israel, EZ 186

(2) *Relationship to Israel at exile and after:* laments in destroyed Temple, ER 149; after Temple's destruction never dwelt in House on high, S 36; weeps for Israel publicly and privately, ER 87; why He weeps secretly, ER 154; chooses not to remember Israelites' iniquities, ER 4; loves Israel everlastingly, ER 8, 31; loves Israel unalteringly, ER 51; king over Israel for ever, ER 159; His holiness, Sabbath's, and Israel's are alike, ER 133; Himself requites nations who distress Israel, S 30; grieves when His children's hunger for Torah is unsatisfied, ER 115

(3) *God and Torah:* His contentment comes only from those who are busy with Torah, ER 4; sits close to disciple of the wise during study, ER 89; studies Torah, imposes judgment, and bestows mercy daily, ER 62, 84, 90, 130, 162; will discourse on Halakot and David will recite 'Aggadah, at feast in Garden of Eden, S 33

(4) *God, mercy of:* evidences of His mercy at Adam's expulsion, ER 164; chooses to see good and not evil, ER 3; had mankind's successive misdeeds which He foresaw pass out of His mind, ER 3; spreads His hands toward those who resolve upon repentance, S 37; physical expressions of His affection, ER 21, 22; out of compassion acts humbly like shepherd, EZ 195; judges in mercy, EZ 194; sides with weak, ER 67; shows no partiality between heathen and Israelites, ER 65; is source of sustenance, ER 70; seeks to make peace, ER 156; makes peace among ministering angels, ER 84; is afflicted when even one person is afflicted, ER 89; His blessing expressed with entire alphabet, His curses with only eight letters, ER 96; welcomes righteous entering eternal world, ER 11; did not create stuff of falsehood or iniquity, EZ 175; has little time for laughter, ER 61; His laughter rare and bittersweet, ER 62; man should imitate His compassion, ER 135, 143–44

(5) *God's powers and manifestations:* is rock of both worlds, ER 91; varieties of His providence, ER 97; His sundry powers as seen in man's life, EZ 199; questioning Him, grave offense, EZ 189; to be praised in midst of grief, ER 97

God-fearers: Ahab's heathen hostages became, ER 49; fought against Aram but left after Ahab's death, ER 49–50

Gog: and allies, sought to exterminate Israel, ER 5; day of, ER 5; punishment of, ER 15; gathered on Israel's mountains for judgment, ER 24; why day of vengeance against, was put off, ER 5

Golden calf: after making of, God replaced ox with cherub in His chariot, ER 161; after, writing on Tables of Commandments vanished, ER 117; after, Israel was doomed to study Torah in distress and banishment, ER 117; Israel after, came to have men and women with discharge and lepers, ER 86 n. 33; made by "mixed multitude," ER 13, n. 66

Good deeds, done without display, cause God to walk with doer, ER 143

Good life, not to be spurned, ER 69

Good wife, is term for Torah, ER 92

Gossip about failings of disciples of wise, equivalent to gossip about God, ER 16
Government, integrity and rational judgment of, in Deborah's time, ER 53
Grace after Meals: meaning of formula of blessing in, ER 141, n. 10; three blessings in, EZ 172
Gratitude for even a salad leaf for dipping should be expressed, ER 89
Great Assembly, definition of, ER 138, n. 16
Greece, God put up with, in reward for Japheth's delicacy, ER 114
Guilt offering, appeases conscience of scrupulously pious, ER 38, n. 78

Hadrian: seized Miriam and her seven sons, ER 151; seized Alexandria, ER 151
Haggai, three rulings of, EZ 169
Ḥallah (dough offering due to priest), ER 97
Hallelujah (response to reader), ER 65
Hallowing name of God, ER 140
Hamor, as convert, ER 146
Hands, are harsh masters, S 1
Harp, David's, north wind blew through strings of, ER 96
Heathen: may have holy spirit suffuse him, ER 48; one should stay away from, ER 113; Jew should not enter into partnership with, ER 45; ritual uncleanness of, S 7, n. 7; restricted with regard to offerings, ER 34; unprovided libations accompanying burnt offerings of, to be purchased out of public funds, ER 35; condemned for mere thought of wicked deed, ER 126. *See also* Gentiles
Heave offering, as fodder for animals, ER 66
Heaven: marriage for the sake of, S 9; reward for marriage for, EZ 177
Heaven and earth: made simultaneously, ER 160; one of five masterpieces in world, ER 187, S 20
Heavens: one visible, six invisible, EZ 188; fit to declare God's glory because they bring about growth of crops, overlook mankind, stars in them are arranged with beauty, speed and silence of sun inspire awe, behold variety of creatures, ER 9–10; their course in time of Moses and Joshua changed to deliver Israel, ER 10; their song deemed by God less desirable than song of Torah, ER 10; their unswerving obedience less desired by God than Israel's merely sporadic obedience, ER 10
Heifers, song of, in praise of Ark, ER 58
Hezekiah and his generation: deliverances of, are of a kind destined for the end of time, ER 88; punished for sitting at table with heathen, ER 47; presumption of, toward God, ER 47; pride of, in matters of Torah, ER 47; given Manasseh in requital, ER 47
Hiel, Ahab doubted that death of his sons resulted from Joshua's curse, EZ 185
High Priest, his daily meal offering was offered out of public funds, ER 35
Holiness, of God, Sabbath, and Israel is alike, ER 133
Holy spirit, rests upon man who has studied entire Lore, ER 8; may suffuse any man or woman in keeping with deeds, ER 48
Horeb, Moses entreated God's mercy at, EZ 186
Horn, sounding of, solely for good news, S 38
Horses of fire, is term for Oral Law, ER 23
Hosea, oldest of four prophets in days of Uzziah, EZ 186; three decrees against Israel issued at birth of three children of, EZ 187
Hoshea: abolished border posts against Jerusalem, EZ 188; should have compelled Israel to go up to Jerusalem, EZ 188

Hospitality, false prophet's, caused Presence to rest on him, ER 61
House on high, God never dwelt in, after Temple's destruction, S 36
Householders, obliged to provide for disciples of wise, ER 139
Humiliation: better to dissemble than to subject another person to, ER 106; willingness to suffer, leads to understanding Torah, ER 64
Humility, ER 103, EZ 197; more desirable than offerings, ER 104; reward of, ER 78
Hushim, cut off Esau's head, S 53
Hypocrisy, ER 106

Idolatry: at Dan, sapped Abraham's strength, ER 28; called "fecal," ER 81; pursued by Israel during 390 of First Temple's 410 years, EZ 185
Imitation, of God's compassion, ER 135, 143–44
Impulse to evil: surrenders to Israel when Israel is occupied with Torah, EZ 167; existence of, cause for joy, ER 81; conquest of, sign of man's love for God, EZ 193; "king" stands for, ER 160; causes God's bittersweet laughter, ER 62; will be requited sevenfold, ER 20; will not exist in time-to-come, ER 81
Impulse to good, "child" stands for, ER 160
Infants, why born crippled, S 41
Iniquities: of Israel, put out of God's mind by Sabbath, ER 4; of Jews, God chooses not to remember, ER 4
Iniquity, God did not create stuff of, EZ 175
Insects, fourteen kinds of, during plague of gnats in Egypt, ER 41
Integrity, lack of, in disciple of wise, S 8
Intercession: deceased forebears delivered from Gehenna by blessings spoken by their children, S 23; by son's study of Torah in behalf of deceased father, EZ 194; by survivors' good deeds which bring forebears to favorable remembrance, ER 88
Intermarriage, ER 116
Intermarriages, no offspring left of, EZ 177
Isaac: thirty-seven at his binding, ER 138; willingness of, to sacrifice himself, EZ 174; binding of, brings to remembrance daily sacrifice, ER 36; exercise of charity by, EZ 170; not subject to sorrow or to Impulse to evil, ER 14; fear of God of, ER 129
Isaiah: reprimanded Hezekiah for effrontery, ER 47; prophesied consolations in Hezekiah's twenty-ninth year, ER 83; knew when not to pacify God, ER 83; prophesied with double portion of Divine Power, ER 82, n. 16; joyfully took upon himself God's decrees, ER 82
Ishmael: rewarded for respect shown to Abraham, ER 65; children of, refused Torah because it prohibited stealing, S 55
Ishmael, R.: slaying of, ER 153; why slain, ER 153
Israel: work of creation done for sake of, S 40; greater than ministering angels because of Torah, ER 116; pace of, in good deeds, compared to swift steeds, EZ 188; holiness of, like that of God and Sabbath ER 133; God provided with Sabbath to put out of His mind their iniquities against Him, ER 4; iniquities of, God chooses not to remember, ER 4; not held accountable until <evil> deed [resulting from evil thought] has actually been committed by, ER 43; virtuous and wicked alike receive God's mercies, ER 89; not required to pay penalty without first being brought to judgment, ER 55; chastened with blows which must be thought of as light, ER 113; chastised only for their own benefit, EZ 191; poverty becomes them, EZ 176; no condition more desirable for, than poverty, EZ 181; merits

of, ER 110, 112; look forward to uttering God's praise, S 56; can never be like nations, ER 159; are one of God's five masterpieces, EZ 187, S 20; lowliest in, who pours out his heart, more acceptable to God than mighty Ahab, ER 98; are God's permanent possession, ER 127; have God's everlasting love, ER 31; God's love for, unaltering, ER 51; are at center of God's concern, ER 25; why God has concern for, ER 9; are heave offering of all the peoples of the world, EZ 173; called large winepress, ER 26; called God's vineyard, ER 43; likened to pebble in sieve, ER 25; called prince or ruler of divine beings, ER 130, n. 6; to be put before Torah, ER 71; learning among, refutation of angels' protest against making man, ER 163; when occupied with Torah, cause Impulse to evil to surrender, EZ 167; four companies of, ER 105

virginity before wedding chamber usual in, ER 116; in Egypt, defiled themselves with idolatry, ER 34, n. 15; in Egypt, did not change their names or language, ER 85, 123; in Egypt, did not learn Egyptian; in Egypt, circumcised sons, ER 123; in Egypt, had sons wed though these would be taken for heavy labor, ER 123; united in Egypt, ER 123, 124; set free from Egypt as reward for conduct of Matriarchs, ER 138; each of them went out of Egypt with but one loaf baked on coals, ER 85; confidence of, first won by God through gifts, then laws concerning injury and exercise of justice set before them, ER 120, 122; of one heart at Mount Sinai, ER 122; but for acceptance of Torah, would have perished, ER 85; after acceptance of Torah, became sound in body, ER 86 n. 33; at giving of Torah angels set crowns upon, EZ 179; crowns forfeited after making of calf, EZ 179; after golden calf, came to have men and women afflicted with discharge and lepers, ER 86 n. 33; readily accepted regulations concerning discharge from private parts, ER 86; in wilderness, were under ban for thirty-eight years, ER 146, n. 18; in wilderness, repented in privacy, ER 86; after golden calf, doomed to study Torah in distress and banishment, ER 117; in Eli's time, not genuine in concern for Ark, ER 57; brought to grief by their own people, ER 143; rejected Prophets, EZ 185; regarded their idols as lovers rivaling God, ER 52; going into exile, asked by God not to walk in silence but to weep, ER 155; dispersion of, sign of God's mercy to, ER 54; pursued by Gog and allies with intent to exterminate them ER 5; plea of, to God for rescue, S 56; foes of, will be requited sevenfold, ER 20; growth to great number brings redemption to, EZ 197; first rejected God's cup of consolation on Judgment Day, S 36

Israel, house of, banished because of brazenness, ER 159

Israel, Land of: God stood and created all lands in, EZ 173; six kinds of terrain of, ER 11, n. 38; greatest understanding of Torah in, ER 11; destroyed only because of wilful neglect [of study] of Torah, EZ 168; at some time in days of Messiah all those who rise to life again will go to, ER 164

Israelite, in Egypt, wed ten wives, ER 43

Israelites: God made His voice vibrate to shatter walls of Egyptian edifices in order to enable escape of those immured alive therein, ER 44; not under suspicion of sodomy or bestiality, ER 101, n. 87

Issachar, princely in knowledge of Torah, ER 60, n. 8

Ithamar, descendants of: High Priests for seventy-two years, ER 57; giving of High Priesthood to, instead of to Phinehas, brought about greater abuse, EZ 190

Jabez: unassuming but conscientious teacher of people of Israel, ER 30; not subject to sorrow or to impulse to evil, ER 14; other name for Othniel, ER 14, n. 38

Jabneh: city of Sages and Rabbis, EZ 168; vineyard of, S 14
Jacob: in womb, offered this world to Esau and asked for world-to-come for himself, S 26; fear of God of, ER 129; merits of, ER 29; exercise of charity by, EZ 170; always frequented house of study, ER 29; begetter of the Fathers of Twelve Tribes, ER 29; feelings of guilt of, ER 29; not subject to sorrow or to impulse to evil, ER 14; no miracle performed for, ER 32; preference of, for Joseph, led to parting from him for twenty-two years, ER 65; reluctance of, to go to Egypt, S 50; sons of, married sisters, S 50
Jael: why deliverance came to Israel through, ER 51; did will of her husband, ER 59
Japheth, delicacy of, reason for God's putting up with Greece, ER 114
Jehoiakim, power of, removed, ER 85
Jehoshaphat: glory and strength of, ER 14; innocent of wrongdoing, ER 77; righteous judges appointed by, ER 14, n. 15; wed his son Joram to Ahab's daughter for social status, EZ 177
Jehoshaphat, valley of, place where Israel will gather on Judgment Day in days of Messiah, S 34
Jehu, God-fearing but became corrupt, EZ 184
Jephthah: pride of, ER 55; should have gone to Phinehas to have himself released from his vow, ER 55; why 42,000 slain during days of, ER 55
Jeremiah: God made ineffective curses of Israel by, EZ 188; concealed Tabernacle and vessels, ER 129, n. 8
Jeroboam son of Joash: accorded honor to Prophets, EZ 184; entire promised Land of Israel given to, ER 88, EZ 184; refused to accept slander of prophet Amos, ER 88
Jeroboam son of Nebat: not condemned until he filled world with transgressions, ER 11; has no portion in the world-to-come, ER 16; spoke properly to Rehoboam, ER 125
Jerusalem: altar in, built in place whence Adam's dust was taken, EZ 173; great academy of, ER 49, 51, 80; men of, cautious concerning company at banquet and co-signer of matrimonial document, ER 147; Hoshea abolished border posts against, EZ 188; destroyed because of wilful neglect of Torah, ER 96
Jesting, grievous consequences of, ER 61, 64
Jethro: one of Egyptian magicians, S 53; why he gave daughter to Moses, S 53; exacted oath from Moses to stay, ER 83; began with shrewdness and ended as true convert, ER 30; transformation of, from idolater into God-fearing man told in seven names of, ER 14, n. 13; not subject to sorrow or to impulse to evil, ER 14; academies of learning never without descendants of, ER 30
Jew: three identifying signs of, ER 84; not to sit at table with heathen, ER 47, 48; not to enter into partnership with heathen, ER 45; watch over, by angels or by God, depends on devotion to study of Torah by, ER 155
Jews: ten classes of different ancestries, ER 100; only ones willing to suffer anguish for Torah and commandments, EZ 173; who devour their own people, ER 133–34
Jezebel, said to Ahab, "Learn idolatry," ER 49
Joash, claim of, to throne, established when crown fit his head, ER 90, n. 5
Jochebed, wed Amram with great display, ER 157, n. 6
Johanan, R., his words spoken at his death, S 43
Johanan ben Zakkai, Rabban, ER 53; rejoiced and made others rejoice in Halakah, ER 136
Jonah, said to have been son of widow of Zarephath, was also incarnation of Messiah son of Joseph, ER 98, n. 59

Leprosy: brought on only because of men's sins, EZ 175; kinds and colors total 72, numerical value of *ḥsd,* "mercy," ER 25, n. 56; of garments and in walls of house, reasons for, ER 77; sign of mercy for Israel, ER 25
Libations, not accompanying burnt offerings of heathen, to be purchased out of public funds, ER 35
Lie, compounding of, ER 76
Light, created on first day, used for three days before creation of luminaries, then hid, will be used again by righteous in time-to-come, S 33–34
Litigant, testimony of one, not to be heard in other's absence, ER 146
Love: which depends on material cause, ER 141; God's, for Israel, is everlasting, ER 31
Love of God, how different from awe of, ER 140
Lust, satisfaction of, as motive for marriage, EZ 177, S 9
Luz, city where death is not, S 14

Maiden, whose father was very friendly with heathen, ER 116
Maidservant, taken to wife then sent away, must continue to be maintained, ER 121
Male member, is harsh master, S 1
Man: set by God to rule world, ER 21; though fashioned in mold of Adam, is never like his fellow, ER 10; inferiority of, to animal, S 42; superior to animals through reverence of God, EZ 193; why God requires service of, EZ 193; ten harsh masters of, S 1; qualities in, which lead to being treasured by God, S 4; should be like ox to yoke, like ass to burden, and like cattle that plows in furrow, in occupying himself with words of Torah, EZ 167; who shares trouble of community, will live to see community's deliverance, EZ 167; should be resourceful in proving fear of God, EZ 167; conduct of, determines his lot in life, ER 115, 164; who studies parts of Torah, is guarded by angels, who studies all of Torah and puts himself under guidance of Sages, is guarded by God Himself, ER 100
Manasseh: end of generation of, began third era in creation, which ended with building of Second Temple, ER 160; given to Hezekiah in requital, ER 47; as king, made image with four faces, EZ 188; left no idol in whole world which he did not worship, EZ 189; not slain because righteous were to issue from, EZ 189; boiled in copper kettle, EZ 188; rebuked for idolatry by prophet, ER 163; not condemned until he filled world with transgressions, ER 11; scorned using his extraordinary powers in love of God, ER 111; has no portion in the world-to-come, ER 16
Mankind: misdeeds of, God foresaw but had pass out of His mind, ER 3; preserved because of reptiles, ER 6; distinction of, ER 86; Torah is for all of, ER 11
Manna: reward for morsel of bread Abraham gave to angels, ER 60; completely absorbed by body, allowed Israel to give all their time to Torah, ER 124, n. 22; differences in tastes of, ER 60; after ceasing of, study of Torah ceased, ER 102
Manoah, totally unlettered in Torah, ER 60
Marriage, for money, lust, status, Heaven, EZ 177, S 9
Masterpieces, God's, five in all: Torah, heaven, Abraham, Israel, Temple, EZ 187, S 20
Matriarchs: reward for conduct of, set Israel free from Egypt, ER 138; why children long withheld from, ER 99
Meal offering: acceptability of, ER 38; baked on griddle, made in stewing pan, significance of, ER 37

Media, God put up with, in reward of Cyrus' weeping, ER 114, 118
Meir, R., greater than his colleagues, ER 36, n. 55
Men, unlettered in Torah: who live by its precepts, ER 138; and immoral, harbor hatred for disciples of wise greater than hatred [heathen] nations harbor for Israel, S 5
Menstruant: spouse may not come near, for seven days after discharge of blood ceases, ER 76; vessels touched by, may not be touched, ER 76; sexual relations with, graver offense than sexual relations with man who has discharge from member, ER 75
Menstruation: sexual relations forbidden during, so that husband's enforced abstinence will make him yearn more for his wife, ER 79; penalty for sexual relations during, ER 79
Mercies, God's, are upon Israel's virtuous and wicked alike, ER 89
Mercy: God's attributes of, are eleven, ER 65; in God's judgment, EZ 194
Merodach-baladan: accorded honor to God, ER 125; deference to God of, reason for God putting up with Nebuchadnezzar, ER 115; four kings descended from him in reward for deference to God, EZ 188, n. 16
Mesha, king of Moab, ER 50
Messiah: called craftsman, ER 96, n. 52; reckoning of year of coming of, linked with anticipated fall of Rome, S 11, n. 43; seven-year period of afflictions preceding coming of, S 11; will come in generation whose leaders will be dog-faced brutes, S 11; signs of coming of, during seven years preceding, S 12; days of, will constitute fifth era of creation, ER 160; reign of, will last two thousand years, ER 6; more than seven hundred years of era of, passed because of sins, ER 7; at some time in days of, all those who rise to life again will go to Land of Israel and never again return to dust, ER 164; character of days of, ER 19; double portion of Torah in days of, EZ 196; nations will enrich Israel in days of, ER 113; nations that have not afflicted Israel will be Israel's farmers and vintagers in days of, ER 121; life in days of, foreshadowed in sundry experiences in this world, ER 14
Messiah, son of Joseph, is son of widow of Zarephath, ER 98
Mĕturgĕman, official who spoke clearly what head of academy whispered to him, S 9, n. 35
Midwife, who inadvertently slew mother or child, penalty for, ER 122
Minyan: benefits of, ER 95; in Torah study, EZ 197; importance of saying Amen in, ER 52
Miriam, daughter of Tanhum: seven sons of, seized by Hadrian, ER 151; age of youngest child of, ER 153
Miriam, well of, travels Saturday night throughout world, S 3, n. 9
Mishnah: Sinaitic origin of, EZ 171; compared to flax out of which fine linen cloth is to be produced, EZ 172; compared to wheat out of which fine flour is to be produced, EZ 172; means double reward in this world and world-to-come, EZ 172
Mixed multitude, had gluttonous craving for meat, ER 60 and n. 15
Money: kinds of earned, S 9; marriage for, S 9; penalty for marriage for, EZ 177
Moon, eclipse of, S 10, 11
Mordecai, acted forgivingly toward Esther, ER 4
Moses: father of wisdom and of Prophets, ER 85; qualities of, ER 83; humility of, ER 33; agonized over profanation of God's and Israel's glory, ER 17; why his hand became leprous, S 54; descendants of, denied royalty, ER 90; returned to Jethro to be released from vow, ER 83, n. 2; spurned comfort when Israel were in distress, EZ 198; made sun stand still on three

occasions, ER 10, n. 30; reluctant to welcome Jethro, ER 30; told untruth to save Israel, ER 17 and n. 14; resistance of, to sending of spies, ER 144; instructions of, to spies, ER 144; and Aaron pursued by spies with evil intent, ER 145; instructed by God in order of prayers for forgiveness, S 41; surpassed all others in interceding in Israel's behalf, ER 33; why credited with writing of Torah, ER 33; God turned over secret of His name to, S 55; set out to make peace, ER 106; meaning of God's communications with, during thirty-eight years' ban, ER 146, n. 18; exercise of charity by, EZ 170; in striking rock made it appear that he, not God, forced rock to give forth water, ER 65; composed Ps. 90 at time of sin in regard to waters of Meribah, ER 65; threat of, that as result of idolatry rain would cease, unfulfilled in days of Ahab, EZ 185; plea of, for prolonged life, S 44; radiance of face of, upon entering into his eternal abode, ER 18
Mother, term for Torah, ER 22
Mountains, asked by God to sing on Day of Atonement, ER 4
Mourning, not to exceed measure prescribed by Sages, ER 18
Mouth, is harsh master, S 1

Nabal: earned death by want of charity, EZ 170; given ten days to repent of churlishness, ER 109
Naphtali: ministered to our father Jacob, ER 51; fetched deed to Cave of Machpelah, S 52
Nathan, R., ER 149
Nations: not only refused Torah, but also spurned Noahide laws, ER 5, n. 36, S 55; admonished by seven Prophets, ER 35, EZ 192; wanted prophet like Moses and were given Balaam, EZ 191; disregarded warning of witnesses who came to them, EZ 192; seek to exterminate Israel, ER 25; ridiculed Israel in regard to possession of Torah, ER 21; will go up to Jerusalem on Sukkot in time-to-come, bringing with them Israel, ER 81; held accountable for [evil] thought <as though> it had in fact been carried out, ER 43; that have not afflicted Israel, will be Israel's farmers and vintagers in days of Messiah, ER 121; why permitted such joy in this world, EZ 174
Nebuchadnezzar, ER 114; short of stature, ER 158; God put up with, in reward of Merodach's deference to God, ER 115; at first feared he would have to reckon with God, whose city he set out to capture, ER 5; why he had Israel tracked down even at night, ER 150; charged Jews with being threat to land, ER 24, n. 46; set exiles up as princes; ER 24; took lives of dead in Valley of Dura, ER 24; ten angels attended punishment of, ER 24; rooted out because of brazenness, ER 74, 158
Needs, man's essential, S 3
Niece, marriage with, regarded by Zoroastrians as laudable, ER 78, n. 53
Nimrod, confronted Abraham, S 48; condemned Abraham to be burned, ER 27
Night, angel who came to help Abraham during war with kings, ER 28
Nine hundred and seventy-four generations that were to have been created: swept away in order to give Torah to twenty-sixth generation from Adam, ER 9; set aside by God to cleave to Israel, ER 130; God sat and pondered, analyzed, tested, and refined all the words of Torah before the world was to be created, ER 130, EZ 189
Ninth of Ab, weeping of, began when Israel without reason wept at spies' report, ER 145
'nky (acronym), ER 130
Noah: upbraided multitudes for 120 years, EZ 174; sustained all his forebears

and forewarned multitudes of flood to come, ER 80; refrained from marital intercourse in ark, ER 162; began, and Manasseh ended, second era of creation, ER 160
Nob, death of city came about because Jonathan denied David two loaves of bread, ER 60
Non-Jew, cheating of, prohibited, ER 74
Norms, for interpreting Scripture, EZ 172

Oath, false, severe penalty for, ER 132
Obadiah, prophet: was Edomite proselyte, ER 125, n. 2; charged by Ahab with not being as righteous as he appeared, ER 125
Occupations, deemed unworthy, S 9
'Ofannim, ER 160, 161
Offenses, should be allowed to pass out of mind, ER 3
Offerings: burnt (also thank offerings) accepted from Gentiles, ER 34, n. 28; restrictions on heathen with regard to, ER 34; require inward preparation, ER 36; meaning of *And* at beginning of regulations concerning certain, ER 38; by converts, opposed by some, ER 146; from hardened Jewish sinners, unacceptable, ER 35
Officer, of court, who inadvertently slew man he was lashing, penalty for, ER 122
Og, ejaculated semen for distance of forty parasangs, S 43
Omri, added large city in Israel; and was first king of Israel who had three descendants occupy throne, ER 49
'Onah, period of, day or night, ER 79, n. 57
One hundred and twenty days, between sixth of Sivan and Day of Atonement, Israel fasted and afflicted themselves, EZ 180
Oppressors, oppress because Israel fail to heed God's precepts, ER 25
Oral Law, called "horses of fire," ER 23
Othniel, Jabez' other name, ER 14, n. 12
Overeating, ER 64; as well as drinking and sleeping, impoverishes, EZ 196; grievous consequences of, ER 103; by Jews at feast of Ahasuerus, ER 4

Palti son of Laish, conquered lustful imaginings, S 51
Parables: daughter of poor family who went to draw water from well, ER 150; foot in well-fitting shoe, ER 84; before creation of Adam God was cheerful like man before he weds and has children, EZ 185; hind giving birth; ER 13; householder who had stubborn heifer, ER 12; householder who hired workmen and kept his eye on them, ER 5; Israel and Judah as two young children, ER 25; king who was angry at his wife, ER 88; king who became angry at his servant, ER 20; king who having become angry at his servant put him behind prison walls, ER 34; king who on certain occasion became angry at his son, EZ 113, 180; king building palace brings foremen, ER 160; king who built four palaces in four different provinces, S 26; king who commanded his son not to come to his feast, EZ 181; king who was about to entrust his son to care of wicked guardian, ER 150; king who found in numerous family only one person who did his will, EZ 174; king who examines his servants, ER 93; king who had lame, mute, and blind children and servants, ER 69, 71; king who had grove of trees near his house, ER 97; king who had solid ingot of gold, ER 9; king who had great palace with barred gate, ER 120; king who had servant he loved, ER 107; king with venerable servant in household, ER 71; king who had servants feasting at banquet, ER 11; king who had servants dwelling beyond iron

wall, EZ 193; king who had sons and servants whom he loved with utter devotion, EZ 194; king who had to go away to city far across the sea, ER 140; king who had wife but wed another, S 29; king who had wife and sons who acted offensively toward him, ER 34; king who had two servants whom he loved with utter love, ER 90, EZ 171; king who had notable sons, ER 12; king who was accompanied by [pack] horses, cavalry, and infantry, ER 164; king who built houses and palaces for his sons and servants, ER 82; king who built palace and decorated it, EZ 173; king who gave his crown to his favorite, ER 125; king married to princess who said to her, "Mix me a cup of wine," ER 149; king who kept precious stones in palace, ER 11; king who learned wisdom from elders in principality, ER 84; king preceded by horses and riders who came to city, ER 119; king who prepared feast, ER 117; king who possessed houses and menservants, ER 55; king who provided each of his servants with shield, ER 162; king who sat on his throne with his servants standing in front of him, ER 31; king of kings who sat reviewing armies of vassal kings, ER 40; king who said to his son, "Fence in my field," ER 159; king who said to his son, "My son, go out and slay all those who are robbers," ER 128; king who sat on his throne with his servant ministering to him, ER 156; king who was seated on throne with elders of realm, ER 11; king who was seated on throne in front of golden salver filled with fruits, ER 100; king who sent emissary to say, "Slaughter many bullocks, eat their flesh and the flesh of many kids of the flock, and drink much wine, so that the prince will sleep and be slothful in cultivating or irrigating fields, should such work be required," ER 82; king who threatens to growl like bear at disobedient servants, ER 6; king who took lash and hung it in his house, ER 6; king who together with his son took road into wilderness, ER 155; king who took wife and traveled with her from kingdom to kingdom, EZ 182; king whose children and wife had so offended him that he proceeded to set his hand against them and drove them out of his house, ER 155; king whose servant got wound on his foot, EZ 191; king who was traveling with son through wilderness, ER 100; king who was visited by his favorite son, ER 135; king who wed woman whom he loved with utter love, EZ 178; king who wed woman having beheld only one of her eyes, ER 29; king whose servant brought wheat as gift, ER 91; king whose servant presented him with seventy jars of oil, ER 49; king whose servant ran away, ER 136; king whose servants were seated before him at table, ER 91; king who wrote out instruction on piece of paper, ER 70; king's daughter whose kin sought to bring her to grief, ER 143; king's servant who was invited to stay with king, ER 69; king's servants who threw palace refuse before his private doorway, ER 4; man who had been confined for nine months in prison, ER 137; man who married his niece, S 36; does man build himself a house for any purpose other than to bring produce, furnishings, and valuables into it?, EZ 175; does man plant vineyard for any purpose other than to eat grapes from it or drink wine from it?, EZ 182; man likened to bag filled with water, ER 62; man who strikes many coins from one die, ER 10; man driven from country to country who hears his fellow speaking same language, ER 158; man who found garment on highway near city, ER 125; man who studies Torah is like lamp which provides light for eyes of many, ER 63; man who studies Torah is like plank over which all pass, ER 63; man who studies Torah is like threshold upon which all step, ER 62; man who studies Torah is like tree into whose shade all come, ER 63; man who was walking in barren land, S 46; master of house who was depositing his vessels, ER 54; nations say, "With how many mighty men will He come at us?" ER 62; olive tree that bears olives for many purposes, ER 92; one who is so poor that he has no roof over his head, EZ 181; one who does his work faithfully and one who does not, ER 5; queen and princes who took edict to people, ER 71; schoolchildren and their teacher who were resorting to blows, ER 114; seller of spices *(rokel)* who carries with him one hundred kinds of spices, ER 106; servant in house who was brought up to manhood, ER 110; ship with one compartment that was split apart, ER 56; son in household who was brought up to manhood, ER 111; son in household who was in burning haste to commit sexual transgressions, ER 111; sun, disk of, is clean upon entering world, unclean upon coming out, ER 11; ten men who assemble for banquet, ER 94; Torah is like beakers filled with [wine], or like cups and tables laden with abundance of all delicacies in entire world, ER 127; Torah is like hide given to man who would tan it, ER 15; two men, one hated by a king and the other by a general, S 28; two servants of mortal king, each of whom was given two sticks of wood, ER 156; grape-bearing vine intermingled with berry-bearing bush, ER 30; grape-bearing vine intermingled with another grape-bearing vine, ER 30; water that goes into river and never returns, ER 105; water that makes purifying pool for all inhabitants of world, ER 105; world in Sennacherib's hand like nest of abandoned eggs, ER 44

Parents, who say things that should not be said, to be reprimanded by sons, ER 115

Parsee priest, interrogates author, ER 5

Patriarch, S 31

Patriarchs: anticipated precepts of Torah, ER 35; given commands which preceded revelation at Sinai, ER 3; entreated God's mercy at Beer-sheba, EZ 186; exercise of charity by, EZ 169; why children long withheld from, ER 99

Pebble in sieve, term for Israel, ER 25

Peki'in, city in southern Palestine, S 7, n. 25

Penitents, God's hands spread toward, S 37

Persia, Jews in, shared immorality which attended Ahasuerus' banquets, ER 4, n. 17

Pharaoh: command of, to cast sons into river, known to all Egyptians, ER 43; rooted out because of brazenness, ER 74, 158

Pharisee, female, S 8

Philistines, priests of, had sense of what was proper in regard to Ark, ER 58

Phinehas: served Israel in Deborah's time as judge and prophet, ER 48; pride of, ER 55; should have gone to Jephthah to release Jephthah from vow, ER 55; giving to Ithamar of High Priesthood, brought greater abuse, EZ 190; responsible for death of Ephraimites, ER 56

Physiognomy, lore of, ER 162

Pity, for three kinds of men, ER 69

Plagiarism, avoidance of, S 19

Plague, that smote Sennacherib, was deliverance of sort destined for end of time, ER 88

Pleiades, beauty of, ER 9

Polemics, with scorner, EZ 196

Poor, given many children to be identified by their proficiency in Torah, ER 99

Population, Israel's, growth of, to great number, leads to redemption, EZ 197

Poverty: becomes Israel, EZ 176; is result of wickedness, ER 120; leads to fear

of God, EZ 181; seven kinds of, EZ 181; in Palestine during fourth century, S 3, n. 8
Prayer(s): injunction in regard to, ER 47; uttered by undistinguished persons, is effective at once, dispensing with need for prayer by great, ER 44; for forgiveness, order of, disclosed by God to Moses, S 41
Privacy, desirability of, in keeping God's precepts, ER 84
Privy, necessity of sitting in, cause for joy, ER 81
Precepts, should be observed in privacy, ER 84
Profaning, of name of God, ER 140
Prophet, false: had Presence rest on him because he provided hospitality, ER 61; caused grief, ER 149
Prophets: make God's plan in world clear, EZ 183; did not subtract from anything that is written in Torah nor did they add anything thereto, ER 82; rejected by Israel, EZ 185; number 48, to correspond to number of cities of refuge, ER 82; seven, admonished nations, ER 35, 142
Proselyte, prophet Obadiah, was an Edomite, ER 125
Proselytes, ER 95, 105; consideration for, ER 106; are to admonish fellow countrymen, ER 35; will sprout in world-to-come, ER 105; not be accepted from among Cutheans until Elijah and Messiah come, EZ 169
Proverbs and sayings: it is an inauspicious sign if adversity comes to a person one year before he reaches old age, ER 30; do not attempt to pacify your fellow in the hour of his anger, ER 83; when the barley is quite gone from the pitcher, strife comes knocking at the door, ER 136, n. 3; he who judges charitably will himself be judged charitably, S 6; always judge a man charitably, not uncharitably, S 6; he who begins performing a commandment, but does not carry it to completion, makes himself, and all that are his, liable to the death penalty, EZ 188; if a disciple of the wise lacks a sense of propriety, an animal is better than he is, ER 33; fear one who has no fear, weep not readily with one who weeps, seek not with anyone who seeks, and do not shame yourself by bowing down with one who keeps bowing down, for he may be a fool and will bring you to folly, S 12; if fire seizes what is moist, what may one expect it to do to what is dry?, ER 65; flesh makes its own stink, ER 143; no man is truly free but the man who occupies himself with the study of Torah, S 17; the good are made agents of blessing, ER 81; through the agency of good men, good things are brought about even to the fourth generation, and through the agency of evil men, evil things are brought about even to the fourth generation, EZ 184; the reward for a good deed is another good deed, ER 76; gossip about failings of disciples of the wise is like gossip about God, ER 16; in my behalf, I own, my heifer broke her leg bone, ER 117, EZ 180; Israel —may I make atonement for them, ER 25; jesting and levity lead a man to lewdness, ER 61; as a man measures, so it is measured out to him, ER 14, 50, 59, 96, 98, 107, 111, 137, 170; a man should do good deeds first and only then ask for Torah from Him whose presence is everywhere, ER 31; a man should first hold fast to the way of humility and only then ask understanding of Torah from Him whose presence is everywhere, ER 31; a man should give his daughter in marriage to a disciple of the wise, ER 30; blessed is the man whose deeds are engendered by his wisdom, ER 84; may So-and-so be remembered for good, for he was the cause of fixing a particular matter of Halakah in my memory, ER 23; he who has the chance to beseech mercy for his fellow man or for a congregation, but does not do so, is called a sinner, ER 87; one man is an altar of atonement for Israel, ER 25; if anyone preserves a single soul, Scripture ascribes it to him

as though he had preserved the entire world, ER 53; one man should not take leave of another without bringing up some matter of Halakah, ER 23; one who desists from transgressing is granted a reward like one who performs a precept, ER 69; it takes the strength of an ox to bring in the crops, ER 121; for the righteous—in their earlier years discord, in their later years concord, EZ 191; Sanhedrin that puts even one man to death in a week [of years] is called a tyrannical tribunal, ER 17; ministering to a scholar can teach us more than studying with him, ER 23; the sentence of the wicked in Gehenna is to endure no more than twelve months, ER 15; if there is no Torah, there is no way for the world [to continue], and if there is no way for the world [to continue], there is no Torah, ER 112; a tree is uprooted only by a tool that is made in part of the tree's own substance, ER 143; he who shares the trouble of his community will live to see the community's deliverance, EZ 167; two are better than three, and alas for one's youth which goes, not to return, S 12; it is an auspicious sign if one's well-being extends to the year before he reaches old age, ER 30; whatever wickedness you seek to fix the blame for, fix it on the man who is notorious for his wickedness, ER 107

Psalm 94, read on fourth day in week, ER 5, n. 39

Public funds: used for daily meal offering of High Priest, ER 35; used to purchase libations which should accompany burnt offerings of heathen, ER 35

Punishment, God's: deferred for three or four generations, ER 98; mild when compared to offense committed, ER 122

Quail, reward for calf served by Abraham to angels, ER 60

Quarrel: calls for interview to reconcile, ER 56; no vengefulness should be harbored after, ER 105

Questioning: of God's justice, S 41; of God, is grave offense, EZ 189

Rachel, entreaty of, prevailed upon God to restore Israel, ER 148

Rahab: received through repentance, S 37; seven kings and eight Prophets issued from, S 37

Ram, symbolic meaning of gait of, ER 36

Rebuke, of neighbor is to be administered privately, ER 109

Red Heifer, ash of, not subject to law of sacrilege, ER 35 n. 36

Redemption, follows growth of Israel's population, EZ 197

Repentance: God's hands spread toward those who resolve upon, S 37; greater than prayer, S 37; greater than charity, S 37; heals Israel of their iniquities, S 38; power of, ER 7, 94; power of, in life of harlot, S 40; even at end of life makes one heir of world-to-come, ER 117; possible for greatest of sinners, ER 121; brings God's instant compassion, ER 18

Reptiles, why created, ER 6

Resignation, in affliction, to God's will, ER 137

Resurrection, ER 21; hint of, in Torah, ER 164; Esau's argument against, S 27; awarded to those who made themselves dwell in humility, ER 22; is God's reward to those who loved Him, ER 22; out of dust of the earth and dust of the dead, S 31; only for Israel, ER 86

Reward and punishment determined by man's conduct, ER 115, 172

Right conduct, specific commands of, preceded revelation at Sinai, ER 3

Righteous: experience discord in earlier years, but concord in later years, EZ 191; radiance of, is their very own, EZ 193; why afflicted with adversity, EZ 181; proof that in the end they will be provided for, ER 120; achieve

share of God's power, ER 8; joys of, in this world, ER 26; punished in this world for trivial offenses, ER 11; no enemy prevails over work of, ER 94; upon entering their eternal world, welcomed by God Himself, ER 11; in time-to-come, will be given radiance of countenance in keeping with Torah in them, ER 16, 20
Ritual slaughter: derived from Torah, ER 72; "misplacing" during, ER 72
Rod: created at twilight, possessors and wonders of, S 53; why turned into serpent and dry stick when Moses cast it to ground, S 54
Roman Emperor, concedes that nations will bow down to Israel, EZ 199
Rome, ER 118; called "small winepress," ER 26; hidden cruelty of, ER 54; anticipated fall of, linked with reckoning of Messiah's coming, S 11, n. 43; God put up with, in reward for Esau's weeping, ER 114
Royalty, denied to Moses' descendants, ER 90
Rudeness, compounding of, ER 77
Rufus, veteran in wickedness, ER 160
Rules of conduct: four in academy, ER 63; twelve, ER 63

Sabbath: holiness of, is like God's and Israel's, ER 133; given to Israel by God, causes Him to put Israel's iniquities out of mind, ER 4; manner of observance of, ER 4, 133; man makes peace on, with his fellows and with God, ER 4; to be given over completely to Torah, ER 4; reading of Scripture on, requires seven men, EZ 172
Sabbath Year (seventh thousand): will have neither sin nor iniquity, neither affliction nor chastisement, ER 7; world will be without affliction and suffused with Sabbath during, ER 7
Safra, R., ER 63
Sage: may not withdraw from congregation in distress, ER 112–13; thoughts of, ER 106; has four qualities of spirit, ER 93
Sages: are blind to temptation, ER 69; are interpreters of Scripture, EZ 183; make expiation for Israel's sins, EZ 173; travel in travail to find doorway into Torah, ER 70; submitting to guidance of, ER 17; ministering to meaning of, ER 37, n. 70; response to needs of, is like bringing first fruits to Temple, EZ 173; called "gardens," ER 117
Saints, EZ 183
Salt, belonging to Sanctuary, use of, by priests, ER 35
Samaria, called "Oholah," ER 49
Samson, S 44
Samuel: given to Elkanah as reward, ER 48; at Gilgal, offered unskinned lamb less than seven days old, ER 87
Sanhedrin: tasks of, ER 54; half of, fell at Ai, ER 103; died because of irreverence of people of Beth-shemesh, ER 58; in days of Gibeah, failed to teach Torah, ER 56; responsible for death of Benjamites in Gibeah, ER 56; that puts even one man to death in a week [of years] is called a tyrannical tribunal, ER 17
Sarah, became young woman again, ER 28
Satan, punishment of, ER 20
Saul: David's sins against, ER 7, n. 8; cherished hostility toward Israel, ER 159; was slain and his line extirpated because of brazenness, ER 159; disregarded regulations concerning marriage, and practiced divination of ghosts, ER 159
Scorner's plea that understanding was not given him, speciousness of, EZ 196
Scorpio, ER 9
Scripture: called chariot of fire, ER 23; precepts repeated in, to intimate that

they are to be obeyed time and again, ER 19; interpreters of, EZ 183; norms for interpreting, EZ 172; reading of, on Sabbath afternoon and on second and fifth day of week requires three men, EZ 172; reading of, on Sabbath requires seven men, EZ 172
Second Temple: stood for 410 years, ER 19; destruction of, began fourth era of creation which is still continuing, ER 160; called "western sea," ER 20
Second tithe, definition of, derived from Scripture, EZ 172
Secret things, term for creation, ER 85
Seir, sons of, rewarded for affably receiving sons of Esau, EZ 174
Seir, won by Esau because of two tears he shed, ER 125, 155
Self-abuse, in city entirely Jewish, ER 101
Semen, involuntary emission of, requires immersion, ER 78
Sennacherib, ER 114; God put up with, in reward of Asshur's virtue, ER 114; was filled with rancor and vengefulness against Israel, ER 44; ordered Jerusalem to be rooted out of earth, ER 44; troops of, so numerous that they soaked up Jordan, ER 45; plague that smote him was deliverance of sort destined for end of time, ER 88; rooted out because of brazenness, ER 74, 158
Seven kinds of poor people, EZ 181
Seven staples of Land of Israel, blessing before and after eating of, EZ 172
Seven years preceding coming of Messiah, S 11
Sexual immorality, Israel guilty of, before entering Land, ER 57
Sexual intercourse with daughter, forbidden in Torah, ER 75
Shem: prophet whom world refused to heed, ER 114; prophesied in vain for four hundred years, ER 142, 174
Sheshai and Talmai, encounter of, with spies, ER 145
Shiloh, pilgrimages to, ER 48
Shinar, name given to Babylon, because it disposed of Israel's sins, that were upon Israel, ER 129
Sibboleth, name of idol in syllables of, ER 56
Sihon and Og, Moses' victory against, proclaimed by sun, ER 10
Simeon, Rabban, why slain, ER 153
Sinai, Mount: lifted itself, and its top penetrated heaven, S 55; Israel of one heart at, ER 122, S 56; during revelation on, God appeared with only one angel, EZ 193; at, God first won with gifts Israel's confidence, then set before them laws concerning injury and exercise of justice, ER 120, 122; Israel's terror at, ER 120
Six commands given to Adam, ER 3, n. 7; not kept by ten generations before flood, ER 162
Six eras in history of creation, ER 160
Six gradations of two levels in God's palace, ER 160
Six things—Torah, Gehenna, Garden of Eden, throne of glory, name of Messiah, and Temple—created in first era of creation, ER 160
Six thousand years, known world intended to exist for, ER 6
Slanderers, seized by angels and thrown into Gehenna, ER 108
Slaves, who are fearers of Heaven, ER 91
Slaying, inadvertent, punishment for, ER 122
Small winepress, term for Rome, ER 26
Social status, penalty for marriage to gain, EZ 177
Sodom: king of, supposed that Abraham wanted to get reward due him, ER 128; people of, rooted out because of shamelessness, ER 74, 158
Sodomy: punished by burning, S 23; Israelites not suspected of, ER 101, n. 81

Solomon: joys of, ER 14; exercise of charity by, EZ 170; Temple of, dedicated when days grew cooler, ER 14, n. 17
Son, righteous: brings deceased wicked father to favorable remembrance, ER 88; studying Torah, able to intercede in behalf of deceased father, EZ 194
Sons, should reprimand parents who say things that should not be said, ER 115
Sorcerers, Pharaoh's, unable to create gnat smaller than lentil seed, ER 41
Spies: what Israel should have said to, ER 144; Moses resisted sending of, ER 144; Moses' instructions to, ER 144; encounter Sheshai and Talmai, ER 145; report of, which led to Israel's weeping without reason, determined day on which ninth of Ab was set, ER 145; pursued Moses and Aaron with evil intent, ER 145; punishment of, ER 145, n. 14
Stories: one of R. 'Aḳiba's pupils who fell in love with harlot, S 39; author accosted by heretic, EZ 171; author accosted by magistrate, ER 95, EZ 167; author accosted by old man, ER 123; author in academy of Jerusalem, ER 49, 51; author in dialogue with Sages about area occupied by mankind, ER 9; author seized during roundup and interrogated by Parsee priest, ER 5; author's encounter with disciple not conversant with Halakah, ER 121; author's encounter with man who had Scripture but no Mishnah, ER 70; author's encounter with man who inquired about reason for first generations' longevity, ER 80; author's encounter with old man, ER 99, 113, 120; author's encounter with scorner, EZ 195; author's encounter with widow of man who died in his middle years, ER 76; blind man who had come forth blind out of his mother's womb, S 41; young child whose father taught him the Book of Genesis, S 21; Dosa ben Orkinas' supposed ruling concerning marriage of co-wife, EZ 168; emperor riding horse and accompanied by notables of Rome, EZ 199; Hadrian's seizure of Miriam and her seven sons, ER 151; Hadrian's capture of Alexandria, ER 151; Rabban Johanan ben Zakkai and two families of priests, ER 53; R. Joshua in marketplace of Babylonian merchants in Peki'in, in southern Palestine, S 7; R. Judah I the Patriarch, dying words of, ER 133; maiden taught fear of sin, S 22; man who was gathering fagots, S 23; man who cried out loudly "Holy, holy, holy!" ER 66; man in synagogue with son who was flippant, ER 65; R. Nathan entered Temple area, ER 149; old woman taught faith in bestowal of reward, S 22; priest without display feared Heaven, ER 90; priest in whose house fire broke out, ER 66; sale of dates to non-Jew with unintentional short-changing, ER 74; slaying of Rabban Simeon and R. Gamaliel, ER 153; visit to city entirely Jewish, ER 100; maiden whose father was very friendly with heathen, ER 116; man who came down from Upper Galilee to work in South, S 6; Rome came and slew all of Bethar, ER 151; Roman commander and R. Judah I the Patriarch, ER 54; R. Zadok entered Temple area, ER 149
Status, social, marriage to gain, S 9
Strangulation, punishment for man who keeps knowledge of Halakah to himself and does not impart it to others, ER 157
Study, in fields other than Torah, disapproved, ER 93
Study of Torah: varieties of, to be pursued, ER 91; need for continuance of, ER 68; how difficulties in comprehension are to be coped with, ER 121
Sukkot, nations will go up to Jerusalem in time-to-come during, and will bring Israel with them, ER 81
Sun: eclipse of, S 10, 11; proclaimed Moses' victory against Sihon and Og, ER 10; travels every day distance of five hundred years at ordinary pace, ER 10
Sustenance, God source of, ER 70

PLAYS ON HEBREW WORDS AND LETTERS*

*In this index all note numbers refer to the notes in this translation.

bĕliyya'al = "ungodly" (*bĕliyya'al* = "worthless") ER 14, n. 9
ben = "among" (*ben* = "out of encounters, disagreements, among") ER 54, n. 18
bĕroš = "cypress" (*ro'š* = "Head") ER 149, n. 13
bĕ-šalom = "in peace" (*bĕ-šalom* = "complete, full complements") ER 52, n. 3
(*bĕ-šalom* = "requital, bestowal [of charity]") ER 52, n. 5
bin Nun = "[Joshua] son of Nun" (*binnun* = "man of understanding") ER 85, n. 23
biṣṣa' = "performed" (*biṣṣa'* = "cut back") ER 7, n. 2
biṣṣaron = "stronghold" (*biṣṣaron* = "abstention") EZ 196, n. 2
bkr = "to treat as first-born" (*kbd* = "to honor") ER 93, n. 22
Buzi (*bzh* = "to abase") ER 34, n. 19
db'k = "thy strength" (*d'bk* = "thy sorrow, thy state of being elderly") ER 52, n. 20
dibber = "spoke" (*dĕḇar* = "word of") ER 8, n. 17
Diblaim (*dibbah* = "ill-fame") (*dĕḇelah* = "pressed fig-cake" EZ 187, n. 4
'dn = "season" (*'dn* = "pleasure") ER 84, n. 21
'dr = "lack" (*'dr* = "flock, band") S 11, n. 48
Eliezer (*'El* = "God," *'ezer* = "whom I would have as my help") ER 31
'ereṣ = "land" (*'eṣah* = "counsel") S 45
'eškol hak-kofer = "cluster of henna" (*'iš šehakkol kofer* = "the One who purges all") ER 81, n. 9
Eznite (*'eznite* [*'ṣ*] = "rough bark of tree") (*'eznite* = "wooden shaft") ER 15, nn. 29, 30
gannim = "gardens" (*gannim* = "enclosures, courtyards") ER 82, n. 14
Gershom (*ger* = "convert," *shom* = "there") ER 30
gibborim = "mighty men" (*gibborim* = "deeds of heroic abnegation") ER 15, n. 22
glh = "show yourselves" (*glh* = "banish [yourselves into freedom]") ER 138, n. 11
grš = "drove out" (*grš* = "separated") ER 3, n. 1
hadar = "majesty" (*ḥazar* = "restorative, gentle") ER 12, n. 59
ḥădarah = "her glory" (*ḥădarim* = "innermost chambers") (*ḥădarah* = "that which men do in secrecy") (*ḥadrah* = "roam about") ER 108
hadraṯ = "beauty" (*ḥerdaṯ* = "awe") ER 12, n. 53
ḥaklili = "red" (*ḥaklili* = "sparkle") EZ 195, n. 4
ḥalĕle = "slain" (*ḥalĕle* = "those who profaned themselves") ER 87
hălikoṯ = "goings" (*hălakoṯ* = "'goings' which ought to be, laws") EZ 173
hălom = "hitherto" (*hălom* = *hlm,* "fitness to wear crown") ER 90

mine [Sages] who determine what is allowed") ER 148
mĕṯim = "men" (*meṯim* = "they who all but slay themselves") ER 22, n. 23
mhr = "hastily" (*mḥr* = "on the morrow") ER 105, n. 123
miḳ-ḳeḏem = "at the east of" (*miḳ-ḳeḏem* = "prior to") ER 3, n. 3
mištolel = "easy mark" (*mištolel* = "fool") S 11
moḵiḥim = "they who decide justly" (*moḵiḥim* = "they who provide guidance") ER 17, n. 39
mor = "myrrh" (*mor* = "bitterness") ER 81, n. 9
ms = *mškn,* "Tabernacle" ER 139, n. 24
naḇalta = "thou hast done foolishly" (*naḇalta* = "thou art humiliated") ER 64, n. 26
naḏiḇ = "prince" (*naḏiḇ* = "that which is princely, generous, warmheartedness") ER 84, n. 7
Nahaliel (*naḥali* = "gift" + *'el* = "God") S 17
(*naḥălu'el* = "possessed themselves of false god") EZ 179
našim = "women" (*našim* = "mother cities") ER 49, n. 6
nassoṯ = "prove" (*nassoṯ* = "exalt") ER 120, n. 6
nḇlh = "dead, corpse" (*bḇl* = "Babylonia") ER 22, n. 22
nĕḏiḇim = "princes" (*nĕḏiḇim* = "those whose hearts have ever been willing") ER 21, n. 11
ne'ĕmanah = "faithful" (*ne'ĕmanah* = "one in which faith is to be put") ER 149, n. 10
[Three letters—*nun, zayin, pe*— in] *nezem zĕhaḇ bĕ-'af* = "ring of gold in a swine's snout" (*nazuf* = "under [Divine] censure") S 17, n. 3
nfš = "hunger" (*nfš* = "soul") ER 62, n. 13
niṣṣaḇim = "stood" (*niṣṣaḇim* = "stood rigid") ER 106
niṯʻalmu = "vanished" (*niṯ'almu* = "were silent") ER 155, n. 37
'nky (*'alef* = *'n',* "I"; *nun* = *nfšy,* "Myself"; *kaf* = *ktbyt,* "I wrote"; *yoḏ* = *yhbyt,* "I gave") ER 130, n. 7
noše' = "pardon" (*nośe'* = "lift up") ER 4, n. 18
'ŏhălim = "tents" (*'ăhalim* = "aloes") ER 117
ʻol = "on high" (*ʻol* = "yoke") ER 7, n. 11
ʻolam = "of old" (*ʻolam* = "world") EZ 173, n. 14
ʻolamoṯ = "spans of fifty years, long periods of time" ER 37
Othniel (*ʻanah 'el* = "God answered him") ER 14, n. 12
pĕsilim = "idols" (*pĕsulim* = "blemished") ER 100, n. 76
pirzono = "His rulers" (*pizrono* = "His scattering, dispersing") ER 54, n. 19
prʻ = "let grow" (*prʻ* = "requite") ER 52
Rachel = *ruaḥ 'el,* "spirit of God" ER 148
Rahab-*rĕḥoḇah* = ["repentance] substantial" S 38
raḥăme = "tender mercies" (*raḥăme* = "issue of womb") ER 111, n. 8

raḵil = "talebearer" (*raḵ* = "soft" + *kil* [*kilai*] = "hard, miserly")	ER 106, n. 116
rawah = "watered" (*rawah* = "that which is to be sated, gut")	ER 72, n. 6
'rb (Arab) = "desert land" (*'rl* [*'Arel*] = "uncircumcised")	ER 156, n. 45
rb' = "stock" (*rb'* = "couching")	ER 116, n. 9
re'aḵa = "thy neighbor" (*re'aḵa* = "thy Friend [above]")	ER 105, n. 123
re-ḡel = "foot" (*reḡel* = "habit, foot's [impulse to evil]")	EZ 167, n. 4
rĕ'iṯem = "discern" (*rĕ'iṯem* = "be looked upon favorably")	ER 88, n. 45
rephaim = "shades" (Rephaim = "[doughty] Rephaim")	ER 22, n. 26
Rephidim (*rfh* = "let go" + *ydym* = "hands")	ER 126
ro'š = "chief" (*roš* = "heir")	ER 15, n. 26
ro'š 'ašmuroṯ = "the beginning of the watches" (*ro'š* = "superior," *'ašmuroṯ* = "Samaria")	ER 98, n. 61
'r'r = "destitute" (*yĕ'o'eru* = "raise")	ER 20, n. 32; EZ 183, n. 3
'rṣ = "earth" (*'rṣ* = "Land of Israel")	EZ 173, n. 15
šaḇtem = "again" (*šaḇtem* = "one of you[r children] returns")	ER 88, n. 45
šaddun = "punishment" (*šed-din* = "there is judgment")	ER 158
ṣafonah = "northward" (*ṣafonah* [*ṣfh*] = "it is seen"; *ṣafonah* [*ṣefunin*] = "laying up of treasure")	ER 36
šaḵanti = "I may dwell" (*škn* = "Temple" + *ti* = letters *taw* [400] + *yoḏ* [10] = 410)	ER 148, n. 2
šamen = "oil" (*šamen* = "rich cream")	ER 60, n. 12
šaniṯi = "I changed" (*šaniṯi* = "I did it again and again")	ER 25, n. 55
śariṯa = "thou hast striven" (*śariṯa* [*śar*] = "thou hast come to have princes")	S 31, n. 8
ṣaw lĕ-ṣaw = "precept by precept" (*ṣaw lo' ṣaw* = "precept became no precept")	ER 19, n. 30
ṣb'ṯ = "hosts [of Israel]" (*ṣade* [90] + *beṯ* [2] + *'alef* [1] + *taw* [400] = 493, the numerical value of the hosts of Israel)	ER 34, n. 25
šbṯ = "rest" (*šbṯ* = "make cease, cause to disappear")	ER 7, n. 3
šb'tym [dual of *šb'*] = "seven" (*šb'tym* = "seven times seven, forty-nine")	ER 105, n. 122; EZ 190
ṣĕfardea = "frog" (*ṣippor* = "bird" + *de'ah* = "knowledge")	ER 41, n. 19
ṣĕfoni = "northern" (*ṣĕfoni* = "hidden")	ER 20, n. 34
šĕlišiyyah = "the third" (*šĕlišiyyah* [*šališ*] = "corps of servitors")	EZ 194, n. 11
Šĕlomoh = "Solomon" (*šĕlomoh* = "peace, makes peace")	ER 84

šělume = "peacable" (*šělume* = "those who perfect") ER 99, n. 69
ṣěme'ah = "dry" (*ṣěme'ah* = "thirsty for moisture") ER 72, n. 6
šě'onah = "their uproar" (*šě'onah* = [*ša'ănan*] "being at ease, comfortable") ER 108, n. 146
ṣěror = "bag" (*ṣrr* = "show hostility, vex") ER 81, n. 9
šfr = "goodly" (*šfr* = "deed") S 52
Shinar [Babylon] = *měna'ereṯ*, "disposed [of the sins that were upon Israel]" ER 129
šḥr = "seek earnestly" (*šḥr* = "seek early in morning") ER 74, n. 16
Sibboleth (*śa' Bul* = "lift up the idol Bul") ER 56
šillaḥti = "I sent" (*šullaḥti* = "I was sent, I had Myself go") EZ 189, n. 18
šinnaim = "teeth" (*šanim* = "years") EZ 195, n. 4
sll = "extol" (*sll* = "being close, intimate") ER 84, n. 12
šlm = "make peace" (*šlm* = "become whole, unite") EZ 178, n. 10
ślyw = "quail" (*slyw* = "thorns") ER 60
'ṣmwt = "bones" (*'ṣ mwṯ* = "tree of death") ER 24
śon'eḵem = "those who hate you" (*šoneḵem* = "those of you who study, who possess [knowledge of] Mishnah") S 5, n. 16
'šrw = "will strengthen" (*'šrw* = "will enrich") ER 113, n. 15
Ṣywn = "Zion" (*ṣywn* = "sign") ER 84
't = particle to indicate that noun following is object (*'t* = "from A to Z, from beginning to end") ER 96
Tachkemoni (*taw* = "Torah's essence" + *chkemoni* = "man's innate wisdom") (*těhe kamoni* = "you are like Me") ER 15
tai'ṣu = "labor" (*těna'aṣu* = "blaspheme") EZ 189, n. 17
tannim = "jackals" (*tannim* = "crocodiles") ER 123, n. 17
tappil = "cause to fall out, bring to life" (*tappil* = "cause to fall") ER 22, n. 26
te'ěsof = "gather" (*te'ěsof* = "allow to be reckoned among") ER 59, n. 2
těḳufah = "circuit" (Arabic *tuḳfa'* = "fierce reproof") ER 11, n. 47
ṭeref = "food" (*ṭeruf* = "wandering, being cast about, trembling") ER 141, n. 8
'tf = "faint" (*'tf* = "wrap oneself" ER 38 and n. 75
tflṣtk = "thy terribleness" (*tfl* = "the least" + *lyṣn* = "scorner") ER 126
'tyrh = "entreaty, yielding to entreaty" (*'tyrh* = "compassion") ER 34, n. 17
u-lě-'immo = "his mother" (*u-lě-'ummo* = "the people which is His very own") ER 85, n. 25
way-ya'ăḇor = "He passed" (*way-ya'ăḇir* = "He had pass") ER 3, nn. 15, 17